THE TIMES

MINI

ATLAS

OF THE

WORLD

TIMES BOOKS
LONDON

THE TIMES MINI ATLAS OF THE WORLD

Times Books, 77-85 Fulham Palace Road,
London W6 8JB

The Times is a registered trademark of
Times Newspapers Ltd

First published 1991
Published as The Times Atlas
of the World Mini Edition 1994
Second Edition 1999
Third Edition 2006
Fourth Edition 2009

Fifth Edition 2012

Printed in Singapore
British Library Cataloguing in Publication Data
A catalogue record for this book is available from the British Library

ISBN 978 0 00 745241 5
Imp 001

All mapping in this atlas is generated from Collins Bartholomew™
digital databases. Collins Bartholomew™, the UK's leading
independent geographical information supplier, can provide a
digital, custom, and premium mapping service to a variety of markets.
For further information:
Tel: +44 (0) 208 307 4515
e-mail: collinsbartholomew@harpercollins.co.uk
or visit our website at: www.collinsbartholomew.com

If you would like to comment on any aspect of this atlas, please write to
Times Atlases, HarperCollins Publishers, Westerhill Road, Bishopbriggs, Glasgow, G64 2QT
email: timesatlases@harpercollins.co.uk
or visit our website at: www.timesatlases.com
or follow us on Twitter @TimesAtlas

Pages	Title	Scale

GEOGRAPHICAL INFORMATION

6–19	**COUNTRIES OF THE WORLD**
20–21	**OCEANIA** Physical Features
22–23	**ASIA** Physical Features
24–25	**EUROPE** Physical Features
26–27	**AFRICA** Physical Features
28–29	**NORTH AMERICA** Physical Features
30–31	**SOUTH AMERICA** Physical Features
32–33	**OCEANS AND POLES** Physical Features
34–35	**CLIMATE**
36–37	**LAND COVER**
38–39	**POPULATION**
40–41	**URBANIZATION**
42–43	**SYMBOLS AND ABBREVIATIONS**

WORLD

Pages	Title	Scale
44–45	**WORLD** Physical Features	1:170 000 000
46–47	**WORLD** Countries	1:170 000 000

OCEANIA

Pages	Title	Scale
48–49	**OCEANIA**	1:70 000 000
50 51	**AUSTRALIA**	1:25 000 000
52–53	**AUSTRALIA** Southeast	1:10 000 000
54	**NEW ZEALAND**	1:10 000 000

ANTARCTICA

Pages	Title	Scale
55	**ANTARCTICA**	1:60 000 000

ASIA

Pages	Title	Scale
56–57	**ASIA**	1:70 000 000
58–59	**SOUTHEAST ASIA**	1:30 000 000
60–61	**MALAYSIA AND INDONESIA** West	1:15 000 000
62–63	**CONTINENTAL SOUTHEAST ASIA**	1:15 000 000
64	**PHILIPPINES**	1:15 000 000

CONTENTS

Pages	Title	Scale
65	**NORTH KOREA and SOUTH KOREA**	1:9 000 000
66–67	**JAPAN**	1:10 000 000
68–69	**CHINA and MONGOLIA**	1:30 000 000
70–71	**CHINA** Central	1:15 000 000
72–73	**SOUTH ASIA**	1:20 000 000
74–75	**PAKISTAN, INDIA and BANGLADESH**	1:15 000 000
76–77	**CENTRAL ASIA**	1:20 000 000
78–79	**ARABIAN PENINSULA**	1:15 000 000
80–81	**EAST MEDITERRANEAN**	1:15 000 000
82–83	**RUSSIAN FEDERATION**	1:42 000 000
84–85	EUROPE	1:40 000 000
86–87	**EUROPEAN RUSSIAN FEDERATION**	1:20 000 000
88–89	**NORTHEAST EUROPE**	1:8 000 000
90–91	**UKRAINE and MOLDOVA**	1:8 000 000
92–93	**SCANDINAVIA and ICELAND**	1:10 000 000
94–95	**BRITISH ISLES**	1:8 000 000
96	**SCOTLAND**	1:4 000 000
97	**IRELAND**	1:4 000 000
98–99	**ENGLAND and WALES**	1:4 000 000
100–101	**NORTHWEST EUROPE**	1:4 000 000
102–103	**CENTRAL EUROPE**	1:8 000 000
104–105	**FRANCE and SWITZERLAND**	1:8 000 000
106–107	**SPAIN and PORTUGAL**	1:8 000 000
108–109	**ITALY and THE BALKANS**	1:8 000 000
110–111	**GREECE, ROMANIA and BULGARIA**	1:8 000 000
112–113	AFRICA	1:60 000 000
114–115	**NORTHWEST AFRICA**	1:26 000 000

CONTENTS

Pages	Title	Scale
116–117	**NORTHEAST AFRICA**	1:26 000 000
118–119	**CENTRAL AFRICA**	1:20 000 000
120–121	**SOUTHERN AFRICA**	1:20 000 000
122–123	**REPUBLIC of SOUTH AFRICA**	1:10 000 000
124–125	NORTH AMERICA	1:70 000 000
126–127	**CANADA**	1:30 000 000
128–129	**CANADA** West	1:15 000 000
130–131	**CANADA** East	1:15 000 000
132–133	**UNITED STATES OF AMERICA**	1:25 000 000
134–135	**USA** West	1:11 000 000
136–137	**USA** North Central	1:11 000 000
138–139	**USA** South Central	1:11 000 000
140–141	**USA** Northeast	1:11 000 000
142–143	**USA** Southeast	1:11 000 000
144–145	**MEXICO**	1:15 000 000
146–147	**CARIBBEAN**	1:20 000 000
148–149	SOUTH AMERICA	1:70 000 000
150–151	**SOUTH AMERICA** North	1:25 000 000
152–153	**SOUTH AMERICA** South	1:25 000 000
154–155	**BRAZIL** Southeast	1:10 000 000
	OCEANS	
156–157	**PACIFIC OCEAN**	1:120 000 000
158	**ATLANTIC OCEAN**	1:120 000 000
159	**INDIAN OCEAN**	1:120 000 000
160	**ARCTIC OCEAN**	1:60 000 000
161–256	INDEX	

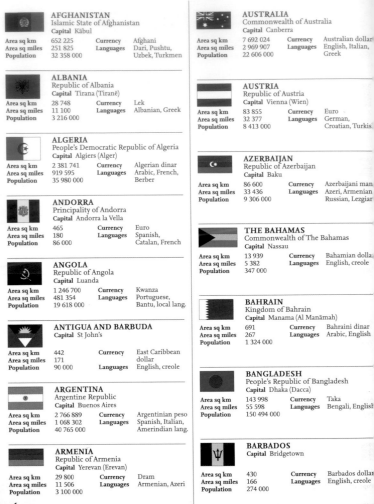

AFGHANISTAN
Islamic State of Afghanistan
Capital Kābul

Area sq km	652 225	**Currency**	Afghani
Area sq miles	251 825	**Languages**	Dari, Pushtu,
Population	32 358 000		Uzbek, Turkmen

ALBANIA
Republic of Albania
Capital Tirana (Tiranë)

Area sq km	28 748	**Currency**	Lek
Area sq miles	11 100	**Languages**	Albanian, Greek
Population	3 216 000		

ALGERIA
People's Democratic Republic of Algeria
Capital Algiers (Alger)

Area sq km	2 381 741	**Currency**	Algerian dinar
Area sq miles	919 595	**Languages**	Arabic, French,
Population	35 980 000		Berber

ANDORRA
Principality of Andorra
Capital Andorra la Vella

Area sq km	465	**Currency**	Euro
Area sq miles	180	**Languages**	Spanish,
Population	86 000		Catalan, French

ANGOLA
Republic of Angola
Capital Luanda

Area sq km	1 246 700	**Currency**	Kwanza
Area sq miles	481 354	**Languages**	Portuguese,
Population	19 618 000		Bantu, local lang.

ANTIGUA AND BARBUDA
Capital St John's

Area sq km	442	**Currency**	East Caribbean
Area sq miles	171		dollar
Population	90 000	**Languages**	English, creole

ARGENTINA
Argentine Republic
Capital Buenos Aires

Area sq km	2 766 889	**Currency**	Argentinian peso
Area sq miles	1 068 302	**Languages**	Spanish, Italian,
Population	40 765 000		Amerindian lang.

ARMENIA
Republic of Armenia
Capital Yerevan (Erevan)

Area sq km	29 800	**Currency**	Dram
Area sq miles	11 506	**Languages**	Armenian, Azeri
Population	3 100 000		

AUSTRALIA
Commonwealth of Australia
Capital Canberra

Area sq km	7 692 024	**Currency**	Australian dollar
Area sq miles	2 969 907	**Languages**	English, Italian,
Population	22 606 000		Greek

AUSTRIA
Republic of Austria
Capital Vienna (Wien)

Area sq km	83 855	**Currency**	Euro
Area sq miles	32 377	**Languages**	German,
Population	8 413 000		Croatian, Turkis

AZERBAIJAN
Republic of Azerbaijan
Capital Baku

Area sq km	86 600	**Currency**	Azerbaijani man
Area sq miles	33 436	**Languages**	Azeri, Armenian
Population	9 306 000		Russian, Lezgiar

THE BAHAMAS
Commonwealth of The Bahamas
Capital Nassau

Area sq km	13 939	**Currency**	Bahamian dolla
Area sq miles	5 382	**Languages**	English, creole
Population	347 000		

BAHRAIN
Kingdom of Bahrain
Capital Manama (Al Manāmah)

Area sq km	691	**Currency**	Bahraini dinar
Area sq miles	267	**Languages**	Arabic, English
Population	1 324 000		

BANGLADESH
People's Republic of Bangladesh
Capital Dhaka (Dacca)

Area sq km	143 998	**Currency**	Taka
Area sq miles	55 598	**Languages**	Bengali, Englist
Population	150 494 000		

BARBADOS
Capital Bridgetown

Area sq km	430	**Currency**	Barbados dollar
Area sq miles	166	**Languages**	English, creole
Population	274 000		

BELARUS
Republic of Belarus
Capital Minsk

Area sq km	207 600	**Currency** Belarus rouble
Area sq miles	80 155	**Languages** Belorussian,
Population	9 559 000	Russian

BELGIUM
Kingdom of Belgium
Capital Brussels (Bruxelles)

Area sq km	30 520	**Currency** Euro
Area sq miles	11 784	**Languages** Dutch (Flemish),
Population	10 754 000	French (Walloon),
		German

BELIZE
Capital Belmopan

Area sq km	22 965	**Currency** Belize dollar
Area sq miles	8 867	**Languages** English, Spanish,
Population	318 000	Mayan, creole

BENIN
Republic of Benin
Capital Porto-Novo

Area sq km	112 620	**Currency** CFA franc*
Area sq miles	43 483	**Languages** French, Fon,
Population	9 100 000	Yoruba, Adja,
		local lang.

BHUTAN
Kingdom of Bhutan
Capital Thimphu

Area sq km	46 620	**Currency** Ngultrum,
Area sq miles	18 000	Indian rupee
Population	738 000	**Languages** Dzongkha,
		Nepali, Assamese

BOLIVIA
Plurinational State of Bolivia
Capital La Paz/Sucre

Area sq km	1 098 581	**Currency** Boliviano
Area sq miles	424 164	**Languages**
Population	10 088 000	Spanish, Quechua,
		Aymara

BOSNIA-HERZEGOVINA
Republic of Bosnia and Herzegovina
Capital Sarajevo

Area sq km	51 130	**Currency** Marka
Area sq miles	19 741	**Languages** Bosnian, Serbian,
Population	3 752 000	Croatian

BOTSWANA
Republic of Botswana
Capital Gaborone

Area sq km	581 370	**Currency** Pula
Area sq miles	224 468	**Languages** English, Setswana,
Population	2 031 000	Shona, local lang.

BRAZIL
Federative Republic of Brazil
Capital Brasília

Area sq km	8 514 879	**Currency** Real
Area sq miles	3 287 613	**Languages** Portuguese
Population	196 655 000	

BRUNEI
State of Brunei Darussalam
Capital Bandar Seri Begawan

Area sq km	5 765	**Currency** Brunei dollar
Area sq miles	2 226	**Languages** Malay, English,
Population	406 000	Chinese

BULGARIA
Republic of Bulgaria
Capital Sofia (Sofiya)

Area sq km	110 994	**Currency** Lev
Area sq miles	42 855	**Languages** Bulgarian,
Population	7 446 000	Turkish, Romany,
		Macedonian

BURKINA FASO
Democratic Republic of Burkina Faso
Capital Ouagadougou

Area sq km	274 200	**Currency** CFA franc*
Area sq miles	105 869	**Languages** French, Moore
Population	16 968 000	(Mossi), Fulani,
		local lang.

BURUNDI
Republic of Burundi
Capital Bujumbura

Area sq km	27 835	**Currency** Burundian franc
Area sq miles	10 747	**Languages** Kirundi (Hutu,
Population	8 575 000	Tutsi), French

CAMBODIA
Kingdom of Cambodia
Capital Phnom Penh

Area sq km	181 035	**Currency** Riel
Area sq miles	69 884	**Languages** Khmer,
Population	14 305 000	Vietnamese

---

* CFA Communauté Financière Africaine

CAMEROON
Republic of Cameroon
Capital Yaoundé

Area sq km	475 442	Currency CFA franc*
Area sq miles	183 569	Languages French, English,
Population	20 030 000	Fang, Bamileke, local lang.

CANADA
Capital Ottawa

Area sq km	9 984 670	Currency Canadian dollar
Area sq miles	3 855 103	Languages English, French
Population	34 350 000	

CAPE VERDE
Republic of Cape Verde
Capital Praia

Area sq km	4 033	Currency Cape Verde
Area sq miles	1 557	escudo
Population	501 000	Languages Portuguese, creole

CENTRAL AFRICAN REPUBLIC
Capital Bangui

Area sq km	622 436	Currency CFA franc*
Area sq miles	240 324	Languages French, Sango,
Population	4 487 000	Banda, Baya, local lang.

CHAD
Republic of Chad
Capital Ndjamena

Area sq km	1 284 000	Currency CFA franc*
Area sq miles	495 755	Languages Arabic, French,
Population	11 525 000	Sara, local lang.

CHILE
Republic of Chile
Capital Santiago

Area sq km	756 945	Currency Chilean peso
Area sq miles	292 258	Languages Spanish,
Population	17 270 000	Amerindian lang.

CHINA
People's Republic of China
Capital Beijing (Peking)

Area sq km	9 584 492	Currency Yuan, HK dollar,
Area sq miles	3 700 593	Macao pataca
Population	1 332 079 000	Languages Mandarin, Hsiang, Cantonese, Wu, regional lang.

COLOMBIA
Republic of Colombia
Capital Bogotá

Area sq km	1 141 748	Currency Colombian peso
Area sq miles	440 831	Languages Spanish,
Population	46 927 000	Amerindian lang.

COMOROS
United Republic of the Comoros
Capital Moroni

Area sq km	1 862	Currency Comoros franc
Area sq miles	719	Languages Shikomor
Population	754 000	(Comorian), French, Arabic

CONGO
Republic of the Congo
Capital Brazzaville

Area sq km	342 000	Currency CFA franc*
Area sq miles	132 047	Languages French, Kongo,
Population	4 140 000	Monokutuba, local lang.

CONGO, DEMOCRATIC REPUBLIC OF THE
Capital Kinshasa

Area sq km	2 345 410	Currency Congolese franc
Area sq miles	905 568	Languages French, Lingala,
Population	67 758 000	Swahili, Kongo, local lang.

COSTA RICA
Republic of Costa Rica
Capital San José

Area sq km	51 100	Currency Costa Rican colón
Area sq miles	19 730	Languages Spanish
Population	4 727 000	

CÔTE D'IVOIRE (IVORY COAST)
Republic of Côte d'Ivoire
Capital Yamoussoukro

Area sq km	322 463	Currency CFA franc*
Area sq miles	124 504	Languages French, creole,
Population	20 153 000	Akan, local lang.

CROATIA
Republic of Croatia
Capital Zagreb

Area sq km	56 538	Currency Kuna
Area sq miles	21 829	Languages Croatian, Serbian
Population	4 396 000	

CUBA
Republic of Cuba
Capital Havana (La Habana)

Area sq km	110 860	**Currency**	Cuban peso
Area sq miles	42 803	**Languages**	Spanish
Population	11 254 000		

CYPRUS
Republic of Cyprus
Capital Nicosia (Lefkosia)

Area sq km	9 251	**Currency**	Euro
Area sq miles	3 572	**Languages**	Greek, Turkish,
Population	1 117 000		English

CZECH REPUBLIC
Capital Prague (Praha)

Area sq km	78 864	**Currency**	Czech koruna
Area sq miles	30 450	**Languages**	Czech, Moravian,
Population	10 534 000		Slovakian

DENMARK
Kingdom of Denmark
Capital Copenhagen (København)

Area sq km	43 075	**Currency**	Danish krone
Area sq miles	16 631	**Languages**	Danish
Population	5 573 000		

DJIBOUTI
Republic of Djibouti
Capital Djibouti

Area sq km	23 200	**Currency**	Djibouti franc
Area sq miles	8 958	**Languages**	Somali, Afar,
Population	906 000		French, Arabic

DOMINICA
Commonwealth of Dominica
Capital Roseau

Area sq km	750	**Currency**	East Caribbean
Area sq miles	290		dollar
Population	68 000	**Languages**	English, creole

DOMINICAN REPUBLIC
Capital Santo Domingo

Area sq km	48 442	**Currency**	Dominican peso
Area sq miles	18 704	**Languages**	Spanish, creole
Population	10 056 000		

EAST TIMOR
Democratic Republic of Timor-Leste
Capital Dili

Area sq km	14 874	**Currency**	US dollar
Area sq miles	5 743	**Languages**	Portuguese, Tetun,
Population	1 154 000		English

ECUADOR
Republic of Ecuador
Capital Quito

Area sq km	272 045	**Currency**	US dollar
Area sq miles	105 037	**Languages**	Spanish, Quechua,
Population	14 666 000		Amerindian lang.

EGYPT
Arab Republic of Egypt
Capital Cairo (Al Qāhirah)

Area sq km	1 000 250	**Currency**	Egyptian pound
Area sq miles	386 199	**Languages**	Arabic
Population	82 537 000		

EL SALVADOR
Republic of El Salvador
Capital San Salvador

Area sq km	21 041	**Currency**	El Salvador colón,
Area sq miles	8 124		US dollar
Population	6 227 000	**Languages**	Spanish

EQUATORIAL GUINEA
Republic of Equatorial Guinea
Capital Malabo

Area sq km	28 051	**Currency**	CFA franc*
Area sq miles	10 831	**Languages**	Spanish, French,
Population	720 000		Fang

ERITREA
State of Eritrea
Capital Asmara

Area sq km	117 400	**Currency**	Nakfa
Area sq miles	45 328	**Languages**	Tigrinya, Tigre
Population	5 415 000		

ESTONIA
Republic of Estonia
Capital Tallinn

Area sq km	45 200	**Currency**	Euro
Area sq miles	17 452	**Languages**	Estonian, Russian
Population	1 341 000		

COUNTRIES OF THE WORLD

ETHIOPIA
Federal Democratic Republic of Ethiopia
Capital Addis Ababa (Ādīs Ābeba)

Area sq km	1 133 880	**Currency** Birr
Area sq miles	437 794	**Languages** Oromo, Amharic,
Population	84 734 000	Tigrinya, local lang.

GEORGIA
Republic of Georgia
Capital Tbilisi

Area sq km	69 700	**Currency** Lari
Area sq miles	26 911	**Languages** Georgian, Russian,
Population	4 329 000	Armenian, Azeri, Ossetian, Abkhaz

FIJI
Republic of Fiji
Capital Suva

Area sq km	18 330	**Currency** Fiji dollar
Area sq miles	7 077	**Languages** English, Fijian,
Population	868 000	Hindi

GERMANY
Federal Republic of Germany
Capital Berlin

Area sq km	357 022	**Currency** Euro
Area sq miles	137 849	**Languages** German, Turkish
Population	82 163 000	

FINLAND
Republic of Finland
Capital Helsinki (Helsingfors)

Area sq km	338 145	**Currency** Euro
Area sq miles	130 559	**Languages** Finnish, Swedish
Population	5 385 000	

GHANA
Republic of Ghana
Capital Accra

Area sq km	238 537	**Currency** Cedi
Area sq miles	92 100	**Languages** English, Hausa,
Population	24 966 000	Akan, local lang.

FRANCE
French Republic
Capital Paris

Area sq km	543 965	**Currency** Euro
Area sq miles	210 026	**Languages** French, Arabic
Population	63 126 000	

GREECE
Hellenic Republic
Capital Athens (Athina)

Area sq km	131 957	**Currency** Euro
Area sq miles	50 949	**Languages** Greek
Population	11 390 000	

GABON
Gabonese Republic
Capital Libreville

Area sq km	267 667	**Currency** CFA franc*
Area sq miles	103 347	**Languages** French, Fang,
Population	1 534 000	local lang.

GRENADA
Capital St George's

Area sq km	378	**Currency** East Caribbean
Area sq miles	146	dollar
Population	105 000	**Languages** English, creole

THE GAMBIA
Republic of The Gambia
Capital Banjul

Area sq km	11 295	**Currency** Dalasi
Area sq miles	4 361	**Languages** English, Malinke,
Population	1 776 000	Fulani, Wolof

GUATEMALA
Republic of Guatemala
Capital Guatemala City

Area sq km	108 890	**Currency** Quetzal, US dollar
Area sq miles	42 043	**Languages** Spanish,
Population	14 757 000	Mayan lang.

Gaza
Semi-autonomous region
Capital Gaza

Area sq km	363	**Currency** Israeli shekel
Area sq miles	140	**Languages** Arabic
Population	1 535 120	

GUINEA
Republic of Guinea
Capital Conakry

Area sq km	245 857	**Currency** Guinea franc
Area sq miles	94 926	**Languages** French, Fulani,
Population	10 222 000	Malinke, local lang.

GUINEA-BISSAU
Republic of Guinea-Bissau
Capital Bissau

Area sq km	36 125	**Currency** CFA franc*
Area sq miles	13 948	**Languages** Portuguese,
Population	1 547 000	crioulo, local lang.

GUYANA
Co-operative Republic of Guyana
Capital Georgetown

Area sq km	214 969	**Currency** Guyana dollar
Area sq miles	83 000	**Languages** English, creole,
Population	756 000	Amerindian lang.

HAITI
Republic of Haiti
Capital Port-au-Prince

Area sq km	27 750	**Currency** Gourde
Area sq miles	10 714	**Languages** French, creole
Population	10 124 000	

HONDURAS
Republic of Honduras
Capital Tegucigalpa

Area sq km	112 088	**Currency** Lempira
Area sq miles	43 277	**Languages** Spanish,
Population	7 755 000	Amerindian lang.

HUNGARY
Republic of Hungary
Capital Budapest

Area sq km	93 030	**Currency** Forint
Area sq miles	35 919	**Languages** Hungarian
Population	9 966 000	

ICELAND
Republic of Iceland
Capital Reykjavik

Area sq km	102 820	**Currency** Icelandic króna
Area sq miles	39 699	**Languages** Icelandic
Population	324 000	

INDIA
Republic of India
Capital New Delhi

Area sq km	3 064 898	**Currency** Indian rupee
Area sq miles	1 183 364	**Languages** Hindi, English,
Population	1 241 492 000	many regional lang.

INDONESIA
Republic of Indonesia
Capital Jakarta

Area sq km	1 919 445	**Currency** Rupiah
Area sq miles	741 102	**Languages** Indonesian,
Population	242 326 000	local lang.

IRAN
Islamic Republic of Iran
Capital Tehrān

Area sq km	1 648 000	**Currency** Iranian rial
Area sq miles	636 296	**Languages** Farsi, Azeri,
Population	74 799 000	Kurdish, regional lang.

IRAQ
Republic of Iraq
Capital Baghdād

Area sq km	438 317	**Currency** Iraqi dinar
Area sq miles	169 235	**Languages** Arabic, Kurdish,
Population	32 665 000	Turkmen

IRELAND
Republic of Ireland
Capital Dublin (Baile Átha Cliath)

Area sq km	70 282	**Currency** Euro
Area sq miles	27 136	**Languages** English, Irish
Population	4 526 000	

ISRAEL
State of Israel
Capital Jerusalem* (Yerushalayim) (El Quds)

Area sq km	20 770	**Currency** Shekel
Area sq miles	8 019	**Languages** Hebrew, Arabic
Population	7 562 000	

* De facto capital. Disputed.

ITALY
Italian Republic
Capital Rome (Roma)

Area sq km	301 245	**Currency** Euro
Area sq miles	116 311	**Languages** Italian
Population	60 789 000	

JAMAICA
Capital Kingston

Area sq km	10 991	**Currency** Jamaican dollar
Area sq miles	4 244	**Languages** English, creole
Population	2 751 000	

JAPAN
Capital Tōkyō

Area sq km	377 727	**Currency**	Yen
Area sq miles	145 841	**Languages**	Japanese
Population	126 497 000		

JORDAN
Hashemite Kingdom of Jordan
Capital 'Ammān

Area sq km	89 206	**Currency**	Jordanian dinar
Area sq miles	34 443	**Languages**	Arabic
Population	6 330 000		

KAZAKHSTAN
Republic of Kazakhstan
Capital Astana (Akmola)

Area sq km	2 717 300	**Currency**	Tenge
Area sq miles	1 049 155	**Languages**	Kazakh, Russian,
Population	16 207 000		Ukrainian, German,
			Uzbek, Tatar

KENYA
Republic of Kenya
Capital Nairobi

Area sq km	582 646	**Currency**	Kenyan shilling
Area sq miles	224 961	**Languages**	Swahili, English,
Population	41 610 000		local lang.

KIRIBATI
Republic of Kiribati
Capital Bairiki

Area sq km	717	**Currency**	Australian dollar
Area sq miles	277	**Languages**	Gilbertese,
Population	101 000		English

KOSOVO
Republic of Kosovo
Capital Prishtinë (Priština)

Area sq km	10 908	**Currency**	Euro
Area sq miles	4 212	**Languages**	Albanian, Serbian
Population	2 180 686		

KUWAIT
State of Kuwait
Capital Kuwait (Al Kuwayt)

Area sq km	17 818	**Currency**	Kuwaiti dinar
Area sq miles	6 880	**Languages**	Arabic
Population	2 818 000		

KYRGYZSTAN
Kyrgyz Republic
Capital Bishkek (Frunze)

Area sq km	198 500	**Currency**	Kyrgyz som
Area sq miles	76 641	**Languages**	Kyrgyz, Russian,
Population	5 393 000		Uzbek

LAOS
Lao People's Democratic Republic
Capital Vientiane (Viangchan)

Area sq km	236 800	**Currency**	Kip
Area sq miles	91 429	**Languages**	Lao, local lang.
Population	6 288 000		

LATVIA
Republic of Latvia
Capital Rīga

Area sq km	64 589	**Currency**	Lats
Area sq miles	24 938	**Languages**	Latvian, Russian
Population	2 243 000		

LEBANON
Republic of Lebanon
Capital Beirut (Beyrouth)

Area sq km	10 452	**Currency**	Lebanese pound
Area sq miles	4 036	**Languages**	Arabic, Armenian
Population	4 259 000		French

LESOTHO
Kingdom of Lesotho
Capital Maseru

Area sq km	30 355	**Currency**	Loti,
Area sq miles	11 720		S. African rand
Population	2 194 000	**Languages**	Sesotho, English,
			Zulu

LIBERIA
Republic of Liberia
Capital Monrovia

Area sq km	111 369	**Currency**	Liberian dollar
Area sq miles	43 000	**Languages**	English, creole,
Population	4 129 000		local lang.

LIBYA
Capital Tripoli (Ṭarābulus)

Area sq km	1 759 540	**Currency**	Libyan dinar
Area sq miles	679 362	**Languages**	Arabic, Berber
Population	6 423 000		

LIECHTENSTEIN
Principality of Liechtenstein
Capital Vaduz

Area sq km	160	**Currency**	Swiss franc
Area sq miles	62	**Languages**	German
Population	36 000		

LITHUANIA
Republic of Lithuania
Capital Vilnius

Area sq km	65 200	**Currency** Litas
Area sq miles	25 174	**Languages** Lithuanian,
Population	3 307 000	Russian, Polish

MALI
Republic of Mali
Capital Bamako

Area sq km	1 240 140	**Currency** CFA franc*
Area sq miles	478 841	**Languages** French, Bambara,
Population	15 840 000	local lang.

LUXEMBOURG
Grand Duchy of Luxembourg
Capital Luxembourg

Area sq km	2 586	**Currency** Euro
Area sq miles	998	**Languages** Letzeburgish,
Population	516 000	German, French

MALTA
Republic of Malta
Capital Valletta

Area sq km	316	**Currency** Euro
Area sq miles	122	**Languages** Maltese, English
Population	418 000	

MACEDONIA (F.Y.R.O.M.)
Republic of Macedonia
Capital Skopje

Area sq km	25 713	**Currency** Macedonian denar
Area sq miles	9 928	**Languages** Macedonian,
Population	2 064 000	Albanian, Turkish

MARSHALL ISLANDS
Republic of the Marshall Islands
Capital Delap-Uliga-Djarrit

Area sq km	181	**Currency** US dollar
Area sq miles	70	**Languages** English,
Population	55 000	Marshallese

MADAGASCAR
Republic of Madagascar
Capital Antananarivo

Area sq km	587 041	**Currency** Malagasy franc
Area sq miles	226 658	Malagasy ariary
Population	21 315 000	**Languages** Malagasy, French

MAURITANIA
Islamic Arab and African Rep. of Mauritania
Capital Nouakchott

Area sq km	1 030 700	**Currency** Ouguiya
Area sq miles	397 955	**Languages** Arabic, French,
Population	3 542 000	local lang.

MALAWI
Republic of Malawi
Capital Lilongwe

Area sq km	118 484	**Currency** Malawian kwacha
Area sq miles	45 747	**Languages** Chichewa,
Population	15 381 000	English, local lang.

MAURITIUS
Republic of Mauritius
Capital Port Louis

Area sq km	2 040	**Currency** Mauritius rupee
Area sq miles	788	**Languages** English, creole,
Population	1 307 000	Hindi, Bhojpuri,
		French

MALAYSIA
Federation of Malaysia
Capital Kuala Lumpur/Putrajaya

Area sq km	332 965	**Currency** Ringgit
Area sq miles	128 559	**Languages** Malay, English,
Population	28 859 000	Chinese, Tamil,
		local lang.

MEXICO
United Mexican States
Capital Mexico City

Area sq km	1 972 545	**Currency** Mexican peso
Area sq miles	761 604	**Languages** Spanish,
Population	114 793 000	Amerindian lang.

MALDIVES
Republic of the Maldives
Capital Male

Area sq km	298	**Currency** Rufiyaa
Area sq miles	115	**Languages** Divehi
Population	320 000	(Maldivian)

MICRONESIA, FEDERATED STATES OF
Capital Palikir

Area sq km	701	**Currency** US dollar
Area sq miles	271	**Languages** English, Chuukese,
Population	112 000	Pohnpeian,
		local lang.

MOLDOVA
Republic of Moldova
Capital Chișinău (Kishinev)

Area sq km	33 700	**Currency**	Moldovan leu
Area sq miles	13 012	**Languages**	Romanian,
Population	3 545 000		Ukrainian,
			Gagauz, Russian

MONACO
Principality of Monaco
Capital Monaco-Ville

Area sq km	2	**Currency**	Euro
Area sq miles	1	**Languages**	French,
Population	35 000		Monégasque,
			Italian

MONGOLIA
Capital Ulan Bator (Ulaanbaatar)

Area sq km	1 565 000	**Currency**	Tugrik (tögrög)
Area sq miles	604 250	**Languages**	Khalka
Population	2 800 000		(Mongolian),
			Kazakh,
			local lang.

MONTENEGRO
Republic of Montenegro
Capital Podgorica

Area sq km	13 812	**Currency**	Euro
Area sq miles	5 333	**Languages**	Serbian
Population	632 000		(Montenegrin),
			Albanian

MOROCCO
Kingdom of Morocco
Capital Rabat

Area sq km	446 550	**Currency**	Moroccan dirham
Area sq miles	172 414	**Languages**	Arabic, Berber,
Population	32 273 000		French

MOZAMBIQUE
Republic of Mozambique
Capital Maputo

Area sq km	799 380	**Currency**	Metical
Area sq miles	308 642	**Languages**	Portuguese,
Population	23 930 000		Makua, Tsonga,
			local lang.

MYANMAR (Burma)
Republic of the Union of Myanmar
Capital Nay Pyi Taw/Rangoon (Yangôn)

Area sq km	676 577	**Currency**	Kyat
Area sq miles	261 228	**Languages**	Burmese, Shan,
Population	48 337 000		Karen, local lang.

NAMIBIA
Republic of Namibia
Capital Windhoek

Area sq km	824 292	**Currency**	Namibian dollar
Area sq miles	318 261	**Languages**	English, Afrikaans,
Population	2 324 000		German, Ovambo,
			local lang.

NAURU
Republic of Nauru
Capital Yaren

Area sq km	21	**Currency**	Australian dollar
Area sq miles	8	**Languages**	Nauruan, English
Population	10 000		

NEPAL
Federal Democratic Republic of Nepal
Capital Kathmandu

Area sq km	147 181	**Currency**	Nepalese rupee
Area sq miles	56 827	**Languages**	Nepali, Maithili,
Population	30 486 000		Bhojpuri, English,
			local lang.

NETHERLANDS
Kingdom of the Netherlands
Capital Amsterdam/The Hague ('s-Gravenhage)

Area sq km	41 526	**Currency**	Euro
Area sq miles	16 033	**Languages**	Dutch, Frisian
Population	16 665 000		

NEW ZEALAND
Capital Wellington

Area sq km	270 534	**Currency**	New Zealand
Area sq miles	104 454		dollar
Population	4 415 000	**Languages**	English, Maori

NICARAGUA
Republic of Nicaragua
Capital Managua

Area sq km	130 000	**Currency**	Córdoba
Area sq miles	50 193	**Languages**	Spanish,
Population	5 870 000		Amerindian lang.

NIGER
Republic of Niger
Capital Niamey

Area sq km	1 267 000	**Currency**	CFA franc*
Area sq miles	489 191	**Languages**	French, Hausa,
Population	16 069 000		Fulani, local lang.

NIGERIA
Federal Republic of Nigeria
Capital Abuja

Area sq km	923 768	**Currency**	Naira
Area sq miles	356 669	**Languages**	English, Hausa,
Population	162 471 000		Yoruba, Ibo,
			Fulani, local lang.

PAPUA NEW GUINEA
Independent State of Papua New Guinea
Capital Port Moresby

Area sq km	462 840	**Currency**	Kina
Area sq miles	178 704	**Languages**	English,
Population	7 014 000		Tok Pisin (creole),
			local lang.

NORTH KOREA
Democratic People's Republic of Korea
Capital P'yŏngyang

Area sq km	120 538	**Currency**	North Korean won
Area sq miles	46 540	**Languages**	Korean
Population	24 451 000		

PARAGUAY
Republic of Paraguay
Capital Asunción

Area sq km	406 752	**Currency**	Guaraní
Area sq miles	157 048	**Languages**	Spanish, Guaraní
Population	6 568 000		

NORWAY
Kingdom of Norway
Capital Oslo

Area sq km	323 878	**Currency**	Norwegian krone
Area sq miles	125 050	**Languages**	Norwegian
Population	4 925 000		

PERU
Republic of Peru
Capital Lima

Area sq km	1 285 216	**Currency**	Nuevo sol
Area sq miles	496 225	**Languages**	Spanish, Quechua,
Population	29 400 000		Aymara

OMAN
Sultanate of Oman
Capital Muscat (Masqaṭ)

Area sq km	309 500	**Currency**	Omani riyal
Area sq miles	119 499	**Languages**	Arabic, Baluchi,
Population	2 846 000		Indian lang.

PHILIPPINES
Republic of the Philippines
Capital Manila

Area sq km	300 000	**Currency**	Philippine peso
Area sq miles	115 831	**Languages**	English, Filipino,
Population	94 852 000		Tagalog, Cebuano,
			local lang.

PAKISTAN
Islamic Republic of Pakistan
Capital Islamabad

Area sq km	803 940	**Currency**	Pakistani rupee
Area sq miles	310 403	**Languages**	Urdu, Punjabi,
Population	176 745 000		Sindhi, Pushtu,
			English

POLAND
Polish Republic
Capital Warsaw (Warszawa)

Area sq km	312 683	**Currency**	Złoty
Area sq miles	120 728	**Languages**	Polish, German
Population	38 299 000		

PALAU
Republic of Palau
Capital Melekeok

Area sq km	497	**Currency**	US dollar
Area sq miles	192	**Languages**	Palauan, English
Population	21 000		

PORTUGAL
Portuguese Republic
Capital Lisbon (Lisboa)

Area sq km	88 940	**Currency**	Euro
Area sq miles	34 340	**Languages**	Portuguese
Population	10 690 000		

PANAMA
Republic of Panama
Capital Panama City

Area sq km	77 082	**Currency**	Balboa
Area sq miles	29 762	**Languages**	Spanish, English,
Population	3 571 000		Amerindian lang.

QATAR
State of Qatar
Capital Doha (Ad Dawḥah)

Area sq km	11 437	**Currency**	Qatari riyal
Area sq miles	4 416	**Languages**	Arabic
Population	1 870 000		

ROMANIA
Capital Bucharest (Bucureşti)

Area sq km	237 500	Currency	Romanian leu
Area sq miles	91 699	Languages	Romanian,
Population	21 436 000		Hungarian

RUSSIAN FEDERATION
Capital Moscow (Moskva)

Area sq km	17 075 400	Currency	Russian rouble
Area sq miles	6 592 849	Languages	Russian, Tatar,
Population	142 836 000		Ukrainian,
			local lang.

RWANDA
Republic of Rwanda
Capital Kigali

Area sq km	26 338	Currency	Rwandan franc
Area sq miles	10 169	Languages	Kinyarwanda,
Population	10 943 000		French, English

ST KITTS AND NEVIS
Federation of St Kitts and Nevis
Capital Basseterre

Area sq km	261	Currency	East Caribbean
Area sq miles	101		dollar
Population	53 000	Languages	English, creole

ST LUCIA
Capital Castries

Area sq km	616	Currency	East Caribbean
Area sq miles	238		dollar
Population	176 000	Languages	English, creole

ST VINCENT AND THE GRENADINES
Capital Kingstown

Area sq km	389	Currency	East Caribbean
Area sq miles	150		dollar
Population	109 000	Languages	English, creole

SAMOA
Independent State of Samoa
Capital Apia

Area sq km	2 831	Currency	Tala
Area sq miles	1 093	Languages	Samoan, English
Population	184 000		

SAN MARINO
Republic of San Marino
Capital San Marino

Area sq km	61	Currency	Euro
Area sq miles	24	Languages	Italian
Population	32 000		

SÃO TOMÉ AND PRÍNCIPE
Democratic Rep. of São Tomé and Príncipe
Capital São Tomé

Area sq km	964	Currency	Dobra
Area sq miles	372	Languages	Portuguese, creole
Population	169 000		

SAUDI ARABIA
Kingdom of Saudi Arabia
Capital Riyadh (Ar Riyāḍ)

Area sq km	2 200 000	Currency	Saudi Arabian
Area sq miles	849 425		riyal
Population	28 083 000	Languages	Arabic

SENEGAL
Republic of Senegal
Capital Dakar

Area sq km	196 720	Currency	CFA franc*
Area sq miles	75 954	Languages	French, Wolof,
Population	12 768 000		Fulani, local lang.

SERBIA
Republic of Serbia
Capital Belgrade (Beograd)

Area sq km	77 453	Currency	Serbian dinar,
Area sq miles	29 904	Languages	Serbian,
Population	7 306 677		Hungarian

SEYCHELLES
Republic of Seychelles
Capital Victoria

Area sq km	455	Currency	Seychelles rupee
Area sq miles	176	Languages	English, French,
Population	87 000		creole

SIERRA LEONE
Republic of Sierra Leone
Capital Freetown

Area sq km	71 740	Currency	Leone
Area sq miles	27 699	Languages	English, creole,
Population	5 997 000		Mende, Temne,
			local lang.

SINGAPORE
Republic of Singapore
Capital Singapore

Area sq km	639	Currency	Singapore dollar
Area sq miles	247	Languages	Chinese, English,
Population	5 188 000		Malay, Tamil

SLOVAKIA
Slovak Republic
Capital Bratislava

Area sq km	49 035	**Currency**	Euro
Area sq miles	18 933	**Languages**	Slovak,
Population	5 472 000		Hungarian, Czech

SLOVENIA
Republic of Slovenia
Capital Ljubljana

Area sq km	20 251	**Currency**	Euro
Area sq miles	7 819	**Languages**	Slovene, Croatian,
Population	2 035 000		Serbian

SOLOMON ISLANDS
Capital Honiara

Area sq km	28 370	**Currency**	Solomon Islands
Area sq miles	10 954		dollar
Population	552 000	**Languages**	English, creole,
			local lang.

SOMALIA
Somali Republic
Capital Mogadishu (Muqdisho)

Area sq km	637 657	**Currency**	Somali shilling
Area sq miles	246 201	**Languages**	Somali, Arabic
Population	9 557 000		

SOUTH AFRICA, REPUBLIC OF
Capital Pretoria (Tshwane)/Cape Town

Area sq km	1 219 090	**Currency**	Rand
Area sq miles	470 693	**Languages**	Afrikaans,
Population	50 460 000		English, nine
			official local lang.

SOUTH KOREA
Republic of Korea
Capital Seoul (Sŏul)

Area sq km	99 274	**Currency**	South Korean
Area sq miles	38 330		won
Population	48 391 000	**Languages**	Korean

SOUTH SUDAN
Republic of South Sudan
Capital Juba

Area sq km	644 329	**Currency**	South Sudan
Area sq miles	248 775		pound
Population	8 260 490	**Languages**	English, Arabic,
			Dinka, Nuer,
			local lang.

SPAIN
Kingdom of Spain
Capital Madrid

Area sq km	504 782	**Currency**	Euro
Area sq miles	194 897	**Languages**	Spanish, Castilian,
Population	46 455 000		Catalan, Galician,
			Basque

SRI LANKA
Democratic Socialist Republic of Sri Lanka
Capital Sri Jayewardenepura Kotte

Area sq km	65 610	**Currency**	Sri Lankan rupee
Area sq miles	25 332	**Languages**	Sinhalese,
Population	21 045 000		Tamil, English

SUDAN
Republic of the Sudan
Capital Khartoum

Area sq km	1 861 484	**Currency**	Sudanese pound
Area sq miles	718 725		(Sudani)
Population	36 371 510	**Languages**	Arabic, Dinka,
			Nubian, Beja,
			Nuer, local lang.

SURINAME
Republic of Suriname
Capital Paramaribo

Area sq km	163 820	**Currency**	Suriname guilder
Area sq miles	63 251	**Languages**	Dutch,
Population	529 000		Surinamese,
			English, Hindi

SWAZILAND
Kingdom of Swaziland
Capital Mbabane

Area sq km	17 364	**Currency**	Emalangeni,
Area sq miles	6 704		South African
Population	1 203 000		rand
		Languages	Swazi, English

SWEDEN
Kingdom of Sweden
Capital Stockholm

Area sq km	449 964	**Currency**	Swedish krona
Area sq miles	173 732	**Languages**	Swedish
Population	9 441 000		

SWITZERLAND
Swiss Confederation
Capital Bern (Berne)

Area sq km	41 293	**Currency**	Swiss franc
Area sq miles	15 943	**Languages**	German, French,
Population	7 702 000		Italian, Romansch

SYRIA
Syrian Arab Republic
Capital Damascus (Dimashq)

Area sq km	185 180	**Currency** Syrian pound
Area sq miles	71 498	**Languages** Arabic, Kurdish,
Population	20 766 000	Armenian

TAIWAN
Republic of China
Capital Taibei

Area sq km	36 179	**Currency** Taiwan dollar
Area sq miles	13 969	**Languages** Mandarin, Min,
Population	23 164 000	Hakka, local lang.

The People's Republic of China claims Taiwan as its 23rd province.

TAJIKISTAN
Republic of Tajikistan
Capital Dushanbe

Area sq km	143 100	**Currency** Somoni
Area sq miles	55 251	**Languages** Tajik, Uzbek,
Population	6 977 000	Russian

TANZANIA
United Republic of Tanzania
Capital Dodoma

Area sq km	945 087	**Currency** Tanzanian shilling
Area sq miles	364 900	**Languages** Swahili, English,
Population	46 218 000	Nyamwezi,
		local lang.

THAILAND
Kingdom of Thailand
Capital Bangkok (Krung Thep)

Area sq km	513 115	**Currency** Baht
Area sq miles	198 115	**Languages** Thai, Lao,
Population	69 519 000	Chinese, Malay,
		Mon-Khmer lang.

TOGO
Republic of Togo
Capital Lomé

Area sq km	56 785	**Currency** CFA franc*
Area sq miles	21 925	**Languages** French, Ewe,
Population	6 155 000	Kabre, local lang.

TONGA
Kingdom of Tonga
Capital Nuku'alofa

Area sq km	748	**Currency** Pa'anga
Area sq miles	289	**Languages** Tongan, English
Population	105 000	

TRINIDAD AND TOBAGO
Republic of Trinidad and Tobago
Capital Port of Spain

Area sq km	5 130	**Currency** Trinidad and
Area sq miles	1 981	Tobago dollar
Population	1 346 000	**Languages** English, creole,
		Hindi

TUNISIA
Republic of Tunisia
Capital Tunis

Area sq km	164 150	**Currency** Tunisian dinar
Area sq miles	63 379	**Languages** Arabic, French
Population	10 594 000	

TURKEY
Republic of Turkey
Capital Ankara

Area sq km	779 452	**Currency** Lira
Area sq miles	300 948	**Languages** Turkish, Kurdish
Population	73 640 000	

TURKMENISTAN
Republic of Turkmenistan
Capital Asgabat (Ashkhabad)

Area sq km	488 100	**Currency** Turkmen manat
Area sq miles	188 456	**Languages** Turkmen, Uzbek,
Population	5 105 000	Russian

TUVALU
Capital Vaiaku

Area sq km	25	**Currency** Australian dollar
Area sq miles	10	**Languages** Tuvaluan, English
Population	10 000	

UGANDA
Republic of Uganda
Capital Kampala

Area sq km	241 038	**Currency** Ugandan shilling
Area sq miles	93 065	**Languages** English, Swahili,
Population	34 509 000	Luganda,
		local lang.

UKRAINE
Capital Kiev (Kyiv)

Area sq km	603 700	**Currency** Hryvnia
Area sq miles	233 090	**Languages** Ukrainian,
Population	45 190 000	Russian

UNITED ARAB EMIRATES
Federation of Emirates
Capital Abu Dhabi (Abū Ẓabī)

Area sq km	77 700	**Currency**	UAE dirham
Area sq miles	30 000	**Languages**	Arabic, English
Population	7 891 000		

UNITED KINGDOM
United Kingdom of Great Britain and
Northern Ireland
Capital London

Area sq km	243 609	**Currency**	Pound sterling
Area sq miles	94 058	**Languages**	English, Welsh,
Population	62 417 000		Gaelic

UNITED STATES OF AMERICA
Capital Washington D.C.

Area sq km	9 826 635	**Currency**	US dollar
Area sq miles	3 794 085	**Languages**	English, Spanish
Population	313 085 000		

URUGUAY
Oriental Republic of Uruguay
Capital Montevideo

Area sq km	176 215	**Currency**	Uruguayan peso
Area sq miles	68 037	**Languages**	Spanish
Population	3 380 000		

UZBEKISTAN
Republic of Uzbekistan
Capital Tashkent

Area sq km	447 400	**Currency**	Uzbek som
Area sq miles	172 742	**Languages**	Uzbek, Russian,
Population	27 760 000		Tajik, Kazakh

VANUATU
Republic of Vanuatu
Capital Port Vila

Area sq km	12 190	**Currency**	Vatu
Area sq miles	4 707	**Languages**	English,
Population	246 000		Bislama (creole),
			French

VATICAN CITY
Vatican City State or Holy See
Capital Vatican City

Area sq km	0.5	**Currency**	Euro
Area sq miles	0.2	**Languages**	Italian
Population	800		

VENEZUELA
Bolivarian Republic of Venezuela
Capital Caracas

Area sq km	912 050	**Currency**	Bolívar fuerte
Area sq miles	352 144	**Languages**	Spanish,
Population	29 437 000		Amerindian lang.

VIETNAM
Socialist Republic of Vietnam
Capital Ha Nôi (Hanoi)

Area sq km	329 565	**Currency**	Dong
Area sq miles	127 246	**Languages**	Vietnamese, Thai,
Population	88 792 000		Khmer, Chinese,
			local lang.

West Bank
Disputed territory

Area sq km	5 860	**Currency**	Jordanian dinar,
Area sq miles	2 263		Israeli shekel
Population	2 513 283	**Languages**	Arabic, Hebrew

Western Sahara
Disputed territory (Morocco)
Capital Laâyoune

Area sq km	266 000	**Currency**	Moroccan dirham
Area sq miles	102 703	**Languages**	Arabic
Population	548 000		

YEMEN
Republic of Yemen
Capital Şan'ā'

Area sq km	527 968	**Currency**	Yemeni riyal
Area sq miles	203 850	**Languages**	Arabic
Population	24 800 000		

ZAMBIA
Republic of Zambia
Capital Lusaka

Area sq km	752 614	**Currency**	Zambian kwacha
Area sq miles	290 586	**Languages**	English, Bemba,
Population	13 475 000		Nyanja, Tonga,
			local lang.

ZIMBABWE
Republic of Zimbabwe
Capital Harare

Area sq km	390 759	**Currency**	Zimbabwean
Area sq miles	150 873		dollar (suspended)
Population	12 754 000	**Languages**	English, Shona,
			Ndebele

Total Land Area 8 844 516 sq km / 3 414 868 sq miles
(includes New Guinea and Pacific Island nations)

HIGHEST MOUNTAIN
Puncak Jaya
5 030 m / 16 502 feet

Oceania cross section

Joseph
Bonaparte Gulf

Arnhem Land

Cape York
Peninsula

Gulf of
Carpentaria

Great Dividing
Range

Cook Strait

North Island

North Cape

Tasman Sea

Oceania cross section and perspective view

HIGHEST MOUNTAINS	metres	feet	Map page
Puncak Jaya, Indonesia	5 030	16 502	59 D3
Puncak Trikora, Indonesia	4 730	15 518	59 D3
Puncak Mandala, Indonesia	4 700	15 420	59 D3
Puncak Yamin, Indonesia	4 595	15 075	—
Mt Wilhelm, Papua New Guinea	4 509	14 793	59 D3
Mt Kubor, Papua New Guinea	4 359	14 301	—

LARGEST ISLAND
New Guinea
808 510 sq km /
312 166 sq miles

LARGEST ISLANDS	sq km	sq miles	Map page
New Guinea	808 510	312 166	59 D3
South Island, New Zealand	151 215	58 384	54 B2
North Island, New Zealand	115 777	44 701	54 B1
Tasmania	67 800	26 178	51 D4

LONGEST RIVERS	km	miles	Map page
Murray-Darling	3 672	2 282	52 B2
Darling	2 844	1 767	52 B2
Murray	2 375	1 476	52 B3
Murrumbidgee	1 485	923	52 B2
Lachlan	1 339	832	53 C2
Cooper Creek	1 113	692	52 B1

LARGEST LAKES	sq km	sq miles	Map page
Lake Eyre	0–8 900	0–3 436	52 A1
Lake Torrens	0–5 780	0–2 232	52 A1

LARGEST LAKE AND LOWEST POINT
Lake Eyre
0–8 900 sq km / 0–3 436 sq miles
16 m / 53 feet below sea level

LONGEST RIVER AND
LARGEST DRAINAGE BASIN
Murray-Darling
3 672 km / 2 282 miles
1 058 000 sq km / 409 000 sq miles

© Collins Bartholomew Ltd

Total Land Area 45 036 492 sq km / 17 388 589 sq miles

LARGEST DRAINAGE BASIN
Ob'-Irtysh
2 990 000 sq km /
1 154 000 sq miles

LARGEST LAKE
Caspian Sea
371 000 sq km /
143 243 sq miles

Asia cross section

LOWEST POINT
Dead Sea
423 m / 1 388 feet
below sea level

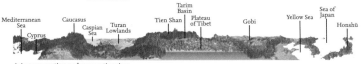

Mediterranean Sea | Caucasus | Caspian Sea | Turan Lowlands | Tien Shan | Tarim Basin | Plateau of Tibet | Gobi | Yellow Sea | Sea of Japan | Honshū
Cyprus

Asia cross section and perspective view

HIGHEST MOUNTAINS	metres	feet	Map page
Mt Everest (Sagarmatha/ Qomolangma Feng), China/Nepal	8 848	29 028	75 C2
K2 (Qogir Feng), China/Pakistan	8 611	28 251	74 B1
Kangchenjunga, India/Nepal	8 586	28 169	75 C2
Lhotse, China/Nepal	8 516	27 939	—
Makalu, China/Nepal	8 463	27 765	—
Cho Oyu, China/Nepal	8 201	26 906	—

LARGEST ISLANDS	sq km	sq miles	Map page
Borneo	745 561	287 861	61 C1
Sumatra (Sumatera)	473 606	182 859	60 A1
Honshū	227 414	87 805	67 B3
Celebes (Sulawesi)	189 216	73 056	58 C3
Java (Jawa)	132 188	51 038	61 B2
Luzon	104 690	40 421	64 B1

LONGEST RIVERS	km	miles	Map page
Yangtze (Chang Jiang)	6 380	3 965	70 C2
Ob'-Irtysh	5 568	3 460	86 F2
Yenisey-Angara-Selenga	5 550	3 449	83 H3
Yellow (Huang He)	5 464	3 395	70 B2
Irtysh	4 440	2 759	86 F2
Mekong	4 425	2 750	63 B2

LARGEST LAKES	sq km	sq miles	Map page
Caspian Sea	371 000	143 243	81 C1
Lake Baikal (Ozero Baykal)	30 500	11 776	69 D1
Lake Balkhash (Ozero Balkash)	17 400	6 718	77 D2
Aral Sea (Aral'skoye More)	17 158	6 625	76 B2
Ysyk-Köl	6 200	2 394	77 D2

LONGEST RIVER
Yangtze (Chang Jiang)
6 380 km /
3 965 miles

HIGHEST MOUNTAIN
Mt Everest
8 848 m / 29 028 feet

LARGEST ISLAND
Borneo
745 561 sq km /
287 861 sq miles

Total Land Area 9 908 599 sq km / 3 825 710 sq miles

LARGEST ISLAND
Great Britain
218 476 sq km /
84 354 sq miles

Europe cross section

HIGHEST MOUNTAIN
El'brus
5 642 m / 18 510 feet

Cordillera Cantabrica | Land's End | Bay of Biscay | Pyrenees | Massif Central | Alps | Adriatic Sea | Carpathian Mountains | Black Sea | Crimea | Sea of Azov | Caucasus

Europe cross section and perspective view

HIGHEST MOUNTAINS	metres	feet	Map pages
El'brus, Russian Federation	5 642	18 510	87 D4
Gora Dykh-Tau, Russian Federation	5 204	17 073	—
Shkhara, Georgia/Russian Federation	5 201	17 063	—
Kazbek, Georgia/Russian Federation	5 047	16 558	76 A2
Mont Blanc, France/Italy	4 810	15 781	105 D2
Dufourspitze, Italy/Switzerland	4 634	15 203	—

LARGEST ISLANDS	sq km	sq miles	Map pages
Great Britain	218 476	84 354	95 C3
Iceland	102 820	39 699	92 A3
Ireland	83 045	32 064	97 C2
Ostrov Severnyy (part of Novaya Zemlya)	47 079	18 177	86 F1
Spitsbergen	37 814	14 600	82 C1

LONGEST RIVER AND
LARGEST DRAINAGE BASIN
Volga
3 688 km / 2 292 miles
1 380 000 sq km / 533 000 sq miles

LONGEST RIVERS	km	miles	Map pages
Volga	3 688	2 292	89 F2
Danube	2 850	1 771	110 A1
Dnieper	2 285	1 420	91 C2
Kama	2 028	1 260	86 E3
Don	1 931	1 200	89 E3
Pechora	1 802	1 120	86 F2

LARGEST LAKE AND LOWEST POINT
Caspian Sea
371 000 sq km / 143 243 sq miles
28m / 92 feet below sea level

LARGEST LAKES	sq km	sq miles	Map pages
Caspian Sea	371 000	143 243	81 C1
Lake Ladoga (Ladozhskoye Ozero)	18 390	7 100	86 C2
Lake Onega (Onezhskoye Ozero)	9 600	3 707	86 C2
Vänern	5 585	2 156	93 F4
Rybinskoye Vodokhranilishche	5 180	2 000	89 E3

Total Land Area 30 343 578 sq km / 11 715 655 sq miles

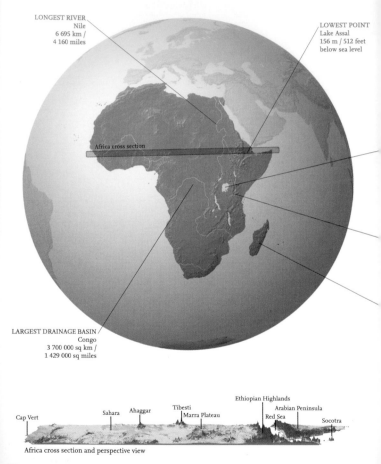

LONGEST RIVER
Nile
6 695 km /
4 160 miles

LOWEST POINT
Lake Assal
156 m / 512 feet
below sea level

Africa cross section

LARGEST DRAINAGE BASIN
Congo
3 700 000 sq km /
1 429 000 sq miles

Cap Vert   Sahara   Ahaggar   Tibesti   Marra Plateau   Ethiopian Highlands   Arabian Peninsula   Red Sea   Socotra

Africa cross section and perspective view

HIGHEST MOUNTAINS	metres	feet	Map page
Kilimanjaro, Tanzania	5 892	19 330	119 D3
Mt Kenya (Kirinyaga), Kenya	5 199	17 057	119 D3
Margherita Peak, Democratic Republic of the Congo/Uganda	5 110	16 765	119 C2
Meru, Tanzania	4 565	14 977	119 D3
Ras Dejen, Ethiopia	4 533	14 872	11/ B3
Mt Karisimbi, Rwanda	4 510	14 796	—

LARGEST ISLANDS	sq km	sq miles	Map page
Madagascar	587 040	226 656	121 D3

LARGEST LAKE
Lake Victoria
68 870 sq km /
26 591 sq miles

LONGEST RIVERS	km	miles	Map page
Nile	6 695	4 160	116 B1
Congo	4 667	2 900	118 B3
Niger	4 184	2 600	115 C4
Zambezi	2 736	1 700	120 C2
Webi Shabeelle	2 490	1 547	117 C4
Ubangi	2 250	1 398	118 B3

HIGHEST MOUNTAIN
Kilimanjaro
5 892 m / 19 330 feet

LARGEST LAKES	sq km	sq miles	Map page
Lake Victoria	68 870	26 591	52 B2
Lake Tanganyika	32 600	12 587	119 C3
Lake Nyasa (Lake Malawi)	29 500	11 390	121 C1
Lake Volta	8 482	3 275	114 C4
Lake Turkana	6 500	2 510	119 D2
Lake Albert	5 600	2 162	119 D2

LARGEST ISLAND
Madagascar
587 040 sq km /
226 656 sq miles

Total Land Area 24 680 331 sq km / 9 529 076 sq miles
(including Hawaiian Islands)

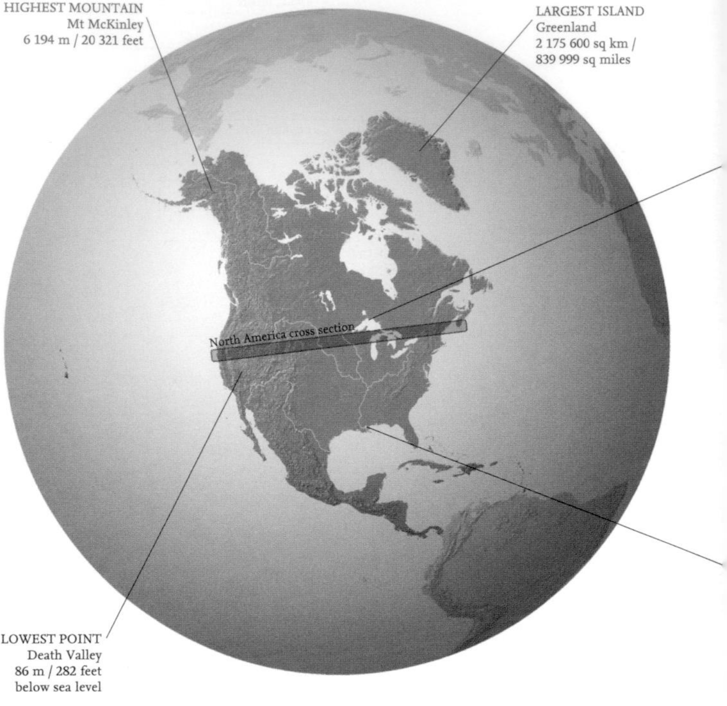

HIGHEST MOUNTAIN
Mt McKinley
6 194 m / 20 321 feet

LARGEST ISLAND
Greenland
2 175 600 sq km /
839 999 sq miles

North America cross section

LOWEST POINT
Death Valley
86 m / 282 feet
below sea level

Coast Ranges

Rocky Mountains

Great Plains

Lake Michigan

Lake Huron

Lake Erie

Chesapeake
Bay

Appalachian
Mountains

Long
Island

Cape
Cod

Nova
Scotia

North America cross section and perspective view

HIGHEST MOUNTAINS	metres	feet	Map page
Mt McKinley, USA	6 194	20 321	124 F2
Mt Logan, Canada	5 959	19 550	126 B2
Pico de Orizaba, Mexico	5 610	18 405	145 C3
Mt St Elias, USA	5 489	18 008	126 B2
Volcán Popocatépetl, Mexico	5 452	17 887	145 C3
Mt Foraker, USA	5 303	17 398	—

LARGEST LAKE
Lake Superior
82 100 sq km /
31 699 sq miles

LARGEST ISLANDS	sq km	sq miles	Map page
Greenland	2 175 600	839 999	127 I2
Baffin Island	507 451	195 927	127 G2
Victoria Island	217 291	83 896	126 D2
Ellesmere Island	196 236	75 767	127 F1
Cuba	110 860	42 803	146 B2
Newfoundland	108 860	42 031	131 E2
Hispaniola	76 192	29 418	147 C2

LONGEST RIVERS	km	miles	Map page
Mississippi-Missouri	5 969	3 709	133 D3
Mackenzie-Peace-Finlay	4 241	2 635	126 C2
Missouri	4 086	2 539	137 E3
Mississippi	3 765	2 340	142 C3
Yukon	3 185	1 979	126 A2
St Lawrence	3 058	1 900	131 D2

LONGEST RIVER AND
LARGEST DRAINAGE BASIN
Mississippi-Missouri
5 969 km / 3 709 miles
3 250 000 sq km / 1 255 000
sq miles

LARGEST LAKES	sq km	sq miles	Map page
Lake Superior	82 100	31 699	140 B1
Lake Huron	59 600	23 012	140 C2
Lake Michigan	57 800	22 317	140 B2
Great Bear Lake	31 328	12 096	126 C2
Great Slave Lake	28 568	11 030	129 C1
Lake Erie	25 700	9 923	140 C2
Lake Winnipeg	24 387	9 416	129 E2
Lake Ontario	18 960	7 320	141 D2

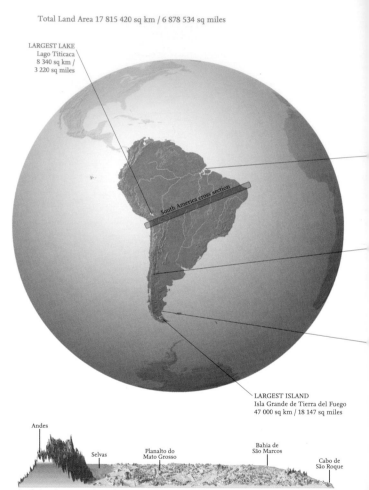

Total Land Area 17 815 420 sq km / 6 878 534 sq miles

LARGEST LAKE
Lago Titicaca
8 340 sq km /
3 220 sq miles

South America cross section

LARGEST ISLAND
Isla Grande de Tierra del Fuego
47 000 sq km / 18 147 sq miles

Andes

Selvas

Planalto do
Mato Grosso

Bahia de
São Marcos

Cabo de
São Roque

South America cross section and perspective view

HIGHEST MOUNTAINS	metres	feet	Map page
Cerro Aconcagua, Argentina	6 959	22 831	153 B4
Nevado Ojos del Salado, Argentina/Chile	6 908	22 664	152 B3
Cerro Bonete, Argentina	6 872	22 546	—
Cerro Pissis, Argentina	6 858	22 500	—
Cerro Tupungato, Argentina/Chile	6 800	22 309	—
Cerro Mercedario, Argentina	6 770	22 211	—

LARGEST ISLANDS	sq km	sq miles	Map page
Isla Grande de Tierra del Fuego	47 000	18 147	153 B6
Isla de Chiloé	8 394	3 241	153 A5
East Falkland	6 760	2 610	153 C6
West Falkland	5 413	2 090	153 B6

LONGEST RIVER AND
LARGEST DRAINAGE BASIN
Amazon
8 516 km / 4 049 miles
7 050 000 sq km / 2 722 000 sq miles

LONGEST RIVERS	km	miles	Map page
Amazon (Amazonas)	6 516	4 049	150 C1
Río de la Plata-Paraná	4 500	2 796	153 C4
Purus	3 218	2 000	150 B2
Madeira	3 200	1 988	150 C2
São Francisco	2 900	1 802	151 E3
Tocantins	2 750	1 709	151 D2

HIGHEST MOUNTAIN
Cerro Aconcagua
6 959 m / 22 831 feet

LARGEST LAKES	sq km	sq miles	Map page
Lake Titicaca	8 340	3 220	152 B2

LOWEST POINT
Laguna del Carbón
105 m / 345 feet below sea level

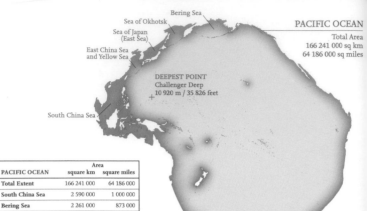

Bering Sea

Sea of Okhotsk

Sea of Japan
(East Sea)

East China Sea
and Yellow Sea

DEEPEST POINT
Challenger Deep
10 920 m / 35 826 feet

South China Sea

	Area	
PACIFIC OCEAN	square km	square miles
Total Extent	166 241 000	64 186 000
South China Sea	2 590 000	1 000 000
Bering Sea	2 261 000	873 000
Sea of Okhotsk	1 392 000	538 000
Sea of Japan (East Sea)	1 013 000	391 000
East China Sea and Yellow Sea	1 202 000	464 000

ANTARCTICA

Total Land Area 12 093 000 sq km /
4 669 107 sq miles (excluding ice shelves)

HIGHEST MOUNTAIN
Vinson Massif
4 897 m / 16 066 feet

HIGHEST MOUNTAINS	Height	
	metres	feet
Vinson Massif	4 897	16 066
Mt Tyree	4 852	15 918
Mt Kirkpatrick	4 528	14 855
Mt Markham	4 351	14 275
Mt Jackson	4 190	13 747
Mt Sidley	4 181	13 717

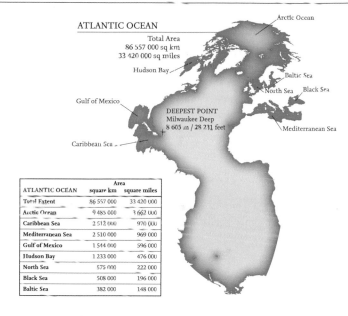

ATLANTIC OCEAN

Total Area
86 557 000 sq km
33 420 000 sq miles

Arctic Ocean

Hudson Bay

Baltic Sea

North Sea   Black Sea

Gulf of Mexico

DEEPEST POINT
Milwaukee Deep
8 605 m / 28 231 feet

Mediterranean Sea

Caribbean Sea

ATLANTIC OCEAN	Area square km	square miles
Total Extent	86 557 000	33 420 000
Arctic Ocean	9 485 000	3 662 000
Caribbean Sea	2 512 000	970 000
Mediterranean Sea	2 510 000	969 000
Gulf of Mexico	1 544 000	596 000
Hudson Bay	1 233 000	476 000
North Sea	575 000	222 000
Black Sea	508 000	196 000
Baltic Sea	382 000	148 000

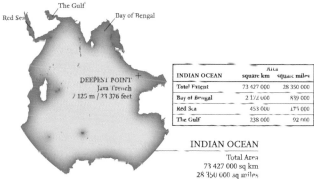

The Gulf

Red Sea

Bay of Bengal

DEEPEST POINT
Java Trench
7 125 m / 23 376 feet

INDIAN OCEAN	Area square km	square miles
Total Extent	73 427 000	28 350 000
Bay of Bengal	2 172 000	839 000
Red Sea	453 000	175 000
The Gulf	238 000	92 000

INDIAN OCEAN

Total Area
73 427 000 sq km
28 350 000 sq miles

MAJOR CLIMATIC REGIONS AND SUB-TYPES

Köppen classification system
Winkel Tripel Projection
scale 1:200 000 000

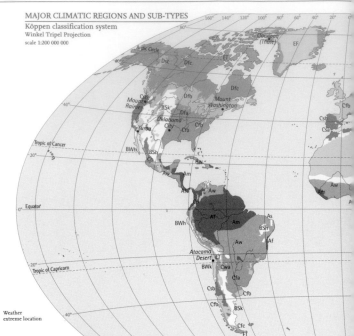

• Weather
  extreme location

WORLD WEATHER EXTREMES

	Location
Highest shade temperature	57.8°C / 136°F Al 'Azīzīyah, Libya (13 September 1922)
Hottest place – Annual mean	34.4°C / 93.9°F Dalol, Ethiopia
Driest place – Annual mean	0.1 mm / 0.004 inches Atacama Desert, Chile
Most sunshine – Annual mean	90% Yuma, Arizona, USA (over 4 000 hours)
Least sunshine	Nil for 182 days each year, South Pole
Lowest screen temperature	-89.2°C / -128.6°F Vostok Station, Antarctica (21 July 1983)
Coldest place – Annual mean	-56.6°C / -69.9°F Plateau Station, Antarctica
Wettest place – Annual mean	11 873 mm / 467.4 inches Meghalaya, India
Highest surface wind speed	
- High altitude	372 km per hour/231 miles per hour Mount Washington, New Hampshire, USA (12 April 1934)
- Low altitude	333 km per hour/207 miles per hour Qaanaaq (Thule), Greenland (8 March 1972)
- Tornado	512 km per hour / 318 miles per hour in a tornado, Oklahoma City, Oklahoma, USA (3 May 1999)
Greatest snowfall	31 102 mm / 1 224.5 inches Mount Rainier, Washington, USA (19 February 1971 – 18 February 1972)

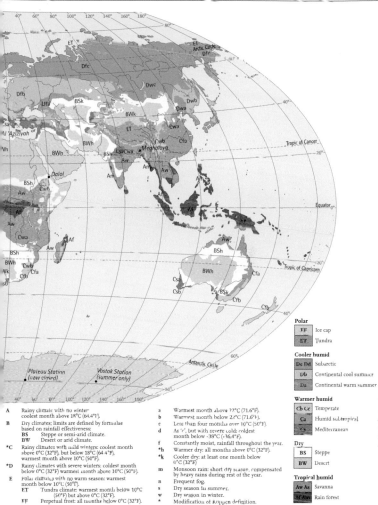

A   Rainy climate with no winter: coolest month above 18°C (64.4°F).

B   Dry climates; limits are defined by formulae based on rainfall effectiveness:
- **BS**   Steppe or semi-arid climate.
- **BW**   Desert or arid climate.

*C   Rainy climates with mild winters: coolest month above 0°C (32°F), but below 18°C (64.4°F), warmest month above 10°C (50°F).

*D   Rainy climates with severe winters: coolest month below 0°C (32°F), warmest month above 10°C (50°F).

E   Polar climates with no warm season: warmest month below 10°C (50°F).
- **ET**   Tundra climate: warmest month below 10°C (50°F) but above 0°C (32°F).
- **EF**   Perpetual frost: all months below 0°C (32°F).

a   Warmest month above 22°C (71.6°F).

b   Warmest month below 22°C (71.6°F).

c   Less than four months over 10°C (50°F).

d   As 'c', but with severe cold: coldest month below -38°C (-36.4°F).

f   Constantly moist, rainfall throughout the year.

*h   Warmer dry: all months above 0°C (32°F).

*k   Cooler dry: at least one month below 0°C (32°F).

m   Monsoon rain: short dry season, compensated by heavy rains during rest of the year.

n   Frequent fog.

s   Dry season in summer.

w   Dry season in winter.

*   Modification of Köppen definition.

Polar
- EF   Ice cap
- ET   Tundra

Cooler humid
- Dc Dd   Subarctic
- Db   Continental cool summer
- Da   Continental warm summer

Warmer humid
- Cb Cc   Temperate
- Ca   Humid subtropical
- Cs   Mediterranean

Dry
- BS   Steppe
- BW   Desert

Tropical humid
- Aw As   Savanna
- Af Am   Rain forest

© Collins Bartholomew Ltd

WORLD LAND COVER

© ESA 2010 and UCLouvain

Winkel Tripel Projection
scale: 1:190 000 000

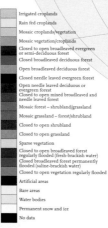

Irrigated croplands
Rain fed croplands
Mosaic croplands/vegetation
Mosaic vegetation/croplands
Closed to open broadleaved evergreen or semi-deciduous forest
Closed broadleaved deciduous forest
Open broadleaved deciduous forest
Closed needle leaved evergreen forest
Open needle leaved deciduous or evergreen forest
Closed to open mixed broadleaved and needle leaved forest
Mosaic forest – shrubland/grassland
Mosaic grassland – forest/shrubland
Closed to open shrubland
Closed to open grassland
Sparse vegetation
Closed to open broadleaved forest regularly flooded (fresh-brackish water)
Closed broadleaved forest permanently flooded (saline-brackish water)
Closed to open vegetation regularly flooded
Artificial areas
Bare areas
Water bodies
Permanent snow and ice
No data

CONTINENTAL LAND COVER COMPOSITION

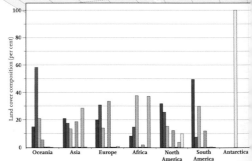

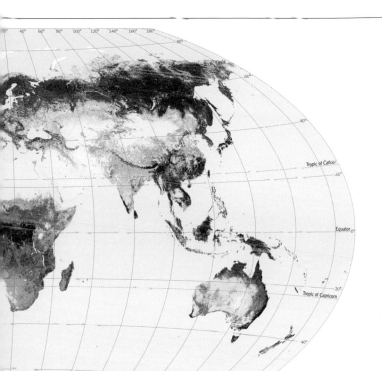

LAND COVER GRAPHS – CLASSIFICATION

Class description	Map classes
Forest/Woodland	Evergreen needleleaf forest
	Evergreen broadleaf forest
	Deciduous needleleaf forest
	Deciduous broadleaf forest
	Mixed forest
Shrubland	Closed shrublands
	Open shrublands
Grass/Savanna	Woody savannas
	Savannas
	Grasslands
Wetland	Permanent wetlands
Crops/Mosaic	Croplands
	Cropland/Natural vegetation mosaic
Urban	Urban and built-up
Snow/Ice	Snow and Ice
Barren	Barren or sparsely vegetated

GLOBAL LAND COVER COMPOSITION

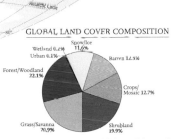

Wetland 0.2%
Urban 0.1%
Snow/Ice 11.6%
Barren 12.3%
Forest/Woodland 22.1%
Crops/Mosaic 12.7%
Grass/Savanna 20.9%
Shrubland 19.9%

© Collins Bartholomew Ltd

WORLD POPULATION DISTRIBUTION
Population Density
Winkel Tripel Projection
scale 1:190 000 000

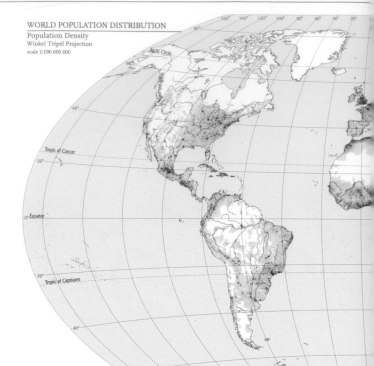

KEY POPULATION STATISTICS FOR MAJOR REGIONS

	Population 2011 (millions)	Growth (per cent)	Infant mortality rate	Total fertility rate	Life expectancy (years)
World	6 974	1.1	42	2.45	69
More developed regions[1]	1 240	0.3	6	1.7	78
Less developed regions[2]	5 774	1.3	46	2.6	67
Africa	1 046	2.3	71	4.4	55
Asia	4 207	1.0	37	2.2	70
Europe[3]	739	0.1	6	1.6	77
Latin America and the Caribbean[4]	597	1.1	19	2.2	75
North America	348	0.9	6	2.0	79
Oceania	37	1.5	19	2.5	78

1. Europe, North America, Australia, New Zealand and Japan.

2. Africa, Asia (excluding Japan), Latin America and the Caribbean, and Oceania (excluding Australia and New Zealand).

3. Includes Russian Federation.

4. South America, Central America (including Mexico) and all Caribbean Islands.

Except for population (2011) the data are annual averages projected for the period 2010–2015.

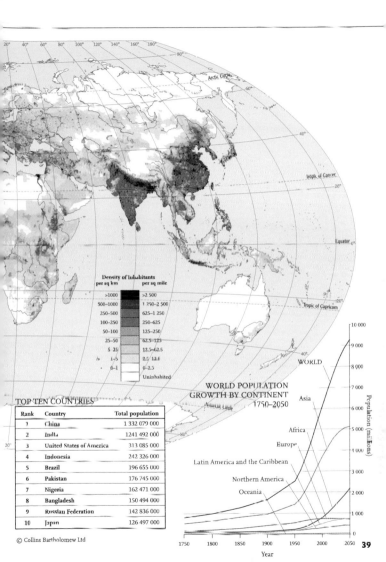

Density of inhabitants

per sq km	per sq mile
>1000	>2 500
500–1000	1 250–2 500
250–500	625–1 250
100–250	250–625
50–100	125–250
25–50	62.5–125
5–25	12.5–62.5
1–5	2.5–12.5
0–1	0–2.5
Uninhabited	

TOP TEN COUNTRIES

Rank	Country	Total population
1	China	1 332 079 000
2	India	1 241 492 000
3	United States of America	313 085 000
4	Indonesia	242 326 000
5	Brazil	196 655 000
6	Pakistan	176 745 000
7	Nigeria	162 471 000
8	Bangladesh	150 494 000
9	Russian Federation	142 836 000
10	Japan	126 497 000

© Collins Bartholomew Ltd

WORLD POPULATION GROWTH BY CONTINENT 1750–2050

WORLD
Asia
Africa
Europe
Latin America and the Caribbean
Northern America
Oceania

Population (millions)

Year

39

THE WORLD'S MAJOR CITIES

Urban agglomerations with over
1 million inhabitants.
Winkel Tripel Projection
scale 1:190 000 000

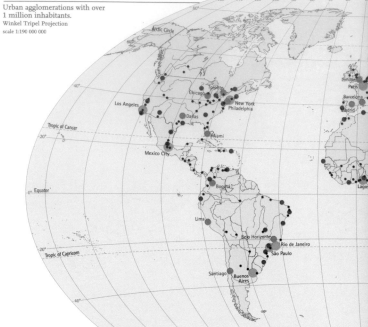

LEVEL OF URBANIZATION BY MAJOR REGION 1970–2030

Urban population as a percentage of total population

	1970	2010	2030
World	36.1	50.5	59.0
More developed regions[1]	64.7	75.2	80.9
Less developed regions[2]	25.3	45.1	55.0
Africa	23.6	40.0	49.9
Asia	22.7	42.2	52.8
Europe[3]	62.8	72.8	78.4
Latin America and the Caribbean[4]	57.1	79.6	84.9
Northern America	73.8	82.1	86.7
Oceania	70.8	70.2	71.4

1. Europe, North America, Australia,
   New Zealand and Japan.
2. Africa, Asia (excluding Japan), Latin
   America and the Caribbean, and
   Oceania (excluding Australia and
   New Zealand).
3. Includes Russian Federation.
4. South America, Central America
   (including Mexico) and all Caribbean
   Islands.

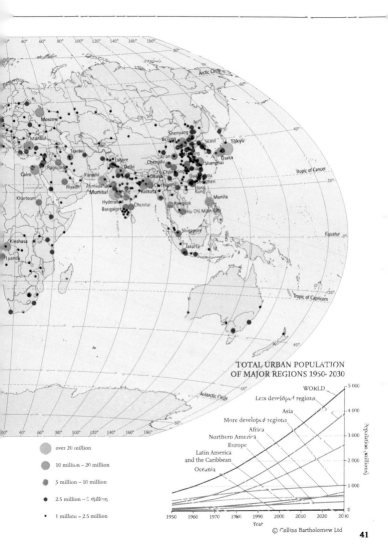

TOTAL URBAN POPULATION
OF MAJOR REGIONS 1950- 2030

WORLD
Less developed regions
Asia
More developed regions
Africa
Northern America
Europe
Latin America
and the Caribbean
Oceania

over 20 million

10 million – 20 million

5 million – 10 million

2.5 million – 5 million

1 million – 2.5 million

© Collins Bartholomew Ltd

SYMBOLS

Map symbols used on the map pages are explained here. The depiction of relief follows the tradition of layer-colouring, with colours depicting altitude bands. Ocean pages have a different contour interval. Settlements are classified in terms of both population and administrative significance. The abbreviations listed are those used in place names on the map pages and within the index.

LAND AND WATER FEATURES

Lake	━━━ River
Impermanent lake	─ ─ ─ Impermanent river
Salt lake or lagoon	Ice cap / Glacier
Impermanent salt lake	⟍¹²³ Pass height in metres
Dry salt lake or salt pan	∴ Site of special interest
	ᴖᴖᴖ Wall

RELIEF

Contour intervals used in layer-colouring for land height and sea depth

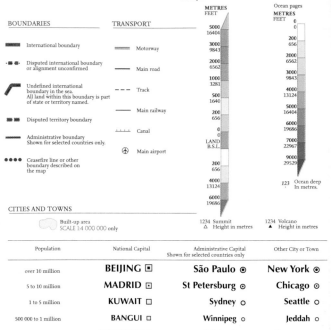

BOUNDARIES

▰▰▰	International boundary
·▰·▰·	Disputed international boundary or alignment unconfirmed
⎛	Undefined international boundary in the sea. All land within this boundary is part of state or territory named.
▰ ▰	Disputed territory boundary
━━	Administrative boundary Shown for selected countries only.
●●●●	Ceasefire line or other boundary described on the map

TRANSPORT

══	Motorway
──	Main road
─ ─ ─	Track
─┼─┼─	Main railway
⊥⊥⊥⊥	Canal
✈	Main airport

CITIES AND TOWNS

Built-up area
SCALE 1:4 000 000 only

1234 Summit
△ Height in metres

1234 Volcano
▲ Height in metres

Population	National Capital	Administrative Capital Shown for selected countries only	Other City or Town
over 10 million	**BEIJING** ▣	**São Paulo** ◉	**New York** ◉
5 to 10 million	**MADRID** ▣	**St Petersburg** ◉	**Chicago** ◉
1 to 5 million	**KUWAIT** ▢	**Sydney** ○	**Seattle** ○
500 000 to 1 million	**BANGUI** ▢	**Winnipeg** ○	**Jeddah** ○
100 000 to 500 000	WELLINGTON ▢	Edinburgh ○	Apucarana ○
50 000 to 100 000	PORT OF SPAIN ▢	Bismarck ○	Invercargill ○
under 50 000	MALABO ▢	Charlottetown ○	Ceres ○

STYLES OF LETTERING

Cities and towns are explained separately

		Physical features	
Country	**FRANCE**	Island	*Gran Canaria*
Overseas Territory/Dependency	**Guadeloupe**	Lake	*Lake Erie*
Disputed Territory	WESTERN SAHARA	Mountain	*Mt Blanc*
Administrative name Shown for selected countries only.	**SCOTLAND**	River	*Thames*
Area name	PATAGONIA	Region	*LAPPLAND*

CONTINENTAL MAPS

BOUNDARIES

————— International boundary

*·-·--·-· Disputed international boundary

········ Ceasefire line

CITIES AND TOWNS

National capital	Other city or town
Kuwait □	Seattle ○

ABBREVIATIONS

Arch.	Archipelago			
B.	Bay			
	Bahia, Baia	Portuguese	bay	
	Bahía	Spanish	bay	
	Baie	French	bay	
C.	Cape			
	Cabo	Portuguese, Spanish	cape, headland	
	Cap	French	cape, headland	
Co	Cerro	Spanish	hill, peak, summit	
E.	East, Eastern			
Est.	Estrecho	Spanish	strait	
Gt	Great			
I.	Island, Isle			
	Ilha	Portuguese	island	
	Isla	Spanish	island	
Is	Islands, Isles			
	Islas	Spanish	islands	
Khr.	Khrebet	Russian	mountain range	
L.	Lake			
	Loch	(Scotland)	lake	
	Lough	(Ireland)	lake	
	Lac	French	lake	
	Lago	Portuguese, Spanish	lake	
M.	Mys	Russian	cape, point	
Mt	Mount			
	Mont	French	hill, mountain	
Mt.	Mountain			

Mts	Mountains			
	Monts	French	hills, mountains	
N.	North, Northern			
O.	Ostrov	Russian	island	
Pt	Point			
Pta	Punta	Italian, Spanish	cape, point	
R.	River			
	Rio	Portuguese	river	
	Río	Spanish	river	
	Rivière	French	river	
Ra.	Range			
S.	South, Southern			
	Salar, Salina, Salinas	Spanish	saltpan, saltpans	
Sa	Serra	Portuguese	mountain range	
	Sierra	Spanish	mountain range	
Sd	Sound			
S.E.	Southeast, Southeastern			
St	Saint			
	Sankt	German	saint	
	Sint	Dutch	saint	
Sta	Santa	Italian, Portuguese, Spanish	saint	
Ste	Sainte	French	saint	
Str.	Strait			
W.	West, Western			
	Wadi, Wâdi	Arabic	watercourse	

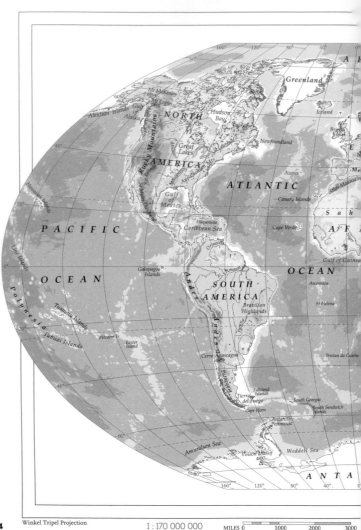

Greenland

Iceland

British

NORTH

Mt McKinley

Mt Logan

Aleutian Islands
Gulf of Alaska

Rocky Mountains

Hudson Bay

Labrador

Newfoundland

AMERICA

Great Lakes

Sierra Madre

Mississippi

Appalachian Mts

ATLANTIC

Azores

Mc

Atlas Mountains

Hawaiian Islands

Gulf of Mexico

PACIFIC

Canary Islands

Sah

Hispaniola
Caribbean Sea

Cape Verde

A F

Line Islands

Orinoco

Gulf of Guinea

OCEAN

Galapagos Islands

OCEAN

Amazon

Polynesia

SOUTH

Ascension

AMERICA

Brazilian Highlands

St Helena

Tuamotu Islands

Andes

Tubuai Islands

Pitcairn Is

Easter Island

Parana

Cerro Aconcagua
6959

Patagonia

Tristan da Cunha

Falkland Islands

Tierra del Fuego

South Georgia

Cape Horn

South Sandwich Islands

Antarctic Peninsula

Amundsen Sea

Vinson Massif
4897

Weddell Sea

ANTA

Winkel Tripel Projection

1 : 170 000 000

MILES 0   1000   2000   3000

ARCTIC OCEAN

40° 80° 120° 160° 80°

Central
Siberian
West Plateau
Siberian Sea of
Plain Okhotsk Bering
Sea
Ural Mountains Ob' Lake
Baikal 60°
North European Amur
Plain Irtysh
EUROPE Gobi Sea
of 40°
Danube Black Sea Volga Japan
Elbrus Aral Sea A S I A Honshu
Terranean Sea Caspian Sea
Mediterranean Sea Tien Shan East PACIFIC
Kunlun Shan China
Arabian Mt Everest Yangtze Sea
8848 OCEAN
Peninsula Himalaya Tropic of Cancer
I C A Deccan
Arabian South
Red Sea Sea Bay China
of Sea Philippines
Ethiopian Bengal Challenger
Highlands Sri Lanka Deep
Congo Lake Maldives 10920 Micronesia
Basin Victoria Bornco Melanesia
Great Kilimanjaro Java Celebes New Equator
Rift 5892 Puncak Jaya Guinea
Valley Seychelles 5030
Zambezi INDIAN Arafura
Sea
Coral
Madagascar Sea
Kalahari OCEAN AUSTRALIA
Desert Tropic of Capricorn
Cape of Great
Good Hope Victoria
Desert Darling
Great Tasman
Australian Sea New Ireland
Bight Great Dividing Range 40°
Îles Kerguélen Tasmania

Davis Sea

Antarctic Circle 60°

CTICA Ross Sea
80°
40° 80° 120° 160°

© Collins Bartholomew Ltd

0 1000 2000 3000 4000 5000 KILOMETRES

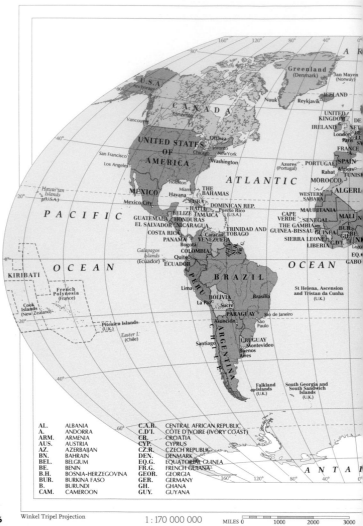

AL. ALBANIA
A. ANDORRA
ARM. ARMENIA
AUS. AUSTRIA
AZ. AZERBAIJAN
BN. BAHRAIN
BEL. BELGIUM
BE. BENIN
B.H. BOSNIA–HERZEGOVINA
BUR. BURKINA FASO
B. BURUNDI
CAM. CAMEROON

C.A.R. CENTRAL AFRICAN REPUBLIC
C.D'I. COTE D'IVOIRE (IVORY COAST)
CR. CROATIA
CYP. CYPRUS
CZ.R. CZECH REPUBLIC
DEN. DENMARK
EQ.G. EQUATORIAL GUINEA
FR.G. FRENCH GUIANA
GEOR. GEORGIA
GER. GERMANY
GH. GHANA
GUY. GUYANA

Winkel Tripel Projection   1 : 170 000 000   MILES 0   1000   2000   3000

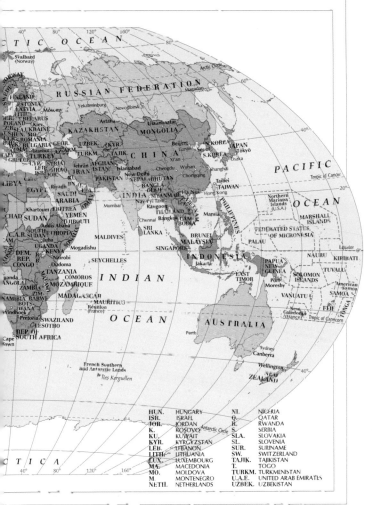

HUN.	HUNGARY	NI.	NIGERIA
ISR.	ISRAEL	Q.	QATAR
JOR.	JORDAN	R.	RWANDA
K.	KOSOVO	S.	SERBIA
KU.	KUWAIT	SLA.	SLOVAKIA
KYR.	KYRGYZSTAN	SL.	SLOVENIA
LEB.	LEBANON	SUR.	SURINAME
LITH.	LITHUANIA	SW.	SWITZERLAND
LUX.	LUXEMBOURG	TAJIK.	TAJIKISTAN
MA.	MACEDONIA	T.	TOGO
MO.	MOLDOVA	TURKM.	TURKMENISTAN
M.	MONTENEGRO	U.A.E.	UNITED ARAB EMIRATES
NETH.	NETHERLANDS	UZBEK.	UZBEKISTAN

0   1000   2000   3000   4000   5000 KILOMETRES

© Collins Bartholomew Ltd

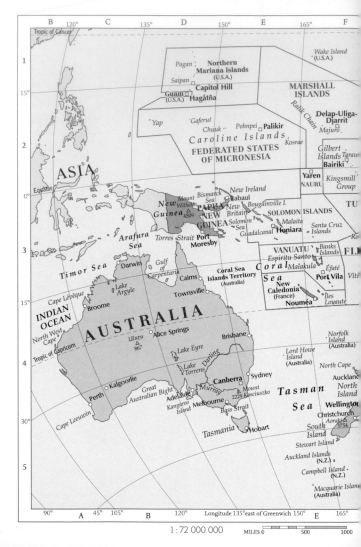

1 : 72 000 000

MILES 0   500   1000

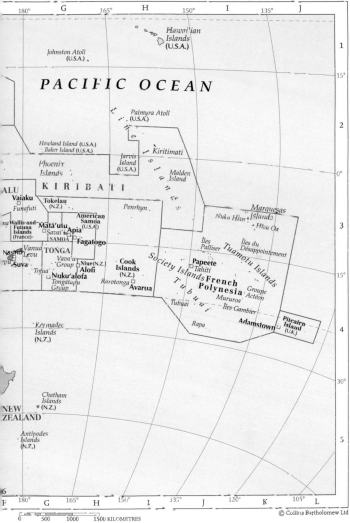

PACIFIC OCEAN

Hawaiian
Islands
(U.S.A.)

Johnston Atoll
(U.S.A.)

Palmyra Atoll
(U.S.A.)

Line Islands

Kiritimati

Howland Island (U.S.A.)
Baker Island (U.S.A.)

Jarvis
Island
(U.S.A.)

Malden
Island

Phoenix
Islands

ALU
Vaiaku

Tokelau
(N.Z.)

Funafuti

na Wallis and
Futuna
Islands
(France)

KIRIBATI

Matā'utu

American
Samoa
(U.S.A.)

Penrhyn

Marquesas
Islands

Nuku Hiva • Hiva Oa

Îles du
Désappointement

Savai'i

Apia

SAMOA

Fagatogo

Vanua
Levu

TONGA

Niue (N.Z.)

Cook
Islands
(N.Z.)

Îles
Palliser

Tuamotu Islands

vu

Nashū
Levu

Suva

Vava'u
Group

Tofua

Alofi

Rarotonga

Society Islands

Papeete
Tahiti

French
Polynesia

Nuku'alofa

Tongatapu
Group

Avarua

Tubuai

Groupe
Actéon

Mururoa

Kermadec
Islands
(N.Z.)

Rapa

Îles Gambier

Tubuai

Adamstown

Pitcairn
Island
(U.K.)

NEW
ZEALAND

Chatham
Islands
(N.Z.)

Antipodes
Islands
(N.Z.)

0   500   1000   1500 KILOMETRES

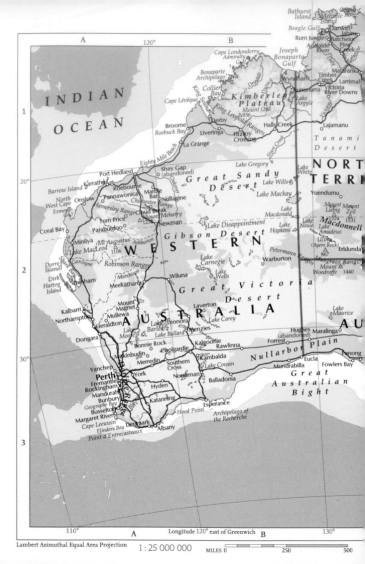

INDIAN

OCEAN

A 120° **B**

Bathurst Island
Melville Island
Beagle Gulf
Rum Jungle
Darwin
Jabiru
Batchelor
Pine Creek
Adelaide River
Cape Londonderry
Admiralty
Joseph Bonaparte Gulf
Bonaparte Archipelago
Collier Bay
Kimberley Plateau
Mount Ord 936
Matarankah
Timber Creek
Larrimah
Victoria River Downs
King Leopold Ranges
Wyndham
Kununurra
Lake Argyle
King Sound
Cape Léveque
Broome
Derby
Halls Creek
Lajamanu
Roebuck Bay
Liveringa
Fitzroy Crossing
Stuart Creek
La Grange
Eighty Mile Beach
T a n a m i D e s e r t

1

NORTH TERRI

Port Hedland
Shay Gap (abandoned)
Great Sandy Desert
Lake Gregory
Lake White
Lake Wills
Lake Mackay
Yuendumu

20°
Barrow Island
Roebourne
Karratha
Marble Bar
Nullagine
North West Cape
Onslow
Pannawonica
Chichester Range
Lake Macdonald
Mount Liebig
Mount Zeil
Exmouth
Hamersley Range
Cloud Break
Mount Meharry
Newman
Lake Disappointment
Lake Hopkins
Lake Neale
1524 1531
Macdonnell
Coral Bay
Tom Price
Paraburdoo
Gibson Desert
Lake Amadeus
Uluru (Ayers Rock)
Erldunda

2
Minilya
Mt Augustus 1106
Ashburton
W E S T E R N
Lake Carnegie
Warburton
Petermann Ranges
867
Musgrave Ranges
Mount Woodroffe 1440
Lake MacLeod
Dorre Island
Gascoyne
Robinson Ranges
Lake Wells
Dirk Hartog Island
Denham
Murchison
Wiluna
Great V i c t o r i a
Meekatharra
A U S T R A L I A
D e s e r t
Lake Maurice

Kalbarri
Mount Magnet
Mullewa
Laverton
Lake Carey
Hughes (abandoned)
Maralinga

AU
Northampton
Geraldton
Leonora
Menzies
Forrest
Lake Moore
Lake Barlee
Lake Ballard
Dongara
Bonnie Rock
Kalgoorlie
Rawlinna
Nullarbor Plain
Eucla
Penong
30°
Mukinbudin
Coolgardie
Fowlers Bay
Yanchep
Merredin
Southern Cross
Kambalda
Mundrabilla
Great
Perth
York
Norseman
Australian
Fremantle
Rockingham
Hyden
Lake Cowan
Bight
Mandurah
Bunbury
Katanning
Balladonia
Geographe Bay
Busselton
Esperance
Margaret River
Hood Point
Archipelago of the Recherche
Cape Leeuwin
Denmark
Flinders Bay
Albany
Point d'Entrecasteaux

3

110° *Longitude 120° east of Greenwich* 130°
A **B**

Lambert Azimuthal Equal Area Projection   1 : 25 000 000   MILES 0   250   500

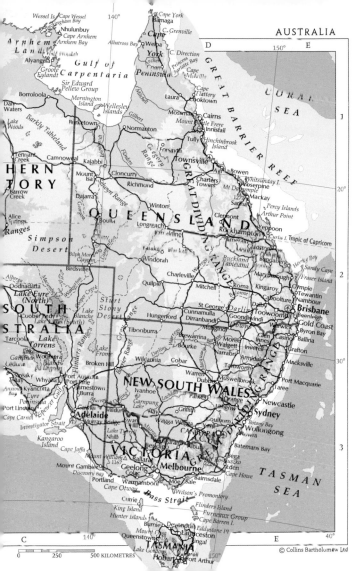

140°

150°

Wessel Is / Cape Wessel
Buckingham Bay
Nhulunbuy
Cape Arnhem
Arnhem Bay
Arnhem
Land
Alyangula
Milingimbi
Groote
Eylandt
Sir Edward
Pellew Group
Mornington
Island
Borroloola
Wellesley
Islands

Cape York
Bamaga
C. Grenville
Cape Weipa
York
Peninsula
Princess
Charlotte Bay
Cape
Melville

Gulf of
Carpenteria

Daly
Waters
Lake
Woods
Barkly Tableland
Burketown
Normanton
Tennant
Creek
Camooweal
Kajabbi

HERN
TORY
Barrow
Creek
Alice
Springs
Ranges

Mount
Isa
Cloncurry
Dajarra
Richmond
Winton
Boulia

QUEENSLAND

Simpson
Desert
Birdsville
Bedourie
Windorah

Laura
C. Flattery
Cooktown
Mossman
Cairns
Mount Bellenden Ker
Innisfail
Tully
Hinchinbrook
Island
Ingham
Townsville
Bowen
Ayr
Whitsunday I.
Charters
Towers
Mt Dalrymple
Mackay
Percy Islands
Arthur Point

GREAT BARRIER REEF

CORAL
SEA

Clermont
Rockhampton
Emerald
Gladstone
Atherton
Tableland
Longreach
Blackall
Charleville
Quilpie
Mitchell
Roma

Bundaberg
Maryborough
Kingaroy
Gympie
Nambour
Maroochydore

Hervey Bay
Sandy Cape
Fraser Island

Tropic of Capricorn

Alberga
Oodnadatta
Lake Eyre
(North)
Coober Pedy
Tarcoola

SOUTH
STRALIA
Lake
Torrens
Gawler
Woomera
Ranges
Ceduna
Streaky
Bay
Whyalla
Anxious
Bay
Kyancutta
Eyre
Peninsula
Port Lincoln
Cape Carnot
Investigator Strait
Kangaroo
Island

Lake
Blanche
Lake
Frome
Broken Hill

Sturt
Stony
Desert
Hungerford
Tibooburra
Wilcannia
Cobar

Cunnamulla
St George
Dirranbandi
Bourke
Brewarrina
Warren
Dubbo
Ivanhoe
Gundagai

NEW SOUTH WALES
Griffith
Wagga Wagga
Albury

Goondiwindi
Moree
Narrabri
Warialda
Inverell
Tamworth
Armidale
Walgett

Toowoomba
Warwick
Glen Innes
Grafton
Macksville
Port Macquarie
Taree
Newcastle
Sydney
Wollongong

Brisbane
Ipswich
Beenleigh
Gold Coast
Byron Bay
Ballina
Casino

GREAT DIVIDING RANGE

Port Augusta
Port Pirie
Jamestown
Burra
Gawler
Adelaide
Murray Bridge

Orange
Bathurst
Goulburn
CANBERRA
Batemans Bay
Bega
Cape Howe

Melbourne
Geelong
Colac
Ballarat
Bendigo
Mildura
Nhill
VICTORIA
Warrnambool
Portland
Cape Otway
Mount Gambier
Discovery Bay

Botany Bay

TASMAN
SEA

Bairnsdale
Moe
Sale
Wilson's Promontory

Bass Strait
Currie
King Island
Hunter Islands
Flinders Island
Furneaux Group
Cape Barren I.

Burnie
Devonport
Launceston
Queenstown
TASMANIA
Hobart
Port Arthur

C
140°

E
150°

40°

© Collins Bartholomew Ltd

0   250   500 KILOMETRES

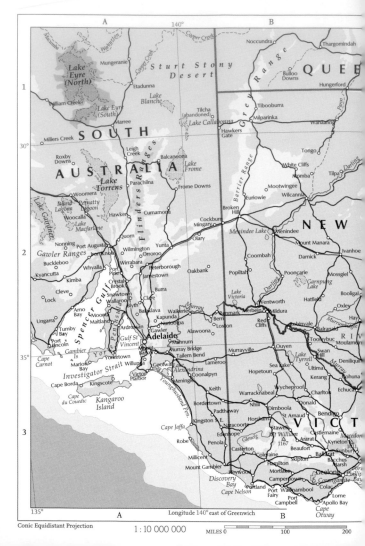

Macumba
Warburton
Coopers Creek
Noccundra
Thargomindah

Mungeranie
Sturt Stony
Desert
Bulloo
Downs
QUEE

Lake
Eyre
(North)
Etadunna
Lake
Blanche
Hungerford

William Creek
Lake Eyre
(South)
Tilcha
(abandoned)
Lake Callabonna
Tibooburra
Milparinka
Wanaaring

Marree
Hawkers
Gate

SOUTH
Leigh
Creek
Balcanoona
Lake
Frome
Tongo

Roxby
Downs
White Cliffs
Wcompah
Tilpa
Darling

AUSTRALIA
Lake
Torrens
Parachilna
Frome Downs
Barrier Range
Mootwingee
Wilcannia

Woomera
Flinders Ranges
Hawker
Cumamona
Euriowie
Broken
Hill

Island
Lagoon
Pernatty
Lagoon
NEW

Woocalla
Lake
Macfarlane
Quorn
Yunta
Cockburn
Mingary
Menindee Lake
Menindee
Mount Manara

Nonning
Port Augusta
Wilmington
Orroroo
Olary
Damrick
Ivanhoe

Gawler Ranges
Iron Knob
Coombah
Popiltah
Poancarie
Garnpung
Lake
Mossgiel

Buckleboo
Whyalla
Port
Pirie
Peterborough
Oakbank
Darling
Hatfield
Booligal

Kyancutta
Kimba
Crystal
Brook
Jamestown
Lake
Victoria
Wentworth
Oxley

Cleve
Lock
Snowtown
Burra
Clare
Merbein
Mildura
Hay

Arno
Bay
Moonta
Wallaroo
Blyth
Balaklava
Waikerie
Renmark
Berri
Red
Cliffs
Robinvale
Balranald
Murrumbidgee
RIV

Ungarra
Maitland
Kapunda
Nuriootpa
Loxon
Tooleybuc
Moulamein

Tumby
Bay
Ardrossan
Gawler
Mannum
Swan
Hill
Deniliqu

Port
Lincoln
Gulf St
Vincent
Adelaide
Murray Bridge
Ouyen
Lake
Tyrrell
Ultima
Kohuna

Gambier
Is
Yorke Peninsula
Yorketown
Tailem Bend
Tameroo
Sea Lake
Kerang
Echuca

Cape
Carnot
Marion
Bay
Investigator Strait
Willunga
Geelwa
Lake
Alexandrina
Coonalpyn
Murrayville
Hopetoun
Wycheproof
Charlton

Cape Borda
Kingscote
Victor
Harbor
Meningie
Keith
Warracknabeal
Donald
Bendigo

Cape
du Couedic
Kangaroo
Island
Coorong
Bordertown
Padthaway
Nhill
Dimboola
St Arnaud
VICT

Cape Jaffa
Kingston S.E.
Naracoorte
Horsham
Stawell
Mt William
1167
Ararat
Castlemaine
Kyneton
Macedon

Robe
Edenhope
Penola
Casterton
Glenelg
Beaufort
Skipton
Ballarat
Sunbury

Millicent
Mount Gambier
Coleraine
Hamilton
Mortlake
Camperdown
Geelong
Bacchus
Marsh

Discovery
Bay
Cape Nelson
Heywood
Portland
Port
Fairy
Warrnambool
Port
Campbell
Colac
Lorne
Apollo Bay
Cape
Otway

Longitude 140° east of Greenwich

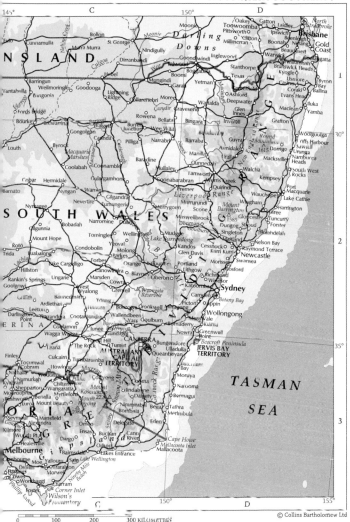

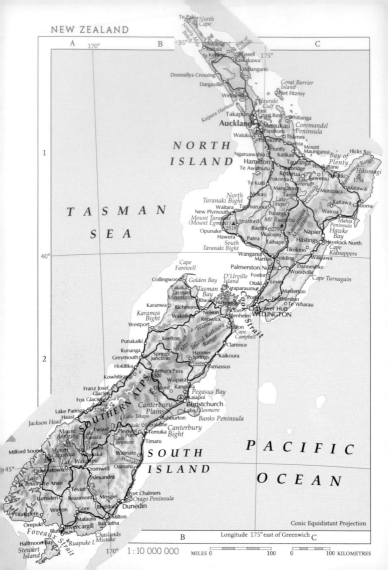

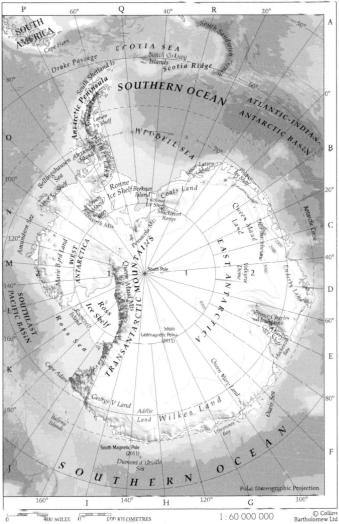

SOUTH AMERICA

Cape Horn

SCOTIA SEA

South Sandwich

South Orkney Islands

Scotia Ridge

Drake Passage

SOUTHERN OCEAN

South Shetland Is.

Antarctic Peninsula

ATLANTIC-INDIAN-ANTARCTIC BASIN

Larsen Ice Shelf

WEDDELL SEA

Bellingshausen Sea

Palmer Land

Alexander Island

Ronne Ice Shelf

Berkner Island

Larsen Ice Shelf

Riiser-Larsen Ice Shelf

Coats Land

Filchner Ice Shelf

Queen Maud Land

Fimbul Ice Shelf

Antarctic Circle

Amundsen Sea

Thurston Island

Ellsworth Mts.

Shackleton Range

Pensacola Mts.

WEST ANTARCTICA

Marie Byrd Land

Valkyrie Dome

EAST ANTARCTICA

Enderby Land

South Pole

SOUTHEAST PACIFIC BASIN

Ross Ice Shelf

Roosevelt Island

Ross Sea

Transantarctic Mountains

Queen Maud Mountains

South Geomagnetic Pole (2011)

Prince Charles Mountains

Amery Ice Shelf

Mac.Robertson Land

Mackenzie Bay

Cape Adare

Queen Mary Land

Davis Sea

Balleny Islands

George V Land

Adélie Land

Wilkes Land

Vincennes Bay

South Magnetic Pole (2011)

Dumont d'Urville Sea

SOUTHERN OCEAN

Polar Stereographic Projection

1 : 60 000 000

© Collins Bartholomew Ltd

0   400 MILES   0   500 KILOMETRES

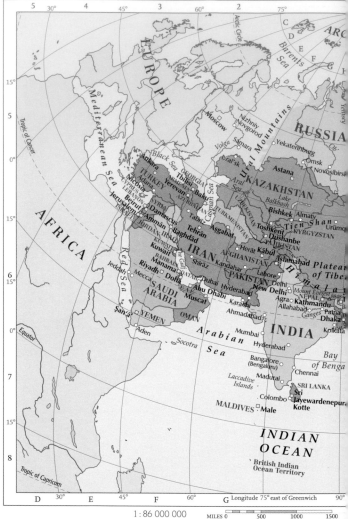

1 : 86 000 000

MILES 0   500   1000   1500

ARCTIC OCEAN

Noril'sk

RUSSIAN FEDERATION

Bering Sea

Magadan

Sea of Okhotsk

Petropavlovsk-Kamchatskiy

Irkutsk Lake Baikal

Ulan Bator

MONGOLIA

Vladivostok

Harbin

Shenyang NORTH KOREA
(East Sea)

Sapporo

Hakodate

Sea of Japan

JAPAN

Dalian P'yŏngyang

Beijing Seoul Tōkyō

SOUTH KOREA

Ōsaka

Tianjin Yellow Fukuoka Hiroshima

Lanzhou Xi'an Sea

CHINA Nanjing Shanghai

Yangtze Wuhan East

Chongdu Hangzhou China

Chongqing Sea

PACIFIC

OCEAN

Kunming Liuzhou Guangzhou Taibei

MYANMAR Nanning TAIWAN

(BURMA) Kaosiung

Nay Pyi Taw Ha Nôi Hong Kong

Hai Phong Luzon Strait

Rangoon Vientiane

THAILAND Quezon City

Bangkok South Manila PHILIPPINES

Andaman CAMBODIA China

Islands Phnom Ho Chi Minh City Sea Davao Melekeok

(India) Penh PALAU

Nicobar Kota

Islands Bandar Seri Kinabalu

(India) Begawan Celebes

Kuala BRUNEI Sea Jayapura

Medan Lumpur Kuching New

Putrajaya MALAYSIA Guinea

SINGAPORE Borneo

Singapore Pontianak

Sumatra INDONESIA

Palembang Banjarmasin Laut Banda

Jakarta Laut Jawa Makassar Dili EAST TIMOR

Bandung Surabaya Semarang Timor

Java Sea OCEANIA

0   1000   2000 KILOMETRES

Albers Equal Area Conic Projection   1 : 30 000 000   MILES 0   200   400   600

PHILIPPINE

PACIFIC

SEA

OCEAN

PHILIPPINES

Northern
Mariana
Islands
(U.S.A.)

CAPITOL HILL

Guam
(U.S.A.)

HAGÅTÑA

Sorsogon
Catarman
Catbalogan
Tacloban

Samar

Surigao
Cagayan de Oro
Davao
Mati
General Santos

Mindanao

Cotabato

More
Gulf

FEDERATED STATES
OF MICRONESIA

Yap

PALAU

MELEKEOK

Caroline
Islands

Kepulauan
Talaud

Kepulauan
Sangir

Morotai

Equator

Hermit Is

Manado
Tobelo
Ternate
Halmahera

Gorontalo

Waigeo

Manokwari
Biak

Sorong
Ransiki

Misool

Jayapura

PAPUA

NEW GUINEA

Seram

Amahai

Ambon

Wewak

Madang

NEW GUINEA

Wau
Lae

Morobe

Nabire

Kepulauan Kai

Amamapare

Merauke

Gulf
of
Papua

PORT
MORESBY

Kalabahi

EAST
TIMOR

Kupang

Melville
Island

Darwin

AUSTRALIA

Croker I.

C. Wessel

Nhulunbuy
C. Arnhem

Gulf
of
Carpentaria

Rote

Bathurst Island

Jabiru

C. York

Coen

© Collins Bartholomew Ltd

0   500   1000 KILOMETRES

59

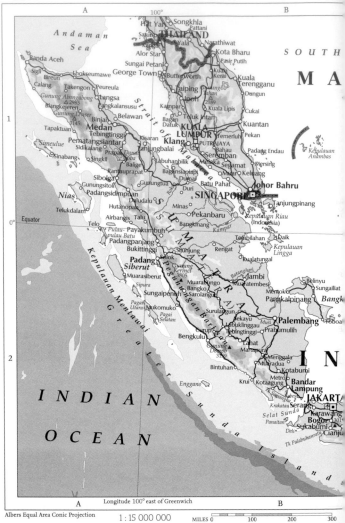

Andaman Sea

SOUTH

MA

Hat Yai Songkhla
Pattani
Sadao THAILAND
Satun Yala Narathiwat

Banda Aceh
Sigli Kota Bharu
Bireun Pasir Putih
Calang Lhokseumawe Kuala Kuala
Takengon Kerai Terengganu
Peureula Sungai Petani Butterworth Dungun
Blangkejeren George Town
Gunung Abongabong Langsa Taiping Kuala Cukai
2985 Pangkalansusu Tapah Lipis
Gunung Leuser Ipoh 2189
3145 Belawan Kampar Teluk Intan Kuantan
Binjai Bagan Pekan
Medan Tebingtinggi Kisaran KUALA LUMPUR Temerluh
Tapaktuan Danau LUMPUR Klang PUTRAJAYA Padang Endau
Pematangsiantar Tanjungbalai Seremban *Kepulauan*
Sidikalang Labuhanbilik Bahau Segamat *Anambas*
Prapat Danau Bagansiapiapi Melaka Segamat
Simeulue Balige Toba Muaro Kelilang
Singkil Rantauprapat Dumai Mersing
Sibolga Duri Batu Pahat
Gunungsitoli Gunungtua Johor Bahru
Padangsidimpuan Daludalu SINGAPORE
Nias Hutanopan Minas Tanjungpinang
Telukdalam Airbangis Pekanbaru *Kepulauan Riau*
Equator Talu Bangkinang *(Indonesia)*
Telo *Pulau-pulau Batu* Payakumbuh Kampar
Padangpanjang Daik
Bukittinggi *Kepulauan Lingga*
Padang Solok Tembilahan
Siberut Shunjung Renggat Kualatungal
Muarasibu *Gunung Kerinci*
Sipura 3805 Muarabungo Jambi
Sungaipenuh Bangko Muaratembesi
Pagai Sarolangun Belinyu
Utara Sukomuko Surulangun Mentok Sungailiat
Pagai Pekayu Pangkalpinang Bangk
Selatan Lubuklinggau Palembang Toboa
Curup Tebingtinggi Prabumulih
Bengkulu Lahat *Musi*
Gunung Dempo Muaraenim
3159 Menggala
Bintuhan Muaradua Kotabumi
Enggano Metro I N
Krui Kotaagung Bandar
Lampung
Gunung JAKARTA
Krakatau Serang Karawang
3301
Selat Sunda Bogor
Sukabumi Cianju
Panaitan
Deli
Tk Palabuhanratu

I N D I A N

O C E A N

Kepulauan Mentawai

S U M A T R A

G r e a t e r S u n d a I s l a n d s

Strait of Malacca

Pegunungan Barisan

Batanghari

Longitude 100° east of Greenwich

A B

1 : 15 000 000 MILES 0 100 200 300

CHINA SEA

LAYSIA

Natuna Besar
Panarik

Kepulauan
Natuna

Kudat
Banggi
Kota Belud
S U L U
S E A
Gunung
Kinabalu
4095
Kota
Kinabalu
Ranau
Sandakan
Beaufort
Labuan
SABAH
BANDAR SERI
BEGAWAN
BRUNEI
Kuala Belait
Lutong
Miri
Seria
Pensiangan
Lumbis
Lamag
Kuamut
Lahad
Datu
Tungku
Tawau
Semporna
CELEBES
SEA
Tarakan
Tanjungselor

Bintulu
Igan Mukah
Sibu
Sarike
Rajang
Kapit
Belaga
Lung
Pakali
Kubuang
Koom
Sambaliung
Sepinang
Datadian
Tanjungredeb

Likau Sematan
Kuching
Saratok
Debak
Sri Aman
Anlu
Lubuk
Putusibau
Sangkulirang
Bontang

Samba
Pemangkat
ingkawang
Kepulauan
Lambem
Mempawah
Pontianak
Bengkayang
Sanggau
Sintang
Semitau
Nangahpinoh
B O R N E O
Mahakam
Longiram
2988
Tenggarong
Samarinda

Balaiberkuak
Telukbatang
Muaralaung
Muarateweh
Balikpapan
Tanahgrogot
Babana
Mamuju

Pulau-pulau
Karimata
Sukadana
Ketapang
Nangatayap
Rantaupanjang
K A L I M A N T A N
Amuntai
Bukit
3074

Kendawangan
Sukaraja
Sampit
Palangkaraya
Vandangan
Kotabaru
Polewali
Majene

Pangkalanbuun
Kualapembuang
Banjarmasin
Martapura
Pagatan
Laut

Tanjung
Puting
Tanjung
Selatan

D O N E S I A
L A U T   J A W A
(J A V A   S E A)
Kepulauan
Laut Kecil

Pulau-pulau
Karimunjawa
Kemujan
Bawean
Kepulauan
Kangean
Sabalana

Tanjung
Indramayu
Tegal Pekalongan
Tuban
Bangkalan
Madura
Sumenep
Laut Bali
(B a l i   S e a)
Kepulauan
Tengah

irebon
Kudus
Bandung
Semarang
Surakarta
Jombang
Pasuruan
Situbondo
S u m b a w a

Garut
iamis
Temanggung
Surabaya
Madiun
Yogyakarta
Malang
Lumajang
Jember
Banyuwangi
Mataram
Alas
Sumbawa
Raba

Cilacap
Kebumen
Singaraja
Klatang
Bali
Dompu

J A V A
(J A W A)
Barung
G. Raung
3142
Denpasar
Praya
Taliwang
L o m b o k

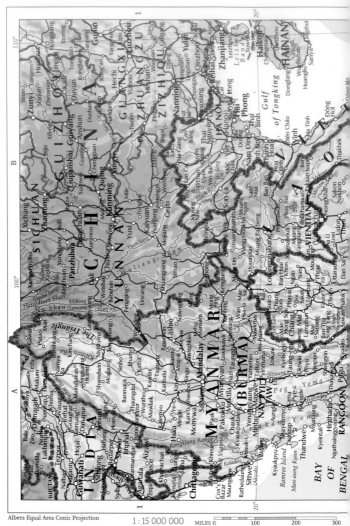

Albers Equal Area Conic Projection

1 : 15 000 000   MILES 0   100   200   300

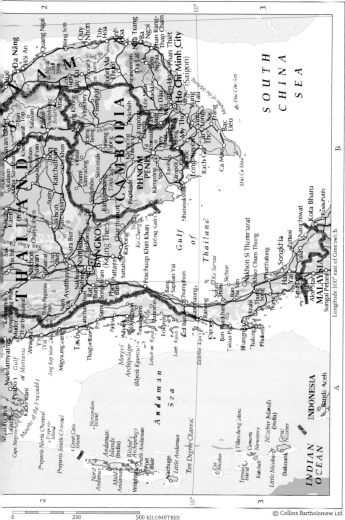

S O U T H

C H I N A

S E A

Dao Côn Son

V I E T N A M

C A M B O D I A

T H A I L A N D

PHNOM
PENH

BANGKOK
(Krung Thep)

Gulf

of

Thailand

Andaman

Sea

MALAYSIA

INDONESIA

Banda Aceh

INDIAN

OCEAN

Da Nẵng

Hôi An

Quang Ngai

Quy Nhơn

Nha Trang

Ho Chi Minh City
(Saigon)

Prepars North Channel

Cape Negrais

Andaman
Islands
(India)

Port
Blair

Little Andaman

Ten Degree Channel

Car
Nicobar

Nicobar Islands
(India)

Great
Nicobar

Kota Bharu

Songkhla

Phuket

Ranong

Chumphon

Prachuap Khiri Khan

Pattaya

Nakhon Ratchasima

Longitude 100° east of Greenwich

PHILIPPINE
SEA

PHILIPPINES

SOUTH

CHINA

SEA

Scarborough
Shoal

LUZON

Laoag City
Aparri
Bangged
Tuguegarao
Vigan
Bontoc
Ilagan
Tagudin
Palanan
San Fernando
Santiago
La Trinidad
Bayombong
Dagupan
Baguio
Lingayen
San Carlos
Tarlac
San Jose
Iba
Cabanatuan
San Fernando
Olongapo
Valenzuela
Polillo Islands
Balanga
Quezon City
MANILA
Pasig
Tagaytay City
Santa Cruz
Batangas
San Pablo
Lucena
Catanduanes
Calapan
Naga
Oas
Virac
Mount
Halcon
Legazpi
Sorsogon
Mindoro
Irosin
Roxas
Sibuyan
Catarman
San Jose
Romblon
Masbate
Calbayog
Samar
New Busuanga
Roxas
Sibuyan Sea
Masbate
Catbalogan
Calamian
Group
Pandan
Visayan
Tacloban
Guiuan
Culion
Roxas
Sea
Leyte
El Nido
Cuyo
Islands
Panay
Cebu
Maasin
Taytay
San Jose de
Iloilo
Pototan
Dinagat
Buenavista
Bacolod
Dumaran
Negros
Talisay
Siargao
Roxas
Cauayan
Tagbilaran
Surigao
Palawan
Puerto Princesa
Panjay
Bohol Sea
Tandag
Quezon
Aborlan
Bayawan
Dumaguete
Butuan
Mount
Presidente
Dapitan
Cagayan
Mantalingajan
Manuel A Roxas
Oroquieta
de Oro
Brooke's Point
Liloy
Iligan
Malaybalay
Bugsuk
Ozamis
Mount
Balabac
Pagadian
Ragang
MINDANAO
Balabac
SULU SEA
Zamboanga
2815
Balabac Strait
Peninsula
Cotabato
Mount
Tagum
Cagayan de
Datu Piang
Apo
Davao
Tawi-Tawi
Zamboanga
Moro
2954
Banggi
Gulf
Isabela
Banga
Digos
Kudat
Basilan
Davao
Gunung
Jolo
Gulf
Kinabalu
General Santos
4095
Sulu
Ranau
Sandakan
Archipelago
Sarangani Islands
MALAYSIA
Lamag
Kepulauan
SABAH
Lahad
Nanusa
Kuamut
Datu
Tumindao
CELEBES
Kepulauan
Pensiangan
SEA
Talaud
INDONESIA
INDONESIA
Sangir
Karakelong
Tawau
Semporna
Kaburuang

Longitude 120° east of Greenwich

Albers Equal Area Conic
Projection

1 : 15 000 000

MILES 0   100

0   250 KILOMETRES

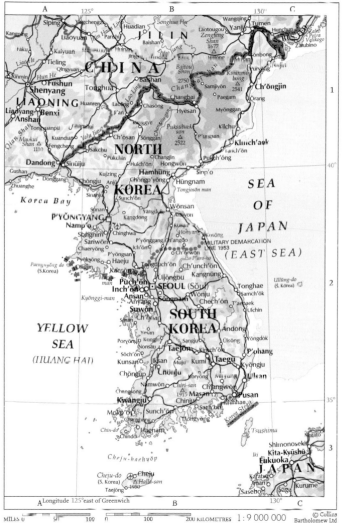

MILES 0   50   100
0   100   200 KILOMETRES   1 : 9 000 000

© Collins
Bartholomew Ltd

Longitude 125° east of Greenwich

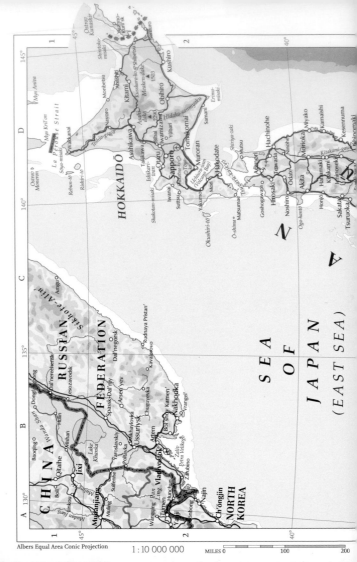

Albers Equal Area Conic Projection

1 : 10 000 000

MILES 0   100   200

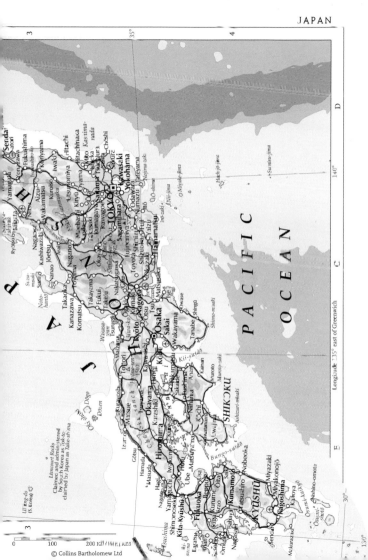

D

140°

C

PACIFIC

OCEAN

E

Longitude 135° east of Greenwich

35°

4

30°

130°

Sendai

TOKYO

Yokohama

NIPPON

Kyōto

Ōsaka

HONSHŪ

SHIKOKU

KYŪSHŪ

Lemnour Rocks
Claimed and administered
by South Korea since 1954,
claimed by Japan as Take-sh·ma

Ullŭng-do
(S.Korea)

0   100   200 KILOMETRES

© Collins Bartholomew Ltd

3

67

75° B 90° C

Longitude 90° east of Greenwich

1 : 30 000 000   MILES 0   200   400   600

A 75° B 90° C

RUSSIAN FE

Astaka Temirtau Yekibastuz Mikhaylovskoye Aleysk Biysk Askiz Batagay Sayan
Karagandy Atasu Karagayly Georgiyevka Rubtsovsk Gorno Teeli Chadan Kyzyl Hatgal Höysgöl

KAZAKHSTAN Moyynty Balkash Kaynar Zharma Ust- Kamenogorsk Agach Altay Ulaangom Tsetserleg Möron Hutag-Ond
Saryshagan Taskesken Ayagoz Kök-pekty Fuyun Har Us Nuur Har Nuur Ulyastay Tsetserleg

Ushtobe Aktogay Manas Hu Karamay Gichgeniyn Nuruu Bayanhongor MON

BISHKEK Almaty Yining Kuytun Shihezi Ürümqi (Ürümchi) Qitaijing Barkol Yiwu Noyön

KYRGYZSTAN **TIEN SHAN** Korla Turpan Toksun Hami Dalain Hob

TAJIK Kashi Bachu Shache Aksu Kuqa Korla Bosten Hu Lop Nur Guazhou Dunhuang Laojunmiao Jiayuguan Jiuquan **Qilian Shan**

Tarim Basin (Tarim Pendi) **Taklimakan Desert (Taklimakan Shamo)** Qiemo Ruoqiang Lao Mangnai Da Qaidam Gangca

Hotan Yutian Minfeng **Qaidam Pendi** Golmud Dulan Xining

KUNLUN SHAN Hoh Xil Shan Madoi

Plateau of Tibet (Qingzang Gaoyuan) **C H I N**

Gêrzê Tanggula Shan Garzê

Hindu Kush **ISLAMABAD** Rawalpindi Jammu Dêrub Siling Co Nagqu Dêgê Dawu

Gujranwala Hoshiarpur **NEPAL** Zhari Namco Nam Co Nyainqêntanglha Shan Yushu Baima

Lahore Ludhiana Chandigarh Gêrzê Cozhê Xigazê Lhasa Zhigang

Sirsa Hisar Meerut Rampur Tingri Qamdo Markam **MYANMAR**

Delhi **NEW DELHI** Bareilly Gorakhpur **KATHMANDU** **THIMPHU** **BHUTAN** Dibrugarh Tezu Putao

Jaipur Agra Lucknow Patna Muzaffarpur Bongaigaon Jorhat **Guwahati** Kohima Myitkyina **Panzhihua**

Ajmer Tonk Kanpur Varanasi Mirzapur Munger Mymensingh Shillong Silchar Imphal Bhamo Dali Chuxiong

Kota Shivpuri Allahabad Rewa Dhanbad **DHAKA** **BANGLADESH** Aizawl Katha Lashio

Bhopal Jabalpur Ranchi Jamshedpur Barisal Wuntho Namtu

INDIA Nagpur Raipur Raurkela **Kolkata** Khulna Jungle Monywa **Mandalay**

Amravati Raigarh Sambalpur Baleshwar Calcutta **Chittagong** Meiktila **MYANMAR**

Jalna Yavatmal Bhubaneshwar Cuttack Mouths of the Ganges Cox's Bazar Taunggyi

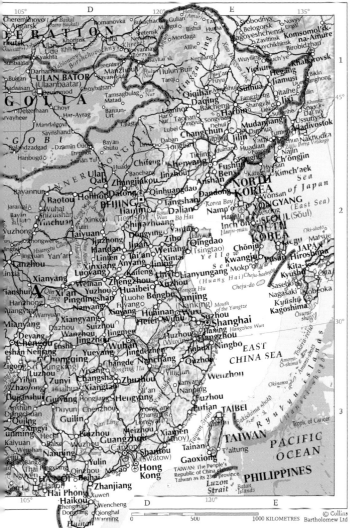

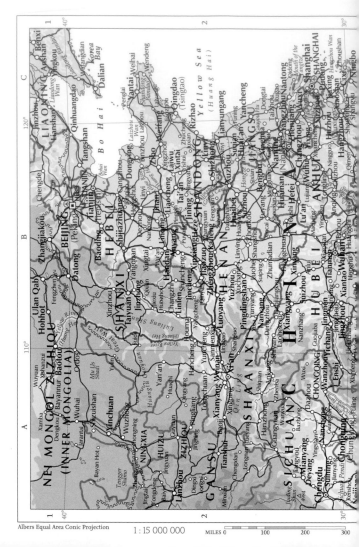

Albers Equal Area Conic Projection

1 : 15 000 000

MILES 0   100   200   300

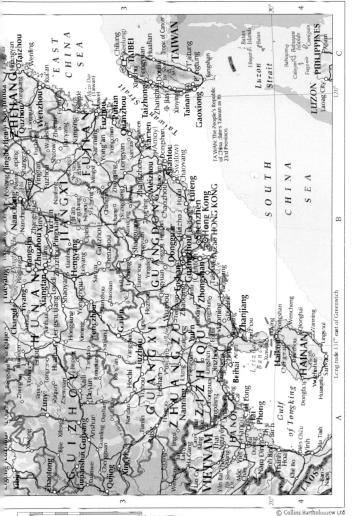

© Collins Bartholomew Ltd

500 KILOMETRES

Longitude 110° east of Greenwich

TAIWAN: The People's Republic
of China claims Taiwan as its
23rd Province.

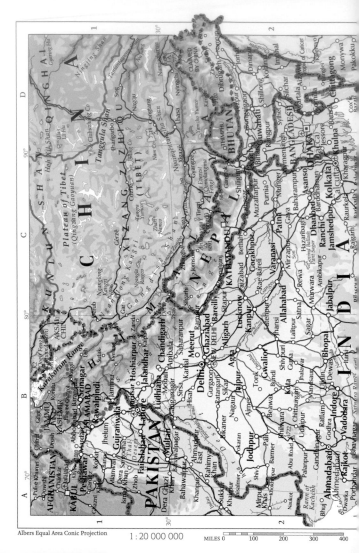

Albers Equal Area Conic Projection

1 : 20 000 000

MILES 0   100   200   300   400

© Collins Bartholomew Ltd

Albers Equal Area Conic Projection

1 : 15 000 000

MILES 0   100   200   300

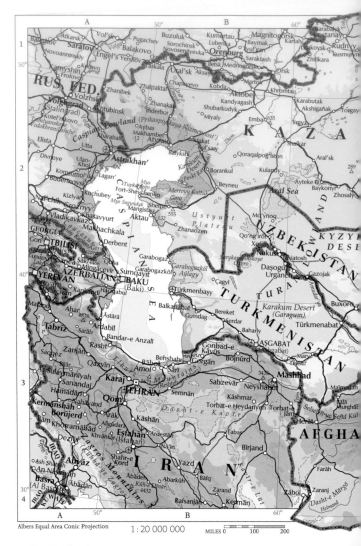

Albers Equal Area Conic Projection

1 : 20 000 000

MILES 0   100   200

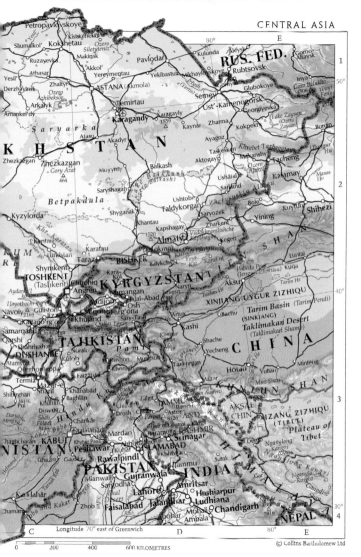

© Collins Bartholomew Ltd

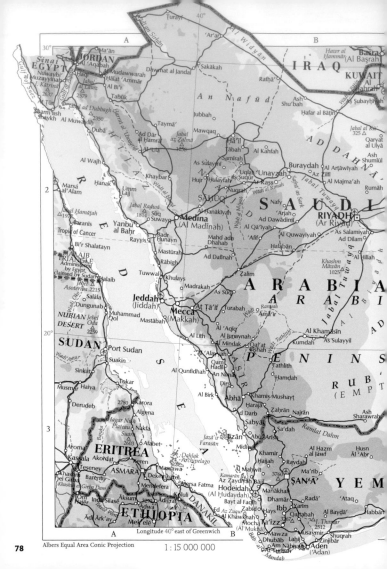

Albers Equal Area Conic Projection

1 : 15 000 000

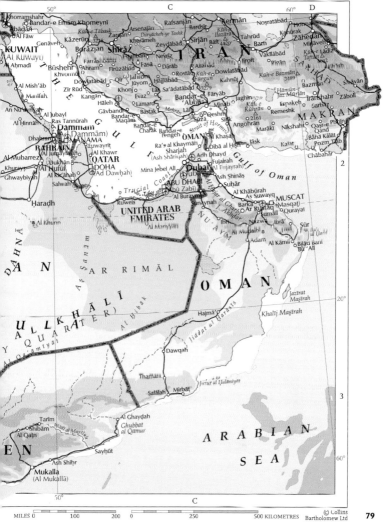

MILES 0   100   200   0   250   500 KILOMETRES   © Collins
                                                                                                  Bartholomew Ltd

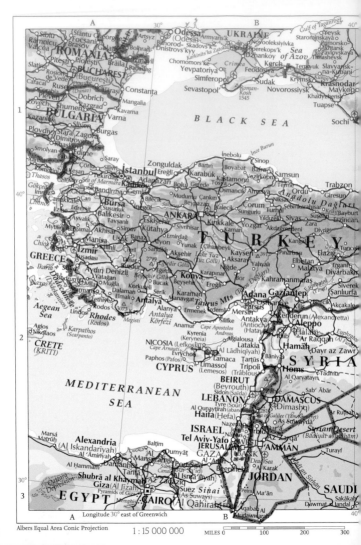

0   250   500 KILOMETRES

Conic Equidistant Projection

1 : 42 000 000

MILES 0   250   500   750

Longitude 75° east of Greenwich

0   500   1000   1500 KILOMETRES

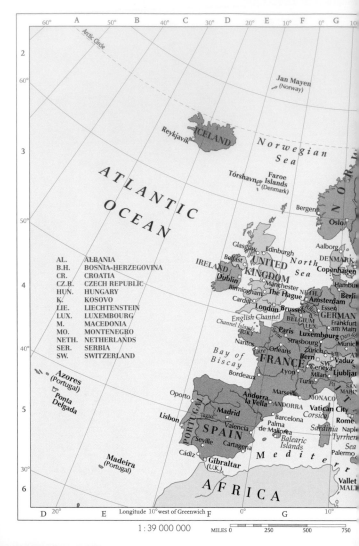

AL.   ALBANIA
B.H.   BOSNIA-HERZEGOVINA
CR.   CROATIA
CZ.R. CZECH REPUBLIC
HUN.   HUNGARY
K.   KOSOVO
LIE.   LIECHTENSTEIN
LUX.   LUXEMBOURG
M.   MACEDONIA
MO.   MONTENEGRO
NETH. NETHERLANDS
SER.   SERBIA
SW.   SWITZERLAND

ATLANTIC OCEAN

Norwegian Sea

Jan Mayen
(Norway)

Reykjavík   ICELAND

Tórshavn   Faroe Islands
(Denmark)

Bergen

Oslo

Glasgow   Edinburgh   *North Sea*
Belfast   Aalborg
IRELAND   UNITED KINGDOM   DENMARK
Dublin   Manchester   Copenhagen
Birmingham   NETH.   Hamburg
Cardiff   The Hague   Amsterdam
London   Brussels   Essen   Berlin
English Channel   BELGIUM   GERMANY
Channel Islands (U.K.)   LUX.   Frankfurt am Main
Paris   Luxembourg
Nantes   Strasbourg   Munich
Orleans   Zürich   SW.   Vaduz
Bay of Biscay   Bern   Geneva   Ljubljana
FRANCE   Lyon   Milan
Bordeaux   Turin   Po
Marseille   MONACO
Oporto   Andorra la Vella   ANDORRA   Vatican City
PORTUGAL   Madrid   Barcelona   Corsica   Rome   Naples
Lisbon   Tagus   SPAIN   Valencia   Palma de Mallorca   Sardinia   *Tyrrhenian Sea*
Seville   Cartagena   *Balearic Islands*   Palermo
Cádiz   Gibraltar (U.K.)   *Mediterr*
Madeira
(Portugal)

Azores
(Portugal)
Ponta Delgada

AFRICA   Valletta   MALTA

Arctic Circle

Longitude 10° west of Greenwich

1 : 39 000 000   MILES 0   250   500   750

© Collins Bartholomew Ltd

0   500   1000 KILOMETRES

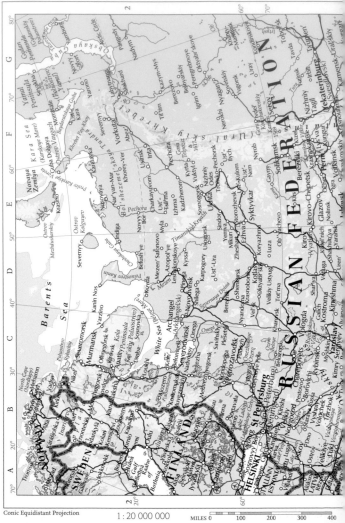

Conic Equidistant Projection   1 : 20 000 000   MILES 0   100   200   300   400

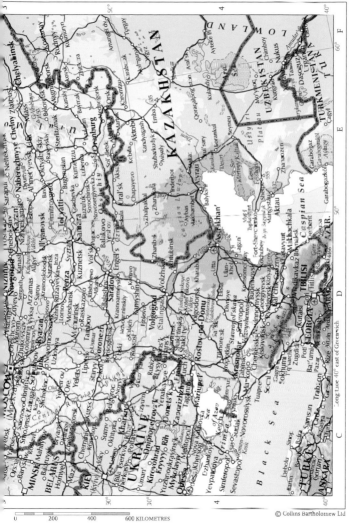

0   200   400   600 KILOMETRES

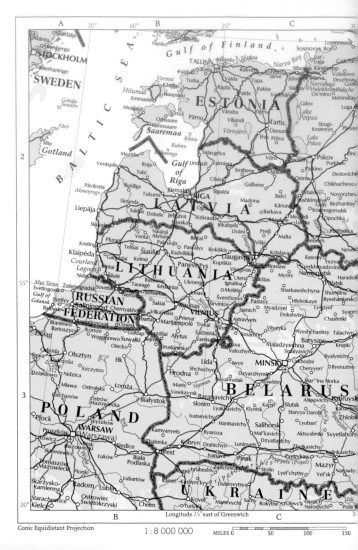

Conic Equidistant Projection

Longitude 25° east of Greenwich

1 : 8 000 000

MILES 0   50   100   150

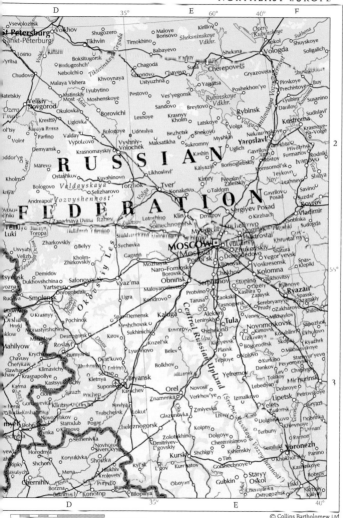

© Collins Bartholomew Ltd

Conic Equidistant Projection 1 : 8 000 000 MILES 0 50 100 150

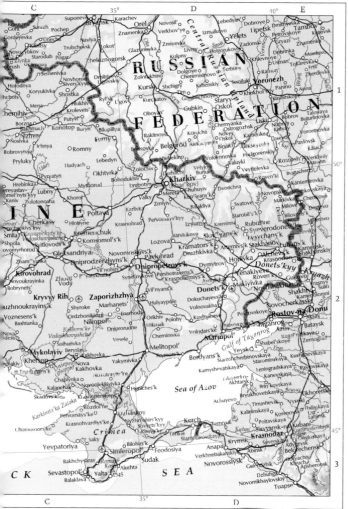

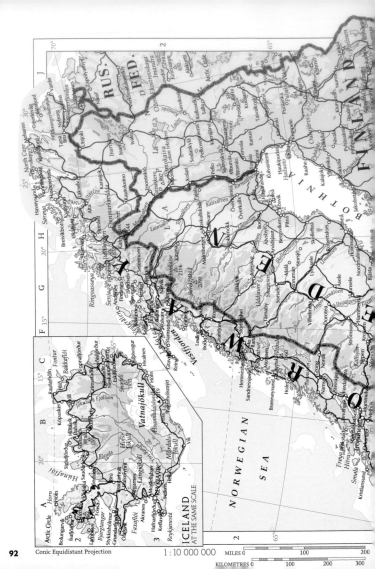

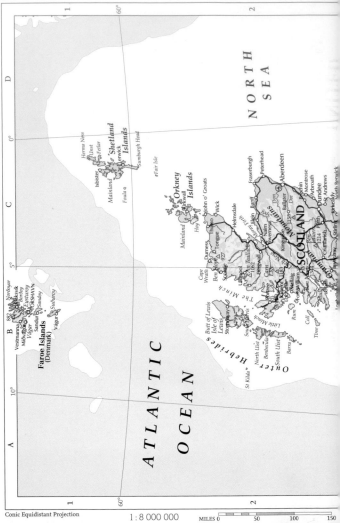

Conic Equidistant Projection

1 : 8 000 000

MILES 0   50   100   150

Map labels

ATLANTIC OCEAN

NORTH SEA

Faroe Islands (Denmark)
- Norðoyar
- Vestmanna
- Mykines
- Borðoy
- Eysturoy
- TÓRSHAVN
- Vágar
- Sandur
- Sandoy
- Vágur
- Suðuroy
- 882

Shetland Islands
- Herma Ness
- Unst
- Fetlar
- Isbister
- Mainland
- Lerwick
- Foula
- Sumburgh Head
- Fair Isle

Orkney Islands
- Mainland
- Kirkwall
- Hoy
- John o' Groats

Outer Hebrides
- Butt of Lewis
- Isle of Lewis
- Stornoway
- North Uist
- Benbecula
- South Uist
- Barra
- St Kilda
- The Minch
- Little Minch

SCOTLAND
- Cape Wrath
- Durness
- Scourie
- Tongue
- Ben Hope 927
- Ben More Assynt 998
- Thurso
- Wick
- Helmsdale
- Ullapool
- Liathach 1062
- Carn Eige 1183
- Ben Nevis 1344
- Fort William
- Mallaig
- Kyle of Lochalsh
- Dingwall
- Inverness
- Nairn
- Elgin
- Banff
- Fraserburgh
- Peterhead
- Grampian Mountains
- Ben Macdui 1309
- Cairn Gorm 1245
- Ballater
- Aberdeen
- Ben Lawers 1214
- Montrose
- Arbroath
- Brechin
- Dundee
- St Andrews
- Stirling
- North Berwick
- Skye
- Rum
- Eigg
- Coll
- Tiree
- Mull
- Don
- Dee

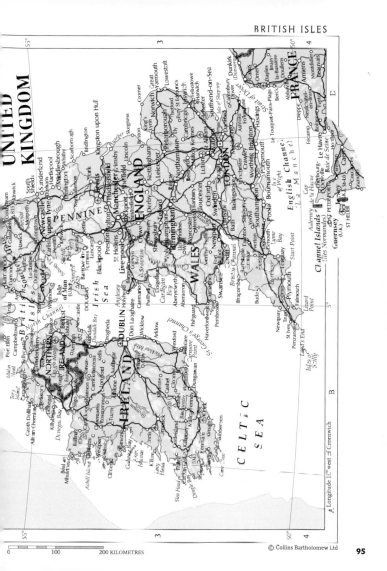

© Collins Bartholomew Ltd

A · B · C · D

North Ronaldsay

Westray
Rousay Sanday
Loth Stronsay
Orkney Papa
Islands Kirkwall
Stromness
Ward Hill Scapa
Hoy *South*
Ronaldsay
Pentland Firth John o'
Dunnet Head o' Groats
Dungansby
Head

Shetland
Herma Ness
Unst
Yell
Fetlar
Ronas Hill Uista
450
Walls *Mainland* Whalsay
Foula Lerwick
Bressay
Shetland
Islands
Sumburgh Sumburgh
Head
60°
Fair Isle

Cape
Wrath Durness
Butt of Lewis
Port of Ness
Thurso Wick
Hope Tongue *Dunbeath*
927
Loch *Naver*
West Stornoway Scourie Ben More Helmsdale
Loch Roag Point of Stoer Assynt Loch
Isle Lochinver 998 Shin Laig
of Ullapool Golspie
58° **Lewis** Dornoch
North An Teallach Dornoch Firth
Harris 1062 Invergordon Lossiemouth
South Loch Ben Black Elgin Buckie Banff Fraserburgh
Harris Gairloch Maree Wyvis Isle Forres Rattray
1046 Dingwall Head
Lochmaddy Achnasheen Inverness Huntly Peterhead
Torridon Strathspey Dufftown Ellon
North Skye Grantown-
Uist Carn on-Spey Inverurie Dyce
Benbecula Portree Eige Aviemore Ben Oldmeldrum Aberdeen
1385 Fort Macdui
South Uist Sgurr Alasdair Augustus Monadhliath Mountains 1309 Ballater Dee
Cuillin Garry Kingussie Braemar Lochnagar Stonehaven
Barra Sound Loch Laggan 1155 North Esk
Canna Mallaig Brechin
Castlebay Rum Lochaber GRAMPIAN MOUNTAINS Montrose
Eigg Ben Blair Atholl Arbroath
Fort Nevis Pitlochry
Point of William 1344 Sidlaw
Ardnamurchan Salen Glen Shiel Ben Kirriemuir Hills
Coll Arinagour Morvern Rannoch Lawers Blairgowrie
Tiree Tobermory Moor 1214 Forth of Tay
Mull Loch Tay Perth Dundee **NORTH**
Ben More Oban Killin St Andrews
966 Loch Awe Crianlarich Crieff **SEA**
Iona Callander Cupar Fife Ness
Fionnphort Colonsay Inveraray Ben Lomond Glenrothes Buckhaven
Loch Stirling Alloa North Berwick
Jura Tarbet Lomond Dunfermline Kirkcaldy Dunbar
Helensburgh Cowdenbeath
56° Lochgilphead Dumbarton Firth of Forth
Islay Greenock Clydebank **Edinburgh** St Abb's Head
Port Johnstone **Glasgow** Musselburgh Berwick-
Askaig Rothesay Paisley Leith upon-Tweed
Gigha Largs Coatbridge Cumbernauld Haddington Holy Island
Port Ellen Goat Fell East Motherwell Penicuik Duns (Lindisfarne)
Mull of Oa 874 Kilbride Hamilton Peebles Galashiels
Arran Ardrossan Biggar Selkirk Newtown
Rathlin Brodick Irvine Kilmarnock Moffat St Boswells 815
Island Prestwick **SOUTHERN UPLANDS** The Cheviot
Giant's Ayr Cumnock Broad Hawick Jedburgh **CHEVIOT**
Causeway Maybole Law Alnwick
Portrush Mull of Kintyre 840 **HILLS**
Coleraine Girvan Thornhill Rothbury
Ballycastle Merrick Moffat Ashington
NORTHERN Ballymoney 843 Dumfries Lockerbie Morpeth
IRELAND Cairnryan Castle Kielder **Newcastle**
Cullybackey Ballymena Newton Douglas Dalbeattie Water **upon Tyne**
Antrim Larne Stranraer Longtown Hexham Blaydon Gateshead
Whitehead Kirkcudbright Carlisle Consett Durham
Ballyclare Luce Annan Spennymoor Wear
Newtownabbey Bay Whithorn Solway Firth Cockermouth Cross **ENGLAND**
Bangor Donaghadee Mull of Galloway Workington Penrith Fell
Belfast Fleetwood 931 893

A · B · C · D

6° 4° Longitude 4° west of Greenwich 2°

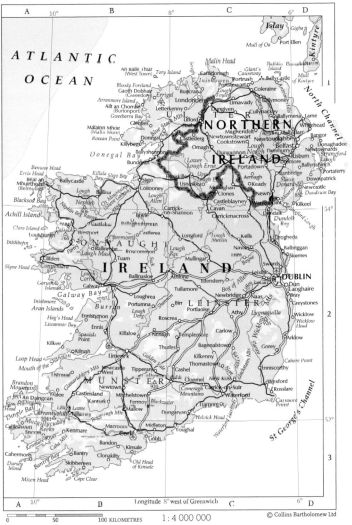

0   50   100 KILOMETRES   1 : 4 000 000   © Collins Bartholomew Ltd

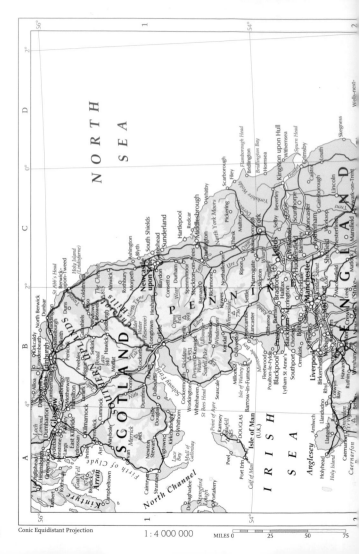

Conic Equidistant Projection

1 : 4 000 000

MILES 0   25   50   75

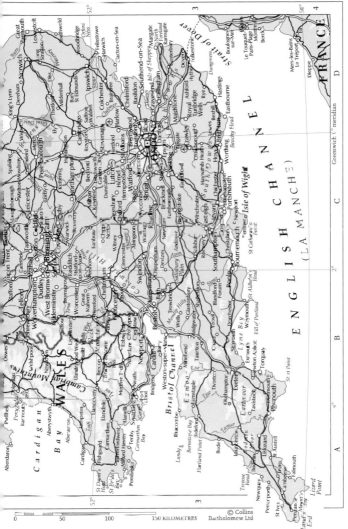

Conic Equidistant Projection

1 : 4 000 000

MILES 0   25   50   75

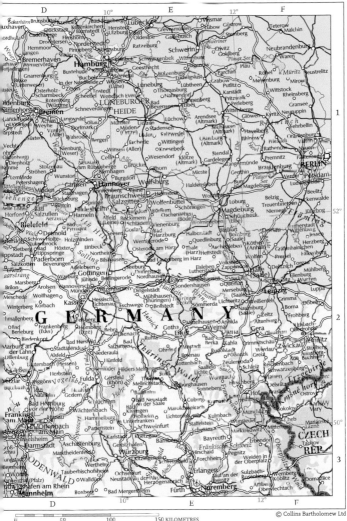

Conic Equidistant Projection

1 : 8 000 000

Longitude 10° east of Greenwich

MILES 0   50   100   150

0   100   200 KILOMETRES

Conic Equidistant Projection

1 : 8 000 000

MILES 0   50   100   150

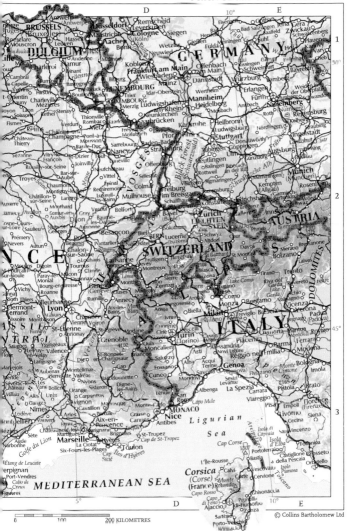

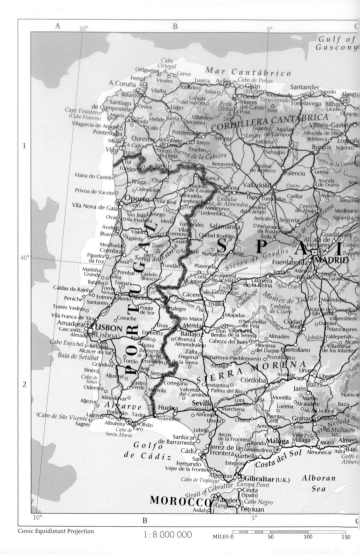

0   100   200 KILOMETRES

Greenwich 0° meridian

MILES 0   50   100   150

Longitude 10° east of Greenwich

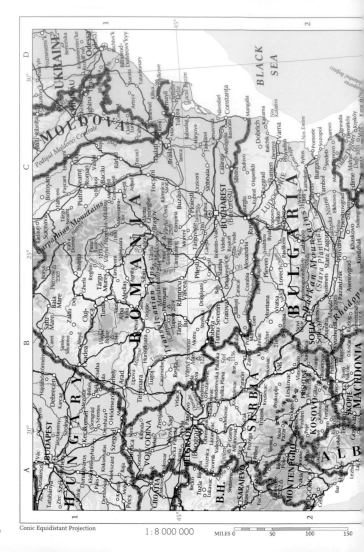

Conic Equidistant Projection

1 : 8 000 000

MILES 0   50   100   150

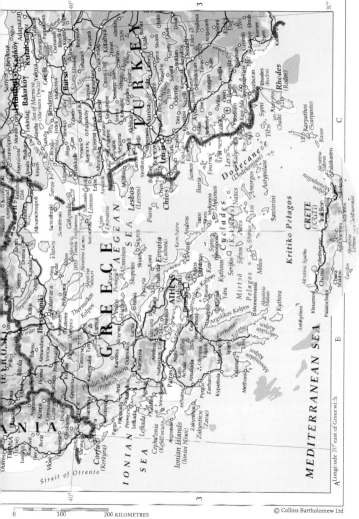

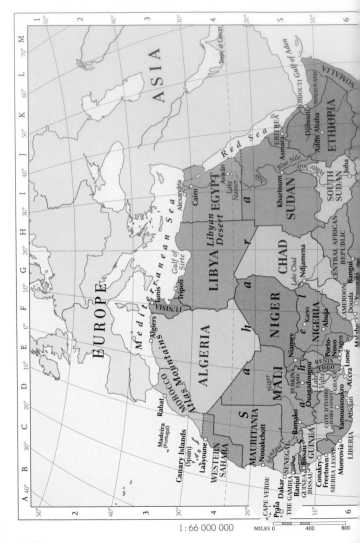

1 : 66 000 000

MILES 0   400   800

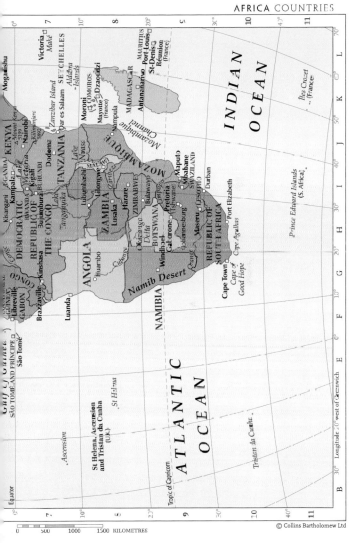

© Collins Bartholomew Ltd

0   500   1000   1500 KILOMETRES

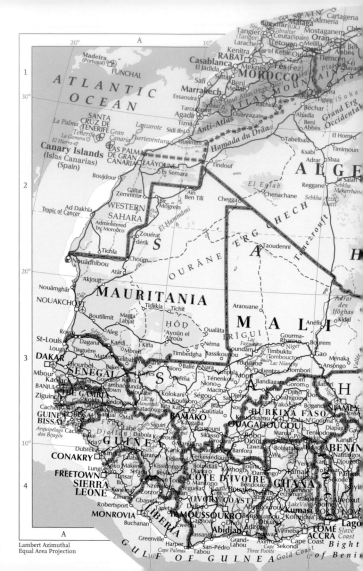

Lambert Azimuthal
Equal Area Projection

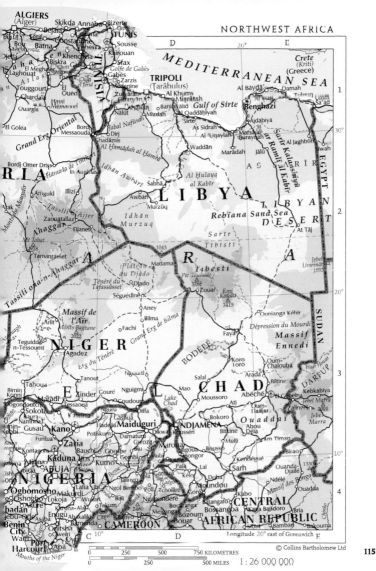

ALGIERS
(Alger)
Skikda Annaba Bizerte
Béjaïa
Guelma
Bou
Saâda Batna Constantine
El Kef
Khenchela Tébessa
Biskra Gafsa TUNIS
Sousse
Kairouan
Sfax
Golfe de Gabès
Gabès
Zarzis

MEDITERRANEAN SEA

Crete
(Kriti)
(Greece)

TRIPOLI
(Ṭarābulus)
Al Khums Miṣrātah
Al Qaddāḥīyah
Banī Walīd
Al Bayḍā Darnah
Tubruq
Marsa

Mizdah
Gulf of Sirte
Sirte
As Sidrah
Al 'Uqaylah Benghazi
Ajdābiyā
Marādah
Burayqah
As Jaghbūb
Siwah

LIBYA

Al Hulayq al Kabīr
Waddān
LIBYAN
DESERT

Sabhā
Awbārī
Murzūq
Idhān Murzūq

Rebiana Sand Sea

Sarir Tibesti

At Tāj
Jebel
Uwaynat
1893

Madama
Tibesti
Pic Toussidé
3265
Zouar
Emi
Koussi
3415

SUDAN

NIGER

Agadez

Bilma
Grand Erg de Bilma

Fachi

Fayā
BODÉLÉ

Ounianga Kébir
Dépression du Mourdi
Massif
Ennedi

DARFUR

CHAD

Lake
Chad

N'DJAMENA

Maiduguri

NIGERIA

ABUJA

CAMEROON

CENTRAL
AFRICAN REPUBLIC

Longitude 20° east of Greenwich

© Collins Bartholomew Ltd

0   250   500   750 KILOMETRES
0   250   500 MILES

1 : 26 000 000

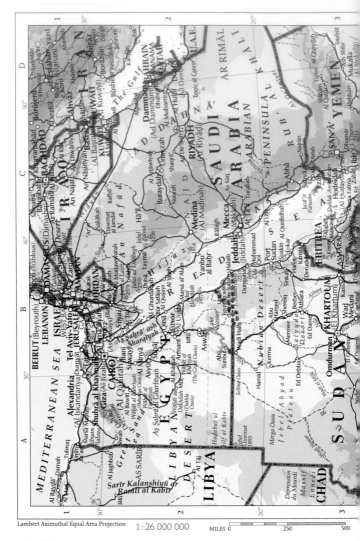

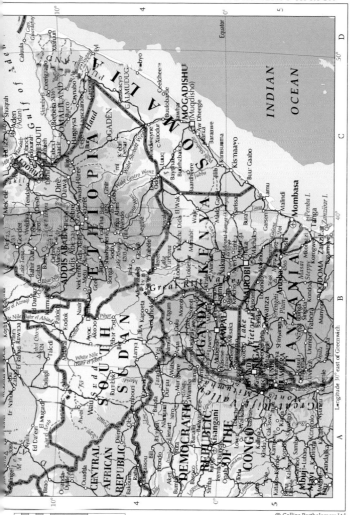

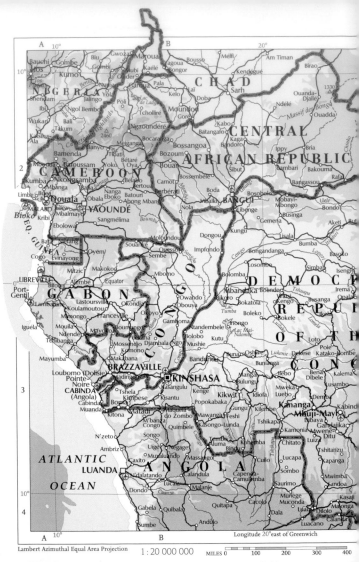

Lambert Azimuthal Equal Area Projection   1 : 20 000 000   MILES 0   100   200   300   400

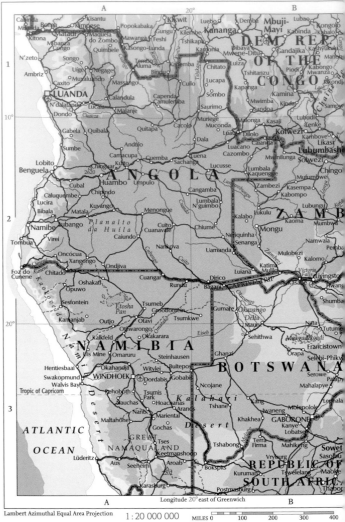

Lambert Azimuthal Equal Area Projection

1 : 20 000 000

MILES 0   100   200   300   400

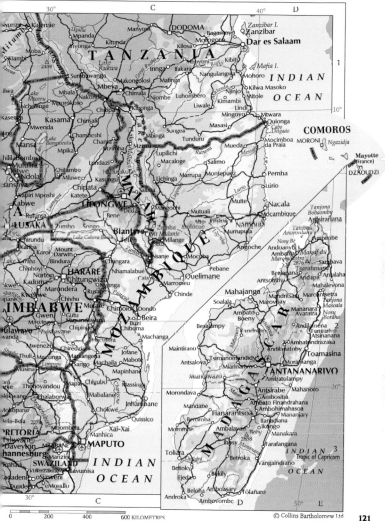

© Collins Bartholomew Ltd

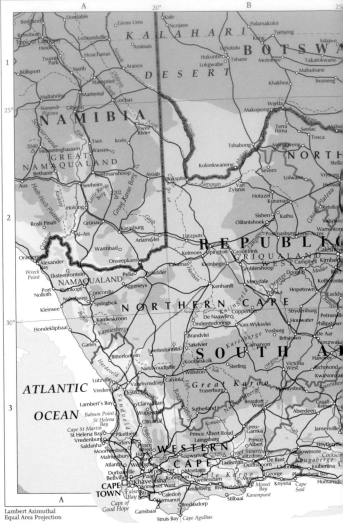

Lambert Azimuthal
Equal Area Projection

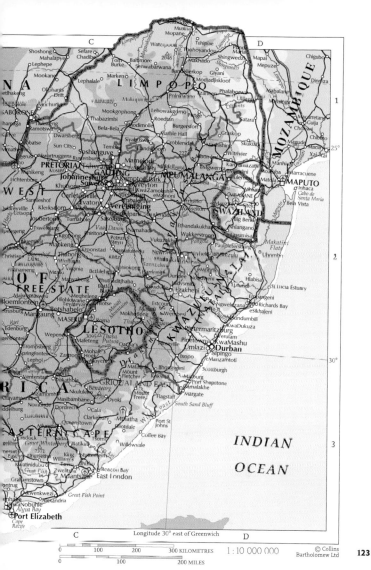

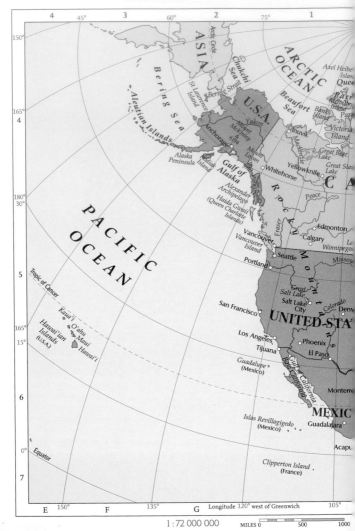

1 : 72 000 000   MILES 0   500   1000

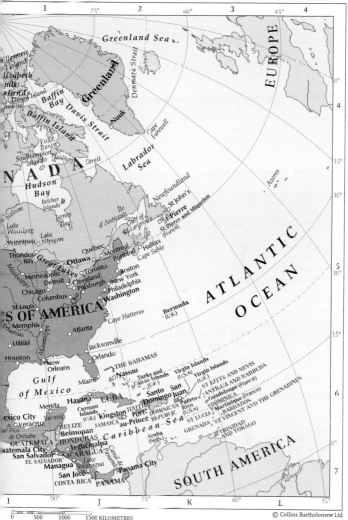

Greenland Sea

EUROPE

Ellesmere Island
lizabeth nds
slands
Devon Island
hannel
Baffin Bay
Greenland
Baffin Island
Davis Strait
Nuuk
Foxe Basin
Southampton Island
Hudson Strait
Denmark Strait
Cape Farewell

Labrador Sea

Azores

ANADA

Hudson Bay
Belcher Islands
James Bay
Île d'Anticosti
Newfoundland
Gulf of St. Lawrence
St-Pierre
St Pierre and Miquelon (France)
St John's

Nelson
Lake Winnipeg
Lake Nipigon
Québec
Montréal
Portland
Halifax
Cape Sable

Thunder Bay
Great Lakes
Ottawa
Toronto
Boston

Minneapolis
Detroit
Cleveland
New York

Chicago
Pittsburgh
Philadelphia
Washington

Columbus

ATLANTIC OCEAN

St Louis
S OF AMERICA
Memphis
Atlanta
Cape Hatteras
Bermuda (U.K.)

Dallas
Houston
New Orleans
Jacksonville
Orlando

Gulf of Mexico
Miami
THE BAHAMAS
Nassau
Turks and Caicos Islands (U.K.)
Virgin Islands
Virgin Islands (U.S.A.)
ANTIGUA AND BARBUDA

Merida
Havana
CUBA
Santo Domingo
San Juan
Puerto Rico (U.S.A.)
Guadeloupe (France)
DOMINICA

exico City
Cayman Islands (U.K.)
Kingston
HAITI
Port-au-Prince
DOMINICAN REPUBLIC
Martinique (France)
ST LUCIA
BARBADOS

Veracruz
Yucatán
JAMAICA
ST VINCENT AND THE GRENADINES

Pico de Orizaba
BELIZE
Belmopan
Caribbean Sea
Aruba (Neth.)
GRENADA
TRINIDAD AND TOBAGO

GUATEMALA
HONDURAS
Tegucigalpa
Canal de Panamá

atemala City
NICARAGUA
EL SALVADOR
Managua
Lake Nicaragua

San Salvador
San José
Panama City
COSTA RICA
PANAMA

SOUTH AMERICA

0   500   1000   1500 KILOMETRES

© Collins Bartholomew Ltd

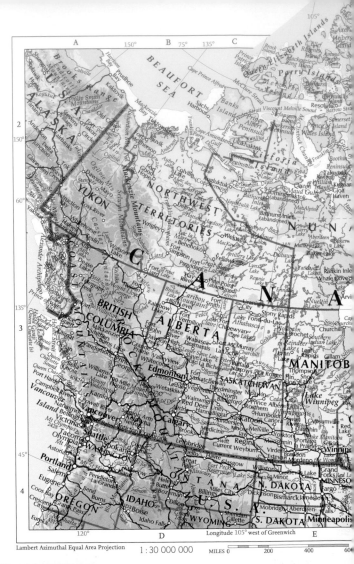

Lambert Azimuthal Equal Area Projection

1 : 30 000 000

MILES 0   200   400   600

Longitude 105° west of Greenwich

© Collins Bartholomew Ltd

Lambert Azimuthal Equal Area Projection

1 : 15 000 000

MILES 0   100   200   300

Longitude 120° west of Greenwich

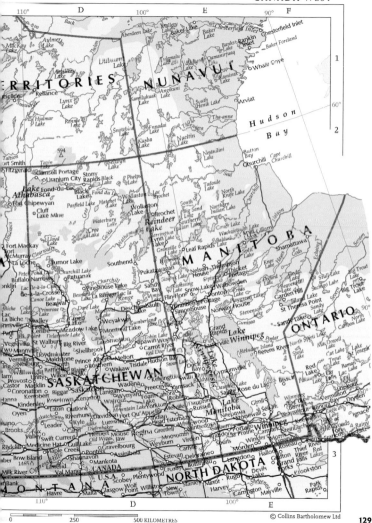

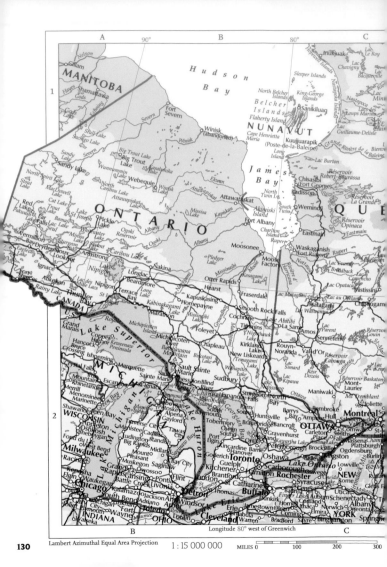

Lambert Azimuthal Equal Area Projection   1 : 15 000 000   MILES 0   100   200   300

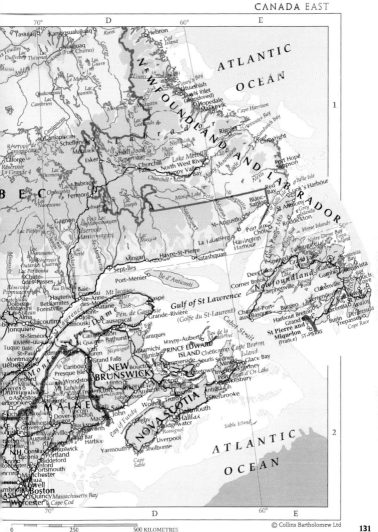

500 KILOMETRES

© Collins Bartholomew Ltd

Lambert Azimuthal Equal Area Projection

1 : 25 000 000

MILES 0   250   500

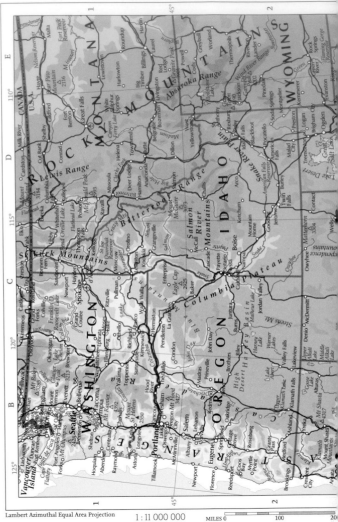

1 : 11 000 000

MILES 0   100   20

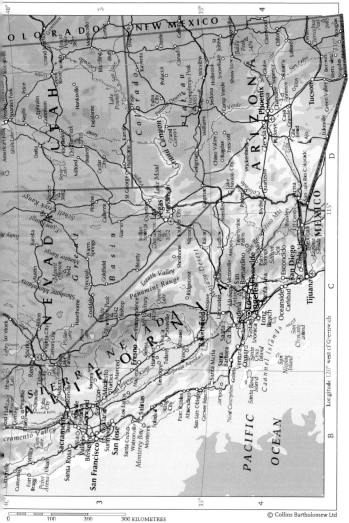

0   100   200   300 KILOMETRES

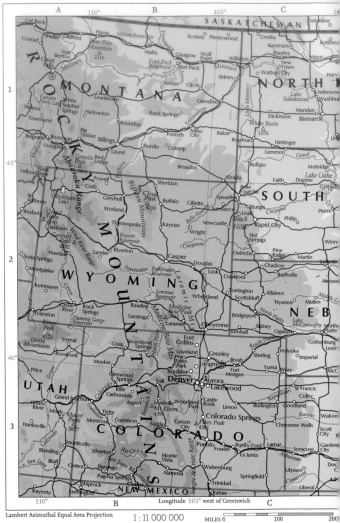

Lambert Azimuthal Equal Area Projection   1 : 11 000 000   MILES 0   100   200

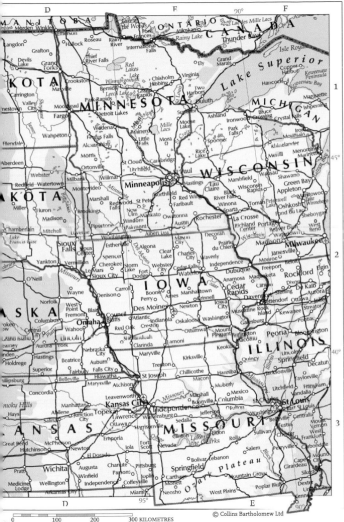

0   100   200   300 KILOMETRES

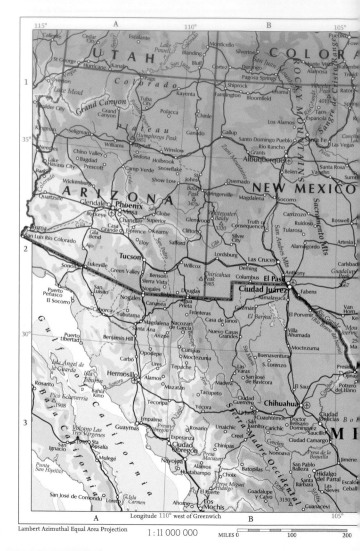

Lambert Azimuthal Equal Area Projection 1 : 11 000 000 MILES 0 100 200

Longitude 110° west of Greenwich

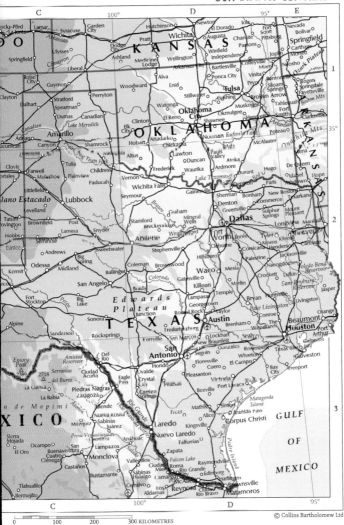

0   100   200   300 KILOMETRES

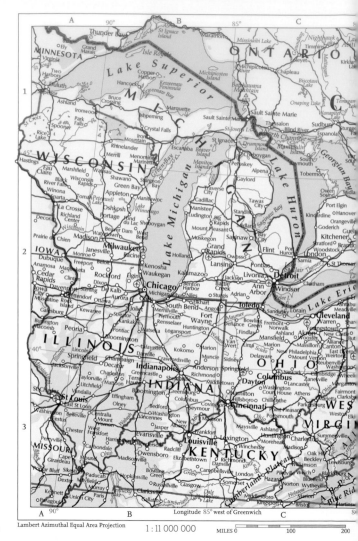

Lambert Azimuthal Equal Area Projection   1 : 11 000 000   MILES 0   100   200

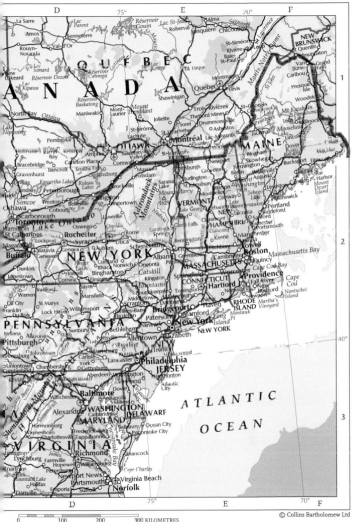

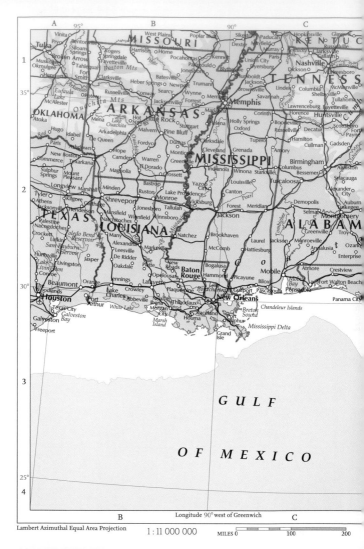

Lambert Azimuthal Equal Area Projection

1 : 11 000 000

MILES 0   100   200

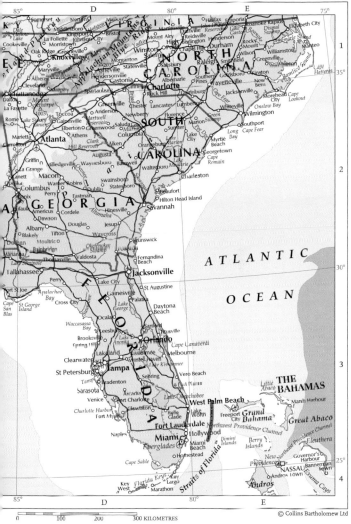

0   100   200   300 KILOMETRES

GULF

OF

MEXICO

GULF OF MEXICO

BAHÍA
DE CAMPECHE

STATES OF AMERICA

TEXAS

MEXICO

SIERRA MADRE DEL SUR

YUCATÁN

BELIZE

GUATEMALA

Gulf of Tehuantepec

Tropic of Cancer

© Collins Bartholomew Ltd

0   250 KILOMETRES

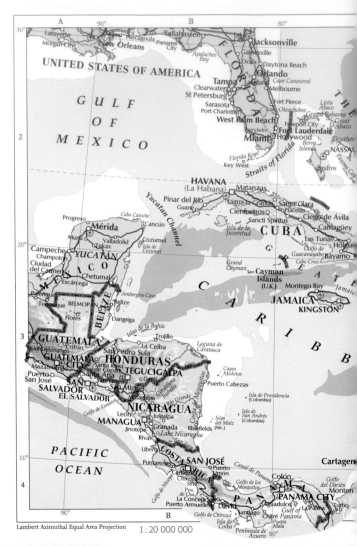

Lambert Azimuthal Equal Area Projection   1 : 20 000 000

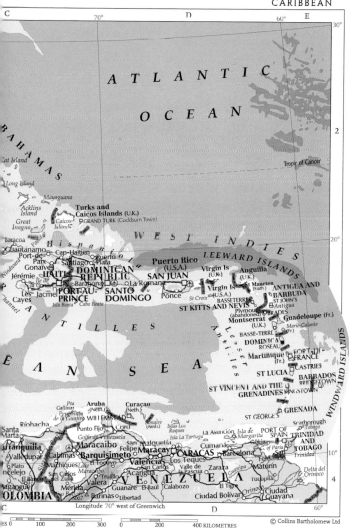

ATLANTIC

OCEAN

Tropic of Cancer

BAHAMAS

Cat Island

Long Island

Mayaguana

Acklins
Island

Great
Inagua

Caicos
Islands

Baracoa

Guantanamo

Port-de-
Paix
Gonaïves

Jérémie

Les
Cayes

Cap-Haïtien

Santiago

Barahona

Jacmel

Turks and
Caicos Islands (U.K.)
GRAND TURK (Cockburn Town)

WEST   INDIES

Hispaniola

Puerto
Plata

HAITI   DOMINICAN
REPUBLIC

PORT-AU-
PRINCE

Isla Beata   Cabo Beata

Puerto Rico
(U.S.A.)

SANTO
DOMINGO

La Romana

SAN JUAN

Ponce

St Croix

LEEWARD ISLANDS

Virgin Is
(U.K.)

Virgin Is
(U.S.A.)

Anguilla
(U.K.)

St Maarten
(Neth.)

BASSETERRE

ST KITTS AND NEVIS

Montserrat
(abandoned)

ANTIGUA AND
BARBUDA

ST JOHN'S

Antigua

BRADES

Guadeloupe (Fr.)

BASSE-TERRE

Marie-Galante

DOMINICA

ROSEAU

Martinique
(Fr.)

FORT-DE-
FRANCE

Ile de
la Gonâve

ANTILLES

Greater   Antilles

Lesser

Antilles

CARIBBEAN   SEA

ST LUCIA

CASTRIES

BARBADOS

BRIDGETOWN

ST VINCENT AND THE
GRENADINES   KINGSTOWN

ST GEORGE'S   GRENADA

WINDWARD ISLANDS

Pta
Gallinas
Península
de la Guajira

Riohacha

Santa
Marta

Barranquilla

Valledupar

Plato

El Banco

Magangué

COLOMBIA

Maicao

Aruba
(Neth.)

Curaçao
(Neth.)

WILLEMSTAD

Bonaire
(Neth.)

Punto Fijo

Coro

San Carlos
del Zulia

Cabimas

Maracaibo

Lake
Maracaibo

Mérida

Barinas

Valera

Trujillo

San
Felipe

Tocuyo

Barquisimeto

Guanare

Acarigua

El Baúl

Islas Los
Roques

Isla La Tortuga

Golfo de Venezuela

Valencia

Los Teques

Valle de
la Pascua

Calabozo

Libertad

Islas Los
Testigos

Isla de
Margarita

La Asunción

Cumaná

CARACAS

Barcelona

Maturín

Zaraza

VENEZUELA

Orinoco

El Tigre

Guanare

PORT OF
SPAIN

Scarborough

Tobago

TRINIDAD
AND
TOBAGO

San
Fernando

G. de Paria

Trinidad

Guanipa

Tucupita

Delta del
Orinoco

Ciudad
Guayana

Ciudad Bolívar

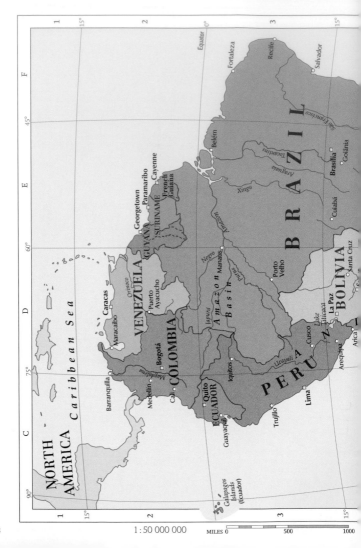

1 : 50 000 000

MILES 0   500   1000

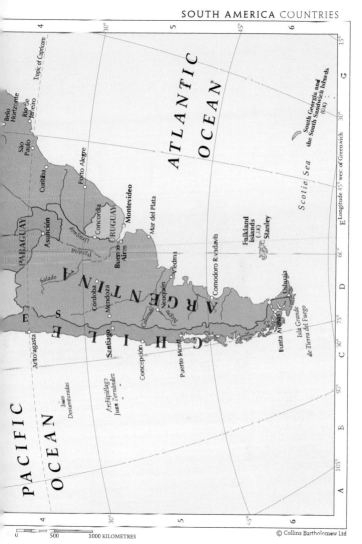

Lambert Azimuthal Equal Area Projection   1 : 25 000 000   MILES 0   250   500

ATLANTIC

OCEAN

GEORGETOWN
New
Amsterdam
Linden
Nickerie
Professor van
Blommestein Meer
PARAMARIBO
St-Laurent-du-Maroni
Kourou
CAYENNE
SURINAME
French
Guiana
Pontoetoe
Oiapoque

Serra Tumucumaque
Lourenço
Calçoene
Ilha de Maracá
Amapá

Mouths of the Amazon
Porto
Santana
Mazagão
Macapá
Cabo
Maguarinho
Arere
Pará
Baía de Marajó
Equator

Oriximiná
Óbidos
Almeirim
Ilha de Marajó
Salinópolis
Bragança
Breves
Chaves
Portel
BELÉM
Vigia
Viseu

Parintins
Monte
Alegre
Santarém
Altamira
Cametá
Acará
Curuçá
Castanhal
Pinheiro
São Luís
Camocim

Itacoatiara
Itaituba
Tucuruí
Represa de
Tucuruí
Jacundá
Marabá
Bacabal
Codó
Itapecuru
Mirim
Fuzilândia
Timbiras
Tianguá
Sobral
Fortaleza
Caucaia

acareacanga
Aruanā
São
Félix
Imperatriz
Tocantinópolis
Grajaú
Barra
do Corda
Caxias
Timon
Pres. Dutra
Campo
Maior
Crateús
Canindé
Quixadá
Aracati

Manuelzinho
Araguaína
Porto
Franco
Balsas
Aldeia Boa
Esperança
Teresina
Piripiri
Tauá
Iguatu
Mossoró
Macau
Natal

R A Z I L
Conceição
do Araguaia
Carolina
Jerumenha
Floriano
Oeiras
Canto do Buriti
Uruçuí
São Raimundo
Picos
Pulastana
Salgueiro
Crato
Juazeiro do Norte
dos Guararapes
Campina
Grande
João
Pessoa
Olinda
Recife

Serra
do Cachimbo
Santa Maria
das Barreiras
Pedro
Afonso
Palmas
Porto
Nacional
Dianópolis
Barragem de
Sobradinho
Corrente
Petrolina
Juazeiro
Senhor do Bonfim
Xique-
Xique
Floresta
Paulo
Afonso
Jacobina
Garanhuns
Caruaru
Maceió

orto José
dos Gaúchos
Óbidos
Porto
Artur
Ilha do
Bananal
São Félix
Natividade
Barreiras
Ibotirama
Santana
Bom Jesus
da Lapa
Irecê
Monte Santo
Serrinha
Feira de
Santana
Aracaju
Estância

Diamantino
Rosário Oeste
barra do
Garças
Aruanã
Goiás
Poranga
Uruaçu
Niquelândia
Formosa
Correntina
Posse
Itaberaba
Brumado
Guanambi
Itabuna
Vitória da
Conquista
Sto.
Antônio
de Jesus
Salvador
Ubaitaba
Ilhéus
Itapetinga

Cáceres
Rondonópolis
Alto Garças
BRASÍLIA
Anápolis
Unaí
Montes
Claros
Janaúba
Januária
Almenara
Porto
Seguro

Puerto
Isabel
Coxim
Itiquira
Jataí
Goiânia
Rio
Verde
Itumbiara
Paraúna
Vianópolis
Paracatu
Jequitaí
Salinas
Teófilo
Otoni
Alcobaça

Rio Verde de Mato Grosso
Araguari
Patos
de Minas

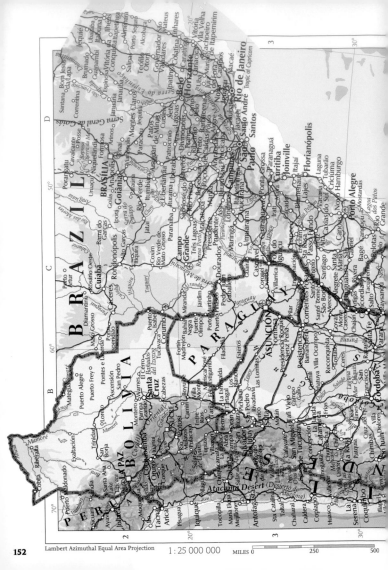

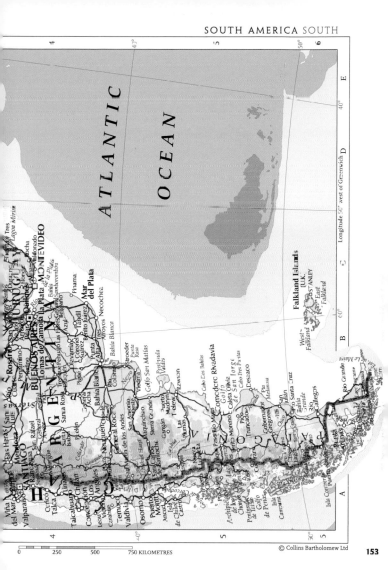

ATLANTIC

OCEAN

URUGUAY

MONTEVIDEO

Mar
del Plata

BUENOS AIRES

ARGENTINA

Bahía Blanca

Península
Valdés

Golfo San Matías

Comodoro Rivadavia

Golfo
de San Jorge

PATAGONIA

Río Gallegos

Falkland Islands
(U.K.)

West
Falkland

East
Falkland

STANLEY

Longitude 50° west of Greenwich D

CHILE

Santiago

Valparaíso

Concepción

Valdivia

Puerto
Montt

Isla de Chiloé

Río Grande

Estrecho de Le Maire

© Collins Bartholomew Ltd

0   250   500   750 KILOMETRES

153

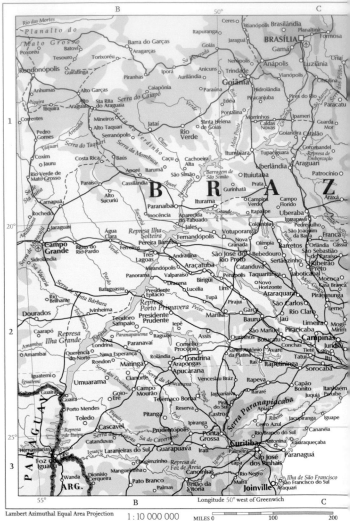

Lambert Azimuthal Equal Area Projection   1 : 10 000 000   MILES 0   100   200

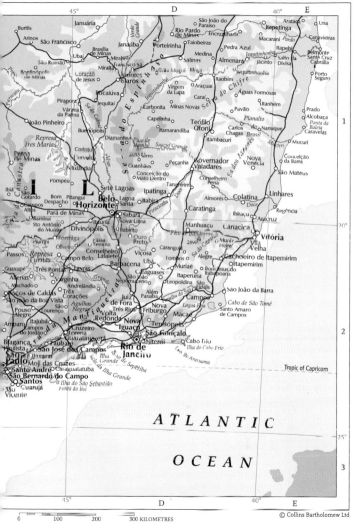

ATLANTIC

OCEAN

Tropic of Capricorn

© Collins Bartholomew Ltd

0   100   200   300 KILOMETRES

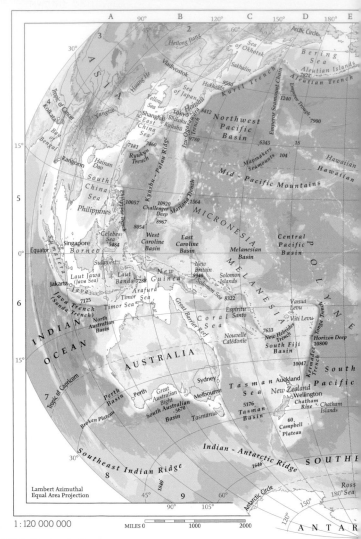

1 : 120 000 000

MILES 0   1000   2000

Lambert Azimuthal
Equal Area Projection

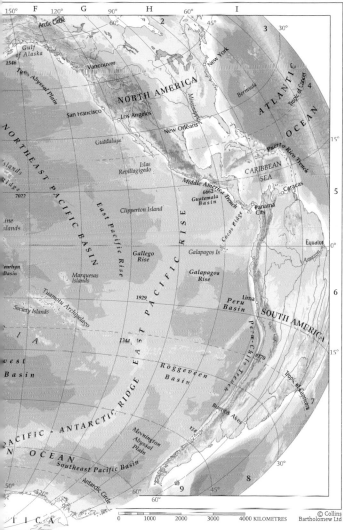

150° F 120° G 90° H 60° I 30°

Arctic Circle

Gulf of Alaska
1546
Turf Abyssal Plain

NORTHEAST PACIFIC BASIN

...lands
...idge
7022

Vancouver

San Francisco
Los Angeles

NORTH AMERICA

Guadalupe

Islas
Revillagigedo

Mississippi

New Orleans

Bermuda

New York

ATLANTIC OCEAN

Tropic of Cancer

...ine
...slands

East Pacific Rise

Clipperton Island

Middle America Trench

6663
Guatemala
Basin

Puerto Rico Trench

CARIBBEAN SEA

15°

...enrhyn
Basin

Gallego
Rise

Marquesas
Islands

1929

Galapagos Is

Galapagos
Rise

Cocos Ridge

Panama
City

Caracas

Equator

Amazon

0°

Tuamotu Archipelago

Society Islands

1344

Lima

Peru
Basin

SOUTH AMERICA

6

...I   A

...west

Basin

EAST PACIFIC RISE

Roggeveen
Basin

Peru-Chile Trench

5170

Buenos Aires

15°

Tropic of Capricorn

7

PACIFIC - ANTARCTIC RIDGE

Mornington
Abyssal
Plain

...N   OCEAN

Southeast Pacific Basin

Antarctic Circle

30°

9

8

50° 120° 60° 45° 30°

60°

...I C A

0   1000   2000   3000   4000 KILOMETRES

© Collins
Bartholomew Ltd

157

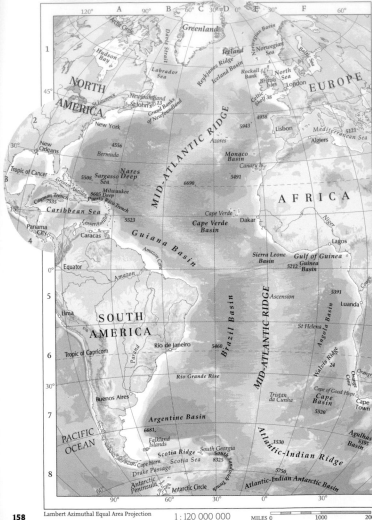

ATLANTIC OCEAN

120°   A   90°   B   60°   C   30°   D   0°   E   30°   F   60°

Arctic Circle

Greenland
Davis Strait   Iceland   Norwegian Basin   Norwegian Sea   Baltic Sea

Hudson Bay   Reykjanes Ridge   Iceland Basin   Rockall Bank   North Sea   British Isles   London

NORTH AMERICA   45°   Labrador Sea   Celtic Shelf 38   EUROPE

St Lawrence   Newfoundland   St John's 13   4938   5943   Lisbon   Mediterranean Sea   5121

New York   Grand Banks of Newfoundland   Azores   Monaco Basin   Algiers

New Orleans   4556   Bermuda   30°   Canary Is.   Canary Is.

Tropic of Cancer   Sargasso Sea   Nares Deep   5508   6690   5491   AFRICA

Greater Antilles   Milwaukee   8605 Deep   Puerto Rico Trench   Cape Verde   Dakar

Cayman Trench   7535   15°   Caribbean Sea   Lesser Antilles   5523   Cape Verde Basin

Panama City   Guiana Basin   Sierra Leone Basin   Gulf of Guinea   Lagos   Niger

Caracas   Amazon Cone   5212   Guinea Basin

Equator   Amazon   0°   Ascension   5391   Cono   Luanda

Lima   SOUTH AMERICA   Brazil Basin   St Helena   Angola Basin

MID-ATLANTIC RIDGE   MID-ATLANTIC RIDGE

Rio de Janeiro   5460   6

Tropic of Capricorn   Paraná   Rio Grande Rise   30°   Walvis Ridge   24   Orange Cone

Buenos Aires   Tristan da Cunha   5520   Cape Basin   Cape of Good Hope   Cape Town

PACIFIC OCEAN   Argentine Basin   7   Agulhas Basin   6195

6681   Falkland Islands   1530   Atlantic-Indian Ridge

Cape Horn   Scotia Ridge   South Georgia   South Sandwich Trench   5750

Drake Passage   Scotia Sea   8325   8

Antarctic Peninsula   Antarctic Circle   Atlantic-Indian Antarctic Basin

90°   60°   30°   0°   30°

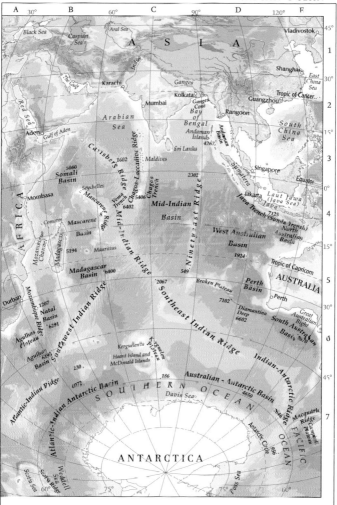

A   30°   B   60°   C   90°   D   120°   E

Black Sea
Caspian Sea
Aral Sea
A   S   I   A
Vladivostok

45°
1

The Gulf
Karachi
Indus
Ganges
Shanghai
East China Sea
Tropic of Cancer

30°

Red Sea
Aden
Gulf of Aden
Arabian Sea
Mumbai
Kolkata
Ganges Cone
Bay of Bengal
Rangoon
Guangzhou

2

Andaman Islands
4267
Sri Lanka
Maldives
South China Sea

15°

Carlsberg Ridge
1602
Chagos-Laccadive Ridge
Andaman Basin

3

AFRICA
Somali Basin
5060
Seychelles
Mascarene Ridge
6402
Vema Trench
Chagos Trench
5406
Chagos Bank
Mid-Indian Basin
2302
Ninetyeast Ridge
Sumatra
Singapore
Equator

0°

Mombasa
Jakarta
Java
Laut Jawa (Java Sea)
Mid-Indian Basin

Comoros
Mascarene Basin
Java Trench (Sunda Trench)
7125
North Australian Basin

4

Madagascar
5194
Mauritius
Mozambique Channel
Mid-Indian Ridge
West Australian Basin
1924

15°

Madagascar Basin
6400
549
Tropic of Capricorn
AUSTRALIA

5

Durban
Mozambique Basin
1207
Natal Basin
6291
Agulhas Plateau
Southwest Indian Ridge
2067
7102
Broken Plateau
Perth Basin
Perth

30°

Agulhas Basin
6195
Southeast Indian Ridge
Diamantina Deep
6602
South Australian Basin
Great Australian Bight

6

Atlantic-Indian Ridge
Kerguelen Plateau
Kerguelen
Heard Island and McDonald Islands
130
Indian-Antarctic Ridge

45°

Atlantic-Indian Antarctic Basin
6071
186
Australian-Antarctic Basin
4650
PACIFIC

Southeast Indian Ridge
Macquarie Ridge

SOUTHERN   OCEAN
Davis Sea
Antarctic Ridge
956
Campbell Plateau

7

Scotia Sea
Weddell Sea
ANTARCTICA
Ross Sea

60°   75°   90°   75°   60°

0   1000   2000   3000   4000 KILOMETRES

© Collins Bartholomew Ltd

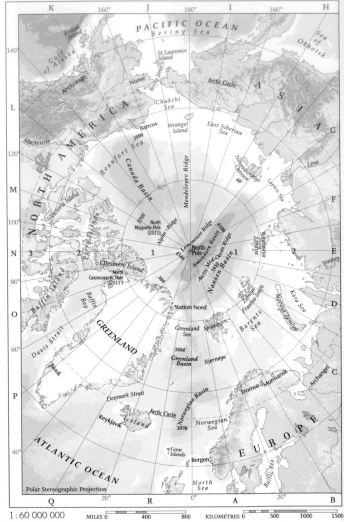

ARCTIC OCEAN

K   160°   J   180°   I   160°   H

PACIFIC OCEAN
Bering Sea

140°   St Lawrence Island
Nome   Bering Strait   Arctic Circle
Gulf of Alaska   Kodiak Island
Anchorage

L   Chukchi Sea   70°   Wrangel Island   East Siberian Sea
Barrow   3990

Mackenzie   Beaufort Sea   Canada Basin   80°   Mendeleyev Ridge   Nautical Mile Chenoyt 60   Laptev Sea   Lena

M   3700   North Magnetic Pole (2011)   Alpha Ridge   Lomonosov Ridge   4100   G   F

Victoria Island   4340   North Pole   Amundsen Basin   Nansen Basin   Khatanga

N   3   2   Ellesmere Island   1   North Geomagnetic Pole (2011)   Arctic Mid-Ocean Ridge   3910   1   2   Yenisey

Baffin Island   Baffin Bay   304   Franz Josef Land   Zemlya   Kara Sea   Novaya Zemlya   D

O   Davis Strait   Station Nord   Greenland Sea   Spitsbergen   Barents Sea

GREENLAND   Greenland Basin   3884   Bjørnøya

Nuuk   C

P   Denmark Strait   Tromsø   Murmansk   Archangel

Reykjavik   Arctic Circle   Norwegian Basin   Norwegian Sea

Iceland   3970   Bergen

ATLANTIC OCEAN   40°   Faroe Islands   North Sea   EUROPE   Baltic Sea

Polar Stereographic Projection

Q   20°   R   0°   A   20°   B

NORTH AMERICA   ASIA

160   1 : 60 000 000   MILES 0   400   800   KILOMETRES 0   500   1000   1500

INTRODUCTION TO THE INDEX

The index includes all names shown on the maps in the Atlas of the World. Names are referenced by page number and by a grid reference. The grid reference correlates to the alphanumeric values which appear within each map frame. Each entry also includes the country or geographical area in which the feature is located. Entries relating to names appearing on insets are indicated by a small box symbol: □, followed by a grid reference if the inset has its own alphanumeric values.

Name forms are as they appear on the maps, with additional alternative names or name forms included as cross-references which refer the user to the entry for the map form of the name. Names beginning with Mc or Mac are alphabetized exactly as they appear. The terms Saint, Sainte, etc., are abbreviated to St, Ste, etc., but alphabetized as if in the full form.

Names of physical features beginning with generic, geographical terms are permuted – the descriptive term is placed after the main part of the name. For example, Lake Superior is indexed as Superior, Lake; Mount Everest as Everest, Mount. This policy is applied to all languages.

Entries, other than those for towns and cities, include a descriptor indicating the type of geographical feature. Descriptors are not included where the type of feature is implicit in the name itself.

Administrative divisions are included to differentiate entries of the same name and feature type within the one country. In such cases, duplicate names are alphabetized in order of administrative division. Additional qualifiers are also included for names within selected geographical areas.

INDEX ABBREVIATIONS

admin. div.	administrative division	g.	gulf	reg.	region
Afgh.	Afghanistan	Ger.	Germany	Rep.	Republic
Alg.	Algeria	Guat.	Guatemala	Rus. Fed.	Russian Federation
Arg.	Argentina	hd	headland	S.	South
Austr.	Australia	Hond.	Honduras	Switz.	Switzerland
aut. reg.	autonomous region	imp. l.	impermanent lake	Tajik.	Tajikistan
aut. rep.	autonomous republic	Indon.	Indonesia	Tanz.	Tanzania
		isth.	isthmus	terr.	territory
Azer.	Azerbaijan	Kazakh.	Kazakhstan	Thai.	Thailand
Bangl.	Bangladesh	Kyrg.	Kyrgyzstan	Trin. and Tob.	Trinidad and Tobago
Bol.	Bolivia	lag.	lagoon		
Bos.-Herz.	Bosnia-Herzegovina	Lith.	Lithuania	Turkm.	Turkmenistan
Bulg.	Bulgaria	Lux.	Luxembourg	U.A.E.	United Arab Emirates
Can.	Canada	Madag.	Madagascar		
C.A.R.	Central African Republic	Maur.	Mauritania	U.K.	United Kingdom
		Mex.	Mexico	Ukr.	Ukraine
Col.	Colombia	Moz.	Mozambique	Uru.	Uruguay
Czech Rep.	Czech Republic	mun.	municipality	U.S.A.	United States of America
Dem. Rep. Congo	Democratic Republic of the Congo	N.	North		
		Neth.	Netherlands	Uzbek.	Uzbekistan
		Nic.	Nicaragua	val.	valley
depr.	depression	N.Z.	New Zealand	Venez.	Venezuela
des.	desert	Pak.	Pakistan		
Dom. Rep.	Dominican Republic	Para.	Paraguay		
		Phil.	Philippines		
		plat.	plateau		
		P.N.G.	Papua New Guinea		
esc.	escarpment				
est.	estuary	Pol.	Poland		
Eth.	Ethiopia	Port.	Portugal		
Fin.	Finland	prov.	province		
for.	forest				

1

128	B2	100 Mile House Can.

A

93	E4	Aabenraa Denmark
100	C2	Aachen Ger.
93	E4	Aalborg Denmark
100	B2	Aalst Belgium
100	B2	Aarschot Belgium
68	C2	Aba China
115	C4	Aba Nigeria
81	C2	Ābādān Iran
81	D2	Ābādeh Iran
114	B1	Abadla Alg.
115	C4	Abakaliki Nigeria
83	H3	Abakan Rus. Fed.
150	A3	Abancay Peru
81	D2	Abarkūh Iran
66	D2	Abashiri Japan
117	B4	Abaya, Lake Eth.
		Ābay Wenz r. Eth./Sudan see Blue Nile
82	G3	Abaza Rus. Fed.
108	A2	Abbasanta Sardegna Italy
104	C1	Abbeville France
142	B3	Abbeville U.S.A.
55	C2	Abbot Ice Shelf Antarctica
74	B1	Abbottabad Pak.
115	E3	Abéché Chad
114	B4	Abengourou Côte d'Ivoire
114	C4	Abeokuta Nigeria
99	A2	Aberaeron U.K.
96	C2	Aberchirder U.K.
99	B3	Aberdare U.K.
99	A2	Aberdaron U.K.
122	B3	Aberdeen S. Africa
96	C2	Aberdeen U.K.
141	D3	Aberdeen MD U.S.A.
137	D1	Aberdeen SD U.S.A.
134	B1	Aberdeen WA U.S.A.
129	E1	Aberdeen Lake Can.
134	B2	Abert, Lake U.S.A.
99	A2	Aberystwyth U.K.
86	F2	Abez' Rus. Fed.
78	B3	Abhā Saudi Arabia
		Abiad, Bahr el r. Sudan/Uganda see White Nile
114	B4	Abidjan Côte d'Ivoire
137	D3	Abilene KS U.S.A.
139	D2	Abilene TX U.S.A.
99	C3	Abingdon U.K.
91	D3	Abinsk Rus. Fed.
130	B2	Abitibi, Lake Can.
		Åbo Fin. see Turku
74	B1	Abohar India
114	C4	Abomey Benin
60	A1	Abongabong, Gunung mt. Indon.
118	B2	Abong Mbang Cameroon
64	A2	Aborlan Phil.
115	D3	Abou Déia Chad
106	B2	Abrantes Port.
152	B3	Abra Pampa Arg.
136	A2	Absaroka Range mts U.S.A.
81	C1	Abşeron Yarımadası pen. Azer.
78	B3	Abū 'Arīsh Saudi Arabia
79	C2	Abu Dhabi U.A.E.
116	B3	Abu Hamed Sudan
115	C4	Abuja Nigeria
81	C2	Abū Kamāl Syria
152	B2	Abunã r. Bol./Brazil
150	B2	Abunã Brazil

74	B2	Abu Road India
116	B2	Abū Sunbul Egypt
117	A3	Abu Zabad Sudan
		Abū Zabī U.A.E. see Abu Dhabi
117	A4	Abyei Sudan
145	B2	Acambaro Mex.
106	B1	A Cañiza Spain
144	B2	Acaponeta Mex.
145	C3	Acapulco Mex.
151	D2	Acará Brazil
150	B1	Acarigua Venez.
145	C3	Acatlán Mex.
145	C3	Acayucán Mex.
114	B4	Accra Ghana
98	B2	Accrington U.K.
74	B2	Achalpur India
97	A2	Achill Island Ireland
101	D1	Achim Ger.
96	B2	Achnasheen U.K.
91	D2	Achuyevo Rus. Fed.
111	C3	Acireale Sicilia Italy
147	C2	Acklins Island Bahamas
153	B4	Aconcagua, Cerro mt. Arg.
106	B1	A Coruña Spain
108	A2	Acqui Terme Italy
103	D2	Ács Hungary
145	C2	Actopán Mex.
139	D2	Ada U.S.A.
79	C2	Adam Oman
80	B2	Adana Turkey
111	D2	Adapazarı Turkey
		Adapazarı Turkey see Adapazarı
108	A1	Adda r. Italy
78	B2	Ad Dafinah Saudi Arabia
78	B2	Ad Dahnā' des. Saudi Arabia
78	B2	Ad Dahnā' des. Saudi Arabia
114	A2	Ad Dakhla Western Sahara
		Ad Dammām Saudi Arabia see Dammam
78	A2	Ad Dār al Ḥamrā' Saudi Arabia
78	B3	Ad Darb Saudi Arabia
78	B2	Ad Dawādimī Saudi Arabia
79	B2	Ad Dawḥah Qatar see Doha
78	B2	Ad Dilam Saudi Arabia
116	C2	Ad Dir'īyah Saudi Arabia
117	B4	Addis Ababa Eth.
81	C2	Ad Dīwānīyah Iraq
52	A2	Adelaide Austr.
50	C1	Adelaide River Austr.
101	D2	Adelebsen Ger.
55	J2	Adélie Land Antarctica
78	B3	Aden Yemen
117	C4	Aden, Gulf of Somalia/Yemen
100	C2	Adenau Ger.
79	C2	Adh Dhayd U.A.E.
59	C3	Adi i. Indon.
78	A3	Ādī Ārk'ay Eth.
116	B3	Ādīgrat Eth.
75	B3	Adilabad India
141	E2	Adirondack Mountains U.S.A.
		Ādīs Ābeba Eth. see Addis Ababa
117	B4	Ādīs Alem Eth.
81	C2	Adıyaman Turkey
110	C1	Adjud Romania
50	B1	Admiralty Gulf Austr.
128	A2	Admiralty Island U.S.A.
104	C2	Adour r. France
106	C2	Adra Spain
114	B2	Adrar Alg.
140	C2	Adrian MI U.S.A.
139	C1	Adrian TX U.S.A.
108	B2	Adriatic Sea Europe

116	B3	Ādwa Eth.
83	K2	Adycha r. Rus. Fed.
91	D3	Adygeysk Rus. Fed.
114	B4	Adzopé Côte d'Ivoire
111	B3	Aegean Sea Greece/Turkey
101	C1	Aerzen Ger.
106	B1	A Estrada Spain
116	B3	Afabet Eritrea
76	C3	Afghanistan country Asia
78	B2	'Afīf Saudi Arabia
80	B2	Afyon Turkey
115	C3	Agadez Niger
114	B1	Agadir Morocco
74	B2	Agar India
75	D2	Agartala India
81	C2	Āgdām (abandoned) Azer.
105	C3	Agde France
104	C3	Agen France
122	A2	Aggeneys S. Africa
111	C3	Agia Varvara Greece
111	B3	Agios Dimitrios Greece
111	C3	Agios Efstratios i. Greece
111	C3	Agios Nikolaos Greece
110	B1	Agnita Romania
75	B2	Agra India
81	C2	Ağrı Turkey
		Ağrı Dağı mt. Turkey see Ararat, Mount
108	B3	Agrigento Sicilia Italy
111	B3	Agrinio Greece
109	B2	Agropoli Italy
154	B2	Água Clara Brazil
146	B4	Aguadulce Panama
144	B2	Aguanaval r. Mex.
144	B1	Agua Prieta Mex.
144	B2	Aguascalientes Mex.
155	D1	Águas Formosas Brazil
106	B1	Águeda Port.
106	C1	Aguilar de Campoo Spain
107	C2	Águilas Spain
144	B3	Aguililla Mex.
122	B3	Agulhas, Cape S. Africa
155	D2	Agulhas Negras mt. Brazil
111	C2	Ağva Turkey
115	C2	Ahaggar plat. Alg.
115	C2	Ahaggar, Tassili oua-n-plat. Alg.
81	C2	Ahar Iran
100	C1	Ahaus Ger.
81	C2	Ahlat Turkey
100	C2	Ahlen Ger.
74	B2	Ahmadabad India
73	B3	Ahmadnagar India
74	B2	Ahmadpur East Pak.
74	B1	Ahmadpur Sial Pak.
		Ahmadabad India see Ahmadabad
		Ahmednagar India see Ahmadnagar
144	B2	Ahome Mex.
79	C2	Ahram Iran
101	E1	Ahrensburg Ger.
104	C2	Ahun France
81	C2	Ahvāz Iran
122	A2	Ai-Ais Namibia
80	B2	Aigialousa Cyprus
111	B3	Aigio Greece
143	D2	Aiken U.S.A.
97	B1	Ailt an Chorráin Ireland
155	D1	Aimorés Brazil
155	D1	Aimorés, Serra dos hills Brazil
114	B2	'Aïn Ben Tili Maur.
107	D2	Aïn Defla Alg.
114	B1	Aïn Sefra Alg.
136	D2	Ainsworth U.S.A.
		Aintab Turkey see Gaziantep

107 D2 Aïn Taya Alg.
107 D2 Aïn Tédélès Alg.
115 C3 Aïr, Massif de l' *mts* Niger
60 A1 Airbangis Indon.
128 C2 Airdrie Can.
104 B3 Aire-sur-l'Adour France
101 E3 Aïsch *r.* Ger.
128 A1 Aishihik Lake Can.
100 A3 Aisne *r.* France
59 D3 Aitape P.N.G.
110 B1 Aiud Romania
105 D3 Aix-en-Provence France
105 D2 Aix-les-Bains France
62 A1 Aizawl India
88 C2 Aizkraukle Latvia
67 C3 Aizu-Wakamatsu Japan
105 D3 Ajaccio *Corse* France
115 E1 Ajdābiyā Libya
115 C2 Ajjer, Tassili n' *plat.* Alg
74 B2 Ajmer India
138 A2 Ajo U.S.A.
77 D2 Akadyr Kazakh.
87 E3 Akbulak Rus. Fed.
80 B2 Akçakale Turkey
80 B2 Akdağmadeni Turkey
88 A2 Åkersberga Sweden
118 C2 Aketi Dem. Rep. Congo
87 D4 Akhalkalaki Georgia
79 C2 Akhḑar, Jabal *mts* Oman
111 C3 Akhisar Turkey
87 D4 Akhtubinsk Rus. Fed.
130 B1 Akimiski Island Can.
66 D3 Akita Japan
114 A3 Aljouil Maur.
77 D1 Akkol' Kazakh.
88 B2 Akmenrags *pt* Latvia
Akmola Kazakh. *see* Astana
117 B4 Akobo S. Sudan
74 B2 Akola India
78 A3 Akordat Eritrea
127 G2 Akpatok Island Can.
92 □A3 Akranes Iceland
140 C2 Akron U.S.A.
75 B1 Aksai Chin *terr.* Asia
80 B2 Aksaray Turkey
76 B1 Aksay Kazakh.
91 D2 Aksay Rus. Fed.
80 B2 Akşehir Turkey
76 C2 Akshiganak Kazakh.
77 E2 Aksu China
74 A3 Āksum Eth.
76 B2 Aktau Kazakh.
76 B1 Aktobe Kazakh.
77 D2 Aktogay Kazakh.
88 C3 Aktsyabrski Belarus
115 C4 Akure Nigeria
92 □B2 Akureyri Iceland
142 C2 Alabama *r.* U.S.A.
142 C2 Alabama *state* U.S.A.
111 C3 Alaçatı Turkey
81 C1 Alagir Rus. Fed.
151 E3 Alagoinhas Brazil
107 C1 Alagón Spain
79 B2 Al Aḥmadi Kuwait
77 F2 Alakol', Ozero *salt l.* Kazakh.
92 J2 Alakurtti Rus. Fed.
78 B3 Al 'Alayyah Saudi Arabia
81 C2 Al 'Amādīyah Iraq
78 A2 Al 'Āmirīyah Egypt
135 C3 Alamo U.S.A.
138 B2 Alamogordo U.S.A.
144 A2 Alamos *Sonora* Mex.
144 B2 Alamos *Sonora* Mex.
138 B3 Alamos *r.* Mex.
136 B3 Alamosa U.S.A.
93 G3 Åland Islands Fin.

80 B2 Alanya Turkey
73 B4 Alappuzha India
80 B3 Al 'Aqabah Jordan
78 B2 Al 'Aqiq Saudi Arabia
107 C2 Alarcón, Embalse de *resr* Spain
80 B2 Al 'Arīsh Egypt
78 B2 Al Arṭāwīyah Saudi Arabia
61 C2 Alas Indon.
111 C3 Alaşehir Turkey
128 A2 Alaska *state* U.S.A.
124 F3 Alaska, Gulf of U.S.A.
81 C2 Älät Azer.
87 D3 Alatyr' Rus. Fed.
150 A2 Alausí Ecuador
93 H3 Alavus Fin.
52 B2 Alawoona Austr.
108 A2 Alba Italy
107 C2 Albacete Spain
110 B1 Alba Iulia Romania
109 C2 Albania *country* Europe
50 A3 Albany Austr.
130 B1 Albany *r.* Can.
143 D2 Albany GA U.S.A.
141 E2 Albany NY U.S.A.
134 B2 Albany OR U.S.A.
Al Başrah Iraq *see* Basra
51 D1 Albatross Bay Austr.
116 A2 Al Bawīṭī Egypt
115 E1 Al Bayḑā' Libya
78 B3 Al Bayḑā' Yemen
143 D1 Albemarle U.S.A.
143 E1 Albemarle Sound *sea chan.* U.S.A.
108 A2 Albenga Italy
51 C2 Alberga *watercourse* Austr.
119 D2 Albert, Lake Dem. Rep. Congo/Uganda
128 C2 Alberta *prov.* Can.
100 A2 Albert Kanaal *canal* Belgium
137 E2 Albert Lea U.S.A.
104 C3 Albi France
78 A2 Al Bi'r Saudi Arabia
78 B3 Al Birk Saudi Arabia
78 B2 Al Biyāḑh *reg.* Saudi Arabia
106 C2 Alboran Sea Europe
Alborz, Reshteh-ye *mts* Iran *see* Elburz Mountains
106 B2 Albufeira Port.
138 B1 Albuquerque U.S.A.
79 C2 Al Buraymī Oman
53 C3 Albury Austr.
106 B2 Alcácer do Sal Port.
106 C1 Alcalá de Henares Spain
106 C2 Alcalá la Real Spain
108 B3 Alcamo *Sicilia* Italy
107 C1 Alcañiz Spain
106 B2 Alcántara Spain
106 C2 Alcaraz Spain
106 C2 Alcaraz, Sierra de *mts* Spain
106 C2 Alcaudete Spain
106 C2 Alcázar de San Juan Spain
91 D2 Alchevs'k Ukr.
155 E1 Alcobaça Brazil
107 C2 Alcoy-Alcoi Spain
107 D2 Alcúdia Spain
145 C2 Aldama Mex.
83 J3 Aldan Rus. Fed.
83 J2 Aldan *r.* Rus. Fed.
95 C4 Alderney *i.* Channel Is
114 A3 Aleg Maur.
155 E3 Alegrete Brazil
152 C3 Alegrete Brazil
83 K3 Aleksandrovsk-Sakhalinskiy Rus. Fed.
91 D1 Alekseyevka *Belgorodskaya Oblast'* Rus. Fed.

91 D1 Alekseyevka *Belgorodskaya Oblast'* Rus. Fed.
89 E3 Aleksin Rus. Fed.
109 D2 Aleksinac Serbia
118 B3 Alèmbé Gabon
155 D2 Além Paraíba Brazil
93 F3 Ålen Norway
104 C2 Alençon France
150 A3 Aleppo Syria
150 A3 Alerta Peru
128 B2 Alert Bay Can.
105 C3 Alès France
110 B1 Aleşd Romania
108 A2 Alessandria Italy
93 E3 Ålesund Norway
124 C3 Aleutian Islands U.S.A.
83 L3 Alevina, Mys *c.* Rus. Fed.
128 A2 Alexander Archipelago *is* U.S.A.
122 A2 Alexander Bay S. Africa
142 C2 Alexander City U.S.A.
55 O2 Alexander Island Antarctica
53 C3 Alexandra Austr.
54 A3 Alexandra N.Z.
111 B2 Alexandreia Greece
Alexandretta Turkey *see* İskenderun
116 A1 Alexandria Egypt
110 C2 Alexandria Romania
123 C3 Alexandria S. Africa
142 B2 Alexandria LA U.S.A.
137 D1 Alexandria MN U.S.A.
141 D3 Alexandria VA U.S.A.
52 A3 Alexandrina, Lake Austr.
111 C2 Alexandroupoli Greece
131 E1 Alexis *r.* Can.
128 B2 Alexis Creek Can.
77 E1 Aleysk Rus. Fed.
107 C1 Alfaro Spain
81 C3 Al Fāw Iraq
101 D2 Alfeld (Leine) Ger.
155 C2 Alfenas Brazil
Al Fujayrah U.A.E. *see* Fujairah
Al Furāt *r.* Iraq/Syria *see* Euphrates
106 B2 Algeciras Spain
107 C2 Algemesí Spain
78 A3 Algena Eritrea
Alger Alg. *see* Algiers
114 C2 Algeria *country* Africa
79 C3 Al Ghaydah Yemen
108 A2 Alghero *Sardegna* Italy
116 B2 Al Ghurdaqah Egypt
79 B2 Al Ghwaybīyah Saudi Arabia
115 C1 Algiers Alg.
123 C3 Algoa Bay S. Africa
137 E2 Algona U.S.A.
106 C1 Algorta Spain
81 C2 Al Ḥajar al Gharbī *mts* Oman
107 C2 Alhama de Murcia Spain
80 A2 Al Ḥammām Egypt
78 B2 Al Ḥanākiyah Saudi Arabia
81 C2 Al Ḥasakah Syria
81 C2 Al Ḥayy Iraq
78 B3 Al Ḥazm al Jawf Yemen
79 C3 Al Ḥibāk *des.* Saudi Arabia
78 B2 Al Ḥillah Saudi Arabia
78 B2 Al Ḥinnāh Saudi Arabia
Al Ḥudaydah Yemen *see* Hodeidah
78 B2 Al Ḥufūf Saudi Arabia
115 D2 Al Ḥulayq al Kabīr *hills* Libya
79 C2 'Alīabad Iran
111 C3 Aliağa Turkey
111 B2 Aliakmonas *r.* Greece

107 C2 Alicante Spain
139 D3 Alice U.S.A.
109 C3 Alice, Punta pt Italy
51 C2 Alice Springs Austr.
75 B2 Aligarh India
81 C2 Aligüdarz Iran
69 E1 Alihe China
118 B3 Alima r. Congo
111 C3 Aliova r. Turkey
117 C3 Ali Sabieh Djibouti
Al Iskandarīyah Egypt see
Alexandria
116 B1 Al Ismā'īlīyah Egypt
123 C3 Aliwal North S. Africa
115 E2 Al Jaghbūb Libya
78 B2 Al Jahrah Kuwait
115 D1 Al Jawsh Libya
106 B2 Aljezur Port.
Al Jīzah Egypt see Giza
79 B2 Al Jubayl Saudi Arabia
79 C2 Al Jumaylīyah Qatar
78 B2 Al Junaynah Saudi Arabia
106 B2 Aljustrel Port.
78 B2 Al Kahfah Saudi Arabia
79 C2 Al Kāmil Oman
80 B2 Al Karak Jordan
79 C2 Al Khabūrah Oman
78 B2 Al Khamāsīn Saudi Arabia
116 B1 Al Khārijah Egypt
79 C2 Al Khaşab Oman
78 B3 Al Khawkhah Yemen
79 C2 Al Khawr Qatar
115 D1 Al Khums Libya
79 B2 Al Khunn Saudi Arabia
79 C2 Al Kir'ānah Qatar
100 B1 Alkmaar Neth.
81 C2 Al Kūt Iraq
Al Kuwayt Kuwait see Kuwait
Al Lādhiqīyah Syria see
Latakia
75 B2 Allahabad India
83 K2 Allakh-Yun' Rus. Fed.
141 D2 Allegheny r. U.S.A.
140 C3 Allegheny Mountains U.S.A.
97 B1 Allen, Lough l. Ireland
145 E2 Allende Coahuila Mex.
145 B2 Allende Nuevo León Mex.
141 D2 Allentown U.S.A.
101 D1 Aller r. Ger.
136 C2 Alliance NE U.S.A.
140 C2 Alliance OH U.S.A.
78 B2 Al Lith Saudi Arabia
96 C2 Alloa U.K.
131 C2 Alma Can.
Alma-Ata Kazakh. see Almaty
106 B2 Almada Port.
106 C2 Almadén Spain
Al Madīnah Saudi Arabia see
Medina
116 B1 Al Mafraq Jordan
78 B3 Al Maḩwīt Yemen
78 B2 Al Majma'ah Saudi Arabia
135 C2 Almanor, Lake U.S.A.
107 C2 Almansa Spain
80 B2 Al Manşūrah Egypt
79 C2 Al Mariyyah U.A.E.
115 E1 Al Marj Libya
77 D2 Almaty Kazakh.
106 C1 Almazán Spain
151 C2 Almeirim Brazil
100 C1 Almelo Neth.
155 D1 Almenara Brazil
106 B1 Almendra, Embalse de resr
Spain
106 B2 Almendralejo Spain
106 C2 Almería Spain
106 C2 Almería, Golfo de b. Spain

87 E3 Al'met'yevsk Rus. Fed.
78 B2 Al Mindak Saudi Arabia
116 B2 Al Minyā Egypt
79 B2 Al Mish'āb Saudi Arabia
106 B2 Almodôvar Port.
106 B2 Almonte Spain
75 B2 Almora India
79 B2 Al Mubarrez Saudi Arabia
79 C2 Al Muḑaibī Oman
80 B3 Al Mukallā Yemen see
Mukalla
Al Mukhā Yemen see Mocha
106 C2 Almuñécar Spain
78 A2 Al Muwayliḩ Saudi Arabia
111 B3 Almyros Greece
96 B2 Alness U.K.
98 C1 Alnwick U.K.
49 G4 Alofi Niue
111 B3 Alonnisos i. Greece
59 C1 Alor i. Indon.
59 C3 Alor, Kepulauan is Indon.
60 B1 Alor Star Malaysia
Alost Belgium see Aalst
86 C2 Alozero (abandoned) Rus. Fed.
140 C1 Alpena U.S.A.
139 C2 Alpine U.S.A.
105 D2 Alps mts Europe
79 B3 Al Qa'āmīyāt reg. Saudi Arabia
115 D1 Al Qaddāḩīyah Libya
Al Qāhirah Egypt see Cairo
78 B2 Al Qā'īyah Saudi Arabia
81 C2 Al Qāmishlī Syria
80 B2 Al Qaryatayn Syria
79 B3 Al Qaţn Yemen
106 B2 Alqueva, Barragem de resr
Port.
80 B2 Al Qunayţirah (abandoned)
Syria
78 B3 Al Qunfidhah Saudi Arabia
116 B2 Al Quşayr Egypt
78 B2 Al Quwayīyah Saudi Arabia
101 D2 Alsfeld Ger.
92 H2 Alta Norway
92 H2 Altaelva r. Norway
68 B1 Altai Mountains Asia
143 D2 Altamaha r. U.S.A.
151 C2 Altamira Brazil
109 C2 Altamura Italy
68 B1 Altay China
68 C1 Altay Mongolia
105 D2 Altdorf Switz.
107 C2 Altea Spain
101 F2 Altenburg Ger.
101 D2 Altenkirchen (Westerwald)
Ger.
111 C3 Altınoluk Turkey
111 D3 Altıntaş Turkey
152 B1 Altiplano plain Bol.
154 B1 Alto Araguaia Brazil
154 B1 Alto Garças Brazil
121 C2 Alto Molócuè Moz.
129 E3 Altona Can.
141 D2 Altoona U.S.A.
154 B1 Alto Sucuriú Brazil
154 B1 Alto Taquari Brazil
102 C2 Altötting Ger.
68 B2 Altun Shan mts China
134 B2 Alturas U.S.A.
139 D1 Altus U.S.A.
88 C2 Alūksne Latvia
78 A2 Al 'Ulā Saudi Arabia
115 D1 Al 'Uqaylah Libya
Al Uqşur Egypt see Luxor
91 C3 Alushta Ukr.
139 D1 Alva U.S.A.
145 C3 Alvarado Mex.

93 F3 Älvdalen Sweden
93 F3 Älvdalen val. Sweden
92 H2 Älvsbyn Sweden
78 A2 Al Wajh Saudi Arabia
74 B2 Alwar India
81 C2 Al Widyān plat. Iraq/
Saudi Arabia
Alxa Youqi China see
Ehen Hudag
Alxa Zuoqi China see Bayan Hot
51 C1 Alyangula Austr.
88 B3 Alytus Lith.
136 C1 Alzada U.S.A.
101 D3 Alzey Ger.
50 C2 Amadeus, Lake imp. l. Austr.
127 G2 Amadjuak Lake Can.
106 B2 Amadora Port.
78 B2 Amā'ir Saudi Arabia
93 F4 Åmål Sweden
111 B3 Amaliada Greece
59 D3 Amamapare Indon.
154 A2 Amambaí Brazil
154 B2 Amambaí r. Brazil
69 E3 Amami-Ō-shima i. Japan
69 E3 Amami-shotō is Japan
77 C1 Amankel'dy Kazakh.
109 C3 Amantea Italy
151 C1 Amapá Brazil
106 B2 Amareleja Port.
139 C1 Amarillo U.S.A.
108 B2 Amaro, Monte mt. Italy
80 B1 Amasya Turkey
150 B1 Amazon r. S. America
151 D1 Amazon, Mouths of the Brazil
Amazonas r. S. America see
Amazon
74 B1 Ambala India
121 □D3 Ambalavao Madag.
121 □D2 Ambanja Madag.
150 A2 Ambato Ecuador
121 □D3 Ambato Boeny Madag.
121 □D3 Ambato Finandrahana Madag.
121 □D2 Ambatolampy Madag.
121 □D2 Ambatondrazaka Madag.
101 E3 Amberg Ger.
146 B3 Ambergris Caye i. Belize
75 C2 Ambikapur India
121 □D2 Ambilobe Madag.
98 B1 Ambleside U.K.
121 □D3 Amboasary Madag.
121 □D2 Ambohimahasoa Madag.
59 C3 Ambon Indon.
59 C3 Ambon i. Indon.
121 □D3 Ambositra Madag.
121 □D3 Ambovombe Madag.
135 C4 Amboy U.S.A.
120 A1 Ambriz Angola
145 B2 Amealco Mex.
144 B2 Ameca Mex.
100 B1 Ameland i. Neth.
134 D2 American Falls U.S.A.
134 D2 American Falls Reservoir U.S.A.
135 D2 American Fork U.S.A.
49 G3 American Samoa terr.
S. Pacific Ocean
142 C2 Americus U.S.A.
100 B1 Amersfoort Neth.
55 F2 Amery Ice Shelf Antarctica
137 E2 Ames U.S.A.
111 B3 Amfissa Greece
83 J2 Amga Rus. Fed.
66 C1 Amgu Rus. Fed.
115 C2 Amguid Alg.
83 K3 Amgun' r. Rus. Fed.
131 D2 Amherst Can.
104 C2 Amiens France
73 B3 Amindivi Islands India

172 A1	Aminuis Namibia	
74 A2	Amir Chah Pak.	
129 D2	Amisk Lake Can.	
139 C3	Amistad Reservoir Mex./U.S.A.	
98 A2	Amlwch U.K.	
80 B2	'Ammān Jordan	
127 I2	Ammassalik Greenland	
78 B3	Am Nabiyah Yemen	
81 D2	Āmol Iran	
111 C3	Amorgos i. Greece	
142 C2	Amory U.S.A.	
130 C2	Amos Can.	
	Amoy China see Xiamen	
155 C4	Amparo Brazil	
107 D1	Amposta Spain	
75 D4	Amravati India	
74 B1	Amritsar India	
100 B1	Amstelveen Neth.	
100 B1	Amsterdam Neth.	
103 C2	Amstetten Austria	
115 E3	Am Timan Chad	
76 B2	Amudar'ya r. Asia	
126 E1	Amund Ringnes Island Can.	
126 C2	Amundsen Gulf Can.	
55 M2	Amundsen Sea Antarctica	
61 C2	Amuntai Indon.	
	Amur r. China see Heilong Jiang	
78 A3	'Amur, Wadi watercourse Sudan	
83 I2	Anabar r. Rus. Fed.	
83 I2	Anabarskiy Zaliv b. Rus. Fed.	
134 D1	Anaconda U.S.A.	
139 D1	Anadarko U.S.A.	
00 D1	Anadolu Dağları mts Turkey	
83 M2	Anadyr' r. Rus. Fed.	
81 C2	'Ānah Iraq	
145 B2	Anáhuac Mex.	
60 B1	Anambas, Kepulauan is Indon.	
137 E2	Anamosa U.S.A.	
80 B2	Anamur Turkey	
67 B4	Anan Japan	
73 B3	Anantapur India	
74 B1	Anantnag India	
90 B2	Anan'yiv Ukr.	
91 D3	Anapa Rus. Fed.	
154 C1	Anápolis Brazil	
152 B3	Añatuya Arg.	
97 B1	An Baile Thiar Ireland	
65 B2	Anbyon N. Korea	
104 B2	Ancenis France	
108 B2	Ancona Italy	
153 A5	Ancud Chile	
	Anda China see Daqing	
97 A2	An Daingean Ireland	
93 E3	Åndalsnes Norway	
142 C2	Andalusia U.S.A.	
73 D3	Andaman Islands India	
63 A2	Andaman Sea Indian Ocean	
121 D2	Andapa Madag.	
100 B1	Andelst Neth.	
92 G2	Andenes Norway	
100 B2	Andenne Belgium	
100 B2	Anderlecht Belgium	
126 C2	Anderson r. Can.	
126 D2	Anderson AK U.S.A.	
140 B2	Anderson IN U.S.A.	
143 D2	Anderson SC U.S.A.	
148 D3	Andes mts S. America	
77 D2	Andijon Uzbek.	
121 D2	Andilamena Madag.	
121 D2	Andilanatoby Madag.	
121 D2	Andoany Madag.	
	Andong China see Dandong	
65 B2	Andong S. Korea	
107 D1	Andorra country Europe	
107 D1	Andorra la Vella Andorra	
99 C3	Andover U.K.	
154 B2	Andradina Brazil	
89 D2	Andreapol' Rus. Fed.	
155 D2	Andrelândia Brazil	
139 C2	Andrews U.S.A.	
109 C2	Andria Italy	
121 D3	Androka Madag.	
146 C2	Andros i. Bahamas	
111 B3	Andros i. Greece	
143 L4	Andros Town Bahamas	
73 B3	Andrott i. India	
90 B1	Andrushivka Ukr.	
92 G2	Andselv Norway	
106 C2	Andújar Spain	
120 A2	Andulo Angola	
114 C3	Anéfis Mali	
115 D3	Aney Niger	
83 H3	Angara r. Rus. Fed.	
69 C1	Angarsk Rus. Fed.	
93 G3	Ånge Sweden	
144 A2	Ángel de la Guarda, Isla i. Mex.	
64 B1	Angeles Phil.	
150 B1	Angel Falls Venez.	
93 F4	Ängelholm Sweden	
92 G3	Ångermanälven r. Sweden	
104 B2	Angers France	
129 E1	Angikuni Lake Can.	
98 A2	Anglesey i. U.K.	
121 C2	Angoche Moz.	
79 C2	Angohrān Iran	
120 A2	Angola country Africa	
140 C2	Angola U.S.A.	
128 A2	Angoon U.S.A.	
104 C2	Angoulême France	
77 D2	Angren Uzbek.	
147 D3	Anguilla terr. West Indies	
75 C2	Angul India	
93 F4	Anholt i. Denmark	
71 B3	Anhua China	
70 B2	Anhui prov. China	
154 B1	Anhumas Brazil	
65 B2	Anju N. Korea	
70 A2	Ankang China	
80 B2	Ankara Turkey	
70 B2	Anlu China	
91 E1	Anna Rus. Fed.	
115 C1	Annaba Alg.	
101 F2	Annaberg-Buchholtz Ger.	
78 B2	An Nafūd des. Saudi Arabia	
81 C2	An Najaf Iraq	
96 C3	Annan U.K.	
141 D3	Annapolis U.S.A.	
75 C2	Annapurna I mt. Nepal	
140 C2	Ann Arbor U.S.A.	
150 C1	Anna Regina Guyana	
81 C2	An Nāşiriyah Iraq	
105 D2	Annecy France	
78 B3	An Nimāş Saudi Arabia	
69 A1	Anning China	
142 C2	Anniston U.S.A.	
105 C2	Annonay France	
79 B2	An Nu'ayriyah Saudi Arabia	
121 D2	Anorotsany, Tanjona hd Madag.	
71 B3	Anpu China	
70 B2	Anqing China	
102 C2	Ansbach Ger.	
70 C1	Anshan China	
71 A3	Anshun China	
150 A3	Ansongo Mali	
150 A3	Antabamba Peru	
80 B2	Antakya Turkey	
121 E2	Antalaha Madag.	
80 B2	Antalya Turkey	
80 B2	Antalya Körfezi g. Turkey	
121 D2	Antananarivo Madag.	
55 Q3	Antarctic Peninsula Antarctica	
96 B2	An Teallach mt. U.K.	
106 C2	Antequera Spain	
138 B2	Anthony U.S.A.	
114 B2	Anti-Atlas mts Morocco	
105 D3	Antibes France	
131 D2	Anticosti, Île d' i. Can.	
131 D2	Antigonish Can.	
147 D3	Antigua i. Antigua	
147 D3	Antigua and Barbuda country West Indies	
145 C2	Antiguo-Morelos Mex.	
111 B3	Antikythira i. Greece	
	Antioch Turkey see Antakya	
49 F6	Antipodes Islands N.Z.	
152 A3	Antofagasta Chile	
154 C3	Antonina Brazil	
97 C1	Antrim U.K.	
97 C1	Antrim Hills U.K.	
	Antwerpen Belgium see Antwerpen	
100 B2	Antwerpen Belgium	
	An Uaimh Ireland see Navan	
74 B2	Anupgarh India	
73 C4	Anuradhapura Sri Lanka	
70 B2	Anyang China	
65 B2	Anyang S. Korea	
108 B2	Anzio Italy	
66 D2	Aomori Japan	
54 B2	Aoraki mt. N.Z.	
108 A1	Aosta Italy	
143 D3	Apalachee Bay U.S.A.	
150 B1	Apaporis r. Col.	
154 B2	Aparecida do Tabuado Brazil	
64 B1	Aparri Phil.	
86 C2	Apatity Rus. Fed.	
144 B3	Apatzingán Mex.	
100 B1	Apeldoorn Neth.	
100 C1	Apen Ger.	
108 A2	Apennines mts Italy	
49 G3	Apia Samoa	
154 C2	Apiaí Brazil	
64 B2	Apo, Mount vol. Phil.	
101 E2	Apolda Ger.	
52 B3	Apollo Bay Austr.	
143 D3	Apopka, Lake U.S.A.	
154 B1	Aporé Brazil	
154 B1	Aporé r. Brazil	
80 B2	Apostolos Andreas, Cape Cyprus	
133 F3	Appalachian Mountains U.S.A.	
53 D2	Appin Austr.	
140 B2	Appleton U.S.A.	
108 B2	Aprilia Italy	
91 D3	Apsheronsk Rus. Fed.	
154 B2	Apucarana Brazil	
154 B2	Apucarana, Serra da hills Brazil	
78 A2	Aqaba, Gulf of Asia	
154 A1	Aquidauana r. Brazil	
75 C2	Ara India	
117 A4	Arab, Bahr el watercourse Sudan	
	Arabian Gulf Asia see The Gulf	
78 B2	Arabian Peninsula Asia	
56 G5	Arabian Sea Indian Ocean	
151 E3	Aracaju Brazil	
151 E2	Aracati Brazil	
154 B2	Araçatuba Brazil	
155 D1	Aracruz Brazil	
155 D1	Araçuaí Brazil	

110 B1 Arad Romania
115 E3 Arada Chad
156 C6 Arafura Sea Austr./Indon.
154 B1 Aragarças Brazil
107 C1 Aragón r. Spain
151 D2 Araguaia r. Brazil
151 E3 Araguaína Brazil
154 C1 Araguari Brazil
67 C3 Arai Japan
115 C2 Arak Alg.
81 C2 Arāk Iran
62 A1 Arakan Yoma mts Myanmar
81 C1 Arak's r. Armenia
76 C2 Aral Sea salt l. Kazakh./Uzbek.
76 C2 Aral'sk Kazakh.
Aral'skoye More salt l.
Kazakh./Uzbek. see Aral Sea
106 C1 Aranda de Duero Spain
109 D2 Arandelovac Serbia
97 B2 Aran Islands Ireland
106 C1 Aranjuez Spain
122 A1 Aranos Namibia
139 D3 Aransas Pass U.S.A.
67 B4 Arao Japan
114 B3 Araouane Mali
151 E2 Arapiraca Brazil
154 B2 Arapongas Brazil
154 C3 Araquari Brazil
78 B1 'Ar'ar Saudi Arabia
154 C2 Araraquara Brazil
151 E2 Araras Brazil
154 B3 Araras, Serra das mts Brazil
52 B3 Ararat Austr.
81 C2 Ararat, Mount Turkey
155 D3 Araruama, Lago de lag. Brazil
155 E1 Arataca Brazil
Aratürük China see Yiwu
150 A1 Arauca Col.
154 C1 Araxá Brazil
81 C2 Arbīl Iraq
96 C2 Arbroath U.K.
74 A2 Arbū-ye Shamālī, Dasht-e des.
Afgh.
104 B3 Arcachon France
143 D3 Arcadia U.S.A.
134 B2 Arcata U.S.A.
145 B3 Arcelia Mex.
86 D2 Archangel Rus. Fed.
51 D1 Archer r. Austr.
134 C2 Arco U.S.A.
106 B2 Arcos de la Frontera Spain
127 F2 Arctic Bay Can.
160 Arctic Ocean World
126 C2 Arctic Red r. Can.
81 C2 Ardabīl Iran
81 C1 Ardahan Turkey
93 E3 Årdalstangen Norway
100 B3 Ardennes plat. Belgium
81 D2 Ardestān Iran
53 C2 Ardlethan Austr.
139 D2 Ardmore U.S.A.
96 A2 Ardnamurchan, Point of U.K.
52 A2 Ardrossan Austr.
96 B3 Ardrossan U.K.
135 B3 Arena, Point U.S.A.
93 E4 Arendal Norway
101 E1 Arendsee (Altmark) Ger.
150 A3 Arequipa Peru
151 E2 Arere Brazil
106 C1 Arévalo Spain
108 B2 Arezzo Italy
104 B2 Argentan France
152 A2 Argentina country S. America
152 A2 Argentino, Lago l. Arg.
104 C2 Argenton-sur-Creuse France
110 C2 Argeş r. Romania
74 A1 Arghandāb Rōd r. Afgh.

111 B3 Argolikos Kolpos b. Greece
111 B3 Argos Greece
111 B3 Argostoli Greece
107 C1 Arguis Spain
69 E1 Argun' r. China/Rus. Fed.
50 B1 Argyle, Lake Austr.
93 F4 Århus Denmark
122 A2 Ariamsvlei Namibia
152 A2 Arica Chile
96 A2 Arinagour U.K.
155 C1 Arinos Brazil
150 C3 Aripuanã Brazil
150 B2 Aripuanã r. Brazil
150 B2 Ariquemes Brazil
154 B1 Ariranhá r. Brazil
138 A2 Arizona state U.S.A.
144 A1 Arizpe Mex.
78 B2 'Arjah Saudi Arabia
92 G2 Arjeplog Sweden
142 B2 Arkadelphia U.S.A.
77 C1 Arkalyk Kazakh.
142 B2 Arkansas r. U.S.A.
142 B1 Arkansas state U.S.A.
137 D3 Arkansas City U.S.A.
Arkhangel'sk Rus. Fed. see
Archangel
97 C2 Arklow Ireland
102 C1 Arkona, Kap c. Ger.
82 G1 Arkticheskogo Instituta,
Ostrova is Rus. Fed.
105 C3 Arles France
115 C3 Arlit Niger
100 B3 Arlon Belgium
97 C1 Armagh U.K.
116 B2 Armant Egypt
81 C1 Armavir Rus. Fed.
81 C1 Armenia country Asia
150 A1 Armenia Col.
144 B3 Armeria Mex.
53 D2 Armidale Austr.
81 C1 Armstrong Can.
80 B1 Armyans'k Ukr.
80 B2 Arnauti, Cape Cyprus
100 B2 Arnhem Neth.
51 C1 Arnhem, Cape Austr.
51 C1 Arnhem Bay Austr.
51 C1 Arnhem Land reg. Austr.
108 B2 Arno r. Italy
52 A2 Arno Bay Austr.
130 C2 Arnprior Can.
100 D2 Arnsberg Ger.
101 E2 Arnstadt Ger.
122 A2 Aroab Namibia
101 D2 Arolsen Ger.
78 A3 Aroma Sudan
108 A1 Arona Italy
144 B2 Aros r. Mex.
81 C2 Ar Ramādī Iraq
96 B3 Arran i. U.K.
97 B1 Arranmore Island Ireland
80 B2 Ar Raqqah Syria
104 C1 Arras France
78 B2 Ar Rass Saudi Arabia
145 C3 Arriagá Mex.
79 C2 Ar Rimāl reg. Saudi Arabia
Ar Riyāḍ Saudi Arabia
see Riyadh
145 C2 Arroyo Seco Mex.
79 C2 Ar Rustāq Oman
80 C2 Ar Ruţbah Iraq
81 D3 Arsenajān Iran
66 B2 Arsen'yev Rus. Fed.
111 B3 Arta Greece
144 B3 Arteaga Mex.
66 B2 Artem Rus. Fed.
91 D2 Artemivs'k Ukr.
104 C2 Artenay France

138 C2 Artesia U.S.A.
51 E2 Arthur Point Austr.
54 B2 Arthur's Pass N.Z.
152 C4 Artigas Uru.
129 D1 Artillery Lake Can.
90 B2 Artsyz Ukr.
77 D3 Artux China
81 C1 Artvin Turkey
59 C3 Aru, Kepulauan is Indon.
119 D2 Arua Uganda
147 D3 Aruba terr. West Indies
119 D3 Arusha Tanz.
69 C1 Arvayheer Mongolia
129 E1 Arviat Can.
92 G2 Arvidsjaur Sweden
93 F4 Arvika Sweden
87 D3 Arzamas Rus. Fed.
107 C2 Arzew Alg.
100 C2 Arzfeld Ger.
101 F2 Aš Czech Rep.
115 C4 Asaba Nigeria
74 B1 Asadābād Afgh.
66 D2 Asahi-dake vol. Japan
66 D2 Asahikawa Japan
78 B3 Asale l. Eth.
75 C2 Asansol India
131 C2 Asbestos Can.
109 C2 Ascea Italy
152 B2 Ascensión Bol.
113 D7 Ascension i. S. Atlantic Ocean
145 C3 Ascensión, Bahía de la b.
Mex.
101 D3 Aschaffenburg Ger.
100 C2 Ascheberg Ger.
101 E2 Aschersleben Ger.
108 B2 Ascoli Piceno Italy
92 G3 Åsele Sweden
110 B2 Asenovgrad Bulg.
76 B3 Aşgabat Turkm.
50 A2 Ashburton watercourse Austr.
54 B2 Ashburton N.Z.
142 B2 Ashdown U.S.A.
143 D1 Asheville U.S.A.
53 D1 Ashford Austr.
99 D3 Ashford U.K.
Ashgabat Turkm. see
Aşgabat
98 C1 Ashington U.K.
67 B4 Ashizuri-misaki pt Japan
136 C3 Ashland KS U.S.A.
140 C3 Ashland KY U.S.A.
140 C2 Ashland OH U.S.A.
134 B2 Ashland OR U.S.A.
140 A1 Ashland WI U.S.A.
88 C3 Ashmyany Belarus
78 B3 Ash Sharawrah Saudi Arabia
Ash Shāriqah U.A.E. see
Sharjah
81 C2 Ash Sharqāt Iraq
81 C2 Ash Shaţrah Iraq
79 B3 Ash Shiḩr Yemen
79 C2 Ash Shināş Oman
78 B2 Ash Shu'bah Saudi Arabia
78 B2 Ash Shumlūl Saudi Arabia
140 C2 Ashtabula U.S.A.
131 C1 Ashuanipi Lake Can.
106 B2 Asilah Morocco
108 A2 Asinara, Golfo dell' b.
Sardegna Italy
82 G3 Asino Rus. Fed.
88 C3 Asipovichy Belarus
78 B2 'Asīr reg. Saudi Arabia
93 F4 Askim Norway
68 C1 Askiz Rus. Fed.
116 B3 Asmara Eritrea
93 F4 Åsnen l. Sweden
116 B2 Asoteriba, Jebel mt. Sudan

103 D2 Aspang-Markt Austria
136 B3 Aspen U.S.A.
54 A2 Aspiring, Mount N.Z.
117 C3 Assab Eritrea
Aş Şaḩrā' al Gharbīyah des.
Egypt see Western Desert
Aş Şaḩrā' ash Sharqīyah des.
Egypt see Eastern Desert
78 B2 As Salamīyah Saudi Arabia
81 C2 As Samāwah Iraq
79 C2 Aş Şanām reg. Saudi Arabia
115 E2 As Sarīr reg. Libya
100 C1 Assen Neth.
100 B2 Assesse Belgium
115 D1 As Sidrah Libya
129 D3 Assiniboia Can.
128 C2 Assiniboine, Mount Can.
154 B2 Assis Brazil
78 B2 Aş Şubayḩīyah Kuwait
81 C2 As Sulaymānīyah Iraq
78 B2 As Sulaymī Saudi Arabia
70 D2 Aş Şulayyil Saudi Arabia
78 B2 As Sūq Saudi Arabia
80 B2 As Suwaydā' Syria
79 C2 As Suwayq Oman
Aswan Egypt see Suez
111 B3 Astakos Greece
77 D1 Astana Kazakh.
81 C2 Āstārā Iran
108 A2 Asti Italy
74 B1 Astor Pak.
106 B1 Astorga Spain
134 B1 Astoria U.S.A.
87 D4 Astrakhan' Rus. Fed.
88 C2 Astravyets Belarus
111 C3 Astypalaia i. Greece
152 C3 Asunción Para.
116 B2 Aswān Egypt
116 B2 Asyūţ Egypt
Atacama, Desierto de des.
Chile see Atacama Desert
152 B3 Atacama, Salar de salt flat
Chile
152 A3 Atacama Desert des. Chile
114 C4 Atakpamé Togo
111 B3 Atalanti Greece
150 A3 Atalaya Peru
77 C2 Atamyrat Turkm.
78 B3 'Ataq Yemen
114 A2 Atâr Maur.
135 B3 Atascadero U.S.A.
77 D2 Atasu Kazakh.
111 C3 Atavyros mt. Greece
116 B3 Athara Sudan
116 B3 Atbara r. Sudan
77 C1 Atbasar Kazakh.
137 D3 Atchison U.S.A.
108 B2 Aterno r. Italy
108 B2 Atessa Italy
100 A2 Ath Belgium
128 C2 Athabasca Can.
129 C2 Athabasca r. Can.
129 D2 Athabasca, Lake Can.
111 B3 Athens Greece
143 D2 Athens GA U.S.A.
140 C3 Athens OH U.S.A.
143 D1 Athens TN U.S.A.
139 D2 Athens TX U.S.A.
Athína Greece see Athens
97 C2 Athlone Ireland
111 B2 Athos mt. Greece
97 C2 Athy Ireland
115 D3 Ati Chad
130 A2 Atikokan Can.
87 D3 Atkarsk Rus. Fed.
143 D2 Atlanta U.S.A.
137 D2 Atlantic U.S.A.

141 E3 Atlantic City U.S.A.
158 Atlantic Ocean World
122 A3 Atlantis S. Africa
114 B1 Atlas Mountains Africa
114 C1 Atlas Saharien mts Alg.
142 C2 Atmore U.S.A.
139 D3 Atoka U.S.A.
75 C2 Atrai r. India
78 B2 Aţ Ţā'if Saudi Arabia
115 E2 Aţ Ţāj Libya
63 B2 Attapu Laos
130 B1 Attawapiskat Can.
130 B1 Attawapiskat r. Can.
130 B1 Attawapiskat Lake Can.
100 C2 Attendorn Ger.
116 B2 Aţ Ţūr Egypt
78 B3 Aţ Turbah Yemen
76 B2 Atyrau Kazakh.
105 C3 Aubenas France
126 C2 Aubry Lake Can.
142 C2 Auburn AL U.S.A.
135 B3 Auburn CA U.S.A.
137 D2 Auburn NE U.S.A.
141 D2 Auburn NY U.S.A.
104 C2 Aubusson France
104 C3 Auch France
54 B1 Auckland N.Z.
48 F6 Auckland Islands is N.Z.
101 F2 Aue Ger.
102 C2 Augsburg Ger.
109 C3 Augusta Sicilia Italy
143 D2 Augusta GA U.S.A.
137 D3 Augusta KS U.S.A.
141 F2 Augusta ME U.S.A.
50 A2 Augustus, Mount Austr.
104 C2 Aulnoye-Aymeries France
62 A2 Aunglan Myanmar
122 B2 Auob watercourse Namibia/
S. Africa
74 B3 Aurangabad India
100 C1 Aurich Ger.
154 C1 Aurilândia Brazil
104 C3 Aurillac France
136 C3 Aurora CO U.S.A.
140 B2 Aurora IL U.S.A.
137 D2 Aurora NE U.S.A.
122 A2 Aus Namibia
137 E2 Austin MN U.S.A.
135 C3 Austin NV U.S.A.
139 D2 Austin TX U.S.A.
50 B2 Australia country Oceania
159 D7 Australian-Antarctic Basin
Southern Ocean
53 C3 Australian Capital Territory
admin. div. Austr.
102 C2 Austria country Europe
144 B3 Autlán Mex.
104 C2 Autun France
105 C2 Auxerre France
105 D2 Auxonne France
105 C2 Avallon France
131 E2 Avalon Peninsula Can.
154 C2 Avaré Brazil
49 H4 Avarua Cook Is
91 D2 Avdiyivka Ukr.
106 B1 Aveiro Port.
109 B2 Avellino Italy
100 A2 Avesnes-sur-Helpe France
93 G3 Avesta Sweden
108 B2 Avezzano Italy
96 C2 Aviemore U.K.
109 C2 Avigliano Italy
105 C3 Avignon France
106 C1 Ávila Spain
106 B1 Avilés Spain

109 C3 Avola Sicilia Italy
99 B2 Avon r. England U.K.
99 C3 Avon r. England U.K.
104 B2 Avranches France
54 B1 Awanui N.Z.
117 C4 Āwash Eth.
117 C3 Āwash r. Eth.
115 D2 Awbārī Libya
115 D2 Awbārī, Idhān des. Libya
117 C4 Aw Dheegle Somalia
96 B2 Awe, Loch l. U.K.
117 A4 Aweil S. Sudan
126 E1 Axel Heiberg Island Can.
114 B4 Axim Ghana
150 A3 Ayacucho Peru
77 E2 Ayagoz Kazakh.
68 B2 Ayakkum Hu salt l. China
106 B2 Ayamonte Spain
83 K3 Ayan Rus. Fed.
150 A3 Ayaviri Peru
76 A2 Aybas Kazakh.
91 D2 Aydar r. Ukr.
77 C2 Aydarko'l ko'li l. Uzbek.
111 C3 Aydın Turkey
Ayers Rock h. Austr. see Uluru
99 C3 Aylesbury U.K.
106 C1 Ayllón Spain
129 D1 Aylmer Lake Can.
117 B4 Ayod S. Sudan
83 M2 Ayon, Ostrov i. Rus. Fed.
114 B3 'Ayoûn el 'Atroûs Maur.
51 D1 Ayr Austr.
96 B3 Ayr U.K.
98 A1 Ayre, Point of Isle of Man
77 C1 Ayteke Bi Kazakh.
110 C2 Aytos Bulg.
145 C3 Ayutla Mex.
63 B2 Ayutthaya Thai.
111 C3 Ayvacık Turkey
111 C3 Ayvalık Turkey
114 C3 Azaouagh, Vallée de
watercourse Mali/Niger
77 C2 Azat, Gory h. Kazakh.
Azbine mts Niger see
Aïr, Massif de l'
81 C1 Azerbaijan country Asia
77 C1 Azhibeksor, Ozero salt l.
Kazakh.
86 D2 Azopol'ye Rus. Fed.
84 D5 Azores aut. reg. Port.
91 D2 Azov Rus. Fed.
91 D2 Azov, Sea of Rus. Fed./Ukr.
Azraq, Baḩr el r. Eth./Sudan
see Blue Nile
106 B2 Azuaga Spain
146 B4 Azuero, Península de pen.
Panama
153 C4 Azul Arg.
80 B2 Az Zaqāzīq Egypt
80 B2 Az Zarqā' Jordan
78 B3 Az Zaydīyah Yemen
114 C2 Azzel Matti, Sebkha salt pan
Alg.
78 B2 Az Zilfī Saudi Arabia
78 B3 Az Zuqur i. Yemen

B

63 B2 Ba, Sông r. Vietnam
117 C4 Baardheere Somalia
77 C3 Bābā, Kōh-e mts Afgh.
110 C2 Babadag Romania
111 C2 Babaeski Turkey
117 C3 Bāb al Mandab str. Africa/Asia
61 C2 Babana Indon.

59 C3	**Babar** i. Indon.	
119 D3	**Babati** Tanz.	
89 E2	**Babayevo** Rus. Fed.	
128 B2	**Babine** r. Can.	
128 B2	**Babine Lake** Can.	
59 C3	**Babo** Indon.	
81 D2	**Bābol** Iran	
122 A3	**Baboon Point** S. Africa	
88 C3	**Babruysk** Belarus	
64 B1	**Babuyan** i. Phil.	
64 B1	**Babuyan Islands** Phil.	
151 D2	**Bacabal** Brazil	
59 C3	**Bacan** i. Indon.	
110 C1	**Bacău** Romania	
52 B3	**Bacchus Marsh** Austr.	
77 D3	**Bachu** China	
129 E1	**Back** r. Can.	
109 C1	**Bačka Palanka** Serbia	
63 B3	**Bac Liêu** Vietnam	
64 B1	**Bacolod** Phil.	
130 C1	**Bacqueville, Lac** l. Can.	
106 B2	**Badajoz** Spain	
62 A1	**Badarpur** India	
101 E2	**Bad Berka** Ger.	
101 E2	**Bad Berleburg** Ger.	
101 E1	**Bad Bevensen** Ger.	
100 C2	**Bad Ems** Ger.	
103 D2	**Baden** Austria	
102 B2	**Baden-Baden** Ger.	
101 E2	**Bad Harzburg** Ger.	
101 E2	**Bad Hersfeld** Ger.	
102 C2	**Bad Hofgastein** Austria	
101 D2	**Bad Homburg vor der Höhe** Ger.	
74 A2	**Badin** Pak.	
	Bādiyat ash Shām des. Asia see Syrian Desert	
101 E2	**Bad Kissingen** Ger.	
100 C3	**Bad Kreuznach** Ger.	
101 E2	**Bad Lauterberg im Harz** Ger.	
101 D2	**Bad Lippspringe** Ger.	
101 D3	**Bad Mergentheim** Ger.	
101 D2	**Bad Nauheim** Ger.	
100 C2	**Bad Neuenahr-Ahrweiler** Ger.	
101 E2	**Bad Neustadt an der Saale** Ger.	
101 E1	**Bad Oldesloe** Ger.	
101 D2	**Bad Pyrmont** Ger.	
78 A2	**Badr Ḥunayn** Saudi Arabia	
101 D1	**Bad Salzuflen** Ger.	
101 E2	**Bad Salzungen** Ger.	
102 C1	**Bad Schwartau** Ger.	
101 E1	**Bad Segeberg** Ger.	
100 C3	**Bad Sobernheim** Ger.	
73 C4	**Badulla** Sri Lanka	
102 B2	**Bad Zwischenahn** Ger.	
106 C2	**Baeza** Spain	
114 A3	**Bafatá** Guinea-Bissau	
160 C2	**Baffin Bay** sea Can./Greenland	
127 G2	**Baffin Island** Can.	
118 B2	**Bafia** Cameroon	
114 A3	**Bafing** r. Africa	
114 A3	**Bafoulabé** Mali	
118 B2	**Bafoussam** Cameroon	
76 B3	**Bāfq** Iran	
80 B1	**Bafra** Turkey	
79 C2	**Bāft** Iran	
119 C3	**Bafwasende** Dem. Rep. Congo	
119 D3	**Bagamoyo** Tanz.	
60 B1	**Bagan Datuk** Malaysia	
120 B2	**Bagani** Namibia	
60 B1	**Bagansiapiapi** Indon.	
138 A2	**Bagdad** U.S.A.	
152 C4	**Bagé** Brazil	
97 C2	**Bagenalstown** Ireland	
81 C2	**Baghdād** Iraq	
77 C3	**Baghlān** Afgh.	
104 C3	**Bagnères-de-Luchon** France	
88 B3	**Bagrationovsk** Rus. Fed.	
	Bagrax China see Bohu	
64 B1	**Baguio** Phil.	
115 C3	**Bagzane, Monts** mts Niger	
79 D2	**Bāhā Kālāt** Iran	
	Bahamas country West Indies see The Bahamas	
146 C2	**Bahamas, The** country West Indies	
75 C2	**Baharampur** India	
	Bahariya Oasis Egypt see Baḥriyah, Wāḥāt al	
76 B3	**Baharly** Turkm.	
60 B1	**Bahau** Malaysia	
72 B2	**Bahawalnagar** Pak.	
74 B2	**Bahawalpur** Pak.	
153 B4	**Bahía Blanca** Arg.	
144 A2	**Bahía Kino** Mex.	
152 C3	**Bahía Negra** Para.	
144 A2	**Bahía Tortugas** Mex.	
117 B3	**Bahir Dar** Eth.	
75 C2	**Bahraich** India	
79 C2	**Bahrain** country Asia	
116 A2	**Baḥriyah, Wāḥāt al** oasis Egypt	
110 B1	**Baia Mare** Romania	
69 E1	**Baicheng** China	
131 D2	**Baie-Comeau** Can.	
	Baie-du-Poste Can. see Mistissini	
131 C2	**Baie-St-Paul** Can.	
65 B1	**Baihe** China	
69 D1	**Baikal, Lake** Rus. Fed.	
110 B2	**Băileşti** Romania	
68 C2	**Baima** China	
143 D2	**Bainbridge** U.S.A.	
48 F2	**Bairiki** Kiribati	
	Bairin Youqi China see Daban	
53 C3	**Bairnsdale** Austr.	
71 A3	**Baise** France	
65 B1	**Baishan** Jilin China	
65 B1	**Baitou Shan** mt. China/N. Korea	
70 A2	**Baiyin** China	
116 B3	**Baiyuda Desert** Sudan	
144 A1	**Baja California** pen. Mex.	
103 D2	**Baja** Hungary	
114 A3	**Bakel** Senegal	
135 C3	**Baker** CA U.S.A.	
136 C1	**Baker** MT U.S.A.	
134 C2	**Baker** OR U.S.A.	
134 B1	**Baker, Mount** vol. U.S.A.	
129 E1	**Baker Foreland** hd Can.	
49 G2	**Baker Island** N. Pacific Ocean	
129 E1	**Baker Lake** Can.	
129 E1	**Baker Lake** l. Can.	
135 C3	**Bakersfield** U.S.A.	
91 C2	**Bakhchysaray** Ukr.	
91 C1	**Bakhmach** Ukr.	
	Bākhtarān Iran see Kermānshāh	
	Bakı Azer. see Baku	
111 C2	**Bakırköy** Turkey	
92 □C2	**Bakkaflói** b. Iceland	
118 C2	**Bakouma** C.A.R.	
81 C1	**Baku** Azer.	
64 A2	**Balabac** Phil.	
64 A2	**Balabac** i. Phil.	
64 A2	**Balabac Strait** Malaysia/Phil.	
61 C2	**Balaikarak** Indon.	
52 A2	**Balaklava** Austr.	
91 C3	**Balaklava** Ukr.	
91 D2	**Balakliya** Ukr.	
87 D3	**Balakovo** Rus. Fed.	
76 C3	**Bālā Murghāb** Afgh.	
145 C3	**Balancán** Mex.	
111 C3	**Balan Dağı** h. Turkey	
64 B1	**Balanga** Phil.	
75 C2	**Balangir** India	
87 D3	**Balashov** Rus. Fed.	
103 D2	**Balaton, Lake** Hungary	
103 D2	**Balatonboglár** Hungary	
150 C2	**Balbina, Represa de** resr Brazil	
97 C2	**Balbriggan** Ireland	
52 A2	**Balcanoona** Austr.	
110 C2	**Balchik** Bulg.	
54 A3	**Balclutha** N.Z.	
129 E2	**Baldock Lake** Can.	
129 D2	**Baldy Mountain** h. Can.	
138 B2	**Baldy Peak** U.S.A.	
	Baleares, Islas is Spain see Balearic Islands	
107 D2	**Balearic Islands** is Spain	
155 E1	**Baleia, Ponta da** pt Brazil	
130 C1	**Baleine, Grande Rivière de la** r. Can.	
131 D1	**Baleine, Rivière à la** r. Can.	
75 C2	**Baleshwar** India	
108 A2	**Balestrieri, Punta** mt. Sardegna Italy	
61 C2	**Bali** i. Indon.	
115 C4	**Bali** Nigeria	
60 A1	**Balige** Indon.	
75 C2	**Baliguda** India	
111 C3	**Balıkesir** Turkey	
61 C2	**Balikpapan** Indon.	
59 D3	**Balimo** P.N.G.	
102 B2	**Balingen** Ger.	
	Bali Sea Indon. see Laut Bali	
76 B3	**Balkanabat** Turkm.	
110 B2	**Balkan Mountains** Bulg./S.M.	
77 D3	**Balkash** Kazakh.	
77 D2	**Balkhash, Lake** Kazakh.	
	Balkash, Ozero l. Kazakh. see Balkhash, Lake	
50 B3	**Balladonia** Austr.	
97 B2	**Ballaghaderreen** Ireland	
92 G2	**Ballangen** Norway	
52 B3	**Ballarat** Austr.	
50 B2	**Ballard, Lake** imp. l. Austr.	
96 C2	**Ballater** U.K.	
114 B3	**Ballé** Mali	
53 D1	**Ballina** Austr.	
97 B1	**Ballina** Ireland	
97 B2	**Ballinasloe** Ireland	
139 D2	**Ballinger** U.S.A.	
97 B1	**Ballinrobe** Ireland	
97 B1	**Ballycastle** Ireland	
97 C1	**Ballycastle** U.K.	
97 D1	**Ballyclare** U.K.	
97 C1	**Ballymena** U.K.	
97 C1	**Ballymoney** U.K.	
97 D1	**Ballynahinch** U.K.	
97 B1	**Ballyshannon** Ireland	
95 C2	**Ballyvoy** U.K.	
51 D2	**Balonne** r. Austr.	
74 B2	**Balotra** India	
75 C2	**Balrampur** India	
52 B2	**Balranald** Austr.	
110 B2	**Balş** Romania	
151 E3	**Balsas** Brazil	
145 C3	**Balsas** Mex.	
90 C2	**Balta** Ukr.	
90 B2	**Bălţi** Moldova	
93 G4	**Baltic Sea** g. Europe	
80 B2	**Baltim** Egypt	
123 C1	**Baltimore** S. Africa	
141 D3	**Baltimore** U.S.A.	
88 B3	**Baltiysk** Rus. Fed.	
62 A1	**Balu** India	
88 C2	**Balvi** Latvia	
77 D2	**Balykchy** Kyrg.	
87 E4	**Balykshi** Kazakh.	

79 C2	Bam Iran	
51 D1	Bamaga Austr.	
130 A1	Bamaji Lake Can.	
114 B3	Bamako Mali	
118 C2	Bambari C.A.R.	
101 E3	Bamberg Ger.	
119 C2	Bambili Dem. Rep. Congo	
119 C2	Bambouti C.A.R.	
155 C2	Bambuí Brazil	
118 B2	Bamenda Cameroon	
74 A1	Bāmyān Afgh.	
119 C2	Banalia Dem. Rep. Congo	
151 C3	Bananal, Ilha do i. Brazil	
74 B2	Banas r. India	
111 C3	Banaz Turkey	
62 B2	Ban Ban Laos	
97 C1	Banbridge U.K.	
99 C2	Banbury U.K.	
130 C2	Bancroft Can.	
119 C2	Banda Dem. Rep. Congo	
75 C2	Banda India	
59 C3	Banda, Kepulauan is Indon.	
59 C3	Banda, Laut sea Indon.	
60 A1	Banda Aceh Indon.	
79 C2	Bandar-e 'Abbās Iran	
81 C2	Bandar-e Anzalī Iran	
79 C2	Bandar-e Chārak Iran	
81 C2	Bandar-e Emām Khomeynī Iran	
79 C2	Bandar-e Lengeh Iran	
79 C2	Bandar-e Maqām Iran	
60 B2	Bandar Lampung Indon.	
61 C1	Bandar Seri Begawan Brunei	
	Banda Sea Indon. see Banda, Laut	
155 D2	Bandeiras, Pico de mt. Brazil	
123 C2	Bandelierkop S. Africa	
144 B2	Banderas, Bahía de b. Mex.	
114 B3	Bandiagara Mali	
111 C2	Bandırma Turkey	
97 B3	Bandon Ireland	
118 B3	Bandundu Dem. Rep. Congo	
61 B2	Bandung Indon.	
128 C2	Banff Can.	
96 C2	Banff U.K.	
114 B3	Banfora Burkina Faso	
64 B2	Banga Phil.	
73 B3	Bangalore India	
118 C2	Bangassou C.A.R.	
59 C3	Banggai Indon.	
59 C3	Banggai, Kepulauan is Indon.	
61 C1	Banggi i. Sabah Malaysia	
60 B2	Bangka i. Indon.	
61 C2	Bangkalan Indon.	
60 B1	Bangkinang Indon.	
60 B2	Bangko Indon.	
63 B2	Bangkok Thai.	
75 C2	Bangladesh country Asia	
63 D2	Ba Ngoi Vietnam	
97 D1	Bangor Northern Ireland U.K.	
98 A2	Bangor Wales U.K.	
141 F2	Bangor U.S.A.	
63 A3	Bang Saphan Yai Thai.	
64 B1	Bangued Phil.	
118 B2	Bangui C.A.R.	
121 B2	Bangweulu, Lake Zambia	
62 B2	Ban Huai Khon Thai.	
116 B2	Banī Suwayf Egypt	
115 D1	Banī Walīd Libya	
80 B2	Bāniyās Syria	
109 C2	Banja Luka Bos.-Herz.	
61 C2	Banjarmasin Indon.	
114 A3	Banjul Gambia	
128 A2	Banks Island B.C. Can.	
126 C2	Banks Island N.W.T. Can.	
48 F3	Banks Islands Vanuatu	
179 F1	Banks Lake Can.	
54 B2	Banks Peninsula N.Z.	
75 C2	Bankura India	
62 A1	Banmauk Myanmar	
62 B2	Ban Mouang Laos	
97 C1	Bann r. U.K.	
62 B2	Ban Napè Laos	
63 A3	Ban Na San Thai.	
143 E4	Bannerman Town Bahamas	
74 B1	Bannu Pak.	
74 B2	Banswara India	
63 A3	Ban Tha Khan Thai.	
62 A2	Ban Tha Song Yang Thai.	
63 B2	Ban Tôp Laos	
97 B3	Bantry Ireland	
97 B3	Bantry Bay Ireland	
118 B2	Banyo Cameroon	
107 D1	Banyoles Spain	
61 C2	Banyuwangi Indon.	
	Bao'an China see Shenzhen	
69 D2	Baochang China	
70 B2	Baoding China	
70 A2	Baoji China	
62 B1	Bao Lac Vietnam	
63 B2	Bao Lôc Vietnam	
66 B1	Baoqing China	
62 A1	Baoshan China	
70 B1	Baotou China	
81 C2	Ba'qūbah Iraq	
109 C2	Bar Montenegro	
117 C4	Baraawe Somalia	
147 C2	Baracoa Cuba	
53 C2	Baradine Austr.	
147 C3	Barahona Dom. Rep.	
116 B3	Baraka watercourse Eritrea/Sudan	
61 C1	Baram r. Sarawak Malaysia	
72 B1	Baramulla India	
74 B1	Baramulla India	
88 C3	Baranavichy Belarus	
78 A2	Baranis Egypt	
90 B1	Baranivka Ukr.	
128 A2	Baranof Island U.S.A.	
59 C3	Barat Daya, Kepulauan is Indon.	
155 D2	Barbacena Brazil	
147 E3	Barbados country West Indies	
107 D1	Barbastro Spain	
104 B2	Barbezieux-St-Hilaire France	
51 D2	Barcaldine Austr.	
107 D1	Barcelona Spain	
150 B1	Barcelona Venez.	
105 D3	Barcelonnette France	
150 B2	Barcelos Brazil	
	Barcoo Creek watercourse Austr. see Cooper Creek	
103 D2	Barcs Hungary	
75 C2	Barddhaman India	
103 E2	Bardejov Slovakia	
79 C2	Bardsīr Iran	
75 B2	Bareilly India	
160 B2	Barents Sea Arctic Ocean	
78 A3	Barentu Eritrea	
75 C2	Barh India	
141 F2	Bar Harbor U.S.A.	
109 C2	Bari Italy	
74 B1	Bari Kōt Afgh.	
150 A1	Barinas Venez.	
75 C2	Baripada India	
75 D2	Barisal Bangl.	
60 B2	Barisan, Pegunungan mts Indon.	
61 C2	Barito r. Indon.	
79 C2	Barkā Oman	
88 C2	Barkava Latvia	
51 C1	Barkly Tableland reg. Austr.	
68 C1	Barkol China	
110 C1	Bârlad Romania	
105 D2	Bar-le-Duc France	
50 A2	Barlee, Lake imp. l. Austr.	
109 C2	Barletta Italy	
53 C2	Barmedman Austr.	
74 B2	Barmer India	
99 A2	Barmouth U.K.	
101 D1	Barmstedt Ger.	
98 C1	Barnard Castle U.K.	
53 B2	Barnato Austr.	
82 G3	Barnaul Rus. Fed.	
127 G2	Barnes Icecap Can.	
100 B1	Barneveld Neth.	
98 C2	Barnsley U.K.	
99 A3	Barnstaple U.K.	
99 A3	Barnstaple Bay U.K.	
143 D2	Barnwell U.S.A.	
	Baroda India see Vadodara	
150 B1	Barquisimeto Venez.	
96 A2	Barra i. U.K.	
53 D2	Barraba Austr.	
151 D2	Barra do Corda Brazil	
134 B1	Barra do Garças Brazil	
150 C2	Barra do São Manuel Brazil	
150 A3	Barranca Lima Peru	
150 A2	Barranca Loreto Peru	
150 A1	Barranqueras Arg.	
150 A1	Barranquilla Col.	
151 D3	Barreiras Brazil	
154 C2	Barretos Brazil	
130 C2	Barrie Can.	
128 B2	Barrière Can.	
52 B2	Barrier Range hills Austr.	
51 D2	Barrington, Mount Austr.	
129 D2	Barrington Lake Can.	
53 C1	Barringun Austr.	
97 C2	Barrow r. Ireland	
51 C2	Barrow Creek Austr.	
98 B1	Barrow-in-Furness U.K.	
50 A2	Barrow Island U.K.	
126 E2	Barrow Strait Can.	
99 B3	Barry U.K.	
130 C2	Barrys Bay Can.	
74 B2	Barsalpur India	
135 C4	Barstow U.S.A.	
105 C2	Bar-sur-Aube France	
80 B1	Bartın Turkey	
51 D1	Bartle Frere, Mount Austr.	
139 D1	Bartlesville U.S.A.	
103 E1	Bartoszyce Pol.	
61 C2	Barung i. Indon.	
69 D1	Baruun-Urt Mongolia	
91 C2	Barvinkove Ukr.	
53 C2	Barwon r. Austr.	
88 C3	Barysaw Belarus	
110 C2	Basarabi Romania	
105 D2	Basel Switz.	
91 C2	Bashtanka Ukr.	
64 B2	Basilan i. Phil.	
99 D3	Basildon U.K.	
99 C3	Basingstoke U.K.	
81 C2	Başkale Turkey	
130 C2	Baskatong, Réservoir resr Can.	
	Basle Switz. see Basel	
118 C2	Basoko Dem. Rep. Congo	
81 C2	Basra Iraq	
128 C2	Bassano Can.	
114 C4	Bassar Togo	
63 A2	Bassein Myanmar	
147 D3	Basse-Terre Guadeloupe	
147 D3	Basseterre St Kitts and Nevis	
114 B3	Bassikounou Maur.	
51 D3	Bass Strait Austr.	
79 C2	Bastak Iran	
101 E2	Bastheim Ger.	
75 C2	Basti India	
105 D3	Bastia Corse France	
100 B2	Bastogne Belgium	

142 B2	Bastrop U.S.A.	
	Basuo China *see* Dongfang	
118 A2	Bata Equat. Guinea	
83 J2	Batagay Rus. Fed.	
154 B2	Bataguassu Brazil	
106 B2	Batalha Port.	
71 C3	Batan *i.* Phil.	
118 B2	Batangafo C.A.R.	
64 B1	Batangas Phil.	
60 B2	Batanghari *r.* Indon.	
71 C3	Batan Islands Phil.	
141 D2	Batavia U.S.A.	
91 D2	Bataysk Rus. Fed.	
130 B2	Batchawana Mountain *h.* Can.	
50 C1	Batchelor Austr.	
63 B2	Bătdâmbâng Cambodia	
53 D3	Batemans Bay Austr.	
142 B1	Batesville U.S.A.	
89 D2	Batetskiy Rus. Fed.	
99 B3	Bath U.K.	
74 B1	Bathinda India	
53 C2	Bathurst Austr.	
131 D2	Bathurst Can.	
126 D2	Bathurst Inlet Can.	
126 D2	Bathurst Inlet (abandoned) Can.	
50 C1	Bathurst Island Austr.	
126 E1	Bathurst Island Can.	
78 B1	Bāṭin, Wādī al *watercourse* Asia	
81 C2	Batman Turkey	
115 C1	Batna Alg.	
142 B2	Baton Rouge U.S.A.	
144 B2	Batopilas Mex.	
118 B2	Batouri Cameroon	
154 B1	Batovi Brazil	
92 I1	Båtsfjord Norway	
73 C4	Batticaloa Sri Lanka	
109 B2	Battipaglia Italy	
129 D2	Battle *r.* Can.	
140 B2	Battle Creek U.S.A.	
135 C2	Battle Mountain U.S.A.	
74 B1	Battura Glacier Pak.	
117 B4	Batu *mt.* Eth.	
60 A2	Batu, Pulau-pulau *is* Indon.	
81 C1	Bat'umi Georgia	
60 B1	Batu Pahat Malaysia	
59 C3	Baubau Indon.	
115 C3	Bauchi Nigeria	
104 B2	Baugé France	
105 D2	Baume-les-Dames France	
154 C2	Bauru Brazil	
154 B1	Baús Brazil	
88 B2	Bauska Latvia	
102 C1	Bautzen Ger.	
144 B2	Bavispe *r.* Mex.	
87 E3	Bavly Rus. Fed.	
62 A1	Bawdwin Myanmar	
61 C2	Bawean *i.* Indon.	
114 B3	Bawku Ghana	
146 C2	Bayamo Cuba	
	Bayan Gol China *see* Dengkou	
68 C1	Bayanhongor Mongolia	
70 A2	Bayan Hot China	
70 A1	Bayannur China	
69 D2	Bayan Shutu China	
69 D1	Bayan-Uul Mongolia	
64 B2	Bayawan Phil.	
80 C1	Bayburt Turkey	
140 C2	Bay City *MI* U.S.A.	
139 D3	Bay City *TX* U.S.A.	
86 F2	Baydaratskaya Guba Rus. Fed.	
117 C4	Baydhabo Somalia	
81 C2	Bayji Iraq	
	Baykal, Ozero *l.* Rus. Fed. *see* Baikal, Lake	
83 I3	Baykal'skiy Khrebet *mts* Rus. Fed.	
76 C2	Baykonyr Kazakh.	
87 E3	Baymak Rus. Fed.	
64 B1	Bayombong Phil.	
104 B3	Bayonne France	
111 C3	Bayramiç Turkey	
101 E3	Bayreuth Ger.	
78 B3	Bayt al Faqīh Yemen	
106 C2	Baza Spain	
106 C2	Baza, Sierra de *mts* Spain	
74 A1	Bārārāk Afgh.	
76 A2	Bazardyuzyu, Gora *mt.* Azer./Rus. Fed.	
104 B3	Bazas France	
74 A2	Bazdar Pak.	
70 A2	Bazhong China	
79 D2	Bazmān Iran	
79 D2	Bazmān, Kūh-e *mt.* Iran	
121 □D2	Bé, Nosy *i.* Madag.	
99 D3	Beachy Head U.K.	
123 C3	Beacon Bay S. Africa	
50 B1	Beagle Gulf Austr.	
121 □D2	Bealanana Madag.	
97 B1	Béal an Mhuirthead Ireland	
130 B2	Beardmore Can.	
	Bear Island Arctic Ocean *see* Bjørnøya	
134 E1	Bear Paw Mountain U.S.A.	
147 C3	Beata, Cabo *c.* Dom. Rep.	
147 C3	Beata, Isla *i.* Dom. Rep.	
137 D2	Beatrice U.S.A.	
135 C3	Beatty U.S.A.	
53 D1	Beaudesert Austr.	
52 B3	Beaufort Austr.	
61 C1	Beaufort *Sabah* Malaysia	
143 D2	Beaufort U.S.A.	
160 L2	Beaufort Sea Can./U.S.A.	
122 B3	Beaufort West S. Africa	
96 B2	Beauly *r.* U.K.	
100 B2	Beaumont Belgium	
54 A3	Beaumont N.Z.	
139 E2	Beaumont U.S.A.	
105 C2	Beaune France	
100 B2	Beauraing Belgium	
129 E2	Beauséjour Can.	
104 C2	Beauvais France	
129 D2	Beauval Can.	
129 D2	Beaver *r.* Can.	
135 D3	Beaver U.S.A.	
126 B2	Beaver Creek Can.	
140 B2	Beaver Dam U.S.A.	
129 E2	Beaver Hill Lake Can.	
140 B1	Beaver Island U.S.A.	
128 C2	Beaverlodge Can.	
74 B2	Beawar India	
154 C2	Bebedouro Brazil	
101 D2	Bebra Ger.	
106 B1	Becerreá Spain	
114 B1	Béchar Alg.	
140 C3	Beckley U.S.A.	
117 B4	Bedelē Eth.	
99 C2	Bedford U.K.	
140 B3	Bedford U.S.A.	
100 C1	Bedum Neth.	
53 D2	Beecroft Peninsula Austr.	
101 F1	Beelitz Ger.	
53 D1	Beenleigh Austr.	
80 B2	Beersheba Israel	
139 D3	Beeville U.S.A.	
53 C3	Bega Austr.	
107 D1	Begur, Cap de *c.* Spain	
128 C2	Behchokǫ̀ Can.	
81 D2	Behshahr Iran	
71 A3	Bei'an China	
71 A3	Beihai China	
70 B2	Beijing China	
100 C1	Beilen Neth.	
96 A2	Beinn Mhòr *h.* U.K.	
121 C2	Beira Moz.	
80 B2	Beirut Lebanon	
123 C1	Beitbridge Zimbabwe	
106 B2	Beja Port.	
115 C1	Bejaïa Alg.	
106 B1	Béjar Spain	
74 A2	Beji *r.* Pak.	
103 E2	Békés Hungary	
103 E2	Békéscsaba Hungary	
121 □D3	Bekily Madag.	
74 A2	Bela Pak.	
123 C1	Bela-Bela S. Africa	
118 B2	Bélabo Cameroon	
109 D2	Bela Crkva Serbia	
61 C1	Belaga *Sarawak* Malaysia	
88 C3	Belarus *country* Europe	
	Belau *country* N. Pacific Ocean *see* Palau	
123 C2	Bela Vista Moz.	
60 A1	Belawan Indon.	
83 M2	Belaya *r.* Rus. Fed.	
103 D1	Bełchatów Pol.	
130 C1	Belcher Islands Can.	
117 C4	Beledweyne Somalia	
151 D2	Belém Brazil	
138 B2	Belen U.S.A.	
89 E3	Belev Rus. Fed.	
97 D1	Belfast U.K.	
141 F2	Belfast U.S.A.	
105 D2	Belfort France	
73 B3	Belgaum India	
100 B2	Belgium *country* Europe	
91 D1	Belgorod Rus. Fed.	
109 D2	Belgrade Serbia	
134 D1	Belgrade U.S.A.	
60 B2	Belinyu Indon.	
61 B2	Belitung *i.* Indon.	
146 B3	Belize Belize	
146 B3	Belize *country* Central America	
83 K1	Bel'kovskiy, Ostrov *i.* Rus. Fed.	
128 B2	Bella Bella Can.	
104 C2	Bellac France	
128 B2	Bella Coola Can.	
53 C1	Bellata Austr.	
136 C2	Belle Fourche U.S.A.	
136 C2	Belle Fourche *r.* U.S.A.	
143 D3	Belle Glade U.S.A.	
104 B2	Belle-Île *i.* France	
131 E1	Belle Isle *i.* Can.	
131 E1	Belle Isle, Strait of Can.	
130 C2	Belleville Can.	
140 B3	Belleville *IL* U.S.A.	
137 D3	Belleville *KS* U.S.A.	
134 B1	Bellevue U.S.A.	
134 B1	Bellingham U.S.A.	
55 O2	Bellingshausen Sea Antarctica	
105 D2	Bellinzona Switz.	
108 B1	Belluno Italy	
122 A3	Bellville S. Africa	
155 E1	Belmonte Brazil	
146 B3	Belmopan Belize	
69 E1	Belogorsk Rus. Fed.	
121 □D3	Beloha Madag.	
155 D1	Belo Horizonte Brazil	
140 B3	Beloit U.S.A.	
86 C2	Belomorsk Rus. Fed.	
91 D3	Belorechensk Rus. Fed.	
87 E3	Beloretsk Rus. Fed.	
	Belorussia *country* Europe *see* Belarus	
86 F2	Beloyarskiy Rus. Fed.	
86 C2	Beloye, Ozero *l.* Rus. Fed.	
	Beloye More *sea* Rus. Fed. *see* White Sea	
86 C2	Belozersk Rus. Fed.	
77 E2	Belukha, Gora *mt.* Kazakh./Rus. Fed.	

86 D2 Belush'ye Rus. Fed.
89 D2 Bely Rus. Fed.
82 F2 Bely, Ostrov *i.* Rus. Fed.
101 F1 Belzig Ger.
137 E1 Bemidji U.S.A.
118 C3 Bena Dibele Dem. Rep. Congo
53 C3 Benalla Austr.
106 B1 Benavente Spain
96 A2 Benbecula *i.* U.K.
134 B2 Bend U.S.A.
123 C3 Bendearg *mt.* S. Africa
52 B3 Bendigo Austr.
121 C2 Bene Moz.
102 C2 Benešov Czech Rep.
109 B2 Benevento Italy
159 C2 Bengal, Bay of *sea* Indian Ocean
    Bengaluru India *see* Bangalore
70 B3 Bengbu China
115 E1 Benghazi Libya
61 B1 Bengkayang Indon.
60 A2 Bengkulu Indon.
120 A2 Benguela Angola
96 B1 Ben Hope *h.* U.K.
152 B2 Beni *r.* Bol.
119 C2 Beni Dem. Rep. Congo
114 B1 Beni Abbès Alg.
107 C2 Benidorm Spain
114 B1 Beni Mellal Morocco
114 C3 Benin *country* Africa
114 C4 Benin, Bight of *g.* Africa
115 C4 Benin City Nigeria
153 C3 Benito Juárez Arg.
150 D2 Benjamin Constant Brazil
144 A1 Benjamín Hill Mex.
59 C3 Benjina Indon.
96 B2 Ben Lawers *mt.* U.K.
96 B2 Ben Lomond *h.* U.K.
96 C2 Ben Macdui *mt.* U.K.
96 A2 Ben More *h.* U.K.
54 B2 Benmore, Lake N.Z.
96 B1 Ben More Assynt *h.* U.K.
128 A2 Bennett Can.
83 K1 Bennetta, Ostrov *i.* Rus. Fed.
96 B2 Ben Nevis *mt.* U.K.
141 E2 Bennington U.S.A.
123 C2 Benoni S. Africa
101 D3 Bensheim Ger.
138 A2 Benson U.S.A.
58 C3 Bentong Malaysia
140 B2 Benton Harbor U.S.A.
142 B1 Bentonville U.S.A.
115 C4 Benue *r.* Nigeria
97 B1 Benwee Head Ireland
96 B2 Ben Wyvis *mt.* U.K.
70 C1 Benxi China
    Beograd Serbia *see* Belgrade
75 C2 Beohari India
67 B4 Beppu Japan
109 C2 Berane Montenegro
109 C2 Berat Albania
116 B3 Berber Sudan
117 C3 Berbera Somalia
118 B2 Berbérati C.A.R.
104 C1 Berck France
91 D2 Berdyans'k Ukr.
90 B2 Berdychiv Ukr.
90 A2 Berehove Ukr.
59 D3 Bereina P.N.G.
76 B3 Bereket Turkm.
129 E2 Berens River Can.
90 A2 Berezhany Ukr.
90 C2 Berezivka Ukr.
90 B1 Berezne Ukr.
86 D2 Bereznik Rus. Fed.
86 E3 Berezniki Rus. Fed.

86 F2 Berezovo Rus. Fed.
107 D1 Berga Spain
111 C3 Bergama Turkey
108 A1 Bergamo Italy
102 C1 Bergen *Mecklenburg-Vorpommern* Ger.
101 D1 Bergen *Niedersachsen* Ger.
93 E3 Bergen Norway
100 B2 Bergen op Zoom Neth.
104 C3 Bergerac France
100 C2 Bergheim (Erft) Ger.
100 C2 Bergisch Gladbach Ger.
122 A1 Bergland Namibia
92 H2 Bergsviken Sweden
83 M3 Beringa, Ostrov *i.* Rus. Fed.
100 B2 Beringen Belgium
75 C3 Bering Sea N. Pacific Ocean
83 N2 Bering Strait Rus. Fed./U.S.A.
135 B3 Berkeley U.S.A.
100 B1 Berkhout Neth.
55 Q2 Berkner Island Antarctica
110 B2 Berkovitsa Bulg.
92 I1 Berlevåg Norway
101 F1 Berlin Ger.
141 E2 Berlin U.S.A.
101 E2 Berlingerode Ger.
53 D3 Bermagui Austr.
144 B2 Bermejillo Mex.
152 B3 Bermejo Bol.
131 D1 Bermen, Lac *l.* Can.
125 K4 Bermuda *terr.* N. Atlantic Ocean
105 D2 Bern Switz.
101 E2 Bernburg (Saale) Ger.
100 C3 Bernkastel-Kues Ger.
126 C2 Bernier Bay Can.
121 □D3 Beroroha Madag.
52 B2 Berri Austr.
107 D2 Berrouaghia Alg.
146 C2 Berry Islands Bahamas
100 C1 Bersenbrück Ger.
90 B2 Bershad' Ukr.
131 D1 Berté, Lac *l.* Can.
118 B2 Bertoua Cameroon
150 B2 Beruri Brazil
98 B1 Berwick-upon-Tweed U.K.
91 C2 Beryslav Ukr.
121 □D2 Besalampy Madag.
105 D2 Besançon France
129 D2 Besnard Lake Can.
142 C2 Bessemer U.S.A.
76 B2 Besshoky, Gora *h.* Kazakh.
118 B2 Bétaré Oya Cameroon
122 A2 Bethanie Namibia
123 C2 Bethlehem S. Africa
141 D2 Bethlehem U.S.A.
121 □D2 Betioky Madag.
77 D2 Betpakdala *plain* Kazakh.
121 □D3 Betroka Madag.
131 D2 Betsiamites Can.
121 □D2 Betsiboka *r.* Madag.
137 E2 Bettendorf U.S.A.
75 C2 Betul India
75 B2 Betwa *r.* India
98 B2 Betws-y-coed U.K.
98 C2 Beverley U.K.
101 D2 Beverungen Ger.
100 B1 Beverwijk Neth.
99 D3 Bexhill U.K.
111 C2 Beykoz Turkey
114 B4 Beyla Guinea
76 B2 Beyneu Kazakh.
80 B1 Beypazarı Turkey
    Beyrouth Lebanon *see* **Beirut**
80 B2 Beyşehir Turkey

80 B2 Beyşehir Gölü *l.* Turkey
91 D2 Beysug *r.* Rus. Fed.
88 C2 Bezhanitsy Rus. Fed.
89 E2 Bezhetsk Rus. Fed.
105 C3 Béziers France
75 C2 Bhadrak India
73 B3 Bhadravati India
75 C2 Bhagalpur India
74 A2 Bhairi Hol *mt.* Pak.
74 B1 Bhakkar Pak.
62 A1 Bhamo Myanmar
74 B2 Bhanjanagar India
74 B2 Bharatpur India
74 B2 Bharuch India
74 B2 Bhavnagar India
75 C3 Bhawanipatna India
123 D2 Bhekuzulu S. Africa
73 B3 Bhima *r.* India
123 C3 Bhisho S. Africa
74 B2 Bhiwani India
123 C3 Bhongweni S. Africa
74 B2 Bhopal India
75 C2 Bhubaneshwar India
74 A2 Bhuj India
74 B2 Bhusawal India
75 D2 Bhutan *country* Asia
62 B2 Bia, Phou *mt.* Laos
59 D3 Biak Indon.
59 D3 Biak *i.* Indon.
103 E1 Biała Podlaska Pol.
103 D1 Białogard Pol.
103 E1 Białystok Pol.
109 C3 Bianco Italy
104 B3 Biarritz France
105 D2 Biasca Switz.
66 D2 Bibai Japan
120 A2 Bibala Angola
102 B2 Biberach an der Riß Ger.
115 C4 Bida Nigeria
141 E2 Biddeford U.S.A.
99 A3 Bideford U.K.
101 D2 Biedenkopf Ger.
105 D2 Biel Switz.
101 D1 Bielefeld Ger.
108 A1 Biella Italy
103 D2 Bielsko-Biała Pol.
63 B2 Biên Hoa Vietnam
130 C1 Bienville, Lac *l.* Can.
100 B3 Bièvre Belgium
118 B3 Bifoun Gabon
111 C3 Biga Turkey
123 D2 Big Bend Swaziland
129 D2 Biggar Can.
96 C3 Biggar U.K.
134 D1 Big Hole *r.* U.S.A.
136 B1 Bighorn *r.* U.S.A.
136 B2 Bighorn Mountains U.S.A.
139 C2 Big Lake U.S.A.
140 B2 Big Rapids U.S.A.
129 D2 Big River Can.
129 E2 Big Sand Lake Can.
137 D2 Big Sioux *r.* U.S.A.
139 C2 Big Spring U.S.A.
134 E1 Big Timber U.S.A.
130 B1 Big Trout Lake Can.
130 A1 Big Trout Lake Can.
109 C2 Bihać Bos.-Herz.
75 C2 Bihar Sharif India
110 B1 Bihor, Vârful *mt.* Romania
114 A3 Bijagós, Arquipélago dos *is* Guinea-Bissau
81 C2 Bijār Iran
109 C2 Bijeljina Bos.-Herz.
109 C2 Bijelo Polje Montenegro
71 A3 Bijie China
74 B2 Bikaner India

69 E1	Bikin Rus. Fed.	
118 B3	Bikoro Dem. Rep. Congo	
79 C2	Bilād Banī Bū 'Alī Oman	
75 C2	Bilaspur India	
90 C2	Bila Tserkva Ukr.	
63 A2	Bilauktaung Range mts	
	Myanmar/Thai.	
106 C1	Bilbao Spain	
111 C2	Bilecik Turkey	
103 E1	Biłgoraj Pol.	
90 C2	Bilhorod-Dnistrovs'kyy Ukr.	
119 C2	Bili Dem. Rep. Congo	
83 M2	Bilibino Rus. Fed.	
134 E1	Billings U.S.A.	
99 B3	Bill of Portland hd U.K.	
115 D3	Bilma Niger	
115 D3	Bilma, Grand Erg de des. Niger	
91 C2	Biloela Austr.	
91 C2	Bilohirs'k Ukr.	
90 B1	Bilohir"ya Ukr.	
91 C1	Bilopillya Ukr.	
91 D2	Bilovods'k Ukr.	
142 C2	Biloxi U.S.A.	
51 C2	Bilpa Morea Claypan salt flat	
	Austr.	
101 E2	Bilshausen Ger.	
115 E3	Biltine Chad	
90 C2	Bilyayivka Ukr.	
143 E3	Bimini Islands Bahamas	
75 B2	Bina-Etawa India	
59 C3	Binaija, Gunung mt. Indon.	
118 B3	Bindu Dem. Rep. Congo	
121 C2	Bindura Zimbabwe	
107 D1	Binéfar Spain	
53 D1	Bingara Austr.	
100 C3	Bingen am Rhein Ger.	
141 F1	Bingham U.S.A.	
141 D2	Binghamton U.S.A.	
81 C2	Bingöl Turkey	
60 A1	Binjai Indon.	
60 B2	Bintuan Indon.	
61 C1	Bintulu Sarawak Malaysia	
70 B2	Binzhou China	
109 C2	Biograd na Moru Croatia	
118 A2	Bioko i. Equat. Guinea	
118 C1	Birao C.A.R.	
75 C2	Biratnagar Nepal	
128 C2	Birch Mountains Can.	
51 C2	Birdsville Austr.	
80 B2	Birecik Turkey	
60 A1	Bireun Indon.	
75 C2	Birganj Nepal	
154 B2	Birigüi Brazil	
76 B3	Birjand Iran	
98 B2	Birkenhead U.K.	
99 C2	Birmingham U.K.	
142 C2	Birmingham U.S.A.	
114 A2	Bîr Mogreïn Maur.	
115 C3	Birnin-Kebbi Nigeria	
115 C3	Birnin Konni Niger	
69 E1	Birobidzhan Rus. Fed.	
97 C2	Birr Ireland	
96 C1	Birsay U.K.	
78 A2	Bi'r Shalatayn Egypt	
91 D1	Biryuch Rus. Fed.	
88 B2	Biržai Lith.	
75 B2	Bisalpur India	
138 B2	Bisbee U.S.A.	
104 A2	Biscay, Bay of sea	
	France/Spain	
102 C2	Bischofshofen Ger.	
130 B2	Biscotasi Lake Can.	
77 D2	Bishkek Kyrg.	
135 C3	Bishop U.S.A.	
69 E1	Bishui China	
150 B1	Bisinaca Col.	
115 C1	Biskra Alg.	

136 C1	Bismarck U.S.A.	
48 D1	Bismarck Sea sea P.N.G.	
107 D2	Bissa, Djebel mt. Alg.	
114 A3	Bissau Guinea-Bissau	
129 E2	Bissett Can.	
128 C2	Bistcho Lake Can.	
110 B1	Bistrița Romania	
110 C1	Bistrița r. Romania	
100 C3	Bitburg Ger.	
105 D2	Bitche France	
115 D3	Bitkine Chad	
109 D2	Bitola Macedonia	
109 C2	Bitonto Italy	
122 A3	Bitterfontein S. Africa	
134 D1	Bitterroot r. U.S.A.	
134 C1	Bitterroot Range mts U.S.A.	
91 D1	Bityug r. Rus. Fed.	
115 D3	Biu Nigeria	
67 C3	Biwa-ko l. Japan	
68 B1	Biysk Rus. Fed.	
115 C1	Bizerte Tunisia	
92 ☐A2	Bjargtangar hd Iceland	
92 G3	Bjästa Sweden	
92 G2	Bjerkvik Norway	
82 C2	Bjørnøya i. Arctic Ocean	
114 B3	Bla Mali	
137 E3	Black r. U.S.A.	
51 D2	Blackall Austr.	
98 B2	Blackburn U.K.	
134 D2	Blackfoot U.S.A.	
102 B2	Black Forest mts Ger.	
136 C2	Black Hills U.S.A.	
96 B2	Black Isle pen. U.K.	
129 D2	Black Lake Can.	
129 D2	Black Lake Can.	
99 B3	Black Mountains hills U.K.	
98 B2	Blackpool U.K.	
62 B1	Black River r. Vietnam	
140 A2	Black River Falls U.S.A.	
140 C3	Blacksburg U.S.A.	
80 B1	Black Sea Asia/Europe	
97 A1	Blacksod Bay Ireland	
97 C2	Blackstairs Mountains	
	hills Ireland	
114 B4	Black Volta r. Africa	
97 C2	Blackwater r. Ireland	
128 B1	Blackwater Lake Can.	
50 A3	Blackwood r. Austr.	
76 A2	Blagodarnyy Rus. Fed.	
110 B2	Blagoevgrad Bulg.	
69 E1	Blagoveshchensk Rus. Fed.	
129 D2	Blaine Lake Can.	
137 D2	Blair U.S.A.	
96 C2	Blair Atholl U.K.	
96 C2	Blairgowrie U.K.	
143 D2	Blakely U.S.A.	
105 D2	Blanc, Mont mt. France/Italy	
153 B4	Blanca, Bahía b. Arg.	
52 A1	Blanche, Lake imp. l. Austr.	
152 B2	Blanco r. Bol.	
131 E1	Blanc-Sablon Can.	
92 ☐A2	Blanda r. Iceland	
99 B3	Blandford Forum U.K.	
135 E3	Blanding U.S.A.	
107 D1	Blanes Spain	
60 A1	Blangkejeren Indon.	
100 C2	Blankenheim Ger.	
100 C2	Blankenrath Ger.	
103 D2	Blansko Czech Rep.	
121 C2	Blantyre Malawi	
98 C1	Blaydon U.K.	
53 C2	Blayney Austr.	
54 B2	Blenheim N.Z.	
115 C1	Blida Alg.	
130 B2	Blind River Can.	
123 C2	Bloemfontein S. Africa	
123 C2	Bloemhof S. Africa	

123 C2	Bloemhof Dam S. Africa	
92 ☐A2	Blönduós Iceland	
97 B1	Bloody Foreland pt Ireland	
138 B1	Bloomfield U.S.A.	
140 B2	Bloomington IL U.S.A.	
140 B3	Bloomington IN U.S.A.	
140 C3	Bluefield U.S.A.	
146 B3	Bluefields Nic.	
53 C2	Blue Mountains Austr.	
134 C1	Blue Mountains U.S.A.	
116 B3	Blue Nile r. Eth./Sudan	
126 D2	Bluenose Lake Can.	
140 C3	Blue Ridge mts U.S.A.	
97 B1	Blue Stack Mountains hills	
	Ireland	
54 A3	Bluff N.Z.	
135 E3	Bluff U.S.A.	
152 D3	Blumenau Brazil	
52 A2	Blyth Austr.	
98 C1	Blyth U.K.	
135 D4	Blythe U.S.A.	
142 C1	Blytheville U.S.A.	
114 A4	Bo Sierra Leone	
64 B1	Boac Phil.	
151 D2	Boa Esperança, Açude resr	
	Brazil	
150 B1	Boa Vista Brazil	
53 C2	Bobadah Austr.	
71 B3	Bobai China	
121 ☐D2	Bobaomby, Tanjona c. Madag.	
114 B3	Bobo-Dioulasso Burkina Faso	
89 F3	Bobrov Rus. Fed.	
91 C1	Bobrovytsya Ukr.	
91 C2	Bobrynets' Ukr.	
121 ☐D3	Boby mt. Madag.	
150 B2	Boca do Acre Brazil	
155 D1	Bocaiúva Brazil	
118 B2	Bocaranga C.A.R.	
103 E2	Bochnia Pol.	
100 C2	Bocholt Ger.	
100 C2	Bochum Ger.	
101 E1	Bockenem Ger.	
118 B2	Boda C.A.R.	
83 I3	Bodaybo Rus. Fed.	
115 D3	Bodélé reg. Chad	
92 H2	Boden Sweden	
99 A3	Bodmin U.K.	
99 A3	Bodmin Moor moorland U.K.	
92 F2	Bodø Norway	
111 C3	Bodrum Turkey	
118 C3	Boende Dem. Rep. Congo	
142 C2	Bogalusa U.S.A.	
114 B3	Bogandé Burkina Faso	
68 B2	Bogda Shan mts China	
53 D1	Boggabilla Austr.	
97 B2	Boggeragh Mountains hills	
	Ireland	
100 B3	Bogny-sur-Meuse France	
97 C2	Bog of Allen reg. Ireland	
53 C3	Bogong, Mount Austr.	
60 B2	Bogor Indon.	
89 E3	Bogoroditsk Rus. Fed.	
150 A1	Bogotá Col.	
82 G3	Bogotol Rus. Fed.	
83 H3	Boguchany Rus. Fed.	
91 E2	Boguchar Rus. Fed.	
70 B2	Bo Hai g. China	
100 A3	Bohain-en-Vermandois	
	France	
70 B2	Bohai Wan b. China	
123 C2	Bohlokong S. Africa	
102 C2	Böhmer Wald mts Ger.	
91 D1	Bohodukhiv Ukr.	
64 B2	Bohol i. Phil.	
64 B2	Bohol Sea Phil.	
68 B2	Bohu China	
155 C2	Boi, Ponta do pt Brazil	

154 B1 **Bois** r. Brazil
126 C2 **Bois, Lac des** l. Can.
134 C2 **Boise** U.S.A.
139 C1 **Boise City** U.S.A.
123 C2 **Boitumelong** S. Africa
101 E1 **Boizenburg** Ger.
76 B3 **Bojnūrd** Iran
118 B3 **Bokatola** Dem. Rep. Congo
114 A3 **Boké** Guinea
118 C3 **Bokele** Dem. Rep. Congo
93 C4 **Boknafjorden** sea chan. Norway
115 D3 **Bokoro** Chad
63 A2 **Bokpyin** Myanmar
89 D2 **Boksitogorsk** Rus. Fed.
122 B2 **Bokspits** Botswana
114 A3 **Bolama** Guinea-Bissau
63 B2 **Bolavén, Phouphiang** plat. Laos
104 C2 **Bolbec** France
77 E2 **Bole** China
118 B3 **Boleko** Dem. Rep. Congo
114 B3 **Bolgatanga** Ghana
90 B2 **Bolhrad** Ukr.
66 B1 **Buli** China
67 B2 **Bolikhamxai** Laos
110 C2 **Bolintin-Vale** Romania
137 E3 **Bolivar** U.S.A.
150 A1 **Bolívar, Pico** mt. Venez.
152 B2 **Bolivia** country S. America
89 E3 **Bolkhov** Rus. Fed.
105 C3 **Bollène** France
93 G3 **Bollnäs** Sweden
53 C1 **Bollon** Austr.
101 E2 **Bollstedt** Ger.
93 F4 **Bolmen** l. Sweden
118 B3 **Bolobo** Dem. Rep. Congo
108 B1 **Bologna** Italy
89 D2 **Bologoye** Rus. Fed.
89 D2 **Bologoye** Rus. Fed.
118 B2 **Bolomba** Dem. Rep. Congo
83 H1 **Bol'shevik, Ostrov** i. Rus. Fed.
86 E2 **Bol'shezemel'skaya Tundra** lowland Rus. Fed.
66 B2 **Bol'shoy Kamen'** Rus. Fed.
Bol'shoy Kavkaz mts Asia/Europe see **Caucasus**
83 K2 **Bol'shoy Lyakhovskiy, Ostrov** i. Rus. Fed.
100 B1 **Bolsward** Neth.
98 B2 **Bolton** U.K.
80 B1 **Bolu** Turkey
92 □A2 **Bolungarvík** Iceland
108 B1 **Bolzano** Italy
118 B3 **Boma** Dem. Rep. Congo
53 D2 **Bomaderry** Austr.
53 C3 **Bombala** Austr.
Bombay India see **Mumbai**
155 D3 **Bom Despacho** Brazil
75 D2 **Bomdila** India
151 D3 **Bom Jesus da Lapa** Brazil
155 D2 **Bom Jesus do Itabapoana** Brazil
115 D1 **Bū, Cap** c. Tunisia
147 D3 **Bonaire** mun. West Indies
50 B1 **Bonaparte Archipelago** is Austr.
131 E2 **Bonavista** Can.
131 E2 **Bonavista Bay** Can.
118 C2 **Bondo** Dem. Rep. Congo
114 B4 **Bondoukou** Côte d'Ivoire
58 C3 **Bonerate, Kepulauan** is Indon.
155 C1 **Bonfinópolis de Minas** Brazil
117 B4 **Bonga** Eth.
75 D2 **Bongaigaon** India
118 C2 **Bonganga** Dem. Rep. Congo
118 C2 **Bongo, Massif des** mts C.A.R.
115 D3 **Bongor** Chad

114 B4 **Bongouanou** Côte d'Ivoire
63 B2 **Rông Sơn** Vietnam
139 D2 **Bonham** U.S.A.
105 D3 **Bonifacio** Corse France
108 A2 **Bonifacio, Strait of** France/Italy
100 C2 **Bonn** Ger.
134 C1 **Bonners Ferry** U.S.A.
50 A3 **Bonnie Rock** Austr.
129 C2 **Bonnyville** Can.
108 A2 **Bonorva** Sardegna Italy
61 C1 **Bontang** Indon.
64 B1 **Bontoc** Phil.
58 B3 **Bontosunggu** Indon.
123 C3 **Bontrug** S. Africa
52 B2 **Booligal** Austr.
53 C1 **Boomi** Austr.
53 D1 **Boonah** Austr.
137 E2 **Boone** U.S.A.
142 C2 **Booneville** U.S.A.
137 E3 **Boonville** U.S.A.
53 C2 **Boorowa** Austr.
128 F2 **Boothia, Gulf of** Can.
126 E2 **Boothia Peninsula** Can.
100 C2 **Boppard** Ger.
144 B2 **Boquilla, Presa de la** resr Mex.
109 D2 **Bor** Serbia
117 B4 **Bor** S. Sudan
80 B2 **Bor** Turkey
121 □E2 **Boraha, Nosy** i. Madag.
76 B2 **Borankul** Kazakh.
93 F4 **Borås** Sweden
79 C2 **Borāzjān** Iran
150 C2 **Borba** Brazil
104 B3 **Bordeaux** France
127 F2 **Borden Peninsula** Can.
52 B3 **Bordertown** Austr.
107 D2 **Bordj Bou Arréridj** Alg.
107 D2 **Bordj Bounaama** Alg.
115 C2 **Bordj Messaouda** Alg.
115 C2 **Bordj Omer Driss** Alg.
94 B1 **Bordoy** i. Faroe Is
92 □A3 **Borgarnes** Iceland
108 A1 **Borgosesia** Italy
87 D3 **Borisoglebsk** Rus. Fed.
89 E2 **Borisoglebskiy** Rus. Fed.
91 D1 **Borisovka** Rus. Fed.
100 C2 **Borken** Ger.
92 G2 **Borkenes** Norway
100 C1 **Borkum** Ger.
100 C1 **Borkum** i. Ger.
93 G3 **Borlänge** Sweden
101 F2 **Borna** Ger.
61 C1 **Borneo** i. Asia
93 F4 **Bornholm** i. Denmark
111 C3 **Bornova** Turkey
90 B1 **Borodyanka** Ukr.
89 D2 **Borovichi** Rus. Fed.
89 E2 **Borovsk** Rus. Fed.
51 C1 **Borroloola** Austr.
110 B1 **Borşa** Romania
90 B2 **Borshchiv** Ukr.
69 D1 **Borshchovochnyy Khrebet** mts Rus. Fed.
101 E1 **Börßum** Ger.
Bortala China see **Bole**
81 C2 **Borūjerd** Iran
90 A2 **Boryslav** Ukr.
90 C1 **Boryspil'** Ukr.
91 C1 **Borzna** Ukr.
69 D1 **Borzya** Rus. Fed.
109 C2 **Bosanska Dubica** Bos.-Herz.
109 C1 **Bosanska Gradiška** Bos.-Herz.
109 C2 **Bosanska Krupa** Bos.-Herz.
109 C1 **Bosanski Novi** Bos.-Herz.
109 C2 **Bosanski Grahovo** Bos. Herz.
123 C2 **Boshof** S. Africa

109 C2 **Bosnia-Herzegovina** country Europe
118 B2 **Bosobolo** Dem. Rep. Congo
110 C2 **Bosporus** str. Turkey
118 B2 **Bossangoa** C.A.R.
118 B2 **Bossembélé** C.A.R.
68 B2 **Bosten Hu** l. China
98 C2 **Boston** U.K.
141 E2 **Boston** U.S.A.
142 B1 **Bosten Mountains** U.S.A.
53 D2 **Botany Bay** Austr.
110 B2 **Botev** mt. Bulg.
93 G3 **Dothnia, Gulf of** Fin./Sweden
110 C1 **Botoşani** Romania
123 C2 **Botshabelo** S. Africa
123 B3 **Botswana** country Africa
109 C3 **Botte Donato, Monte** mt. Italy
136 C1 **Bottineau** U.S.A.
100 C2 **Bottrop** Ger.
154 C2 **Botucatu** Brazil
114 D4 **Duuaké** Côte d'Ivoire
118 B2 **Bouar** C.A.R.
114 B1 **Bou Arfa** Morocco
131 D2 **Bouctouche** Can.
107 E2 **Bougaa** Alg.
114 B3 **Bougouni** Mali
100 B3 **Bouillon** Belgium
107 D2 **Bouira** Alg.
114 A2 **Boujdour** Western Sahara
136 B2 **Boulder** U.S.A.
135 D3 **Boulder City** U.S.A.
51 C2 **Boulia** Austr.
104 C2 **Boulogne-Billancourt** France
99 D3 **Boulogne-sur-Mer** France
118 B3 **Boumango** Gabon
118 B2 **Boumba** r. Cameroon
107 D2 **Boumerdes** Alg.
114 B4 **Bouna** Côte d'Ivoire
114 B4 **Boundiali** Côte d'Ivoire
134 D2 **Bountiful** U.S.A.
114 B3 **Bourem** Mali
104 C2 **Bourganeuf** France
105 D2 **Bourg-en-Bresse** France
104 C2 **Bourges** France
53 C2 **Bourke** Austr.
99 C3 **Bournemouth** U.K.
115 C1 **Bou Saâda** Alg.
115 D3 **Bousso** Chad
114 A3 **Boutilimit** Maur.
129 C3 **Bow** r. Can.
51 D2 **Bowen** Austr.
123 C3 **Bowe Island** Can.
140 B3 **Bowling Green** KY U.S.A.
140 C2 **Bowling Green** OH U.S.A.
136 C1 **Bowman** U.S.A.
101 D3 **Boxberg** Ger.
100 B2 **Boxtel** Neth.
80 B1 **Boyabat** Turkey
97 B2 **Boyle** Ireland
97 C2 **Boyne** r. Ireland
136 B2 **Boysen Reservoir** U.S.A.
152 B3 **Boyuibe** Bol.
111 C3 **Bozburun** Turkey
111 C3 **Dozcaada** i. Turkey
111 C3 **Bozdağ** mt. Turkey
111 C3 **Boz Dağları** mts Turkey
111 C3 **Bozdoğan** Turkey
134 D1 **Bozeman** U.S.A.
118 B2 **Bozoum** C.A.R.
111 D3 **Büyüyük** Turkey
109 C2 **Brač** i. Croatia
130 C2 **Bracebridge** Can.
99 C3 **Bracknell** U.K.
143 D3 **Bradenton** U.S.A.
98 C2 **Bradford** U.K.
141 D2 **Bradford** U.S.A.

139 D2 Brady U.S.A.
96 C2 Braemar U.K.
106 B1 Braga Port.
151 D2 Bragança Brazil
106 B1 Bragança Port.
155 C2 Bragança Paulista Brazil
89 D3 Brahin Belarus
73 C3 Brahmapur India
62 A1 Brahmaputra r. China/India
110 C1 Brăila Romania
137 E1 Brainerd U.S.A.
99 D3 Braintree U.K.
100 B2 Braives Belgium
101 C1 Brake (Unterweser) Ger.
100 D1 Bramsche Ger.
150 B2 Branco r. Brazil
101 F1 Brandenburg Ger.
129 E3 Brandon Can.
97 A2 Brandon Mountain h. Ireland
122 B3 Brandvlei S. Africa
103 D1 Braniewo Pol.
130 B2 Brantford Can.
131 D2 Bras d'Or Lake Can.
155 C3 Brasil, Planalto do plat. Brazil
154 C1 Brasilândia Brazil
155 D1 Brasília Brazil
155 D1 Brasília de Minas Brazil
88 C2 Braslaw Belarus
110 C1 Braşov Romania
103 D2 Bratislava Slovakia
83 H3 Bratsk Rus. Fed.
102 C2 Braunau am Inn Austria
101 E1 Braunschweig Ger.
92 □A2 Brautarholt Iceland
Bravo del Norte, Río r. Mex./U.S.A. see Rio Grande
135 C4 Brawley U.S.A.
97 C2 Bray Ireland
150 C2 Brazil country S. America
139 D3 Brazos r. U.S.A.
118 B3 Brazzaville Congo
96 C2 Brčko Bos.-Herz.
96 C2 Brechin U.K.
100 B2 Brecht Belgium
139 D2 Breckenridge U.S.A.
103 D2 Břeclav Czech Rep.
99 B3 Brecon U.K.
99 B3 Brecon Beacons reg. U.K.
100 B2 Breda Neth.
122 B3 Bredasdorp S. Africa
102 B2 Bregenz Austria
92 H1 Breivikbotn Norway
92 E3 Brekstad Norway
101 D1 Bremen Ger.
101 D1 Bremerhaven Ger.
134 B1 Bremerton U.S.A.
101 D1 Bremervörde Ger.
139 D2 Brenham U.S.A.
108 B1 Brennero Italy
102 C2 Brenner Pass Austria/Italy
99 D3 Brentwood U.K.
108 B1 Brescia Italy
108 B1 Bressanone Italy
96 □ Bressay i. U.K.
104 B2 Bressuire France
88 B3 Brest Belarus
104 B2 Brest France
142 C3 Breton Sound b. U.S.A.
151 C2 Breves Brazil
53 C1 Brewarrina Austr.
134 C1 Brewster U.S.A.
89 E2 Breytovo Rus. Fed.
109 C1 Brezovo Polje plain Croatia
118 C2 Bria C.A.R.
105 D3 Briançon France
90 B2 Briceni Moldova
99 B3 Bridgend U.K.

141 E2 Bridgeport CT U.S.A.
136 C2 Bridgeport NE U.S.A.
147 E3 Bridgetown Barbados
131 D2 Bridgewater Can.
99 B3 Bridgwater U.K.
98 C1 Bridlington U.K.
98 C1 Bridlington Bay U.K.
105 D2 Brig Switz.
134 D2 Brigham City U.S.A.
54 B3 Brighton N.Z.
99 C3 Brighton U.K.
105 D3 Brignoles France
101 D2 Brilon Ger.
109 C2 Brindisi Italy
91 D2 Brin'kovskaya Rus. Fed.
53 D1 Brisbane Austr.
99 B3 Bristol U.K.
143 D1 Bristol U.S.A.
99 A3 Bristol Channel est. U.K.
128 B2 British Columbia prov. Can.
56 G7 British Indian Ocean Territory terr. Indian Ocean
95 B2 British Isles is Europe
123 C2 Brits S. Africa
122 B3 Britstown S. Africa
104 C2 Brive-la-Gaillarde France
106 C1 Briviesca Spain
103 D2 Brno Czech Rep.
143 D2 Broad r. U.S.A.
130 C1 Broadback r. Can.
96 C3 Broad Law h. U.K.
136 B1 Broadus U.S.A.
129 D2 Brochet Can.
129 D2 Brochet, Lac l. Can.
131 D2 Brochet, Lac au l. Can.
101 E1 Bröckel Ger.
126 D1 Brock Island Can.
130 C2 Brockville Can.
127 F2 Brodeur Peninsula Can.
96 B3 Brodick U.K.
103 D1 Brodnica Pol.
90 B1 Brody Ukr.
139 D1 Broken Arrow U.S.A.
137 D2 Broken Bow U.S.A.
52 B2 Broken Hill Austr.
99 B2 Bromsgrove U.K.
93 E4 Brønderslev Denmark
92 F2 Brønnøysund Norway
64 A2 Brooke's Point Phil.
142 B2 Brookhaven U.S.A.
134 B2 Brookings OR U.S.A.
137 D2 Brookings SD U.S.A.
129 C2 Brooks Can.
126 B2 Brooks Range mts U.S.A.
143 D3 Brooksville U.S.A.
96 B2 Broom, Loch inlet U.K.
50 B1 Broome Austr.
134 B2 Brothers U.S.A.
Broughton Island Can. see Qikiqtarjuaq
90 C1 Brovary Ukr.
139 C2 Brownfield U.S.A.
128 C3 Browning U.S.A.
142 C1 Brownsville TN U.S.A.
139 D3 Brownsville TX U.S.A.
139 D2 Brownwood U.S.A.
92 □A2 Brú Iceland
104 C1 Bruay-la-Bussière France
140 B1 Bruce Crossing U.S.A.
103 D2 Bruck an der Mur Austria
Bruges Belgium see Brugge
100 A2 Brugge Belgium
128 C2 Brûlé Can.
151 D3 Brumado Brazil
93 F3 Brumunddal Norway
61 C1 Brunei country Asia
102 C2 Brunico Italy

101 D1 Brunsbüttel Ger.
143 D2 Brunswick GA U.S.A.
141 F2 Brunswick ME U.S.A.
53 D1 Brunswick Heads Austr.
136 C2 Brush U.S.A.
100 B2 Brussels Belgium
Bruxelles Belgium see Brussels
139 D2 Bryan U.S.A.
89 D3 Bryansk Rus. Fed.
91 D2 Bryukhovetskaya Rus. Fed.
103 D1 Brzeg Pol.
114 A3 Buba Guinea-Bissau
80 B2 Bucak Turkey
150 A1 Bucaramanga Col.
53 C3 Buchan Austr.
114 A4 Buchanan Liberia
110 C2 Bucharest Romania
101 D1 Bucholz in der Nordheide Ger.
110 C1 Bucin, Pasul pass Romania
101 D1 Bückeburg Ger.
138 A2 Buckeye U.S.A.
96 C2 Buckhaven U.K.
96 C2 Buckie U.K.
51 C1 Buckingham Bay Austr.
51 D2 Buckland Tableland reg. Austr.
52 A2 Buckleboo Austr.
141 F2 Bucksport U.S.A.
Bucureşti Romania see Bucharest
89 D3 Buda-Kashalyova Belarus
103 D2 Budapest Hungary
75 B2 Budaun India
108 A2 Buddusò Sardegna Italy
99 A3 Bude U.K.
87 D4 Budennovsk Rus. Fed.
89 D2 Budogoshch' Rus. Fed.
108 A2 Budoni Sardegna Italy
118 A2 Buea Cameroon
144 B3 Buenaventura Mex.
106 C1 Buendía, Embalse de resr Spain
155 C1 Buenópolis Brazil
153 C4 Buenos Aires Arg.
153 A5 Buenos Aires, Lago l. Arg./Chile
141 D2 Buffalo NY U.S.A.
136 C1 Buffalo SD U.S.A.
136 B2 Buffalo WY U.S.A.
129 D2 Buffalo Narrows Can.
122 A2 Buffels watercourse S. Africa
110 C2 Buftea Romania
103 E1 Bug r. Pol.
61 C2 Bugel, Tanjung pt Indon.
109 C2 Bugojno Bos.-Herz.
64 A2 Bugsuk i. Phil.
87 E3 Buguruslan Rus. Fed.
110 C1 Buhuşi Romania
99 B2 Builth Wells U.K.
69 D1 Buir Nur l. Mongolia
120 A3 Buitepos Namibia
109 D2 Bujanovac Serbia
119 C3 Bujumbura Burundi
69 D1 Bukachacha Rus. Fed.
119 C3 Bukavu Dem. Rep. Congo
60 B2 Bukittinggi Indon.
119 D3 Bukoba Tanz.
53 D2 Bulahdelah Austr.
121 B3 Bulawayo Zimbabwe
111 C3 Buldan Turkey
123 D2 Bulembu Swaziland
69 C1 Bulgan Mongolia
110 C2 Bulgaria country Europe
54 B2 Buller r. N.Z.
52 B1 Bulloo Downs Austr.
122 A1 Büllsport Namibia
58 C3 Bulukumba Indon.
118 B3 Bulungu Dem. Rep. Congo
118 C2 Bumba Dem. Rep. Congo

62 A1 **Bumhkang** Myanmar
118 B3 **Buna** Dem. Rep. Congo
50 A3 **Bunbury** Austr.
97 C1 **Buncrana** Ireland
113 D3 **Bunda Tanz.**
51 E2 **Bundaberg** Austr.
53 D2 **Bundarra** Austr.
74 B2 **Bundi** India
97 B1 **Bundoran** Ireland
53 C3 **Bungendore** Austr.
67 B4 **Bungo-suidō** sea chan. Japan
119 D2 **Bunia** Dem. Rep. Congo
118 C3 **Bunianga** Dem. Rep. Congo
63 B2 **Buôn Ma Thuôt** Vietnam
119 D3 **Bura** Kenya
78 B2 **Buraydah** Saudi Arabia
100 D2 **Burco** Somalia
117 C4 **Burco** Somalia
100 B1 **Burdaard** Neth.
80 B2 **Burdur** Turkey
117 B3 **Burē** Eth.
99 D2 **Bure** r. U.K.
74 B1 **Burewala** Pak.
110 C2 **Burgas** Bulg.
101 E1 **Burg bei Magdeburg** Ger.
101 E1 **Burgdorf** Niedersachsen Ger.
101 E1 **Burgdorf** Niedersachsen Ger.
131 E2 **Burgeo** Can.
123 D1 **Burgersfort** S. Africa
100 A2 **Burgh-Haamstede** Neth.
145 C2 **Burgos** Mex.
106 C1 **Burgos** Spain
111 C3 **Burhaniye** Turkey
74 B2 **Burhanpur** India
101 D1 **Burhave (Butjadingen)** Ger.
131 E2 **Burin** Can.
151 D2 **Buriti Bravo** Brazil
155 C1 **Buritis** Brazil
51 C1 **Burketown** Austr.
114 B3 **Burkina Faso** country Africa
134 D2 **Burley** U.S.A.
136 C3 **Burlington** CO U.S.A.
137 E2 **Burlington** IA U.S.A.
143 E1 **Burlington** NC U.S.A.
141 E2 **Burlington** VT U.S.A.
Burma country Asia see Myanmar
134 B2 **Burney** U.S.A.
51 D4 **Burnie** Austr.
98 B2 **Burnley** U.K.
134 C3 **Burns** U.S.A.
128 B2 **Burns Lake** Can.
77 C2 **Burqin** China
52 A2 **Burra** Austr.
109 D2 **Burrel** Albania
97 B2 **Burren** reg. Ireland
53 C2 **Burrendong, Lake** resr Austr.
53 C2 **Burrinjuck Reservoir** Austr.
107 C2 **Burriana** Spain
53 C2 **Burrinjuck Reservoir** Austr.
144 B3 **Burro, Serranías del** mts Mex.
111 C2 **Bursa** Turkey
116 B2 **Bûr Safâjah** Egypt
Bûr Sa'îd Egypt see **Port Said**
130 C1 **Burton, Lac** l. Can.
99 C2 **Burton upon Trent** U.K.
59 C3 **Buru** i. Indon.
119 C3 **Burundi** country Africa
119 C3 **Bururi** Burundi
91 C1 **Buryn'** Ukr.
99 D2 **Bury St Edmunds** U.K.
118 C3 **Busanga** Dem. Rep. Congo
79 C2 **Büshehr** Iran
119 D3 **Bushenyi** Uganda
118 C2 **Businga** Dem. Rep. Congo
50 A3 **Busselton** Austr.
139 C3 **Bustamante** Mex.

118 C2 **Buta** Dem. Rep. Congo
119 C3 **Butare** Rwanda
123 C2 **Butha-Buthe** Lesotho
140 D2 **Butler** U.S.A.
59 C3 **Butoa** i. Indon.
134 D1 **Butte** U.S.A.
60 B1 **Butterworth** Malaysia
96 A1 **Butt of Lewis** hd U.K.
129 E2 **Button Bay** Can.
64 B2 **Butuan** Phil.
91 E1 **Buturlinovka** Rus. Fed.
75 C2 **Butwal** Nepal
101 D2 **Butzbach** Ger.
117 C4 **Buulobarde** Somalia
117 C5 **Buur Gaabo** Somalia
117 C4 **Buurhabaka** Somalia
76 C3 **Buxoro** Uzbek.
101 D1 **Buxtehude** Ger.
89 F2 **Buy** Rus. Fed.
87 D4 **Buynaksk** Rus. Fed.
111 C3 **Büyükmenderes** r. Turkey
110 C1 **Buzău** Romania
121 C2 **Búzi** Moz.
87 F3 **Buzuluk** Rus. Fed.
110 C2 **Byala** Bulg.
88 C3 **Byalynichy** Belarus
88 D3 **Byarezina** r. Belarus
88 C2 **Byaroza** Belarus
103 D1 **Bydgoszcz** Pol.
88 C3 **Byerazino** Belarus
88 C2 **Byeshankovichy** Belarus
89 D3 **Bykhaw** Belarus
127 F2 **Bylot Island** Can.
53 C2 **Byrock** Austr.
53 D1 **Byron Bay** Austr.
83 J2 **Bytantay** r. Rus. Fed.
103 D1 **Bytom** Pol.
103 D1 **Bytów** Pol.

C

154 B2 **Caarapó** Brazil
64 B1 **Cabanatuan** Phil.
117 C3 **Cabdul Qaadir** Somalia
106 B2 **Cabeza del Buey** Spain
152 B2 **Cabezas** Bol.
150 A1 **Cabimas** Venez.
120 A1 **Cabinda** Angola
118 B3 **Cabinda** prov. Angola
155 D2 **Cabo Frio** Brazil
155 D2 **Cabo Frio, Ilha do** i. Brazil
130 C2 **Cabonga, Réservoir** resr Can.
51 E2 **Caboolture** Austr.
150 A2 **Cabo Pantoja** Peru
144 A1 **Caborca** Mex.
144 B2 **Cabo San Lucas** Mex.
131 D2 **Cabot Strait** Can.
155 D1 **Cabral, Serra do** mts Brazil
107 D2 **Cabrera, Illa de** i. Spain
106 B1 **Cabrera, Sierra de la** mts Spain
129 D2 **Cabri** Can.
107 C2 **Cabriel** r. Spain
152 C3 **Caçador** Brazil
109 D2 **Čačak** Serbia
108 A2 **Caccia, Capo** c. Sardegna Italy
151 C3 **Cáceres** Brazil
106 B2 **Cáceres** Spain
128 B2 **Cache Creek** Can.
114 A3 **Cacheu** Guinea-Bissau
151 C2 **Cachimbo, Serra do** hills Brazil
154 B1 **Cachoeira Alta** Brazil
155 D2 **Cachoeiro de Itapemirim** Brazil
114 A3 **Cacine** Guinea-Bissau
120 A2 **Cacolo** Angola

154 B1 **Caçu** Brazil
103 D2 **Čadca** Slovakia
101 D1 **Cadenberge** Ger.
145 B2 **Cadereyta** Mex.
140 B2 **Cadillac** U.S.A.
106 B2 **Cádiz** Spain
106 B2 **Cádiz, Golfo de** g. Spain
128 C2 **Cadotte Lake** Can.
104 B2 **Caen** France
98 A2 **Caernarfon** U.K.
98 A2 **Caernarfon Bay** U.K.
152 B3 **Cafayate** Arg.
64 B2 **Cagayan de Oro** Phil.
64 A2 **Cagayan de Tawi-Tawi** i. Phil.
108 B2 **Cagli** Italy
108 A3 **Cagliari** Sardegna Italy
108 A3 **Cagliari, Golfo di** b. Sardegna Italy
76 B2 **Çagyl** Turkm.
97 B3 **Caha Mountains** hills Ireland
97 A3 **Cahermore** Ireland
97 C2 **Cahir** Ireland
97 A3 **Cahirsiveen** Ireland
97 C2 **Cahore Point** Ireland
104 C3 **Cahors** France
90 B2 **Cahul** Moldova
121 C2 **Caia** Moz.
151 C3 **Caiabis, Serra dos** hills Brazil
120 B2 **Caianda** Angola
154 B1 **Caiapó, Serra do** mts Brazil
154 B1 **Caiapônia** Brazil
147 C2 **Caicos Islands** Turks and Caicos Is
96 C2 **Cairngorm Mountains** U.K.
98 A1 **Cairnryan** U.K.
51 D1 **Cairns** Austr.
116 B1 **Cairo** Egypt
98 C2 **Caistor** U.K.
120 A2 **Caiundo** Angola
150 A2 **Cajamarca** Peru
109 C1 **Čakovec** Croatia
123 C3 **Cala** S. Africa
150 B1 **Calabozo** Venez.
110 B2 **Calafat** Romania
153 A6 **Calafate** Arg.
107 C1 **Calahorra** Spain
104 C1 **Calais** France
141 F1 **Calais** U.S.A.
152 B3 **Calama** Chile
64 A1 **Calamian Group** is Phil.
107 C2 **Calamocha** Spain
120 A1 **Calandula** Angola
60 A1 **Calang** Indon.
64 B1 **Calapan** Phil.
110 C2 **Călăraşi** Romania
107 C1 **Calatayud** Spain
64 B1 **Calayan** i. Phil.
64 B1 **Calbayog** Phil.
151 F2 **Calcanhar, Ponta do** pt Brazil
151 C1 **Calçoene** Brazil
Calcutta India see **Kolkata**
106 B2 **Caldas da Rainha** Port.
154 C1 **Caldas Novas** Brazil
152 A3 **Caldera** Chile
134 C2 **Caldwell** U.S.A.
123 C3 **Caledon** r. Lesotho/S. Africa
122 A3 **Caledon** S. Africa
153 B5 **Caleta Olivia** Arg.
98 A1 **Calf of Man** i. Isle of Man
128 C2 **Calgary** Can.
150 A1 **Cali** Col.
Calicut India see **Kozhikode**
135 C3 **Caliente** U.S.A.
135 B2 **California** state U.S.A.
144 A1 **California, Gulf of** Mex.
135 B3 **California Aqueduct** canal U.S.A.

122 B3 Calitzdorp S. Africa
145 C2 Calkini Mex.
52 B1 Callabonna, Lake imp. l. Austr.
96 B2 Callander U.K.
150 A3 Callao Peru
108 B3 Caltagirone Sicilia Italy
108 B3 Caltanissetta Sicilia Italy
120 A2 Caluquembe Angola
117 D3 Caluula Somalia
105 D3 Calvi Corse France
107 D2 Calviá Spain
144 B2 Calvillo Mex.
122 A3 Calvinia S. Africa
109 C2 Calvo, Monte mt. Italy
144 B2 Camacho Mex.
120 A2 Camacupa Angola
146 C2 Camagüey Cuba
150 A3 Camana Peru
154 B1 Camapuã Brazil
145 C2 Camargo Mex.
63 B3 Ca Mau Vietnam
63 B3 Ca Mau, Mui c. Vietnam
63 B2 Cambodia country Asia
99 A3 Camborne U.K.
105 C1 Cambrai France
99 B2 Cambrian Mountains hills U.K.
54 C1 Cambridge N.Z.
99 D2 Cambridge U.K.
141 E2 Cambridge MA U.S.A.
141 D3 Cambridge MD U.S.A.
137 E1 Cambridge MN U.S.A.
140 C2 Cambridge OH U.S.A.
131 D1 Cambrien, Lac l. Can.
53 D2 Camden Austr.
142 B2 Camden AR U.S.A.
141 F2 Camden ME U.S.A.
118 B2 Cameroon country Africa
118 B2 Cameroon Highlands slope Cameroon/Nigeria
151 D2 Cametá Brazil
64 B1 Camiguin i. Phil.
152 B3 Camiri Bol.
151 D2 Camocim Brazil
51 C1 Camooweal Austr.
63 A3 Camorta i. India
153 A5 Campana, Isla i. Chile
122 B2 Campbell S. Africa
54 B2 Campbell, Cape N.Z.
48 F6 Campbell Island N.Z.
128 B2 Campbell River Can.
140 B3 Campbellsville U.S.A.
131 D2 Campbellton Can.
96 B3 Campbeltown U.K.
145 C3 Campeche Mex.
145 C3 Campeche, Bahía de g. Mex.
52 B3 Camperdown Austr.
110 C1 Câmpina Romania
151 E2 Campina Grande Brazil
154 C2 Campinas Brazil
154 C1 Campina Verde Brazil
108 B2 Campobasso Italy
155 C2 Campo Belo Brazil
154 C1 Campo Florido Brazil
152 B3 Campo Gallo Arg.
154 B2 Campo Grande Brazil
151 D2 Campo Maior Brazil
106 B2 Campo Maior Port.
154 B2 Campo Mourão Brazil
155 D2 Campos Brazil
155 C1 Campos Altos Brazil
155 C2 Campos do Jordão Brazil
110 C1 Câmpulung Romania
138 A2 Camp Verde U.S.A.
128 C2 Camrose Can.
129 D2 Camsell Portage Can.
111 C2 Çan Turkey
126 F2 Canada country N. America

139 C1 Canadian U.S.A.
139 D1 Canadian r. U.S.A.
111 C2 Çanakkale Turkey
144 A1 Cananea Mex.
154 C2 Cananéia Brazil
Canarias, Islas terr. N. Atlantic Ocean see Canary Islands
114 A2 Canary Islands terr. N. Atlantic Ocean
155 C1 Canastra, Serra da mts Brazil
144 B2 Canatlán Mex.
143 D3 Canaveral, Cape U.S.A.
155 E1 Canavieiras Brazil
53 C3 Canberra Austr.
145 D2 Cancún Mex.
111 C3 Çandarlı Turkey
145 C3 Candelaria Mex.
129 D2 Candle Lake Can.
120 A2 Cangamba Angola
106 B1 Cangas del Narcea Spain
152 C4 Canguçu Brazil
70 B2 Cangzhou China
131 D1 Caniapiscau Can.
131 D1 Caniapiscau r. Can.
131 C1 Caniapiscau, Réservoir de resr Can.
108 B3 Canicattì Sicilia Italy
151 E2 Canindé Brazil
144 B2 Cañitas de Felipe Pescador Mex.
80 B1 Çankırı Turkey
128 C2 Canmore Can.
96 A2 Canna i. U.K.
105 D3 Cannes France
99 B2 Cannock U.K.
53 C3 Cann River Austr.
152 C3 Canoas Brazil
129 D2 Canoe Lake Can.
154 B3 Canoinhas Brazil
136 B3 Canon City U.S.A.
129 D2 Canora Can.
53 C2 Canowindra Austr.
106 B1 Cantábrica, Cordillera mts Spain
106 B1 Cantábrico, Mar sea Spain
99 D3 Canterbury U.K.
54 B2 Canterbury Bight b. N.Z.
54 B2 Canterbury Plains N.Z.
63 B2 Cần Thơ Vietnam
151 D2 Canto do Buriti Brazil
Canton China see Guangzhou
142 C2 Canton MS U.S.A.
140 C2 Canton OH U.S.A.
139 C1 Canyon U.S.A.
134 D1 Canyon Ferry Lake U.S.A.
62 B1 Cao Bằng Vietnam
154 C2 Capão Bonito Brazil
155 D2 Caparaó, Serra do mts Brazil
51 D4 Cape Barren Island Austr.
52 A3 Cape Borda Austr.
131 D2 Cape Breton Island Can.
114 B4 Cape Coast Ghana
141 E2 Cape Cod Bay U.S.A.
127 F2 Cape Dorset Can.
143 E2 Cape Fear r. U.S.A.
137 F3 Cape Girardeau U.S.A.
155 D1 Capelinha Brazil
100 B2 Capelle aan den IJssel Neth.
120 A1 Capenda-Camulemba Angola
122 A3 Cape Town S. Africa
112 C5 Cape Verde country N. Atlantic Ocean
51 D1 Cape York Peninsula Austr.
147 C3 Cap-Haïtien Haiti
151 D2 Capim r. Brazil
58 D1 Capitol Hill N. Mariana Is.
109 C2 Čapljina Bos.-Herz.

109 B3 Capo d'Orlando Sicilia Italy
108 A2 Capraia, Isola di i. Italy
108 A2 Caprara, Punta pt Sardegna Italy
108 B2 Capri, Isola di i. Italy
120 B2 Caprivi Strip reg. Namibia
150 B2 Caquetá r. Col.
110 B2 Caracal Romania
150 B1 Caracas Venez.
151 D2 Caracol Brazil
155 C2 Caraguatatuba Brazil
153 A4 Carahue Chile
151 D1 Caraí Brazil
155 D2 Carangola Brazil
110 B1 Caransebeş Romania
131 D2 Caraquet Can.
146 B3 Caratasca, Laguna de lag. Hond.
155 D1 Caratinga Brazil
150 B2 Carauari Brazil
107 C2 Caravaca de la Cruz Spain
155 E1 Caravelas Brazil
129 E3 Carberry Can.
144 A2 Carbó Mex.
107 C2 Carbon, Cap c. Alg.
153 B5 Carbón, Laguna del l. Arg.
108 A3 Carbonara, Capo c. Sardegna Italy
136 B3 Carbondale CO U.S.A.
140 B3 Carbondale IL U.S.A.
131 E2 Carbonear Can.
155 D1 Carbonita Brazil
107 C2 Carcaixent Spain
104 C3 Carcassonne France
128 A1 Carcross Can.
145 C3 Cárdenas Mex.
99 B3 Cardiff U.K.
99 A2 Cardigan U.K.
99 A2 Cardigan Bay U.K.
128 C3 Cardston Can.
110 B1 Carei Romania
104 B2 Carentan France
50 B2 Carey, Lake imp. l. Austr.
155 D2 Cariacica Brazil
146 B3 Caribbean Sea N. Atlantic Ocean
141 F1 Caribou U.S.A.
130 B2 Caribou Lake Can.
128 C2 Caribou Mountains Can.
144 B2 Carichic Mex.
100 B3 Carignan France
53 C2 Carinda Austr.
107 C1 Cariñena Spain
130 C2 Carleton Place Can.
123 C2 Carletonville S. Africa
97 C1 Carlingford Lough inlet Ireland/U.K.
98 B1 Carlisle U.K.
141 D2 Carlisle U.S.A.
155 D1 Carlos Chagas Brazil
97 C2 Carlow Ireland
135 C4 Carlsbad CA U.S.A.
138 C2 Carlsbad NM U.S.A.
129 D3 Carlyle Can.
128 A1 Carmacks Can.
129 E3 Carman Can.
99 A3 Carmarthen U.K.
99 A3 Carmarthen Bay U.K.
104 C3 Carmaux France
145 C3 Carmelita Guat.
144 A2 Carmen, Isla i. Mex.
104 B2 Carnac France
122 B3 Carnarvon S. Africa
97 C1 Carndonagh Ireland
50 B2 Carnegie, Lake imp. l. Austr.
96 B2 Carn Eige mt. U.K.
63 A3 Car Nicobar i. India

118 B2	Carnot C.A.R.	
52 A2	Carnot, Cape Austr.	
97 C2	Carnsore Point Ireland	
151 D2	Carolina Brazil	
48 D2	Caroline Islands *is*	
	N. Pacific Ocean	
59 D2	Caroline Islands	
	N. Pacific Ocean	
103 D2	Carpathian Mountains Europe	
	Carpaţii Meridionali *mts*	
	Romania *see* Transylvanian Alps	
51 C1	Carpentaria, Gulf of Austr.	
105 D3	Carpentras France	
97 B3	Carrantuohill *mt.* Ireland	
105 E3	Carrara Italy	
97 C2	Carrickmacross Ireland	
97 B2	Carrick-on-Shannon Ireland	
97 C2	Carrick-on-Suir Ireland	
137 D1	Carrington U.S.A.	
139 D3	Carrizo Springs U.S.A.	
129 B2	Carrizo U.S.A.	
137 E2	Carroll U.S.A.	
143 C2	Carrollton U.S.A.	
129 D2	Carrot River Can.	
135 C3	Carson City U.S.A.	
150 A1	Cartagena Col.	
107 C2	Cartagena Spain	
146 B4	Cartago Costa Rica	
137 E3	Carthage MO U.S.A.	
139 E2	Carthage TX U.S.A.	
131 E1	Cartwright Can.	
151 E2	Caruaru Brazil	
114 B1	Casablanca Morocco	
154 C2	Casa Branca Brazil	
144 B3	Casa de Janos Mex.	
138 A2	Casa Grande U.S.A.	
108 A1	Casale Monferrato Italy	
109 C2	Casarano Italy	
134 C2	Cascade U.S.A.	
134 B2	Cascade Range *mts* Can./U.S.A.	
106 B2	Cascais Port.	
154 B2	Cascavel Brazil	
108 B2	Caserta Italy	
97 C2	Cashel Ireland	
53 C1	Casino Austr.	
107 C1	Caspe Spain	
136 B2	Casper U.S.A.	
76 A2	Caspian Lowland Kazakh./ Rus. Fed.	
81 C1	Caspian Sea Asia/Europe	
154 C2	Cássia Brazil	
128 D1	Cassiar Can.	
128 A2	Cassiar Mountains Can.	
154 B1	Cassilândia Brazil	
108 B2	Cassino Italy	
96 B2	Cassley *r.* U.K.	
151 D2	Castanhal Brazil	
152 B4	Castaño *r.* Arg.	
144 B2	Castaños Mex.	
104 C3	Casteljaloux France	
107 C2	Castellón de la Plana Spain	
106 B2	Castelo Branco Port.	
108 B3	Castelvetrano *Sicilia* Italy	
52 D3	Casterton Austr.	
108 B2	Castiglione della Pescaia Italy	
97 C1	Castlebar Ireland	
96 A2	Castlebay U.K.	
97 C1	Castleblayney Ireland	
97 C1	Castlederg U.K.	
96 C3	Castle Douglas U.K.	
128 C3	Castlegar Can.	
97 B2	Castleisland Ireland	
52 B3	Castlemaine Austr.	
97 B2	Castlerea Ireland	
96 C2	Castlereagh *r.* Austr.	
126 C3	Castle Rock U.S.A.	
129 C2	Castor Can.	
104 C3	Castres France	
100 B1	Castricum Neth.	
147 D3	Castries St Lucia	
154 C2	Castro Brazil	
153 A5	Castro Chile	
106 B2	Castro Verde Port.	
109 C3	Castrovillari Italy	
150 A2	Catacaos Peru	
155 D2	Cataguases Brazil	
154 C1	Catalão Brazil	
152 B3	Catamarca Arg.	
64 B1	Catanduanes *i.* Phil.	
154 C2	Catanduva Brazil	
154 B3	Catanduvas Brazil	
109 C3	Catania *Sicilia* Italy	
109 C3	Catanzaro Italy	
64 B1	Catarman Phil.	
64 B1	Catbalogan Phil.	
145 C3	Catemaco Mex.	
147 C2	Cat Island Bahamas	
130 A1	Cat Lake Can.	
141 F2	Catskill Mountains U.S.A.	
64 B2	Cauayan Phil.	
150 A1	Cauca *r.* Col.	
151 E2	Caucaia Brazil	
81 C1	Caucasus *mts* Asia/Europe	
100 A2	Caudry France	
109 C3	Caulonia Italy	
131 D2	Causapscal Can.	
105 D3	Cavaillon France	
151 D3	Cavalcante Brazil	
97 C2	Cavan Ireland	
154 B3	Cavernoso, Serra do *mts* Brazil	
151 D2	Caxias Brazil	
152 C3	Caxias do Sul Brazil	
120 A1	Caxito Angola	
151 C1	Cayenne Fr. Guiana	
146 B3	Cayman Islands *terr.* West Indies	
117 C4	Caynabo Somalia	
120 D2	Casombo Angola	
144 B2	Ceballos Mex.	
64 B1	Cebu Phil.	
64 B1	Cebu *i.* Phil.	
108 B2	Cecina Italy	
137 F2	Cedar *r.* U.S.A.	
135 D3	Cedar City U.S.A.	
137 E2	Cedar Falls U.S.A.	
130 D2	Cedar Lake Can.	
137 E2	Cedar Rapids U.S.A.	
144 A1	Cedros, Isla *i.* Mex.	
51 C3	Ceduna Austr.	
117 C4	Ceeldheere Somalia	
117 C3	Ceerigaabo Somalia	
108 B3	Cefalù *Sicilia* Italy	
145 B2	Celaya Mex.	
58 C3	Celebes *i.* Indon.	
156 B5	Celebes Sea Indon./Phil.	
145 C2	Celestún Mex.	
101 E1	Celle Ger.	
95 B3	Celtic Sea Ireland/U.K.	
59 D3	Cenderawasih, Teluk *b.* Indon.	
150 A1	Central, Cordillera *mts* Col.	
150 A3	Central, Cordillera *mts* Peru	
64 B1	Central, Cordillera *mts* Phil.	
118 C2	Central African Republic *country* Africa	
74 A2	Central Brahui Range *mts* Pak.	
137 D2	Central City U.S.A.	
140 B3	Centralia IL U.S.A.	
134 B1	Centralia WA U.S.A.	
74 A2	Central Makran Range *mts* Pak.	
59 D3	Central Range *mts* P.N.G.	
89 E3	Central Russian Upland *hills* Rus. Fed.	
83 I2	Central Siberian Plateau Rus. Fed.	
111 B3	Cephalonia *i.* Greece	
	Ceram Sea Indon. *see* Seram, Laut	
152 B3	Ceres Arg.	
154 C1	Ceres Brazil	
122 A3	Ceres S. Africa	
104 C3	Céret France	
106 C1	Cerezo de Abajo Spain	
109 C2	Cerignola Italy	
110 C2	Cernavodă Romania	
145 C2	Cerralvo Mex.	
144 B2	Cerralvo, Isla *i.* Mex.	
145 B2	Cerritos Mex.	
154 C2	Cerro Azul Brazil	
145 B2	Cerro Azul Mex.	
150 A3	Cerro de Pasco Peru	
105 D3	Cervione *Corse* France	
106 B1	Cervo Spain	
108 B2	Cesena Italy	
88 C2	Cēsis Latvia	
102 C2	České Budějovice Czech Rep.	
101 F3	Český les *mts* Czech Rep.	
111 C3	Çeşme Turkey	
53 D2	Cessnock Austr.	
109 C2	Cetinje Montenegro	
109 C3	Cetraro Italy	
106 B2	Ceuta N. Africa	
105 C3	Cévennes *mts* France	
	Ceylon *country* Asia *see* Sri Lanka	
79 D2	Chābahār Iran	
150 A2	Chachapoyas Peru	
89 D3	Chachersk Belarus	
63 B2	Chachoengsao Thai.	
115 D3	Chad *country* Africa	
115 D3	Chad, Lake Africa	
69 C1	Chadaasan Mongolia	
68 C1	Chadan Rus. Fed.	
123 C1	Chadibe Botswana	
136 C2	Chadron U.S.A.	
65 B2	Chaeryŏng N. Korea	
74 A2	Chagai Pak.	
77 C3	Chaghcharān Afgh.	
89 E2	Chagoda Rus. Fed.	
75 C2	Chaibasa India	
63 B2	Chainat Thai.	
63 B2	Chaiyaphum Thai.	
152 C4	Chajari Arg.	
131 D1	Chakonipau, Lac *l.* Can.	
150 A3	Chala Peru	
74 A1	Chalap Dalan *mts* Afgh.	
131 D2	Chaleur Bay *inlet* Can.	
74 B2	Chalisgaon India	
111 C3	Chalki *i.* Greece	
111 B3	Chalkida Greece	
104 B2	Challans France	
134 D2	Challis U.S.A.	
105 C2	Châlons-en-Champagne France	
105 C2	Chalon-sur-Saône France	
138 B1	Chama U.S.A.	
121 C2	Chama Zambia	
74 A1	Chaman Pak.	
74 B1	Chamba India	
74 B2	Chambal *r.* India	
137 D2	Chamberlain U.S.A.	
141 D3	Chambersburg U.S.A.	
105 D2	Chambéry France	
121 C2	Chambeshi Zambia	
140 B2	Champaign U.S.A.	
141 E2	Champlain, Lake Can./U.S.A.	
145 C3	Champotón Mex.	
152 A3	Chañaral Chile	
126 B2	Chandalar *r.* U.S.A.	
142 C3	Chandeleur Islands U.S.A.	

74	B1	Chandigarh India
138	A2	Chandler U.S.A.
75	B3	Chandrapur India
63	B3	Chang, Ko *i.* Thai.
		Chang'an China *see* Rong'an
121	C3	Changane *r.* Moz.
121	C2	Changara Moz.
65	B1	Changbai China
65	B1	Changbai Shan *mts* China/ N. Korea
69	E2	Changchun China
71	B3	Changde China
65	B2	Ch'angdo N. Korea
65	B3	Changhŭng S. Korea
		Chang Jiang *r.* China *see* Yangtze
65	B1	Changjin N. Korea
65	B1	Changjin-gang *r.* N. Korea
71	B3	Changsha China
65	B2	Changsŏng S. Korea
71	B3	Changting China
65	B2	Ch'angwŏn S. Korea
70	B2	Changyuan China
70	B2	Changzhi China
70	B2	Changzhou China
111	B3	Chania Greece
95	C4	Channel Islands English Chan.
135	C4	Channel Islands U.S.A.
131	E2	Channel-Port-aux-Basques Can.
63	B2	Chanthaburi Thai.
104	C2	Chantilly France
137	D3	Chanute U.S.A.
82	G3	Chany, Ozero *salt l.* Rus. Fed.
71	B3	Chaoyang China
		Chaoyang China *see* Huinan
71	B3	Chaozhou China
144	B2	Chapala, Laguna de *l.* Mex.
76	B1	Chapayevo Kazakh.
152	C3	Chapecó Brazil
143	E1	Chapel Hill U.S.A.
130	B2	Chapleau Can.
89	E3	Chaplygin Rus. Fed.
91	C2	Chaplynka Ukr.
145	B2	Charcas Mex.
99	B3	Chard U.K.
104	B2	Charente *r.* France
77	C3	Chārīkār Afgh.
86	E2	Charkayuvom Rus. Fed.
100	B2	Charleroi Belgium
141	D3	Charles, Cape U.S.A.
137	E2	Charles City U.S.A.
140	B3	Charleston *IL* U.S.A.
143	E2	Charleston *SC* U.S.A.
140	C3	Charleston *WV* U.S.A.
135	C3	Charleston Peak U.S.A.
52	D2	Charleville Austr.
105	C2	Charleville-Mézières France
143	D1	Charlotte U.S.A.
143	D3	Charlotte Harbor *b.* U.S.A.
141	D3	Charlottesville U.S.A.
131	D2	Charlottetown Can.
52	B3	Charlton Austr.
130	C1	Charlton Island Can.
51	D2	Charters Towers Austr.
104	C2	Chartres France
128	C2	Chase Can.
88	C3	Chashniki Belarus
54	A3	Chaslands Mistake *c.* N.Z.
65	B1	Chasŏng N. Korea
104	B2	Chassiron, Pointe de *pt* France
104	B2	Châteaubriant France
104	C2	Château-du-Loir France
104	C2	Châteaudun France
104	B2	Châteaulin France

105	D3	Châteauneuf-les-Martigues France
104	C2	Châteauneuf-sur-Loire France
105	C2	Château-Thierry France
128	C2	Chateh Can.
100	B3	Châtelet Belgium
104	C2	Châtellerault France
140	C2	Chatham Ont. Can.
49	G5	Chatham Islands *is* N.Z.
105	C2	Châtillon-sur-Seine France
143	D2	Chattahoochee *r.* U.S.A.
143	C1	Chattanooga U.S.A.
63	B2	Châu Đốc Vietnam
62	A1	Chauk Myanmar
105	D2	Chaumont France
104	C2	Chauny France
151	D2	Chaves Brazil
106	B1	Chaves Port.
130	C1	Chavigny, Lac *l.* Can.
89	D3	Chavusy Belarus
89	E2	Chayevo Rus. Fed.
86	E3	Chaykovskiy Rus. Fed.
102	C1	Cheb Czech Rep.
87	D3	Cheboksary Rus. Fed.
140	C1	Cheboygan U.S.A.
65	B2	Chech'ŏn S. Korea
114	B2	Chegga Maur.
134	B1	Chehalis U.S.A.
65	B3	Cheju S. Korea
65	B3	Cheju-do *i.* S. Korea
65	B3	Cheju-haehyŏp *sea chan.* S. Korea
89	E2	Chekhov Rus. Fed.
134	B1	Chelan, Lake U.S.A.
103	E1	Chełm Pol.
99	D3	Chelmer *r.* U.K.
103	D1	Chełmno Pol.
99	D3	Chelmsford U.K.
99	B3	Cheltenham U.K.
87	F3	Chelyabinsk Rus. Fed.
101	F2	Chemnitz Ger.
114	B2	Chenachane Alg.
70	B1	Chengde China
70	A2	Chengdu China
71	A3	Chengguan China
71	B4	Chengmai China
		Chengshou China *see* Yingshan
70	A2	Chengxian China
		Chengyang China *see* Juxian
73	C3	Chennai India
71	B3	Chenzhou China
99	B3	Chepstow U.K.
104	B2	Cherbourg-Octeville France
89	E3	Cheremisinovo Rus. Fed.
69	C1	Cheremkhovo Rus. Fed.
89	E2	Cherepovets Rus. Fed.
91	C2	Cherkasy Ukr.
87	D4	Cherkessk Rus. Fed.
91	C1	Chernihiv Ukr.
91	C2	Cherninivka Ukr.
90	B2	Chernivtsi Ukr.
91	C1	Chernyakhiv Ukr.
88	B3	Chernyakhovsk Rus. Fed.
89	E3	Chernyanka Rus. Fed.
83	I2	Chernyshevskiy Rus. Fed.
137	D2	Cherokee U.S.A.
83	K2	Cherskogo, Khrebet *mts* Rus. Fed.
91	E2	Chertkovo Rus. Fed.
90	A1	Chervonohrad Ukr.
88	C3	Chervyen' Belarus
89	D3	Cherykaw Belarus
141	D3	Chesapeake Bay U.S.A.
86	D2	Cheshskaya Guba *b.* Rus. Fed.
98	B2	Chester U.K.
140	B3	Chester *IL* U.S.A.

143	D2	Chester *SC* U.S.A.
98	C2	Chesterfield U.K.
129	E1	Chesterfield Inlet Can.
129	E1	Chesterfield Inlet Can.
141	F1	Chesuncook Lake U.S.A.
131	D2	Chéticamp Can.
145	D3	Chetumal Mex.
128	B2	Chetwynd Can.
98	B1	Cheviot Hills U.K.
136	C2	Cheyenne *r.* U.S.A.
136	C2	Cheyenne U.S.A.
136	C3	Cheyenne Wells U.S.A.
75	C2	Chhapra India
75	B2	Chhatarpur India
62	A2	Chiang Dao Thai.
62	A2	Chiang Mai Thai.
62	A2	Chiang Rai Thai.
108	A1	Chiavenna Italy
70	B3	Chibi China
121	C3	Chiboma Moz.
130	C2	Chibougamau Can.
123	D1	Chibuto Moz.
75	D1	Chibuzhang Co *l.* China
140	B2	Chicago U.S.A.
128	A2	Chichagof Island U.S.A.
99	C3	Chichester U.K.
50	A2	Chichester Range *mts* Austr.
139	D1	Chickasha U.S.A.
150	A2	Chiclayo Peru
153	B5	Chico *r.* Arg.
135	B3	Chico U.S.A.
131	C2	Chicoutimi Can.
108	B2	Chieti Italy
145	C3	Chietla Mex.
69	D2	Chifeng China
155	F1	Chifre, Serra do *mts* Brazil
145	C3	Chignahuapán Mex.
121	C3	Chigubo Moz.
144	B2	Chihuahua Mex.
88	C2	Chikhachevo Rus. Fed.
67	C3	Chikuma-gawa *r.* Japan
128	B2	Chilanko *r.* Can.
74	B1	Chilas Pak.
139	C2	Childress U.S.A.
153	A4	Chile *country* S. America
152	B3	Chilecito Arg.
75	C3	Chilika Lake India
121	B2	Chililabombwe Zambia
128	B2	Chilko *r.* Can.
128	B2	Chilko Lake Can.
153	A4	Chillán Chile
137	E3	Chillicothe *MO* U.S.A.
140	C3	Chillicothe *OH* U.S.A.
128	B3	Chilliwack Can.
153	A5	Chiloé, Isla de *i.* Chile
145	C3	Chilpancingo Mex.
53	C3	Chiltern Austr.
71	C3	Chilung Taiwan
119	D3	Chimala Tanz.
152	B4	Chimbas Arg.
150	A2	Chimborazo *mt.* Ecuador
150	A2	Chimbote Peru
87	E4	Chimboy Uzbek.
		Chimkent Kazakh. *see* Shymkent
121	C3	Chimoio Moz.
77	C3	Chimtargha, Qullai *mt.* Tajik.
68	C2	China *country* Asia
145	C2	China Mex.
150	A3	Chincha Alta Peru
128	C2	Chinchaga *r.* Can.
145	D3	Chinchorro, Banco Mex.
121	C2	Chinde Moz.
65	B3	Chindo S. Korea
65	B3	Chin-do *i.* S. Korea
68	C2	Chindu China
62	A1	Chindwin *r.* Myanmar

65 B2	**Chinghwa** N. Korea
120 B2	**Chingola** Zambia
120 A2	**Chinguar** Angola
65 B2	**Chinhae** S. Korea
121 C2	**Chinhoyi** Zimbabwe
74 B1	**Chiniot** Pak.
144 B2	**Chinipas** Mex.
65 B2	**Chinju** S. Korea
118 C2	**Chinko** r. C.A.R.
138 B1	**Chinle** U.S.A.
71 B3	**Chinmen** Taiwan
67 C3	**Chino** Japan
104 C2	**Chinon** France
138 A2	**Chino Valley** U.S.A.
121 C2	**Chinsali** Zambia
108 B1	**Chioggia** Italy
111 C3	**Chios** Greece
111 C3	**Chios** i. Greece
121 C2	**Chipata** Zambia
120 A2	**Chipindo** Angola
121 C2	**Chipinge** Zimbabwe
73 B3	**Chiplun** India
99 B3	**Chippenham** U.K.
99 C3	**Chipping Norton** U.K.
77 C2	**Chirchiq** Uzbek.
121 C3	**Chiredzi** Zimbabwe
138 B2	**Chiricahua Peak** U.S.A.
146 B4	**Chiriquí, Golfo de** b. Panama
65 B2	**Chiri-san** mt. S. Korea
146 B4	**Chirripó** mt. Costa Rica
121 B2	**Chirundu** Zimbabwe
130 C1	**Chisasibi** Can.
137 E1	**Chisholm** U.S.A.
90 B2	**Chişinău** Moldova
87 E3	**Chistopol'** Rus. Fed.
69 D1	**Chita** Rus. Fed.
120 A2	**Chitado** Angola
121 C2	**Chitambo** Zambia
120 B1	**Chitato** Angola
121 C1	**Chitipa** Malawi
73 B3	**Chitradurga** India
74 B1	**Chitral** Pak.
146 B4	**Chitré** Panama
75 D2	**Chittagong** Bangl.
74 B2	**Chittaurgarh** India
121 C2	**Chitungwiza** Zimbabwe
120 B2	**Chiume** Angola
121 C2	**Chivhu** Zimbabwe
70 B2	**Chizhou** China
114 C1	**Chlef** Alg.
107 D2	**Chlef, Oued** r. Alg.
153 B4	**Choele Choel** Arg.
144 B2	**Choix** Mex.
103 D1	**Chojnice** Pol.
117 B3	**Ch'ok'ē Mountains** Eth.
117 B3	**Ch'ok'ē Terara** mt. Eth.
83 K2	**Chokurdakh** Rus. Fed.
121 C3	**Chókwé** Moz.
104 B2	**Cholet** France
102 C1	**Chomutov** Czech Rep.
83 I2	**Chona** r. Rus. Fed.
65 B2	**Ch'ŏnan** S. Korea
150 A2	**Chone** Ecuador
65 B1	**Ch'ŏngjin** N. Korea
65 B2	**Chŏngju** N. Korea
65 B2	**Ch'ŏngju** N. Korea
65 B2	**Ch'ŏngp'yŏng** N. Korea
70 A3	**Chongqing** China
70 A3	**Chongqing** mun. China
71 A3	**Chongzuo** China
65 B2	**Chŏnju** S. Korea
153 A5	**Chonos, Archipiélago de los** is Chile
154 B3	**Chopimzinho** Brazil
111 B3	**Chora Sfakion** Greece
98 B2	**Chorley** U.K.
91 C2	**Chornomors'ke** Ukr.
90 B2	**Chortkiv** Ukr.
65 B2	**Ch'ŏrwŏn** S. Korea
65 B1	**Ch'osan** N. Korea
67 D3	**Chōshi** Japan
103 D1	**Choszczno** Pol.
114 A2	**Choûm** Maur.
69 D1	**Choybalsan** Mongolia
69 D1	**Choyr** Mongolia
54 B2	**Christchurch** N.Z.
99 C3	**Christchurch** U.K.
127 G2	**Christian, Cape** Can.
123 C2	**Christiana** S. Africa
54 A2	**Christina, Mount** N.Z.
153 B5	**Chubut** r. Arg.
90 B1	**Chudniv** Ukr.
89 D2	**Chudovo** Rus. Fed.
	Chudskoye Ozero l. Estonia/Rus. Fed. see Peipus, Lake
126 B2	**Chugach Mountains** U.S.A.
67 B4	**Chūgoku-sanchi** mts Japan
66 B2	**Chuguyevka** Rus. Fed.
91 D2	**Chuhuyiv** Ukr.
160 J3	**Chukchi Sea** Rus. Fed./U.S.A.
83 N2	**Chukotskiy Poluostrov** pen. Rus. Fed.
135 C4	**Chula Vista** U.S.A.
82 G3	**Chulym** Rus. Fed.
152 B3	**Chumbicha** Arg.
83 K3	**Chumikan** Rus. Fed.
63 A2	**Chumphon** Thai.
65 B2	**Ch'unch'ŏn** S. Korea
83 H2	**Chunya** r. Rus. Fed.
150 A3	**Chuquibamba** Peru
152 B3	**Chuquicamata** Chile
105 D2	**Chur** Switz.
62 A1	**Churachandpur** India
129 E2	**Churchill** Can.
129 E2	**Churchill** r. Man. Can.
131 D1	**Churchill** r. Nfld. and Lab. Can.
129 E2	**Churchill, Cape** Can.
131 D1	**Churchill Falls** Can.
129 D2	**Churchill Lake** Can.
74 B2	**Churu** India
131 C2	**Chute-des-Passes** Can.
62 B1	**Chuxiong** China
90 B2	**Ciadîr-Lunga** Moldova
61 B2	**Ciamis** Indon.
60 B2	**Cianjur** Indon.
154 B2	**Cianorte** Brazil
103 E1	**Ciechanów** Pol.
146 C2	**Ciego de Ávila** Cuba
146 B2	**Cienfuegos** Cuba
107 C2	**Cieza** Spain
106 C2	**Cigüela** r. Spain
80 B2	**Cihanbeyli** Turkey
144 B3	**Cihuatlán** Mex.
106 C2	**Cíjara, Embalse de** resr Spain
61 B2	**Cilacap** Indon.
139 C1	**Cimarron** r. U.S.A.
90 B2	**Cimişlia** Moldova
108 B2	**Cimone, Monte** mt. Italy
141 D3	**Cincinnati** U.S.A.
111 C3	**Çine** Turkey
100 B2	**Ciney** Belgium
145 C3	**Cintalapa** Mex.
71 B3	**Ciping** China
126 B3	**Circle** AK U.S.A.
134 E1	**Circle** MT U.S.A.
58 B3	**Cirebon** Indon.
99 C3	**Cirencester** U.K.
108 A1	**Ciriè** Italy
109 C3	**Cirò Marina** Italy
109 C2	**Citluk** Bos.-Herz.
122 A3	**Citrusdal** S. Africa
145 B2	**Ciudad Acuña** Mex.
145 B3	**Ciudad Altamirano** Mex.
150 B1	**Ciudad Bolívar** Venez.
144 B2	**Ciudad Camargo** Mex.
144 A2	**Ciudad Constitución** Mex.
144 B2	**Ciudad del Carmen** Mex.
145 C2	**Ciudad Delicias** Mex.
145 C2	**Ciudad de Valles** Mex.
150 B1	**Ciudad Guayana** Venez.
138 B3	**Ciudad Guerrero** Mex.
144 B3	**Ciudad Guzmán** Mex.
145 C3	**Ciudad Hidalgo** Mex.
145 C3	**Ciudad Ixtepec** Mex.
144 B1	**Ciudad Juárez** Mex.
145 C2	**Ciudad Mante** Mex.
145 C2	**Ciudad Mier** Mex.
144 B2	**Ciudad Obregón** Mex.
106 C2	**Ciudad Real** Spain
145 C2	**Ciudad Río Bravo** Mex.
106 B1	**Ciudad Rodrigo** Spain
145 C2	**Ciudad Victoria** Mex.
107 D1	**Ciutadella** Spain
111 C3	**Civan Dağ** mt. Turkey
108 B1	**Cividale del Friuli** Italy
108 B2	**Civitanova Marche** Italy
108 B2	**Civitavecchia** Italy
104 C2	**Civray** France
111 C3	**Çivril** Turkey
70 C2	**Cixi** China
99 D3	**Clacton-on-Sea** U.K.
128 C2	**Claire, Lake** Can.
105 C2	**Clamecy** France
122 A3	**Clanwilliam** S. Africa
52 A2	**Clare** Austr.
97 A2	**Clare Island** Ireland
141 F2	**Claremont** U.S.A.
97 B2	**Claremorris** Ireland
54 B2	**Clarence** N.Z.
131 F2	**Clarenville** Can.
128 C2	**Claresholm** Can.
137 D2	**Clarinda** U.S.A.
123 C3	**Clarkebury** S. Africa
134 C1	**Clark Fork** r. U.S.A.
143 D2	**Clark Hill Reservoir** U.S.A.
140 C3	**Clarksburg** U.S.A.
142 B2	**Clarksdale** U.S.A.
142 C1	**Clarksville** AR U.S.A.
142 C1	**Clarksville** TN U.S.A.
154 B1	**Claro** r. Brazil
139 C1	**Clayton** U.S.A.
97 B3	**Clear, Cape** Ireland
137 E2	**Clear Lake** U.S.A.
135 B3	**Clear Lake** U.S.A.
128 C2	**Clearwater** Can.
129 C2	**Clearwater** r. Can.
143 D3	**Clearwater** U.S.A.
134 C1	**Clearwater** r. U.S.A.
139 D2	**Cleburne** U.S.A.
51 D2	**Clermont** Austr.
105 C2	**Clermont-Ferrand** France
52 A2	**Cleve** Austr.
142 B2	**Cleveland** MS U.S.A.
142 C2	**Cleveland** OH U.S.A.
143 D1	**Cleveland** TN U.S.A.
134 D1	**Cleveland, Mount** U.S.A.
143 D3	**Clewiston** U.S.A.
97 A2	**Clifden** Ireland
53 D1	**Clifton** Austr.
138 B2	**Clifton** U.S.A.
128 B2	**Clinton** Can.
137 E2	**Clinton** IA U.S.A.
137 E3	**Clinton** MO U.S.A.
139 D1	**Clinton** OK U.S.A.
96 A2	**Clisham** h. U.K.
98 B2	**Clitheroe** U.K.
97 B3	**Clonakilty** Ireland
51 D2	**Cloncurry** Austr.
97 C1	**Clones** Ireland
97 C2	**Clonmel** Ireland

100	D1	Cloppenburg Ger.
50	A2	Cloud Break Austr.
136	B2	Cloud Peak U.S.A.
139	C2	Clovis U.S.A.
129	D2	Cluff Lake Mine Can.
110	B1	Cluj-Napoca Romania
51	C2	Cluny U.K.
105	D2	Cluses France
54	A3	Clutha r. N.Z.
96	B3	Clyde r. U.K.
96	B3	Clyde, Firth of est. U.K.
96	B3	Clydebank U.K.
127	G2	Clyde River Can.
144	B3	Coalcomán Mex.
135	C3	Coaldale U.S.A.
128	B2	Coal River Can.
150	B2	Coari Brazil
150	B2	Coari r. Brazil
142	B2	Coastal Plain U.S.A.
128	B2	Coast Mountains Can.
135	B2	Coast Ranges mts U.S.A.
96	B3	Coatbridge U.K.
127	F2	Coats Island Can.
55	R2	Coats Land reg. Antarctica
145	C3	Coatzacoalcos Mex.
146	A3	Cobán Guat.
53	C2	Cobar Austr.
97	B3	Cobh Ireland
152	B2	Cobija Bol.
141	D2	Cobourg Can.
50	C1	Cobourg Peninsula Austr.
53	C3	Cobram Austr.
101	E2	Coburg Ger.
152	B2	Cochabamba Bol.
100	C2	Cochem Ger.
		Cochin India see Kochi
128	C2	Cochrane Alta Can.
130	B2	Cochrane Ont. Can.
153	A5	Cochrane Chile
52	B2	Cockburn Austr.
		Cockburn Town Turks and
		Caicos Is see Grand Turk
98	B3	Cockermouth U.K.
122	B1	Cockscomb mt. S. Africa
146	B3	Coco r. Hond./Nic.
144	B2	Cocula Mex.
150	A1	Cocuy, Sierra Nevada del mt. Col.
141	E2	Cod, Cape U.S.A.
108	B2	Codigoro Italy
131	D1	Cod Island Can.
151	D2	Codó Brazil
136	B2	Cody U.S.A.
51	D1	Coen Austr.
100	C2	Coesfeld Ger.
134	C1	Coeur d'Alene U.S.A.
123	C3	Coffee Bay S. Africa
137	D3	Coffeyville U.S.A.
53	D2	Coffs Harbour Austr.
104	B2	Cognac France
118	A2	Cogo Equat. Guinea
52	B3	Cohuna Austr.
146	B4	Coiba, Isla de i. Panama
153	A5	Coihaique Chile
73	B3	Coimbatore India
106	B1	Coimbra Port.
52	B3	Colac Austr.
155	D1	Colatina Brazil
136	C3	Colby U.S.A.
99	D3	Colchester U.K.
129	C2	Cold Lake Can.
96	C3	Coldstream U.K.
139	D2	Coleman U.S.A.
52	B3	Coleraine Austr.
97	C1	Coleraine U.K.
123	C3	Colesberg S. Africa
144	B3	Colima Mex.

144	B3	Colima, Nevado de vol. Mex.
96	A2	Coll i. U.K.
53	C1	Collarenebri Austr.
50	B1	Collier Bay Austr.
54	B2	Collingwood N.Z.
97	B1	Collooney Ireland
105	D2	Colmar France
100	C2	Cologne Ger.
154	C2	Colômbia Brazil
150	A1	Colombia country S. America
73	B4	Colombo Sri Lanka
104	C3	Colomiers France
152	C4	Colón Arg.
146	C4	Colón Panama
109	C3	Colonna, Capo c. Italy
96	A2	Colonsay i. U.K.
153	B4	Colorado r. Arg.
138	A2	Colorado r. Mex./U.S.A.
139	D3	Colorado r. U.S.A.
136	B3	Colorado state U.S.A.
135	E3	Colorado Plateau U.S.A.
136	C3	Colorado Springs U.S.A.
144	B2	Colotlán Mex.
136	B1	Colstrip U.S.A.
137	E3	Columbia MO U.S.A.
143	D2	Columbia SC U.S.A.
142	C1	Columbia TN U.S.A.
134	B1	Columbia r. U.S.A.
128	C2	Columbia, Mount Can.
134	D1	Columbia Falls U.S.A.
128	B2	Columbia Mountains Can.
134	C1	Columbia Plateau U.S.A.
143	D2	Columbus GA U.S.A.
140	B3	Columbus IN U.S.A.
142	C2	Columbus MS U.S.A.
137	D2	Columbus NE U.S.A.
138	B2	Columbus NM U.S.A.
140	C3	Columbus OH U.S.A.
134	C1	Colville U.S.A.
126	A2	Colville r. U.S.A.
126	C2	Colville Lake Can.
98	B2	Colwyn Bay U.K.
108	B2	Comacchio Italy
145	C3	Comalcalco Mex.
110	C1	Comănești Romania
130	C1	Comencho, Lac l. Can.
97	C2	Comeragh Mountains hills Ireland
75	D2	Comilla Bangl.
108	A2	Comino, Capo c. Sardegna Italy
145	C3	Comitán de Domínguez Mex.
104	C2	Compiègne France
144	B2	Compostela Mex.
90	B2	Comrat Moldova
114	A4	Conakry Guinea
155	E1	Conceição da Barra Brazil
151	D2	Conceição do Araguaia Brazil
155	D1	Conceição do Mato Dentro Brazil
152	B3	Concepción Arg.
153	A4	Concepción Chile
144	B2	Concepción Mex.
135	B4	Conception, Point U.S.A.
154	C2	Conchas Brazil
138	C1	Conchas U.S.A.
144	B2	Conchos r. Chihuahua Mex.
145	C2	Conchos r. Nuevo León/Tamaulipas Mex.
135	B3	Concord CA U.S.A.
141	E2	Concord NH U.S.A.
152	C4	Concordia Arg.

122	A2	Concordia S. Africa
137	D3	Concordia U.S.A.
53	C2	Condobolin Austr.
104	C3	Condom France
134	B1	Condon U.S.A.
108	B1	Conegliano Italy
104	C2	Confolens France
75	C2	Congdü China
118	B3	Congo country Africa
118	B3	Congo r. Congo/Dem. Rep. Congo
118	C3	Congo, Democratic Republic of the country Africa
129	C2	Conklin Can.
97	B1	Conn, Lough l. Ireland
97	B2	Connaught reg. Ireland
141	E2	Connecticut r. U.S.A.
141	E2	Connecticut state U.S.A.
97	B2	Connemara reg. Ireland
134	D1	Conrad U.S.A.
139	D2	Conroe U.S.A.
155	D2	Conselheiro Lafaiete Brazil
155	D1	Conselheiro Pena Brazil
98	C1	Consett U.K.
63	B3	Côn Sơn, Đảo i. Vietnam
110	C2	Constanţa Romania
106	B2	Constantina Spain
115	C1	Constantine Alg.
134	D2	Contact U.S.A.
150	A2	Contamana Peru
153	A6	Contreras, Isla i. Chile
126	D2	Contwoyto Lake Can.
142	B1	Conway AR U.S.A.
141	E2	Conway NH U.S.A.
51	C2	Coober Pedy Austr.
		Cook, Mount mt. N.Z. see Aoraki
143	C1	Cookeville U.S.A.
49	H4	Cook Islands S. Pacific Ocean
131	E1	Cook's Harbour Can.
97	C1	Cookstown U.K.
54	B2	Cook Strait N.Z.
51	D1	Cooktown Austr.
53	C2	Coolabah Austr.
53	C2	Coolamon Austr.
53	D1	Coolangatta Austr.
50	B3	Coolgardie Austr.
53	C3	Cooma Austr.
52	B2	Coombah Austr.
53	C2	Coonabarabran Austr.
52	A3	Coonalpyn Austr.
53	C2	Coonamble Austr.
52	A1	Cooper Creek watercourse Austr.
134	B2	Coos Bay U.S.A.
53	C2	Cootamundra Austr.
145	C3	Copainalá Mex.
145	C3	Copala Mex.
93	F4	Copenhagen Denmark
109	C2	Copertino Italy
152	A3	Copiapó Chile
140	B1	Copper Harbor U.S.A.
		Coppermine Can. see Kugluktuk
126	D2	Coppermine r. Can.
122	B2	Copperton S. Africa
152	A3	Coquimbo Chile
110	B2	Corabia Romania
155	D1	Coração de Jesus Brazil
150	A3	Coracora Peru
53	D1	Coraki Austr.
50	A2	Coral Bay Austr.
127	F2	Coral Harbour Can.
156	D7	Coral Sea S. Pacific Ocean
48	D4	Coral Sea Islands Territory Austr.
52	B3	Corangamite, Lake Austr.
99	C2	Corby U.K.

153 A5 **Corcovado, Golfo de** *sea chan.* Chile
143 D2 **Cordele** U.S.A.
64 B1 **Cordilleras Range** *mts* Phil.
152 B4 **Córdoba** Arg.
145 C3 **Córdoba** Mex.
111 C2 **Córdoba** Spain
153 B4 **Córdoba, Sierras de** *mts* Arg.
111 A3 **Corfu** *i.* Greece
106 B2 **Coria** Spain
111 B3 **Corinth** Greece
142 C2 **Corinth** U.S.A.
155 D1 **Corinto** Brazil
97 B3 **Cork** Ireland
111 C2 **Çorlu** Turkey
154 C1 **Cornélio Procópio** Brazil
131 E2 **Corner Brook** Can.
53 C3 **Corner Inlet** *b* Austr.
145 B3 **Corning** *CA* U.S.A.
141 D2 **Corning** *NY* U.S.A.
       Corn Islands *is* Nic. see **Maíz, Islas del**
108 B2 **Corno Grande** *mt.* Italy
130 C2 **Cornwall** Can.
126 E1 **Cornwallis Island** Can.
150 B1 **Coro** Venez.
154 B1 **Coromandel** Brazil
54 C1 **Coromandel Peninsula** N.Z.
129 C2 **Coronation** Can.
126 D2 **Coronation Gulf** Can.
152 C3 **Coronel Oviedo** Para.
153 B4 **Coronel Suárez** Arg.
150 A3 **Coropuna, Nudo** *mt.* Peru
109 D2 **Çorovodë** Albania
139 D3 **Corpus Christi** U.S.A.
152 B2 **Corque** Bol.
151 D3 **Corrente** Brazil
154 B1 **Correntes** Brazil
151 D3 **Correntina** Brazil
97 B2 **Corrib, Lough** *l.* Ireland
152 C3 **Corrientes** Arg.
144 B2 **Corrientes, Cabo** *c.* Mex.
53 C3 **Corryong** Austr.
105 D3 **Corse** *i.* France see **Corsica**
105 D3 **Corse, Cap** *c. Corse* France
105 D3 **Corsica** *i.* France
139 D2 **Corsicana** U.S.A.
105 D3 **Corte** *Corse* France
106 B2 **Cortegana** Spain
136 B3 **Cortez** U.S.A.
108 B1 **Cortina d'Ampezzo** Italy
141 D2 **Cortland** U.S.A.
108 B2 **Cortona** Italy
106 B2 **Coruche** Port.
       Çoruh Turkey see **Artvin**
80 D1 **Çorum** Turkey
152 C2 **Corumbá** Brazil
154 C1 **Corumbá** *r.* Brazil
134 B2 **Corvallis** U.S.A.
98 A2 **Corwen** U.K.
144 B2 **Cosalá** Mex.
145 C3 **Cosamaloapan** Mex.
109 C3 **Cosenza** Italy
105 C2 **Cosne-Cours-sur-Loire** France
107 C2 **Costa Blanca** *coastal area* Spain
107 D1 **Costa Brava** *coastal area* Spain
106 B2 **Costa del Sol** *coastal area* Spain
154 B1 **Costa Rica** Brazil
146 B3 **Costa Rica** *country* Central America
144 B2 **Costa Rica** Mex.
110 B2 **Costeşti** Romania
64 B2 **Cotabato** Phil.
114 B4 **Côte d'Ivoire** *country* Africa

150 A2 **Cotopaxi, Volcán** *vol.* Ecuador
99 B3 **Cotswold Hills** U.K.
134 B2 **Cottage Grove** U.S.A.
102 C1 **Cottbus** Ger.
104 B2 **Coubre, Pointe de la** *pt* France
52 A3 **Couedic, Cape du** Austr.
137 D2 **Council Bluffs** U.S.A.
88 B2 **Courland Lagoon** *b.* Lith./Rus. Fed.
128 B3 **Courtenay** Can.
104 B2 **Coutances** France
104 B2 **Coutras** France
100 B2 **Couvin** Belgium
99 C2 **Coventry** U.K.
140 C3 **Covington** U.S.A.
50 B3 **Cowan, Lake** *imp. l.* Austr.
96 C2 **Cowdenbeath** U.K.
53 C3 **Cowes** Austr.
134 B1 **Cowlitz** *r.* U.S.A.
53 C2 **Cowra** Austr.
154 B1 **Coxim** Brazil
75 D2 **Cox's Bazar** Bangl.
145 B3 **Coyuca de Benítez** Mex.
75 C1 **Cozhê** China
145 D2 **Cozumel** Mex.
145 D2 **Cozumel, Isla de** *i.* Mex.
123 C3 **Cradock** S. Africa
136 B2 **Craig** U.S.A.
102 C2 **Crailsheim** Ger.
110 B2 **Craiova** Romania
129 D2 **Cranberry Portage** Can.
53 C3 **Cranbourne** Austr.
128 C3 **Cranbrook** Can.
151 D2 **Crateús** Brazil
151 E2 **Crato** Brazil
136 C2 **Crawford** U.S.A.
140 B2 **Crawfordsville** U.S.A.
99 C3 **Crawley** U.K.
134 D1 **Crazy Mountains** U.S.A.
129 C2 **Cree** *r.* Can.
144 B2 **Creel** Mex.
129 C2 **Cree Lake** Can.
100 B1 **Creil** Neth.
105 D2 **Crema** Italy
108 B1 **Cremona** Italy
108 B2 **Cres** *i.* Croatia
134 B2 **Crescent City** U.S.A.
128 C3 **Creston** Can.
137 E2 **Creston** U.S.A.
142 C2 **Crestview** U.S.A.
111 B3 **Crete** *i.* Greece
107 D1 **Creus, Cabo de** *c.* Spain
98 B2 **Crewe** U.K.
96 B2 **Crianlarich** U.K.
152 D3 **Criciúma** Brazil
96 C2 **Crieff** U.K.
108 B1 **Crikvenica** Croatia
91 C2 **Crimea** *pen.* Ukr.
101 F2 **Crimmitschau** Ger.
154 C1 **Cristalina** Brazil
101 E1 **Crivitz** Ger.
       Crna Gora *country* Europe see **Montenegro**
109 D2 **Črnomelj** Slovenia
97 B2 **Croagh Patrick** *h.* Ireland
109 C1 **Croatia** *country* Europe
61 C1 **Crocker, Banjaran** *mts* Malaysia
139 D2 **Crockett** U.S.A.
59 C3 **Croker Island** Austr.
99 D2 **Cromer** U.K.
54 A3 **Cromwell** N.Z.
137 D2 **Crookston** U.S.A.
53 C2 **Crookwell** Austr.
138 C1 **Crosby** U.S.A.
143 D3 **Cross City** U.S.A.

142 B2 **Crossett** U.S.A.
98 B1 **Cross Fell** *h.* U.K.
129 E2 **Cross Lake** Can.
143 C1 **Crossville** U.S.A.
109 C3 **Crotone** Italy
99 D3 **Crowborough** U.K.
142 B2 **Crowley** U.S.A.
128 C3 **Crowsnest Pass** Can.
146 C3 **Cruz, Cabo** *c.* Cuba
151 D2 **Cruz Alta** Brazil
152 B4 **Cruz del Eje** Arg.
155 D2 **Cruzeiro** Brazil
150 A2 **Cruzeiro do Sul** Brazil
52 A2 **Crystal Brook** Austr.
139 D3 **Crystal City** U.S.A.
140 B1 **Crystal Falls** U.S.A.
103 E2 **Csongrád** Hungary
120 B2 **Cuando** *r.* Angola/Zambia
120 A2 **Cuangar** Angola
118 B3 **Cuango** *r.* Angola/Dem. Rep. Congo
120 A1 **Cuanza** *r.* Angola
120 C2 **Cuatro Ciénegas** Mex.
144 B2 **Cuauhtémoc** Mex.
145 C3 **Cuautla** Mex.
146 B2 **Cuba** *country* West Indies
120 A2 **Cubal** Angola
120 B2 **Cubango** *r.* Angola/Namibia
150 A1 **Cúcuta** Col.
73 B3 **Cuddalore** India
73 B3 **Cuddapah** India
106 C1 **Cuéllar** Spain
120 A2 **Cuemba** Angola
150 A2 **Cuenca** Ecuador
107 C1 **Cuenca** Spain
107 C1 **Cuenca, Serranía de** *mts* Spain
145 C3 **Cuernavaca** Mex.
139 D3 **Cuero** U.S.A.
151 C3 **Cuiabá** Brazil
151 C3 **Cuiabá** *r.* Brazil
96 A2 **Cuillin Sound** *sea chan.* U.K.
120 A1 **Cuilo** *r.* Angola
120 B2 **Cuito** *r.* Angola
120 A2 **Cuito Cuanavale** Angola
60 B1 **Cukai** Malaysia
53 C3 **Culcairn** Austr.
53 C1 **Culgoa** *r.* Austr.
144 B2 **Culiacán** Mex.
64 A1 **Culion** *i.* Phil.
107 C2 **Cullera** Spain
142 C2 **Cullman** U.S.A.
97 C1 **Cullybackey** U.K.
151 C3 **Culuene** *r.* Brazil
150 B1 **Cumaná** Venez.
141 D3 **Cumberland** U.S.A.
140 C3 **Cumberland** *r.* U.S.A.
129 D2 **Cumberland Lake** Can.
127 G2 **Cumberland Peninsula** Can.
142 C1 **Cumberland Plateau** U.S.A.
127 G2 **Cumberland Sound** *sea chan.* Can.
96 C3 **Cumbernauld** U.K.
135 B3 **Cummings** U.S.A.
96 B3 **Cumnock** U.K.
144 B1 **Cumpas** Mex.
145 C3 **Cunduacán** Mex.
120 A2 **Cunene** *r.* Angola
108 A2 **Cuneo** Italy
53 C1 **Cunnamulla** Austr.
108 A1 **Cuorgnè** Italy
96 C2 **Cupar** U.K.
147 D3 **Curaçao** *terr.* West Indies
150 A2 **Curaray** *r.* Ecuador
153 A4 **Curicó** Chile
154 C3 **Curitiba** Brazil
52 A2 **Curnamona** Austr.

Currie

51 D3 Currie Austr.
51 E2 Curtis Island Austr.
151 C2 Curuá r. Brazil
60 B2 Curup Indon.
151 D2 Cururupu Brazil
155 D1 Curvelo Brazil
150 A3 Cusco Peru
139 D1 Cushing U.S.A.
134 D1 Cut Bank U.S.A.
75 C2 Cuttack India
101 D1 Cuxhaven Ger.
64 B1 Cuyo Islands Phil.
Cuzco Peru see Cusco
119 C3 Cyangugu Rwanda
111 B3 Cyclades is Greece
129 C3 Cypress Hills Can.
80 B2 Cyprus country Asia
102 C2 Czech Republic country Europe
103 D1 Czersk Pol.
103 D1 Częstochowa Pol.

D

Đa, Sông r. Vietnam see
Black River
69 D3 Daban China
114 A3 Dabola Guinea
Dacca Bangl. see Dhaka
102 C2 Dachau Ger.
74 A2 Dadu Pak.
64 B1 Daet Phil.
114 A3 Dagana Senegal
64 B1 Dagupan Phil.
73 B3 Dahanu India
69 D2 Da Hinggan Ling mts China
116 C3 Dahlak Archipelago is Eritrea
100 C2 Dahlen Ger.
78 B3 Dahm, Ramlat des. audi Arabia/Yemen
60 B2 Daik Indon.
106 C2 Daimiel Spain
51 C2 Dajarra Austr.
114 A3 Dakar Senegal
116 A2 Dākhilah, Wāḩat ad oasis Egypt
Dakhla Oasis Egypt see Dākhilah, Wāḩat ad
63 A3 Dakoank India
88 C3 Dakol'ka r. Belarus
Dakovica Kosovo see Gjakovë
109 C3 Đakovo Croatia
120 B2 Dala Angola
68 C2 Dalain Hob China
93 G3 Dalälven r. Sweden
111 C3 Dalaman Turkey
111 C3 Dalaman r. Turkey
69 C2 Dalandzadgad Mongolia
63 B2 Đa Lat Vietnam
74 A2 Dalbandin Pak.
96 C3 Dalbeattie U.K.
51 E2 Dalby Austr.
143 C1 Dale Hollow Lake U.S.A.
53 C3 Dalgety Austr.
131 C1 Dalhart U.S.A.
131 D2 Dalhousie Can.
62 B1 Dali China
70 C2 Dalian China
96 C3 Dalkeith U.K.
139 D2 Dallas U.S.A.
128 A2 Dall Island U.S.A.
109 C2 Dalmatia reg. Bos.-Herz./Croatia
66 C2 Dal'negorsk Rus. Fed.
66 B1 Dal'nerechensk Rus. Fed.
114 B4 Daloa Côte d'Ivoire

51 D2 Dalrymple, Mount Austr.
92 □A3 Dalsmynni Iceland
75 C2 Daltenganj India
143 D2 Dalton U.S.A.
60 B1 Daludalu Indon.
92 □B2 Dalvík Iceland
50 C1 Daly r. Austr.
51 C1 Daly Waters Austr.
74 B2 Daman India
80 B2 Damanhūr Egypt
59 C3 Damar i. Indon.
80 B2 Damascus Syria
115 D3 Damaturu Nigeria
76 B3 Damāvand, Qolleh-ye mt. Iran
81 D2 Dāmghān Iran
79 C2 Dammam Saudi Arabia
101 D1 Damme Ger.
75 B2 Damoh India
114 B4 Damongo Ghana
59 C3 Dampir, Selat sea chan. Indon.
75 C2 Dampoǀ Zangbo r. China
117 C3 Danakil reg. Africa
114 B4 Danané Côte d'Ivoire
63 B2 Đa Nẵng Vietnam
141 E2 Danbury U.S.A.
65 A1 Dandong China
146 B3 Dangriga Belize
70 B2 Dangshan China
89 F2 Danilov Rus. Fed.
89 E2 Danilovskaya Vozvyshennost' hills Rus. Fed.
70 B2 Danjiangkou China
89 E3 Dankov Rus. Fed.
146 B3 Danlí Hond.
101 E2 Dannenberg (Elbe) Ger.
54 C2 Dannevirke N.Z.
62 B2 Dan Sai Thai.
Dantu China see Zhenjiang
110 A1 Danube r. Europe
110 C1 Danube Delta Romania/Ukr.
140 B2 Danville IL U.S.A.
140 C3 Danville KY U.S.A.
141 D3 Danville VA U.S.A.
71 A4 Danzhou China
71 B3 Daoxian China
114 C3 Dapaong Togo
64 B2 Dapitan Phil.
68 C2 Da Qaidam China
69 E1 Daqing China
80 B2 Dar'ā Syria
79 C2 Dārāb Iran
81 D2 Dārān Iran
75 C2 Darbhanga India
119 D3 Dar es Salaam Tanz.
117 A3 Darfur reg. Sudan
74 B1 Dargai Pak.
54 B1 Dargaville N.Z.
53 C3 Dargo Austr.
69 D1 Darhan Mongolia
150 A1 Darién, Golfo del g. Col.
75 C2 Darjiling India
52 B2 Darling r. Austr.
53 C2 Darling Downs hills Austr.
50 A3 Darling Range hills Austr.
98 C1 Darlington U.K.
53 C2 Darlington Point Austr.
103 D1 Darłowo Pol.
101 D3 Darmstadt Ger.
115 E1 Darnah Libya
52 B2 Darnick Austr.
107 C1 Daroca Spain
99 D3 Dartford U.K.
99 A3 Dartmoor hills U.K.
131 D2 Dartmouth Can.
99 B3 Dartmouth U.K.
59 D3 Daru P.N.G.
50 C1 Darwin Austr.

74 A2 Dasht r. Pak.
76 B2 Daşoguz Turkm.
61 C1 Datadian Indon.
111 C3 Datça Turkey
70 B1 Datong China
64 B2 Datu Piang Phil.
74 B1 Daud Khel Pak.
88 C2 Daugava r. Latvia
88 C2 Daugavpils Latvia
100 C2 Daun Ger.
129 D2 Dauphin Can.
129 E2 Dauphin Lake Can.
73 B3 Davangere India
64 B2 Davao Phil.
64 B2 Davao Gulf Phil.
137 E2 Davenport U.S.A.
99 C2 Daventry U.K.
123 C2 Daveyton S. Africa
146 B4 David Panama
129 D2 Davidson Can.
126 E3 Davidson Lake Can.
135 B3 Davis U.S.A.
131 D1 Davis Inlet (abandoned) Can.
159 F3 Davis Sea Antarctica
160 P3 Davis Strait Can./Greenland
105 D2 Davos Switz.
78 A2 Dawmat al Jandal Saudi Arabia
79 C3 Dawqah Oman
126 B2 Dawson r. Can.
143 D2 Dawson U.S.A.
128 B2 Dawson Creek Can.
128 B2 Dawsons Landing Can.
68 C2 Dawu China
Dawukou China see Shizuishan
104 B3 Dax France
68 C2 Da Xueshan mts China
80 C2 Dayr az Zawr Syria
140 C3 Dayton U.S.A.
143 D3 Daytona Beach U.S.A.
70 A2 Dazhou China
122 B3 De Aar S. Africa
80 B2 Dead Sea salt l. Asia
71 B3 De'an China
152 B4 Deán Funes Arg.
128 B2 Dease Lake Can.
126 D2 Dease Strait Can.
135 C3 Death Valley depr. U.S.A.
104 C2 Deauville France
61 C1 Debak Sarawak Malaysia
109 D2 Debar Macedonia
103 E2 Debrecen Hungary
117 B3 Debre Markos Eth.
117 B3 Debre Tabor Eth.
117 B4 Debre Zeyit Eth.
142 C2 Decatur AL U.S.A.
140 B3 Decatur IL U.S.A.
73 B3 Deccan plat. India
102 C1 Děčín Czech Rep.
137 E2 Decorah U.S.A.
88 C2 Dedovichi Rus. Fed.
121 C2 Dedza Malawi
98 B2 Dee r. England/Wales U.K.
96 C2 Dee r. Scotland U.K.
53 D1 Deepwater Austr.
131 E2 Deer Lake Can.
134 D1 Deer Lodge U.S.A.
140 C2 Defiance U.S.A.
68 C2 Dêgê China
117 C4 Degeh Bur Eth.
102 C2 Deggendorf Ger.
91 E2 Degtevo Rus. Fed.
75 B1 Dehra Dun India
75 C2 Dehri India
69 E2 Dehui China
100 A2 Deinze Belgium
110 B1 Dej Romania

140 B2 De Kalb U.S.A.
78 A3 Dekemhare Eritrea
118 C3 Dekese Dem. Rep. Congo
135 C3 Delano U.S.A.
135 D3 Delano Peak U.S.A.
123 D2 Delareyville S. Africa
129 D2 Delaroche Lake Can.
140 C2 Delaware U.S.A.
141 D3 Delaware r. U.S.A.
141 D3 Delaware state U.S.A.
141 D3 Delaware Bay U.S.A.
53 C3 Delegate Austr.
105 D2 Delémont Switz.
100 B1 Delft Neth.
100 C1 Delfzijl Neth.
121 D2 Delgado, Cabo c. Moz.
69 C1 Delgerhaan Mongolia
75 B2 Delhi India
66 D2 Deli i. Indon.
126 A3 Déline Can.
101 F2 Delitzsch Ger.
107 C2 Dellys Alg.
101 D1 Delmenhorst Ger.
109 B1 Delnice Croatia
83 I1 De-Longa, Ostrova is Rus. Fed.
129 D3 Deloraine Can.
111 B3 Delphi tourist site Greece
139 C3 Del Rio U.S.A.
136 B3 Delta CO U.S.A.
135 D3 Delta UT U.S.A.
126 B2 Delta Junction U.S.A.
109 D3 Delvinë Albania
106 C1 Demanda, Sierra de la mts Spain
118 C3 Demba Dem. Rep. Congo
117 B4 Dembi Dolo Eth.
89 D2 Demidov Rus. Fed.
138 B2 Deming U.S.A.
111 B3 Demirci Turkey
110 C2 Demirköy Turkey
102 C1 Demmin Ger.
142 C2 Demopolis U.S.A.
60 B2 Dempo, Gunung vol. Indon.
89 D2 Demyansk Rus. Fed.
122 B3 De Naawte S. Africa
100 B1 Den Burg Neth.
100 B2 Dendermonde Belgium
70 A1 Dengkou China
70 B2 Dengzhou China
Den Haag Neth. see The Hague
50 A2 Denham Austr.
100 B1 Den Helder Neth.
52 B3 Deniliquin Austr.
134 C2 Denio U.S.A.
137 D2 Denison IA U.S.A.
139 D2 Denison TX U.S.A.
111 C3 Denizli Turkey
53 D2 Denman Austr.
50 A3 Denmark Austr.
93 E4 Denmark country Europe
160 Q3 Denmark Strait Greenland/Iceland
61 C2 Denpasar Indon.
139 D2 Denton U.S.A.
50 A3 D'Entrecasteaux, Point Austr.
136 B3 Denver U.S.A.
75 C2 Deogarh Orissa India
74 B2 Deogarh Rajasthan India
75 C2 Deoghar India
83 K2 Deputatskiy Rus. Fed.
68 C3 Dêqên China
142 B2 De Queen U.S.A.
74 A2 Dera Bugti Pak.
74 B1 Dera Ghazi Khan Pak.
74 B1 Dera Ismail Khan Pak.
87 D4 Derbent Rus. Fed.

50 B1 Derby Austr.
99 C2 Derby U.K.
99 D2 Dereham U.K.
97 B2 Derg, Lough l. Ireland
91 D1 Derhachi Ukr.
142 B2 De Ridder U.S.A.
91 D2 Derkul r. Rus. Fed./Ukr.
73 B1 Dêrub China
116 B3 Derudeb Sudan
122 B3 De Rust S. Africa
109 C2 Derventa Bos. Herz.
98 C2 Derwent r. U.K.
98 B1 Derwent Water l. U.K.
77 C1 Derzhavinsk Kazakh.
152 B2 Desaguadero r. Bol.
129 D2 Deschambault Lake Can.
134 B1 Deschutes r. U.S.A.
117 B3 Desē Eth.
153 B5 Deseado Arg.
153 B5 Deseado r. Arg.
137 E2 Des Moines U.S.A.
137 E2 Des Moines r. U.S.A.
91 C1 Desna r. Rus. Fed./Ukr.
89 D3 Desnogorsk Rus. Fed.
101 F2 Dessau Ger.
126 B2 Destruction Bay Can.
149 C3 Desventuradas, Islas is S. Pacific Ocean
128 C2 Detah Can.
101 D2 Detmold Ger.
140 D2 Detroit U.S.A.
137 D1 Detroit Lakes U.S.A.
100 B2 Deurne Neth.
110 B1 Deva Romania
100 C1 Deventer Neth.
96 C2 Deveron r. U.K.
103 D2 Devét skal h. Czech Rep.
137 D1 Devils Lake U.S.A.
128 A2 Devils Paw mt. U.S.A.
99 C3 Devizes U.K.
74 B2 Devli India
89 B2 Devnya Bulg.
128 C2 Devon Can.
126 E1 Devon Island Can.
51 D4 Devonport Austr.
74 B2 Dewas India
137 F3 Dexter U.S.A.
70 A2 Deyang China
59 D3 Deyong, Tanjung pt Indon.
81 C2 Dezful Iran
70 B2 Dezhou China
79 C2 Dhahran Saudi Arabia
75 C2 Dhaka Bangl.
78 B3 Dhamār Yemen
75 C2 Dhamtari India
75 C2 Dhanbad India
74 B2 Dhankuta Nepal
62 A1 Dharmanagar India
75 C2 Dharmjaygarh India
73 B3 Dharwad India
74 B2 Dhasa India
78 B3 Dhubāb Yemen
74 B2 Dhule India
144 A1 Diablo, Picacho del mt. Mex.
51 C2 Diamantina watercourse Austr.
151 D1 Diamantina Brazil
151 C3 Diamantina, Chapada plat. Brazil
151 C3 Diamantino Brazil
71 B3 Dianbai China
151 D3 Dianópolis Brazil
114 B4 Dianra Côte d'Ivoire
113 C4 Diapaga Burkina Faso
79 C2 Dibā al Ḩişn U.A.E.
118 C3 Dibaya Dem. Rep. Congo
62 A1 Dibrugarh India
136 C1 Dickinson U.S.A.

142 C1 Dickson U.S.A.
Dicle r. Turkey see Tigris
105 D3 Die France
129 D2 Diefenbaker, Lake Can.
114 B3 Diéma Mali
62 B2 Diên Châu Vietnam
101 D1 Diepholz Ger.
104 C2 Dieppe France
115 D3 Diffa Niger
131 D2 Digby Can.
105 D3 Digne-les-Bains France
105 C2 Digoin France
64 B2 Digos Phil.
59 D3 Digul r. Indon.
Dihang r. China/India see Brahmaputra
Dihang r. China/India see Yarlung Zangbo
105 C2 Dijon France
117 C3 Dikhil Djibouti
111 C3 Dikili Turkey
100 A2 Diksmuide Belgium
115 D3 Dikwa Nigeria
117 B4 Dila Eth.
74 A1 Dilārām Afgh.
59 C3 Dili East Timor
101 D2 Dillenburg Ger.
134 D1 Dillon U.S.A.
118 C4 Dilolo Dem. Rep. Congo
62 A1 Dimapur India
72 D2 Dimapur India
72 D2 Dimapur India
Dimashq Syria see Damascus
52 B2 Dimboola Austr.
110 C2 Dimitrovgrad Bulg.
87 D3 Dimitrovgrad Rus. Fed.
64 B1 Dinagat i. Phil.
104 B2 Dinan France
100 B2 Dinant Belgium
111 D3 Dinar Turkey
81 C2 Dīnār, Kūh-e mt. Iran
73 B3 Dindigul India
123 D1 Dindiza Moz.
101 E2 Dingelstädt Ger.
75 C2 Dinggyê China
97 A2 Dingle Ireland
96 B2 Dingle Bay Ireland
70 A2 Dingxi China
154 B3 Dionísio Cerqueira Brazil
114 A3 Diourbel Senegal
74 B1 Dir Pak.
51 D1 Direction, Cape Austr.
117 C4 Dirē Dawa Eth.
120 B2 Dirico Angola
115 D1 Dirj Libya
50 A2 Dirk Hartog Island Austr.
53 C1 Dirranbandi Austr.
78 B3 Dirs Saudi Arabia
53 C1 Disappointment, Lake imp. l. Austr.
52 B3 Discovery Bay Austr.
143 C1 Dismal Swamp U.S.A.
99 D2 Diss U.K.
108 B3 Dittaino r. Sicilia Italy
74 B2 Diu India
155 D2 Divinópolis Brazil
87 D4 Divnoye Rus. Fed.
114 B4 Divo Côte d'Ivoire
80 B2 Divriği Turkey
140 B2 Dixon U.S.A.
128 A2 Dixon Entrance sea chan. Can./U.S.A.
80 C2 Diyarbakır Turkey
74 A2 Diz Pak.
115 D2 Djado Niger
115 D2 Djado, Plateau du Niger
118 B3 Djambala Congo

115 C2 Djanet Alg.
115 C1 Djelfa Alg.
119 C2 Djéma C.A.R.
114 B3 Djenné Mali
114 B3 Djibo Burkina Faso
117 C3 Djibouti *country* Africa
117 C3 Djibouti Djibouti
114 C4 Djougou Benin
□□ C3 Djúpivogur Iceland
91 E1 Dmitriyevka Rus. Fed.
89 E3 Dmitriyev-L'govskiy Rus. Fed.
89 E2 Dmitrov Rus. Fed.
Dnepr *r.* Ukr. *see* Dnieper
91 C2 Dnieper *r.* Ukr.
90 B2 Dniester *r.* Ukr.
Dnipro *r.* Ukr. *see* Dnieper
91 C2 Dniprodzerzhyns'k Ukr.
91 D2 Dnipropetrovs'k Ukr.
91 C2 Dniprorudne Ukr.
Dnister *r.* Ukr. *see* Dniester
88 C2 Dno Rus. Fed.
115 D4 Doba Chad
88 B2 Dobele Latvia
101 F2 Döbeln Ger.
59 C3 Doberai, Jazirah *pen.* Indon.
59 C3 Dobo Indon.
109 C2 Doboj Bos.-Herz.
110 C2 Dobrich Bulg.
89 F3 Dobrinka Rus. Fed.
89 E3 Dobroye Rus. Fed.
89 D3 Dobrush Belarus
155 E1 Doce *r.* Brazil
145 B2 Doctor Arroyo Mex.
144 B2 Doctor Belisario Domínguez Mex.
111 C3 Dodecanese *is* Greece
Dodekanisos *is* Greece *see* Dodecanese
136 C3 Dodge City U.S.A.
119 D3 Dodoma Tanz.
100 C2 Doetinchem Neth.
59 C3 Dofa Indon.
75 C2 Dogai Coring *salt l.* China
128 B2 Dog Creek Can.
67 B3 Dōgo *i.* Japan
115 C3 Dogondoutchi Niger
81 C2 Doğubeyazıt Turkey
79 C2 Doha Qatar
62 A2 Doi Saket Thai.
100 B1 Dokkum Neth.
88 C3 Dokshytsy Belarus
91 D2 Dokuchayevs'k Ukr.
131 C2 Dolbeau-Mistassini Can.
104 B2 Dol-de-Bretagne France
105 D2 Dole France
99 B2 Dolgellau U.K.
89 E3 Dolgorukovo Rus. Fed.
89 E3 Dolgoye Rus. Fed.
Dolisie Congo *see* Loubomo
59 D3 Dolok, Pulau *i.* Indon.
108 B1 Dolomites *mts* Italy
117 C4 Dolo Odo Eth.
126 D2 Dolphin and Union Strait Can.
90 A2 Dolyna Ukr.
102 C2 Domažlice Czech Rep.
93 E3 Dombås Norway
103 D2 Dombóvár Hungary
128 B2 Dome Creek Can.
147 D3 Dominica *country* West Indies
147 C3 Dominican Republic *country* West Indies
89 E2 Domodedovo Rus. Fed.
111 B3 Domokos Greece
61 C2 Dompu Indon.
89 E3 Don *r.* Rus. Fed.
96 C2 Don *r.* U.K.
97 D1 Donaghadee U.K.

52 B3 Donald Austr.
Donau *r.* Austria/Ger. *see* Danube
102 C2 Donauwörth Ger.
106 B2 Don Benito Spain
98 C2 Doncaster U.K.
120 A1 Dondo Angola
121 C2 Dondo Moz.
73 C4 Dondra Head Sri Lanka
97 B1 Donegal Ireland
97 B1 Donegal Bay Ireland
91 D2 Donets'k Ukr.
91 D2 Donets'kyy Kryazh *hills* Rus. Fed./Ukr.
50 A2 Dongara Austr.
62 B1 Dongchuan China
71 A4 Dongfang China
66 B1 Dongfanghong China
58 B3 Donggala Indon.
65 A2 Donggang China
71 B3 Dongguan China
62 B2 Đông Ha Vietnam
Dong Hai *sea* N. Pacific Ocean *see* East China Sea
62 B2 Đông Hơi Vietnam
118 B2 Dongou Congo
71 B3 Dongshan China
70 C2 Dongtai China
71 B3 Dongting Hu *l.* China
Dong Ujimqin Qi China *see* Uliastai
70 B2 Dongying China
54 B1 Donnellys Crossing N.Z.
Donostia Spain *see* San Sebastián
99 B3 Dorchester U.K.
122 A1 Dordabis Namibia
104 B2 Dordogne *r.* France
100 B2 Dordrecht Neth.
123 C3 Dordrecht S. Africa
129 D2 Doré Lake Can.
101 D1 Dörfmark Ger.
114 B3 Dori Burkina Faso
122 A3 Doring *r.* S. Africa
96 B2 Dornoch U.K.
96 B2 Dornoch Firth *est.* U.K.
89 D3 Dorogobuzh Rus. Fed.
90 B2 Dorohoi Romania
68 C1 Döröö Nuur *salt l.* Mongolia
92 G3 Dorotea Sweden
50 A2 Dorre Island Austr.
53 D2 Dorrigo Austr.
100 C2 Dortmund Ger.
100 C2 Dortmund-Ems-Kanal *canal* Ger.
153 B5 Dos Bahías, Cabo *c.* Arg.
101 F1 Dosse *r.* Ger.
114 C3 Dosso Niger
143 C2 Dothan U.S.A.
101 D1 Dötlingen Ger.
105 C1 Douai France
118 A2 Douala Cameroon
104 B2 Douarnenez France
114 B3 Douentza Mali
98 A1 Douglas Isle of Man
122 B2 Douglas S. Africa
128 A2 Douglas AK U.S.A.
138 B2 Douglas AZ U.S.A.
143 D2 Douglas GA U.S.A.
136 B2 Douglas WY U.S.A.
71 C3 Douliu Taiwan
104 C1 Doullens France
154 B1 Dourada, Serra *hills* Brazil
154 B2 Dourados Brazil
154 B2 Dourados, Serra dos *hills* Brazil
106 B1 Douro *r.* Port.

99 D3 Dover U.K.
141 D3 Dover U.S.A.
95 D3 Dover, Strait of France/U.K.
141 F1 Dover-Foxcroft U.S.A.
79 C2 Dowlatābād *Būshehr* Iran
79 C2 Dowlatābād *Kermān* Iran
97 D1 Downpatrick U.K.
77 C3 Dowshī Afgh.
67 B3 Dōzen *is* Japan
130 C2 Dozois, Réservoir *resr* Can.
114 B2 Drâa, Hamada du *plat.* Alg.
154 B2 Dracena Brazil
100 C1 Drachten Neth.
110 B2 Drăgănești-Olt Romania
110 B2 Drăgășani Romania
88 C3 Drahichyn Belarus
123 C2 Drakensberg *mts* Lesotho/S. Africa
123 C2 Drakensberg *mts* S. Africa
158 B8 Drake Passage S. Atlantic Ocean
111 B2 Drama Greece
93 F4 Drammen Norway
109 C1 Drava *r.* Europe
128 C2 Drayton Valley Can.
101 D2 Dreieich Ger.
102 C1 Dresden Ger.
104 C2 Dreux France
100 B1 Driemond Neth.
109 C2 Drina *r.* Bosnia-Herzegovina/Serbia
109 C2 Drniš Croatia
110 B2 Drobeta-Turnu Severin Romania
101 D1 Drochtersen Ger.
97 C2 Drogheda Ireland
90 A2 Drohobych Ukr.
97 C1 Dromore U.K.
74 B1 Drosh Pak.
53 C3 Drouin Austr.
128 C2 Drumheller Can.
140 C1 Drummond Island U.S.A.
131 C2 Drummondville Can.
88 B3 Druskininkai Lith.
91 D2 Druzhkivka Ukr.
88 C2 Druzhnaya Gorka Rus. Fed.
130 A2 Dryden Can.
50 B1 Drysdale *r.* Austr.
78 A2 Ḏuḇā Saudi Arabia
79 C2 Dubai U.A.E.
129 D1 Dubawnt Lake Can.
Dubayy U.A.E. *see* Dubai
78 A2 Dubbagh, Jabal ad *mt.* Saudi Arabia
53 C2 Dubbo Austr.
97 C2 Dublin Ireland
143 D2 Dublin U.S.A.
90 B1 Dubno Ukr.
141 D2 Du Bois U.S.A.
114 A4 Dubréka Guinea
109 C2 Dubrovnik Croatia
90 B1 Dubrovytsya Ukr.
89 D3 Dubrowna Belarus
137 E2 Dubuque U.S.A.
129 D2 Duck Bay Can.
101 E2 Duderstadt Ger.
82 G2 Dudinka Rus. Fed.
99 B2 Dudley U.K.
106 B1 Duero *r.* Spain
131 C1 Duffreboy, Lac *l.* Can.
96 C2 Dufftown U.K.
109 C2 Dugi Rat Croatia
100 C2 Duisburg Ger.
123 C3 Dukathole S. Africa
79 C2 Dukhān Qatar
89 D2 Dukhovshchina Rus. Fed.
Dukou China *see* Panzhihua

88 C2 Dükstas Lith.
68 C2 Dulan China
152 B4 Dulce *r.* Arg.
100 C2 Dülmen Ger.
110 C2 Dulovo Bulg.
137 E1 Duluth U.S.A.
61 D3 Dumaguete Phil.
60 B1 Dumai Indon.
64 B1 Dumaran *i.* Phil.
142 B2 Dumas AR U.S.A.
139 C1 Dumas TX U.S.A.
96 B3 Dumbarton U.K.
103 D2 Ďumbier *mt.* Slovakia
96 C3 Dumfries U.K.
55 J3 Dumont d'Urville Sea Antarctica
116 B1 Dumyât Egypt
Duna *r.* Hungary see Danube
Dunaj *r.* Slovakia see Danube
102 D2 Dunakeszi Hungary
Dunărea *r.* Romania see Danube
103 D2 Dunaújváros Hungary
Dunav *r.* Yugo. see Danube
90 B2 Dunayivtsi Ukr.
96 C2 Dunbar U.K.
96 C1 Dunbeath U.K.
128 B3 Duncan Can.
139 D2 Duncan U.S.A.
96 C1 Duncansby Head U.K.
97 C1 Dundalk Ireland
97 C2 Dundalk Bay Ireland
127 G1 Dundas Greenland
123 D2 Dundas S. Africa
96 C2 Dundee U.K.
97 D1 Dundrum Bay U.K.
54 B3 Dunedin N.Z.
96 C2 Dunfermline U.K.
97 C1 Dungannon U.K.
74 B2 Dungarpur India
97 C2 Dungarvan Ireland
99 D3 Dungeness *hd* U.K.
97 C1 Dungiven U.K.
53 C2 Dungog Austr.
119 C2 Dungu Dem. Rep. Congo
60 B1 Dungun Malaysia
116 B2 Dungunab Sudan
69 E2 Dunhua China
68 C2 Dunhuang China
Dunkerque France see Dunkirk
104 C1 Dunkirk France
141 D2 Dunkirk U.S.A.
97 C2 Dún Laoghaire Ireland
97 B1 Dunmurry U.K.
96 C1 Dunnet Head U.K.
96 C3 Duns U.K.
99 C3 Dunstable U.K.
110 B2 Dupnitsa Bulg.
136 C1 Dupree U.S.A.
50 B1 Durack *r.* Austr.
144 B2 Durango Mex.
106 C1 Durango Spain
136 B3 Durango U.S.A.
139 D2 Durant U.S.A.
153 C4 Durazno Uru.
123 D2 Durban S. Africa
104 C3 Durban-Corbières France
122 A3 Durbanville S. Africa
100 B2 Durbuy Belgium
100 C2 Düren Ger.
73 C2 Durg India
98 C1 Durham U.K.
143 E1 Durham U.S.A.
60 B1 Duri Indon.
109 C2 Durmitor *mt.* Montenegro
96 B1 Durness U.K.

109 C2 Durrës Albania
97 A3 Dursey Island Ireland
111 C3 Dursunbey Turkey
59 D3 D'Urville, Tanjung *pt* Indon.
54 B2 D'Urville Island N.Z.
71 A3 Dushan China
77 C3 Dushanbe Tajik.
100 C2 Düsseldorf Ger.
71 A3 Duyun China
91 D2 Dvorichna Ukr.
74 A2 Dwarka India
123 C1 Dwarsberg S. Africa
134 C1 Dworshak Reservoir U.S.A.
89 D3 Dyat'kovo Rus. Fed.
96 C2 Dyce U.K.
127 G2 Dyer, Cape Can.
142 C1 Dyersburg U.S.A.
103 D2 Dyje *r.* Austria/Czech Rep.
103 D1 Dylewska Góra *h.* Pol.
91 D2 Dymytrov Ukr.
123 C3 Dyoki S. Africa
87 E3 Dzamin Üüd Mongolia
69 D2 Dzamin Üüd Mongolia
120 D2 Dzaoudzi Mayotte
82 C1 Dzhambul Kazakh. see Taraz
91 C2 Dzhankoy Ukr.
91 D3 Dzhubga Rus. Fed.
83 K3 Dzhugdzhur, Khrebet *mts* Rus. Fed.
103 E1 Działdowo Pol.
69 D1 Dzuunmod Mongolia
88 C3 Dzyarzhynsk Belarus
88 C3 Dzyatlavichy Belarus

E

131 E1 Eagle *r.* Can.
134 C1 Eagle Cap *mt.* U.S.A.
130 A2 Eagle Lake Can.
134 B2 Eagle Lake U.S.A.
139 C3 Eagle Pass U.S.A.
126 B2 Eagle Plain Can.
130 A1 Ear Falls Can.
99 D3 Eastbourne U.K.
156 C3 East China Sea N. Pacific Ocean
54 B1 East Coast Bays N.Z.
129 D3 Eastend Can.
123 C3 Eastern Cape *prov.* S. Africa
116 B2 Eastern Desert Egypt
73 B3 Eastern Ghats *mts* India
129 E2 Easterville Can.
153 C6 East Falkland *i.* Falkland Is.
100 C1 East Frisian Islands Ger.
96 B3 East Kilbride U.K.
99 C3 Eastleigh U.K.
140 C2 East Liverpool U.S.A.
123 C3 East London S. Africa
130 C1 Eastmain Can.
130 C1 Eastmain *r.* Can.
143 D2 Eastman U.S.A.
140 A3 East St Louis U.S.A.
East Sea N. Pacific Ocean see Japan, Sea of
83 K2 East Siberian Sea Rus. Fed.
59 C3 East Timor *country* Asia
140 A2 Eau Claire U.S.A.
130 C1 Eau Claire, Lac à l' *l.* Can.
59 D2 Eauripik *atoll* Micronesia
145 C2 Ebano Mex.
99 B3 Ebbw Vale U.K.
102 C1 Eberswalde-Finow Ger.
109 C2 Eboli Italy
118 B2 Ebolowa Cameroon
107 D1 Ebro *r.* Spain

144 A2 Echeverria, Pico *mt.* Mex.
129 E2 Echoing *r.* Can.
100 C3 Echternach Lux.
52 B3 Echuca Austr.
106 B2 Écija Spain
102 B1 Eckernförde Ger.
127 F2 Eclipse Sound *sea chan.* Can.
150 A2 Ecuador *country* S. America
116 C3 Ed Eritrea
117 A3 Ed Da'ein Sudan
117 B3 Ed Damazin Sudan
116 B3 Ed Damer Sudan
116 B3 Ed Debba Sudan
116 B3 Ed Dueim Sudan
51 D4 Eddystone Point Austr.
100 B1 Ede Neth.
118 B2 Edéa Cameroon
154 C1 Edéia Brazil
53 C3 Eden Austr.
98 B1 Eden *r.* U.K.
123 C2 Edenburg S. Africa
97 C2 Edenderry Ireland
52 A3 Edenhope Austr.
111 B3 Edessa Greece
82 C1 Edgeøya *i.* Svalbard
139 D3 Edinburg U.S.A.
96 C3 Edinburgh U.K.
110 C2 Edirne Turkey
128 C2 Edmonton Can.
131 D2 Edmundston Can.
111 C3 Edremit Turkey
111 C3 Edremit Körfezi *b.* Turkey
128 C2 Edson Can.
119 C3 Edward, Lake Dem. Rep. Congo/Uganda
139 C2 Edwards Plateau TX U.S.A.
100 C1 Eenrum Neth.
48 F4 Éfaté *i.* Vanuatu
140 B3 Effingham U.S.A.
135 C3 Egan Range *mts* U.S.A.
103 E2 Eger Hungary
93 E4 Egersund Norway
92 □C2 Egilsstaðir Iceland
80 B2 Eğirdir Turkey
80 B2 Eğirdir Gölü *l.* Turkey
104 C2 Égletons France
83 M2 Egvekinot Rus. Fed.
116 A2 Egypt *country* Africa
68 C2 Ehen Hudag China
100 C1 Eibergen Neth.
100 C2 Eifel *hills* Ger.
96 A2 Eigg *i.* U.K.
73 B4 Eight Degree Channel India/Maldives
50 B1 Eighty Mile Beach Austr.
80 B3 Eilat Israel
101 F2 Eilenburg Ger.
101 D2 Einbeck Ger.
100 B2 Eindhoven Neth.
150 B2 Eirunepé Brazil
120 B2 Eiseb *watercourse* Namibia
101 E2 Eisenach Ger.
102 C1 Eisenhüttenstadt Ger.
103 D2 Eisenstadt Austria
101 E2 Eisleben Lutherstadt Ger.
Eivissa Spain see Ibiza
107 C2 Eivissa *i.* Spain see Ibiza
107 C2 Ejea de los Caballeros Spain
121 □D3 Ejeda Madag.
Ejin Qi China see Dalain Hob
93 H4 Ekenäs Fin.
92 J2 Ekostrovskaya Imandra, Ozero *i.* Rus. Fed.
93 F4 Eksjö Sweden
122 A2 Eksteenfontein S. Africa
130 B1 Ekwan *r.* Can.
62 A2 Ela Myanmar

123 C2 Elandsdoorn S. Africa
111 B3 Elassona Greece
80 B2 Elazığ Turkey
108 B2 Elba, Isola d' i. Italy
150 A1 El Banco Col.
138 B2 El Barreal salt l. Mex.
144 B1 El Barreal salt l. Mex.
109 D2 Elbasan Albania
150 B1 El Baúl Venez.
114 C1 El Bayadh Alg.
101 D1 Elbe r. Ger.
136 B3 Elbert, Mount U.S.A.
143 D2 Elberton U.S.A.
104 C2 Elbeuf France
80 B2 Elbistan Turkey
103 D1 Elblag Pol.
87 D4 El'brus mt. Rus. Fed.
81 C2 Elburz Mountains Iran
150 B1 El Callao Venez.
139 D2 El Campo U.S.A.
135 C4 El Centro U.S.A.
152 B2 El Cerro Bol.
107 C2 Elche-Elx Spain
107 C2 Elda Spain
137 E3 Eldon U.S.A.
144 B2 El Dorado Mex.
142 B2 El Dorado AR U.S.A.
137 D3 El Dorado KS U.S.A.
114 B2 El Eglab plat. Alg.
106 C2 El Ejido Spain
89 E2 Elektrostal' Rus. Fed.
150 A2 El Encanto Col.
146 C2 Eleuthera i. Bahamas
117 A3 El Fasher Sudan
144 B2 El Fuerte Mex.
117 A3 El Geneina Sudan
116 B3 El Geteina Sudan
96 C2 Elgin U.K.
138 A2 Elgin U.S.A.
115 C1 El Goléa Alg.
144 A1 El Golfo de Santa Clara Mex.
119 D2 Elgon, Mount Kenya/Uganda
114 A2 El Ḥammâmi reg. Maur.
114 A2 El Hierro i. Islas Canarias
145 C2 El Higo Mex.
114 C2 El Homr Alg.
87 D4 Elista Rus. Fed.
141 E2 Elizabeth U.S.A.
143 E1 Elizabeth City U.S.A.
140 B3 Elizabethtown U.S.A.
114 B1 El Jadida Morocco
103 E1 Ełk Pol.
139 D1 Elk City U.S.A.
128 C2 Elkford Can.
140 B2 Elkhart U.S.A.
         El Khartum Sudan see
         Khartoum
110 C2 Elkhovo Bulg.
140 D3 Elkins U.S.A.
128 C3 Elko Can.
134 C2 Elko U.S.A.
129 C2 Elk Point Can.
126 E1 Ellef Ringnes Island Can.
137 D3 Ellendale U.S.A.
134 B1 Ellensburg U.S.A.
54 B2 Ellesmere, Lake N.Z.
127 F1 Ellesmere Island Can.
98 B2 Ellesmere Port U.K.
126 E2 Ellice r. Can.
         Ellice Islands country S. Pacific
         Ocean see Tuvalu
123 C3 Elliotdale S. Africa
96 C2 Ellon U.K.
141 F2 Ellsworth U.S.A.
55 O2 Ellsworth Mountains
         Antarctica
111 C3 Elmalı Turkey

115 C1 El Meghaïer Alg.
141 D2 Elmira U.S.A.
107 C2 El Moral Spain
101 D1 Elmshorn Ger.
117 A3 El Muglad Sudan
64 A1 El Nido Phil.
117 B3 El Obeid Sudan
144 B2 El Oro Mex.
115 C1 El Oued Alg.
138 A2 Eloy U.S.A.
138 B2 El Paso U.S.A.
144 B1 El Porvenir Mex.
107 D1 El Prat de Llobregat Spain
139 D1 El Reno U.S.A.
145 B2 El Salado Mex.
144 B2 El Salto Mex.
146 B3 El Salvador country Central
         America
145 B2 El Salvador Mex.
138 B3 El Sauz Mex.
144 A1 El Socorro Mex.
145 C2 El Temascal Mex.
150 B1 El Tigre Venez.
147 D4 El Tocuyo Venez.
88 C2 Elva Estonia
106 B2 Elvas Port.
93 F3 Elverum Norway
119 E2 El Wak Kenya
99 D2 Ely U.K.
137 E1 Ely MN U.S.A.
135 D3 Ely NV U.S.A.
123 C2 eMalahleni S. Africa
81 D2 Emāmrūd Iran
93 G4 Emån r. Sweden
123 D2 eManzamtoti S. Africa
76 B2 Emba Kazakh.
123 C2 Embalenhle S. Africa
154 C1 Emborcação, Represa de resr
         Brazil
119 D3 Embu Kenya
100 C1 Emden Ger.
51 D2 Emerald Austr.
129 E3 Emerson Can.
111 C3 Emet Turkey
123 D2 eMgwenya S. Africa
115 D3 Emi Koussi mt. Chad
110 C2 Emine, Nos pt Bulg.
80 B2 Emirdağ Turkey
123 D2 eMjindini S. Africa
88 B2 Emmaste Estonia
100 B1 Emmeloord Neth.
100 C2 Emmelshausen Ger.
100 C1 Emmen Neth.
123 D2 eMondlo S. Africa
139 C3 Emory Peak U.S.A.
144 A2 Empalme Mex.
123 D2 Empangeni S. Africa
108 B2 Empoli Italy
137 D3 Emporia KS U.S.A.
141 D3 Emporia VA U.S.A.
         Empty Quarter des. Saudi
         Arabia see Rub' al Khālī
100 C1 Ems r. Ger.
100 C1 Emsdetten Ger.
123 C2 eMzinoni S. Africa
59 D3 Enarotali Indon.
144 B2 Encarnación Mex.
152 C3 Encarnación Para.
155 D1 Encruzilhada Brazil
58 C3 Ende Indon.
126 A2 Endicott Mountains U.S.A.
91 C2 Enerhodar Ukr.
87 D3 Engel's Rus. Fed.
60 B2 Enggano i. Indon.
98 C2 England admin. div. U.K.
130 A1 English r. Can.
95 C4 English Channel France/U.K.

139 D1 Enid U.S.A.
100 B1 Enkhuizen Neth.
93 G4 Enköping Sweden
108 B3 Enna Sicilia Italy
129 D1 Ennadai Lake Can.
117 A3 En Nahud Sudan
115 E3 Ennedi, Massif mts Chad
53 C1 Enngonia Austr.
97 B2 Ennis Ireland
139 D2 Ennis U.S.A.
97 C2 Enniscorthy Ireland
97 C1 Enniskillen U.K.
97 B2 Ennistymon Ireland
102 C2 Enns r. Austria
92 H2 Enontekiö Fin.
53 C3 Ensay Austr.
100 C1 Enschede Neth.
144 A1 Ensenada Mex.
70 A2 Enshi China
128 C1 Enterprise Can.
142 C2 Enterprise AL U.S.A.
134 C1 Enterprise OR U.S.A.
152 B3 Entre Ríos Bol.
106 B2 Entroncamento Port.
115 C4 Enugu Nigeria
150 A2 Envira Brazil
135 D3 Ephraim U.S.A.
134 C1 Ephrata U.S.A.
105 D2 Épinal France
99 C3 Epsom U.K.
118 A2 Equatorial Guinea country
         Africa
101 F3 Erbendorf Ger.
100 C3 Erbeskopf h. Ger.
81 C2 Erciş Turkey
65 B1 Erdao Jiang r. China
111 C2 Erdek Turkey
80 B2 Erdemli Turkey
155 D2 Erechim Brazil
69 D1 Ereentsav Mongolia
80 B2 Ereğli Turkey
80 B1 Ereğli Zonguldak Turkey
69 D2 Erenhot China
         Erevan Armenia see Yerevan
101 E2 Erfurt Ger.
80 B2 Ergani Turkey
114 B2 'Erg Chech des. Alg./Mali
111 C2 Ergene r. Turkey
140 C2 Erie U.S.A.
140 C2 Erie, Lake Can./U.S.A.
66 D2 Erimo-misaki c. Japan
116 B3 Eritrea country Africa
101 E3 Erlangen Ger.
50 C2 Erldunda Austr.
123 C2 Ermelo S. Africa
80 B2 Ermenek Turkey
111 B3 Ermoupoli Greece
73 B4 Ernakulam India
73 B3 Erode India
100 B2 Erp Neth.
114 B1 Er Rachidia Morocco
117 B3 Er Rahad Sudan
97 B1 Errigal h. Ireland
97 A1 Erris Head Ireland
109 D2 Ersekë Albania
91 E1 Ertil' Rus. Fed.
101 D2 Erwitte Ger.
102 C1 Erzgebirge mts
         Czech Rep./Ger.
80 B2 Erzincan Turkey
81 C2 Erzurum Turkey
93 E4 Esbjerg Denmark
135 D3 Escalante U.S.A.
144 B2 Escalón Mex.
140 B1 Escanaba U.S.A.
145 C3 Escárcega Mex.
107 C1 Escatrón Spain

100 A2	Escaut r. Belgium/France	
101 E1	Eschede Ger.	
100 B3	Esch-sur-Alzette Lux.	
101 E2	Eschwege Ger.	
100 C2	Eschweiler Ger.	
135 C4	Escondido U.S.A.	
144 B2	Escuinapa Mex.	
111 C3	Eşen Turkey	
81 D2	Eşfahān Iran	
123 D2	eSikhaleni S. Africa	
98 B1	Esk r. U.K.	
131 D1	Esker Can.	
92 □C2	Eskifjörður Iceland	
93 G4	Eskilstuna Sweden	
	Eskimo Point Can. see Arviat	
80 B2	Eskişehir Turkey	
81 C2	Eslāmābād-e Gharb Iran	
111 C3	Esler Dağı mt. Turkey	
111 C3	Eşme Turkey	
150 A1	Esmeraldas Ecuador	
79 D2	Espakeh Iran	
104 C3	Espalion France	
130 B2	Espanola Can.	
138 B1	Espanola U.S.A.	
50 B3	Esperance Austr.	
144 B2	Esperanza Mex.	
106 B2	Espichel, Cabo c. Port.	
155 D1	Espinhaço, Serra de mts Brazil	
151 D3	Espinosa Brazil	
48 F4	Espíritu Santo i. Vanuatu	
144 A2	Espíritu Santo, Isla i. Mex.	
92 H3	Espoo Fin.	
153 A5	Esquel Arg.	
114 B1	Essaouira Morocco	
114 A2	Es Semara Western Sahara	
100 C2	Essen Ger.	
150 C1	Essequibo r. Guyana	
83 L3	Esso Rus. Fed.	
79 C2	Eştahbān Iran	
151 D3	Estância Brazil	
123 C2	Estcourt S. Africa	
107 C1	Estella Spain	
106 C1	Estepona Spain	
106 C1	Esteras de Medinaceli Spain	
129 D2	Esterhazy Can.	
152 B3	Esteros Para.	
136 B2	Estes Park U.S.A.	
129 D3	Estevan Can.	
137 E2	Estherville U.S.A.	
129 D2	Eston Can.	
88 C2	Estonia country Europe	
106 B2	Estrela, Serra da mts Port.	
106 B2	Estremoz Port.	
52 M3	Etadunna Austr.	
104 C2	Étampes France	
104 C1	Étaples France	
88 B4	Etawah India	
123 D2	Ethandakukhanya S. Africa	
117 B4	Ethiopia country Africa	
109 C3	Etna, Mount vol. Sicilia Italy	
128 A2	Etolin Island U.S.A.	
120 A2	Etosha Pan salt pan Namibia	
100 C3	Ettelbruck Lux.	
100 B2	Etten-Leur Neth.	
107 C1	Etxarri-Aranatz Spain	
99 D3	Eu France	
53 C2	Euabalong Austr.	
	Euboea i. Greece see Evvoia	
50 B3	Eucla Austr.	
143 C2	Eufaula U.S.A.	
139 D2	Eufaula Lake resr U.S.A.	
134 B2	Eugene U.S.A.	
144 A2	Eugenia, Punta pt Mex.	
53 C1	Eulo Austr.	
53 C2	Eumungerie Austr.	
142 C2	Eunice U.S.A.	
80 C2	Euphrates r. Asia	
134 B2	Eureka CA U.S.A.	
134 C1	Eureka MT U.S.A.	
135 C1	Eureka NV U.S.A.	
52 B2	Euriowie Austr.	
53 C2	Euroa Austr.	
106 B2	Europa Point Gibraltar	
128 B2	Eutsuk Lake Can.	
130 C1	Evans, Lac l. Can.	
53 D1	Evans Head Austr.	
127 F2	Evans Strait Can.	
136 A2	Evanston U.S.A.	
140 B3	Evansville U.S.A.	
123 C2	Evaton S. Africa	
79 C2	Evaz Iran	
83 L2	Evensk Rus. Fed.	
50 C2	Everard Range hills Austr.	
75 C2	Everest, Mount China/Nepal	
134 B1	Everett U.S.A.	
100 A2	Evergem Belgium	
143 D3	Everglades swamp U.S.A.	
118 B2	Evinayong Equat. Guinea	
93 E4	Evje Norway	
106 B2	Évora Port.	
104 C2	Évreux France	
111 C2	Evros r. Greece/Turkey	
111 B3	Evrotas r. Greece	
80 B2	Evrychou Cyprus	
111 B3	Evvoia i. Greece	
119 E2	Ewaso Ngiro r. Kenya	
152 B2	Exaltación Bol.	
99 B3	Exe r. U.K.	
99 B3	Exeter U.K.	
99 B3	Exmoor hills U.K.	
99 B3	Exmouth U.K.	
50 A2	Exmouth Gulf Austr.	
146 C2	Exuma Cays is Bahamas	
117 C4	Eyl Somalia	
52 A1	Eyre (North), Lake imp. l. Austr.	
51 C3	Eyre Peninsula Austr.	
94 B1	Eysturoy i. Faroe Is	
123 D2	Ezakheni S. Africa	
123 C2	Ezenzeleni S. Africa	
70 B2	Ezhou China	
86 E2	Ezhva Rus. Fed.	
111 C3	Ezine Turkey	

F

138 B2	Fabens U.S.A.	
108 B2	Fabriano Italy	
115 D3	Fachi Niger	
114 C3	Fada-N'Gourma Burkina Faso	
108 B2	Faenza Italy	
59 C3	Fafanlap Indon.	
110 B1	Făgăraş Romania	
49 G3	Fagatogo American Samoa	
93 E3	Fagernes Norway	
93 G4	Fagersta Sweden	
153 B6	Fagnano, Lago l. Arg./Chile	
114 B3	Faguibine, Lac l. Mali	
92 □B3	Fagurhólsmýri Iceland	
126 B2	Fairbanks U.S.A.	
137 D2	Fairbury U.S.A.	
135 B3	Fairfield U.S.A.	
96 □	Fair Isle i. U.K.	
137 E2	Fairmont MN U.S.A.	
140 C3	Fairmont WV U.S.A.	
128 C2	Fairview Can.	
59 D2	Fais i. Micronesia	
74 B1	Faisalabad Pak.	
136 C1	Faith U.S.A.	
77 D3	Faizabad Afgh.	
75 C2	Faizabad India	
59 C3	Faktai Indon.	
65 A1	Faku China	
114 A4	Falaba Sierra Leone	
139 D3	Falcon Lake Mex./U.S.A.	
139 D3	Falfurrias U.S.A.	
128 C2	Falher Can.	
101 F2	Falkenberg Ger.	
93 F4	Falkenberg Sweden	
101 F1	Falkensee Ger.	
96 C3	Falkirk U.K.	
153 C6	Falkland Islands terr. S. Atlantic Ocean	
93 F4	Falköping Sweden	
135 C3	Fallon U.S.A.	
141 E2	Fall River U.S.A.	
137 D2	Falls City U.S.A.	
99 A3	Falmouth U.K.	
122 A3	False Bay S. Africa	
93 F4	Falster i. Denmark	
110 C1	Fălticeni Romania	
93 G3	Falun Sweden	
71 A3	Fangcheng China	
71 C3	Fangshan Taiwan	
69 E1	Fangzheng China	
108 B2	Fano Italy	
119 C2	Faradje Dem. Rep. Congo	
121 □D3	Farafangana Madag.	
116 A2	Farāfirah, Wāḩāt al oasis Egypt	
76 C3	Farāh Afgh.	
114 A3	Faranah Guinea	
78 B3	Farasān, Jazā'ir is Saudi Arabia	
127 J3	Farewell, Cape Greenland	
54 B2	Farewell, Cape N.Z.	
137 D1	Fargo U.S.A.	
77 D2	Farg'ona Uzbek.	
137 E2	Faribault U.S.A.	
141 E2	Farmington ME U.S.A.	
138 B1	Farmington NM U.S.A.	
141 D3	Farmville U.S.A.	
99 C3	Farnborough U.K.	
128 C2	Farnham, Mount Can.	
128 A1	Faro Can.	
106 B2	Faro Port.	
88 A2	Fårö i. Sweden	
94 B1	Faroe Islands terr. N. Atlantic Ocean	
79 C2	Farrāshband Iran	
139 C2	Farwell U.S.A.	
79 C2	Fāryāb Iran	
79 C2	Fasā Iran	
109 C2	Fasano Italy	
90 B1	Fastiv Ukr.	
75 B2	Fatehgarh India	
75 C2	Fatehpur India	
92 G2	Fauske Norway	
92 □A3	Faxaflói b. Iceland	
92 G3	Faxälven r. Sweden	
115 D3	Faya Chad	
142 B1	Fayetteville AR U.S.A.	
143 E1	Fayetteville NC U.S.A.	
142 C1	Fayetteville TN U.S.A.	
74 B1	Fazilka India	
114 A2	Fdérik Maur.	
143 E2	Fear, Cape U.S.A.	
54 C2	Featherston N.Z.	
104 C2	Fécamp France	
102 C1	Fehmarn i. Ger.	
101 F1	Fehrbellin Ger.	
155 D2	Feia, Lagoa lag. Brazil	
150 A2	Feijó Brazil	
54 C2	Feilding N.Z.	
151 E3	Feira de Santana Brazil	
107 C2	Felanitx Spain	
145 D3	Felipe C. Puerto Mex.	
155 C1	Felixlândia Brazil	
99 D3	Felixstowe U.K.	
101 D2	Felsberg Ger.	
108 B1	Feltre Italy	
93 F3	Femunden l. Norway	

71 B3 **Fengcheng** *Jiangxi* China
65 A1 **Fengcheng** *Liaoning* China
62 A1 **Fengqing** China
70 B2 **Fengxian** China
Fengxiang China *see* Lincang
71 C3 **Fengyuan** Taiwan
70 B1 **Fengzhen** China
105 D3 **Feno, Capo di** *c. Corse* France
121 □D2 **Fenoarivo Atsinanana** Madag.
91 D2 **Feodosiya** Ukr.
108 A3 **Fer, Cap de** *c.* Alg.
137 D1 **Fergus Falls** U.S.A.
109 D2 **Ferizaj** Kosovo
114 B4 **Ferkessédougou** Côte d'Ivoire
108 B2 **Fermo** Italy
131 D1 **Fermont** Can.
106 B1 **Fermoselle** Spain
97 C2 **Fermoy** Ireland
143 D2 **Fernandina Beach** U.S.A.
154 B2 **Fernandópolis** Brazil
128 C3 **Fernie** Can.
108 B2 **Ferrara** Italy
154 B2 **Ferreiros** Brazil
108 A2 **Ferro, Capo** *c. Sardegna* Italy
106 B1 **Ferrol** Spain
100 B1 **Ferwert** Neth.
114 B1 **Fès** Morocco
118 B3 **Feshi** Dem. Rep. Congo
137 E3 **Festus** U.S.A.
111 C3 **Fethiye** Turkey
96 □ **Fetlar** *i.* U.K.
130 C1 **Feuilles, Rivière aux** *r.* Can.
Fez Morocco *see* **Fès**
121 □D3 **Fianarantsoa** Madag.
117 B4 **Fichē** Eth.
109 C2 **Fier** Albania
96 C2 **Fife Ness** *pt* U.K.
104 C3 **Figeac** France
106 B1 **Figueira da Foz** Port.
107 D1 **Figueres** Spain
114 B1 **Figuig** Morocco
48 F3 **Fiji** *country* S. Pacific Ocean
152 B3 **Filadelfia** Para.
55 Q2 **Filchner Ice Shelf** Antarctica
98 C1 **Filey** U.K.
111 B3 **Filippiada** Greece
93 F4 **Filipstad** Sweden
96 C2 **Findhorn** *r.* U.K.
140 C2 **Findlay** U.S.A.
51 D4 **Fingal** Austr.
141 D2 **Finger Lakes** U.S.A.
106 B1 **Finisterre, Cape** Spain
92 13 **Finland** *country* Europe
93 H4 **Finland, Gulf of** Europe
128 B2 **Finlay** *r.* Can.
53 C3 **Finley** Austr.
101 E2 **Finne** *ridge* Ger.
92 H2 **Finnmarksvidda** *reg.* Norway
92 G2 **Finnsnes** Norway
93 G4 **Finspång** Sweden
96 A2 **Fionnphort** U.K.
Firat *r.* Turkey *see* **Euphrates**
Firenze Italy *see* **Florence**
105 C2 **Firminy** France
75 B2 **Firozabad** India
74 B1 **Firozpur** India
79 C2 **Fīrūzābād** Iran
122 A2 **Fish** *watercourse* Namibia
122 B3 **Fish** *r.* S. Africa
99 A3 **Fishguard** U.K.
105 C2 **Fismes** France
Fisterra, Cabo *c.* Spain *see*
Finisterre, Cape
141 E2 **Fitchburg** U.S.A.
129 C2 **Fitzgerald** Can.
50 B1 **Fitzroy Crossing** Austr.
108 B2 **Fivizzano** Italy

119 C3 **Fizi** Dem. Rep. Congo
92 G3 **Fjällsjöälven** *r.* Sweden
123 C3 **Flagstaff** S. Africa
138 A1 **Flagstaff** U.S.A.
130 C1 **Flaherty Island** Can.
98 C1 **Flamborough Head** U.K.
101 F1 **Fläming** *hills* Ger.
136 B2 **Flaming Gorge Reservoir**
U.S.A.
134 D1 **Flathead** *r.* U.S.A.
134 D1 **Flathead Lake** U.S.A.
51 D1 **Flattery, Cape** Austr.
134 B1 **Flattery, Cape** U.S.A.
98 B2 **Fleetwood** U.K.
93 E4 **Flekkefjord** Norway
102 B1 **Flensburg** Ger.
104 B2 **Flers** France
51 D1 **Flinders** *r.* Austr.
50 A3 **Flinders Bay** Austr.
51 D3 **Flinders Island** Austr.
52 A2 **Flinders Ranges** *mts* Austr.
129 D2 **Flin Flon** Can.
140 C2 **Flint** U.S.A.
107 D1 **Florac** France
108 B2 **Florence** Italy
142 C2 **Florence** AL U.S.A.
138 A2 **Florence** AZ U.S.A.
143 C2 **Florence** OR U.S.A.
143 E2 **Florence** SC U.S.A.
150 A1 **Florencia** Col.
146 B3 **Flores** Guat.
58 C3 **Flores** *i.* Indon.
58 B3 **Flores, Laut** *sea* Indon.
Flores Sea Indon. *see*
Flores, Laut
151 E3 **Floresta** Brazil
139 D3 **Floresville** U.S.A.
151 D2 **Floriano** Brazil
152 B3 **Florianópolis** Brazil
153 C4 **Florida** Uru.
143 D2 **Florida** *state* U.S.A.
143 D4 **Florida, Straits of** N. Atlantic
Ocean
143 D4 **Florida Keys** *is* U.S.A.
111 B2 **Florina** Greece
93 E3 **Florø** Norway
129 D2 **Foam Lake** Can.
109 C2 **Foča** Bos.-Herz.
110 C1 **Focşani** Romania
71 B3 **Fogang** China
109 C2 **Foggia** Italy
131 E2 **Fogo Island** Can.
104 C3 **Foix** France
89 D3 **Fokino** Rus. Fed.
130 B2 **Foleyet** Can.
108 B2 **Foligno** Italy
99 D3 **Folkestone** U.K.
143 D2 **Folkston** U.S.A.
108 B2 **Follonica** Italy
129 D2 **Fond-du-Lac** Can.
129 D2 **Fond du Lac** *r.* Can.
140 B2 **Fond du Lac** U.S.A.
106 B1 **Fondevila** Spain
108 B2 **Fondi** Italy
146 B3 **Fonseca, Golfo do** *b.* Central
America
150 B2 **Fonte Boa** Brazil
104 B2 **Fontenay-le-Comte** France
92 □C2 **Fontur** *pt* Iceland
53 C2 **Forbes** Austr.
101 E3 **Forchheim** Ger.
93 E3 **Førde** Norway
53 C1 **Fords Bridge** Austr.
142 B2 **Fordyce** U.S.A.
142 C2 **Forest** U.S.A.
53 C3 **Forest Hill** Austr.
131 D2 **Forestville** Can.

96 C2 **Forfar** U.K.
134 B1 **Forks** U.S.A.
108 B2 **Forlì** Italy
107 D2 **Formentera** *i.* Spain
107 D2 **Formentor, Cap de** *c.* Spain
155 C2 **Formiga** Brazil
152 C3 **Formosa** Arg.
Formosa *country* Asia *see*
Taiwan
154 C1 **Formosa** Brazil
96 C2 **Forres** U.K.
50 B3 **Forrest** Austr.
142 B1 **Forrest City** U.S.A.
51 D1 **Forsayth** Austr.
93 H3 **Forssa** Fin.
53 D2 **Forster** Austr.
136 B1 **Forsyth** U.S.A.
74 B2 **Fort Abbas** Pak.
130 B1 **Fort Albany** Can.
151 E2 **Fortaleza** Brazil
128 C2 **Fort Assiniboine** Can.
96 B2 **Fort Augustus** U.K.
134 D1 **Fort Benton** U.S.A.
135 B3 **Fort Bragg** U.S.A.
Fort Chimo Can. *see* **Kuujjuaq**
129 C2 **Fort Chipewyan** Can.
136 B2 **Fort Collins** U.S.A.
147 D3 **Fort-de-France** Martinique
137 E2 **Fort Dodge** U.S.A.
130 A2 **Fort Frances** Can.
Fort Franklin Can. *see* **Déline**
Fort George Can. *see* **Chisasibi**
126 C2 **Fort Good Hope** Can.
96 C2 **Forth** *r.* U.K.
96 C2 **Forth, Firth of** *est.* U.K.
152 C3 **Fortín Madrejón** Para.
143 D3 **Fort Lauderdale** U.S.A.
128 B1 **Fort Liard** Can.
129 C2 **Fort Mackay** Can.
129 C2 **Fort McMurray** Can.
126 C2 **Fort McPherson** Can.
136 C2 **Fort Morgan** U.S.A.
143 D3 **Fort Myers** U.S.A.
128 B2 **Fort Nelson** Can.
128 B2 **Fort Nelson** *r.* Can.
142 C2 **Fort Payne** U.S.A.
136 B1 **Fort Peck** U.S.A.
136 B1 **Fort Peck Reservoir** U.S.A.
143 D3 **Fort Pierce** U.S.A.
128 C1 **Fort Providence** Can.
129 D2 **Fort Qu'Appelle** Can.
128 C1 **Fort Resolution** Can.
Fort Rupert Can. *see*
Waskaganish
128 B2 **Fort St James** Can.
128 B2 **Fort St John** Can.
128 C2 **Fort Saskatchewan** Can.
137 E3 **Fort Scott** U.S.A.
130 B1 **Fort Severn** Can.
76 B2 **Fort-Shevchenko** Kazakh.
128 B1 **Fort Simpson** Can.
129 C1 **Fort Smith** Can.
142 B1 **Fort Smith** U.S.A.
139 C2 **Fort Stockton** U.S.A.
138 C2 **Fort Sumner** U.S.A.
128 C2 **Fort Vermilion** Can.
142 C2 **Fort Walton Beach** U.S.A.
140 B2 **Fort Wayne** U.S.A.
96 B2 **Fort William** U.K.
139 D2 **Fort Worth** U.S.A.
126 B2 **Fort Yukon** U.S.A.
71 B3 **Foshan** China
92 F3 **Fosna** *pen.* Norway
93 E3 **Fosnavåg** Norway
92 □B3 **Foss** Iceland
92 □A2 **Fossá** Iceland
108 A2 **Fossano** Italy

53 C3 Foster Austr.
104 B2 Fougères France
96 ☐ Foula i. U.K.
111 C3 Fournoi i. Greece
114 A3 Fouta Djallon reg. Guinea
54 A3 Foveaux Strait N.Z.
126 C3 Fowler U.S.A.
50 C3 Fowlers Bay Austr.
128 C2 Fox Creek Can.
127 F2 Foxe Basin g. Can.
127 F2 Foxe Channel Can.
127 F2 Foxe Peninsula Can.
54 B2 Fox Glacier N.Z.
128 C2 Fox Lake Can.
128 A1 Fox Mountain Can.
54 C3 Foxton N.Z.
129 D2 Fox Valley Can.
97 C1 Foyle, Lough b. Ireland/U.K.
154 B3 Foz de Areia, Represa de resr
Brazil
120 A2 Foz do Cunene Angola
154 B3 Foz do Iguaçu Brazil
107 D1 Fraga Spain
154 C2 Franca Brazil
109 C2 Francavilla Fontana Italy
104 C2 France country Europe
118 B3 Franceville Gabon
137 D2 Francis Case, Lake U.S.A.
155 F1 Francisco Sá Brazil
120 B3 Francistown Botswana
128 C2 François Lake Can.
101 D2 Frankenberg (Eder) Ger.
101 D3 Frankenthal (Pfalz) Ger.
101 D2 Frankenwald mts Ger.
140 D3 Frankfort U.S.A.
101 D2 Frankfurt am Main Ger.
102 C1 Frankfurt an der Oder Ger.
102 C2 Fränkische Alb hills Ger.
101 E3 Fränkische Schweiz reg. Ger.
141 D2 Franklin U.S.A.
126 C2 Franklin Bay Can.
134 C1 Franklin D. Roosevelt Lake
U.S.A.
128 B1 Franklin Mountains Can.
126 E2 Franklin Strait Can.
82 E1 Frantsa-Iosifa, Zemlya is
Rus. Fed.
54 B2 Franz Josef Glacier N.Z.
Franz Josef Land is Rus. Fed.
see Frantsa-Iosifa, Zemlya
108 A2 Frasca, Capo della c. Sardegna
Italy
128 B3 Fraser r. B.C. Can.
131 D1 Fraser r. Nfld. and Lab. Can.
122 B7 Fraserburg S. Africa
96 C2 Fraserburgh U.K.
130 B2 Fraserdale Can.
51 E2 Fraser Island Austr.
128 B2 Fraser Lake Can.
153 C4 Fray Bentos Uru.
93 E4 Fredericia Denmark
139 D2 Frederick U.S.A.
139 D2 Fredericksburg TX U.S.A.
141 D3 Fredericksburg VA U.S.A.
128 A2 Frederick Sound sea chan.
U.S.A.
131 D2 Fredericton Can.
93 F4 Frederikshavn Denmark
Frederikshamn Fin. see Hamina
93 F4 Fredrikstad Norway
140 B2 Freeport IL U.S.A.
139 D3 Freeport TX U.S.A.
146 C2 Freeport City Bahamas
139 D3 Freer U.S.A.
123 C2 Free State prov. S. Africa
114 A4 Freetown Sierra Leone
106 B2 Fregenal de la Sierra Spain

104 B2 Fréhel, Cap c. France
102 B2 Freiburg im Breisgau Ger.
102 C2 Freising Ger.
102 C2 Freistadt Austria
105 D3 Fréjus France
50 A3 Fremantle Austr.
137 D2 Fremont NE U.S.A.
140 C2 Fremont OH U.S.A.
151 C1 French Guiana terr. S. America
134 E1 Frenchman r. U.S.A.
49 I4 French Polynesia terr.
S. Pacific Ocean
144 B2 Fresnillo Mex.
135 C3 Fresno U.S.A.
107 D2 Freu, Cap des c. Spain
105 D2 Freyming-Merlebach France
114 A3 Fria Guinea
152 B3 Frias Arg.
102 B2 Friedrichshafen Ger.
101 F1 Friesack Ger.
100 C1 Friesoythe Ger.
Frobisher Bay Can. see
Iqaluit
127 G2 Frobisher Bay Can.
101 F2 Frohburg Ger.
87 D4 Frolovo Rus. Fed.
52 A2 Frome, Lake imp. l. Austr.
52 A2 Frome Downs Austr.
100 C2 Fröndenberg Ger.
145 C3 Frontera Mex.
144 B1 Fronteras Mex.
108 B2 Frosinone Italy
92 E3 Frøya i. Norway
Frunze Kyrg. see Bishkek
105 D2 Frutigen Switz.
103 D2 Frýdek-Místek Czech Rep.
71 B3 Fu'an China
106 C1 Fuenlabrada Spain
152 C3 Fuerte Olimpo Para.
114 A2 Fuerteventura i. Islas
Canarias
64 B1 Fuga i. Phil.
79 C2 Fujairah U.A.E.
67 C3 Fuji Japan
71 B3 Fujian prov. China
67 C3 Fujinomiya Japan
67 C3 Fuji-san vol. Japan
67 C3 Fukui Japan
67 B4 Fukuoka Japan
67 D3 Fukushima Japan
101 D2 Fulda Ger.
101 D2 Fulda r. Ger.
70 A3 Fuling China
137 E3 Fulton U.S.A.
105 C2 Fumay France
114 A1 Funchal Arquipélago da
Madeira
106 B1 Fundão Port.
131 D2 Fundy, Bay of g. Can.
70 B2 Funing Jiangsu China
71 A3 Funing Yunnan China
115 C3 Funtua Nigeria
79 C2 Fürgun, Küh-e mt. Iran
89 F2 Furmanov Rus. Fed.
155 C2 Furnas, Represa resr Brazil
51 D4 Furneaux Group is Austr.
100 C1 Fürstenau Ger.
101 E3 Fürth Ger.
66 D3 Furukawa Japan
127 F2 Fury and Hecla Strait Can.
65 A1 Fushun China
65 B1 Fusong China
79 C2 Fuwayrit Qatar
70 B2 Fuyang China
69 E1 Fuyu China
68 B1 Fuyun China

71 B3 Fuzhou China
71 B3 Fuzhou China
Fuzhou China see Fuzhou
93 F4 Fyn i. Denmark
F.Y.R.O.M. country Europe see
Macedonia

G

117 C4 Gaalkacyo Somalia
120 A2 Gabela Angola
115 D1 Gabès Tunisia
115 D1 Gabès, Golfe de g. Tunisia
118 B3 Gabon country Africa
123 C1 Gaborone Botswana
110 C2 Gabrovo Bulg.
114 A3 Gabú Guinea-Bissau
73 D3 Gadag India
75 C2 Gadchiroli India
101 E1 Gadebusch Ger.
142 C2 Gadsden U.S.A.
110 C2 Găeşti Romania
108 B2 Gaeta Italy
143 D1 Gaffney U.S.A.
115 C1 Gafsa Tunisia
89 E2 Gagarin Rus. Fed.
114 B4 Gagnoa Côte d'Ivoire
131 D1 Gagnon Can.
81 C1 Gagra Georgia
122 A2 Galab watercourse Namibia
111 C3 Gaidouronisi i. Greece
104 C3 Gaillac France
143 D3 Gainesville FL U.S.A.
142 D2 Gainesville GA U.S.A.
139 D2 Gainesville TX U.S.A.
98 C2 Gainsborough U.K.
52 A2 Gairdner, Lake imp. l. Austr.
96 B2 Gairloch U.K.
119 E3 Galana r. Kenya
103 D2 Galanta Slovakia
148 B3 Galapagos Islands Ecuador
96 C3 Galashiels U.K.
110 C1 Galaţi Romania
93 E3 Galdhøpiggen mt. Norway
145 B2 Galeana Mex.
128 C2 Galena Bay Can.
140 A2 Galesburg U.S.A.
122 B2 Galeshewe S. Africa
80 D3 Galich Rus. Fed.
116 B1 Galilee, Sea of l. Israel
142 C1 Gallatin U.S.A.
73 C4 Galle Sri Lanka
150 A1 Gallinas, Punta pt Col.
109 C2 Gallipoli Italy
111 C2 Gallipoli Turkey
92 H2 Gällivare Sweden
138 B1 Gallup U.S.A.
117 C4 Galmudug reg. Somalia
114 A2 Galtat Zemmour Western
Sahara
97 B2 Galtymore h. Ireland
139 E3 Galveston U.S.A.
139 E3 Galveston Bay U.S.A.
97 B2 Galway Ireland
97 B2 Galway Bay Ireland
154 C1 Gamá Brazil
123 D3 Gamalakhe S. Africa
Gambia country Africa see
The Gambia
114 A3 Gambia, The country Africa
52 A3 Gambier Islands Austr.
131 E2 Gambo Can.
118 B3 Gamboma Congo
128 C1 Gamètì Can.
138 B1 Ganado U.S.A

Gäncä

81 C1 Gäncä Azer.
Gand Belgium see Ghent
61 C2 Gandadiwata, Bukit mt. Indon.
118 C3 Gandajika Dem. Rep. Congo
131 E2 Gander Can.
131 E2 Gander r. Can.
101 N1 Ganderkesee Ger.
107 D1 Gandesa Spain
74 B2 Gandhidham India
74 B2 Gandhinagar India
74 B2 Gandhi Sagar resr India
107 C2 Gandia Spain
Ganga r. Bangl./India see
Ganges
153 B5 Gangán Arg.
74 B2 Ganganagar India
68 C2 Gangca China
75 C1 Gangdisê Shan mts China
75 D2 Ganges r. Bangl./India
105 C3 Ganges France
75 C2 Ganges, Mouths of the
Bangl./India
75 C2 Gangtok India
105 C2 Gannat France
136 B2 Gannett Peak U.S.A.
122 A3 Gansbaai S. Africa
70 A1 Gansu prov. China
71 B3 Ganzhou China
114 B3 Gao Mali
97 B1 Gaoth Dobhair Ireland
114 A3 Gaoual Guinea
71 C3 Gaoxiong Taiwan
70 B2 Gaoyou China
70 B2 Gaoyou Hu l. China
105 D3 Gap France
75 C1 Gar China
76 B2 Garabogaz Turkm.
76 B2 Garabogazköl Turkm.
76 B2 Garabogazköl Aýlagy b.
Turkm.
53 C1 Garah Austr.
151 E2 Garanhuns Brazil
135 B2 Garberville U.S.A.
101 D2 Garbsen Ger.
154 C2 Garça Brazil
101 E1 Gardelegen Ger.
136 C3 Garden City U.S.A.
129 E2 Garden Hill Can.
77 C3 Gardēz Afgh.
88 B2 Gargždai Lith.
123 C3 Gariep Dam dam S. Africa
122 A3 Garies S. Africa
119 D3 Garissa Kenya
102 C2 Garmisch-Partenkirchen Ger.
52 B2 Garnpung Lake imp. l. Austr.
104 B3 Garonne r. France
117 C4 Garoowe Somalia
74 B1 Garoth India
118 B2 Garoua Cameroon
96 B2 Garry r. U.K.
126 E2 Garry Lake Can.
119 E3 Garsen Kenya
61 C2 Garut Indon.
140 B2 Gary U.S.A.
145 B2 Garza García Mex.
68 C2 Garzê China
104 B3 Gascony, Gulf of France
50 A2 Gascoyne r. Austr.
115 D3 Gashua Nigeria
131 D2 Gaspé Can.
131 D2 Gaspésie, Péninsule de la pen.
Can.
143 E1 Gaston, Lake U.S.A.
143 D1 Gastonia U.S.A.
107 C2 Gata, Cabo de c. Spain
88 D2 Gatchina Rus. Fed.
98 C1 Gateshead U.K.

139 D2 Gatesville U.S.A.
130 C2 Gatineau r. Can.
53 D1 Gatton Austr.
129 E2 Gauer Lake Can.
93 E4 Gausta mt. Norway
123 C2 Gauteng prov. S. Africa
79 C2 Gävbandi Iran
111 B3 Gavdos i. Greece
93 G3 Gävle Sweden
89 E2 Gavrilov Posad Rus. Fed.
89 E2 Gavrilov-Yam Rus. Fed.
62 A1 Gawai Myanmar
52 A2 Gawler Austr.
52 A2 Gawler Ranges hills Austr.
75 C2 Gaya India
114 C3 Gaya Niger
140 C1 Gaylord U.S.A.
86 E2 Gayny Rus. Fed.
80 B2 Gaza terr. Asia
80 B2 Gaziantep Turkey
76 C2 Gazojak Turkm.
114 B4 Gbarnga Liberia
103 D1 Gdańsk Pol.
88 A3 Gdańsk, Gulf of Pol./Rus. Fed.
88 C2 Gdov Rus. Fed.
103 D1 Gdynia Pol.
116 B3 Gedaref Sudan
101 D2 Gedern Ger.
111 C3 Gediz r. Turkey
102 C1 Gedser Denmark
100 B2 Geel Belgium
52 B3 Geelong Austr.
101 E1 Geesthacht Ger.
75 C1 Gê'gyai China
129 D2 Geikie r. Can.
93 E3 Geilo Norway
62 B1 Gejiu China
108 B3 Gela Sicilia Italy
91 D3 Gelendzhik Rus. Fed.
Gelibolu Turkey see Gallipoli
100 C2 Gelsenkirchen Ger.
118 C3 Gemena Dem. Rep. Congo
111 C2 Gemlik Turkey
117 C4 Genalē Wenz r. Eth.
81 D3 Genäveh Iran
153 B4 General Acha Arg.
153 B4 General Alvear Arg.
153 C4 General Belgrano Arg.
144 B2 General Cepeda Mex.
153 B4 General Pico Arg.
153 B4 General Roca Arg.
64 B2 General Santos Phil.
100 C2 Genesee r. U.S.A.
141 D2 Geneseo U.S.A.
105 D2 Geneva Switz.
141 D2 Geneva U.S.A.
105 D2 Geneva, Lake France/Switz.
Genève Switz. see Geneva
106 B2 Genil r. Spain
100 B2 Genk Belgium
108 A2 Genoa Italy
Genova Italy see Genoa
101 F1 Genthin Ger.
50 A3 Geographe Bay Austr.
131 D1 George r. Can.
122 B3 George S. Africa
143 D3 George, Lake FL U.S.A.
141 E2 George, Lake NY U.S.A.
114 A3 Georgetown Gambia
151 C1 Georgetown Guyana
60 B1 George Town Malaysia
143 E2 Georgetown SC U.S.A.
139 D2 Georgetown TX U.S.A.
55 I2 George V Land reg. Antarctica
81 C1 Georgia country Asia
143 D2 Georgia state U.S.A.
130 B2 Georgian Bay Can.

51 C2 Georgina watercourse Austr.
77 E2 Georgiyevka Kazakh.
87 D4 Georgiyevsk Rus. Fed.
101 F2 Gera Ger.
151 D3 Geral de Goiás, Serra hills
Brazil
54 B2 Geraldine N.Z.
50 A2 Geraldton Austr.
80 B1 Gerede Turkey
135 C2 Gerlach U.S.A.
103 E2 Gerlachovský štít mt. Slovakia
102 C1 Germany country Europe
100 C2 Gerolstein Ger.
101 E3 Gerolzhofen Ger.
101 D2 Gersfeld (Rhön) Ger.
75 C1 Gêrzê China
141 D3 Gettysburg PA U.S.A.
136 D1 Gettysburg SD U.S.A.
109 D2 Gevgelija Macedonia
111 C3 Geyikli Turkey
122 B2 Ghaap Plateau S. Africa
115 C1 Ghadāmis Libya
75 C2 Ghaghara r. India
114 B4 Ghana country Africa
120 B3 Ghanzi Botswana
115 C1 Ghardaïa Alg.
115 D1 Gharyān Libya
75 C2 Ghatal India
75 B2 Ghaziabad India
75 C2 Ghazipur India
77 C3 Ghaznī Afgh.
100 A2 Ghent Belgium
110 B1 Gherla Romania
105 D3 Ghisonaccia Corse France
74 B2 Ghotaru India
74 A2 Ghotki Pak.
91 E3 Giaginskaya Rus. Fed.
97 C1 Giant's Causeway lava field U.K.
61 C2 Gianyar Indon.
109 C3 Giarre Sicilia Italy
108 A1 Giaveno Italy
122 A2 Gibeon Namibia
106 B2 Gibraltar Gibraltar
106 B2 Gibraltar, Strait of
Morocco/Spain
50 B2 Gibson Desert Austr.
68 C1 Gichgeniyn Nuruu mts
Mongolia
117 B4 Gīdolē Eth.
104 C2 Gien France
101 D2 Gießen Ger.
101 E1 Gifhorn Ger.
128 C2 Gift Lake Can.
67 C3 Gifu Japan
96 B3 Gigha i. U.K.
106 B1 Gijón Spain
138 A2 Gila r. U.S.A.
138 A2 Gila Bend U.S.A.
51 D1 Gilbert r. Austr.
49 F2 Gilbert Islands is Kiribati
134 D1 Gildford U.S.A.
53 C2 Gilgandra Austr.
74 B1 Gilgit Pak.
74 B1 Gilgit r. Pak.
53 C2 Gilgunnia Austr.
129 E2 Gillam Can.
136 B2 Gillette U.S.A.
99 D3 Gillingham U.K.
129 E2 Gimli Can.
117 C4 Gīnīr Eth.
109 C2 Ginosa Italy
53 C3 Gippsland reg. Austr.
74 A2 Girdar Dhor r. Pak.
80 B1 Giresun Turkey
74 A1 Girishk Afgh.
107 D1 Girona Spain
96 B3 Girvan U.K.

54 C1 Gisborne N.Z.
93 F4 Gislaved Sweden
119 C3 Gitarama Rwanda
108 B2 Giulianova Italy
110 C2 Giurgiu Romania
110 C3 Giuvala, Pasul pass Romania
105 C2 Givors France
123 D1 Giyani S. Africa
116 B2 Giza Egypt
109 D4 Gjakovë Kosovo
109 D2 Gjilan Kosovo
109 D2 Gjirokastër Albania
126 C2 Gjoa Haven Can.
93 F3 Gjøvik Norway
131 E2 Glace Bay Can.
134 B1 Glacier Peak vol. U.S.A.
51 E2 Gladstone Austr.
92 □A2 Gláma mts Iceland
107 C1 Glamoč Bos.-Herz.
100 C3 Glan r. Ger.
97 B2 Glanaruddery Mountains hills Ireland
96 B3 Glasgow U.K.
140 B3 Glasgow KY U.S.A.
136 B1 Glasgow MT U.S.A.
99 B3 Glastonbury U.K.
101 F2 Glauchau Ger.
86 E3 Glazov Rus. Fed.
89 E3 Glazunovka Rus. Fed.
96 B2 Glen Coe val. U.K.
138 A2 Glendale U.S.A.
53 D2 Glen Davis Austr.
136 C1 Glendive U.S.A.
96 C2 Glenelg r. Austr.
53 D1 Glen Innes Austr.
126 B2 Glennallen U.S.A.
96 C2 Glenrothes U.K.
141 E2 Glens Falls U.S.A.
96 C2 Glen Shee val. U.K.
97 B1 Glenties Ireland
138 B2 Glenwood U.S.A.
136 B3 Glenwood Springs U.S.A.
103 D1 Gliwice Pol.
138 A2 Globe U.S.A.
103 D1 Głogów Pol.
92 F2 Glomfjord Norway
93 F4 Glomma r. Norway
52 B2 Gloucester Austr.
99 B3 Gloucester U.K.
101 F1 Glöwen Ger.
77 E1 Glubokoye Kazakh.
101 D1 Glückstadt Ger.
103 C2 Gmünd Austria
102 C2 Gmunden Austria
101 E1 Gnarrenburg Ger.
103 D1 Gniezno Pol.
75 D2 Goalpara India
96 B3 Goat Fell h. U.K.
117 C4 Goba Eth.
120 A3 Gobabis Namibia
153 A5 Gobernador Gregores Arg.
69 D2 Gobi des. China/Mongolia
100 C2 Goch Ger.
122 A1 Gochas Namibia
74 B3 Godavari r. India
73 C3 Godavari, Mouths of the India
130 B2 Goderich Can.
74 B2 Godhra India
129 E2 Gods r. Can.
129 E2 Gods Lake Can.
Godthåb Greenland see Nuuk
Godwin-Austen, Mount China/Pakistan see K2
130 C2 Goéland, Lac au l. Can.
131 D1 Goélands, Lac aux l. Can.
100 A2 Goes Neth.
154 C1 Goiandira Brazil

154 C1 Goiânia Brazil
154 B1 Goiás Brazil
154 B2 Goio-Erê Brazil
111 C2 Gökçeada i. Turkey
111 C3 Gökçedağ Turkey
121 B2 Gokwe Zimbabwe
93 E3 Gol Norway
62 A1 Golaghat India
111 C2 Gölcük Turkey
103 E1 Goldap Pol.
101 F1 Goldberg Ger.
53 D1 Gold Coast Austr.
114 B4 Gold Coast Ghana
128 C2 Golden Can.
54 B2 Golden Bay N.Z.
128 B3 Golden Hinde mt. Can.
97 B2 Golden Vale lowland Ireland
135 C3 Goldfield U.S.A.
128 B3 Gold River Can.
143 E1 Goldsboro U.S.A.
135 C4 Goleta U.S.A.
68 C2 Golmud China
81 D2 Golpāyegān Iran
96 C2 Golspie U.K.
119 C3 Goma Dem. Rep. Congo
75 C2 Gomati r. India
115 D3 Gombe Nigeria
115 D3 Gombi Nigeria
Gomel' Belarus see Homyel'
144 B2 Gómez Palacio Mex.
147 C3 Gonaïves Haiti
147 C3 Gonâve, Île de la i. Haiti
81 D2 Gonbad-e Kavus Iran
117 B3 Gonder Eth.
75 C2 Gondia India
111 C2 Gönen Turkey
115 D4 Gongola r. Nigeria
53 C2 Gongolgon Austr.
75 D1 Gongtang China
145 C2 Gonzáles Mex.
139 D3 Gonzales U.S.A.
122 A3 Good Hope, Cape of S. Africa
134 D2 Gooding U.S.A.
136 C3 Goodland U.S.A.
53 C1 Goodooga Austr.
98 C2 Goole U.K.
53 C2 Goolgowi Austr.
52 A3 Goolwa Austr.
53 D1 Goondiwindi Austr.
134 B2 Goose Lake U.S.A.
102 B2 Göppingen Ger.
75 C2 Gorakhpur India
109 C2 Goražde Bos.-Herz.
111 C3 Gördes Turkey
89 D3 Gordeyevka Rus. Fed.
51 D4 Gordon, Lake Austr.
115 D4 Goré Chad
117 B4 Gorē Eth.
54 A3 Gore N.Z.
97 C2 Gorey Ireland
81 D2 Gorgān Iran
81 C1 Gori Georgia
108 B1 Gorizia Italy
Gor'kiy Rus. Fed. see Nizhniy Novgorod
103 E2 Gorlice Pol.
103 C1 Görlitz Ger.
109 D2 Gornji Milanovac Serbia
109 C2 Gornji Vakuf Bos.-Herz.
77 E1 Gorno-Altaysk Rus. Fed.
110 C2 Gornotrakiyska Nizina lowland Bulg.
77 E1 Gornyak Rus. Fed.
59 D3 Goroka P.N.G.
114 B3 Gorom Gorom Burkina Faso
59 C2 Gorontalo Indon.
89 E3 Gorshechnoye Rus. Fed.

97 B2 Gorumna Island Ireland
91 D1 Goryachiy Klyuch Rus. Fed.
103 D1 Gorzów Wielkopolski Pol.
53 D2 Gosford Austr.
66 D2 Goshogawara Japan
101 E2 Goslar Ger.
109 C2 Gospić Croatia
99 C3 Gosport U.K.
109 D2 Gostivar Macedonia
Göteborg Sweden see Gothenburg
101 E2 Gotha Ger.
93 F4 Gothenburg Sweden
136 C2 Gothenburg U.S.A.
93 G4 Gotland i. Sweden
111 B2 Gotse Delchev Bulg.
93 G4 Gotska Sandön i. Sweden
67 B4 Gōtsu Japan
101 D2 Göttingen Ger.
128 B2 Gott Peak Can.
100 B1 Gouda Neth.
114 A3 Goudiri Senegal
115 D3 Goudoumaria Niger
130 C2 Gouin, Réservoir resr Can.
53 C2 Goulburn Austr.
53 D3 Goulburn r. N.S.W. Austr.
53 B3 Goulburn r. Vic. Austr.
114 B3 Goundam Mali
107 D2 Gouraya Alg.
104 C3 Gourdon France
115 D3 Gouré Niger
122 B3 Gourits r. S. Africa
114 B3 Gourma-Rharous Mali
53 C3 Gourock Range mts Austr.
155 D1 Governador Valadares Brazil
143 E3 Governor's Harbour Bahamas
68 C2 Govi Altayn Nuruu mts Mongolia
75 C2 Govind Ballash Pant Sagar resr India
99 A3 Gower pen. U.K.
152 C3 Goya Arg.
81 C1 Göyçay Azer.
75 C1 Gozha Co salt l. China
122 B3 Graaff-Reinet S. Africa
101 E1 Grabow Ger.
109 C2 Gračac Croatia
87 F3 Grachevka Rus. Fed.
101 F2 Gräfenhainichen Ger.
53 D1 Grafton Austr.
137 D1 Grafton U.S.A.
139 D2 Graham U.S.A.
128 A2 Graham Island Can.
55 P3 Graham Land pen. Antarctica
123 C3 Grahamstown S. Africa
151 D2 Grajaú Brazil
111 B2 Grammos mt. Greece
96 B2 Grampian Mountains U.K.
146 B3 Granada Nic.
106 C2 Granada Spain
141 E1 Granby Can.
114 A2 Gran Canaria i. Islas Canarias
152 B3 Gran Chaco reg. Arg./Para.
136 C1 Grand r. U.S.A.
146 C2 Grand Bahama i. Bahamas
131 E2 Grand Bank Can.
158 C2 Grand Banks of Newfoundland N. Atlantic Ocean
138 A1 Grand Canyon U.S.A.
138 A1 Grand Canyon gorge U.S.A.
146 D3 Grand Cayman i. Cayman Is
129 C2 Grand Centre Can.
134 C1 Grand Coulee U.S.A.
152 B2 Grande r. Bol.
154 B2 Grande r. Brazil
153 B6 Grande, Bahía b. Arg.

155 D2 Grande, Ilha i. Brazil
128 C2 Grande Cache Can.
128 C2 Grande Prairie Can.
114 B1 Grand Erg Occidental des. Alg.
115 C2 Grand Erg Oriental des. Alg.
131 D2 Grande-Rivière Can.
152 B4 Grandes, Salinas salt flat Arg.
131 D2 Grand Falls Can.
131 E2 Grand Falls-Windsor Nfld.
and Lab. Can.
128 C3 Grand Forks Can.
137 D3 Grand Forks U.S.A.
128 C1 Grandin, Lac l. Can.
137 D2 Grand Island U.S.A.
142 B3 Grand Isle U.S.A.
136 B3 Grand Junction U.S.A.
114 B4 Grand-Lahou Côte d'Ivoire
131 D2 Grand Lake N.B. Can.
131 E2 Grand Lake Nfld. and Lab. Can.
137 E1 Grand Marais U.S.A.
106 B2 Grândola Port.
129 E2 Grand Rapids Can.
140 B2 Grand Rapids MI U.S.A.
137 E1 Grand Rapids MN U.S.A.
136 A2 Grand Teton mt. U.S.A.
147 C2 Grand Turk Turks and
Caicos Is
134 C1 Grangeville U.S.A.
128 C2 Granisle Can.
134 E1 Granite Peak U.S.A.
108 B3 Granitola, Capo c. Sicilia Italy
93 F4 Gränna Sweden
101 F1 Gransee Ger.
99 C2 Grantham U.K.
96 C2 Grantown-on-Spey U.K.
138 B1 Grants U.S.A.
134 B2 Grants Pass U.S.A.
104 B2 Granville France
129 D2 Granville Lake Can.
155 D1 Grão Mogol Brazil
123 D1 Graskop S. Africa
105 D3 Grasse France
107 D1 Grassy Japan
92 F2 Gravdal Norway
104 B2 Grave, Pointe de pt France
129 D3 Gravelbourg Can.
130 C2 Gravenhurst Can.
53 D1 Gravesend Austr.
99 D3 Gravesend U.K.
105 D2 Gray France
103 D2 Graz Austria
146 C2 Great Abaco i. Bahamas
50 B3 Great Australian Bight g.
Austr.
54 C1 Great Barrier Island N.Z.
51 D1 Great Barrier Reef Austr.
135 C3 Great Basin U.S.A.
126 D2 Great Bear Lake Can.
93 F4 Great Belt sea chan. Denmark
137 D3 Great Bend U.S.A.
63 A2 Great Coco Island Cocos Is
53 B3 Great Dividing Range mts
Austr.
146 B2 Greater Antilles is
Caribbean Sea
58 A3 Greater Sunda Islands is
Indon.
60 A3 Greater Sunda Islands is
Indon.
61 A3 Greater Sunda Islands is
Indon.
134 D1 Great Falls U.S.A.
123 C3 Great Fish r. S. Africa
123 C3 Great Fish Point S. Africa
147 C2 Great Inagua i. Bahamas
122 B3 Great Karoo plat. S. Africa
123 C3 Great Kei r. S. Africa

99 B2 Great Malvern U.K.
122 A2 Great Namaqualand reg.
Namibia
63 A3 Great Nicobar i. India
99 D2 Great Ouse r. U.K.
119 D3 Great Rift Valley Africa
119 D3 Great Ruaha r. Tanz.
134 D2 Great Salt Lake U.S.A.
135 D2 Great Salt Lake Desert U.S.A.
116 A2 Great Sand Sea des.
Egypt/Libya
50 B2 Great Sandy Desert Austr.
128 C1 Great Slave Lake Can.
143 D1 Great Smoky Mountains
U.S.A.
50 B2 Great Victoria Desert Austr.
70 B1 Great Wall tourist site China
99 D2 Great Yarmouth U.K.
111 B3 Greece country Europe
136 C2 Greeley U.S.A.
82 F1 Greem-Bell, Ostrov i. Rus. Fed.
140 B3 Green r. KY U.S.A.
136 B3 Green r. WY U.S.A.
140 B2 Green Bay U.S.A.
140 B1 Green Bay b. U.S.A.
140 C3 Greenbrier r. U.S.A.
140 B3 Greencastle U.S.A.
143 D1 Greeneville U.S.A.
141 E2 Greenfield U.S.A.
129 D2 Green Lake Can.
127 I2 Greenland terr. N. America
160 R2 Greenland Sea
Greenland/Svalbard
96 B3 Greenock U.K.
135 D3 Green River UT U.S.A.
136 B2 Green River WY U.S.A.
140 B3 Greensburg IN U.S.A.
141 D2 Greensburg PA U.S.A.
143 E2 Green Swamp U.S.A.
138 A2 Green Valley U.S.A.
114 B4 Greenville Liberia
142 C2 Greenville AL U.S.A.
142 B2 Greenville MS U.S.A.
143 E1 Greenville NC U.S.A.
143 D2 Greenville SC U.S.A.
139 D2 Greenville TX U.S.A.
53 D2 Greenwell Point Austr.
143 D2 Greenwood U.S.A.
50 B2 Gregory, Lake imp. l. Austr.
51 D1 Gregory Range hills Austr.
101 F2 Greifswald Ger.
93 F4 Grenaa Denmark
142 C2 Grenada U.S.A.
147 D3 Grenada country West Indies
104 C3 Grenade France
53 C2 Grenfell Austr.
129 D2 Grenfell Can.
105 D2 Grenoble France
51 D1 Grenville, Cape Austr.
134 B1 Gresham U.S.A.
100 C1 Greven Ger.
111 B2 Grevena Greece
100 C2 Grevenbroich Ger.
101 E1 Grevesmühlen Ger.
138 B2 Greybull U.S.A.
128 A1 Grey Hunter Peak Can.
131 E1 Grey Islands Can.
54 B2 Greymouth N.Z.
52 B1 Grey Range hills Austr.
97 C2 Greystones Ireland
143 D2 Griffin U.S.A.
53 C2 Griffith Austr.
101 F2 Grimma Ger.
102 C1 Grimmen Ger.
98 C2 Grimsby U.K.

128 C2 Grimshaw Can.
92 □B2 Grímsstaðir Iceland
93 E4 Grimstad Norway
131 E2 Grinnell U.S.A.
122 B3 Griqualand East reg. S. Africa
122 B3 Griqualand West reg. S. Africa
127 F1 Grise Fiord Can.
96 C1 Gritley U.K.
123 C2 Groblersdal S. Africa
122 B2 Groblershoop S. Africa
Grodno Belarus see Hrodna
104 B2 Groix, Île de i. France
100 C1 Gronau (Westfalen) Ger.
92 F3 Grong Norway
100 C1 Groningen Neth.
122 B2 Grootdrink S. Africa
51 C1 Groote Eylandt i. Austr.
120 A2 Grootfontein Namibia
122 A2 Groot Karas Berg plat.
Namibia
122 B3 Groot Swartberge mts S. Africa
123 C3 Groot Winterberg mt. S. Africa
101 D2 Großenlüder Ger.
102 C2 Großer Rachel mt. Ger.
102 C2 Grosser Speikkogel mt. Austria
108 B2 Grosseto Italy
101 D3 Groß-Gerau Ger.
102 C2 Großglockner mt. Austria
100 C1 Groß-Hesepe Ger.
101 E2 Großlohra Ger.
122 A1 Gross Ums Namibia
131 E1 Groswater Bay Can.
130 B2 Groundhog r. Can.
49 I4 Groupe Actéon is Fr. Polynesia
135 B3 Grover Beach U.S.A.
141 E2 Groveton U.S.A.
87 D4 Groznyy Rus. Fed.
109 C1 Grubišno Polje Croatia
103 D1 Grudziądz Pol.
122 A2 Grünau Namibia
92 □A3 Grundarfjörður Iceland
89 E3 Gryazi Rus. Fed.
89 F2 Gryazovets Rus. Fed.
103 D1 Gryfice Pol.
102 C1 Gryfino Pol.
146 C2 Guacanayabo, Golfo de b. Cuba
144 B2 Guadalajara Mex.
106 C1 Guadalajara prov. Spain
49 E3 Guadalcanal i. Solomon Is
107 C1 Guadalope r. Spain
106 B2 Guadalquivir r. Spain
132 B4 Guadalupe i. Mex.
106 B2 Guadalupe, Sierra de mts
Spain
138 C2 Guadalupe Peak U.S.A.
144 B2 Guadalupe Victoria Mex.
144 B2 Guadalupe y Calvo Mex.
106 C1 Guadarrama, Sierra de mts
Spain
147 D3 Guadeloupe terr. West Indies
106 B2 Guadiana r. Port./Spain
106 C2 Guadix Spain
154 B2 Guaíra Brazil
147 C3 Guajira, Península de la pen.
Col.
150 A2 Gualaceo Ecuador
59 D2 Guam terr. N. Pacific Ocean
144 B2 Guamúchil Mex.
144 B2 Guanacevi Mex.
151 D3 Guanambi Brazil
150 B1 Guanare Venez.
146 B2 Guane Cuba
70 A2 Guang'an China
71 B3 Guangchang China
71 B3 Guangdong prov. China
71 A3 Guangxi Zhuangzu Zizhiqu
aut. reg. China

70 A2	Guangyuan China	
71 B3	Guangzhou China	
155 D1	Guanhães Brazil	
147 D4	Guanipa r. Venez.	
71 A3	Guanling China	
65 A1	Guanshui China	
	Guansuo China see Guanling	
147 A2	Guantánamo Cuba	
150 B3	Guaporé r. Bol./Brazil	
154 B3	Guarapuava Brazil	
154 C3	Guaraqueçaba Brazil	
155 C2	Guaratinguetá Brazil	
106 B1	Guarda Port.	
106 C1	Guarda Spain	
155 C2	Guarda Mor Brazil	
144 B2	Guardo Spain	
146 A3	Guarujá Brazil	
	Guasave Mex.	
146 A3	Guatemala country Central America	
	Guatemala City Guat.	
150 B2	Guaviare r. Col.	
155 C2	Guaxupé Brazil	
150 A2	Guayaquil Ecuador	
150 B3	Guayaramerín Bol.	
144 A2	Guaymas Mex.	
68 C2	Guazhou China	
117 B3	Guba Eth.	
86 E1	Guba Dolgaya Rus. Fed.	
89 E3	Gubkin Rus. Fed.	
115 C1	Guelma Alg.	
114 A2	Guelmim Morocco	
130 B2	Guelph Can.	
145 C2	Guémez Mex.	
104 C3	Guéret France	
95 C4	Guernsey terr. Channel Is.	
144 A2	Guerrero Negro Mex.	
131 D1	Guers, Lac l. Can.	
118 B3	Guider Cameroon	
108 B2	Guidonia-Montecelio Italy	
71 A3	Guigang China	
100 A3	Guignicourt France	
123 D1	Guija Moz.	
99 C3	Guildford U.K.	
71 B3	Guilin China	
130 C1	Guillaume-Delisle, Lac l. Can.	
106 B1	Guimarães Port.	
114 A3	Guinea country Africa	
113 F6	Guinea, Gulf of Africa	
114 A3	Guinea-Bissau country Africa	
104 B2	Guingamp France	
104 B2	Guipavas France	
154 B1	Guiratinga Brazil	
150 B1	Güiria Venez.	
100 A3	Guise France	
64 B1	Guiuan Phil.	
71 A3	Guiyang China	
71 A3	Guizhou prov. China	
74 B1	Gujranwala Pak.	
74 B1	Gujrat Pak.	
91 C2	Gukovo Rus. Fed.	
53 C2	Gulargambone Austr.	
73 B3	Gulbarga India	
88 C2	Gulbene Latvia	
79 C2	Gulf, the Asia	
111 B3	Gulf of Corinth sea chan Greece	
142 C2	Gulfport U.S.A.	
69 E1	Gulian China	
77 C2	Guliston Uzbek.	
	Gulja China see Yining	
129 D2	Gull Lake Can.	
111 C3	Güllük Turkey	
119 D2	Gulu Uganda	
120 B2	Gumare Botswana	
76 B3	Gumdag Turkm.	
75 C2	Gumla India	
100 C2	Gummersbach Ger.	
74 B2	Guna India	
53 C3	Gundagai Austr.	
111 C3	Güney Turkey	
118 B3	Gungu Dem. Rep. Congo	
129 E2	Gunisao r. Can.	
53 D2	Gunnedah Austr.	
136 B3	Gunnison CO U.S.A.	
135 D3	Gunnison UT U.S.A.	
136 B3	Gunnison r. U.S.A.	
73 B3	Guntakal India	
60 A1	Gunungsitoli Indon.	
60 A1	Gunungtua Indon.	
102 C2	Günzburg Ger.	
102 C2	Gunzenhausen Ger.	
70 B2	Guojiaba China	
74 B2	Guoyang China	
151 D2	Gurgueia r. Brazil	
150 B1	Guri, Embalse de resr Venez.	
154 C1	Gurinhatã Brazil	
151 D2	Gurupi r. Brazil	
74 B2	Guru Sikhar mt. India	
	Gur'yev Kazakh. see Atyrau	
115 C3	Gusau Nigeria	
65 A2	Gushan China	
70 B2	Gushi China	
83 I3	Gusinoozersk Rus. Fed.	
89 F2	Gus'-Khrustal'nyy Rus. Fed.	
108 A3	Guspini Sardegna Italy	
128 A2	Gustavus U.S.A.	
101 F1	Güstrow Ger.	
101 D2	Gütersloh Ger.	
121 C2	Gutu Mupandawana Zimbabwe	
75 D2	Guwahati India	
150 C1	Guyana country S. America	
	Guyi China see Sanjiang	
139 C1	Guymon U.S.A.	
53 D2	Guyra Austr.	
70 A2	Guyuan China	
144 B1	Guzmán Mex.	
74 A2	Gwadar Pak.	
128 A2	Gwaii Haanas Can.	
75 B2	Gwalior India	
121 B3	Gwanda Zimbabwe	
117 D3	Gwardafuy, Gees c. Somalia	
97 B1	Gweebarra Bay Ireland	
121 B2	Gweru Zimbabwe	
115 D3	Gwoza Nigeria	
53 D2	Gwydir r. Austr.	
75 C2	Gyangzê Co l. China	
68 C2	Gyaring Hu l. China	
86 G1	Gydan Peninsula Rus. Fed.	
	Gydanskiy Poluostrov pen. Rus. Fed. see Gydan Peninsula	
	Gyêgu China see Yushu	
51 F2	Gympie Austr.	
103 D2	Gyöngyös Hungary	
103 D2	Győr Hungary	
129 E2	Gypsumville Can.	
103 E2	Gyula Hungary	
81 C1	Gyumri Armenia	

H

88 B2	Haapsalu Estonia	
100 B1	Haarlem Neth.	
101 C2	Haarstrang ridge Ger.	
54 A2	Haast N.Z.	
78 B3	Habbān Yemen	
81 C2	Habbānīyah, Hawr al l. Iraq	
67 C4	Hachijō-jima i. Japan	
66 D2	Hachinohe Japan	
81 C1	Hacıqabul Azer.	
121 C3	Hacufera Moz.	
79 C2	Hadd, Ra's al pt Oman	
96 C3	Haddington U.K.	
115 D3	Hadejia Nigeria	
93 E4	Haderslev Denmark	
91 C1	Hadyach Ukr.	
65 B2	Haeju N. Korea	
65 B2	Haeju-man b. N. Korea	
65 B3	Haenam S. Korea	
78 B2	Hafar al Bāţin Saudi Arabia	
	Haflong India	
92 □A3	Hafnarfjörður Iceland	
78 A3	Hagar Nish Plateau Eritrea/Sudan	
48 D2	Hagåtña Guam	
100 C2	Hagen Ger.	
101 E1	Hagenow Ger.	
128 B2	Hagensborg Can.	
141 D3	Hagerstown U.S.A.	
93 F3	Hagfors Sweden	
67 B4	Hagi Japan	
62 B1	Hà Giang Vietnam	
97 B2	Hag's Head Ireland	
104 B2	Hague, Cap de la c. France	
119 D3	Hai Tanz.	
128 A2	Haida Gwaii Can.	
62 B1	Hai Duong Vietnam	
80 B2	Haifa Israel	
71 B3	Haifeng China	
71 B3	Haikou China	
78 B2	Hā'il Saudi Arabia	
92 H2	Hailuoto i. Fin.	
71 A4	Hainan prov. China	
69 D3	Hainan Dao i. China	
128 A2	Haines U.S.A.	
128 A1	Haines Junction Can.	
101 E2	Hainich ridge Ger.	
101 E2	Hainleite ridge Ger.	
62 B1	Hai Phong Vietnam	
147 C3	Haiti country West Indies	
116 B3	Haiya Sudan	
103 E2	Hajdúböszörmény Hungary	
78 B3	Hajjah Yemen	
79 C2	Hajjiābād Iran	
62 A1	Haka Myanmar	
81 C2	Hakkâri Turkey	
66 D2	Hakodate Japan	
	Halab Syria see Aleppo	
78 B2	Halabān Saudi Arabia	
81 C2	Halabja Iraq	
116 B2	Halaib Sudan	
79 C3	Halāniyāt, Juzur al is Oman	
78 A2	Halā'ib 'Azamia Saudi Arabia	
101 E2	Halberstadt Ger.	
64 B1	Halcon, Mount Phil.	
93 F4	Halden Norway	
101 E1	Haldensleben Ger.	
75 B2	Haldwani India	
79 C2	Hāleh Iran	
54 A3	Halfmoon Bay N.Z.	
131 D2	Halifax Can.	
98 C2	Halifax U.K.	
141 D3	Halifax U.S.A.	
65 B3	Halla-san mt. S. Korea	
127 H2	Hall Beach Can.	
100 B2	Halle Belgium	
101 E2	Halle (Saale) Ger.	
103 C2	Hallein Austria	
137 D1	Hallock U.S.A.	
50 B1	Halls Creek Austr.	
60 C2	Halmahera i. Indon.	
93 F4	Halmstad Sweden	
62 B1	Ha Long Vietnam	
67 B4	Hamada Japan	
81 C2	Hamadān Iran	
80 B2	Ḩamāh Syria	
67 C4	Hamamatsu Japan	

Hamar

93 F3 Hamar Norway
116 B2 Ḥamāṭah, Jabal mt. Egypt
73 C4 Hambantota Sri Lanka
101 D1 Hamburg Ger.
78 A2 Ḥamd, Wādī al watercourse Saudi Arabia
78 B3 Ḥamḍah Saudi Arabia
93 H3 Hämeenlinna Fin.
101 D1 Hameln Ger.
50 A2 Hamersley Range mts Austr.
65 B2 Hamhŭng N. Korea
68 C2 Hami China
116 B2 Hamid Sudan
52 B3 Hamilton Austr.
130 C2 Hamilton Can.
54 C1 Hamilton N.Z.
96 B3 Hamilton U.K.
142 C2 Hamilton AL U.S.A.
134 D1 Hamilton MT U.S.A.
140 C3 Hamilton OH U.S.A.
93 I3 Hamina Fin.
100 C2 Hamm Ger.
81 C2 Ḥammār, Hawr al imp. l. Iraq
101 D3 Hammelburg Ger.
92 G3 Hammerdal Sweden
92 H1 Hammerfest Norway
142 B2 Hammond U.S.A.
141 E3 Hammonton U.S.A.
115 D2 Ḥamrā', Al Ḥamādah al plat. Libya
78 A2 Ḥanak Saudi Arabia
66 D3 Hanamaki Japan
101 D2 Hanau Ger.
69 D2 Hanbogd Mongolia
70 B2 Hancheng China
140 B1 Hancock U.S.A.
70 B2 Handan China
135 C3 Hanford U.S.A.
68 C1 Hangayn Nuruu mts Mongolia
Hanggin Houqi China see Xamba
Hangö Fin. see Hanko
70 C2 Hangzhou China
70 C2 Hangzhou Wan b. China
Hanjia China see Pengshu
Hanjiang China see Yangzhou
93 H4 Hanko Fin.
135 D3 Hanksville U.S.A.
54 B2 Hanmer Springs N.Z.
129 C2 Hanna Can.
137 E3 Hannibal U.S.A.
101 D1 Hannover Ger.
101 D2 Hannoversch Münden Ger.
93 F4 Hanöbukten b. Sweden
62 B1 Ha Nôi Vietnam
Hanoi China see Ha Nôi
130 C2 Hanover Can.
122 B3 Hanover S. Africa
93 E4 Hanstholm Denmark
88 C3 Hantsavichy Belarus
75 C2 Hanumana India
74 B2 Hanumangarh India
70 A2 Hanzhong China
92 H2 Haparanda Sweden
100 B2 Hapert Neth.
131 D1 Happy Valley-Goose Bay Can.
78 A2 Ḥaql Saudi Arabia
79 B3 Ḥaraḍh Saudi Arabia
88 C2 Haradok Belarus
78 B3 Harajā Saudi Arabia
121 C2 Harare Zimbabwe
79 C3 Ḥarāsīs, Jiddat al des. Oman
69 D1 Har-Ayrag Mongolia
69 E1 Harbin China
131 E2 Harbour Breton Can.

74 B2 Harda India
Hardangerfjorden sea chan. Norway
100 C1 Hardenberg Neth.
100 B1 Harderwijk Neth.
122 A3 Hardeveld mts S. Africa
134 E1 Hardin U.S.A.
128 C1 Hardisty Lake Can.
100 C1 Haren (Ems) Ger.
117 C4 Härer Eth.
117 C4 Hargeysa Somalia
110 C1 Harghita-Mădăraş, Vârful mt. Romania
68 C2 Har Hu l. China
74 B1 Haripur Pak.
74 A1 Hari Rūd r. Afgh./Iran
100 B1 Harlingen Neth.
139 D3 Harlingen U.S.A.
99 D3 Harlow U.K.
134 E1 Harlowton U.S.A.
134 C1 Harney Basin U.S.A.
134 C2 Harney Lake U.S.A.
93 G3 Härnösand Sweden
69 E1 Har Nur China
68 C1 Har Nuur l. Mongolia
114 B4 Harper Liberia
101 D1 Harpstedt Ger.
53 D2 Harrington Austr.
131 E1 Harrington Harbour Can.
96 A2 Harris, Sound of sea chan. U.K.
140 B3 Harrisburg IL U.S.A.
141 D2 Harrisburg PA U.S.A.
123 C2 Harrismith S. Africa
142 B1 Harrison U.S.A.
131 E1 Harrison, Cape Can.
126 A2 Harrison Bay U.S.A.
141 D3 Harrisonburg U.S.A.
137 E3 Harrisonville U.S.A.
98 C2 Harrogate U.K.
110 C2 Hârşova Romania
92 G2 Harstad Norway
122 B2 Hartbees watercourse S. Africa
103 D2 Hartberg Austria
141 E2 Hartford U.S.A.
99 A3 Hartland Point U.K.
98 C1 Hartlepool U.K.
128 B2 Hartley Bay Can.
123 D2 Harts r. S. Africa
131 D2 Hartwell Reservoir U.S.A.
68 C1 Har Us Nuur l. Mongolia
136 C1 Harvey U.S.A.
99 D3 Harwich U.K.
101 E2 Harz hills Ger.
73 B3 Hassan India
100 B2 Hasselt Belgium
115 C1 Hassi Messaoud Alg.
93 F4 Hässleholm Sweden
100 B2 Hastière-Lavaux Belgium
53 C3 Hastings Austr.
54 C1 Hastings N.Z.
99 D3 Hastings U.K.
137 D2 Hastings MN U.S.A.
137 D2 Hastings NE U.S.A.
Hatay Turkey see Antakya
129 D2 Hatchet Lake Can.
52 B2 Hatfield Austr.
68 C1 Hatgal Mongolia
62 B2 Ha Tinh Vietnam
143 E1 Hatteras, Cape U.S.A.
142 C2 Hattiesburg U.S.A.
100 C2 Hattingen Ger.
63 B2 Hat Yai Thai.
117 C4 Haud reg. Eth.
93 E4 Haugesund Norway
93 E4 Haukeligrend Norway
92 I2 Haukipudas Fin.

54 C1 Hauraki Gulf N.Z.
114 B1 Haut Atlas mts Morocco
131 D2 Hauterive Can.
114 B1 Hauts Plateaux Alg.
146 B2 Havana Cuba
99 C3 Havant U.K.
101 E1 Havel r. Ger.
101 F1 Havelberg Ger.
54 B2 Havelock N.Z.
54 C1 Havelock North N.Z.
99 A3 Haverfordwest U.K.
103 D2 Havlíčkův Brod Czech Rep.
92 H1 Havøysund Norway
111 C3 Havran Turkey
134 E1 Havre U.S.A.
131 D2 Havre-Aubert Can.
131 D1 Havre-St-Pierre Can.
124 E5 Hawai'i i. U.S.A.
124 E5 Hawai'ian Islands N. Pacific Ocean
98 B2 Hawarden U.K.
54 A2 Hawea, Lake N.Z.
54 B1 Hawera N.Z.
98 B1 Hawes U.K.
96 C3 Hawick U.K.
54 C1 Hawke Bay N.Z.
52 A2 Hawker Austr.
52 B1 Hawkers Gate Austr.
135 C3 Hawthorne U.S.A.
52 B2 Hay Austr.
128 C1 Hay r. Can.
134 C1 Hayden U.S.A.
129 E2 Hayes r. Man. Can.
126 E2 Hayes r. Nunavut Can.
79 C3 Haymā' Oman
77 C2 Hayotboshi tog'i mt. Uzbek.
111 C2 Hayrabolu Turkey
128 C1 Hay River Can.
137 D3 Hays U.S.A.
78 B3 Hays Yemen
90 B2 Haysyn Ukr.
99 C3 Haywards Heath U.K.
74 A1 Hazārah Jāt reg. Afgh.
140 C3 Hazard U.S.A.
75 C2 Hazaribagh India
75 C2 Hazaribagh Range mts India
128 B2 Hazelton Can.
141 D2 Hazleton U.S.A.
53 C3 Healesville Austr.
130 B2 Hearst Can.
70 B2 Hebei prov. China
53 C1 Hebel Austr.
142 B1 Heber Springs U.S.A.
131 D1 Hebron Can.
128 A2 Hecate Strait Can.
71 A3 Hechi China
93 F3 Hede Sweden
100 B1 Heerenveen Neth.
100 B1 Heerhugowaard Neth.
100 B2 Heerlen Neth.
Hefa Israel see Haifa
70 B2 Hefei China
70 B3 Hefeng China
69 E1 Hegang China
102 B1 Heide Ger.
122 A1 Heide Namibia
102 B2 Heidelberg Ger.
122 B3 Heidelberg S. Africa
102 B2 Heilbronn Ger.
69 E1 Heilong Jiang r. China
93 I3 Heinola Fin.
92 F3 Helagsfjället mt. Sweden
142 B2 Helena AR U.S.A.
134 D1 Helena MT U.S.A.
96 C3 Helensburgh U.K.
102 B1 Helgoland i. Ger.

102 B1	Helgoländer Bucht g. Ger.	
	Helixi China see Ningguo	
92 □A3	Hella Iceland	
100 B2	Hellevoetsluis Neth.	
107 C2	Hellín Spain	
76 C3	Helmand r. Afgh.	
101 A1	Helmbrechts Ger.	
122 A2	Helmeringhausen Namibia	
100 B2	Helmond Neth.	
96 C1	Helmsdale U.K.	
96 C1	Helmsdale r. U.K.	
101 E1	Helmstedt Ger.	
65 B1	Helong China	
93 F4	Helsingborg Sweden	
	Helsingfors Fin. see Helsinki	
93 F4	Helsingør Denmark	
93 H3	Helsinki Fin.	
97 C2	Helvick Head Ireland	
99 C3	Hemel Hempstead U.K.	
101 D1	Hemmoor Ger.	
92 F2	Hemnesberget Norway	
70 B2	Henan prov. China	
140 B3	Henderson KY U.S.A.	
143 F1	Henderson NC U.S.A.	
135 D3	Henderson NV U.S.A.	
139 E2	Henderson TX U.S.A.	
143 D1	Hendersonville U.S.A.	
99 C3	Hendon U.K.	
62 A1	Hengduan Shan mts China	
100 C1	Hengelo Neth.	
	Hengnan China see Hengyang	
70 B2	Hengshan China	
71 A3	Hengxian China	
71 B3	Hengyang China	
	Hengzhou China see Hengxian	
91 C2	Heniches'k Ukr.	
100 C2	Hennef (Sieg) Ger.	
130 B1	Henrietta Maria, Cape Can.	
139 D1	Henryetta U.S.A.	
127 G2	Henry Kater, Cape Can.	
101 D1	Henstedt-Ulzburg Ger.	
120 A3	Hentiesbaai Namibia	
71 A3	Hepu China	
76 C3	Herāt Afgh.	
129 D2	Herbert Can.	
101 D2	Herbstein Ger.	
99 D2	Hereford U.K.	
139 C2	Hereford U.S.A.	
101 D1	Herford Ger.	
100 C2	Herkenbosch Neth.	
96 □	Herma Ness hd U.K.	
122 A3	Hermanus S. Africa	
53 C2	Hermidale Austr.	
134 C1	Hermiston U.S.A.	
59 D3	Hermit Islands P.N.G.	
144 A2	Hermosillo Mex.	
154 B3	Hernandarias Para.	
100 C2	Herne Ger.	
93 E4	Herning Denmark	
99 C3	Hertford U.K.	
123 C2	Hertzogville S. Africa	
51 F2	Hervey Bay Austr.	
101 F2	Herzberg Ger.	
101 E3	Herzogenaurach Ger.	
71 A3	Heshan China	
128 A1	Hess r. U.S.A.	
101 D2	Hessisch Lichtenau Ger.	
136 C1	Hettinger U.S.A.	
101 E2	Hettstedt Ger.	
98 B1	Hexham U.K.	
71 B3	Heyuan China	
53 C3	Heywood Austr.	
70 B2	Heze China	
71 B3	Hezhou China	
137 D3	Hiawatha U.S.A.	
137 E1	Hibbing U.S.A.	

54 C1	Hicks Bay N.Z.	
66 D2	Hidaka-sanmyaku mts Japan	
145 C2	Hidalgo Mex.	
144 B2	Hidalgo del Parral Mex.	
154 C1	Hidrolândia Brazil	
	High Atlas mts Morocco see Haut Atlas	
134 B2	High Desert U.S.A.	
128 C2	High Level Can.	
143 E1	High Point U.S.A.	
128 C2	High Prairie Can.	
128 C2	High River Can.	
129 D2	Highrock Lake Can.	
99 C3	High Wycombe U.K.	
88 B2	Hiiumaa i. Estonia	
78 A2	Hijaz reg. Saudi Arabia	
54 C1	Hikurangi mt. N.Z.	
101 E2	Hildburghausen Ger.	
101 E2	Hilders Ger.	
101 D1	Hildesheim Ger.	
81 C2	Hillah Iraq	
100 C2	Hillesheim Ger.	
140 C3	Hillsboro OH U.S.A.	
139 D2	Hillsboro TX U.S.A.	
53 C2	Hillston Austr.	
143 D2	Hilton Head Island U.S.A.	
100 B1	Hilversum Neth.	
68 B2	Himalaya mts Asia	
67 B4	Himeji Japan	
123 C2	Himeville S. Africa	
51 D1	Hinchinbrook Island Austr.	
74 A1	Hindu Kush mts Afgh./Pak.	
73 B3	Hindustan i. India	
73 B3	Hindupur India	
81 C2	Hīnis Turkey	
92 G2	Hinnøya i. Norway	
106 B2	Hinojosa del Duque Spain	
62 A2	Hinthada Myanmar	
128 C2	Hinton Can.	
75 C2	Hirakud Reservoir India	
66 D2	Hirosaki Japan	
67 B4	Hiroshima Japan	
101 E3	Hirschaid Ger.	
101 E2	Hirschberg Ger.	
105 C2	Hirson France	
93 E4	Hirtshals Denmark	
74 B2	Hisar India	
147 C2	Hispaniola i. Caribbean Sea	
81 C2	Hīt Iraq	
67 D3	Hitachi Japan	
67 D3	Hitachinaka Japan	
92 E3	Hitra i. Norway	
49 I3	Hiva Oa i. Fr. Polynesia	
93 G4	Hjälmaren l. Sweden	
129 D1	Hjalmar Lake Can.	
92 F4	Hjørring Denmark	
123 D2	Hlabisa S. Africa	
92 □B2	Hlíð Iceland	
91 C2	Hlobyne Ukr.	
123 C2	Hlohlowane S. Africa	
123 C2	Hlotse Lesotho	
91 C1	Hlukhiv Ukr.	
88 C2	Hlybokaye Belarus	
114 C4	Ho Ghana	
62 B2	Hoa Binh Vietnam	
122 A1	Hoachanas Namibia	
51 D4	Hobart Austr.	
139 D1	Hobart U.S.A.	
139 C2	Hobbs U.S.A.	
93 E4	Hobro Denmark	
117 C4	Hobyo Somalia	
63 B2	Ho Chi Minh City Vietnam	
114 B3	Hodh reg. Maur.	
78 B3	Hodeidah Yemen	
103 E2	Hódmezővásárhely Hungary	
	Hoek van Holland Neth. see Hook of Holland	

65 B2	Hoeyang N. Korea	
101 E2	Hof Ger.	
101 E2	Hofheim in Unterfranken Ger.	
92 □B3	Höfn Austurland Iceland	
92 □A2	Höfn Vestfirðir Iceland	
92 □B2	Hofsjökull Iceland	
67 B4	Hōfu Japan	
93 G4	Högsby Sweden	
101 D2	Hohe Rhön mts Ger.	
100 C2	Hohe Venn moorland Belgium	
70 B1	Hohhot China	
75 C3	Hoh Xil Shan mts China	
63 B2	Hôi An Vietnam	
62 A1	Hojai India	
54 B2	Hokitika N.Z.	
66 D2	Hokkaidō i. Japan	
128 B2	Holberg Can.	
138 A2	Holbrook U.S.A.	
137 D2	Holdrege U.S.A.	
146 C2	Holguín Cuba	
92 □B2	Hóll Iceland	
	Holland country Europe see Netherlands	
140 B2	Holland U.S.A.	
100 B1	Hollum Neth.	
142 C2	Holly Springs U.S.A.	
134 C4	Hollywood U.S.A.	
143 D3	Hollywood U.S.A.	
92 F2	Holm Norway	
92 H3	Holmsund Sweden	
122 A2	Holoog Namibia	
93 E4	Holstebro Denmark	
98 A2	Holston r. U.S.A.	
98 A2	Holyhead U.K.	
98 C1	Holy Island England U.K.	
98 A2	Holy Island Wales U.K.	
136 C2	Holyoke U.S.A.	
101 D2	Holzminden Ger.	
62 A1	Homalin Myanmar	
101 D2	Homberg (Efze) Ger.	
114 B3	Hombori Mali	
127 G2	Home Bay Can.	
143 D3	Homestead U.S.A.	
92 F3	Hommelvik Norway	
80 B2	Homs Syria	
89 D3	Homyel' Belarus	
122 A3	Hondeklipbaai S. Africa	
145 C3	Hondo r. Belize/Mex.	
139 D3	Hondo U.S.A.	
146 B3	Honduras country Central America	
93 F3	Hønefoss Norway	
135 B3	Honey Lake U.S.A.	
104 C2	Honfleur France	
70 B3	Honghu China	
71 A3	Hongjiang China	
69 D3	Hong Kong China	
71 B3	Hong Kong aut. reg. China	
65 B1	Hongwŏn N. Korea	
70 B2	Hongze Hu l. China	
49 E3	Honiara Solomon Is	
66 D3	Honjō Japan	
97 I1	Honningsvåg Norway	
67 B3	Honshū i. Japan	
134 B1	Hood, Mount vol. U.S.A.	
134 B1	Hood River U.S.A.	
100 C1	Hoogeveen Neth.	
100 C1	Hoogezand-Sappemeer Neth.	
100 C2	Hoog-Keppel Neth.	
100 B2	Hook of Holland Neth.	
128 A2	Hoonah U.S.A.	
100 B1	Hoorn Neth.	
128 B3	Hope Can.	
142 B2	Hope U.S.A.	
83 N2	Hope, Point U.S.A.	
131 D1	Hopedale Can.	

131 D1 Hope Mountains Can.
52 B3 Hopetoun Austr.
122 B2 Hopetown S. Africa
141 D3 Hopewell U.S.A.
130 C1 Hopewell Islands Can.
50 B2 Hopkins, Lake imp. l. Austr.
140 B3 Hopkinsville U.S.A.
134 B1 Hoquiam U.S.A.
81 C1 Horasan Turkey
93 F4 Hörby Sweden
89 D3 Horki Belarus
91 D2 Horlivka Ukr.
79 D2 Hormak Iran
79 C2 Hormuz, Strait of Iran/Oman
103 D2 Horn Austria
92 □A2 Horn c. Iceland
153 B6 Horn, Cape Chile
141 D2 Hornell U.S.A.
130 B2 Hornepayne Can.
98 C2 Hornsea U.K.
90 B2 Horodenka Ukr.
91 C1 Horodnya Ukr.
90 B2 Horodok Khmel'nyts'ka Oblast' Ukr.
90 A2 Horodok L'vivs'ka Oblast' Ukr.
90 A1 Horokhiv Ukr.
Horqin Youyi Qianqi China see Ulanhot
131 E1 Horse Islands Can.
52 B3 Horsham Austr.
126 C2 Horton r. Can.
117 B4 Hosa'ina Eth.
74 A2 Hoshab Pak.
74 B1 Hoshiarpur India
77 E3 Hotan China
122 B2 Hotazel S. Africa
142 B2 Hot Springs AR U.S.A.
136 C2 Hot Springs SD U.S.A.
128 C1 Hottah Lake Can.
62 B1 Houayxay Laos
100 B2 Houffalize Belgium
70 B2 Houma China
142 B3 Houma U.S.A.
128 B2 Houston Can.
139 D3 Houston U.S.A.
122 B3 Houwater S. Africa
68 C1 Hovd Mongolia
99 C3 Hove U.K.
68 C1 Hövsgöl Nuur l. Mongolia
116 A3 Howar, Wadi watercourse Sudan
53 C3 Howe, Cape Austr.
49 G2 Howland Island N. Pacific Ocean
53 C3 Howlong Austr.
101 D2 Höxter Ger.
96 C1 Hoy i. U.K.
93 E3 Høyanger Norway
102 C1 Hoyerswerda Ger.
62 A2 Hpapun Myanmar
103 D1 Hradec Králové Czech Rep.
109 C2 Hrasnica Bos.-Herz.
91 C1 Hrebinka Ukr.
88 B3 Hrodna Belarus
62 A1 Hsi-hseng Myanmar
62 A1 Hsipaw Myanmar
70 A2 Huachi China
150 A3 Huacho Peru
69 D2 Huade China
65 B1 Huadian China
70 B2 Huai'an China
70 B2 Huaibei China
71 A3 Huaihua China
70 B2 Huainan China
70 B2 Huaiyang China
145 C3 Huajuápan de León Mex.
59 C3 Huaki Indon.
71 C3 Hualian Taiwan

150 A2 Huallaga r. Peru
120 A2 Huambo Angola
150 A3 Huancayo Peru
Huangcaoba China see Xingyi
70 B2 Huangchuan China
Huang Hai sea N. Pacific Ocean see Yellow Sea
Huang He r. China see Yellow River
71 A4 Huangliu China
70 B3 Huangshan China
70 B2 Huangshi China
70 A2 Huangtu Gaoyuan plat. China
71 C3 Huangyan China
65 B1 Huanren China
150 A2 Huánuco Peru
152 B2 Huanuni Bol.
150 A2 Huaráz Peru
150 A3 Huarmey Peru
152 A3 Huasco Chile
152 A3 Huasco r. Chile
144 B2 Huatabampo Mex.
145 C3 Huatusco Mex.
71 A3 Huayuan China
70 B2 Hubei China
73 B3 Hubli India
Hubballi India see Hubli
100 C2 Hückelhoven Ger.
98 C2 Hucknall U.K.
98 C2 Huddersfield U.K.
93 G3 Hudiksvall Sweden
141 E2 Hudson r. U.S.A.
129 D2 Hudson Bay Can.
127 F3 Hudson Bay sea Can.
128 B2 Hudson's Hope Can.
127 G2 Hudson Strait Can.
63 B2 Huê Vietnam
146 A3 Huehuetenango Guat.
144 B2 Huehueto, Cerro mt. Mex.
145 C2 Huejutla Mex.
106 B2 Huelva Spain
107 C2 Huércal-Overa Spain
107 C1 Huesca Spain
106 C2 Huéscar Spain
50 B3 Hughes (abandoned) Austr.
139 D2 Hugo U.S.A.
122 B2 Huhudi S. Africa
122 A2 Huib-Hoch Plateau Namibia
71 B3 Huichang China
65 B1 Huich'ŏn N. Korea
120 A2 Huila, Planalto da Angola
71 B3 Huilai China
62 B1 Huili China
65 B1 Huinan China
93 H3 Huittinen Fin.
145 C3 Huixtla Mex.
Huiyang China see Huizhou
71 B3 Huize China
71 B3 Huizhou China
78 B2 Hujr Saudi Arabia
122 B1 Hukuntsi Botswana
78 B2 Hulayfah Saudi Arabia
66 B1 Hulin China
130 C2 Hull Can.
Hulun China see Hulun Buir
69 D1 Hulun Buir China
69 D1 Hulun Nur l. China
91 D2 Hulyaypole Ukr.
69 E1 Huma China
150 B2 Humaitá Brazil
122 B3 Humansdorp S. Africa
98 C2 Humber est. U.K.
126 D3 Humboldt Can.
142 C1 Humboldt U.S.A.
135 C2 Humboldt r. U.S.A.
103 E2 Humenné Slovakia
53 C3 Hume Reservoir Austr.

138 A1 Humphreys Peak U.S.A.
92 □A2 Húnaflói b. Iceland
71 B3 Hunan prov. China
65 C1 Hunchun China
110 B1 Hunedoara Romania
101 D2 Hünfeld Ger.
103 D2 Hungary country Europe
52 B1 Hungerford Austr.
65 B2 Hüngnam N. Korea
65 A1 Hun He r. China
99 D2 Hunstanton U.K.
101 D1 Hunte r. Ger.
51 D4 Hunter Islands Austr.
99 C2 Huntingdon U.K.
140 B2 Huntington IN U.S.A.
140 C3 Huntington WV U.S.A.
54 C1 Huntly N.Z.
96 C2 Huntly U.K.
130 C2 Huntsville Can.
142 C2 Huntsville AL U.S.A.
139 D2 Huntsville TX U.S.A.
59 D3 Huon Peninsula P.N.G.
70 B2 Huozhou China
137 D2 Huron U.S.A.
140 C2 Huron, Lake Can./U.S.A.
135 D3 Hurricane U.S.A.
92 □B2 Húsavík Iceland
110 C1 Huşi Romania
126 A2 Huslia U.S.A.
78 B3 Ḥuşn Āl 'Abr Yemen
102 B1 Husum Ger.
69 C1 Hutag-Öndör Mongolia
60 A1 Hutanopan Indon.
137 D3 Hutchinson U.S.A.
70 C2 Huzhou China
92 □C3 Hvalnes Iceland
92 □B3 Hvannadalshnúkur vol. Iceland
109 C2 Hvar i. Croatia
120 B2 Hwange Zimbabwe
136 C2 Hyannis U.S.A.
68 C1 Hyargas Nuur salt l. Mongolia
50 A3 Hyden Austr.
73 B3 Hyderabad India
74 A2 Hyderabad Pak.
105 D3 Hyères France
105 D3 Hyères, Îles d' France
65 B1 Hyesan N. Korea
128 B2 Hyland Post Can.
67 B3 Hyōno-sen mt. Japan
99 D3 Hythe U.K.
93 H3 Hyvinkää Fin.

I

150 B2 Iaco r. Brazil
110 C2 Ialomiţa r. Romania
110 C1 Ianca Romania
110 C1 Iaşi Romania
64 A1 Iba Phil.
115 C4 Ibadan Nigeria
150 A1 Ibagué Col.
150 A1 Ibarra Ecuador
78 B3 Ibb Yemen
100 C1 Ibbenbüren Ger.
115 C4 Ibi Nigeria
155 C1 Ibiá Brazil
155 D1 Ibiraçu Brazil
107 D2 Ibiza Spain
107 D2 Ibiza i. Spain
151 D3 Ibotirama Brazil
79 C2 Ibrā' Oman
79 C2 Ibrī Oman
150 A3 Ica Peru
92 □B2 Iceland country Europe
66 D3 Ichinoseki Japan

91 C1	Ichnya Ukr.	
65 A3	Ich'ŏn N. Korea	
139 E2	Idabel U.S.A.	
134 D1	Idaho state U.S.A.	
134 D2	Idaho Falls U.S.A.	
100 C3	Idar-Oberstein Ger.	
116 B2	Idfu Egypt	
115 D2	Idhān Murzuq des. Libya	
118 B3	Idiofa Dem. Rep. Congo	
80 B2	Idlib Syria	
154 B2	Iepê Brazil	
100 A2	Ieper Belgium	
119 D3	Ifakara Tanz.	
121 □D3	Ifanadiana Madag.	
115 C4	Ife Nigeria	
114 C1	Ifôghas, Adrar des hills Mali	
61 C1	Igan Sarawak Malaysia	
154 C1	Igarapava Brazil	
82 G2	Igarka Rus. Fed.	
74 B3	Igatpuri India	
81 C2	Iğdır Turkey	
108 A3	Iglesias Sardegna Italy	
127 F2	Igloolik Can.	
	Igluligaarjuk Can. see	
	Chesterfield Inlet	
130 A2	Ignace Can.	
88 C2	Ignalina Lith.	
110 C2	İğneada Turkey	
111 B3	Igoumenitsa Greece	
86 E3	Igra Rus. Fed.	
86 F2	Igrim Rus. Fed.	
154 B3	Iguaçu r. Brazil	
154 B3	Iguaçu Falls Arg./Brazil	
145 C3	Iguala Mex.	
107 D1	Igualada Spain	
154 C2	Iguape Brazil	
154 B2	Iguatemi Brazil	
154 E2	Iguatu Brazil	
151 E2	Iguatu Brazil	
118 A3	Iguéla Gabon	
119 D3	Igunga Tanz.	
121 □D3	Ihosy Madag.	
92 I3	Iisalmi Fin.	
115 C4	Ijebu-Ode Nigeria	
100 B1	IJmuiden Neth.	
100 B1	IJssel r. Neth.	
100 B1	IJsselmeer l. Neth.	
123 G2	Ikageng S. Africa	
111 C3	Ikaria i. Greece	
118 C3	Ikela Dem. Rep. Congo	
110 B2	Ikhtiman Bulg.	
67 A4	Iki-shima i. Japan	
121 □D3	Ikongo Madag.	
65 B2	Iksan S. Korea	
64 B1	Ilagan Phil.	
81 C2	Ïlâm Iran	
75 C2	Ilam Nepal	
103 D1	Iława Pol.	
77 D2	Ilazārān, Kūh-e mt. Iran	
129 D2	Île-à-la-Crosse Can.	
129 D2	Île-à-la-Crosse, Lac l. Can.	
118 C3	Ilebo Dem. Rep. Congo	
124 H6	Île Clipperton terr. N. Pacific Ocean	
119 D2	Ilemi Triangle terr. Kenya	
119 D2	Ileret Kenya	
113 K11	Îles Crozet is Indian Ocean	
49 I3	Îles du Désappointement is Fr. Polynesia	
49 I4	Îles Gambier is Fr. Polynesia	
99 D3	Ilford U.K.	
99 A3	Ilfracombe U.K.	
155 D2	Ilha Grande, Baía da b. Brazil	
154 B2	Ilha Grande, Represa resr Brazil	
154 B2	Ilha Solteíra, Represa resr Brazil	
106 B1	Ílhavo Port.	
151 E3	Ilhéus Brazil	
64 B2	Iligan Phil.	
152 A4	Illapel Chile	
90 C2	Illichivs'k Ukr.	
140 A3	Illinois r. U.S.A.	
140 B3	Illinois state U.S.A.	
90 B?	Illintsi Ukr.	
115 C2	Illizi Alg.	
89 D2	Il'men', Ozero l. Rus. Fed.	
101 E2	Ilmenau Ger.	
150 A3	Ilo Peru	
64 B1	Iloilo Phil.	
92 J3	Ilomantsi Fin.	
115 C4	Ilorin Nigeria	
53 D1	Iluka Austr.	
127 H2	Ilulissat Greenland	
67 A4	Imari Japan	
117 C4	Īmī Eth.	
108 B2	Imola Italy	
151 D?	Imperatriz Brazil	
136 C2	Imperial U.S.A	
118 B2	Impfondo Congo	
62 A1	Imphal India	
111 C2	Imroz Turkey	
150 B3	Inambari r. Peru	
115 C2	In Aménas Alg.	
59 C3	Inanwatan Indon.	
92 I2	Inari Fin.	
92 I2	Inarijärvi l. Fin.	
67 D3	Inawashiro-ko l. Japan	
80 B1	Înea Burun pt Turkey	
65 B2	Inch'ŏn S. Korea	
123 D2	Incomati r. Moz.	
78 A3	Inda Silasē Eth.	
144 B2	Indé Mex.	
135 C3	Independence CA U.S.A.	
137 E2	Independence IA U.S.A.	
137 D3	Independence KS U.S.A.	
137 E3	Independence MO U.S.A.	
134 C2	Independence Mountains U.S.A.	
76 B2	Inderbor Kazakh.	
72 B2	India country Asia	
141 D2	Indiana U.S.A.	
140 B2	Indiana state U.S.A.	
140 B3	Indianapolis U.S.A.	
129 D2	Indian Head Can.	
159	Indian Ocean World	
137 E2	Indianola IA U S A	
142 B2	Indianola MS U.S.A.	
135 C3	Indian Springs U.S.A.	
86 D2	Indiga Rus. Fed.	
83 K2	Indigirka r. Rus. Fed.	
109 D1	Indija Serbia	
135 C4	Indio U.S.A.	
58 B3	Indonesia country Asia	
74 B2	Indore India	
61 B2	Indramayu, Tanjung pt Indon.	
104 C2	Indre r. France	
74 A2	Indus r. China/Pak	
74 A2	Indus, Mouths of the Pak.	
80 B1	İnebolu Turkey	
111 C2	İneğöl Turkey	
144 B3	Infiernillo, Presa resr Mex.	
53 D1	Inglewood Austr.	
102 C2	Ingolstadt Ger.	
75 C2	Ingraj Bazar India	
123 D2	Inhaca Moz.	
121 C3	Inhambane Moz.	
97 A2	Inishbofin i. Ireland	
97 B1	Inishmore i. Ireland	
97 C1	Inishowen pen. Ireland	
54 E2	Inland Kaikoura Range mts N.Z.	
102 C2	Inn r. Europe	
127 G1	Innaanganeq c. Greenland	
96 B?	Inner Sound sea chan. U.K.	
51 D1	Innisfail Austr.	
102 C2	Innsbruck Austria	
154 B1	Inocência Brazil	
118 B3	Inongo Dem. Rep. Congo	
103 D1	Inowrocław Pol.	
114 C2	In Salah Alg.	
67 A2	Insein Myanmar	
86 F2	Inta Rus. Fed.	
137 F1	International Falls U.S.A.	
130 C1	Inukjuak Can.	
126 C2	Inuvik Can.	
96 B2	Inveraray U.K.	
54 A3	Invercargill N.Z.	
53 D1	Inverell Austr.	
96 B2	Invergordon U.K.	
128 C2	Invermere Can.	
131 D2	Inverness Can.	
96 B2	Inverness U.K.	
96 C2	Inverurie U.K.	
52 A3	Investigator Strait Austr.	
77 E1	Ioya Rus. Fed.	
119 D3	Inyonga Tanz.	
87 D3	Inza Rus. Fed.	
111 B3	Ioannina Greece	
137 D3	Iola U.S.A.	
96 A2	Iona i. U.K.	
111 B3	Ionian Islands Greece	
109 C3	Ionian Sea Greece/Italy	
	Ionioi Nisoi is Greece see	
	Ionian Islands	
111 C3	Ios i. Greece	
137 E2	Iowa state U.S.A.	
137 E2	Iowa City U.S.A.	
154 C1	Ipameri Brazil	
155 D1	Ipatinga Brazil	
81 C1	Ipatovo Rus. Fed.	
123 C2	Ipelegeng S. Africa	
150 A1	Ipiales Col.	
154 B3	Ipiranga Brazil	
60 B1	Ipoh Malaysia	
154 B1	Iporá Brazil	
118 C2	Ippy C.A.R.	
111 C2	Ipsala Turkey	
53 D1	Ipswich Austr.	
99 D2	Ipswich U.K.	
127 G2	Iqaluit Can.	
152 A3	Iquique Chile	
150 A2	Iquitos Peru	
	Irakleio Greece see Iraklion	
76 B3	Iran country Asia	
61 C1	Iran, Pegunungan mts Indon.	
79 D2	Īrānshahr Iran	
144 B2	Irapuato Mex.	
81 C2	Iraq country Asia	
154 B3	Irati Brazil	
80 B2	Irbid Jordan	
86 F3	Irbit Rus. Fed.	
151 D3	Irecê Brazil	
97 C2	Ireland country Europe	
118 C3	Irema Dem. Rep. Congo	
114 B3	Irîgui reg. Mali/Maur.	
119 D3	Iringa Tanz.	
151 D2	Iriri r. Brazil	
95 B3	Irish Sea Ireland/U.K.	
69 C1	Irkutsk Rus. Fed.	
52 A2	Iron Knob Austr.	
140 B1	Iron Mountain U.S.A.	
140 A1	Ironwood U.S.A.	
64 B1	Irosin Phil.	
67 C4	Irō-zaki pt Japan	
90 C1	Irpin' Ukr.	
62 A2	Irrawaddy r. Myanmar	
63 A2	Irrawaddy, Mouths of the Myanmar	
86 F2	Irtysh r. Kazakh./Rus. Fed.	

107 C1 Irun Spain
96 B3 Irvine U.K.
64 B2 Isabela Phil.
146 B3 Isabela, Cordillera mts Nic.
92 CA2 Ísafjördur Iceland
67 B4 Isahaya Japan
105 E2 Isar r. Ger.
96 □ Isbister U.K.
108 B2 Ischia, Isola d' i. Italy
67 C4 Ise Japan
118 C2 Isengi Dem. Rep. Congo
100 C2 Iserlohn Ger.
101 D1 Isernhagen Ger.
67 C4 Ise-wan b. Japan
114 C4 Iseyin Nigeria
Isfahan Iran see Eşfahān
66 D3 Ishikari-wan b. Japan
66 D3 Ishinomaki Japan
67 D3 Ishioka Japan
140 B1 Ishpeming U.S.A.
111 C2 Işıklar Dağı mts Turkey
111 C3 Işıklı Turkey
123 D2 Isipingo S. Africa
119 C2 Isiro Dem. Rep. Congo
80 B2 İskenderun Turkey
82 S3 Iskitim Rus. Fed.
110 B2 Iskür r. Bulg.
128 A2 Iskut r. Can.
74 B1 Islamabad Pak.
52 A2 Island Lagoon imp. l. Austr.
129 E2 Island Lake Can.
54 B1 Islands, Bay of N.Z.
96 A3 Islay i. U.K.
77 D3 Ismoili Somoní, Qullai mt.
        Tajik.
109 C3 Isola di Capo Rizzuto Italy
110 C2 Isperikh Bulg.
80 B2 Israel country Asia
105 C2 Issoire France
111 C2 İstanbul Turkey
        İstanbul Boğazı str. Turkey see
        Bosporus
111 B3 Istiaia Greece
105 C3 Istres France
108 B1 Istria pen. Croatia
151 D3 Itaberaba Brazil
155 D1 Itabira Brazil
155 D2 Itabirito Brazil
151 E3 Itabuna Brazil
150 D2 Itacoatiara Brazil
154 B2 Itaguajé Brazil
151 D3 Itaí Brazil
154 B3 Itaipu, Represa de resr Brazil
151 C2 Itaituba Brazil
152 D3 Itajaí Brazil
155 C2 Itajubá Brazil
108 B2 Italy country Europe
155 D1 Itamarandiba Brazil
155 D1 Itambacuri Brazil
155 D1 Itambé, Pico de mt. Brazil
62 D4 Itanagar India
154 C2 Itanhaém Brazil
155 D1 Itanhém Brazil
155 D1 Itaobím Brazil
154 C1 Itapajipe Brazil
155 E1 Itapebi Brazil
155 D2 Itapecuru Mirim Brazil
155 D2 Itapemirim Brazil
155 D2 Itaperuna Brazil
155 D1 Itapetinga Brazil
154 C2 Itapetininga Brazil
154 C2 Itapeva Brazil
151 E3 Itapicuru r. Brazil
154 C1 Itapuranga Brazil
154 C2 Itararé Brazil
75 B4 Itarsi India
154 B1 Itarumã Brazil

155 D2 Itaúna Brazil
71 C3 Itbayat i. Phil.
141 D2 Ithaca U.S.A.
101 D1 Ith Hils ridge Ger.
118 C2 Itimbiri r. Dem. Rep. Congo
155 D1 Itinga Brazil
154 B1 Itiquira Brazil
154 A1 Itiquira r. Brazil
67 C4 Itō Japan
154 C2 Itu Brazil
150 A2 Itui r. Brazil
154 C1 Ituiutaba Brazil
119 C3 Itula Dem. Rep. Congo
154 C1 Itumbiara Brazil
154 B1 Iturama Brazil
101 D1 Itzehoe Ger.
83 N2 Iul'tin Rus. Fed.
154 B2 Ivai r. Brazil
92 I2 Ivalo Fin.
88 C3 Ivanava Belarus
52 B2 Ivanhoe Austr.
90 B1 Ivankiv Ukr.
90 A2 Ivano-Frankivs'k Ukr.
89 F2 Ivanovo Rus. Fed.
88 C3 Ivatsevichy Belarus
111 C2 Ivaylovgrad Bulg.
86 F2 Ivdel' Rus. Fed.
154 B2 Ivinheima Brazil
154 B2 Ivinheima r. Brazil
127 H2 Ivittuut Greenland
        Ivory Coast country Africa see
        Côte d'Ivoire
108 A1 Ivrea Italy
111 C3 İvrindi Turkey
127 F2 Ivujivik Can.
67 D3 Iwaki Japan
67 B4 Iwakuni Japan
66 D3 Iwamizawa Japan
66 D2 Iwanai Japan
88 C3 Iwye Belarus
123 D3 Ixopo S. Africa
144 B3 Ixtlán Mex.
145 D2 Izamal Mex.
81 C1 Izberbash Rus. Fed.
86 E3 Izhevsk Rus. Fed.
86 E2 Izhma Rus. Fed.
89 E3 Izmalkovo Rus. Fed.
111 C3 İzmir Turkey
111 C3 İznik Gölü l. Turkey
152 B2 Izozog, Bañados del swamp
        Bol.
67 B3 Izumo Japan
90 B1 Izyaslav Ukr.
91 D2 Izyum Ukr.

J

        Jabal, Bahr el r. S. Sudan/
        Uganda see White Nile
106 C2 Jabalón r. Spain
75 B2 Jabalpur India
50 C1 Jabiru Austr.
109 C2 Jablanica Bos.-Herz.
151 E2 Jaboatão dos Guararapes
        Brazil
154 C2 Jaboticabal Brazil
107 C1 Jaca Spain
145 C2 Jacala Mex.
151 C2 Jacareacanga Brazil
155 C2 Jacareí Brazil
155 D1 Jacinto Brazil
141 E1 Jackman U.S.A.
142 C2 Jackson AL U.S.A.
140 C2 Jackson MI U.S.A.

142 B2 Jackson MS U.S.A.
142 C1 Jackson TN U.S.A.
136 A2 Jackson WY U.S.A.
54 A2 Jackson Head N.Z.
142 B2 Jacksonville FL U.S.A.
143 D2 Jacksonville IL U.S.A.
140 A3 Jacksonville IL U.S.A.
143 E2 Jacksonville NC U.S.A.
139 D2 Jacksonville TX U.S.A.
147 C3 Jacmel Haiti
74 A2 Jacobabad Pak.
151 D3 Jacobina Brazil
131 D2 Jacques-Cartier, Mont mt.
        Can.
151 D2 Jacundá Brazil
154 C2 Jacupiranga Brazil
109 C2 Jadovnik mt. Bos.-Herz.
106 A2 Jaén Peru
106 C2 Jaén Spain
52 A3 Jaffa, Cape Austr.
73 B4 Jaffna Sri Lanka
73 C3 Jagdalpur India
123 C2 Jagersfontein S. Africa
79 C2 Jaghīn Iran
154 C2 Jaguariaíva Brazil
79 C2 Jahrom Iran
74 B2 Jaipur India
74 B2 Jaisalmer India
75 C2 Jajarkot Nepal
60 B2 Jakarta Indon.
128 A1 Jakes Corner Can.
92 G2 Jäkkvik Sweden
92 H3 Jakobstad Fin.
77 D3 Jalālābād Afgh.
77 D2 Jalal-Abad Kyrg.
74 B1 Jalandhar India
        Jalapa Mex. see Xalapa
154 B2 Jales Brazil
74 B2 Jalgaon India
115 D4 Jalingo Nigeria
74 B3 Jalna India
144 B2 Jalpa Mex.
75 C2 Jalpaiguri India
145 C2 Jalpan Mex.
115 E2 Jālū Libya
146 C3 Jamaica country West Indies
146 C3 Jamaica Channel
        Haiti/Jamaica
75 C2 Jamalpur Bangl.
60 B2 Jambi Indon.
137 D2 James r. N. Dakota/S. Dakota
        U.S.A.
141 D3 James r. VA U.S.A.
130 B1 James Bay Can.
52 A2 Jamestown Austr.
137 D2 Jamestown ND U.S.A.
141 D2 Jamestown NY U.S.A.
74 B1 Jammu India
74 B1 Jammu and Kashmir terr. Asia
74 B2 Jamnagar India
93 I3 Jämsä Fin.
75 C2 Jamshedpur India
75 C2 Jamuna r. Bangl.
75 C2 Janakpur Nepal
155 D1 Janaúba Brazil
81 D2 Jandaq Iran
140 B2 Janesville U.S.A.
84 F1 Jan Mayen terr. Arctic Ocean
81 D1 Jañña Turkm.
122 B3 Jansenville S. Africa
155 D1 Januária Brazil
74 B2 Jaora India
67 C3 Japan country Asia
156 C3 Japan, Sea of N. Pacific Ocean
150 B2 Japurá Brazil
154 C1 Jaraguá Brazil

154 B2 Jaraguari Brazil
70 A2 Jarantai China
152 C3 Jardim Brazil
103 D1 Jarocin Pol.
103 E1 Jarosław Pol.
92 F3 Järpen Sweden
150 B3 Jarú Brazil
Jarud China see Lubei
49 H3 Jarvis Island
S. Pacific Ocean
79 C2 Jāsk Iran
103 E2 Jasło Pol.
128 C2 Jasper Can.
140 B3 Jasper IN U.S.A.
139 E2 Jasper TX U.S.A.
103 D2 Jastrzębie-Zdrój Pol.
103 D2 Jászberény Hungary
154 B1 Jataí Brazil
74 A2 Jati Pak.
154 C2 Jaú Brazil
150 B2 Jaú r. Brazil
145 C2 Jaumave Mex.
75 C2 Jaunpur India
154 B1 Jauru Brazil
61 B2 Java i. Indon.
Java i. Indon. see Java
Java Sea Indon. see Jawa, Laut
159 D4 Jawa, Laut sea Indon.
117 C4 Jawhar Somalia
103 D1 Jawor Pol.
103 D1 Jaworzno Pol.
59 D3 Jaya, Puncak mt. Indon.
59 D3 Jayapura Indon.
79 C2 Jaz Mūrīān, Hāmūn-e imp. l.
Iran
128 B1 Jean Marie River Can.
131 D1 Jeannin, Lac l. Can.
116 A3 Jebel Abyad Plateau Sudan
96 C3 Jedburgh U.K.
78 A2 Jeddah Saudi Arabia
101 E1 Jeetze r. Ger.
135 C3 Jefferson, Mount U.S.A.
137 E3 Jefferson City U.S.A.
88 C2 Jēkabpils Latvia
103 D1 Jelenia Góra Pol.
88 B2 Jelgava Latvia
61 C2 Jember Indon.
101 E2 Jena Ger.
Jengish Chokusu mt. China/
Kyrg. see Pobeda Peak
80 B2 Jenin West Bank
142 B2 Jennings U.S.A.
151 D3 Jequié Brazil
155 D1 Jequitaí Brazil
155 D1 Jequitinhonha Brazil
155 E1 Jequitinhonha r. Brazil
147 C3 Jérémie Haiti
144 B2 Jerez Mex.
106 B2 Jerez de la Frontera Spain
109 D3 Jergucat Albania
115 C1 Jerid, Chott el salt l.
Tunisia
134 D2 Jerome U.S.A.
95 C4 Jersey terr. Channel Is
151 D2 Jerumenha Brazil
80 B2 Jerusalem Israel/West Bank
53 D3 Jervis Bay Territory admin. div.
Austr.
108 B1 Jesenice Slovenia
108 B2 Jesi Italy
101 F2 Jessen Ger.
75 C2 Jessore Bangl.
143 D2 Jesup U.S.A.
145 C3 Jesús Carranza Mex.
109 C2 Jezercë, Maja mt. Albania
74 B2 Jhalawar India
74 B1 Jhang Pak.

75 B2 Jhansi India
75 C2 Jharsuguda India
74 B1 Jhelum Pak.
70 C2 Jiading China
69 E1 Jiamusi China
71 B3 Ji'an Jiangxi China
65 B1 Ji'an Jilin China
62 A1 Jianchuan China
Jiandaoyu China see Guojiaba
70 B2 Jiangsu prov. China
71 B3 Jiangxi prov. China
70 A2 Jiangyou China
70 B3 Jianli China
70 B2 Jianqiao China
71 B3 Jianyang Fujian China
70 A2 Jianyang Sichuan China
70 C2 Jiaozhou China
70 C2 Jiaozuo China
70 C2 Jiaxing China
71 C3 Jiayi Taiwan
68 C2 Jiayuguan China
Jiddah Saudi Arabia see Jeddah
92 G2 Jiehkkevárri mt. Norway
70 B2 Jiexiu China
68 C2 Jigzhi China
103 D2 Jihlava Czech Rep.
117 C4 Jilib Somalia
116 A2 Jilf al Kabīr, Hadabat al plat.
Egypt
117 C4 Jilib Somalia
69 E2 Jilin China
65 B1 Jilin prov. China
65 A1 Jilin Hada Ling mts China
117 B4 Jīma Eth.
144 B2 Jiménez Chihuahua Mex.
145 C2 Jiménez Tamaulipas Mex.
70 B2 Jinan China
70 B2 Jincheng China
53 C3 Jindabyne Austr.
103 D2 Jindřichův Hradec Czech Rep.
71 B3 Jingdezhen China
70 B2 Jinghong China
Jinghang Yunhe canal China
Jinghang Yunhe canal China
see Jinghang Yunhe
62 B1 Jinghe China
70 B2 Jingmen China
70 A2 Jingning China
70 A2 Jingtai China
71 A3 Jingxi China
65 B1 Jingyu China
70 A2 Jingyuan China
70 B2 Jingzhou China
70 B2 Jingzhou China
71 B3 Jinhua China
70 B2 Jining Shandong China
119 D2 Jinja Uganda
117 B4 Jinka Eth.
146 B3 Jinotepe Nic.
71 A3 Jinping China
Jinsha Jiang r. China see
Yangtze
70 B3 Jiushi China
70 B2 Jinzhong China
70 C1 Jinzhou China
150 B3 Jiparaná r. Brazil
75 C1 Jirang China
79 C2 Jīroft Iran
71 A3 Jishou China
110 B2 Jiu r. Romania
70 A2 Jiuding Shan mt. China
70 B3 Jiujiang China
66 B1 Jixi China
78 B3 Jīzān Saudi Arabia
77 C2 Jizzax Uzbek.
151 E2 João Pessoa Brazil
155 C1 João Pinheiro Brazil
74 B2 Jodhpur India

92 I3 Joensuu Fin.
67 C3 Jōetsu Japan
121 C3 Jofane Moz.
88 C2 Jōgeva Estonia
123 C2 Johannesburg S. Africa
134 C2 John Day U.S.A.
134 B1 John Day r. U.S.A.
128 C2 John D'Or Prairie Can.
143 E1 John H. Kerr Reservoir U.S.A.
96 C1 John o' Groats U.K.
143 D1 Johnson City U.S.A.
128 A1 Johnson's Crossing Can.
49 H1 Johnston Atoll N. Pacific
Ocean
96 B3 Johnstone U.K.
141 D2 Johnstown U.S.A.
60 B1 Johor Bahru Malaysia
88 C2 Jõhvi Estonia
154 C3 Joinville Brazil
105 D2 Joinville France
92 G2 Jokkmokk Sweden
92 □B2 Jökulsá á Fjöllum r. Iceland
140 B2 Joliet U.S.A.
130 C2 Joliette Can.
64 B2 Jolo Phil.
64 B2 Jolo i. Phil.
61 C2 Jombang Indon.
75 C2 Jomsom Nepal
88 B2 Jonava Lith.
142 B1 Jonesboro AR U.S.A.
142 B2 Jonesboro LA U.S.A.
127 F1 Jones Sound sea chan. Can.
93 F4 Jönköping Sweden
131 C2 Jonquière Can.
145 C3 Jonuta Mex.
137 E3 Joplin U.S.A.
80 B2 Jordan country Asia
80 B2 Jordan r. Asia
136 B1 Jordan U.S.A.
134 C2 Jordan Valley U.S.A.
62 A1 Jorhat India
93 E4 Jørpeland Norway
115 C4 Jos Nigeria
145 C3 José Cardel Mex.
131 D1 Joseph, Lac l. Can.
50 B1 Joseph Bonaparte Gulf Austr.
115 C4 Jos Plateau Nigeria
93 E3 Jotunheimen mts Norway
122 B3 Joubertina S. Africa
123 C2 Jouberton S. Africa
93 I3 Joutseno Fin.
134 B1 Juan de Fuca Strait
Can./U.S.A.
Juanshui China see
Tongcheng
145 B2 Juárez Mex.
151 D2 Juazeiro Brazil
151 E2 Juazeiro do Norte Brazil
117 B4 Juba S. Sudan
117 C5 Jubba r. Somalia
78 B2 Jubbah Saudi Arabia
145 C3 Juchitán Mex.
102 C2 Judenburg Austria
101 D2 Jühnde Ger.
146 B3 Juigalpa Nic.
100 C1 Juist i. Ger.
155 D2 Juiz de Fora Brazil
150 A3 Juliaca Peru
75 C2 Jumla Nepal
74 B2 Junagadh India
139 D2 Junction U.S.A.
137 D3 Junction City U.S.A.
154 C2 Jundiaí Brazil
128 A2 Juneau U.S.A.
53 C2 Junee Austr.
105 D2 Jungfrau mt. Switz.
141 D2 Juniata r. U.S.A.

92 G3	Junsele Sweden	
134 C2	Juntura U.S.A.	
154 C2	Juquiá Brazil	
117 A4	Jur r. S. Sudan	
105 D3	Jura mts France/Switz.	
96 B2	Jura i. U.K.	
96 B3	Jura, Sound of sea chan. U.K.	
88 B2	Jurbarkas Lith.	
88 B2	Jūrmala Latvia	
152 E1	Juruá r. Brazil	
150 C2	Juruena r. Brazil	
150 B2	Jutaí r. Brazil	
101 F2	Jüterbog Ger.	
146 B2	Juventud, Isla de la i. Cuba	
70 B2	Juxian China	
79 C2	Jūyom Iran	
122 B1	Jwaneng Botswana	
93 I3	Jyväskylä Fin.	

K

74 B1	K2 mt. China/Pakistan	
119 C3	Kabalo Dem. Rep. Congo	
119 C3	Kabare Dem. Rep. Congo	
130 B2	Kabinakagami Lake Can.	
118 C3	Kabinda Dem. Rep. Congo	
118 B2	Kabo C.A.R.	
120 B2	Kabompo Zambia	
119 C3	Kabongo Dem. Rep. Congo	
77 C3	Kābul Afgh.	
64 B2	Kaburuang i. Indon.	
121 B2	Kabwe Zambia	
74 A2	Kachchh, Gulf of India	
74 B2	Kachchh, Rann of marsh India	
83 I3	Kachug Rus. Fed.	
81 C1	Kaçkar Dağı mt. Turkey	
	Kadapa India see Cuddapah	
111 C2	Kadıköy Turkey	
114 B3	Kadiolo Mali	
73 B3	Kadmat atoll India	
121 B2	Kadoma Zimbabwe	
63 A2	Kadonkani Myanmar	
117 A3	Kadugli Sudan	
115 C3	Kaduna Nigeria	
89 E2	Kaduy Rus. Fed.	
86 E2	Kadzherom Rus. Fed.	
114 A3	Kaédi Maur.	
118 B1	Kaélé Cameroon	
65 B2	Kaesŏng N. Korea	
114 A3	Kaffrine Senegal	
121 B2	Kafue Zambia	
120 B2	Kafue r. Zambia	
118 B2	Kaga Bandoro C.A.R.	
91 E2	Kagal'nitskaya Rus. Fed.	
67 B4	Kagoshima Japan	
90 C2	Kaharlyk Ukr.	
61 C2	Kahayan r. Indon.	
118 B3	Kahemba Dem. Rep. Congo	
101 E2	Kahla Ger.	
79 C2	Kahnūj Iran	
92 H2	Kahperusvaarat mts Fin.	
80 B2	Kahramanmaraş Turkey	
79 C2	Kahūrak Iran	
59 C3	Kai, Kepulauan is Indon.	
115 C4	Kaiama Nigeria	
54 B2	Kaiapoi N.Z.	
59 C3	Kai Besar i. Indon.	
70 B2	Kaifeng China	
	Kaihua China see Wenshan	
122 B2	Kaiingveld reg. S. Africa	
59 C3	Kai Kecil i. Indon.	
54 B2	Kaikoura N.Z.	
114 A4	Kailahun Sierra Leone	
71 A3	Kaili China	
59 C3	Kaimana Indon.	

54 C1	Kaimanawa Mountains N.Z.	
67 C4	Kainan Japan	
115 C3	Kainji Reservoir Nigeria	
54 B1	Kaipara Harbour N.Z.	
74 B2	Kairana India	
115 D1	Kairouan Tunisia	
54 B1	Kaitaia N.Z.	
54 C1	Kaitawa N.Z.	
	Kaitong China see Tongyu	
59 C3	Kaiwatu Indon.	
65 A1	Kaiyuan Liaoning China	
62 B1	Kaiyuan Yunnan China	
92 I3	Kajaani Fin.	
51 D2	Kajabbi Austr.	
122 B2	Kakamas S. Africa	
119 D2	Kakamega Kenya	
91 C2	Kakhovka Ukr.	
91 C2	Kakhovs'ke Vodoskhovyshche resr Ukr.	
73 C3	Kakinada India	
128 C1	Kakisa Can.	
119 C3	Kakoswa Dem. Rep. Congo	
126 B2	Kaktovik U.S.A.	
	Kalaallit Nunaat terr. N. America see Greenland	
59 C3	Kalabahi Indon.	
120 B2	Kalabo Zambia	
91 E1	Kalach Rus. Fed.	
119 D2	Kalacha Dida Kenya	
62 A1	Kaladan r. India/Myanmar	
120 B3	Kalahari Desert Africa	
92 H3	Kalajoki Fin.	
111 B2	Kalamaria Greece	
111 B3	Kalamata Greece	
140 B2	Kalamazoo U.S.A.	
111 B3	Kalampaka Greece	
91 C2	Kalanchak Ukr.	
115 E1	Kalanshiyū ar Ramlī al Kabīr, Sarīr des. Libya	
63 B2	Kalasin Thai.	
79 C2	Kalāt Iran	
74 A2	Kalat Pak.	
50 A2	Kalbarri Austr.	
	Kalburgi India see Gulbarga	
111 C3	Kale Turkey	
80 B1	Kalecik Turkey	
118 C3	Kalema Dem. Rep. Congo	
119 C3	Kalemie Dem. Rep. Congo	
62 A1	Kalemyo Myanmar	
	Kalgan China see Zhangjiakou	
50 B3	Kalgoorlie Austr.	
109 C2	Kali Croatia	
110 C2	Kaliakra, Nos pt Bulg.	
119 C3	Kalima Dem. Rep. Congo	
61 C2	Kalimantan reg. Indon.	
88 B3	Kaliningrad Rus. Fed.	
91 D2	Kalininskaya Rus. Fed.	
88 C3	Kalinkavichy Belarus	
134 D1	Kalispell U.S.A.	
103 D1	Kalisz Pol.	
91 E2	Kalitva r. Rus. Fed.	
92 H2	Kalix Sweden	
92 H2	Kalixälven r. Sweden	
111 C3	Kalkan Turkey	
120 A3	Kalkfeld Namibia	
92 I3	Kallavesi l. Fin.	
92 F3	Kallsjön l. Sweden	
93 G4	Kalmar Sweden	
93 G4	Kalmarsund sea chan. Sweden	
120 B2	Kalomo Zambia	
128 B2	Kalone Peak Can.	
75 B1	Kalpa India	
73 B3	Kalpeni atoll India	
75 B2	Kalpi India	
101 D1	Kaltenkirchen Ger.	
89 E3	Kaluga Rus. Fed.	
93 F4	Kalundborg Denmark	

90 A2	Kalush Ukr.	
89 E2	Kalyazin Rus. Fed.	
111 C3	Kalymnos i. Greece	
119 C3	Kama Dem. Rep. Congo	
62 A2	Kama Myanmar	
86 E3	Kama r. Rus. Fed.	
66 D3	Kamaishi Japan	
80 B2	Kaman Turkey	
120 A2	Kamanjab Namibia	
78 B3	Kamarān i. Yemen	
74 A2	Kamarod Pak.	
50 B3	Kambalda Austr.	
119 C4	Kambove Dem. Rep. Congo	
183 L3	Kamchatka Peninsula Rus. Fed.	
110 C2	Kamchiya r. Bulg.	
110 B2	Kamenitsa mt. Bulg.	
108 B2	Kamenjak, Rt pt Croatia	
91 D1	Kamenka Rus. Fed.	
91 E2	Kamenolomni Rus. Fed.	
83 M2	Kamenskoye Rus. Fed.	
91 E2	Kamensk-Shakhtinskiy Rus. Fed.	
86 F3	Kamensk-Ural'skiy Rus. Fed.	
122 A3	Kamiesberg mts S. Africa	
122 A3	Kamieskroon S. Africa	
129 D1	Kamilukuak Lake Can.	
119 C3	Kamina Dem. Rep. Congo	
129 E1	Kaminak Lake Can.	
90 A1	Kamin'-Kashyrs'kyy Ukr.	
128 B2	Kamloops Can.	
118 C3	Kamonia Dem. Rep. Congo	
119 D2	Kampala Uganda	
60 B1	Kampar r. Indon.	
60 B1	Kampar Malaysia	
100 B1	Kampen Neth.	
119 C3	Kampene Dem. Rep. Congo	
63 A2	Kamphaeng Phet Thai.	
63 B2	Kâmpóng Cham Cambodia	
63 B2	Kâmpóng Chhnăng Cambodia	
	Kâmpóng Saôm Cambodia see Sihanoukville	
63 B2	Kâmpóng Spœ Cambodia	
63 B2	Kâmpôt Cambodia	
129 D2	Kamsack Can.	
86 E3	Kamskoye Vodokhranilishche resr Rus. Fed.	
117 C4	Kamsuuma Somalia	
90 B2	Kam"yanets'-Podil's'kyy Ukr.	
90 A1	Kam"yanka-Buz'ka Ukr.	
88 B3	Kamyanyets Belarus	
91 D2	Kamyshevatskaya Rus. Fed.	
87 D3	Kamyshin Rus. Fed.	
135 D3	Kanab U.S.A.	
118 C3	Kananga Dem. Rep. Congo	
87 D3	Kanash Rus. Fed.	
140 C3	Kanawha r. U.S.A.	
67 C3	Kanazawa Japan	
62 A1	Kanbalu Myanmar	
63 A2	Kanchanaburi Thai.	
73 B3	Kanchipuram India	
77 C3	Kandahār Afgh.	
86 C2	Kandalaksha Rus. Fed.	
61 C2	Kandangan Indon.	
74 A2	Kandh Kot Pak.	
114 C3	Kandi Benin	
74 B2	Kandla India	
53 C2	Kandos Austr.	
121 □D2	Kandreho Madag.	
73 C4	Kandy Sri Lanka	
76 B3	Kandyagash Kazakh.	
127 G1	Kane Basin b. Greenland	
91 D2	Kanevskaya Rus. Fed.	
122 B1	Kang Botswana	
127 H2	Kangaatsiaq Greenland	
114 B3	Kangaba Mali	
80 B2	Kangal Turkey	

79 C2 Kangān Iran
60 B1 Kangar Malaysia
52 A3 Kangaroo Island Austr.
75 C2 Kangchenjunga mt. India/Nepal
65 B2 Kangdong N. Korea
61 C3 Kangean, Kepulauan is Indon.
127 I2 Kangeq c. Greenland
127 H2 Kangerlussuaq inlet Greenland
127 I2 Kangerlussuaq inlet Greenland
127 H2 Kangersuatsiaq Greenland
65 B1 Kangye N. Korea
131 D1 Kangiqsualujjuaq Can.
127 I2 Kangiqsujuaq Can.
127 G2 Kangirsuk Can.
75 C2 Kangmar China
65 B2 Kangnŭng S. Korea
65 A1 Kangping China
72 D2 Kangto mt. China/India
62 A1 Kani Myanmar
86 D2 Kanin, Poluostrov pen. Rus. Fed.
86 D2 Kanin Nos Rus. Fed.
91 C2 Kaniv Ukr.
93 H3 Kankaanpää Fin.
140 B2 Kankakee U.S.A.
114 B3 Kankan Guinea
75 C2 Kanker India
Kannur India see Kannur
73 B3 Kannur India
115 C3 Kano Nigeria
122 B3 Kanonpunt pt S. Africa
67 B4 Kanoya Japan
73 C2 Kanpur India
136 C3 Kansas r. U.S.A.
137 D3 Kansas state U.S.A.
137 E3 Kansas City U.S.A.
83 H3 Kansk Rus. Fed.
114 C4 Kantchari Burkina Faso
91 D2 Kantemirovka Rus. Fed.
97 B2 Kanturk Ireland
123 D2 Kanyamazane S. Africa
123 C1 Kanye Botswana
120 A2 Kaokoveld plat. Namibia
114 A3 Kaolack Senegal
120 B2 Kaoma Zambia
118 C3 Kapanga Dem. Rep. Congo
100 B2 Kapellen Belgium
121 B2 Kapiri Mposhi Zambia
127 H2 Kapisillit Greenland
130 B1 Kapiskau r. Can.
61 C1 Kapit Sarawak Malaysia
63 A3 Kapoe Thai.
117 B4 Kapoeta S. Sudan
103 D2 Kaposvár Hungary
77 D2 Kapshagay Kazakh.
77 D2 Kapshagay, Vodokhranilishche resr Kazakh.
61 B2 Kapuas r. Indon.
52 A2 Kapunda Austr.
130 B2 Kapuskasing Can.
103 D2 Kapuvár Hungary
88 C3 Kapyl' Belarus
114 C4 Kara Togo
111 C3 Kara Ada i. Turkey
76 C1 Karabalyk Kazakh.
80 B1 Karabük Turkey
76 C2 Karabutak Kazakh.
110 C2 Karacaköy Turkey
89 D3 Karachev Rus. Fed.
74 A2 Karachi Pak.
Kara Deniz sea Asia/Europe see Black Sea
77 D2 Karagandy Kazakh.
77 D2 Karagayly Kazakh.
83 L3 Karaginskiy Zaliv b. Rus. Fed.

81 D2 Karaj Iran
64 B2 Karakelong i. Indon.
77 D2 Kara-Köl Kyrg.
77 D2 Karakol Kyrg.
74 B1 Karakoram Range mts Asia
Karakum, Peski des. Kazakh. see Karakum Desert
76 B2 Karakum Desert Kazakh.
78 C3 Karakum Desert Turkm.
Karakumy, Peski des. Turkm. see Karakum Desert
80 B2 Karaman Turkey
77 E2 Karamay China
54 B2 Karamea N.Z.
54 B2 Karamea Bight b. N.Z.
80 B2 Karapınar Turkey
122 A2 Karasburg Namibia
Kara Sea Rus. Fed.
92 I2 Karasjok Norway
82 G3 Karasuk Rus. Fed.
77 D2 Karatau Kazakh.
77 C2 Karatau, Khrebet mts Kazakh.
86 F2 Karatayka Rus. Fed.
67 A4 Karatsu Japan
60 B2 Karawang Indon.
81 C2 Karbala' Iraq
103 E2 Karcag Hungary
111 B3 Karditsa Greece
88 B2 Kärdla Estonia
122 B3 Kareeberge mts S. Africa
75 B2 Kareli India
74 B1 Kargil India
121 C2 Kariba Zimbabwe
121 B2 Kariba, Lake resr Zambia/Zimbabwe
61 B2 Karimata, Pulau-pulau is Indon.
61 B2 Karimata, Selat str. Indon.
73 B3 Karimnagar India
61 C2 Karimunjawa, Pulau-pulau is Indon.
91 C2 Karkinit-s'ka Zatoka g. Ukr.
91 D2 Karlivka Ukr.
109 C1 Karlovac Croatia
102 C1 Karlovy Vary Czech Rep.
93 F4 Karlshamn Sweden
93 G4 Karlskrona Sweden
102 B2 Karlsruhe Ger.
93 F4 Karlstad Sweden
101 D3 Karlstadt Ger.
89 D3 Karma Belarus
93 E4 Karmøy i. Norway
75 D2 Karnafuli Reservoir Bangl.
74 B2 Karnal India
110 C2 Karnobat Bulg.
74 A2 Karodi Pak.
121 B2 Karoi Zimbabwe
121 C1 Karonga Malawi
116 B3 Karora Eritrea
111 C3 Karpathos i. Greece
111 B3 Karpenisi Greece
86 D2 Karpogory Rus. Fed.
50 A2 Karratha Austr.
81 C1 Kars Turkey
88 C2 Kārsava Latvia
86 E2 Karskiye Vorota, Proliv str. Rus. Fed.
Karskoye More sea Rus. Fed. see Kara Sea
101 E1 Karstädt Ger.
111 C2 Kartal Turkey
87 F3 Kartaly Rus. Fed.
73 B3 Karwar India
83 I3 Karymskoye Rus. Fed.
111 B3 Karystos Greece
80 A2 Kaş Turkey
130 B1 Kasabonika Lake Can.

118 C4 Kasaji Dem. Rep. Congo
121 C2 Kasama Zambia
120 B2 Kasane Botswana
118 B3 Kasangulu Dem. Rep. Congo
73 B3 Kasaragod India
129 D1 Kasba Lake Can.
121 B2 Kasempa Zambia
118 C4 Kasenga Dem. Rep. Congo
119 C3 Kasenye Dem. Rep. Congo
119 C3 Kasese Dem. Rep. Congo
119 D2 Kasese Uganda
81 D2 Kāshān Iran
Kashgar China see Kashi
77 D3 Kashi China
67 D3 Kashima-nada b. Japan
89 E2 Kashin Rus. Fed.
89 E3 Kashira Rus. Fed.
89 E3 Kashirskoye Rus. Fed.
67 C3 Kashiwazaki Japan
76 B3 Kāshmar Iran
74 A2 Kashmore Pak.
119 C3 Kashyukulu Dem. Rep. Congo
89 F2 Kasimov Rus. Fed.
93 H3 Kaskinen Fin.
119 C3 Kasongo Dem. Rep. Congo
118 B3 Kasongo-Lunda Dem. Rep. Congo
111 C3 Kasos i. Greece
Kaspiyskoye More i. Asia/Europe see Caspian Sea
116 B3 Kassala Sudan
101 D2 Kassel Ger.
80 B1 Kastamonu Turkey
111 B2 Kastoria Greece
89 D3 Kastsyukovichy Belarus
119 D3 Kasulu Tanz.
121 C2 Kasungu Malawi
141 F1 Katahdin, Mount U.S.A.
118 C3 Katako-Kombe Dem. Rep. Congo
50 A3 Katanning Austr.
63 A3 Katchall i. India
111 B2 Katerini Greece
128 A2 Kate's Needle mt. Can./U.S.A.
121 C2 Katete Zambia
62 A1 Katha Myanmar
50 C1 Katherine r. Austr.
74 B2 Kathiawar pen. India
75 C2 Kathmandu Nepal
122 B2 Kathu S. Africa
74 B1 Kathua India
114 B3 Kati Mali
75 C2 Katihar India
54 C1 Katikati N.Z.
123 C3 Katikati S. Africa
120 B3 Katima Mulilo Namibia
123 C2 Katlehong S. Africa
111 B3 Kato Achaia Greece
53 D2 Katoomba Austr.
103 D1 Katowice Pol.
78 A2 Kātrīnā, Jabal mt. Egypt
93 G4 Katrineholm Sweden
115 C3 Katsina Nigeria
115 C4 Katsina-Ala Nigeria
77 C3 Kattaqo'rg'on Uzbek.
93 F4 Kattegat str. Denmark/Sweden
100 B1 Katwijk aan Zee Neth.
124 E5 Kaua'i i. U.S.A.
93 H3 Kauhajoki Fin.
88 B3 Kaunas Lith.
115 C3 Kaura-Namoda Nigeria
92 H2 Kautokeino Norway
111 B3 Kavala Greece
66 C2 Kavalerovo Rus. Fed.
73 C3 Kavali India
73 B3 Kavaratti atoll India
110 C2 Kavarna Bulg.
81 D2 Kavīr, Dasht-e des. Iran

67 C3	Kawagoe Japan	
54 B1	Kawakawa N.Z.	
67 C3	Kawanishi Japan	
130 C2	Kawartha Lakes Can.	
67 C3	Kawasaki Japan	
54 C1	Kawerau N.Z.	
63 A2	Kawkareik Myanmar	
62 A1	Kawlin Myanmar	
63 A2	Kawmapyin Myanmar	
63 A2	Kawthaung Myanmar	
77 D3	Kaxgar He r. China	
114 B3	Kaya Burkina Faso	
61 C1	Kayan r. Indon.	
136 B2	Kaycee U.S.A.	
138 A1	Kayenta U.S.A.	
114 A3	Kayes Mali	
77 D2	Kaynar Kazakh.	
80 B2	Kayseri Turkey	
61 D1	Kazakhskiy Zaliv b. Kazakh.	
76 C2	Kazakhstan country Asia	
87 D3	Kazan' Rus. Fed.	
80 A1	Kazanlŭk Bulg.	
76 A2	Kazbek mt. Georgia/Rus. Fed.	
81 D3	Kāzerūn Iran	
103 E2	Kazincbarcika Hungary	
86 F2	Kazym-Mys Rus. Fed.	
111 B3	Kea i. Greece	
97 C1	Keady U.K.	
137 D2	Kearney U.S.A.	
138 A2	Kearny U.S.A.	
116 A3	Kebkabiya Sudan	
92 G2	Kebnekaise mt. Sweden	
117 C4	K'ebri Dehar Eth.	
61 B2	Kebumen Indon.	
128 B2	Kechika r. Can.	
103 D2	Kecskemét Hungary	
88 B2	Kėdainiai Lith.	
114 A3	Kédougou Senegal	
103 D1	Kędzierzyn-Koźle Pol.	
128 B1	Keele r. Can.	
128 A1	Keele Peak Can.	
	Keeling Taiwan see Chilung	
141 E2	Keene U.S.A.	
122 A2	Keetmanshoop Namibia	
129 E3	Keewatin Can.	
	Kefallonia i. Greece see Cephalonia	
59 C3	Kefamenanu Indon.	
92 □A3	Keflavík Iceland	
77 D2	Kegen Kazakh.	
128 C2	Keg River Can.	
62 A1	Kehsi Mansam Myanmar	
98 C2	Keighley U.K.	
88 B2	Keila Estonia	
122 B2	Keimoes S. Africa	
92 I3	Keitele l. Fin.	
52 B3	Keith Austr.	
103 E2	Kékes mt. Hungary	
92 J2	Kelesuayv, Gora h. Rus. Fed.	
102 C2	Kelheim Ger.	
80 B1	Kelkit r. Turkey	
128 B1	Keller Lake Can.	
134 C1	Kellogg U.S.A.	
92 I2	Kelloselkä Fin.	
97 C2	Kells Ireland	
88 B2	Kelmė Lith.	
115 D4	Kélo Chad	
128 C3	Kelowna Can.	
96 C3	Kelso U.K.	
134 B1	Kelso U.S.A.	
60 B1	Keluang Malaysia	
129 D2	Kelvington Can.	
86 C2	Kem' Rus. Fed.	
128 B2	Kemano (abandoned) Can.	
111 C3	Kemer Turkey	
82 G3	Kemerovo Rus. Fed.	
92 H2	Kemi Fin.	
92 I2	Kemijärvi Fin.	
92 I2	Kemijoki r. Fin.	
136 A2	Kemmerer U.S.A.	
92 I3	Kempele Fin.	
53 D2	Kempsey Austr.	
130 C2	Kempt, Lac l. Can.	
102 C2	Kempten (Allgäu) Ger.	
123 C2	Kempton Park S. Africa	
61 C2	Kemujan i. Indon.	
129 D2	Kenaston Can.	
98 B1	Kendal U.K.	
59 C3	Kendari Indon.	
61 C2	Kendawangan Indon.	
115 D3	Kendégué Chad	
114 A4	Kenema Sierra Leone	
118 B3	Kenge Dem. Rep. Congo	
62 A1	Kengtung Myanmar	
122 B2	Kenhardt S. Africa	
114 B1	Kenitra Morocco	
97 B3	Kenmare Ireland	
136 C1	Kenmare U.S.A.	
97 A3	Kenmare River inlet Ireland	
100 C3	Kenn Ger.	
137 E3	Kennett U.S.A.	
134 C1	Kennewick U.S.A.	
129 E3	Kenora Can.	
140 B2	Kenosha U.S.A.	
138 C2	Kent U.S.A.	
77 C2	Kentau Kazakh.	
140 B3	Kentucky r. U.S.A.	
140 C3	Kentucky state U.S.A.	
140 B3	Kentucky Lake U.S.A.	
119 D3	Kenya country Africa	
119 D3	Kenya, Mount Kenya	
137 E2	Keokuk U.S.A.	
75 C2	Keonjhar India	
111 C3	Kepsut Turkey	
52 B3	Kerang Austr.	
91 D2	Kerch Ukr.	
59 D3	Kerema P.N.G.	
123 C3	Keremeos Can.	
116 B3	Keren Eritrea	
81 C2	Kerend Iran	
	Kerepakupai Merú Venez. see Angel Falls	
159 C7	Kerguelen Plateau Indian Ocean	
119 D3	Kericho Kenya	
54 B1	Kerikeri N.Z.	
60 B2	Kerinci, Gunung vol. Indon.	
111 A3	Kerkyra Greece	
	Kerkyra i. Greece see Corfu	
116 B3	Kerma Sudan	
49 G4	Kermadec Islands S. Pacific Ocean	
79 C1	Kermān Iran	
81 C2	Kermānshāh Iran	
139 C2	Kermit U.S.A.	
135 C3	Kern r. U.S.A.	
100 C2	Kerpen Ger.	
129 D2	Kerrobert Can.	
139 D2	Kerrville U.S.A.	
	Keryneia Cyprus see Kyrenia	
130 B1	Kesagami Lake Can.	
111 C2	Keşan Turkey	
66 D3	Kesennuma Japan	
74 B2	Keshod India	
100 C2	Kessel Neth.	
98 B1	Keswick U.K.	
103 D2	Keszthely Hungary	
82 G3	Ket' r. Rus. Fed.	
61 C2	Ketapang Indon.	
128 A2	Ketchikan U.S.A.	
134 D2	Ketchum U.S.A.	
99 C2	Kettering U.K.	
93 H3	Keuruu Fin.	
100 C2	Kevelaer Ger.	
140 B2	Kewanee U.S.A.	
140 B1	Keweenaw Bay U.S.A.	
140 B1	Keweenaw Peninsula U.S.A.	
143 D3	Key Largo U.S.A.	
141 D3	Keyser U.S.A.	
143 D4	Key West U.S.A.	
123 C2	Kgotsong S. Africa	
69 E1	Khabarovsk Rus. Fed.	
80 B1	Khadyzhensk Rus. Fed.	
62 A1	Khagrachari Bangl.	
74 A2	Khairpur Pak.	
122 B1	Khakhea Botswana	
68 C1	Khamar-Daban, Khrebet mts Rus. Fed.	
74 B2	Khambhat India	
73 B3	Khambhat, Gulf of India	
74 B2	Khamgaon India	
78 B3	Khamir Yemen	
78 B3	Khamis Mushayt Saudi Arabia	
77 C3	Khānābād Afgh.	
74 B2	Khandwa India	
83 K2	Khandyga Rus. Fed.	
74 B1	Khanewal Pak.	
66 B2	Khanka, Lake China/Rus. Fed.	
74 B2	Khanpur Pak.	
77 D2	Khantau Kazakh.	
83 H2	Khantayskoye, Ozero l. Rus. Fed.	
86 F2	Khanty-Mansiysk Rus. Fed.	
63 A3	Khao Chum Thong Thai.	
63 A2	Khao Laem, Ang Kep Nam Thai.	
87 D4	Kharabali Rus. Fed.	
75 C2	Kharagpur India	
79 C2	Khārān r. Iran	
116 B2	Khārijah, Wāḥāt al oasis Egypt	
91 D2	Kharkiv Ukr.	
	Khar'kov Ukr. see Kharkiv	
110 C2	Kharmanli Bulg.	
86 D3	Kharovsk Rus. Fed.	
116 B3	Khartoum Sudan	
87 D4	Khasavyurt Rus. Fed.	
79 D2	Khāsh Iran	
78 A3	Khashm el Girba Sudan	
78 A3	Khashm el Girba Dam Sudan	
74 D2	Khasi Hills India	
110 C2	Khaskovo Bulg.	
123 C3	Khayamnandi S. Africa	
78 A2	Khaybar Saudi Arabia	
122 A3	Khayelitsha S. Africa	
107 D2	Khemis Miliana Alg.	
63 B2	Khemmarat Thai.	
115 C1	Khenchela Alg.	
81 D3	Kherāmeh Iran	
91 C2	Kherson Ukr.	
83 H2	Kheta r. Rus. Fed.	
69 D1	Khilok Rus. Fed.	
89 E2	Khimki Rus. Fed.	
74 A2	Khipro Pak.	
89 E3	Khlevnoye Rus. Fed.	
90 B2	Khmel'nyts'kyy Ukr.	
89 E3	Khokhol'skiy Rus. Fed.	
74 B2	Khokhropar Pak.	
89 D2	Kholm Rus. Fed.	
89 D2	Kholm-Zhirkovskiy Rus. Fed.	
79 C2	Khonj Iran	
63 B2	Khon Kaen Thai.	
62 A1	Khonsa India	
83 K2	Khonuu Rus. Fed.	
86 E2	Khorey-Ver Rus. Fed.	
69 D1	Khorinsk Rus. Fed.	
91 C2	Khorol Ukr.	
81 C2	Khorramābād Iran	
81 C2	Khorramshahr Iran	
77 D3	Khorugh Tajik.	
74 A1	Khōst Afgh.	
62 A1	Khreum Myanmar	

76 B1 Khromtau Kazakh.
90 B2 Khrystynivka Ukr.
77 C2 Khujand Tajik.
63 B2 Khu Khan Thai.
78 A2 Khulays Saudi Arabia
75 C2 Khulna Bangl.
79 B2 Khurayş Saudi Arabia
74 B1 Khushab Pak.
90 A2 Khust Ukr.
123 C2 Khutsong S. Africa
74 A2 Khuzdar Pak
81 D2 Khvānsār Iran
79 C2 Khvormūj Iran
81 C2 Khvoy Iran
89 D2 Khvoynaya Rus. Fed.
77 D3 Khyber Pass Afgh./Pak.
53 D2 Kiama Austr.
119 C3 Kiambi Dem. Rep. Congo
119 D3 Kibiti Tanz.
109 D2 Kičevo Macedonia
114 C3 Kidal Mali
99 B2 Kidderminster U.K.
114 A3 Kidira Senegal
54 C1 Kidnappers, Cape N.Z.
102 C1 Kiel Ger.
103 E1 Kielce Pol.
98 B1 Kielder Water U.K.
90 C1 Kiev Ukr.
114 A3 Kiffa Maur.
119 D3 Kigali Rwanda
119 C3 Kigoma Tanz.
88 B2 Kihnu i. Estonia
92 I2 Kiiminki Fin.
67 B4 Kii-suidō sea chan. Japan
109 D1 Kikinda Serbia
119 C3 Kikondja Dem. Rep. Congo
59 D3 Kikori P.N.G.
59 D3 Kikori r. P.N.G.
118 B3 Kikwit Dem. Rep. Congo
65 B1 Kilchu N. Korea
118 B3 Kilembe Dem. Rep. Congo
139 E2 Kilgore U.S.A.
119 D3 Kilimanjaro vol. Tanz.
80 B2 Kilis Turkey
90 B2 Kiliya Ukr.
97 B2 Kilkee Ireland
97 D1 Kilkeel U.K.
97 C2 Kilkenny Ireland
111 B2 Kilkis Greece
97 B1 Killala Bay Ireland
97 B2 Killaloe Ireland
129 C2 Killam Can.
97 B2 Killarney Ireland
139 D2 Killeen U.S.A.
96 B2 Killin U.K.
97 B1 Killybegs Ireland
96 B3 Kilmarnock U.K.
53 B3 Kilmore Austr.
119 D3 Kilosa Tanz.
97 B2 Kilrush Ireland
119 C3 Kilwa Dem. Rep. Congo
119 D3 Kilwa Masoko Tanz.
119 D3 Kimambi Tanz.
52 A2 Kimba Austr.
136 C2 Kimball U.S.A.
128 C3 Kimberley Can.
122 B3 Kimberley S. Africa
50 B1 Kimberley Plateau Austr.
65 B1 Kimch'aek N. Korea
65 B2 Kimch'ŏn S. Korea
127 G2 Kimmirut Can.
89 E3 Kimovsk Rus. Fed.
118 B3 Kimpese Dem. Rep. Congo
89 E2 Kimry Rus. Fed.
61 C1 Kinabalu, Gunung mt. Sabah Malaysia
128 C2 Kinbasket Lake Can.

130 B2 Kincardine Can.
62 A1 Kinchang Myanmar
119 C3 Kinda Dem. Rep. Congo
98 C2 Kinder Scout h. U.K.
129 D2 Kindersley Can.
114 A3 Kindia Guinea
119 C3 Kindu Dem. Rep. Congo
86 D3 Kineshma Rus. Fed.
51 E2 Kingaroy Austr.
135 B3 King City U.S.A.
130 C1 King George Islands Can.
88 C2 Kingisepp Rus. Fed.
51 D3 King Island Austr.
50 B1 King Leopold Ranges hills Austr.
138 A1 Kingman U.S.A.
135 B3 Kings r. U.S.A.
52 A3 Kingscote Austr.
99 D2 King's Lynn U.K.
48 F3 Kingsmill Group is Kiribati
50 B1 King Sound b. Austr.
134 D2 Kings Peak U.S.A.
143 D1 Kingsport U.S.A.
130 C2 Kingston Can.
146 C3 Kingston Jamaica
141 E2 Kingston U.S.A.
52 A3 Kingston South East Austr.
98 C2 Kingston upon Hull U.K.
147 D3 Kingstown St Vincent
139 D3 Kingsville U.S.A.
99 B3 Kingswood U.K.
96 B2 Kingussie U.K.
126 E2 King William Island Can.
123 C3 King William's Town S. Africa
67 D3 Kinka-san i. Japan
93 F4 Kinna Sweden
97 B3 Kinsale Ireland
118 B3 Kinshasa Dem. Rep. Congo
143 E1 Kinston U.S.A.
88 B2 Kintai Lith.
114 B4 Kintampo Ghana
96 B3 Kintyre pen. U.K.
62 A1 Kin-U Myanmar
130 C2 Kipawa, Lac l. Can.
83 I3 Kirensk Rus. Fed.
89 E3 Kireyevsk Rus. Fed.
        Kirghizia country Asia see Kyrgyzstan
49 G3 Kiribati country Pacific Ocean
80 B2 Kırıkkale Turkey
89 E2 Kirillov Rus. Fed.
        Kirin China see Jilin
        Kirinyaga mt. Kenya see Kenya, Mount
89 D2 Kirishi Rus. Fed.
49 H2 Kiritimati atoll Kiribati
111 C3 Kırkağaç Turkey
96 C2 Kirkcaldy U.K.
96 B3 Kirkcudbright U.K.
92 J2 Kirkenes Norway
130 B2 Kirkland Lake Can.
137 F2 Kirksville U.S.A.
81 C2 Kirkūk Iraq
96 C1 Kirkwall U.K.
89 D3 Kirov Kaluzhskaya Oblast' Rus. Fed.
86 D3 Kirov Rus. Fed.
        Kirovabad Azer. see Gäncä
86 E3 Kirovo-Chepetsk Rus. Fed.
91 C2 Kirovohrad Ukr.
86 C2 Kirovsk Rus. Fed.
91 D2 Kirovs'ke Ukr.
96 C2 Kirriemuir U.K.
86 E3 Kirs Rus. Fed.
74 A2 Kirthar Range mts Pak.
92 H2 Kiruna Sweden
67 C3 Kiryū Japan

89 E2 Kirzhach Rus. Fed.
119 C2 Kisangani Dem. Rep. Congo
118 B3 Kisantu Dem. Rep. Congo
60 A1 Kisaran Indon.
82 G3 Kiselevsk Rus. Fed.
75 C2 Kishangarh India
115 C4 Kishi Nigeria
        Kishinev Moldova see Chişinău
77 D1 Kishkenekol' Kazakh.
74 B1 Kishtwar India
119 D3 Kisii Kenya
103 D2 Kiskőrös Hungary
103 D2 Kiskunhalas Hungary
87 D4 Kislovodsk Rus. Fed.
117 C5 Kismaayo Somalia
119 C3 Kisoro Uganda
111 B3 Kissamos Greece
114 A4 Kissidougou Guinea
143 D3 Kissimmee U.S.A.
143 D3 Kissimmee, Lake U.S.A.
129 D2 Kississing Lake Can.
119 D3 Kisumu Kenya
114 B3 Kita Mali
66 D3 Kitakami Japan
66 D3 Kitakami-gawa r. Japan
67 B4 Kita-Kyūshū Japan
119 D2 Kitale Kenya
66 D2 Kitami Japan
130 B2 Kitchener Can.
93 J3 Kitee Fin.
119 D2 Kitgum Uganda
128 B2 Kitimat Can.
118 B3 Kitona Dem. Rep. Congo
119 D3 Kitunda Tanz.
128 B2 Kitwanga Can.
121 B2 Kitwe Zambia
101 E3 Kitzingen Ger.
92 I3 Kiuruvesi Fin.
119 C3 Kivu, Lac l. Dem. Rep. Congo/Rwanda
110 C2 Kıyıköy Turkey
86 E3 Kizel Rus. Fed.
111 C3 Kızılca Dağ mt. Turkey
87 D4 Kizlyar Rus. Fed.
92 I1 Kjøllefjord Norway
92 G2 Kjøpsvik Norway
102 C1 Kladno Czech Rep.
102 C2 Klagenfurt Austria
88 B2 Klaipėda Lith.
94 B1 Klaksvík Faroe Is
134 D2 Klamath r. U.S.A.
134 B2 Klamath Falls U.S.A.
134 B2 Klamath Mountains U.S.A.
60 B1 Klang Malaysia
102 C2 Klatovy Czech Rep.
122 A3 Klawer S. Africa
128 A2 Klawock U.S.A.
128 B2 Kleena Kleene Can.
122 D2 Kleinbegin S. Africa
122 A2 Kleinsee S. Africa
123 C2 Klerksdorp S. Africa
89 D3 Kletnya Rus. Fed.
100 C2 Kleve Ger.
89 D3 Klimavichy Belarus
89 D3 Klimovo Rus. Fed.
89 E2 Klimovsk Rus. Fed.
89 E2 Klin Rus. Fed.
101 F2 Klínovec mt. Czech Rep.
93 G4 Klintehamn Sweden
89 D3 Klintsy Rus. Fed.
109 C2 Ključ Bos.-Herz.
103 D1 Kłodzko Pol.
100 C1 Kloosterhaar Neth.
103 D2 Klosterneuburg Austria
101 E1 Klötze (Altmark) Ger.
103 D1 Kluczbork Pol.
128 A2 Klukwan U.S.A.

Klyetsk

88 C3 Klyetsk Belarus
98 C1 Knaresborough U.K.
93 F3 Knästen h. Sweden
129 E2 Knee Lake Can.
101 E1 Knesebeck Ger.
101 E3 Knetzgau Ger.
109 C2 Knin Croatia
103 C2 Knittelfeld Austria
109 D2 Knjaževac Serbia
100 A2 Knokke-Heist Belgium
143 D1 Knoxville U.S.A.
122 B3 Knysna S. Africa
76 B1 Kobda Kazakh.
67 C4 Kōbe Japan
København Denmark see Copenhagen
100 C2 Koblenz Ger.
88 B3 Kobroör i. Indon.
88 B3 Kobryn Belarus
109 D2 Kočani Macedonia
111 C2 Kocasu r. Turkey
75 C2 Koch Bihar India
73 B4 Kochi India
67 B4 Kōchi Japan
87 D4 Kochubey Rus. Fed.
75 C2 Kodarma India
117 B4 Kodok S. Sudan
90 B2 Kodyma Ukr.
111 C2 Kodzhaele mt. Bulg./Greece
122 A2 Koës Namibia
122 C2 Koffiefontein S. Africa
114 B4 Koforidua Ghana
67 C3 Kōfu Japan
131 D1 Kogaluk r. Can.
117 B5 Kogelo Kenya
74 B1 Kohat Pak.
62 A1 Kohima India
88 C2 Kohtla-Järve Estonia
92 H3 Kokkola Fin.
140 B2 Kokomo U.S.A.
77 E2 Kokpekty Kazakh.
77 C1 Kokshetau Kazakh.
131 D1 Koksoak r. Can.
123 C3 Kokstad S. Africa
Koktokay China see Fuyun
58 C3 Kolaka Indon.
86 C2 Kola Peninsula Rus. Fed.
92 H2 Kolari Fin.
114 A3 Kolda Senegal
93 E4 Kolding Denmark
107 D2 Koléa Alg.
86 D2 Kolguyev, Ostrov i. Rus. Fed.
73 B3 Kolhapur India
88 B2 Kolkasrags pt Latvia
75 C2 Kolkata India
Kollam India see Kollam
73 B4 Kollam India
Köln Ger. see Cologne
103 D1 Kołobrzeg Pol.
114 B3 Kolokani Mali
89 E2 Kolomna Rus. Fed.
90 B2 Kolomyya Ukr.
122 B2 Kolonkwaneng Botswana
82 G3 Kolpashevo Rus. Fed.
89 E3 Kolpny Rus. Fed.
Kol'skiy Poluostrov pen. Rus. Fed. see Kola Peninsula
78 B3 Koluli Eritrea
119 C4 Kolwezi Dem. Rep. Congo
83 L2 Kolyma r. Rus. Fed.
83 L2 Kolymskaya Nizmennost' lowland Rus. Fed.
83 M2 Kolymskiy, Khrebet mts Rus. Fed.
67 C3 Komaki Japan
83 M3 Komandorskiye Ostrova is Rus. Fed.

103 D2 Komárno Slovakia
123 D2 Komati r. S. Africa/Swaziland
67 C3 Komatsu Japan
119 C3 Kombe Dem. Rep. Congo
90 C2 Kominternivs'ke Ukr.
109 C2 Komiža Croatia
103 D2 Komló Hungary
118 B3 Komono Congo
111 C2 Komotini Greece
122 B3 Komsberg mts S. Africa
83 H1 Komsomolets, Ostrov i. Rus. Fed.
89 F2 Komsomol'sk Rus. Fed.
91 C2 Komsomol's'k Ukr.
87 D4 Komsomol'skiy Rus. Fed.
69 E1 Komsomol'sk-na-Amure Rus. Fed.
89 E2 Konakovo Rus. Fed.
75 C3 Kondagaon India
86 F2 Kondinskoye Rus. Fed.
119 D3 Kondoa Tanz.
86 C2 Kondopoga Rus. Fed.
89 E3 Kondrovo Rus. Fed.
127 I2 Kong Christian IX Land reg. Greenland
127 I2 Kong Frederik VI Kyst coastal area Greenland
65 B2 Kongju S. Korea
119 C3 Kongolo Dem. Rep. Congo
93 E4 Kongsberg Norway
93 F3 Kongsvinger Norway
77 D3 Kongur Shan mt. China
100 C2 Königswinter Ger.
103 D1 Konin Pol.
109 C2 Konjic Bos.-Herz.
122 A2 Konkiep watercourse Namibia
91 C1 Konotop Ukr.
102 B2 Konstanz Ger.
115 C3 Kontagora Nigeria
63 B2 Kon Tum Vietnam
63 B2 Kon Tum, Cao Nguyên plat. Vietnam
80 B2 Konya Turkey
100 C3 Konz Ger.
86 E3 Konzhakovskiy Kamen', Gora mt. Rus. Fed.
134 C1 Kooskia U.S.A.
128 C3 Kootenay Lake Can.
122 B3 Kootjieskolk S. Africa
92 □B2 Kópasker Iceland
108 B1 Koper Slovenia
93 G4 Kopparberg Sweden
109 C1 Koprivnica Croatia
73 C3 Korablino Rus. Fed.
101 D2 Korbach Ger.
109 D2 Korçë Albania
109 C2 Korčula Croatia
109 C2 Korčula i. Croatia
70 C2 Korea Bay g. China/N. Korea
65 B3 Korea Strait Japan/S. Korea
91 D2 Korenovsk Rus. Fed.
90 B1 Korets' Ukr.
111 C2 Körfez Turkey
114 B4 Korhogo Côte d'Ivoire
Korinthos Greece see Corinth
103 D2 Kőris-hegy h. Hungary
109 D2 Koritnik mt. Albania/Kosovo
67 C3 Kōriyama Japan
80 B2 Korkuteli Turkey
68 B2 Korla China
103 D2 Körmend Hungary
114 B3 Koro Mali
131 D1 Koroc r. Can.
91 D1 Korocha Rus. Fed.
119 D3 Korogwe Tanz.
59 C2 Koror Palau

90 B1 Korosten' Ukr.
90 B1 Korostyshiv Ukr.
115 D3 Koro Toro Chad
91 C2 Korsun'-Shevchenkivs'kyy Ukr.
103 E1 Korsze Pol.
100 A2 Kortrijk Belgium
83 L3 Koryakskaya, Sopka vol. Rus. Fed.
83 M2 Koryakskoye Nagor'ye mts Rus. Fed.
86 D2 Koryazhma Rus. Fed.
65 B2 Koryŏng S. Korea
91 C1 Koryukivka Ukr.
111 C3 Kos Greece
111 C3 Kos i. Greece
65 B2 Kosan N. Korea
103 D1 Kościan Pol.
53 C3 Kościuszko, Mount Austr.
68 B1 Kosh-Agach Rus. Fed.
103 E2 Košice Slovakia
92 H2 Koskullskulle Sweden
65 B2 Kosŏng N. Korea
103 D2 Kosovo country Europe
Kosovska Mitrovica Kosovo see Mitrovicë
48 E2 Kosrae atoll Micronesia
114 B4 Kossou, Lac de l. Côte d'Ivoire
76 C1 Kostanay Kazakh.
110 B2 Kostenets Bulg.
123 C2 Koster S. Africa
117 B3 Kosti Sudan
86 C2 Kostomuksha Rus. Fed.
90 B2 Kostopil' Ukr.
89 F2 Kostroma Rus. Fed.
89 F2 Kostroma r. Rus. Fed.
102 C1 Kostrzyn Pol.
103 D1 Koszalin Pol.
103 D2 Kőszeg Hungary
74 B2 Kota India
61 C2 Kotaagung Indon.
61 C2 Kotabaru Indon.
61 C1 Kota Belud Sabah Malaysia
60 B1 Kota Bharu Malaysia
61 C2 Kotabumi Indon.
61 C1 Kota Kinabalu Sabah Malaysia
61 C1 Kota Samarahan Sarawak Malaysia
86 D3 Kotel'nich Rus. Fed.
87 D4 Kotel'nikovo Rus. Fed.
83 K1 Kotel'nyy, Ostrov i. Rus. Fed.
101 E2 Köthen (Anhalt) Ger.
93 I3 Kotka Fin.
86 D2 Kotlas Rus. Fed.
109 C2 Kotor Varoš Bos.-Herz.
87 D3 Kotovo Rus. Fed.
91 E1 Kotovsk Rus. Fed.
90 B2 Kotovs'k Ukr.
83 H2 Kotuy r. Rus. Fed.
100 A2 Koudekerke Neth.
114 B3 Koudougou Burkina Faso
122 B3 Kougaberge mts S. Africa
118 B3 Koulamoutou Gabon
114 B3 Koulikoro Mali
114 A3 Koundâra Guinea
151 C3 Kourou Fr. Guiana
114 B3 Kouroussa Guinea
115 D3 Kousséri Cameroon
114 B3 Koutiala Mali
93 I3 Kouvola Fin.
92 J2 Kovdor Rus. Fed.
90 A1 Kovel' Ukr.
89 F2 Kovrov Rus. Fed.
54 B2 Kowhitirangi N.Z.
Koyamutthoor India see Coimbatore
111 C3 Köyceğiz Turkey
86 D2 Koyda Rus. Fed.

126 A2 **Koyukuk** r. U.S.A.
111 B2 **Kozani** Greece
90 C1 **Kozelets'** Ukr.
89 E3 **Kozel'sk** Rus. Fed.
73 B3 **Kozhikode** India
90 B2 **Kozyatyn** Ukr.
63 A3 **Krabi** Thai.
63 A2 **Kra Buri** Thai.
63 B3 **Krâchéh** Cambodia
93 E4 **Kragerø** Norway
100 B1 **Kragenburg** Neth.
109 D2 **Kragujevac** Serbia
60 B2 **Krakatau** i. Indon.
103 D1 **Kraków** Pol.
91 D2 **Kramators'k** Ukr.
93 G3 **Kramfors** Sweden
111 B3 **Kranidi** Greece
86 E1 **Krasino** Rus. Fed.
88 C2 **Krāslava** Latvia
101 F2 **Kraslice** Czech Rep.
89 D3 **Krasnapollye** Belarus
89 D3 **Krasnaya Gora** Rus. Fed.
87 D3 **Krasnoarmeysk** Rus. Fed.
91 D2 **Krasnoarmiys'k** Ukr.
86 D2 **Krasnoborsk** Rus. Fed.
91 D2 **Krasnodar** Rus. Fed.
91 D2 **Krasnodarskoye**
         Vodokhranilishche *resr*
         Rus. Fed.
91 D2 **Krasnodon** Ukr.
88 C2 **Krasnogorodsk** Rus. Fed.
91 D2 **Krasnohrad** Ukr.
91 C2 **Krasnohvardiys'ke** Ukr.
86 F3 **Krasnokamsk** Rus. Fed.
89 D2 **Krasnomayskiy** Rus. Fed.
91 C2 **Krasnoperekops'k** Ukr.
87 D3 **Krasnoslobodsk** Rus. Fed.
86 E3 **Krasnoufimsk** Rus. Fed.
83 H3 **Krasnoyarsk** Rus. Fed.
89 F2 **Krasnoye-na-Volge** Rus. Fed.
89 D3 **Krasnyy** Rus. Fed.
89 F2 **Krasnyy Kholm** Rus. Fed.
87 C4 **Krasnyy Luch** Ukr.
91 E2 **Krasnyy Sulin** Rus. Fed.
90 B2 **Krasyliv** Ukr.
100 C2 **Krefeld** Ger.
91 C2 **Kremenchuk** Ukr.
91 C2 **Kremenchuts'ke**
         Vodoskhovyshche *resr* Ukr.
102 D2 **Křemešník** h. Czech Rep.
91 D2 **Kreminna** Ukr.
103 D2 **Krems an der Donau** Austria
89 D2 **Kresttsy** Rus. Fed.
88 D2 **Kretinga** Lith.
100 C2 **Kreuzau** Ger.
100 C2 **Kreuztal** Ger.
118 A2 **Kribi** Cameroon
111 B3 **Krikellos** Greece
66 D1 **Kril'on, Mys** c. Rus. Fed.
73 C3 **Krishna** r. India
73 C3 **Krishna, Mouths of the** India
75 C2 **Krishnanagar** India
93 E4 **Kristiansand** Norway
93 F4 **Kristianstad** Sweden
92 E3 **Kristiansund** Norway
93 F4 **Kristinehamn** Sweden
111 C3 **Kriti** i. Greece *see* **Crete**
111 C3 **Kritiko Pelagos** *sea* Greece
          Krivoy Rog Ukr. *see* **Kryvyy Rih**
109 C1 **Križevci** Croatia
108 D1 **Krk** i. Croatia
92 F3 **Krokom** Sweden
91 C1 **Krolevets'** Ukr.
101 E2 **Kronach** Ger.
63 B2 **Krŏng Kaôh Kŏng** Cambodia
127 I2 **Kronprins Frederik Bjerge**
          nunataks Greenland

122 C2 **Kroonstad** S. Africa
87 D4 **Kropotkin** Rus. Fed.
103 E2 **Krosno** Pol.
103 D1 **Krotoszyn** Pol.
60 B2 **Krui** Indon.
109 C2 **Krujë** Albania
111 C2 **Krumovgrad** Bulg.
          Krung Thep Thai. *see* **Bangkok**
88 C3 **Krupki** Belarus
109 D2 **Kruševac** Serbia
101 F2 **Krušné hory** *mts* Czech Rep.
128 A2 **Kruzof Island** U.S.A.
89 D3 **Krychaw** Belarus
91 D3 **Krymsk** Rus. Fed.
91 C2 **Kryvyy Rih** Ukr.
114 B2 **Ksabi** Alg.
107 D2 **Ksar el Boukhari** Alg.
114 B1 **Ksar el Kebir** Morocco
89 E3 **Kshenskiy** Rus. Fed.
78 B2 **Kŭ', Jabal al** *h.* Saudi Arabia
61 C1 **Kuala Belait** Brunei
60 D1 **Kuala Kerai** Malaysia
60 B1 **Kuala Lipis** Malaysia
60 B1 **Kuala Lumpur** Malaysia
61 C2 **Kualapembuang** Indon.
60 B1 **Kuala Terengganu** Malaysia
60 B2 **Kualatungal** Indon.
61 C1 **Kuamut** *Sabah* Malaysia
65 A1 **Kuandian** China
60 B1 **Kuantan** Malaysia
91 D2 **Kuban'** r. Rus. Fed.
89 E2 **Kubenskoye, Ozero** l. Rus. Fed.
110 C2 **Kubrat** Bulg.
61 C1 **Kubuang** Indon.
61 C1 **Kuching** *Sarawak* Malaysia
109 C2 **Kuçovë** Albania
61 C1 **Kudat** *Sabah* Malaysia
61 C2 **Kudus** Indon.
102 C2 **Kufstein** Austria
127 F2 **Kugaaruk** Can.
67 C3 **Kughtuk** Can.
92 I3 **Kuhmo** Fin.
79 C2 **Kührän, Küh-e** *mt.* Iran
          Kuitin China *see* **Kuytun**
120 A2 **Kuito** Angola
92 I2 **Kuivaniemi** Fin.
65 B2 **Kujang** N. Korea
109 D2 **Kukës** Albania
111 C3 **Kula** Turkey
75 D2 **Kula Kangri** *mt.* Bhutan/China
76 B2 **Kulandy** Kazakh.
88 B2 **Kuldiga** Latvia
122 B1 **Kule** Botswana
101 E2 **Kulmbach** Ger.
77 C3 **Külob** Tajik.
76 B2 **Kul'sary** Kazakh.
77 D1 **Kulunda** Rus. Fed.
127 I2 **Kulusuk** Greenland
67 C3 **Kumagaya** Japan
67 B4 **Kumamoto** Japan
109 D2 **Kumanovo** Macedonia
114 B4 **Kumasi** Ghana
118 A2 **Kumba** Cameroon
78 B2 **Kumdah** Saudi Arabia
87 E3 **Kumertau** Rus. Fed.
65 B2 **Kumi** S. Korea
93 G4 **Kumla** Sweden
115 D3 **Kumo** Nigeria
62 A1 **Kumon Range** *mts* Myanmar
62 B2 **Kumphawapi** Thai.
          Kumul China *see* **Hami**
66 D2 **Kunashir, Ostrov** i. Rus. Fed.
120 A2 **Kunene** r. Angola/Namibia
77 D2 **Kungei Alatau** *mts* Kazakh./
          Kyrg.
93 F4 **Kungsbacka** Sweden
118 B2 **Kungu** Dem. Rep. Congo

86 E3 **Kungur** Rus. Fed.
62 A1 **Kunhing** Myanmar
77 D3 **Kunlun Shan** *mts* China
62 B1 **Kunming** China
65 B2 **Kunsan** S. Korea
50 B1 **Kununurra** Austr.
92 I3 **Kuopio** Fin.
109 C1 **Kupa** r. Croatia/Slovenia
59 C3 **Kupang** Indon.
88 B2 **Kupiškis** Lith.
111 C2 **Küplü** Turkey
128 A2 **Kupreanof Island** U.S.A.
91 D2 **Kup"yans'k** Ukr.
77 E2 **Kuqa** China
67 B4 **Kurashiki** Japan
67 C4 **Kurayoshi** Japan
89 E3 **Kurchatov** Rus. Fed.
110 C2 **Kürdzhali** Bulg.
67 B4 **Kure** Japan
88 B2 **Kuressaare** Estonia
86 F2 **Kurgan** Rus. Fed.
93 H3 **Kurikka** Fin.
156 C3 **Kuril Trench** N. Pacific Ocean
89 F3 **Kurkino** Rus. Fed.
117 B3 **Kurmuk** Sudan
73 B3 **Kurnool** India
67 D3 **Kuroiso** Japan
53 D2 **Kurri Kurri** Austr.
89 E3 **Kursk** Rus. Fed.
122 B2 **Kuruman** S. Africa
122 B2 **Kuruman** *watercourse* S. Africa
67 B4 **Kurume** Japan
83 I3 **Kurumkan** Rus. Fed.
73 C4 **Kurunegala** Sri Lanka
111 C3 **Kuşadası** Turkey
111 C3 **Kuşadası Körfezi** b. Turkey
111 C2 **Kuş Gölü** l. Turkey
91 D2 **Kushchevskaya** Rus. Fed.
66 D2 **Kushiro** Japan
62 A1 **Kushtia** Bangl.
76 C1 **Kusmuryn** Kazakh.
66 D2 **Kussharo-ko** l. Japan
111 C3 **Kütahya** Turkey
81 C1 **Kutaisi** Georgia
109 C1 **Kutjevo** Croatia
103 D1 **Kutno** Pol.
118 B3 **Kutu** Dem. Rep. Congo
126 D2 **Kuujjua** r. Can.
131 D1 **Kuujjuaq** Can.
130 C1 **Kuujjuarapik** Can.
92 I2 **Kuusamo** Fin.
120 A2 **Kuvango** Angola
89 D2 **Kuvshinovo** Rus. Fed.
78 B2 **Kuwait** *country* Asia
79 B2 **Kuwait** Kuwait
          Kuybyshev Rus. Fed. *see*
          Samara
91 D2 **Kuybyshev** Ukr.
87 D3 **Kuybyshevskoye**
          Vodokhranilishche *resr*
          Rus. Fed
77 E2 **Kuytun** China
111 C3 **Kuyucak** Turkey
87 D3 **Kuznetsk** Rus. Fed.
90 B1 **Kuznetsov's'k** Ukr.
97 H1 **Kvalsund** Norway
123 D2 **KwaDukuza** S. Africa
123 D2 **KwaMashu** S. Africa
65 B2 **Kwangju** S. Korea
65 B1 **Kwanmo-bong** *mt.* N. Korea
123 D2 **KwaNobuhle** S. Africa
122 B3 **KwaNonzame** S. Africa
123 C3 **Kwatinidubu** S. Africa
123 C3 **KwaZamokuhle** S. Africa
123 D2 **KwaZulu-Natal** *prov.* S. Africa
121 B2 **Kwekwe** Zimbabwe
118 D3 **Kwenge** r. Dem. Rep. Congo

103	D1	Kwidzyn Pol.
118	B3	Kwilu r. Angola/Dem. Rep. Congo
59	C3	Kwoka mt. Indon.
53	C3	Kyabram Austr.
62	A2	Kyaikto Myanmar
69	D1	Kyakhta Rus. Fed.
52	A2	Kyancutta Austr.
62	A1	Kyaukpadaung Myanmar
62	A2	Kyaukpyu Myanmar
88	B3	Kybartai Lith.
62	A2	Kyebogyi Myanmar
62	A2	Kyeintali Myanmar
74	B1	Kyelang India
		Kyiv Ukr. see Kiev
90	C1	Kyivs'ke Vodoskhovyshche resr Ukr.
		Kyklades is Greece see Cyclades
129	D2	Kyle Can.
96	C3	Kyle of Lochalsh U.K.
100	C3	Kyll r. Ger.
111	B3	Kyllini mt. Greece
111	B3	Kymi Greece
52	B3	Kyneton Austr.
119	D2	Kyoga, Lake Uganda
53	D1	Kyogle Austr.
65	B2	Kyŏnggi-man b. S. Korea
65	B2	Kyŏngju S. Korea
67	C4	Kyōto Japan
111	B3	Kyparissia Greece
111	B3	Kyra Panagia i. Greece
80	B2	Kyrenia Cyprus
77	D2	Kyrgyzstan country Asia
101	F1	Kyritz Ger.
92	H3	Kyrönjoki r. Fin.
86	E2	Kyrta Rus. Fed.
86	D2	Kyssa Rus. Fed.
111	B3	Kythira i. Greece
111	B3	Kythnos i. Greece
128	B2	Kyuquot Can.
67	B4	Kyūshū i. Japan
110	B2	Kyustendil Bulg.
92	H3	Kyyjärvi Fin.
68	C1	Kyzyl Rus. Fed.
76	C2	Kyzylkum Desert Kazakh./Uzbek.
77	C2	Kyzylorda Kazakh.

L

145	C3	La Angostura, Presa de resr Mex.
117	C4	Laascaanood Somalia
150	B1	La Asunción Venez.
114	A2	Laâyoune Western Sahara
87	D4	Laba r. Rus. Fed.
144	B2	La Babia Mex.
146	B3	La Bahía, Islas de is Hond.
152	B3	La Banda Arg.
104	B2	La Baule-Escoublac France
114	A3	Labé Guinea
128	A1	Laberge, Lake Can.
129	C2	La Biche, Lac l. Can.
87	D4	Labinsk Rus. Fed.
64	B1	Labo Phil.
104	B3	Labouheyre France
131	D1	Labrador reg. Can.
131	D1	Labrador City Can.
158	C1	Labrador Sea Can./Greenland
150	B2	Lábrea Brazil
61	C1	Labuan Malaysia
60	B1	Labuhanbilik Indon.
59	C3	Labuna Indon.
63	A2	Labutta Myanmar
86	F2	Labytnangi Rus. Fed.

109	C2	Laç Albania
105	C2	La Capelle France
73	B3	Laccadive Islands India
129	E2	Lac du Bonnet Can.
146	B3	La Ceiba Hond.
53	B2	Lachlan r. Austr.
141	E1	Lachute Can.
105	D3	La Ciotat France
129	C2	Lac La Biche Can.
		Lac la Martre Can. see Whatì
141	E1	Lac-Mégantic Can.
128	C2	Lacombe Can.
146	B4	La Concepción Panama
145	C3	La Concordia Mex.
108	A3	Laconi Sardegna Italy
141	E2	Laconia U.S.A.
128	C2	La Crete Can.
140	A2	La Crosse U.S.A.
144	B2	La Cruz Mex.
144	B2	La Cuesta Mex.
75	B1	Ladakh Range mts India/Pak.
122	B3	Ladismith S. Africa
79	D2	Lādīz Iran
86	C2	Ladoga, Lake Rus. Fed.
		Ladozhskoye Ozero l. Rus. Fed. see Ladoga, Lake
128	B3	Ladysmith Can.
123	C2	Ladysmith S. Africa
59	D3	Lae P.N.G.
152	B3	La Esmeralda Bol.
93	F4	Læsø i. Denmark
143	C2	La Fayette U.S.A.
140	B2	Lafayette IN U.S.A.
142	B2	Lafayette LA U.S.A.
115	C4	Lafia Nigeria
104	B2	La Flèche France
143	D1	La Follette U.S.A.
131	C1	Laforge Can.
79	C2	Lāft Iran
108	A3	La Galite i. Tunisia
91	E1	Lagan' Rus. Fed.
118	B2	Lagdo, Lac de l. Cameroon
115	C1	Laghouat Alg.
155	D1	Lagoa Santa Brazil
114	A2	La Gomera i. Islas Canarias
114	C4	Lagos Nigeria
106	B2	Lagos Port.
134	C1	La Grande U.S.A.
130	C1	La Grande 3, Réservoir resr Can.
131	C1	La Grande 4, Réservoir resr Can.
50	B1	La Grange Austr.
143	C2	La Grange U.S.A.
150	B1	La Gran Sabana plat. Venez.
152	D3	Laguna Brazil
144	A2	Laguna, Picacho de la mt. Mex.
150	A2	Lagunas Peru
		La Habana Cuba see Havana
61	C1	Lahad Datu Sabah Malaysia
60	B2	Lahat Indon.
78	B3	Laḥij Yemen
81	C2	Lāhījān Iran
100	C2	Lahnstein Ger.
74	B1	Lahore Pak.
74	A2	Lahri Pak.
93	I3	Lahti Fin.
115	D4	Laï Chad
53	D1	Laidley Austr.
104	C2	L'Aigle France
111	B3	Laimos, Akrotirio pt Greece
122	B3	Laingsburg S. Africa
92	H2	Lainioälven r. Sweden
96	B1	Lairg U.K.
108	B1	Laives Italy
70	B2	Laiwu China
70	C2	Laiyang China

70	B2	Laizhou China
70	B2	Laizhou Wan b. China
50	C1	Lajamanu Austr.
152	C3	Lajes Brazil
144	B2	La Junta Mex.
136	C3	La Junta U.S.A.
121	C2	Lake Cabora Bassa resr Moz.
53	C2	Lake Cargelligo Austr.
53	D2	Lake Cathie Austr.
142	B2	Lake Charles U.S.A.
143	D2	Lake City FL U.S.A.
143	E2	Lake City SC U.S.A.
108	A1	Lake Como Can.
128	B3	Lake Cowichan Can.
108	B1	Lake Garda Italy
138	A2	Lake Havasu City U.S.A.
143	D3	Lakeland U.S.A.
128	C2	Lake Louise Can.
134	B1	Lake Oswego U.S.A.
54	A2	Lake Paringa N.Z.
142	B2	Lake Providence U.S.A.
54	B2	Lake Pukaki N.Z.
53	C3	Lakes Entrance Austr.
134	B2	Lakeview U.S.A.
136	B3	Lakewood CO U.S.A.
141	E2	Lakewood NJ U.S.A.
143	D3	Lake Worth U.S.A.
74	A2	Lakhpat India
74	B1	Lakki Marwat Pak.
111	B3	Lakonikos Kolpos b. Greece
92	H1	Lakselv Norway
107	C1	L'Alcora Spain
145	C3	La Libertad Guat.
106	B1	Lalín Spain
75	B2	Lalitpur India
129	D2	La Loche Can.
100	B2	La Louvière Belgium
108	A2	La Maddalena Sardegna Italy
61	C1	Lamag Sabah Malaysia
		La Manche str. France/U.K. see English Channel
136	C3	Lamar U.S.A.
79	C2	Lamard Iran
108	A3	La Marmora, Punta mt. Sardegna Italy
128	C1	La Martre, Lac l. Can.
118	B3	Lambaréné Gabon
122	A3	Lambert's Bay S. Africa
92	☐A2	Lambeyri Iceland
106	B2	Lamego Port.
150	A3	La Merced Peru
52	B3	Lameroo Austr.
139	C2	Lamesa U.S.A.
111	B3	Lamia Greece
137	E2	Lamoni U.S.A.
62	A2	Lampang Thai.
139	D2	Lampasas U.S.A.
145	B2	Lampazos Mex.
99	A2	Lampeter U.K.
62	A2	Lamphun Thai.
119	E3	Lamu Kenya
62	A2	Lan, Loi mt. Myanmar/Thai.
96	C3	Lanark U.K.
62	A2	Lanbi Kyun i. Myanmar
		Lancang Jiang r. China see Mekong
98	B1	Lancaster U.K.
135	C4	Lancaster CA U.S.A.
140	C3	Lancaster OH U.S.A.
141	D2	Lancaster PA U.S.A.
143	D2	Lancaster SC U.S.A.
127	F2	Lancaster Sound str. Can.
		Lanchow China see Lanzhou
102	C2	Landeck Austria
136	B2	Lander U.S.A.
99	A3	Land's End pt U.K.
102	C2	Landshut Ger.

93 F4 Landskrona Sweden
143 C2 Lanett U.S.A.
122 B2 Langberg mts S. Africa
137 D1 Langdon U.S.A.
93 F4 Langeland i. Denmark
101 D1 Langen Ger.
100 C1 Langeoog Ger.
100 C1 Langeoog i. Ger.
101 D2 Langgöns Ger.
92 □A3 Langjökull Iceland
105 C3 Langogne France
104 B3 Langon France
105 D2 Langres France
60 A1 Langsa Indon.
62 B1 Lang Son Vietnam
101 D1 Langwedel Ger.
129 D2 Lanigan Can.
153 A4 Lanín, Volcán vol. Arg./Chile
81 C2 Länkäran Azer.
104 B2 Lannion France
119 C3 Lanping China
71 B3 Lanxi China
117 B4 Lanya S. Sudan
114 A2 Lanzarote i. Islas Canarias
70 A2 Lanzhou China
64 B1 Laoag City Phil.
62 B1 Lao Cai Vietnam
70 B2 Laohekou China
68 C2 Laojunmiao China
65 B1 Laoling China
65 B1 Lao Ling mts China
68 C2 Lao Mangnai China
105 C2 Laon France
62 B2 Laos country Asia
65 B1 Laotougou China
154 C3 Lapa Brazil
114 A2 La Palma i. Islas Canarias
146 C4 La Palma Panama
150 B1 La Paragua Venez.
152 B2 La Paz Bol.
144 A2 La Paz Mex.
150 B2 La Pedrera Col.
66 D1 La Pérouse Strait Japan/Rus. Fed.
145 C2 La Pesca Mex.
144 B2 La Piedad Mex.
153 C4 La Plata Arg.
153 C4 La Plata, Río de sea chan. Arg./Uru.
106 B1 La Pola Spain
93 I3 Lappeenranta Fin.
92 G2 Lapland reg. Europe
111 C2 Lâpseki Turkey
83 J1 Laptev Sea Rus. Fed.
Laptevykh, More sea Rus. Fed. see Laptev Sea
92 H3 Lapua Fin.
152 B3 La Quiaca Arg.
79 C2 Lār Iran
114 B1 Larache Morocco
136 B2 Laramie U.S.A.
136 B2 Laramie Mountains U.S.A.
154 B3 Laranjeiras do Sul Brazil
59 C3 Larantuka Indon.
59 C3 Larat i. Indon.
92 D2 Larba Alg.
106 C1 Laredo Spain
139 D3 Laredo U.S.A.
96 B3 Largs U.K.
152 B3 La Rioja Arg.
111 B3 Larisa Greece
74 A2 Larkana Pak.
80 B2 Larnaca Cyprus
97 D1 Larne U.K.
100 B2 La Roche-en-Ardenne Belgium

104 B2 La Rochelle France
104 B2 La Roche-sur-Yon France
107 C2 La Roda Spain
147 D3 La Romana Dom. Rep.
129 D2 La Ronge Can.
129 D2 La Ronge, Lac l. Can.
50 C1 Larrimah Austr.
55 P3 Larsen Ice Shelf Antarctica
93 F4 Larvik Norway
130 □2 Las Cuevas Can.
158 B2 Las Cruces Arg.
153 C4 Las Flores Arg.
153 B4 Las Heras Arg.
62 A1 Lashio Myanmar
74 A1 Lashkar Gāh Afgh.
109 C3 La Sila reg. Italy
152 B3 Las Lomitas Arg.
144 B2 Las Nieves Mex.
114 A2 Las Palmas de Gran Canaria Islas Canarias
108 A2 La Spezia Italy
152 B5 Las Plumas Arg.
129 D2 Last Mountain Lake Can.
152 B3 Las Tórtolas, Cerro mt. Arg./Chile
118 B3 Lastoursville Gabon
109 C2 Lastovo i. Croatia
144 A2 Las Tres Vírgenes, Volcán vol. Mex.
146 C2 Las Tunas Cuba
144 B2 Las Varas Chihuahua Mex.
144 B2 Las Varas Nayarit Mex.
138 B1 Las Vegas NM U.S.A.
135 C3 Las Vegas NV U.S.A.
131 F1 La Tabatière Can.
80 B2 Latakia Syria
101 D3 La Teste-de-Buch France
108 B2 Latina Italy
147 D3 La Tortuga, Isla i. Venez.
64 B1 La Trinidad Phil.
89 E2 Latskoye Rus. Fed.
131 C2 La Tuque Can.
88 B2 Latvia country Europe
101 F2 Lauchhammer Ger.
106 C1 Laudio Spain
101 E3 Lauf an der Pegnitz Ger.
105 D2 Laufen Switz.
51 D4 Launceston Austr.
99 A3 Launceston U.K.
62 A1 Laungyyaung Myanmar
142 C2 Laurel MS U.S.A.
134 E1 Laurel MT U.S.A.
109 C2 Lauria Italy
143 E2 Laurinburg U.S.A.
105 D2 Lausanne Switz.
61 C2 Laut i. Indon.
61 C2 Laut Bali sea Indon.
101 D2 Lautersbach (Hessen) Ger.
61 C2 Laut Kecil, Kepulauan is Indon.
100 C1 Lauwersmeer l. Neth.
104 B2 Laval France
107 C2 La Vall d'Uixó Spain
50 B2 Laverton Austr.
155 D2 Lavras Brazil
123 D2 Lavumisa Swaziland
61 C1 Lawas Sarawak Malaysia
62 A1 Lawksawk Myanmar
114 B3 Lawra Ghana
137 D3 Lawrence U.S.A.
142 C1 Lawrenceburg U.S.A.
139 D2 Lawton U.S.A.
78 A2 Lawz, Jabal al mt. Saudi Arabia
93 F4 Laxå Sweden
74 B1 Layyah Pak.

109 D2 Lazarevac Serbia
144 A1 Lázaro Cárdenas Baja California Mex.
144 B3 Lázaro Cárdenas Michoacán Mex.
88 B3 Lazdijai Lith.
136 C2 Lead U.S.A.
129 D2 Leader Can.
136 B3 Leadville U.S.A.
Leaf Bay Can. see Tasiujaq
129 D2 Leaf Rapids Can.
97 B2 Leane, Lough l. Ireland
137 E3 Leavenworth U.S.A.
80 B2 Lebanon country Asia
137 E3 Lebanon MO U.S.A.
141 E2 Lebanon NH U.S.A.
134 B2 Lebanon OR U.S.A.
141 D2 Lebanon PA U.S.A.
89 E3 Lebedyan' Rus. Fed.
91 C1 Lebedyn Ukr.
104 C2 Le Blanc France
103 D1 Lębork Pol.
123 C1 Lebowakgomo S. Africa
106 B2 Lebrija Spain
153 A4 Lebu Chile
104 C3 Le Bugue France
109 C2 Lecce Italy
108 A1 Lecco Italy
102 C2 Lech r. Austria/Ger.
111 B3 Lechaina Greece
71 B3 Lechang China
102 B1 Leck Ger.
104 C3 Lectoure France
106 B1 Ledesma Spain
104 C2 Le Dorat France
128 C2 Leduc Can.
137 E1 Leech Lake U.S.A.
98 C2 Leeds U.K.
98 B2 Leek U.K.
100 C1 Leer (Ostfriesland) Ger.
143 D3 Leesburg U.S.A.
142 B2 Leesville U.S.A.
53 C2 Leeton Austr.
122 B3 Leeu-Gamka S. Africa
100 B1 Leeuwarden Neth.
50 A3 Leeuwin, Cape Austr.
147 D3 Leeward Islands Caribbean Sea
111 B3 Lefkada Greece
111 B3 Lefkada i. Greece
Lefkosia Cyprus see Nicosia
64 B1 Legazpi Phil.
108 B1 Legnago Italy
103 D1 Legnica Pol.
75 B1 Leh India
104 C2 Le Havre France
123 B1 Lehututu Botswana
103 D2 Leibnitz Austria
99 C2 Leicester U.K.
51 C1 Leichhardt r. Austr.
100 B1 Leiden Neth.
100 A2 Leie r. Belgium
52 A2 Leigh Creek Austr.
93 E3 Leikanger Norway
101 D1 Leine r. Ger.
97 C2 Leinster reg. Ireland
101 F2 Leipzig Ger.
92 F2 Leiranger Norway
106 B2 Leiria Port.
93 C4 Leirvik Norway
97 C2 Leixlip Ireland
71 B3 Lelyang China
71 B3 Leizhou China
71 A3 Leizhou Bandao pen. China
118 B3 Lékana Congo
100 B1 Lelystad Neth.

153	B6	**Le Maire, Estrecho de** sea chan. Arg.
		Léman, Lac l. France/Switz. see Geneva, Lake
104	C2	Le Mans France
137	D2	Le Mars U.S.A.
154	C2	Leme Brazil
		Lemesos Cyprus see Limassol
101	D1	Lemförde Ger.
127	G2	Lemieux Islands Can.
136	C1	Lemmon U.S.A.
135	C3	Lemoore U.S.A.
131	D1	Le Moyne, Lac l. Can.
62	A1	Lemro r. Myanmar
109	C3	Le Murge hills Italy
83	J2	Lena r. Rus. Fed.
100	C1	Lengerich Ger.
71	B3	Lengshuijiang China
91	D2	Lenine Ukr.
		Leningrad Rus. Fed. see St Petersburg
91	D2	Leningradskaya Rus. Fed.
77	D3	Lenin Peak Kyrg./Tajik.
		Leninsk Kazakh. see Baykonyr
89	E3	Leninskiy Rus. Fed.
100	A2	Lens Belgium
104	A2	Lens France
83	I2	Lensk Rus. Fed.
103	D2	Lenti Hungary
109	C3	Lentini Sicilia Italy
114	B3	Léo Burkina Faso
103	D2	Leoben Austria
99	B2	Leominster U.K.
144	B2	Leominster U.S.A.
146	B3	León Nic.
106	B1	León Spain
122	A1	Leonardville Namibia
50	B2	Leonora Austr.
155	D2	Leopoldina Brazil
123	C1	Lephalale S. Africa
123	C1	Lephepe Botswana
123	C3	Lephoi S. Africa
71	B3	Leping China
105	C2	Le Puy-en-Velay France
150	A2	Lérida Col.
106	C1	Lerma Spain
111	C3	Leros i. Greece
130	C1	Le Roy, Lac l. Can.
93	F4	Lerum Sweden
96	□	Lerwick U.K.
111	C3	Lesbos i. Greece
147	C3	Les Cayes Haiti
69	C3	Leshan China
86	D2	Leshukonskoye Rus. Fed.
109	D2	Leskovac Serbia
104	B2	Lesneven France
89	E2	Lesnoye Rus. Fed.
83	H3	Lesosibirsk Rus. Fed.
123	C2	Lesotho country Africa
66	B1	Lesozavodsk Rus. Fed.
104	B2	Les Sables-d'Olonne France
147	D3	Lesser Antilles is Caribbean Sea
81	C1	Lesser Caucasus mts Asia
128	C2	Lesser Slave Lake Can.
58	B3	Lesser Sunda Islands is Indon.
105	C3	Les Vans France
		Lesvos i. Greece see Lesbos
103	D1	Leszno Pol.
99	C3	Letchworth Garden City U.K.
128	C3	Lethbridge Can.
150	C1	Lethem Guyana
58	C3	Leti, Kepulauan is Indon.
150	B2	Leticia Col.
123	C1	Letlhakeng Botswana

104	C1	Le Touquet-Paris-Plage France
99	D3	Le Tréport France
63	A2	Letsok-aw Kyun i. Myanmar
123	C2	Letsopa S. Africa
97	C1	Letterkenny Ireland
105	C3	Leucate, Étang de l. France
60	A1	Leuser, Gunung mt. Indon.
100	B2	Leuven Belgium
92	F3	Levanger Norway
139	C2	Levelland U.S.A.
50	B1	Lévêque, Cape Austr.
100	C2	Leverkusen Ger.
103	D2	Levice Slovakia
54	C2	Levin N.Z.
89	E3	Lev Tolstoy Rus. Fed.
99	D3	Lewes U.K.
96	A1	Lewis, Isle of i. U.K.
140	C3	Lewisburg U.S.A.
134	D1	Lewis Range mts U.S.A.
134	C1	Lewiston ID U.S.A.
141	E2	Lewiston ME U.S.A.
134	E1	Lewistown U.S.A.
140	C3	Lexington KY U.S.A.
136	D2	Lexington NE U.S.A.
141	D3	Lexington VA U.S.A.
64	B1	Leyte i. Phil.
109	C2	Lezhë Albania
89	F2	Lezhnevo Rus. Fed.
89	E3	L'gov Rus. Fed.
75	C2	Lhagoi Kangri mt. China
68	C2	Lharigarbo China
75	D2	Lhasa China
75	C2	Lhazê China
60	A1	Lhokseumawe Indon.
111	B3	Liakoura mt. China
67	B3	Liancourt Rocks i. N. Pacific Ocean
71	B3	Lianhua China
71	B3	Lianjiang China
70	C1	Lianshan China
70	B2	Lianyungang China
71	B3	Lianzhou China
70	B2	Liaocheng China
70	C1	Liaodong Bandao pen. China
70	C1	Liaodong Wan b. China
65	A1	Liao He r. China
70	C1	Liaoning prov. China
65	A1	Liaoyang China
65	B1	Liaoyuan China
128	B1	Liard r. Can.
134	C1	Libby U.S.A.
118	B2	Libenge Dem. Rep. Congo
136	C3	Liberal U.S.A.
103	D1	Liberec Czech Rep.
114	B4	Liberia country Africa
146	B3	Liberia Costa Rica
150	B1	Libertad Venez.
100	B3	Libin Belgium
104	B3	Libourne France
118	A2	Libreville Gabon
115	D2	Libya country Africa
115	E2	Libyan Desert Egypt/Libya
116	A1	Libyan Plateau Egypt/Libya
108	B3	Licata Sicilia Italy
		Licheng China see Lipu
121	C2	Lichinga Moz.
101	E2	Lichte Ger.
123	C2	Lichtenburg S. Africa
101	E2	Lichtenfels Ger.
88	C3	Lida Belarus
93	F4	Lidköping Sweden
50	C2	Liebig, Mount Austr.
105	D2	Liechtenstein country Europe
100	B2	Liège Belgium
92	J3	Lieksa Fin.

119	C2	Lienart Dem. Rep. Congo
63	B2	Liên Nghia Vietnam
102	C2	Lienz Austria
88	B2	Liepāja Latvia
102	C2	Liezen Austria
97	C1	Liffey r. Ireland
97	C1	Lifford Ireland
53	C1	Lightning Ridge Austr.
121	C2	Ligonha r. Moz.
105	D3	Ligurian Sea France/Italy
119	C4	Likasi Dem. Rep. Congo
128	B2	Likely Can.
89	E2	Likhoslavl' Rus. Fed.
61	B1	Liku Indon.
105	D3	L'Île-Rousse Corse France
71	B3	Liling China
93	F4	Lilla Edet Sweden
100	B2	Lille Belgium
105	C1	Lille France
		Lille Bælt sea chan. Denmark see Little Belt
93	F3	Lillehammer Norway
93	F4	Lillestrøm Norway
128	B2	Lillooet Can.
121	C2	Lilongwe Malawi
64	B2	Liloy Phil.
150	A3	Lima Peru
140	C2	Lima U.S.A.
80	B2	Limassol Cyprus
97	C1	Limavady U.K.
153	B4	Limay r. Arg.
101	F2	Limbach-Oberfrohna Ger.
88	B2	Limbaži Latvia
118	A2	Limbe Cameroon
100	C2	Limburg an der Lahn Ger.
122	B2	Lime Acres S. Africa
154	C2	Limeira Brazil
97	B2	Limerick Ireland
93	E4	Limfjorden sea chan. Denmark
111	C3	Limnos i. Greece
104	C2	Limoges France
136	C3	Limon U.S.A.
104	C3	Limoux France
123	C1	Limpopo prov. S. Africa
121	C3	Limpopo r. S. Africa/Zimbabwe
64	A1	Linapacan i. Phil.
153	A4	Linares Chile
145	C2	Linares Mex.
106	C2	Linares Spain
62	B1	Lincang China
98	C2	Lincoln U.K.
140	B2	Lincoln IL U.S.A.
141	F1	Lincoln ME U.S.A.
137	D2	Lincoln NE U.S.A.
151	C1	Linden Guyana
142	C1	Linden U.S.A.
119	C2	Lindi r. Dem. Rep. Congo
119	D3	Lindi Tanz.
		Lindisfarne i. U.K. see Holy Island
80	A2	Lindos Greece
141	D2	Lindsay Can.
49	H2	Line Islands Kiribati
70	B2	Linfen China
64	B1	Lingayen Phil.
70	B2	Lingbao China
123	C3	Lingelethu S. Africa
123	C3	Lingelihle S. Africa
100	C1	Lingen (Ems) Ger.
60	B2	Lingga, Kepulauan is Indon.
71	A3	Lingshan China
71	A4	Lingshui China
114	A3	Linguère Senegal
63	B2	Linh, Ngok mt. Vietnam
155	D1	Linhares Brazil
93	G4	Linköping Sweden

66 B1 Linkou China
70 D2 Linqing China
154 C2 Lins Brazil
136 C1 Linton U.S.A.
69 D2 Linxi China
69 C2 Linxia China
70 B2 Linyi *Shandong* China
70 B2 Linyi *Shandong* China
70 C2 Linying China
102 C2 Linz Austria
105 C3 Lion, Golfe du *g.* France
109 B3 Lipari Italy
108 B3 Lipari, isole *is* Italy
89 E3 Lipetsk Rus. Fed.
110 B1 Lipova Romania
101 D2 Lippstadt Ger.
71 B3 Lipu China
76 C1 Lisakovsk Kazakh.
118 C2 Lisala Dem. Rep. Congo
        Lisboa Port. *see* Lisbon
106 B2 Lisbon Port.
97 C1 Lisburn U.K.
97 B2 Liscannor Bay Ireland
104 C2 Lisieux France
99 A3 Liskeard U.K.
89 E3 Liski Rus. Fed.
53 D1 Lismore Austr.
97 C1 Lisnaskea U.K.
97 B2 Listowel Ireland
71 A3 Litang *Guangxi* China
68 C2 Litang *Sichuan* China
140 B3 Litchfield *IL* U.S.A.
137 E1 Litchfield *MN* U.S.A.
53 D2 Lithgow Austr.
111 B3 Lithino, Akrotirio *pt* Greece
88 B3 Lithuania *country* Europe
102 C1 Litoměřice Czech Rep.
146 C2 Little Abaco *i.* Bahamas
73 B3 Little Andaman *i.* India
83 E4 Little Belt *sea chan.* Denmark
137 E1 Little Falls U.S.A.
139 C2 Littlefield U.S.A.
99 C3 Littlehampton U.K.
122 A2 Little Karas Berg *plat.*
        Namibia
122 B3 Little Karoo *plat.* S. Africa
96 A2 Little Minch *sea chan.* U.K.
136 C1 Little Missouri *r.* U.S.A.
63 A3 Little Nicobar *i.* India
142 B2 Little Rock U.S.A.
141 E2 Littleton U.S.A.
70 B2 Liujiachang China
71 A3 Liupanshui China
71 A3 Liuzhou China
111 B3 Livadeia Greece
88 C2 Līvāni Latvia
50 B1 Livernge Austr.
128 C2 Livermore, Mount U.S.A.
131 D2 Liverpool Can.
98 B2 Liverpool U.K.
127 F2 Liverpool, Cape Can.
53 C2 Liverpool Range *mts* Austr.
134 D1 Livingston *MT* U.S.A.
139 E2 Livingston *TX* U.S.A.
139 C2 Livingston, Lake U.S.A.
120 B2 Livingstone Zambia
109 C2 Livno Bos.-Herz.
89 E3 Livny Rus. Fed.
140 C2 Livonia U.S.A.
108 B2 Livorno Italy
119 D3 Liwale Tanz.
70 B2 Liyang China
99 A4 Lizard Point U.K.
108 B1 Ljubljana Slovenia
92 F3 Ljungan *r.* Sweden
93 F4 Ljungby Sweden
93 G3 Ljusdal Sweden

93 G3 Ljusnan *r.* Sweden
99 B3 Llandeilo U.K.
99 B3 Llandovery U.K.
99 B2 Llandrindod Wells U.K.
98 B2 Llandudno U.K.
99 A3 Llanelli U.K.
98 A2 Llangefni U.K.
139 C2 Llano Estacado *plain* U.S.A.
150 B1 Llanos *plain* Col./Venez.
107 D1 Lleida Spain
99 A2 Lleyn Peninsula U.K.
107 C2 Lliria Spain
128 B2 Lloyd George, Mount Can.
129 D2 Lloyd Lake Can.
129 C2 Lloydminster Can.
152 B3 Llullaillaco, Volcán *vol.* Chile
123 C2 Lobatse Botswana
120 A2 Lobito Angola
101 F1 Loburg Ger.
96 B2 Lochaber *reg.* U.K.
104 C2 Loches France
96 B2 Lochgilphead U.K.
96 B2 Lochinver U.K.
96 A2 Lochmaddy U.K.
96 C2 Lochnagar *mt.* U.K.
57 A2 Lock Austr.
96 C3 Lockerbie U.K.
139 D3 Lockhart U.S.A.
141 D2 Lock Haven U.S.A.
141 D2 Lockport U.S.A.
63 B2 Lôc Ninh Vietnam
105 C3 Lodève France
86 C2 Lodeynoye Pole Rus. Fed.
92 F2 Lødingen Norway
119 D2 Lodwar Kenya
103 D1 Łódź Pol.
62 B2 Loei Thai.
122 A3 Loeriesfontein S. Africa
92 F2 Lofoten *is* Norway
134 D2 Logan U.S.A.
126 B2 Logan, Mount Can.
140 B2 Logansport U.S.A.
108 B1 Logatec Slovenia
106 C1 Logroño Spain
101 D1 Löhne Ger.
101 D1 Lohne (Oldenburg) Ger.
62 A2 Loikaw Myanmar
104 B2 Loire *r.* France
150 A2 Loja Ecuador
106 C2 Loja Spain
92 I2 Lokan tekojärvi *resr* Fin.
74 B1 Lokar Afgh.
100 B2 Lokeren Belgium
122 B1 Lokgwabe Botswana
119 D2 Lokichar Kenya
119 D2 Lokichokio Kenya
89 D2 Loknya Rus. Fed.
115 C4 Lokoja Nigeria
89 D3 Lokot' Rus. Fed.
88 C2 Loksa Estonia
127 G2 Loks Land *i.* Can.
93 F4 Lolland *i.* Denmark
119 D3 Lollondo Tanz.
122 B2 Lolwane S. Africa
93 E3 Lom Bulg.
93 E3 Lom Norway
119 C2 Lomami *r.* Dem. Rep. Congo
153 C4 Lomas de Zamora Arg.
61 C2 Lombok *i.* Indon.
61 C2 Lombok, Selat *sea chan.* Indon.
114 C4 Lomé Togo
118 C3 Lomela *r.* Dem. Rep. Congo
100 B2 Lommel Belgium
96 B2 Lomond, Loch *l.* U.K.
88 C2 Lomonosov Rus. Fed.
135 B4 Lompoc U.S.A.
63 B2 Lom Sak Thai.

103 E1 Łomża Pol.
130 B2 London Can.
99 C3 London U.K.
140 C3 London U.S.A.
97 C1 Londonderry U.K.
50 B1 Londonderry, Cape Austr.
154 B2 Londrina Brazil
83 M2 Longa, Proliv *sea chan.*
        Rus. Fed.
61 C1 Long Akah *Sarawak* Malaysia
143 E2 Long Bay U.S.A.
135 C4 Long Beach U.S.A.
97 C2 Longford Ireland
61 C2 Longiram Indon.
147 C2 Long Island Bahamas
130 C1 Long Island Can.
59 D3 Long Island P.N.G.
141 E2 Long Island U.S.A.
130 B2 Longlac Can.
130 B2 Long Lake Can.
136 B2 Longmont U.S.A.
70 A2 Longnan China
140 C2 Long Point Can.
71 B3 Longquan China
131 E2 Long Range Mountains Can.
51 D2 Longreach Austr.
99 D2 Long Stratton U.K.
98 B1 Longtown U.K.
105 D2 Longuyon France
139 E2 Longview *TX* U.S.A.
134 B1 Longview *WA* U.S.A.
70 A2 Longxi China
71 B3 Longxi Shan *mt.* China
63 B2 Long Xuyên Vietnam
71 B3 Longyan China
82 C1 Longyearbyen Svalbard
105 D2 Lons-le-Saunier France
143 E2 Lookout, Cape U.S.A.
97 D2 Loop Head Ireland
63 B2 Lop Buri Thai.
64 B1 Lopez Phil.
68 C2 Lop Nur *salt flat* China
118 B3 Lopori *r.* Dem. Rep. Congo
74 A2 Lora, Hāmūn-i- *dry lake*
        Afgh./Pak.
106 B2 Lora del Río Spain
140 C2 Lorain U.S.A.
74 A1 Loralai Pak.
107 C2 Lorca Spain
48 E5 Lord Howe Island Austr.
138 B2 Lordsburg U.S.A.
155 C2 Lorena Brazil
152 B2 Loreto Bol.
144 A2 Loreto Mex.
104 B2 Lorient France
52 B3 Lorne Austr.
130 D1 Los Alamos U.S.A.
139 D3 Los Aldamas Mex.
153 A4 Los Angeles Chile
135 C4 Los Angeles U.S.A.
135 B3 Los Banos U.S.A.
152 B3 Los Blancos Arg.
91 E1 Losevo Rus. Fed.
108 B2 Lošinj *i.* Croatia
144 B2 Los Mochis Mex.
118 B2 Losombo Dem. Rep. Congo
147 D3 Los Roques, Islas *is* Venez.
96 C2 Lossiemouth U.K.
150 B1 Los Teques Venez.
152 A4 Los Vilos Chile
104 C3 Lot *r.* France
96 C1 Loth U.K.
119 D2 Lotikipi Plain Kenya/Sudan
118 C3 Loto Dem. Rep. Congo
89 E2 Lotoshino Rus. Fed.
62 B1 Louangnamtha Laos

62 B2 Louangphabang Laos
118 B3 Loubomo Congo
104 B2 Loudéac France
71 B3 Loudi China
118 B3 Loudima Congo
114 A3 Louga Senegal
99 C2 Loughborough U.K.
97 B2 Loughrea Ireland
105 D2 Louhans France
97 B2 Louisburgh Ireland
142 B2 Louisiana *state* U.S.A.
140 B3 Louisville *KY* U.S.A.
142 C2 Louisville *MS* U.S.A.
86 C2 Loukhi Rus. Fed.
130 C1 Loups Marins, Lacs des *lakes* Can.
104 B3 Lourdes France
151 E1 Lourenço Brazil
106 B1 Lousã Port.
53 C2 Louth Austr.
98 C2 Louth U.K.
Louvain Belgium *see* Leuven
89 D2 Lovat' *r.* Rus. Fed.
110 B2 Lovech Bulg.
136 B2 Loveland U.S.A.
135 C2 Lovelock U.S.A.
139 C2 Lovington U.S.A.
119 C3 Lowa Dem. Rep. Congo
141 E2 Lowell U.S.A.
128 C3 Lower Arrow Lake Can.
54 B2 Lower Hutt N.Z.
97 C1 Lower Lough Erne *l.* U.K.
128 B2 Lower Post Can.
99 D2 Lowestoft U.K.
103 D1 Łowicz Pol.
141 D2 Lowville U.S.A.
52 B2 Loxton Austr.
Loyang China *see* Luoyang
48 F4 Loyauté, Îles *is* New Caledonia
89 D3 Loyew Belarus
92 F2 Løypskardtinden *mt.* Norway
109 C2 Loznica Serbia
91 D2 Lozova Ukr.
120 B2 Luacano Angola
70 B2 Lu'an China
120 A1 Luanda Angola
121 C2 Luangwa *r.* Zambia
121 B2 Luanshya Zambia
106 B1 Luarca Spain
120 B2 Luau Angola
103 E1 Lubaczów Pol.
120 A2 Lubango Angola
119 C3 Lubao Dem. Rep. Congo
103 E1 Lubartów Pol.
101 D1 Lübbecke Ger.
139 C2 Lubbock U.S.A.
101 E1 Lübeck Ger.
69 E2 Lubei China
87 E3 Lubenka Kazakh.
103 D1 Lubin Pol.
103 E1 Lublin Pol.
91 C1 Lubny Ukr.
61 C1 Lubok Antu *Sarawak* Malaysia
101 E1 Lübow Ger.
101 E1 Lübtheen Ger.
119 C3 Lubudi Dem. Rep. Congo
60 B2 Lubuklinggau Indon.
119 C4 Lubumbashi Dem. Rep. Congo
120 B2 Lubungu Zambia
119 C3 Lubutu Dem. Rep. Congo
120 A1 Lucala Angola
97 C2 Lucan Ireland
120 B1 Lucapa Angola
96 B3 Luce Bay U.K.
154 B3 Lucélia Brazil
64 B1 Lucena Phil.

106 C2 Lucena Spain
103 D2 Lučenec Slovakia
109 C2 Lucera Italy
105 D2 Lucerne Switz.
101 F1 Lüchow Ger.
120 A2 Lucira Angola
101 F1 Luckenwalde Ger.
122 B2 Luckhoff S. Africa
75 C2 Lucknow India
120 B2 Lucusse Angola
Lüda China *see* Dalian
100 C2 Lüdenscheid Ger.
101 E1 Lüder Ger.
120 A3 Lüderitz Namibia
74 B1 Ludhiana India
140 B2 Ludington U.S.A.
99 B2 Ludlow U.K.
135 C3 Ludlow U.S.A.
110 C2 Ludogorie *reg.* Bulg.
93 G3 Ludvika Sweden
102 B2 Ludwigsburg Ger.
101 F1 Ludwigsfelde Ger.
101 D3 Ludwigshafen am Rhein Ger.
101 E1 Ludwigslust Ger.
88 C2 Ludza Latvia
118 C3 Luebo Dem. Rep. Congo
120 A2 Luena Angola
70 A2 Lüeyang China
71 B3 Lufeng China
139 E2 Lufkin U.S.A.
88 C2 Luga Rus. Fed.
88 C2 Luga *r.* Rus. Fed.
105 D2 Lugano Switz.
121 C2 Lugenda *r.* Moz.
97 C2 Lugnaquilla *h.* Ireland
106 B1 Lugo Spain
110 B1 Lugoj Romania
91 D2 Luhans'k Ukr.
119 D3 Luhombero Tanz.
90 B1 Luhyny Ukr.
120 B2 Luiana Angola
118 C3 Luilaka *r.* Dem. Rep. Congo
105 D2 Luino Italy
92 I2 Luiro *r.* Fin.
118 C3 Luiza Dem. Rep. Congo
70 B2 Lujiang China
109 C2 Lukavac Bos.-Herz.
118 B3 Lukenie *r.* Dem. Rep. Congo
138 A2 Lukeville U.S.A.
89 E3 Lukhovitsy Rus. Fed.
103 E1 Łuków Pol.
120 B2 Lukulu Zambia
92 H2 Luleå Sweden
92 H2 Luleälven *r.* Sweden
110 C2 Lüleburgaz Turkey
70 B2 Lüliang Shan *mts* China
75 C1 Lumajang Indon.
75 C1 Lumajangdong Co *salt l.* China
120 B2 Lumbala Kaquengue Angola
120 B2 Lumbala N'guimbo Angola
143 E2 Lumberton U.S.A.
61 C1 Lumbis Indon.
106 B1 Lumbrales Spain
63 B3 Lumphät Cambodia
129 D2 Lumsden Can.
54 A3 Lumsden N.Z.
93 F4 Lund Sweden
121 C2 Lundazi Zambia
99 A3 Lundy *i.* U.K.
101 E1 Lüneburg Ger.
101 E1 Lüneburger Heide *reg.* Ger.
100 C2 Lünen Ger.
105 D2 Lunéville France
120 B2 Lunga *r.* Zambia
114 A4 Lungi Sierra Leone
62 A1 Lunglei India

120 B2 Lungwebungu *r.* Zambia
74 B2 Luni *r.* India
88 C3 Luninyets Belarus
114 A4 Lunsar Sierra Leone
77 E2 Luntai China
71 A3 Luodian China
71 B3 Luoding China
70 B2 Luohe China
70 B2 Luoyang China
121 B3 Lupane Zimbabwe
110 B1 Lupeni Romania
121 C2 Lupilichi Moz.
101 F2 Luppa Ger.
121 D2 Lúrio Moz.
121 D2 Lurio *r.* Moz.
121 C2 Lusaka Zambia
118 C3 Lusambo Dem. Rep. Congo
109 C2 Lushnjë Albania
136 C2 Lusk U.S.A.
76 B3 Lüt, Kavir-e *des.* Iran
99 C3 Luton U.K.
61 C1 Lutong *Sarawak* Malaysia
129 C1 Łutselk'e Can.
90 B1 Luts'k Ukr.
122 B2 Lutzputs S. Africa
122 A3 Lutzville S. Africa
117 C4 Luuq Somalia
137 D2 Luverne U.S.A.
119 C3 Luvua *r.* Dem. Rep. Congo
123 D1 Luvuvhu *r.* S. Africa
119 D2 Luwero Uganda
59 C3 Luwuk Indon.
100 C3 Luxembourg *country* Europe
100 C3 Luxembourg Lux.
105 D2 Luxeuil-les-Bains France
123 C3 Luxolweni S. Africa
116 B2 Luxor Egypt
100 B2 Luyksgestel Neth.
86 D2 Luza Rus. Fed.
Luzern Switz. *see* Lucerne
71 A3 Luzhou China
154 C1 Luziânia Brazil
151 D2 Luzilândia Brazil
64 B1 Luzon *i.* Phil.
71 C3 Luzon Strait Phil./Taiwan
90 A2 L'viv Ukr.
L'vov Ukr. *see* L'viv
88 C3 Lyakhavichy Belarus
92 G3 Lycksele Sweden
88 C3 Lyel'chytsy Belarus
88 C3 Lyepyel' Belarus
99 B3 Lyme Bay U.K.
141 D3 Lynchburg U.S.A.
129 D2 Lynn Lake Can.
129 D1 Lynx Lake Can.
105 C2 Lyon France
89 D2 Lyozna Belarus
86 E3 Lys'va Rus. Fed.
91 D2 Lysychans'k Ukr.
98 B2 Lytham St Anne's U.K.
88 C3 Lyuban' Belarus
89 E2 Lyubertsy Rus. Fed.
90 B1 Lyubeshiv Ukr.
89 F2 Lyubim Rus. Fed.
91 D2 Lyubotyn Ukr.
89 D2 Lyubytino Rus. Fed.
89 D3 Lyudinovo Rus. Fed.

M

80 B2 Ma'ān Jordan
88 C2 Maardu Estonia
100 B2 Maas *r.* Neth.
100 B2 Maaseik Belgium
64 B1 Maasin Phil.

100 B2 Maastricht Neth.
121 C3 Mabalane Moz.
150 C1 Mabaruma Guyana
121 C3 Mabote Moz.
122 A2 Mabule Botswana
122 B1 Mabutsane Botswana
155 D2 Macaé Brazil
121 C2 Macaloge Moz.
126 E2 MacAlpine Lake Can.
71 D3 Macau aut. reg. China
61 C2 Macau mun. China
151 C1 Macapá Brazil
150 A2 Macará Ecuador
155 D1 Macarani Brazil
123 D1 Macarretane Moz.
151 E2 Macau Brazil
98 B2 Macclesfield U.K.
50 B2 Macdonald, Lake imp. l. Austr.
50 C2 Macdonnell Ranges mts Austr.
130 A1 MacDowell Lake Can.
106 B1 Macedo de Cavaleiros Port
52 B3 Macedon mt. Austr.
109 D2 Macedonia country Europe
151 E3 Maceió Brazil
108 A3 Macerata Italy
52 A2 Macfarlane, Lake imp. l. Austr.
97 B3 Macgillycuddy's Reeks mts Ireland
74 A2 Mach Pak.
155 A2 Machado Brazil
121 C3 Machaila Moz.
119 D3 Machakos Kenya
150 A2 Machala Ecuador
68 C2 Machali China
121 C3 Machaze Moz.
70 B2 Macheng China
141 F2 Machias U.S.A.
150 A1 Machiques Venez.
150 A3 Machu Picchu tourist site Peru
123 D2 Macia Moz.
110 C1 Măcin Romania
114 B3 Macina Mali
53 D1 Macintyre r. Austr.
51 D2 Mackay Austr.
50 B2 Mackay, Lake imp. l. Austr.
129 C1 MacKay Lake Can.
128 B2 Mackenzie r. Can.
128 A1 Mackenzie r. Can.
126 B2 Mackenzie Bay Can.
126 D1 Mackenzie King Island Can.
128 A1 Mackenzie Mountains Can.
129 D2 Macklin Can.
53 D2 Macksville Austr.
53 D1 Maclean Austr.
50 A2 MacLeod, Lake dry lake Austr.
140 A2 Macomb U.S.A.
108 A2 Macomer Sardegna Italy
105 C2 Mâcon France
143 D2 Macon GA U.S.A.
137 E3 Macon MO U.S.A.
53 C2 Macquarie r. Austr.
48 E6 Macquarie Island S. Pacific Ocean
53 C2 Macquarie Marshes Austr.
97 B3 Macroom Ireland
52 A1 Macumba watercourse Austr.
145 C3 Macuspana Mex.
144 B2 Macuzari, Presa resr Mex.
123 D2 Madadeni S. Africa
121 □D3 Madagascar country Africa
115 D2 Madama Niger
111 B2 Madan Bulg.
59 D3 Madang P.N.G.
150 A2 Madeira r. Brazil
114 A1 Madeira terr. N. Atlantic Ocean
131 D2 Madeleine, Îles de la is Can.
144 B2 Madera Mex.

135 B3 Madera U.S.A.
73 B3 Madgaon India
118 B3 Madingou Congo
140 B3 Madison IN U.S.A.
137 D2 Madison SD U.S.A.
140 B2 Madison WI U.S.A.
140 C3 Madison WV U.S.A.
134 D1 Madison r. U.S.A.
140 B3 Madisonville U.S.A.
61 C2 Madoi China
119 D2 Mado Gashi Kenya
88 C2 Madona Latvia
78 A2 Madrakah Saudi Arabia
134 B2 Madras India see Chennai
134 B2 Madras U.S.A.
145 C2 Madre, Laguna lag. Mex.
145 B3 Madre del Sur, Sierra mts Mex.
144 B2 Madre Occidental, Sierra mts Mex.
145 B2 Madre Oriental, Sierra mts Mex.
106 C1 Madrid Spain
106 C2 Madridejos Spain
61 C2 Madura i. Indon.
61 C2 Madura, Selat sea chan. Indon.
73 B4 Madurai India
67 C3 Maebashi Japan
62 A2 Mae Hong Son Thai.
62 A1 Mae Sai Thai.
62 A2 Mae Sariang Thai.
62 A1 Mae Suai Thai.
123 C2 Mafeteng Lesotho
119 D3 Mafia Island Tanz.
119 D3 Mafinga Tanz.
154 C3 Mafra Port.
83 L3 Magadan Rus. Fed.
147 C4 Magangué Col.
142 B2 Magdalena Mex.
138 B2 Magdalena U.S.A.
144 A2 Magdalena, Bahía b. Mex.
101 E1 Magdeburg Ger.
153 A6 Magellan, Strait of Chile
97 C1 Magherafelt U.K.
87 E3 Magnitogorsk Rus. Fed.
142 B2 Magnolia U.S.A.
131 D1 Magpie, Lac l. Can.
114 A3 Magta' Lahjar Maur.
151 D2 Maguarinho, Cabo c. Brazil
123 D2 Magude Moz.
62 A1 Magwe Myanmar
81 C2 Mahābād Iran
74 B2 Mahajan India
121 □D2 Mahajanga Madag.
61 C2 Mahakam r. Indon.
123 C1 Mahalapye Botswana
121 □D2 Mahalevona Madag.
75 C2 Mahanadi r. India
121 □D2 Mahanoro Madag.
63 B2 Maha Sarakham Thai.
121 □D2 Mahavavy r. Madag.
78 B2 Mahd adh Dhahab Saudi Arabia
150 C1 Mahdia Guyana
113 K7 Mahé i. Seychelles
74 B2 Mahesana India
74 B2 Mahi r. India
54 C1 Mahia Peninsula N.Z.
120 B3 Mahikeng S. Africa
123 C2 Mahikeng S. Africa
89 D3 Mahilyow Belarus
74 B2 Mahi r. India
110 C2 Mahya Dağı mt. Turkey
74 A1 Maïdan Shahr Afgh.
129 D2 Maidstone Can.
99 D3 Maidstone U.K.
115 D3 Maiduguri Nigeria

75 C2 Mailani India
76 C3 Maïmanah Afgh.
101 D2 Main r. Ger.
118 B3 Mai-Ndombe, Lac l. Dem. Rep. Congo
101 E3 Main-Donau-Kanal canal Ger.
141 F1 Maine state U.S.A.
62 A1 Maingkwan Myanmar
96 C1 Mainland i. Scotland U.K.
96 □ Mainland i. Scotland U.K.
121 □D2 Maintirano Madag.
101 D2 Mainz Ger.
150 B1 Maiquetía Venez.
53 D2 Maitland N.S.W. Austr.
52 A2 Maitland S.A. Austr.
146 B3 Maíz, Islas del is Nic.
67 C3 Maizuru Japan
61 C2 Majene Indon.
107 D2 Majorca i. Spain
40 F2 Majuro atoll Marshall Is
123 C2 Majwemasweu S. Africa
118 B3 Makabana Congo
58 B3 Makale Indon.
77 E2 Makanshy Kazakh.
109 C2 Makarska Croatia
58 B3 Makassar Indon.
61 C2 Makassar, Selat str. Indon.
Makassar Strait Indon. see Makassar, Selat
76 B2 Makat Kazakh.
123 D2 Makatini Flats lowland S. Africa
114 A4 Makeni Sierra Leone
120 B3 Makgadikgadi depr. Botswana
87 D4 Makhachkala Rus. Fed.
123 C1 Makhado S. Africa
76 B2 Makhambet Kazakh.
119 D3 Makindu Kenya
77 D1 Makinsk Kazakh.
91 D2 Makiyivka Ukr.
Makkah Saudi Arabia see Mecca
131 E1 Makkovik Can.
103 E2 Makó Hungary
118 B2 Makokou Gabon
119 D3 Makongolosi Tanz.
122 B2 Makopong Botswana
79 D2 Makran reg. Iran/Pak.
74 A2 Makran Coast Range mts Pak.
89 E2 Maksatikha Rus. Fed.
81 C2 Makū Iran
62 A1 Makum India
67 B4 Makurazaki Japan
115 C4 Makurdi Nigeria
92 G2 Malå Sweden
146 B4 Mala, Punta pt Panama
118 A2 Malabo Equat. Guinea
60 A1 Malacca, Strait of Indon./Malaysia
134 D2 Malad City U.S.A.
88 C3 Maladzyechna Belarus
106 C2 Málaga Spain
97 B1 Malahide Ireland
48 E3 Malaita i. Solomon Is
117 B4 Malakal S. Sudan
48 F4 Malakula i. Vanuatu
61 C2 Malang Indon.
120 A1 Malanje Angola
93 G4 Mälaren l. Sweden
153 B4 Malargüe Arg.
80 B2 Malatya Turkey
121 C2 Malawi country Africa
Malawi, Lake Africa see Nyasa, Lake
89 D2 Malaya Vishera Rus. Fed.
64 B2 Malaybalay Phil.
81 C2 Malāyer Iran

Malaysia

60 B1 Malaysia *country* Asia
81 C2 Malazgirt Turkey
103 D1 Malbork Pol.
101 F1 Malchin Ger.
100 A4 Maldegem Belgium
49 H3 Malden Island Kiribati
56 G6 Maldives *country* Indian Ocean
153 C4 Maldonado Uru.
56 G6 Male Maldives
111 B3 Maleas, Akrotirio *pt* Greece
103 D2 Malá Karpaty *hills* Slovakia
134 C2 Malheur Lake U.S.A.
114 B3 Mali *country* Africa
114 A3 Mali Guinea
58 C3 Malili Indon.
119 E3 Malindi Kenya
97 C1 Malin Head Ireland
111 C2 Malkara Turkey
88 C3 Mal'kavichy Belarus
110 C2 Malko Tŭrnovo Bulg.
53 C3 Mallacoota Austr.
53 C3 Mallacoota Inlet *b.* Austr.
96 B2 Mallaig U.K.
129 E1 Mallery Lake Can.
Mallorca *i.* Spain see Majorca
97 B2 Mallow Ireland
92 H2 Malmberget Sweden
100 C2 Malmédy Belgium
122 A3 Malmesbury S. Africa
93 F4 Malmö Sweden
62 B1 Malong China
118 C4 Malonga Dem. Rep. Congo
93 E3 Måløy Norway
89 E2 Maloyaroslavets Rus. Fed.
89 E2 Maloye Borisovo Rus. Fed.
8 H5 Malta *country* Europe
88 C2 Malta Latvia
134 E1 Malta U.S.A.
122 A1 Maltahöhe Namibia
98 C1 Malton U.K.
Maluku *is* Indon. *see* Moluccas
59 C3 Maluku, Laut *sea* Indon.
93 F3 Malung Sweden
123 C2 Maluti Mountains Lesotho
73 B3 Malvan India
142 B2 Malvern U.S.A.
90 B1 Malyn Ukr.
83 L2 Malyy Anyuy *r.* Rus. Fed.
83 K2 Malyy Lyakhovskiy, Ostrov *i.* Rus. Fed.
122 C2 Mamafubedu S. Africa
119 C2 Mambasa Dem. Rep. Congo
118 B2 Mambéré *r.* C.A.R.
123 C2 Mamelodi S. Africa
150 B3 Mamoré *r.* Bol./Brazil
114 A3 Mamou Guinea
61 C2 Mamuju Indon.
114 B4 Man Côte d'Ivoire
98 A1 Man, Isle of *i.* Irish Sea
150 B2 Manacapuru Brazil
107 D2 Manacor Spain
59 C2 Manado Indon.
146 B3 Managua Nic.
121 □D3 Manakara Madag.
78 B3 Manākhah Yemen
79 C2 Manama Bahrain
59 D3 Manam Island P.N.G.
121 □D3 Mananara *r.* Madag.
121 □D2 Mananara Avaratra Madag.
121 □D3 Mananjary Madag.
114 A3 Manantali, Lac de *l.* Mali
77 E2 Manas Hu *l.* China
59 C3 Manatuto East Timor
62 A2 Man-aung Kyun *i.* Myanmar
150 B2 Manaus Brazil

80 B2 Manavgat Turkey
98 B2 Manchester U.K.
141 E2 Manchester U.S.A.
121 □D3 Mandabe Madag.
93 E4 Mandal Norway
59 D3 Mandalā, Puncak *mt.* Indon.
62 A1 Mandalay Myanmar
69 D1 Mandalgovi Mongolia
136 C1 Mandan U.S.A.
118 B1 Mandara Mountains Cameroon/Nigeria
108 A3 Mandas *Sardegna* Italy
100 C2 Manderscheid Ger.
74 B1 Mandi India
114 B3 Mandiana Guinea
75 C2 Mandla India
121 □D2 Mandritsara Madag.
74 B2 Mandsaur India
50 A3 Mandurah Austr.
73 B3 Mandya India
108 B1 Manerbio Italy
90 B1 Manevychi Ukr.
109 C2 Manfredonia Italy
114 B3 Manga Burkina Faso
118 B3 Mangai Dem. Rep. Congo
54 C1 Mangakino N.Z.
110 C2 Mangalia Romania
73 B3 Mangalore India
123 C2 Mangaung S. Africa
61 B2 Manggar Indon.
76 B2 Mangistau Kazakh.
121 C2 Mangochi Malawi
59 C3 Mangole *i.* Indon.
154 B3 Mangueirinha Brazil
69 E1 Mangui China
137 D3 Manhattan U.S.A.
121 C3 Manhica Moz.
155 D2 Manhuaçu Brazil
121 □D2 Mania *r.* Madag.
108 B1 Maniago Italy
150 B2 Manicoré Brazil
131 D2 Manicouagan *r.* Can.
131 D1 Manicouagan, Petit Lac *l.* Can.
131 D1 Manicouagan, Réservoir *resr* Can.
79 B2 Manifah Saudi Arabia
64 B1 Manila Phil.
53 D2 Manilla Austr.
111 C3 Manisa Turkey
140 B2 Manistee U.S.A.
129 E2 Manitoba *prov.* Can.
129 E2 Manitoba, Lake Can.
140 B1 Manitou Islands U.S.A.
130 B2 Manitoulin Island Can.
140 B2 Manitowoc U.S.A.
130 C2 Maniwaki Can.
150 A1 Manizales Col.
142 C2 Mankato U.S.A.
114 B4 Mankono Côte d'Ivoire
129 D3 Mankota Can.
73 C4 Mankulam Sri Lanka
74 B2 Manmad India
73 B3 Mannar, Gulf of India/Sri Lanka
101 D3 Mannheim Ger.
128 C2 Manning Can.
52 A2 Mannum Austr.
129 C2 Mannville Can.
59 C3 Manokwari Indon.
119 C3 Manono Dem. Rep. Congo
63 A2 Manoron Myanmar
105 D3 Manosque France
131 C1 Manouane, Lac *l.* Can.
107 D1 Manresa Spain
121 B2 Mansa Zambia
127 F2 Mansel Island Can.
92 I2 Mansel'kya *ridge* Fin./Rus. Fed.

53 C3 Mansfield Austr.
98 C2 Mansfield U.K.
142 B2 Mansfield *LA* U.S.A.
140 C2 Mansfield *OH* U.S.A.
141 D2 Mansfield *PA* U.S.A.
150 A2 Manta Ecuador
143 E1 Manteo U.S.A.
104 C2 Mantes-la-Jolie France
155 C2 Mantiqueira, Serra da *mts* Brazil
Mantova Italy *see* Mantua
108 B1 Mantua Italy
151 C2 Manuelzinho Brazil
59 C3 Manui *r.* Indon.
54 B1 Manukau N.Z.
142 B2 Many U.S.A.
119 D3 Manyoni Tanz.
106 C2 Manzanares Spain
144 B3 Manzanillo Mex.
69 D1 Manzhouli China
123 D2 Manzini Swaziland
115 D3 Mao Chad
107 D2 Mao Spain
59 D3 Maoke, Pegunungan *mts* Indon.
123 C2 Maokeng S. Africa
65 A1 Maokui Shan *mt.* China
71 B3 Maoming China
121 C3 Mapai Moz.
75 C1 Mapam Yumco *l.* China
145 C3 Mapastepec Mex.
144 B2 Mapimí Mex.
144 B2 Mapimí, Bolsón de *des.* Mex.
121 C3 Mapinhane Moz.
129 D3 Maple Creek Can.
121 C3 Maputo Moz.
123 D2 Maputo *r.* Moz./S. Africa
120 A1 Maquela do Zombo Angola
153 B5 Maquinchao Arg.
137 E2 Maquoketa U.S.A.
150 B2 Maraã Brazil
151 D2 Marabá Brazil
151 C1 Maracá, Ilha de *i.* Brazil
150 A1 Maracaibo Venez.
150 A1 Maracaibo, Lake Venez.
152 C3 Maracaju, Serra de *hills* Brazil
154 A2 Maracaju, Serra de *hills* Brazil
150 B1 Maracay Venez.
115 D2 Marādah Libya
115 C3 Maradi Niger
81 C2 Marāgheh Iran
151 C1 Marajó, Baía de *est.* Brazil
151 C2 Marajó, Ilha de *i.* Brazil
79 C2 Maraki Iran
119 D2 Maralal Kenya
50 C3 Maralinga Austr.
81 C2 Marand Iran
150 A2 Marañón *r.* Peru
130 B2 Marathon Can.
143 D4 Marathon U.S.A.
106 C2 Marbella Spain
50 A2 Marble Bar Austr.
123 C1 Marble Hall S. Africa
123 D3 Marburg S. Africa
101 D2 Marburg an der Lahn Ger.
99 D2 March U.K.
100 B2 Marche-en-Famenne Belgium
106 B2 Marchena Spain
152 B4 Mar Chiquita, Laguna *l.* Arg.
141 E2 Marcy, Mount U.S.A.
74 B1 Mardan Pak.
153 C4 Mar del Plata Arg.
81 C2 Mardin Turkey
96 B2 Maree, Loch *l.* U.K.
108 B3 Marettimo, Isola *i. Sicilia* Italy
89 D2 Marevo Rus. Fed.
138 C2 Marfa U.S.A.

50 A3 **Margaret River** Austr.
147 D2 **Margarita, Isla de** i. Venez.
123 D3 **Margate** S. Africa
99 D3 **Margate** U.K.
119 C2 **Margherita Peak** Dem. Rep.
Congo/Uganda
76 C3 **Märgö, Dasht-e** des. Afgh.
91 C2 **Marhanets'** Ukr.
62 A1 **Mari** Myanmar
152 B3 **María Elena** Chile
156 C5 **Mariana Trench** N. Pacific
Ocean
142 B2 **Marianna** AR U.S.A.
143 D2 **Marianna** FL U.S.A.
102 C2 **Mariánské Lázně** Czech Rep.
144 B2 **Marías, Islas** is Mex.
78 B3 **Ma'rib** Yemen
109 C1 **Maribor** Slovenia
117 A4 **Maridi** watercourse S. Sudan
55 M2 **Marie Byrd Land** reg.
Antarctica
147 D3 **Marie-Galante** i. Guadeloupe
93 G3 **Mariehamn** Fin.
122 A1 **Mariental** Namibia
93 F4 **Mariestad** Sweden
143 D2 **Marietta** GA U.S.A.
140 C3 **Marietta** OH U.S.A.
105 D3 **Marignane** France
83 K3 **Marii, Mys** pt Rus. Fed.
88 B3 **Marijampolė** Lith.
154 C2 **Marília** Brazil
106 B1 **Marín** Spain
109 C3 **Marina di Gioiosa Ionica**
Italy
88 C3 **Mar"ina Horka** Belarus
140 B1 **Marinette** U.S.A.
154 B2 **Maringá** Brazil
106 B2 **Marinha Grande** Port.
140 B2 **Marion** IN U.S.A.
140 C2 **Marion** OH U.S.A.
143 E2 **Marion** SC U.S.A.
140 C3 **Marion** VA U.S.A.
143 D2 **Marion, Lake** U.S.A.
52 A3 **Marion Bay** Austr.
152 B3 **Mariscal José Félix
Estigarribia** Para.
110 C2 **Maritsa** r. Bulg.
91 D2 **Mariupol'** Ukr.
117 C4 **Marka** Somalia
123 C3 **Marken** S. Africa
100 B1 **Markermeer** l. Neth.
83 I2 **Markha** r. Rus. Fed.
91 D2 **Markivka** Ukr.
142 B2 **Marksville** U.S.A.
101 D3 **Marktheidenfeld** Ger.
101 F2 **Marktredwitz** Ger.
100 C2 **Marl** Ger.
100 A3 **Marle** France
139 D2 **Marlin** U.S.A.
104 C3 **Marmande** France
111 C2 **Marmara, Sea of** g. Turkey
Marmara Denizi g. Turkey see
Marmara, Sea of
111 C3 **Marmaris** Turkey
104 C2 **Marne à la Vallée** France
121 □D2 **Maroantsetra** Madag.
101 E2 **Maroldsweisach** Ger.
121 □D2 **Maromokotro** mt. Madag.
121 C3 **Marondera** Zimbabwe
151 C1 **Maroni** r. Fr. Guiana
118 B3 **Maroua** Cameroon
121 □D2 **Marovoay** Madag.
49 I3 **Marquesas Islands** is Fr.
Polynesia
140 B1 **Marquette** U.S.A.
117 A3 **Marra, Jebel** mt. Sudan
117 A3 **Marra, Jebel** plat. Sudan

173 D2 **Marraquene** Moz.
114 B1 **Marrakech** Morocco
52 A1 **Marree** Austr.
121 C2 **Marromeu** Moz.
121 C2 **Marrupa** Moz.
116 B2 **Marsá al 'Alam** Egypt
115 D1 **Marsá al Burayqah** Libya
119 D2 **Marsabit** Kenya
108 B3 **Marsala** Sicilia Italy
116 A1 **Marsá Maṭrūḥ** Egypt
101 D2 **Marsberg** Ger.
108 B2 **Marsciano** Italy
53 C2 **Marsden** Austr.
105 D3 **Marseille** France
137 D2 **Marshall** MN U.S.A.
137 E3 **Marshall** MO U.S.A.
137 E2 **Marshall** TX U.S.A.
48 F2 **Marshall Islands** country
N. Pacific Ocean
137 E2 **Marshalltown** U.S.A.
140 A2 **Marshfield** U.S.A.
143 E3 **Marsh Harbour** Bahamas
142 B3 **Marsh Island** U.S.A.
88 A2 **Märsta** Sweden
61 C2 **Martapura** Kalimantan Selatan
Indon.
60 B2 **Martapura** Sumatera Selatan
Indon.
141 E2 **Martha's Vineyard** i. U.S.A.
105 D2 **Martigny** Switz.
103 D2 **Martin** Slovakia
136 C2 **Martin** U.S.A.
145 C2 **Martínez** Mex.
147 D3 **Martinique** terr. West Indies
141 D3 **Martinsburg** U.S.A.
140 D3 **Martinsville** U.S.A.
76 B1 **Martok** Kazakh.
54 C2 **Marton** N.Z.
107 D1 **Martorell** Spain
106 C2 **Martos** Spain
76 C3 **Mary** Turkm.
51 E2 **Maryborough** Austr.
122 B2 **Marydale** S. Africa
141 D3 **Maryland** state U.S.A.
137 D3 **Maryville** MO U.S.A.
143 D1 **Maryville** TN U.S.A.
119 D3 **Masai Steppe** plain Tanz.
119 D3 **Masaka** Uganda
65 B2 **Masan** S. Korea
119 D4 **Masasi** Tanz.
64 B1 **Masbate** Phil.
64 B1 **Masbate** i. Phil.
123 C2 **Maseru** Lesotho
76 B3 **Mashhad** Iran
123 D3 **Mashishing** S. Africa
74 A2 **Mashkel, Hamun-i-** salt flat
Pak.
123 C3 **Masibambane** S. Africa
79 C3 **Masilah, Wādī al** watercourse
Yemen
123 C2 **Masilo** S. Africa
119 D2 **Masindi** Uganda
79 C3 **Maṣīrah, Jazīrat** i. Oman
79 C3 **Maṣīrah, Khalīj** b. Oman
81 C2 **Masjed-e Soleymān** Iran
97 B2 **Mask, Lough** l. Ireland
121 □E2 **Masoala, Tanjona** c. Madag.
137 E2 **Mason City** U.S.A.
Masqat Oman see **Muscat**
108 B2 **Massa** Italy
141 E2 **Massachusetts** state U.S.A.
141 E2 **Massachusetts Bay** U.S.A.
121 C3 **Massangena** Moz.
120 A1 **Massango** Angola
116 B3 **Massawa** Eritrea

141 E2 **Massena** U.S.A.
128 A2 **Masset** Can.
105 C2 **Massif Central** mts France
140 C2 **Massillon** U.S.A.
121 C3 **Massinga** Moz.
123 D1 **Massingir** Moz.
78 A2 **Mastābah** Saudi Arabia
54 C2 **Masterton** N.Z.
74 A2 **Mastung** Pak.
78 A2 **Mastūrah** Saudi Arabia
88 B3 **Masty** Belarus
67 B4 **Masuda** Japan
Masuku Gabon see **Franceville**
121 C3 **Masvingo** Zimbabwe
69 D1 **Matad** Mongolia
118 B3 **Matadi** Dem. Rep. Congo
146 B3 **Matagalpa** Nic.
130 C2 **Matagami** Can.
130 C2 **Matagami, Lac** l. Can.
139 D3 **Matagorda Island** U.S.A.
120 A2 **Matala** Angola
114 A3 **Matam** Senegal
144 B2 **Matamoros** Coahuila Mex.
145 C2 **Matamoros** Tamaulipas Mex.
119 D3 **Matandu** r. Tanz.
131 D2 **Matane** Can.
146 B2 **Matanzas** Cuba
73 C4 **Matara** Sri Lanka
61 C2 **Mataram** Indon.
50 C1 **Mataranka** Austr.
107 D1 **Mataró** Spain
123 C3 **Matatiele** S. Africa
54 A3 **Mataura** N.Z.
49 G3 **Mata'utu** Wallis and Futuna Is
54 C1 **Matawai** N.Z.
152 B2 **Mategua** Bol.
145 B2 **Matehuala** Mex.
109 C2 **Matera** Italy
139 D3 **Mathis** U.S.A.
75 B2 **Mathura** India
64 B2 **Mati** Phil.
98 C2 **Matlock** U.K.
150 C3 **Mato Grosso** Brazil
154 B1 **Mato Grosso, Planalto do** plat.
Brazil
123 D2 **Matola** Moz.
Matou China see **Pingguo**
67 B3 **Matsue** Japan
66 D2 **Matsumae** Japan
67 C4 **Matsusaka** Japan
67 B4 **Matsuyama** Japan
130 B1 **Mattagami** r. Can.
105 D2 **Matterhorn** mt. Italy/Switz.
134 C2 **Matterhorn** mt. U.S.A.
140 B3 **Mattoon** U.S.A.
150 B1 **Maturín** Venez.
123 C2 **Matwabeng** S. Africa
100 A2 **Maubeuge** France
104 C3 **Maubourguet** France
124 E5 **Maui** i. U.S.A.
140 C2 **Maumee** r. U.S.A.
120 B2 **Maun** Botswana
62 A1 **Maungdaw** Myanmar
50 C2 **Maurice, Lake** imp. l.
Austr.
114 A3 **Mauritania** country Africa
113 K9 **Mauritius** country Indian
Ocean
78 B2 **Māwān, Khashm** mt.
Saudi Arabia
118 B3 **Mawanga** Dem. Rep. Congo
71 B3 **Mawei** China
62 A1 **Mawkmai** Myanmar
62 A1 **Mawlaik** Myanmar
63 A2 **Mawlamyaing** Myanmar
78 B2 **Mawqaq** Saudi Arabia
78 B3 **Mawza** Yemen

108 A3 Maxia, Punta *mt. Sardegna* Italy
83 J2 Maya *r.* Rus. Fed.
147 C2 Mayaguana *i.* Bahamas
96 B3 Maybole U.K.
104 B2 Mayenne France
104 B2 Mayenne *r.* France
128 C2 Mayerthorpe Can.
140 B3 Mayfield U.S.A.
87 D4 Maykop Rus. Fed.
126 B2 Mayo Can.
118 B3 Mayoko Congo
121 D2 Mayotte *terr.* Africa
83 J3 Mayskiy Rus. Fed.
140 C3 Maysville U.S.A.
118 B3 Mayumba Gabon
137 D1 Mayville U.S.A.
151 C2 Mazagão Brazil
104 C3 Mazamet France
77 C3 Mazar China
108 B3 Mazara del Vallo *Sicilia* Italy
77 C3 Mazār-e Sharīf Afgh.
144 A2 Mazatán Mex.
146 A3 Mazatenango Guat.
144 B2 Mazatlán Mex.
88 B2 Mažeikiai Lith.
88 B2 Mazirbe Latvia
71 C3 Mazu Dao *i.* Taiwan
121 B3 Mazunga Zimbabwe
88 C3 Mazyr Belarus
123 D2 Mbabane Swaziland
118 B3 Mbaïki C.A.R.
121 C1 Mbala Zambia
119 D2 Mbale Uganda
118 B2 Mbalmayo Cameroon
118 B3 Mbandaka Dem. Rep. Congo
118 A2 Mbanga Cameroon
120 A1 M'banza Congo Angola
119 D3 Mbeya Tanz.
119 D4 Mbinga Tanz.
123 D2 Mbombela S. Africa
118 B2 Mbomo Congo
118 B2 Mbouda Cameroon
114 A3 Mbour Senegal
114 A3 Mbout Maur.
118 C3 Mbuji-Mayi Dem. Rep. Congo
119 D3 Mbuyuni Tanz.
139 D2 McAlester U.S.A.
139 D3 McAllen U.S.A.
128 B3 McBride Can.
134 C2 McCall U.S.A.
126 E2 McClintock Channel Can.
126 D2 McClure Strait Can.
142 D2 McComb U.S.A.
136 C2 McConaughy, Lake U.S.A.
136 C2 McCook U.S.A.
134 C2 McDermitt U.S.A.
134 D1 McDonald Peak U.S.A.
134 D1 McGuire, Mount U.S.A.
128 C2 McLennan Can.
128 B2 McLeod Lake Can.
134 B1 McMinnville OR U.S.A.
142 C1 McMinnville TN U.S.A.
137 D3 McPherson U.S.A.
123 C3 Mdantsane S. Africa
135 D3 Mead, Lake *resr* U.S.A.
129 D2 Meadow Lake Can.
140 C2 Meadville U.S.A.
66 D2 Meaken-dake *vol.* Japan
106 B1 Mealhada Port.
131 E1 Mealy Mountains Can.
128 C2 Meander River Can.
78 A2 Mecca Saudi Arabia
100 B2 Mechelen Belgium
100 B2 Mechelen Neth.
100 C2 Mechernich Ger.
100 C2 Meckenheim Ger.

106 B1 Meda Port.
60 A1 Medan Indon.
153 B5 Medanosa, Punta *pt* Arg.
73 C4 Medawachchiya Sri Lanka
107 D2 Médéa Alg.
150 A1 Medellín Col.
115 D1 Medenine Tunisia
134 B2 Medford U.S.A.
110 C2 Medgidia Romania
110 B1 Mediaş Romania
136 B2 Medicine Bow Mountains U.S.A.
136 B2 Medicine Bow Peak U.S.A.
129 C2 Medicine Hat Can.
137 D3 Medicine Lodge U.S.A.
155 D1 Medina Brazil
78 A2 Medina Saudi Arabia
106 C1 Medinaceli Spain
106 B1 Medina del Campo Spain
106 B1 Medina de Rioseco Spain
84 G5 Mediterranean Sea World
129 C2 Medley U.S.A.
87 E3 Mednogorsk Rus. Fed.
83 L2 Medvezh'i, Ostrova *is* Rus. Fed.
86 C2 Medvezh'yegorsk Rus. Fed.
50 A2 Meekatharra Austr.
136 B2 Meeker U.S.A.
75 B2 Meerut India
100 A2 Meetkerke Belgium
111 B3 Megalopoli Greece
75 C2 Meghasani *mt.* India
80 A2 Megisti *i.* Greece
92 I1 Mehamn Norway
50 A2 Meharry, Mount Austr.
81 D2 Mehrān *watercourse* Iran
74 B1 Mehtar Lām Afgh.
154 C1 Meia Ponte *r.* Brazil
118 B2 Meiganga Cameroon
65 B1 Meihekou China
Meijiang China see Ningdu
62 A1 Meiktila Myanmar
101 E2 Meiningen Ger.
102 C1 Meißen Ger.
71 B3 Meizhou China
152 B3 Mejicana *mt.* Arg.
152 A3 Mejillones Chile
117 B3 Mek'elē Eth.
114 C2 Mekerrhane, Sebkha *salt pan* Alg.
114 B1 Meknès Morocco
63 B2 Mekong *r.* Asia
63 B3 Mekong, Mouths of the Vietnam
60 B1 Melaka Malaysia
53 B3 Melbourne Austr.
143 D3 Melbourne U.S.A.
108 A2 Mele, Capo *c.* Italy
131 C1 Mélèzes, Rivière aux *r.* Can.
115 D3 Melfi Chad
109 C2 Melfi Italy
129 D2 Melfort Can.
92 F3 Melhus Norway
106 B1 Melide Spain
114 B1 Melilla N. Africa
91 D2 Melitopol' Ukr.
101 D1 Melle Ger.
93 F4 Mellerud Sweden
101 E2 Mellrichstadt Ger.
100 D1 Mellum *i.* Ger.
152 C4 Melo Uru.
115 C1 Melrhir, Chott *salt l.* Alg.
99 C2 Melton Mowbray U.K.
104 C2 Melun France
129 D2 Melville Can.
51 D1 Melville, Cape Austr.
131 E1 Melville, Lake Can.

50 C1 Melville Island Austr.
126 D1 Melville Island Can.
127 F2 Melville Peninsula Can.
102 C2 Memmingen Ger.
61 B1 Mempawah Indon.
80 B3 Memphis *tourist site* Egypt
142 B1 Memphis TN U.S.A.
139 C2 Memphis TX U.S.A.
91 C1 Mena Ukr.
142 B2 Mena U.S.A.
114 C3 Ménaka Mali
Menam Khong *r.* Laos/Thai. *see* Mekong
105 C3 Mende France
116 B3 Mendefera Eritrea
145 C2 Méndez Mex.
119 D2 Mendī Eth.
59 D3 Mendi P.N.G.
99 B3 Mendip Hills U.K.
153 B4 Mendoza Arg.
111 C3 Menemen Turkey
60 B2 Menggala Indon.
62 B1 Mengzi China
131 D1 Menihek Can.
52 B2 Menindee Austr.
52 B2 Menindee Lake Austr.
52 A3 Meningie Austr.
104 C2 Mennecy France
140 B1 Menominee U.S.A.
120 A2 Menongue Angola
Menorca *i.* Spain *see* Minorca
60 A2 Mentawai, Kepulauan *is* Indon.
60 B2 Mentok Indon.
50 B2 Menzies Austr.
100 C1 Meppel Neth.
100 C1 Meppen Ger.
123 D1 Mepuze Moz.
123 C2 Meqheleng S. Africa
108 B1 Merano Italy
59 D3 Merauke Indon.
52 B2 Merbein Austr.
135 B3 Merced U.S.A.
152 C3 Mercedes Arg.
127 G2 Mercy, Cape Can.
139 C1 Meredith, Lake U.S.A.
91 D2 Merefa Ukr.
116 A3 Merga Oasis Sudan
63 A2 Mergui Archipelago *is* Myanmar
110 C2 Meriç *r.* Greece/Turkey
145 D2 Mérida Mex.
106 B2 Mérida Spain
150 A1 Mérida Venez.
142 C2 Meridian U.S.A.
53 C3 Merimbula Austr.
116 B3 Merowe Sudan
50 A3 Merredin Austr.
96 B3 Merrick *h.* U.K.
140 B1 Merrill U.S.A.
140 B2 Merrillville U.S.A.
128 B2 Merritt Can.
53 C2 Merrygoen Austr.
116 C3 Mersa Fatma Eritrea
100 C3 Mersch Lux.
101 E2 Merseburg (Saale) Ger.
98 B2 Mersey *r.* U.K.
80 B2 Mersin Turkey
60 B1 Mersing Malaysia
99 D4 Mers-les-Bains France
74 B2 Merta India
99 B3 Merthyr Tydfil U.K.
106 B2 Mértola Port.
76 B2 Mertvyy Kultuk, Sor *dry lake* Kazakh.
119 D3 Meru *vol.* Tanz.
100 C3 Merzig Ger.
138 A2 Mesa U.S.A.

109 C2 Mesagne Italy
101 D2 Meschede Ger.
89 E3 Meshchovsk Rus. Fed.
91 E2 Meshkovskaya Rus. Fed.
111 B2 Mesimeri Greece
111 B3 Mesolongi Greece
121 D2 Messaló r. Moz.
109 C3 Messina Sicilia Italy
109 C3 Messina, Strait of Italy
111 B3 Messiniakós Kolpos g. Greece
110 B2 Mesta r. Bulg.
150 B1 Meta r. Col./Venez.
127 G2 Meta Incognita Peninsula Can.
152 B2 Metán Arg.
111 B3 Methoni Greece
109 C2 Metković Croatia
60 B2 Metro Indon.
117 B4 Metu Eth.
105 D2 Metz France
100 B2 Meuse r. Belgium/France
139 D2 Mexia U.S.A.
144 A1 Mexicali Mex.
144 B2 Mexico country Central
America
137 E3 Mexico U.S.A.
125 I5 Mexico, Gulf of Mex./U.S.A.
145 C3 Mexico City Mex.
101 F1 Meyenburg Ger.
86 D2 Mezen' Rus. Fed.
86 D2 Mezen' r. Rus. Fed.
86 E1 Mezhdusharskiy, Ostrov i.
Rus. Fed.
103 E2 Mezőtúr Hungary
144 B2 Mezquitic Mex.
88 C2 Mežvidi Latvia
121 C2 Mfuwe Zambia
123 D2 Mhlume Swaziland
74 B2 Mhow India
145 C3 Miahuatlán Mex.
106 B2 Miajadas Spain
143 D3 Miami FL U.S.A.
139 E1 Miami OK U.S.A.
143 D3 Miami Beach U.S.A.
81 C2 Miāndowāb Iran
121 □D2 Miandrivazo Madag.
81 C2 Mīāneh Iran
74 B1 Mianwali Pak.
70 A2 Mianyang China
121 □D2 Miarinarivo Madag.
87 F3 Miass Rus. Fed.
128 C2 Mica Creek Can.
103 E2 Michalovce Slovakia
140 B1 Michigan state U.S.A.
140 B2 Michigan, Lake U.S.A.
140 B2 Michigan U.S.A.
130 B2 Michipicoten Island Can.
130 B2 Michipicoten River Can.
89 F3 Michurinsk Rus. Fed.
48 D2 Micronesia, Federated States
of country N. Pacific Ocean
100 A2 Middelburg Neth.
123 C3 Middelburg E. Cape S. Africa
123 C2 Middelburg Mpumalanga
S. Africa
100 B2 Middelharnis Neth.
134 B2 Middle Alkali Lake U.S.A.
73 D3 Middle Andaman i. India
136 D2 Middle Loup r. U.S.A.
140 C3 Middlesboro U.S.A.
98 C1 Middlesbrough U.K.
141 E2 Middletown NY U.S.A.
140 C3 Middletown OH U.S.A.
78 B3 Midi Yemen
130 C2 Midland Can.
140 C2 Midland MI U.S.A.
139 C2 Midland TX U.S.A.
97 B3 Midleton Ireland

94 B1 Miðvágur Faroe Is
109 D2 Midzhur mt. Bulg./S.M.
103 E1 Mielec Pol.
110 C1 Miercurea-Ciuc Romania
106 B1 Mieres del Camín Spain
101 E1 Mieste Ger.
145 C3 Miguel Alemán, Presa resr
Mex.
144 B2 Miguel Auza Mex.
144 B2 Miguel Hidalgo, Presa resr
Mex.
63 A2 Migyaunglaung Myanmar
89 E3 Mikhaylov Rus. Fed.
Mikhaylovgrad Bulg. see
Montana
66 B2 Mikhaylovka Rus. Fed.
77 D1 Mikhaylovskoye Rus. Fed.
93 I3 Mikkeli Fin.
86 E2 Mikun' Rus. Fed.
67 C3 Mikuni-sanmyaku mts Japan
108 A1 Milan Italy
121 C2 Milange Moz.
Milan Italy see Milan
111 C3 Milas Turkey
137 D1 Milbank U.S.A.
99 D2 Mildenhall U.K.
52 B2 Mildura Austr.
62 B1 Mile China
136 B1 Miles City U.S.A.
141 D3 Milford DE U.S.A.
135 D3 Milford UT U.S.A.
99 A3 Milford Haven U.K.
54 A3 Milford Sound N.Z.
107 D2 Miliana Alg.
116 D3 Milk, Wadi el watercourse
Sudan
83 L3 Mil'kovo Rus. Fed.
129 C3 Milk River Can.
105 C3 Millau France
143 D2 Milledgeville U.S.A.
137 E1 Mille Lacs lakes U.S.A.
130 A2 Mille Lacs, Lac des l. Can.
137 D2 Miller U.S.A.
91 E2 Millerovo Rus. Fed.
52 A2 Millers Creek Austr.
52 B3 Millicent Austr.
141 F1 Millinocket U.S.A.
53 D1 Millmerran Austr.
98 B1 Millom U.K.
128 C1 Mills Lake Can.
111 B3 Milos i. Greece
89 E3 Miloslavskoye Rus. Fed.
91 E2 Milove Ukr.
52 B1 Milparinka Austr.
54 A3 Milton N.Z.
99 C3 Milton Keynes U.K.
140 B2 Milwaukee U.S.A.
104 B3 Mimizan France
79 C2 Mimongo Gabon
79 C2 Mīnāb Iran
58 C2 Minahasa, Semenanjung pen.
Indon.
79 C2 Mina Jebel Ali U.A.E.
60 B1 Minas Indon.
153 C4 Minas Uru.
155 D1 Minas Novas Brazil
145 C3 Minatitlán Mex.
62 A1 Minbu Myanmar
64 B2 Mindanao i. Phil.
101 D1 Minden Ger.
142 B2 Minden LA U.S.A.
137 D2 Minden NE U.S.A.
64 B1 Mindoro i. Phil.
64 A1 Mindoro Strait Phil.
118 B3 Mindouli Congo
99 B3 Minehead U.K.
154 B1 Mineiros Brazil

139 D2 Mineral Wells U.S.A.
77 E1 Minfeng China
119 C4 Minga Dem. Rep. Congo
81 C1 Mingäçevir Azer.
131 D1 Mingan Can.
52 B2 Mingary Austr.
70 B2 Mingguang China
62 A1 Mingin Myanmar
107 C2 Minglanilla Spain
119 D4 Mingoyo Tanz.
69 E1 Mingshui China
71 B3 Mingxi China
73 B4 Minicoy atoll India
50 A2 Minilya Austr.
131 D1 Minipi Lake Can.
130 A1 Miniss Lake Can.
115 C4 Minna Nigeria
137 E2 Minneapolis U.S.A.
129 E2 Minnedosa Can.
137 E2 Minnesota r. U.S.A.
137 F1 Minnesota state U.S.A.
106 B1 Miño r. Port./Spain
107 D1 Minorca i. Spain
136 C1 Minot U.S.A.
88 C3 Minsk Belarus
103 E1 Mińsk Mazowiecki Pol.
131 D2 Minto Can.
130 C1 Minto, Lac l. Can.
70 A2 Minxian China
155 D1 Mirabela Brazil
155 D1 Miralta Brazil
131 D2 Miramichi N.B. Can.
111 C3 Mirampellou, Kolpos b.
Greece
152 C3 Miranda Brazil
152 C2 Miranda r. Brazil
106 C1 Miranda de Ebro Spain
106 B1 Mirandela Port.
154 B2 Mirandópolis Brazil
79 C3 Mirbāţ Oman
61 C1 Miri Sarawak Malaysia
153 C4 Mirim, Lagoa l. Brazil/Uru.
79 D2 Mīrjāveh Iran
83 I2 Mirnyy Rus. Fed.
101 F1 Mirow Ger.
74 A2 Mirpur Khas Pak.
111 B3 Mirtoö Pelagos sea Greece
65 B2 Miryang S. Korea
75 C2 Mirzapur India
66 B1 Mishan China
146 B3 Miskitos, Cayos is Nic.
103 E2 Miskolc Hungary
59 C3 Misoöl i. Indon.
115 D1 Mişrātah Libya
130 B1 Missinaibi r. Can.
130 B2 Missinaibi Lake Can.
128 B3 Mission Can.
130 B1 Missisa Lake Can.
118 C2 Mississippi r. Gabon
142 C2 Mississippi r. U.S.A.
142 C2 Mississippi state U.S.A.
134 D1 Missoula U.S.A.
137 E3 Missouri r. U.S.A.
137 E3 Missouri state U.S.A.
131 C2 Mistassibi r. Can.
130 C1 Mistassini, Lac l. Can.
131 D1 Mistastin Lake Can.
103 D2 Mistelbach Austria
131 D1 Mistinibi, Lac l. Can.
130 C1 Mistissini Can.
51 D2 Mitchell Austr.
51 D1 Mitchell r. Austr.
137 D2 Mitchell U.S.A.
97 B2 Mitchelstown Ireland
74 A2 Mithi Pak.
67 D3 Mito Japan
119 D3 Mitole Tanz.

109 D2 Mitrovicë Kosovo
53 D2 Mittagong Austr.
101 E2 Mittelhausen Ger.
101 D1 Mittellandkanal canal Ger.
101 F3 Mitterteich Ger.
150 A1 Mitú Col.
119 C4 Mitumba, Chaîne des mts Dem. Rep. Congo
119 C3 Mitumba, Monts mts Dem. Rep. Congo
118 B2 Mitzic Gabon
78 B2 Miyah, Wādī al watercourse Saudi Arabia
67 C4 Miyake-jima i. Japan
66 D3 Miyako Japan
67 B4 Miyakonojō Japan
76 B2 Miyaly Kazakh.
67 B4 Miyazaki Japan
115 D1 Mizdah Libya
97 B3 Mizen Head Ireland
90 A2 Mizhhirr''ya Ukr.
93 G4 Mjölby Sweden
93 F3 Mjøsa l. Norway
119 D3 Mkomazi Tanz.
103 C1 Mladá Boleslav Czech Rep.
109 D2 Mladenovac Serbia
103 E1 Mława Pol.
123 C3 Mlungisi S. Africa
90 B1 Mlyniv Ukr.
123 C2 Mmabatho S. Africa
123 C2 Mmathethe Botswana
135 E3 Moab U.S.A.
123 D2 Moamba Moz.
119 C3 Moba Dem. Rep. Congo
118 C2 Mobayi-Mbongo Dem. Rep. Congo
137 E3 Moberly U.S.A.
142 C2 Mobile U.S.A.
142 C2 Mobile Bay U.S.A.
136 C1 Mobridge U.S.A.
121 D2 Moçambique Moz.
62 B1 Môc Châu Vietnam
78 B3 Mocha Yemen
123 C1 Mochudi Botswana
121 D2 Mocímboa da Praia Moz.
150 A1 Mocoa Col.
154 C2 Mococa Brazil
144 B2 Mocorito Mex.
144 B1 Moctezuma Chihuahua Mex.
145 B2 Moctezuma San Luis Potosí Mex.
144 B2 Moctezuma Sonora Mex.
121 C2 Mocuba Moz.
105 C2 Modane France
122 B2 Modder r. S. Africa
108 B2 Modena Italy
135 B3 Modesto U.S.A.
123 C1 Modimolle S. Africa
123 C2 Modjadjiskloof S. Africa
53 C3 Moe Austr.
100 C2 Moers Ger.
96 C3 Moffat U.K.
117 C4 Mogadishu Somalia
123 C1 Mogalakwena r. S. Africa
62 A1 Mogaung Myanmar
Mogilev Belarus see Mahilyow
154 C2 Mogi-Mirim Brazil
83 I3 Mogocha Rus. Fed.
62 A1 Mogok Myanmar
103 D2 Mohács Hungary
123 C3 Mohale's Hoek Lesotho
74 B1 Mohali India
107 D2 Mohammadia Alg.
141 E2 Mohawk r. U.S.A.
119 D3 Mohoro Tanz.
90 B2 Mohyliv-Podil's'kyy Ukr.

110 C1 Moineşti Romania
92 F2 Mo i Rana Norway
104 C3 Moissac France
135 C3 Mojave U.S.A.
135 C3 Mojave Desert U.S.A.
62 B1 Mojiang China
155 C2 Moji das Cruzes Brazil
154 C2 Moji-Guaçu r. Brazil
54 B1 Mokau N.Z.
123 C2 Mokhotlong Lesotho
123 C1 Mokopane S. Africa
65 B3 Moko'p S. Korea
145 C2 Molango Mex.
Moldavia country Europe see Moldova
92 E3 Molde Norway
90 B2 Moldova country Europe
110 B1 Moldoveanu, Vârful mt. Romania
90 B2 Moldovei Centrale, Podişul plat. Moldova
123 C1 Molepolole Botswana
88 C2 Molėtai Lith.
109 C2 Molfetta Italy
107 C1 Molina de Aragón Spain
150 A3 Mollendo Peru
53 C2 Molong Austr.
122 B2 Molopo watercourse Botswana/S. Africa
118 B2 Moloundou Cameroon
59 C3 Moluccas is Indon.
Molucca Sea Indon. see Maluku, Laut
52 B2 Momba Austr.
119 D3 Mombasa Kenya
154 B1 Mombuca, Serra da hills Brazil
93 F4 Møn i. Denmark
105 D3 Monaco country Europe
96 B2 Monadhliath Mountains U.K.
97 C1 Monaghan Ireland
89 D3 Monastyrshchina Rus. Fed.
90 B2 Monastyryshche Ukr.
66 D2 Monbetsu Japan
108 A1 Moncalieri Italy
107 C1 Moncayo mt. Spain
86 C1 Monchegorsk Rus. Fed.
100 C2 Mönchengladbach Ger.
144 B2 Monclova Mex.
131 D2 Moncton Can.
106 B1 Mondego r. Port.
118 B2 Mondjoku Dem. Rep. Congo
108 A2 Mondovì Italy
111 B3 Monemvasia Greece
66 D1 Moneron, Ostrov i. Rus. Fed.
137 E3 Monett U.S.A.
108 B1 Monfalcone Italy
106 B1 Monforte de Lemos Spain
62 B1 Mông Cai Vietnam
62 B1 Mong Lin Myanmar
68 C1 Mongolia country Asia
62 A1 Mong Pawk Myanmar
62 A1 Mong Ping Myanmar
120 B2 Mongu Zambia
135 C3 Monitor Range mts U.S.A.
114 C4 Mono r. Benin/Togo
135 C3 Mono Lake U.S.A.
109 C2 Monopoli Italy
107 C1 Monreal del Campo Spain
142 B2 Monroe LA U.S.A.
140 B2 Monroe WI U.S.A.
142 C2 Monroeville U.S.A.
114 A4 Monrovia Liberia
100 A2 Mons Belgium
122 B3 Montagu S. Africa
109 C3 Montalto mt. Italy
110 B2 Montana Bulg.
134 E1 Montana state U.S.A.
104 C2 Montargis France

104 C3 Montauban France
141 E2 Montauk Point U.S.A.
123 C2 Mont-aux-Sources mt. Lesotho
105 C2 Montbard France
105 C2 Montbrison France
100 B3 Montcornet France
104 B3 Mont-de-Marsan France
104 C2 Montdidier France
151 C2 Monte Alegre Brazil
105 D3 Monte-Carlo Monaco
152 C4 Monte Caseros Arg.
146 C3 Montego Bay Jamaica
105 C3 Montélimar France
109 C2 Montella Italy
145 C2 Montemorelos Mex.
104 B2 Montendre France
109 C2 Montenegro country Europe
121 C2 Montepuez Moz.
108 B2 Montepulciano Italy
135 B3 Monterey U.S.A.
135 B3 Monterey Bay U.S.A.
150 A1 Montería Col.
152 B2 Montero Bol.
145 B2 Monterrey Mex.
109 C2 Montesano sulla Marcellana Italy
109 C2 Monte Sant'Angelo Italy
151 E3 Monte Santo Brazil
108 A2 Monte Santu, Capo di c. Sardegna Italy
155 D1 Montes Claros Brazil
153 C4 Montevideo Uru.
137 D2 Montevideo U.S.A.
136 B3 Monte Vista U.S.A.
142 C2 Montgomery U.S.A.
105 D2 Monthey Switz.
142 B2 Monticello AR U.S.A.
135 E3 Monticello UT U.S.A.
104 C2 Montignac France
105 D2 Montigny-le-Roi France
106 C2 Montilla Spain
131 D2 Mont-Joli Can.
130 C2 Mont-Laurier Can.
104 C2 Montluçon France
131 C2 Montmagny Can.
104 C2 Montmorillon France
51 E2 Monto Austr.
134 D2 Montpelier ID U.S.A.
141 E2 Montpelier VT U.S.A.
105 C3 Montpellier France
130 C2 Montréal Can.
129 D2 Montreal Lake Can.
129 D2 Montreal Lake l. Can.
99 D3 Montreuil France
105 D2 Montreux Switz.
96 C2 Montrose U.K.
136 B3 Montrose U.S.A.
147 D3 Montserrat terr. West Indies
62 A1 Monywa Myanmar
108 A1 Monza Italy
107 C1 Monzón Spain
123 C1 Mookane Botswana
123 C1 Mookgophong S. Africa
53 D1 Moonie Austr.
53 C1 Moonie r. Austr.
52 A2 Moonta Austr.
50 A2 Moore, Lake imp. l. Austr.
137 D1 Moorhead U.S.A.
53 C3 Mooroopna Austr.
122 A3 Moorreesburg S. Africa
130 B1 Moose r. Can.
130 B1 Moose Factory Can.
141 F1 Moosehead Lake U.S.A.
129 D2 Moose Jaw Can.
137 E1 Moose Lake U.S.A.
129 D2 Moosomin Can.
130 B1 Moosonee Can.

52 B2 Mootwingee Austr.
123 C1 Mopane S. Africa
114 B3 Mopti Mali
150 A3 Moquegua Peru
93 F3 Mora Sweden
137 E1 Mora U.S.A.
75 D2 Moradabad India
121 □D2 Moramanga Madag.
103 D2 Morava r. Europe
96 B2 Moray Firth b. U.K.
100 C3 Morbach Ger.
74 B2 Morbi India
104 B3 Morcenx France
69 E1 Mordaga China
129 E3 Morden Can.
91 E1 Mordovo Rus. Fed.
98 B1 Morecambe U.K.
98 B1 Morecambe Bay U.K.
53 C1 Moree Austr.
59 D3 Morehead P.N.G.
140 C3 Morehead U.S.A.
143 E2 Morehead City U.S.A.
145 B3 Morelia Mex.
107 C1 Morella Spain
106 B2 Morena, Sierra mts Spain
110 C2 Moreni Romania
128 A2 Moresby, Mount Can.
142 B3 Morgan City U.S.A.
143 D1 Morganton U.S.A.
140 D3 Morgantown U.S.A.
105 D2 Morges Switz.
77 C3 Morghāb, Daryā-ye r. Afgh.
66 D2 Mori Japan
128 B2 Morice Lake Can.
66 D3 Morioka Japan
53 D2 Morisset Austr.
104 B2 Morlaix France
51 C1 Mornington Island Austr.
59 D3 Morobe P.N.G.
114 B1 Morocco country Africa
119 D3 Morogoro Tanz.
64 B2 Moro Gulf Phil.
122 B2 Morokweng S. Africa
121 □D3 Morombe Madag.
68 C1 Mörön Mongolia
121 □D3 Morondava Madag.
121 D2 Moroni Comoros
59 C2 Morotai i. Indon.
119 D2 Moroto Uganda
98 B1 Morpeth U.K.
86 F2 Morrasala Rus. Fed.
154 C1 Morrinhos Brazil
129 E3 Morris Can.
137 D2 Morris U.S.A.
143 D1 Morristown U.S.A.
87 D3 Morshansk Rus. Fed.
154 B1 Mortes, Rio das r. Brazil
52 B3 Mortlake Austr.
53 D3 Moruya Austr.
96 B2 Morvern reg. U.K.
53 C3 Morwell Austr.
102 B2 Mosbach Ger.
89 F2 Moscow Rus. Fed.
134 C1 Moscow U.S.A.
100 C2 Mosel r. Ger.
105 D2 Moselle r. France
134 C1 Moses Lake U.S.A.
92 □A3 Mosfellsbær Iceland
54 B3 Mosgiel N.Z.
89 D2 Moshenskoye Rus. Fed.
119 D3 Moshi Tanz.
92 F2 Mosjøen Norway
Moskva Rus. Fed. see Moscow
103 D2 Mosonmagyaróvár Hungary
146 B3 Mosquitos, Costa de coastal area Nic.

146 B4 Mosquitos, Golfo de los b. Panama
93 F4 Moss Norway
122 B3 Mossel Bay S. Africa
122 B3 Mossel Bay S. Africa
118 B3 Mossendjo Congo
52 B2 Mossgiel Austr.
51 D1 Mossman Austr.
151 E2 Mossoró Brazil
53 D2 Moss Vale Austr.
102 C1 Most Czech Rep.
114 C1 Mostaganem Alg.
109 C2 Mostar Bos.-Herz.
152 C4 Mostardas Brazil
81 C2 Mosul Iraq
93 G4 Motala Sweden
96 C3 Motherwell U.K.
107 C2 Motilla del Palancar Spain
122 B1 Motokwe Botswana
106 C2 Motril Spain
110 B2 Motru Romania
63 A2 Mottama, Gulf of Myanmar
145 D2 Motul Mex.
111 C3 Moudros Greece
118 B3 Mouila Gabon
52 B3 Moulamein Austr.
105 C2 Moulins France
143 D2 Moultrie U.S.A.
143 E2 Moultrie, Lake U.S.A.
140 B3 Mound City U.S.A.
115 D4 Moundou Chad
137 E3 Mountain Grove U.S.A.
142 B1 Mountain Home AR U.S.A.
134 C2 Mountain Home ID U.S.A.
142 D1 Mount Airy U.S.A.
52 A3 Mount Barker Austr.
53 C3 Mount Beauty Austr.
121 C2 Mount Darwin Zimbabwe
141 F2 Mount Desert Island U.S.A.
123 C3 Mount Fletcher S. Africa
123 C3 Mount Frere S. Africa
52 B3 Mount Gambier Austr.
59 D3 Mount Hagen P.N.G.
52 A2 Mount Hope Austr.
51 C2 Mount Isa Austr.
50 A2 Mount Magnet Austr.
52 B2 Mount Manara Austr.
54 C1 Mount Maunganui N.Z.
111 B2 Mount Olympus Greece
137 E2 Mount Pleasant IA U.S.A.
140 C2 Mount Pleasant MI U.S.A.
139 E2 Mount Pleasant TX U.S.A.
99 A3 Mount's Bay U.K.
134 B1 Mount Shasta U.S.A.
140 B3 Mount Vernon IL U.S.A.
140 C2 Mount Vernon OH U.S.A.
134 B1 Mount Vernon WA U.S.A.
51 C2 Moura Austr.
115 E3 Mourdi, Dépression du depr. Chad
97 C1 Mourne Mountains hills U.K.
100 A2 Mouscron Belgium
115 D3 Moussoro Chad
58 C2 Moutong Indon.
115 C2 Mouydir, Monts du plat. Alg.
100 D3 Mouzon France
97 B1 Moy r. Ireland
117 B4 Moyale Eth.
123 C3 Moyeni Lesotho
76 B2 Mo'ynoq Uzbek.
77 D2 Moyynty Kazakh.
121 C3 Mozambique country Africa
113 I9 Mozambique Channel Africa
89 E2 Mozhaysk Rus. Fed.
119 D3 Mpanda Tanz.
121 C2 Mpika Zambia
121 C1 Mporokoso Zambia

173 C2 Mpumalanga prov. S. Africa
62 A1 Mrauk-U Myanmar
88 C2 Mshinskaya Rus. Fed.
107 D2 M'Sila Alg.
89 D2 Msta r. Rus. Fed.
89 D2 Mstinskiy Most Rus. Fed.
89 D3 Mstsislaw Belarus
123 C3 Mthatha S. Africa
89 E3 Mtsensk Rus. Fed.
119 E4 Mtwara Tanz.
118 B3 Muanda Dem. Rep. Congo
63 B2 Muang Không Laos
62 B1 Muang Ngoy Laos
62 B2 Muang Pakbeng Laos
62 B1 Muang Sing Laos
62 B2 Muang Vangviang Laos
60 B1 Muar Malaysia
60 B2 Muarabungo Indon.
60 B2 Muaradua Indon.
61 C2 Muaralaung Indon.
60 A2 Muarasiberut Indon.
60 B2 Muaratembesi Indon.
61 C2 Muarateweh Indon.
119 D2 Mubende Uganda
115 D3 Mubi Nigeria
120 B2 Muconda Angola
155 E1 Mucuri Brazil
155 F1 Mucuri r. Brazil
66 A2 Mudanjiang China
66 A1 Mudan Jiang r. China
111 C2 Mudanya Turkey
101 E1 Müden (Örtze) Ger.
53 C2 Mudgee Austr.
63 A2 Mudon Myanmar
80 B1 Mudurnu Turkey
121 C2 Mueda Moz.
121 B2 Mufulira Zambia
120 B2 Mufumbwe Zambia
111 C3 Muğla Turkey
116 B2 Muhammad Qol Sudan
101 F2 Mühlberg Ger.
101 E2 Mühlhausen (Thüringen) Ger.
121 C2 Muite Moz.
65 B2 Muju S. Korea
90 A2 Mukacheve Ukr.
61 C1 Mukah Sarawak Malaysia
79 B3 Mukalla Yemen
63 B2 Mukdahan Thai.
50 A3 Mukinbudin Austr.
60 B2 Mukomuko Indon.
121 C2 Mulanje, Mount Malawi
101 F2 Mulde r. Ger.
144 A2 Mulegé Mex.
139 C2 Muleshoe U.S.A.
106 C2 Mulhacén mt. Spain
100 C2 Mülheim an der Ruhr Ger.
105 D2 Mulhouse France
66 B2 Muling China
66 B1 Muling He r. China
96 B2 Mull i. U.K.
53 C2 Mullaley Austr.
138 C2 Mullen U.S.A.
61 C1 Mullen, Pegunungan mts Indon.
50 A2 Mullewa Austr.
97 C2 Mullingar Ireland
96 B3 Mull of Galloway c. U.K.
96 B3 Mull of Kintyre hd U.K.
96 A3 Mull of Oa hd U.K.
120 B2 Mulobezi Zambia
74 B1 Multan Pak.
73 B3 Mumbai India
120 B2 Mumbwa Zambia
143 D2 Muna Mex.
101 E2 Münchberg Ger.
München Ger. see Munich
140 B2 Muncie U.S.A.

50 B3 Mundrabilla Austr.
119 C2 Mungbere Dem. Rep. Congo
75 C2 Munger India
52 A1 Mungeranie Austr.
53 C1 Mungindi Austr.
102 C2 Munich Ger.
155 D2 Muniz Freire Brazil
101 E1 Münster Niedersachsen Ger.
100 C2 Münster Nordrhein-Westfalen Ger.
97 B2 Munster reg. Ireland
100 C2 Münsterland reg. Ger.
62 B1 Mường Nhe Vietnam
92 H2 Muonio Fin.
92 H2 Muonioälven r. Fin./Sweden
Muqdisho Somalia see Mogadishu
103 D2 Mur r. Austria
119 C3 Muramvya Burundi
119 D3 Murang'a Kenya
81 B2 Murat r. Turkey
111 C2 Murath Turkey
50 A2 Murchison watercourse Austr.
107 C2 Murcia Spain
111 C2 Mürefte Turkey
110 B1 Mureșul r. Romania
104 C3 Muret France
142 C1 Murfreesboro U.S.A.
77 D3 Murghob Tajik.
155 D2 Muriaé Brazil
120 B1 Muriege Angola
101 F1 Müritz l. Ger.
86 C2 Murmansk Rus. Fed.
87 D3 Murom Rus. Fed.
66 D2 Muroran Japan
106 B1 Muros Spain
67 B4 Muroto Japan
67 B4 Muroto-zaki pt Japan
143 D1 Murphy U.S.A.
53 C1 Murra Murra Austr.
52 A3 Murray r. Austr.
128 B2 Murray r. Can.
140 B3 Murray U.S.A.
143 D2 Murray, Lake U.S.A.
52 A3 Murray Bridge Austr.
122 B3 Murraysburg S. Africa
52 B3 Murrayville Austr.
53 C2 Murrumbidgee r. Austr.
121 C2 Murrupula Moz.
53 D2 Murrurundi Austr.
109 C1 Murska Sobota Slovenia
54 C1 Murupara N.Z.
49 I4 Mururoa atoll Fr. Polynesia
75 C2 Murwara India
53 D1 Murwillumbah Austr.
115 D2 Murzuq Libya
81 C2 Muş Turkey
110 B2 Musala mt. Bulg.
65 B1 Musan N. Korea
78 B3 Musaymir Yemen
79 C2 Muscat Oman
137 E2 Muscatine U.S.A.
50 C2 Musgrave Ranges mts Austr.
118 B3 Mushie Dem. Rep. Congo
60 B2 Musi r. Indon.
123 D1 Musina S. Africa
140 B2 Muskegon U.S.A.
139 D1 Muskogee U.S.A.
128 B2 Muskwa r. Can.
74 A1 Muslimbagh Pak.
78 A3 Musmar Sudan
119 D3 Musoma Tanz.
96 C3 Musselburgh U.K.
88 B2 Mustjala Estonia
53 D2 Muswellbrook Austr.
116 A2 Mūṭ Egypt
121 C2 Mutare Zimbabwe

66 D2 Mutsu Japan
121 C2 Mutuali Moz.
92 I2 Muurola Fin.
70 A2 Mu Us Shadi des. China
120 A1 Muxaluando Angola
86 C2 Muyezerskiy Rus. Fed.
119 D3 Muyinga Burundi
74 B1 Muzaffargarh Pak.
75 C2 Muzaffarpur India
144 B2 Múzquiz Mex.
75 C1 Muz Shan mt. China
119 C3 Mwanza Dem. Rep. Congo
119 D3 Mwanza Tanz.
118 C3 Mweka Dem. Rep. Congo
121 B2 Mwenda Zambia
118 C3 Mwene-Ditu Dem. Rep. Congo
121 C3 Mwenezi Zimbabwe
119 C3 Mweru, Lake Dem. Rep. Congo/Zambia
118 C3 Mwimba Dem. Rep. Congo
120 B2 Mwinilunga Zambia
88 C3 Myadzyel Belarus
62 A1 Myanaung Myanmar
62 A1 Myanmar country Asia
63 A2 Myaungmya Myanmar
63 A2 Myeik Myanmar
Myeik Kyunzu is Myanmar see Mergui Archipelago
62 A1 Myingyan Myanmar
62 A1 Myitkyina Myanmar
91 C2 Mykolayiv Ukr.
111 C3 Mykonos Greece
111 C3 Mykonos i. Greece
86 E2 Myla Rus. Fed.
75 D2 Mymensingh Bangl.
65 B1 Myŏnggan N. Korea
88 C2 Myory Belarus
92 □B3 Mýrdalsjökull Iceland
91 C2 Myrhorod Ukr.
90 C2 Myronivka Ukr.
143 E2 Myrtle Beach U.S.A.
53 C1 Myrtleford Austr.
134 B2 Myrtle Point U.S.A.
89 E2 Myshkin Rus. Fed.
103 C1 Myślibórz Pol.
73 B3 Mysore India
83 N2 Mys Shmidta Rus. Fed.
Mysuru India see Mysore
63 B2 My Tho Vietnam
111 C3 Mytilini Greece
89 E3 Mytishchi Rus. Fed.
123 C3 Mzamomhle S. Africa
121 C2 Mzimba Malawi
121 C2 Mzuzu Malawi

97 C2 Naas Ireland
122 A2 Nababeep S. Africa
87 E3 Naberezhnyye Chelny Rus. Fed.
59 D3 Nabire Indon.
80 B2 Nāblus West Bank
121 D2 Nacala Moz.
63 A2 Nachuge India
139 E2 Nacogdoches U.S.A.
144 B1 Nacozari de García Mex.
74 B2 Nadiad India
90 A2 Nadvirna Ukr.
86 C2 Nadvoitsy Rus. Fed.
86 G2 Nadym Rus. Fed.
93 F4 Næstved Denmark
111 B3 Nafpaktos Greece
111 B3 Nafplio Greece

115 D1 Nafūsah, Jabal hills Libya
78 B2 Nafy Saudi Arabia
64 B1 Naga Phil.
130 B1 Nagagami r. Can.
67 C3 Nagano Japan
67 C3 Nagaoka Japan
75 D2 Nagaon India
74 B1 Nagar India
74 B2 Nagar Parkar Pak.
67 A4 Nagasaki Japan
67 B4 Nagato Japan
74 B2 Nagaur India
73 B4 Nagercoil India
74 A2 Nagha Kalat Pak.
75 B2 Nagina India
67 C3 Nagoya Japan
75 B2 Nagpur India
68 C2 Nagqu China
103 D2 Nagyatád Hungary
103 D2 Nagykanizsa Hungary
128 B1 Nahanni Butte Can.
76 A3 Nahāvand Iran
101 C1 Nahrendorf Ger.
153 A5 Nahuel Huapí, Lago l. Arg.
131 D1 Nain Can.
81 D2 Nā'īn Iran
96 C2 Nairn U.K.
119 D3 Nairobi Kenya
119 D3 Naivasha Kenya
81 D2 Najafābād Iran
78 B2 Najd reg. Saudi Arabia
106 C1 Nájera Spain
65 C1 Najin N. Korea
78 B3 Najrān Saudi Arabia
Nakambé r. Burkina/Ghana see White Volta
67 C3 Nakatsugawa Japan
78 A3 Nakfa Eritrea
66 B2 Nakhodka Rus. Fed.
63 B2 Nakhon Pathom Thai.
63 B2 Nakhon Ratchasima Thai.
63 B2 Nakhon Sawan Thai.
63 A3 Nakhon Si Thammarat Thai.
130 B1 Nakina Can.
121 C1 Nakonde Zambia
93 F4 Nakskov Denmark
119 D3 Nakuru Kenya
128 C2 Nakusp Can.
75 D2 Nalbari India
87 D4 Nal'chik Rus. Fed.
115 D1 Nālūt Libya
123 C2 Namahadi S. Africa
77 D2 Namangan Uzbek.
122 A2 Namaqualand reg. S. Africa
51 E2 Nambour Austr.
53 C2 Nambucca Heads Austr.
75 D1 Nam Co salt l. China
62 B1 Nam Đinh Vietnam
120 A3 Namib Desert Namibia
120 A2 Namibe Angola
120 A3 Namibia country Africa
72 D2 Namjagbarwa Feng mt. China
59 C3 Namlea Indon.
53 C2 Namoi r. Austr.
134 C2 Nampa U.S.A.
114 B3 Nampala Mali
65 B2 Namp'o N. Korea
121 C2 Nampula Moz.
62 A1 Namrup India
62 A1 Namsang Myanmar
92 F3 Namsos Norway
63 A2 Nam Tok Thai.
83 J2 Namtsy Rus. Fed.
62 A1 Namtu Myanmar
100 B2 Namur Belgium
120 B2 Namwala Zambia
65 B2 Namwŏn S. Korea

62 A1 Namya Ra Myanmar
62 B2 Nan Thai.
128 B3 Nanaimo Can.
71 B3 Nan'an China
122 A1 Nananib Plateau Namibia
67 C3 Nanao Japan
71 B3 Nanchang *Jiangxi* China
71 B3 Nanchang *Jiangxi* China
70 A2 Nanchong China
63 A3 Nancowry i. India
105 D2 Nancy France
75 C1 Nanda Devi *mt.* India
71 A3 Nandan China
73 B3 Nanded India
74 B2 Nandurbar India
73 B3 Nandyal India
71 B3 Nanfeng China
118 B2 Nanga Eboko Cameroon
61 C2 Nangapinoh Indon.
74 B1 Nanga Parbat *mt.* Pak.
61 C2 Nangatayap Indon.
70 B2 Nangong China
119 D3 Nangulangwa Tanz.
70 C2 Nanhui China
70 B2 Nanjing China
Nanjing China *see* Nanjing
120 A2 Nankova Angola
71 B3 Nan Ling *mts* China
71 A3 Nanning China
127 H2 Nanortalik Greenland
71 A3 Nanpan Jiang *r.* China
75 C2 Nanpara India
71 B3 Nanping China
Nansei-shotō *is* Japan *see*
Ryukyu Islands
104 B2 Nantes France
70 C2 Nantong China
141 F2 Nantucket Island U.S.A.
155 D1 Nanuque Brazil
64 B2 Nanusa, Kepulauan *is*
Indon.
71 B3 Nanxiong China
70 B2 Nanyang China
70 B2 Nanzhang China
107 D2 Nao, Cabo de la *c.* Spain
131 C1 Naococane, Lac *l.* Can.
135 B3 Napa U.S.A.
126 D2 Napaktulik Lake Can.
127 H2 Napasoq Greenland
54 C1 Napier N.Z.
108 B2 Naples Italy
143 D3 Naples U.S.A.
150 A2 Napo *r.* Ecuador/Peru
Napoli Italy *see* Naples
114 B3 Nara Mali
93 I4 Narach Belarus
52 B3 Naracoorte Austr.
145 C3 Naranjos Mex.
63 D3 Narathiwat Thai.
105 C3 Narbonne France
63 A2 Narcondam Island India
127 G1 Nares Strait Can./Greenland
122 A1 Narib Namibia
87 D4 Narimanov Rus. Fed.
67 D3 Narita Japan
74 B2 Narmada *r.* India
74 B2 Narnaul India
108 B2 Narni Italy
90 B1 Narodychi Ukr.
89 E2 Naro-Fominsk Rus. Fed.
53 D3 Narooma Austr.
88 C3 Narowlya Belarus
53 C2 Narrabri Austr.
53 C2 Narrandera Austr.
53 C2 Narromine Austr.
88 C2 Narva Estonia
88 C2 Narva Bay Estonia/Rus. Fed.

92 G2 Narvik Norway
88 C2 Narvskoye vodokhranilishche
resr Estonia/Rus. Fed.
86 E2 Nar'yan-Mar Rus. Fed.
77 D2 Naryn Kyrg.
74 B2 Nashik India
141 E2 Nashua U.S.A.
142 C1 Nashville U.S.A.
49 I5 Nasinu Fiji
117 B4 Nasir S. Sudan
128 B2 Nass *r.* Can.
146 C2 Nassau Bahamas
116 B2 Nasser, Lake *resr* Egypt
93 F4 Nässjö Sweden
130 C1 Nastapoca *r.* Can.
130 C1 Nastapoka Islands Can.
120 B3 Nata Botswana
151 E2 Natal Brazil
131 D1 Natashquan Can.
131 D1 Natashquan *r.* Can.
142 B2 Natchez U.S.A.
142 B2 Natchitoches U.S.A.
53 C3 Nathalia Austr.
107 D1 Nati, Punta *pt* Spain
114 C3 Natitingou Benin
151 D3 Natividade Brazil
67 D3 Natori Japan
131 D1 Natuashish Can.
61 B1 Natuna, Kepulauan *is* Indon.
61 B1 Natuna Besar *i.* Indon.
120 A3 Nauchas Namibia
101 F1 Nauen Ger.
88 B2 Naujoji Akmenė Lith.
74 A2 Naukot Pak.
101 E2 Naumburg (Saale) Ger.
48 F3 Nauru *country* S. Pacific Ocean
145 C2 Nautla Mex.
88 C3 Navahrudak Belarus
106 B2 Navalmoral de la Mata Spain
106 B2 Navalvillar de Pela Spain
97 C2 Navan Ireland
88 C2 Navapolatsk Belarus
83 M2 Navarin, Mys *c.* Rus. Fed.
153 B6 Navarino, Isla *i.* Chile
96 B1 Naver *r.* U.K.
73 B3 Navi Mumbai India
89 D3 Navlya Rus. Fed.
110 C2 Năvodari Romania
77 C2 Navoiy Uzbek.
144 B2 Navojoa Mex.
144 B2 Navolato Mex.
74 A2 Nawabshah Pak.
62 A1 Nawnghkio Myanmar
62 A1 Nawngleng Myanmar
111 C3 Naxos Greece
111 C3 Naxos *i.* Greece
144 B2 Nayar Mex.
66 D2 Nayoro Japan
144 B2 Nazas Mex.
144 B2 Nazas *r.* Mex.
150 A3 Nazca Peru
80 B2 Nazerat Israel
111 C3 Nazilli Turkey
117 B4 Nazrēt Eth.
79 C2 Nazwá Oman
121 B1 Nchelenge Zambia
122 B1 Ncojane Botswana
120 A1 N'dalatando Angola
118 C2 Ndélé C.A.R.
118 B3 Ndendé Gabon
115 D3 Ndjamena Chad
121 B2 Ndola Zambia
97 C1 Neagh, Lough *l.* U.K.
50 C1 Neale, Lake *imp. l.* Austr.
111 B2 Nea Roda Greece
99 B3 Neath U.K.
53 C1 Nebine Creek *r.* Austr.

150 B1 Neblina, Pico da *mt.* Brazil
89 D2 Nebolchi Rus. Fed.
136 C2 Nebraska *state* U.S.A.
137 D2 Nebraska City U.S.A.
108 B3 Nebrodi, Monti *mts* Sicilia Italy
153 C4 Necochea Arg.
131 C1 Nedlouc, Lac *l.* Can.
135 D4 Needles U.S.A.
71 B3 Neemuch India
129 E2 Neepawa Can.
87 E3 Neftekamsk Rus. Fed.
82 F2 Nefteyugansk Rus. Fed.
120 A1 Negage Angola
117 B4 Negēlē Eth.
150 A2 Negra, Punta *pt* Peru
63 A2 Negrais, Cape Myanmar
153 B5 Negro *r.* Arg.
150 C2 Negro *r.* S. America
152 C4 Negro *r.* Uru.
106 B2 Negro, Cabo *c.* Morocco
64 B2 Negros *i.* Phil.
69 E1 Nehe China
70 A2 Neijiang China
129 D2 Neilburg Can.
150 A1 Neiva Col.
129 E2 Nejanilini Lake Can.
117 B4 Nek'emtē Eth.
89 F2 Nekrasovskoye Rus. Fed.
89 D2 Nelidovo Rus. Fed.
73 B3 Nellore India
128 C3 Nelson Can.
129 E2 Nelson *r.* Can.
54 B2 Nelson N.Z.
52 B3 Nelson, Cape Austr.
53 C2 Nelson Bay Austr.
129 E2 Nelson House Can.
134 F1 Nelson Reservoir U.S.A.
88 B2 Néma Maur.
114 B3 Neman Rus. Fed.
104 C2 Nemours France
66 D2 Nemuro Japan
90 B2 Nemyriv Ukr.
97 B2 Nenagh Ireland
99 D2 Nene *r.* U.K.
69 E1 Nenjiang China
137 E3 Neosho U.S.A.
75 C2 Nepal *country* Asia
75 C2 Nepalganj Nepal
135 D3 Nephi U.S.A.
97 B1 Nephin *h.* Ireland
97 B1 Nephin Beg Range *hills* Ireland
131 D2 Nepisiguit *r.* Can.
119 C2 Nepoko *r.* Dem. Rep. Congo
104 C3 Nérac France
53 D1 Nerang Austr.
69 D1 Nerchinsk Rus. Fed.
89 F2 Nerekhta Rus. Fed.
109 C2 Neretva *r.* Bos.-Herz./Croatia
120 B2 Neriquinha Angola
88 B3 Neris *r.* Lith.
89 E2 Nerl' *r.* Rus. Fed.
86 F2 Nerokhi Rus. Fed.
154 C1 Nerópolis Brazil
83 J3 Neryungri Rus. Fed.
92 □C2 Neskaupstaður Iceland
96 B2 Ness, Loch *l.* U.K.
136 D3 Ness City U.S.A.
111 B2 Nestos *r.* Greece
100 B1 Netherlands *country* Europe
Netherlands Antilles *terr.* West Indies *see* Aruba, Bonaire, Curaçao, Saba, Sint Eustatius, Sint Maarten
127 G2 Nettilling Lake Can.
101 F1 Neubrandenburg Ger.

Neuchâtel

105 D2 Neuchâtel Switz.
100 C2 Neuerburg Ger.
100 B3 Neufchâteau Belgium
105 D2 Neufchâteau France
104 C2 Neufchâtel-en-Bray France
101 D2 Neuhof Ger.
102 B1 Neumünster Ger.
102 B2 Neunkirchen Ger.
153 B4 Neuquén Arg.
153 B4 Neuquén r. Arg.
101 F1 Neuruppin Ger.
100 C2 Neuss Ger.
101 D1 Neustadt am Rübenberge Ger.
101 E3 Neustadt an der Aisch Ger.
101 F1 Neustrelitz Ger.
100 C2 Neuwied Ger.
137 E3 Nevada U.S.A.
135 C3 Nevada state U.S.A.
106 C2 Nevada, Sierra mts Spain
135 B2 Nevada, Sierra mts U.S.A.
88 C2 Nevel' Rus. Fed.
105 C2 Nevers France
53 C2 Nevertire Austr.
109 C2 Nevesinje Bos.-Herz.
87 D4 Nevinnomyssk Rus. Fed.
128 B2 New Aiyansh Can.
140 B3 New Albany U.S.A.
151 C1 New Amsterdam Guyana
141 E2 Newark NJ U.S.A.
140 C2 Newark OH U.S.A.
98 C2 Newark-on-Trent U.K.
141 E2 New Bedford U.S.A.
143 E1 New Bern U.S.A.
143 D2 Newberry U.S.A.
139 E2 New Boston U.S.A.
139 D3 New Braunfels U.S.A.
97 C2 Newbridge Ireland
48 E3 New Britain i. P.N.G.
131 D2 New Brunswick prov. Can.
99 C3 Newbury U.K.
64 A1 New Busuanga Phil.
48 E4 New Caledonia terr. S. Pacific Ocean
53 D2 Newcastle Austr.
123 C2 Newcastle S. Africa
97 D1 Newcastle U.K.
140 C2 New Castle U.S.A.
136 C2 Newcastle U.S.A.
98 B2 Newcastle-under-Lyme U.K.
98 C1 Newcastle upon Tyne U.K.
97 B2 Newcastle West Ireland
74 B2 New Delhi India
128 C3 New Denver Can.
53 D2 New England Range mts Austr.
131 E2 Newfoundland i. Can.
131 E1 Newfoundland and Labrador prov. Can.
131 D2 New Glasgow Can.
59 D3 New Guinea i. Indon./P.N.G.
141 E2 New Hampshire state U.S.A.
141 E2 New Haven U.S.A.
128 B2 New Hazelton Can.
New Hebrides country S. Pacific Ocean see Vanuatu
142 B2 New Iberia U.S.A.
48 E3 New Ireland i. P.N.G.
141 E3 New Jersey state U.S.A.
130 C2 New Liskeard Can.
50 A2 Newman Austr.
138 B2 New Mexico state U.S.A.
142 B3 New Orleans U.S.A.
140 C2 New Philadelphia U.S.A.
54 B1 New Plymouth N.Z.
99 C3 Newport England U.K.
99 B3 Newport Wales U.K.
142 B1 Newport AR U.S.A.

134 B2 Newport OR U.S.A.
141 E2 Newport RI U.S.A.
141 E2 Newport VT U.S.A.
134 C1 Newport WA U.S.A.
141 D3 Newport News U.S.A.
143 E3 New Providence i. Bahamas
99 A3 Newquay U.K.
142 B2 New Roads U.S.A.
97 C2 New Ross Ireland
97 C1 Newry U.K.
83 K1 New Siberia Islands Rus. Fed.
52 B2 New South Wales state Austr.
137 E2 Newton IA U.S.A.
137 D3 Newton KS U.S.A.
99 B3 Newton Abbot U.K.
96 B3 Newton Stewart U.K.
97 B2 Newtown Ireland
99 B2 Newtown U.K.
136 C1 New Town U.S.A.
97 D1 Newtownabbey U.K.
97 D1 Newtownards U.K.
96 C3 Newtown St Boswells U.K.
97 C1 Newtownstewart U.K.
137 E2 New Ulm U.S.A.
141 E2 New York U.S.A.
141 D2 New York state U.S.A.
54 B2 New Zealand country Oceania
79 C2 Neyrīz Iran
76 B3 Neyshābūr Iran
145 C3 Nezahualcóyotl Mex.
145 C3 Nezahualcóyotl, Presa resr Mex.
61 B1 Ngabang Indon.
75 C2 Ngamring China
75 C1 Ngangla Ringco salt l. China
77 E3 Nganglong Kangri mt. China
75 C1 Nganglong Kangri mts China
75 C1 Ngangzê Co salt l. China
62 A2 Ngao Thai.
118 B2 Ngaoundéré Cameroon
54 C1 Ngaruawahia N.Z.
62 A2 Ngathainggyaung Myanmar
121 D2 Ngazidja i. Comoros
118 B3 Ngo Congo
115 D4 Ngol Bembo Nigeria
68 C2 Ngoring Hu l. China
115 D3 Ngourti Niger
115 D3 Nguigmi Niger
59 D2 Ngulu atoll Micronesia
115 D3 Nguru Nigeria
123 D2 Ngwelezana S. Africa
121 C2 Nhamalabué Moz.
63 B2 Nha Trang Vietnam
52 B3 Nhill Austr.
123 D2 Nhlangano Swaziland
51 C1 Nhulunbuy Austr.
141 D2 Niagara Falls Can.
114 C3 Niamey Niger
119 C2 Niangara Dem. Rep. Congo
114 B3 Niangay, Lac l. Mali
60 A1 Nias i. Indon.
146 B3 Nicaragua country Central America
146 B3 Nicaragua, Lake Nic.
105 D3 Nice France
73 D4 Nicobar Islands India
80 B2 Nicosia Cyprus
146 B4 Nicoya, Golfo de b. Costa Rica
88 B2 Nida Lith.
103 E1 Nidzica Pol.
102 B1 Niebüll Ger.
101 D2 Niederaula Ger.
118 B2 Niefang Equat. Guinea
101 F1 Niemegk Ger.
101 D1 Nienburg (Weser) Ger.

100 B1 Nieuwe-Niedorp Neth.
151 C1 Nieuw Nickerie Suriname
122 A3 Nieuwoudtville S. Africa
100 A2 Nieuwpoort Belgium
80 B2 Niğde Turkey
115 C3 Niger country Africa
115 C4 Niger r. Africa
115 C4 Niger, Mouths of the Nigeria
115 C4 Nigeria country Africa
130 B2 Nighthawk Lake Can.
111 B2 Nigrita Greece
67 C3 Niigata Japan
67 B4 Niihama Japan
67 C4 Nii-jima i. Japan
67 C3 Niitsu Japan
100 B2 Nijmegen Neth.
100 C1 Nijverdal Neth.
92 J2 Nikel' Rus. Fed.
83 M3 Nikol'skoye Rus. Fed.
91 C2 Nikopol' Ukr.
80 B1 Niksar Turkey
79 D2 Nikshahr Iran
109 C2 Nikšić Montenegro
116 B1 Nile r. Africa
140 B2 Niles U.S.A.
74 A1 Nīlī Afgh.
105 C3 Nîmes France
53 C3 Nimmitabel Austr.
117 B4 Nimule Sudan
53 C1 Nindigully Austr.
73 B4 Nine Degree Channel India
53 C3 Ninety Mile Beach Austr.
54 B1 Ninety Mile Beach N.Z.
70 C2 Ningbo China
71 B3 Ningde China
70 B2 Ningguo China
71 C3 Ninghai China
Ningjiang China see Songyuan
68 C2 Ningjing Shan mts China
70 A2 Ningxia Huizu Zizhiqu aut. reg. China
70 B2 Ningyang China
62 B1 Ninh Binh Vietnam
63 B2 Ninh Hoa Vietnam
66 D2 Ninohe Japan
137 D2 Niobrara r. U.S.A.
114 B3 Niono Mali
104 B2 Niort France
129 D2 Nipawin Can.
130 B2 Nipigon Can.
130 B2 Nipigon, Lake Can.
131 D1 Nipishish Lake Can.
130 C2 Nipissing, Lake Can.
135 C3 Nipton U.S.A.
151 D3 Niquelândia Brazil
73 B3 Nirmal India
109 D2 Niš Serbia
109 D2 Nišava r. Serbia
108 B3 Niscemi Sicilia Italy
67 B4 Nishino-omote Japan
155 C2 Niterói Brazil
96 C3 Nith r. U.K.
103 D2 Nitra Slovakia
49 G4 Niue terr. S. Pacific Ocean
92 H3 Nivala Fin.
100 B2 Nivelles Belgium
73 B3 Nizamabad India
87 E3 Nizhnekamsk Rus. Fed.
83 H3 Nizhneudinsk Rus. Fed.
82 G2 Nizhnevartovsk Rus. Fed.
89 F3 Nizhniy Kislyay Rus. Fed.
87 D3 Nizhniy Lomov Rus. Fed.
87 D3 Nizhniy Novgorod Rus. Fed.
86 E2 Nizhniy Odes Rus. Fed.
86 E3 Nizhniy Tagil Rus. Fed.

83 G2 **Nizhnyaya Tunguska** r. Rus. Fed.
91 C1 **Nizhyn** Ukr.
119 D3 **Njinjo** Tanz.
119 D3 **Njombe** Tanz.
121 C2 **Nkhotakota** Malawi
118 A2 **Nkongsamba** Cameroon
123 C3 **Nkululeko** S. Africa
123 C3 **Nkwenkwezi** S. Africa
67 B4 **Nobeoka** Japan
52 B1 **Noccundra** Austr.
144 A1 **Nogales** Mex.
138 A2 **Nogales** U.S.A.
104 C2 **Nogent-le-Rotrou** France
89 E2 **Noginsk** Rus. Fed.
74 B2 **Nohar** India
100 C4 **Nohfelden** Ger.
104 B2 **Noirmoutier, Île de** i. France
104 B2 **Noirmoutier-en-l'Île** France
67 C4 **Nojima-zaki** c. Japan
74 B2 **Nokha** India
93 H3 **Nokia** Fin.
74 A2 **Nok Kundi** Pak.
118 B2 **Nola** C.A.R.
86 D3 **Nolinsk** Rus. Fed.
123 C3 **Nomonde** S. Africa
123 D2 **Nondweni** S. Africa
62 B2 **Nong Khai** Thai.
52 A2 **Nonning** Austr.
144 B2 **Nonoava** Mex.
65 B2 **Nonsan** S. Korea
63 B2 **Nonthaburi** Thai.
122 B3 **Nonzwakazi** S. Africa
77 C3 **Nnrak Tajik.**
141 D1 **Noranda** Can.
82 C1 **Nordaustlandet** i. Svalbard
128 C2 **Nordegg** Can.
100 C1 **Norden** Ger.
83 H1 **Nordenshel'da, Arkhipelag** is Rus. Fed.
100 C1 **Norderney** Ger.
100 C1 **Norderney** i. Ger.
101 E1 **Norderstedt** Ger.
93 E3 **Nordfjordeid** Norway
101 E2 **Nordhausen** Ger.
101 D1 **Nordholz** Ger.
100 C1 **Nordhorn** Ger.
Nordkapp c. Norway see North Cape
92 F3 **Nordli** Norway
102 C2 **Nördlingen** Ger.
92 G3 **Nordmaling** Sweden
94 B1 **Nordoyar** is Faroe Is
97 L3 **Nore** r. Ireland
137 D2 **Norfolk** NE U.S.A.
141 D3 **Norfolk** VA U.S.A.
48 F4 **Norfolk Island** terr. S. Pacific Ocean
93 E3 **Norheimsund** Norway
82 G3 **Noril'sk** Rus. Fed.
75 C2 **Norkyung** China
130 D1 **Norman** U.S.A.
Normandes, Îles is English Chan. see Channel Islands
51 D1 **Normanton** Austr.
93 G4 **Norrköping** Sweden
93 G4 **Norrtälje** Sweden
50 B3 **Norseman** Austr.
92 G3 **Norsjö** Sweden
98 C1 **Northallerton** U.K.
50 A2 **Northampton** Austr.
99 C2 **Northampton** U.K.
73 D3 **North Andaman** i. India
129 D2 **North Battleford** Can.
130 C2 **North Bay** Can.
130 C1 **North Belcher Islands** Can.
96 C2 **North Berwick** U.K.

92 I1 **North Cape** Norway
54 B1 **North Cape** N.Z.
130 A1 **North Caribou Lake** Can.
143 E1 **North Carolina** state U.S.A.
130 B2 **North Channel** lake channel Can.
96 A3 **North Channel** U.K.
128 B3 **North Cowichan** Can.
136 C1 **North Dakota** state U.S.A.
99 C3 **North Downs** hills U.K.
143 E3 **Northeast Providence Channel** Bahamas
101 D2 **Northeim** Ger.
122 A2 **Northern Cape** prov. S. Africa
129 E2 **Northern Indian Lake** Can.
97 C1 **Northern Ireland** prov. U.K.
48 D1 **Northern Mariana Islands** terr. N. Pacific Ocean
50 C1 **Northern Territory** admin. div. Austr.
96 C2 **North Esk** r. U.K.
137 E2 **Northfield** U.S.A.
99 D3 **North Foreland** c. U.K.
54 B1 **North Island** N.Z.
129 E2 **North Knife Lake** Can.
65 B1 **North Korea** country Asia
62 A1 **North Lakhimpur** India
128 B1 **North Nahanni** r. Can.
136 C2 **North Platte** U.S.A.
136 C2 **North Platte** r. U.S.A.
96 C1 **North Ronaldsay** i. U.K.
94 D2 **North Sea** Europe
130 A1 **North Spirit Lake** Can.
53 D1 **North Stradbroke Island** Austr.
54 B1 **North Taranaki Bight** b. N.Z.
130 C1 **North Twin Island** Can.
98 B1 **North Tyne** r. U.K.
96 A2 **North Uist** i. U.K.
131 D2 **Northumberland Strait** Can.
122 C2 **North West** prov. S. Africa
50 A2 **North West Cape** Austr.
143 E3 **Northwest Providence Channel** Bahamas
131 E1 **North West River** Can.
128 B1 **Northwest Territories** admin. div. Can.
98 C1 **North York Moors** moorland U.K.
140 C3 **Norton** U.S.A.
121 C2 **Norton** Zimbabwe
140 C2 **Norwalk** U.S.A.
92 F3 **Norway** country Europe
129 E2 **Norway House** Can.
160 A3 **Norwegian Sea** N Atlantic Ocean
99 D2 **Norwich** U.K.
141 E2 **Norwich** CT U.S.A.
141 D2 **Norwich** NY U.S.A.
66 D2 **Noshiro** Japan
91 C1 **Nosivka** Ukr.
122 D2 **Nosop** watercourse Africa
86 E2 **Nosovaya** Rus. Fed.
79 C2 **Noşratābād** Iran
Nossob watercourse Africa see Nosop
103 D1 **Noteć** r. Pol.
93 E4 **Notodden** Norway
67 C3 **Noto-hantō** pen. Japan
131 E2 **Notre-Dame, Monts** mts Can.
131 E2 **Notre Dame Bay** Can.
130 C1 **Nottaway** r. Can.
99 C2 **Nottingham** U.K.
114 A2 **Nouâdhibou** Maur.
114 A3 **Nouakchott** Maur.
114 A3 **Nouâmghâr** Maur.
48 F4 **Nouméa** New Caledonia

114 B3 **Nouna** Burkina Faso
154 B2 **Nova Esperança** Brazil
155 D2 **Nova Friburgo** Brazil
109 C1 **Nova Gradiška** Croatia
154 B2 **Nova Granada** Brazil
155 D2 **Nova Iguaçu** Brazil
91 C2 **Nova Kakhovka** Ukr.
155 D1 **Nova Lima** Brazil
154 B2 **Nova Londrina** Brazil
91 C2 **Nova Odesa** Ukr.
131 D2 **Nova Scotia** prov. Can.
155 D1 **Nova Venécia** Brazil
83 K1 **Novaya Sibir', Ostrov** i. Rus. Fed.
86 E1 **Novaya Zemlya** is Rus. Fed.
103 D2 **Nové Zámky** Slovakia
91 C1 **Novhorod-Sivers'kyy** Ukr.
110 B2 **Novi Iskŭr** Bulg.
108 A2 **Novi Ligure** Italy
109 D2 **Novi Pazar** Serbia
109 C1 **Novi Sad** Serbia
87 D3 **Novoanninskiy** Rus. Fed.
150 B2 **Novo Aripuanã** Brazil
91 D2 **Novoazovs'k** Ukr.
91 E2 **Novocherkassk** Rus. Fed.
86 D2 **Novodvinsk** Rus. Fed.
152 C3 **Novo Hamburgo** Brazil
154 C2 **Novo Horizonte** Brazil
90 B1 **Novohrad-Volyns'kyy** Ukr.
103 D2 **Novo mesto** Slovenia
91 D3 **Novomikhaylovskiy** Rus. Fed.
89 E3 **Novomoskovsk** Rus. Fed.
91 D2 **Novomoskovs'k** Ukr.
91 C2 **Novomyrhorod** Ukr.
91 C2 **Novooleksiyivka** Ukr.
91 D3 **Novo Paraíso** Brazil
91 C2 **Novopskov** Ukr.
91 D3 **Novorossiysk** Rus. Fed.
88 C2 **Novorzhev** Rus. Fed.
87 E3 **Novosergiyevka** Rus. Fed.
91 D2 **Novoshakhtinsk** Rus. Fed.
82 G3 **Novosibirsk** Rus. Fed.
Novosibirskiye Ostrova is Rus. Fed. see New Siberia Islands
89 E3 **Novosil'** Rus. Fed.
89 D2 **Novosokol'niki** Rus. Fed.
91 C2 **Novotroyits'ke** Ukr.
91 C2 **Novoukrayinka** Ukr.
90 A1 **Novovolyns'k** Ukr.
89 D2 **Novozybkov** Rus. Fed.
103 D2 **Nový Jičín** Czech Rep.
86 E2 **Nvy Bor** Rus. Fed.
91 D1 **Novyi Oskol** Rus. Fed.
86 G2 **Novyy Port** Rus. Fed.
82 G2 **Novyy Urengoy** Rus. Fed.
69 E1 **Novyy Urgal** Rus. Fed.
103 D1 **Nowogard** Pol.
53 D2 **Nowra** Austr.
81 D2 **Nowshahr** Iran
74 B1 **Nowshera** Pak.
103 E2 **Nowy Sącz** Pol.
103 E2 **Nowy Targ** Pol.
87 G2 **Noyabr'sk** Rus. Fed.
105 C2 **Noyon** France
68 C2 **Noyon** Mongolia
121 C2 **Nsanje** Malawi
118 B3 **Ntandembele** Dem. Rep. Congo
111 B3 **Ntoro, Kavo** pt Greece
119 D3 **Ntungamo** Uganda
79 C2 **Nu'aym** reg. Oman
116 B2 **Nubian Desert** Sudan
129 E1 **Nueltin Lake** Can.
153 A5 **Nueva Lubecka** Arg.
145 B2 **Nueva Rosita** Mex.
144 B1 **Nuevo Casas Grandes** Mex.
144 B2 **Nuevo Ideal** Mex.

145 C2 Nuevo Laredo Mex.
117 C4 Nugaal watercourse Somalia
117 C4 Nugaaleed, Dooxo val.
        Somalia
105 C2 Nuits-St-Georges France
        Niu Jiang r. China/Myanmar
        see Salween
49 G4 Nuku'alofa Tonga
49 I3 Nuku Hiva i. Fr. Polynesia
76 B2 Nukus Uzbek.
50 B2 Nullagine Austr.
50 B3 Nullarbor Plain Austr.
115 D4 Numan Nigeria
67 C3 Numazu Japan
93 E3 Numedal val. Norway
59 C3 Numfoor i. Indon.
53 C3 Numurkah Austr.
        Nunap Isua c. Greenland see
        Farewell, Cape
127 G3 Nunavik reg. Can.
129 E1 Nunavut admin. div. Can.
99 C2 Nuneaton U.K.
106 B1 Nuñomoral Spain
108 A2 Nuoro Sardegna Italy
78 B2 Nuqrah Saudi Arabia
101 E3 Nuremberg Ger.
52 A2 Nuriootpa Austr.
92 I3 Nurmes Fin.
        Nürnberg Ger. see Nuremberg
62 A1 Nu Shan mts China
74 A2 Nushki Pak.
127 H2 Nuuk Greenland
127 H3 Nuussuaq Greenland
127 H2 Nuussuaq pen. Greenland
78 A2 Nuwaybi' al Muzayyinah
        Egypt
122 B3 Nuwveldberge mts S. Africa
86 F2 Nyagan' Rus. Fed.
75 D1 Nyainqêntanglha Feng mt.
        China
75 D2 Nyainqêntanglha Shan mts
        China
117 A3 Nyala Sudan
86 D2 Nyandoma Rus. Fed.
118 B3 Nyanga r. Gabon
121 C2 Nyanga Zimbabwe
        Nyang'oma Kenya see Kogelo
121 C2 Nyasa, Lake Africa
93 F4 Nyborg Denmark
92 I1 Nyborg Norway
93 G4 Nybro Sweden
119 D3 Nyeri Kenya
68 C3 Nyingchi China
103 E2 Nyíregyháza Hungary
93 F4 Nykøbing Denmark
93 G4 Nyköping Sweden
53 C2 Nymagee Austr.
93 G4 Nynäshamn Sweden
53 C2 Nyngan Austr.
88 B3 Nyoman r. Belarus/Lith.
105 D3 Nyons France
86 E2 Nyrob Rus. Fed.
134 C2 Nyssa U.S.A.
119 C3 Nyunzu Dem. Rep. Congo
91 C2 Nyzh'ohirs'kyy Ukr.
119 D3 Nzega Tanz.
114 B4 Nzérékoré Guinea
120 A1 N'zeto Angola

53 D1 Oakey Austr.
134 B1 Oak Harbor U.S.A.
140 C3 Oak Hill U.S.A.
135 B3 Oakland U.S.A.
50 B2 Oakover r. Austr.
134 B2 Oakridge U.S.A.
143 D1 Oak Ridge U.S.A.
54 B3 Oamaru N.Z.
64 B1 Oas Phil.
145 C3 Oaxaca Mex.
86 F2 Ob' r. Rus. Fed.
118 B2 Obala Cameroon
96 B2 Oban U.K.
106 B1 O Barco Spain
53 C2 Oberon Austr.
101 F3 Oberpfälzer Wald mts Ger.
101 F3 Oberviechtach Ger.
59 C3 Obi i. Indon.
151 C2 Óbidos Brazil
66 D2 Obihiro Japan
69 E1 Obluch'ye Rus. Fed.
89 E2 Obninsk Rus. Fed.
119 C2 Obo C.A.R.
117 C3 Obock Djibouti
118 B3 Bouya Congo
89 E3 Oboyan' Rus. Fed.
144 B2 Obregón, Presa resr Mex.
109 D2 Obrenovac Serbia
87 E3 Obshchiy Syrt hills
        Kazakh./Rus. Fed.
86 G2 Obskaya Guba sea chan.
        Rus. Fed.
114 B4 Obuasi Ghana
90 C1 Obukhiv Ukr.
86 D2 Ob'yachevo Rus. Fed.
143 D3 Ocala U.S.A.
144 B2 Ocampo Mex.
106 C2 Ocaña Spain
150 A1 Occidental, Cordillera mts Col.
150 A3 Occidental, Cordillera mts
        Peru
141 D3 Ocean City U.S.A.
128 B2 Ocean Falls Can.
135 C4 Oceanside U.S.A.
91 C2 Ochakiv Ukr.
86 E3 Ocher Rus. Fed.
101 E3 Ochsenfurt Ger.
143 D2 Oconee r. U.S.A.
145 C3 Ocosingo Mex.
59 D3 Oussi enclave East Timor
116 B2 Oda, Jebel mt. Sudan
66 D2 Ōdate Japan
67 C3 Odawara Japan
93 E3 Odda Norway
106 B2 Odemira Port.
111 C3 Ödemiş Turkey
93 F4 Odense Denmark
101 D3 Odenwald reg. Ger.
102 C1 Oderbucht b. Ger.
        Odesa Ukr. see Odessa
90 C2 Odessa Ukr.
139 C2 Odessa U.S.A.
114 B4 Odienné Côte d'Ivoire
103 D2 Odra r. Ger./Pol.
151 D2 Oeiras Brazil
100 D2 Oelde Ger.
136 C2 Oelrichs U.S.A.
101 F2 Oelsnitz Ger.
100 B1 Oenkerk Neth.
109 C2 Ofanto r. Italy
101 D2 Offenbach am Main Ger.
102 B2 Offenburg Ger.
117 C4 Ogadēn reg. Eth.
66 C3 Oga-hantō pen. Japan
67 C3 Ōgaki Japan
136 C2 Ogallala U.S.A.
115 C4 Ogbomosho Nigeria

134 D2 Ogden U.S.A.
141 D2 Ogdensburg U.S.A.
126 B2 Ogilvie r. Can.
126 B2 Ogilvie Mountains Can.
143 D2 Oglethorpe, Mount U.S.A.
130 B1 Ogoki r. Can.
130 B1 Ogoki Reservoir Can.
88 B2 Ogre Latvia
109 C1 Ogulin Croatia
140 B3 Ohio r. U.S.A.
140 C2 Ohio state U.S.A.
101 E2 Ohrdruf Ger.
109 D2 Ohrid Macedonia
151 C1 Oiapoque Brazil
141 D2 Oil City U.S.A.
100 A3 Oise r. France
67 B4 Ōita Japan
144 B2 Ojinaga Mex.
152 B3 Ojos del Salado, Nevado mt.
        Arg./Chile
89 F3 Oka r. Rus. Fed.
120 A3 Okahandja Namibia
120 A3 Okakarara Namibia
128 C3 Okanagan Falls Can.
128 C3 Okanagan Lake Can.
134 C1 Okanogan U.S.A.
134 C1 Okanogan r. U.S.A.
74 B1 Okara Pak.
120 B2 Okavango r. Africa
120 B2 Okavango Delta swamp
        Botswana
67 C3 Okaya Japan
67 B4 Okayama Japan
67 C4 Okazaki Japan
143 D3 Okeechobee, Lake U.S.A.
143 D2 Okefenokee Swamp U.S.A.
99 A3 Okehampton U.K.
74 A2 Okha India
83 K3 Okha Rus. Fed.
75 C2 Okhaldhunga Nepal
83 K3 Okhota r. Rus. Fed.
83 K3 Okhotsk Rus. Fed.
156 C2 Okhotsk, Sea of Japan/
        Rus. Fed.
91 C1 Okhtyrka Ukr.
69 E3 Okinawa i. Japan
67 B3 Oki-shotō is Japan
139 D1 Oklahoma state U.S.A.
139 D1 Oklahoma City U.S.A.
139 D1 Okmulgee U.S.A.
78 A2 Oko, Wadi watercourse Sudan
118 B3 Okondja Gabon
128 C2 Okotoks Can.
89 D3 Okovskiy Les for. Rus. Fed.
118 B3 Okoyo Congo
92 H1 Øksfjord Norway
62 A1 Oktwin Myanmar
86 D2 Oktyabr'skiy Arkhangel'skaya
        Oblast' Rus. Fed.
        Oktyabr'skiy Kamchatskiy Kray
        Rus. Fed.
87 E3 Oktyabr'skiy Respublika
        Bashkortostan Rus. Fed.
86 F2 Oktyabr'skoye Rus. Fed.
83 H1 Oktyabr'skoy Revolyutsii,
        Ostrov i. Rus. Fed.
89 D2 Okulovka Rus. Fed.
66 C2 Okushiri-tō i. Japan
92 □A3 Ólafsvík Iceland
93 G4 Öland i. Sweden
52 B2 Olary Austr.
153 B4 Olavarría Arg.
103 D1 Oława Pol.
108 A2 Olbia Sardegna Italy
126 B2 Old Crow Can.
101 D1 Oldenburg Ger.
102 C1 Oldenburg in Holstein Ger.

100 C1	Oldenzaal Neth.	
97 B3	Old Head of Kinsale Ireland	
128 C2	Olds Can.	
129 D2	Old Wives Lake Can.	
141 D2	Olean U.S.A.	
103 E1	Olecko Pol.	
83 J2	Olekminsk Rus. Fed.	
91 C2	Oleksandriya Ukr.	
86 C2	Olenegorsk Rus. Fed.	
83 I2	Olenek Rus. Fed.	
83 I2	Olenek r. Rus. Fed.	
89 D2	Olenino Rus. Fed.	
90 B1	Oleve't Ukr.	
106 B2	Olhão Port.	
122 A2	Olifants watercourse Namibia	
123 D1	Olifants S. Africa	
123 D1	Olifants r. Northern S. Africa	
122 A3	Olifants r. W. Cape S. Africa	
122 B2	Olifantshoek S. Africa	
154 C2	Olímpia Brazil	
151 E2	Olinda Brazil	
123 C1	Oliphants Drift Botswana	
107 C2	Oliva Spain	
155 D2	Oliveira Brazil	
106 B2	Olivenza Spain	
152 B3	Ollagüe Chile	
150 A2	Olmos Peru	
140 B3	Olney U.S.A.	
103 B3	Olomouc Czech Rep.	
64 B1	Olongapo Phil.	
104 B3	Oloron-Ste-Marie France	
107 D1	Olot Spain	
69 D1	Olovyannaya Rus. Fed.	
83 I2	Oloy r. Rus. Fed.	
100 F3	Olpe Ger.	
103 E1	Olsztyn Pol.	
110 B2	Olt r. Romania	
81 C1	Oltu Turkey	
111 B3	Olympia tourist site Greece	
134 B1	Olympia U.S.A.	
134 B1	Olympus, Mount U.S.A.	
83 M3	Olyutorskiy, Mys c. Rus. Fed.	
97 C1	Omagh U.K.	
137 D2	Omaha U.S.A.	
79 C2	Oman country Asia	
79 C2	Oman, Gulf of Asia	
120 A3	Omaruru Namibia	
120 B2	Omatako watercourse Namibia	
116 B3	Omdurman Sudan	
53 C3	Omeo Austr.	
145 C3	Ometepec Mex.	
78 A3	Om Hajer Eritrea	
128 B2	Omineca Mountains Can.	
67 C3	Ōmiya Japan	
100 C1	Ommen Neth.	
83 L2	Omolon r. Rus. Fed.	
100 B3	Omont France	
82 F3	Omsk Rus. Fed.	
83 L2	Omsukchan Rus. Fed.	
110 C1	Omu, Vârful mt. Romania	
67 A4	Ōmura Japan	
141 D2	Onancock U.S.A.	
140 C1	Onaping Lake Can.	
121 C2	Onatchiway, Lac l. Can.	
120 A2	Oncócua Angola	
122 B3	Onderstedorings S. Africa	
120 A2	Ondjiva Angola	
86 C2	Onega Rus. Fed.	
86 C2	Onega r. Rus. Fed.	
141 D2	Oneida Lake U.S.A.	
137 D2	O'Neill U.S.A.	
141 D2	Oneonta U.S.A.	
110 C1	Oneşti Romania	
86 C2	Onezhskoye, Ozero l. Rus. Fed. see Onezhskoye Ozero	
86 C2	Onezhskoye Ozero l. Rus. Fed.	
122 B2	Ongers watercourse S. Africa	

65 B2	Ongjin N. Korea	
73 C3	Ongole India	
121 □D3	Onilahy r. Madag.	
115 C4	Onitsha Nigeria	
122 A2	Onseepkans S. Africa	
50 A2	Onslow Austr.	
143 E2	Onslow Bay U.S.A.	
130 A1	Ontario prov. Can.	
134 C2	Ontario U.S.A.	
141 D2	Ontario, Lake Can./U.S.A.	
51 C2	Oodnadatta Austr.	
100 B2	Oostburg Neth.	
100 A2	Oosterhout Neth.	
100 B1	Oosterschelde est. Neth.	
100 B1	Oost-Vlieland Neth.	
128 B2	Ootsa Lake Can.	
128 B2	Ootsa Lake l. Can.	
118 C3	Opala Dem. Rep. Congo	
130 C1	Opataca, Lac l. Can.	
103 D2	Opava Czech Rep.	
143 C2	Opelika U.S.A.	
142 B2	Opelousas U.S.A.	
130 C1	Opinaca, Réservoir resr Can.	
131 D1	Opiscotéo, Lac l. Can.	
88 D1	Opochka Rus. Fed.	
144 A2	Opodepe Mex.	
103 D1	Opole Pol.	
106 B1	Oporto Port.	
54 C1	Opotiki N.Z.	
93 E3	Oppdal Norway	
54 B2	Opunake N.Z.	
120 A2	Opuwo Namibia	
110 B1	Oradea Romania	
	Orahovac Kosovo see Rahovec	
114 B1	Oran Alg.	
152 B3	Orán Arg.	
65 B1	Orang N. Korea	
53 C2	Orange Austr.	
105 C3	Orange France	
122 A2	Orange r. Namibia/S. Africa	
139 E2	Orange U.S.A.	
143 D2	Orangeburg U.S.A.	
140 C2	Orangeville Can.	
101 F1	Oranienburg Ger.	
122 A2	Oranjemund Namibia	
120 B3	Orapa Botswana	
110 B1	Orăştie Romania	
108 B2	Orbetello Italy	
53 C3	Orbost Austr.	
50 B1	Ord, Mount h. Austr.	
106 B1	Ordes Spain	
70 B2	Ordos China	
80 B1	Ordu Turkey	
	Ordzhonikidze Rus. Fed. see Vladikavkaz	
91 C2	Ordzhonikidze Ukr.	
93 G4	Örebro Sweden	
134 B2	Oregon state U.S.A.	
134 B1	Oregon City U.S.A.	
87 D3	Orekhovo-Zuyevo Rus. Fed.	
89 E3	Orel Rus. Fed.	
	Orel, Ozero l. Rus. Fed.	
135 D3	Orem U.S.A.	
111 C3	Ören Turkey	
87 E3	Orenburg Rus. Fed.	
54 A3	Orepuki N.Z.	
93 F4	Öresund str. Denmark/ Sweden	
99 D2	Orford Ness hd U.K.	
111 C3	Orhaneli Turkey	
111 C2	Orhangazi Turkey	
83 I3	Orhon Gol r. Mongolia	
152 B2	Oriental, Cordillera mts Bol.	
150 A1	Oriental, Cordillera mts Col.	
150 A3	Oriental, Cordillera mts Peru	
107 C2	Orihuela Spain	
91 D2	Orikhiv Ukr.	

130 C2	Orillia Can.	
150 B1	Orinoco r. Col./Venez.	
150 B1	Orinoco, Delta del Venez.	
93 H4	Orissaare Estonia	
108 A3	Oristano Sardegna Italy	
93 I3	Orivesi l. Fin.	
151 C2	Oriximiná Brazil	
145 C3	Orizaba Mex.	
145 C3	Orizaba, Pico de vol. Mex.	
92 E3	Orkanger Norway	
93 F4	Örkelljunga Sweden	
92 E3	Orkla r. Norway	
96 C1	Orkney Islands U.K.	
154 C2	Orlândia Brazil	
143 D3	Orlando U.S.A.	
104 C2	Orléans France	
74 A2	Ormara Pak.	
64 B1	Ormoc Phil.	
98 B2	Ormskirk U.K.	
92 G3	Örnsköldsvik Sweden	
114 B3	Orodara Burkina Faso	
134 C1	Orofino U.S.A.	
	Oroqen Zizhiqi China see Alihe	
64 B2	Oroquieta Phil.	
108 A2	Orosei Sardegna Italy	
108 A2	Orosei, Golfo di b. Sardegna Italy	
103 E2	Orosháza Hungary	
135 B3	Oroville U.S.A.	
52 A2	Orroroo Austr.	
89 D3	Orsha Belarus	
87 E3	Orsk Rus. Fed.	
93 E3	Ørsta Norway	
106 B1	Ortegal, Cabo c. Spain	
104 B3	Orthez France	
106 B1	Ortigueira Spain	
137 D1	Ortonville U.S.A.	
83 J2	Orulgan, Khrebet mts Rus. Fed.	
	Orümïyeh, Daryächeh-ye salt l. Iran see Urmia, Lake	
152 B2	Oruro Bol.	
108 B2	Orvieto Italy	
146 B4	Osa, Península de pen. Costa Rica	
137 E3	Osage r. U.S.A.	
67 C4	Ōsaka Japan	
101 E1	Oschersleben (Bode) Ger.	
108 A2	Oschiri Sardegna Italy	
89 E3	Osetr r. Rus. Fed.	
77 D2	Osh Kyrg.	
120 A2	Oshakati Namibia	
130 C2	Oshawa Can.	
66 C2	O-shima i. Japan	
67 C4	Ō-shima i. Japan	
140 B2	Oshkosh U.S.A.	
81 C2	Oshnovīyeh Iran	
115 C4	Oshogbo Nigeria	
118 B3	Oshwe Dem. Rep. Congo	
109 C1	Osijek Croatia	
128 B2	Osilinka r. Can.	
108 B2	Osimo Italy	
123 D2	oSizweni S. Africa	
137 D2	Oskaloosa U.S.A.	
93 G4	Oskarshamn Sweden	
89 E3	Oskol r. Rus. Fed.	
93 F4	Oslo Norway	
93 F4	Oslofjorden sea chan. Norway	
80 B1	Osmancık Turkey	
111 C2	Osmaneli Turkey	
80 B2	Osmaniye Turkey	
88 C2	Os'mino Rus. Fed.	
100 D1	Osnabrück Ger.	
153 A5	Osorno Chile	
106 C1	Osorno Spain	
128 C3	Osoyoos Can.	

Oss

100	B2	Oss Neth.
51	D4	Oss, Mount Austr.
83	L3	Ossora Rus. Fed.
89	D2	Ostashkov Rus. Fed.
101	D1	Oste r. Ger.
100	A2	Ostend Belgium
111	E1	Osterburg (Altmark) Ger.
93	F3	Österdälven r. Sweden
101	D1	Osterholz-Scharmbeck Ger.
101	E2	Osterode am Harz Ger.
92	F3	Östersund Sweden
		Ostfriesische Inseln is Ger. see East Frisian Islands
100	C1	Ostfriesland reg. Ger.
93	G3	Östhammar Sweden
103	D2	Ostrava Czech Rep.
103	D1	Ostróda Pol.
89	E3	Ostrogozhsk Rus. Fed.
103	E1	Ostrołęka Pol.
101	F2	Ostrov Czech Rep.
88	C2	Ostrov Rus. Fed.
103	E1	Ostrowiec Świętokrzyski Pol.
103	E1	Ostrów Mazowiecka Pol.
103	D1	Ostrów Wielkopolski Pol.
110	B2	Osŭm r. Bulg.
67	B4	Ōsumi-kaikyō sea chan. Japan
67	B4	Ōsumi-shotō is Japan
106	B2	Osuna Spain
141	D2	Oswego U.S.A.
99	C3	Oswestry U.K.
67	C3	Ōta Japan
54	B3	Otago Peninsula N.Z.
54	C2	Otaki N.Z.
66	D2	Otaru Japan
120	A2	Otavi Namibia
134	C1	Othello U.S.A.
120	A3	Otjiwarongo Namibia
117	B3	Otoro, Jebel mt. Sudan
93	E4	Otra r. Norway
109	C2	Otranto, Strait of Albania/Italy
67	C3	Ōtsu Japan
93	E3	Otta Norway
130	C2	Ottawa Can.
130	C2	Ottawa r. Can.
140	B2	Ottawa IL U.S.A.
137	D3	Ottawa KS U.S.A.
130	B1	Otter Rapids Can.
100	B1	Ottignies Belgium
137	E2	Ottumwa U.S.A.
150	A2	Otuzco Peru
52	B3	Otway, Cape Austr.
142	C1	Ouachita r. U.S.A.
142	B2	Ouachita, Lake U.S.A.
142	B2	Ouachita Mountains U.S.A.
118	C2	Ouadda C.A.R.
115	D3	Ouaddaï reg. Chad
114	B3	Ouagadougou Burkina Faso
114	B3	Ouahigouya Burkina Faso
114	B3	Oualâta Maur.
118	C2	Ouanda-Djallé C.A.R.
114	B2	Ouarâne reg. Maur.
115	C1	Ouargla Alg.
114	B1	Ouarzazate Morocco
100	A2	Oudenaarde Belgium
122	B3	Oudtshoorn S. Africa
107	C2	Oued Tlélat Alg.
104	A2	Ouessant, Île d' i. France
118	B2	Ouesso Congo
114	B1	Oujda Morocco
107	D2	Ouled Farès Alg.
92	I2	Oulu Fin.
92	I3	Oulujärvi l. Fin.
108	A1	Ouse Italy
115	E3	Oum-Chalouba Chad
115	D3	Oum-Hadjer Chad
115	E3	Ouianga Kébir Chad
100	B2	Oupeye Belgium
106	B1	Ourense Spain
154	C2	Ourinhos Brazil
155	D2	Ouro Preto Brazil
100	B2	Ourthe r. Belgium
98	C2	Ouse r. U.K.
131	D2	Outardes, Rivière aux r. Can.
131	D1	Outardes Quatre, Réservoir resr Can.
96	A2	Outer Hebrides is U.K.
120	A3	Outjo Namibia
129	D2	Outlook Can.
92	I3	Outokumpu Fin.
52	B3	Ouyen Austr.
106	B1	Ovar Port.
92	H2	Överkalix Sweden
135	D3	Overton U.S.A.
92	H2	Övertorneå Sweden
106	B1	Oviedo Spain
93	E3	Øvre Årdal Norway
93	F3	Øvre Rendal Norway
90	B1	Ovruch Ukr.
118	B3	Owando Congo
67	C4	Owase Japan
137	E2	Owatonna U.S.A.
140	B3	Owensboro U.S.A.
135	C3	Owens Lake U.S.A.
130	B2	Owen Sound Can.
115	C4	Owerri Nigeria
140	C2	Owosso U.S.A.
134	C2	Owyhee U.S.A.
134	C2	Owyhee r. U.S.A.
54	B2	Oxford N.Z.
99	C3	Oxford U.K.
142	C2	Oxford U.S.A.
129	E2	Oxford Lake Can.
52	B2	Oxley Austr.
97	B1	Ox Mountains hills Ireland
135	C4	Oxnard U.S.A.
67	C3	Oyama Japan
118	B2	Oyem Gabon
129	C2	Oyen Can.
105	D2	Oyonnax France
64	B2	Ozamis Phil.
142	C2	Ozark U.S.A.
137	E3	Ozark Plateau U.S.A.
137	E3	Ozarks, Lake of the U.S.A.
83	L3	Ozernovskiy Rus. Fed.
88	B3	Ozersk Rus. Fed.
89	E3	Ozery Rus. Fed.
87	D3	Ozinki Rus. Fed.

P

127	H2	Paamiut Greenland
122	A3	Paarl S. Africa
103	D1	Pabianice Pol.
75	C2	Pabna Bangl.
74	A2	Pab Range mts Pak.
109	C3	Pachino Sicilia Italy
145	C2	Pachuca Mex.
156		Pacific Ocean World
103	D1	Paczków Pol.
60	B2	Padang Indon.
60	B1	Padang Endau Malaysia
60	B2	Padangpanjang Indon.
60	A1	Padangsidimpuan Indon.
101	D2	Paderborn Ger.
		Padova Italy see Padua
139	D3	Padre Island U.S.A.
52	B3	Padthaway Austr.
108	B1	Padua Italy
140	B3	Paducah KY U.S.A.
139	C2	Paducah TX U.S.A.
65	B1	Paegam N. Korea
65	A2	Paengnyŏng-do i. S. Korea
54	C1	Paeroa N.Z.
		Pafos Cyprus see Paphos
109	C2	Pag Croatia
64	B2	Pagadian Phil.
60	B2	Pagai Selatan i. Indon.
60	B2	Pagai Utara i. Indon.
59	D1	Pagan i. N. Mariana Is
61	C2	Pagatan Indon.
138	A1	Page U.S.A.
88	B2	Pagėgiai Lith.
136	B3	Pagosa Springs U.S.A.
88	C2	Paide Estonia
93	I3	Päijänne l. Fin.
75	C2	Paikü Co l. China
138	A1	Painted Desert U.S.A.
96	B3	Paisley U.K.
92	H2	Pajala Sweden
150	B1	Pakaraima Mountains S. America
150	C1	Pakaraima Mountains S. America
74	A2	Pakistan country Asia
62	A1	Pakokku Myanmar
88	B2	Pakruojis Lith.
103	D2	Paks Hungary
130	A1	Pakwash Lake Can.
62	B2	Pakxan Laos
63	B2	Pakxé Laos
115	D4	Pala Chad
60	B2	Palabuhanratu, Teluk b. Indon.
111	C3	Palaikastro Greece
111	B3	Palaiochora Greece
122	B1	Palamakoloi Botswana
107	D1	Palamós Spain
83	L3	Palana Rus. Fed.
64	B1	Palanan Phil.
61	C2	Palangkaraya Indon.
74	B2	Palanpur India
120	B3	Palapye Botswana
83	L2	Palatka Rus. Fed.
143	D3	Palatka U.S.A.
59	C2	Palau country N. Pacific Ocean
63	A2	Palaw Myanmar
64	A2	Palawan i. Phil.
93	H4	Paldiski Estonia
60	B2	Palembang Indon.
106	C1	Palencia Spain
145	C3	Palenque Mex.
108	B3	Palermo Sicilia Italy
139	D2	Palestine U.S.A.
62	A1	Paletwa Myanmar
74	B2	Pali India
48	E2	Palikir Micronesia
109	C2	Palinuro, Capo c. Italy
111	B3	Paliouri, Akrotirio pt Greece
100	B3	Paliseul Belgium
92	I3	Paljakka h. Fin.
88	C2	Palkino Rus. Fed.
73	B4	Palk Strait India/Sri Lanka
54	C2	Palliser, Cape N.Z.
49	I3	Palliser, Îles is Fr. Polynesia
106	B2	Palma del Río Spain
107	D2	Palma de Mallorca Spain
154	B3	Palmas Brazil
151	D3	Palmas Brazil
114	B4	Palmas, Cape Liberia
154	C3	Palmeira Brazil
151	D2	Palmeirais Brazil
55	P2	Palmer Land reg. Antarctica
54	C2	Palmerston North N.Z.
109	C3	Palmi Italy
145	C2	Palmillas Mex.
150	A1	Palmira Col.

135 C4 Palm Springs U.S.A.
49 H2 Palmyra Atoll N. Pacific Ocean
117 B3 Paloich S. Sudan
145 C3 Palomares Mex.
107 C2 Palos, Cabo de c. Spain
92 I3 Paltamo Fin.
58 B3 Palu Indon.
83 M2 Palyavaam r. Rus. Fed.
104 C3 Pamiers France
77 D3 Pamir mts Asia
143 E1 Pamlico Sound sea chan. U.S.A.
152 B2 Pampa Grande Bol.
153 B4 Pampas reg. Arg.
150 A1 Pamplona Col.
107 C1 Pamplona Spain
111 D2 Pamukova Turkey
60 B2 Panaitan i. Indon.
73 B3 Panaji India
146 B4 Panama country Central America
146 L4 Panamá, Canal de Panama
146 C4 Panama, Gulf of Panama
146 C4 Panama City Panama
142 C2 Panama City U.S.A.
135 C3 Panamint Range mts U.S.A.
61 B1 Panarik Indon.
64 B3 Panay i. Phil.
109 D2 Pančevo Serbia
64 B1 Pandan Phil.
75 C2 Pandaria India
73 B3 Pandharpur India
88 A2 Panevėžys Lith.
61 C2 Pangkalanbuun Indon.
60 A1 Pangkalansusu Indon.
60 B2 Pangkalpinang Indon.
127 G2 Pangnirtung Can.
86 G2 Pangody Rus. Fed.
89 F3 Panino Rus. Fed.
74 B2 Panipat India
74 A2 Panjgur Pak.
65 C1 Pan Ling mts China
75 C2 Panna India
50 A2 Pannawonica Austr.
154 B2 Panorama Brazil
65 B1 Panshi China
145 C2 Pánuco Mex.
62 B1 Panzhihua China
109 C3 Paola Italy
63 B2 Paôy Pêt Cambodia
103 D2 Pápa Hungary
54 B1 Papantla Mex.
145 C2 Papantla Mex.
49 I4 Papeete Fr. Polynesia
100 C1 Papenburg Ger.
80 B2 Paphos Cyprus
59 F3 Papua, Gulf of P.N.G.
59 D3 Papua New Guinea country Oceania
50 A2 Paraburdoo Austr.
141 L1 Paracatu Brazil
155 C1 Paracatu r. Brazil
52 A2 Parachilna Austr.
109 D2 Paraćin Serbia
155 D1 Pará de Minas Brazil
135 B3 Paradise U.S.A.
142 B1 Paragould U.S.A.
151 B2 Paraguai r. Brazil
152 C3 Paraguay r. Arg./Para.
152 C3 Paraguay country S. America
155 D2 Paraíba do Sul r. Brazil
154 B1 Paraíso Brazil
145 C3 Paraíso Mex.
114 C4 Parakou Benin
151 C1 Paramaribo Suriname
83 L3 Paramushir, Ostrov i. Rus. Fed.

152 B4 Paraná Arg.
154 A3 Paraná r. S. America
154 C3 Paranaguá Brazil
154 B1 Paranaíba Brazil
154 B2 Paranaíba r. Brazil
154 B2 Paranapanema r. Brazil
154 B2 Paranapiacaba, Serra mts Brazil
154 B2 Paranavaí Brazil
54 B2 Paraparaumu N.Z.
155 D2 Parati Brazil
154 B1 Paraúna Brazil
105 C2 Paray-le-Monial France
73 B3 Parbhani India
101 E1 Parchim Ger.
155 E1 Pardo r. Bahia Brazil
154 B2 Pardo r. Mato Grosso do Sul Brazil
154 C2 Pardo r. São Paulo Brazil
103 D1 Pardubice Czech Rep.
150 B3 Parecis, Serra dos hills Brazil
130 C2 Parent, Lac l. Can.
58 B3 Parepare Indon.
89 D2 Parfino Rus. Fed.
111 B3 Parga Greece
109 C3 Parghelia Italy
147 D3 Paria, Gulf of Trin. and Tob./Venez.
150 B1 Parima, Serra mts Brazil
151 C2 Parintins Brazil
104 C2 Paris France
142 C1 Paris TN U.S.A.
139 D2 Paris TX U.S.A.
93 H3 Parkano Fin.
138 A2 Parker U.S.A.
140 C3 Parkersburg U.S.A.
53 C2 Parkes Austr.
140 A1 Park Falls U.S.A.
137 D1 Park Rapids U.S.A.
108 B2 Parma Italy
151 D2 Parnaíba Brazil
151 D2 Parnaíba r. Brazil
54 B2 Parnassus N.Z.
111 B3 Parnonas mts Greece
88 B2 Pärnu Estonia
65 B2 P'aro-ho l. S. Korea
52 B2 Paroo watercourse Austr.
111 C3 Paros i. Greece
144 B2 Parras Mex.
126 C2 Parry, Cape Can.
126 D1 Parry Islands Can.
130 C2 Parry Sound Can.
137 D3 Parsons U.S.A.
101 D2 Partenstein Ger.
104 B2 Parthenay France
97 B2 Partry Mountains hills Ireland
151 C2 Paru r. Brazil
135 C4 Pasadena U.S.A.
62 A1 Pasawng Myanmar
142 C2 Pascagoula U.S.A.
110 C1 Paşcani Romania
134 C1 Pasco U.S.A.
102 C1 Pasewalk Ger.
129 D2 Pasfield Lake Can.
64 B1 Pasig Phil.
60 B1 Pasir Putih Malaysia
74 A2 Pasni Pak.
153 A5 Paso Río Mayo Arg.
135 B3 Paso Robles U.S.A.
155 D2 Passa Tempo Brazil
102 C2 Passau Ger.
152 C3 Passo Fundo Brazil
155 C2 Passos Brazil
88 C2 Pastavy Belarus
150 A2 Pastaza r. Peru
150 A1 Pasto Col.
61 C2 Pasuruan Indon.

88 B2 Pasvalys Lith.
153 A6 Patagonia reg. Arg.
75 C2 Patan Nepal
54 B1 Patea N.Z.
141 E2 Paterson U.S.A.
Pathein Myanmar see Bassein
136 B2 Pathfinder Reservoir U.S.A.
61 C2 Pati Indon.
81 A1 Patkai Bum hills India/Myanmar
111 C3 Patmos i. Greece
75 C2 Patna India
81 C2 Patnos Turkey
154 B3 Pato Branco Brazil
152 C4 Patos, Lagoa dos l. Brazil
155 C1 Patos de Minas Brazil
152 B4 Patquía Arg.
111 B3 Patras Greece
75 C2 Patratu India
154 C1 Patrocínio Brazil
63 B2 Pattani Thai.
63 B2 Pattaya Thai.
128 B2 Pattullo, Mount Can.
129 D2 Patuanak Can.
144 B3 Pátzcuaro Mex.
104 B3 Pau France
104 B3 Pauillac France
62 A1 Pauk Myanmar
151 D2 Paulistana Brazil
151 E2 Paulo Afonso Brazil
123 D2 Paulpietersburg S. Africa
139 D1 Pauls Valley U.S.A.
62 A2 Paungde Myanmar
155 D1 Pavão Brazil
108 A1 Pavia Italy
88 B2 Pāvilosta Latvia
110 C2 Pavlikeni Bulg.
77 D1 Pavlodar Kazakh.
91 D2 Pavlohrad Ukr.
91 E1 Pavlovsk Rus. Fed.
91 D2 Pavlovskaya Rus. Fed.
60 B2 Payakumbuh Indon.
134 C2 Payette U.S.A.
134 C2 Payette r. U.S.A.
86 F2 Pay-Khoy, Khrebet hills Rus. Fed.
152 C4 Paysandú Uru.
81 C1 Pazar Turkey
110 B2 Pazardzhik Bulg.
111 C3 Pazarköy Turkey
108 B1 Pazin Croatia
63 A2 Pe Myanmar
128 C2 Peace r. Can.
128 C2 Peace River Can.
135 E3 Peale, Mount U.S.A.
142 C2 Pearl r. U.S.A.
139 D3 Pearsall U.S.A.
121 C2 Pebane Moz.
Peć Kosovo see Pejë
155 D1 Peçanha Brazil
86 E2 Pechora Rus. Fed.
88 C2 Pechory Rus. Fed.
139 C2 Pecos U.S.A.
139 C3 Pecos r. U.S.A.
103 D2 Pécs Hungary
155 D1 Pedra Azul Brazil
154 C2 Pedregulho Brazil
151 D2 Pedreiras Brazil
73 C4 Pedro, Point Sri Lanka
151 D2 Pedro Afonso Brazil
154 B1 Pedro Gomes Brazil
152 C3 Pedro Juan Caballero Para.
96 C3 Peebles U.K.
143 E2 Pee Dee r. U.S.A.
126 C2 Peel r. Can.
98 A1 Peel Isle of Man

128 C2 Peerless Lake Can.
54 B2 Pegasus Bay N.Z.
101 E3 Pegnitz Ger.
62 A2 Pegu Myanmar
62 A2 Pegu Yoma mts Myanmar
153 B4 Pehuajó Arg.
101 C1 Peine Ger.
88 C2 Peipus, Lake Estonia/Rus. Fed.
154 B2 Peixe r. Brazil
109 D2 Pejë Kosovo
61 B1 Pekalongan Indon.
60 B1 Pekan Malaysia
60 B1 Pekanbaru Indon.
Peking China see Beijing
130 B2 Pelee Island Can.
59 C3 Peleng i. Indon.
92 I2 Pelkosenniemi Fin.
122 A2 Pella S. Africa
59 D3 Pelleluhu Islands P.N.G.
92 H2 Pello Fin.
128 A1 Pelly r. Can.
128 A1 Pelly Mountains Can.
152 C4 Pelotas Brazil
152 C3 Pelotas, Rio das r. Brazil
141 F1 Pemadumcook Lake U.S.A.
61 B1 Pemangkat Indon.
60 A1 Pematangsiantar Indon.
121 D2 Pemba Moz.
120 B2 Pemba Zambia
119 D3 Pemba Island Tanz.
128 B2 Pemberton Can.
137 D1 Pembina r. Can./U.S.A.
130 C2 Pembroke Can.
99 A3 Pembroke U.K.
145 C2 Peña Nevada, Cerro mt. Mex.
154 B2 Penápolis Brazil
106 B1 Peñaranda de Bracamonte Spain
107 C1 Peñarroya mt. Spain
106 B2 Peñarroya-Pueblonuevo Spain
106 B1 Peñas, Cabo de c. Spain
153 A5 Penas, Golfo de g. Chile
134 C1 Pendleton U.S.A.
128 B2 Pendleton Bay Can.
134 C1 Pend Oreille Lake U.S.A.
74 B3 Penganga r. India
123 D1 Penge S. Africa
70 C2 Penglai China
71 A3 Pengshui China
106 B2 Peniche Port.
98 B1 Penicuik U.K.
108 B2 Penne Italy
98 B1 Pennines hills U.K.
141 D2 Pennsylvania state U.S.A.
127 G2 Penny Icecap Can.
141 F2 Penobscot r. U.S.A.
52 B3 Penola Austr.
50 C3 Penong Austr.
49 H3 Penrhyn atoll Cook Is
98 B1 Penrith U.K.
142 C2 Pensacola U.S.A.
55 Q1 Pensacola Mountains Antarctica
61 C1 Pensiangan Sabah Malaysia
128 C3 Penticton Can.
96 C1 Pentland Firth sea chan. U.K.
99 B2 Penygadair h. U.K.
87 D3 Penza Rus. Fed.
99 A3 Penzance U.K.
140 B2 Peoria U.S.A.
107 C1 Perales del Alfambra Spain
51 E2 Percy Isles Austr.
86 F2 Peregrebnoye Rus. Fed.
150 A1 Pereira Col.
154 B2 Pereira Barreto Brazil
90 A2 Peremyshlyany Ukr.
89 E2 Pereslavl'-Zalesskiy Rus. Fed.

91 C1 Pereyaslav-Khmel'nyts'kyy Ukr.
153 B4 Pergamino Arg.
92 H3 Perhonjoki r. Fin.
131 C2 Péribonka, Lac l. Can.
152 B3 Perico Arg.
144 B2 Pericos Mex.
104 C2 Périgueux France
147 C4 Perijá, Sierra de mts Venez.
153 A5 Perito Moreno Arg.
101 E1 Perleberg Ger.
86 E3 Perm' Rus. Fed.
52 A2 Pernatty Lagoon imp. l. Austr.
105 C2 Péronne France
145 C3 Perote Mex.
104 C3 Perpignan France
99 A3 Perranporth U.K.
143 D2 Perry FL U.S.A.
143 D2 Perry GA U.S.A.
137 E2 Perry IA U.S.A.
139 C1 Perryton U.S.A.
137 F3 Perryville U.S.A.
99 B2 Pershore U.K.
91 D2 Pershotravens'k Ukr.
Persian Gulf Asia see The Gulf
50 A3 Perth Austr.
96 C2 Perth U.K.
105 D3 Pertuis France
108 A2 Pertusato, Capo c. Corse France
150 A2 Peru country S. America
157 H4 Peru-Chile Trench S. Pacific Ocean
108 B2 Perugia Italy
154 C2 Peruíbe Brazil
100 A2 Péruwelz Belgium
90 C2 Pervomays'k Ukr.
89 F3 Pervomayskiy Rus. Fed.
91 D2 Pervomays'kyy Ukr.
108 B2 Pesaro Italy
108 B2 Pescara Italy
108 B2 Pescara r. Italy
74 B1 Peshawar Pak.
109 D2 Peshkopi Albania
109 C1 Pesnica Slovenia
89 E2 Pestovo Rus. Fed.
144 B3 Petatlán Mex.
140 B2 Petenwell Lake U.S.A.
52 A2 Peterborough Austr.
130 C2 Peterborough Can.
99 C2 Peterborough U.K.
96 D2 Peterhead U.K.
50 B2 Petermann Ranges mts Austr.
129 D2 Peter Pond Lake Can.
128 A2 Petersburg AK U.S.A.
141 D3 Petersburg VA U.S.A.
101 D1 Petershagen Ger.
131 E1 Petit Mécatina r. Can.
145 D2 Peto Mex.
140 C1 Petoskey U.S.A.
80 B2 Petra tourist site Jordan
66 B2 Petra Velikogo, Zaliv b. Rus. Fed.
111 B2 Petrich Bulg.
151 D2 Petrolina Brazil
83 L3 Petropavlovsk-Kamchatskiy Rus. Fed.
77 C1 Petropavlovskoye Kazakh.
110 B1 Petroșani Romania
89 F3 Petrovskoye Rus. Fed.
86 C2 Petrozavodsk Rus. Fed.
123 C2 Petrusburg S. Africa
123 C2 Petrus Steyn S. Africa
89 E2 Petushki Rus. Fed.
60 A1 Peureula Indon.

83 M2 Pevek Rus. Fed.
102 B2 Pforzheim Ger.
102 C2 Pfunds Austria
101 D3 Pfungstadt Ger.
123 C2 Phahameng S. Africa
123 D1 Phalaborwa S. Africa
74 B2 Phalodi India
63 B2 Phang Hoei, San Khao mts Thai.
63 A3 Phangnga Thai.
62 B1 Phăng Xi Păng mt. Vietnam
62 B2 Phan Rang-Thap Cham Vietnam
63 B2 Phan Thiêt Vietnam
63 B3 Phatthalung Thai.
62 A2 Phayao Thai.
129 D2 Phelps Lake Can.
143 C2 Phenix City U.S.A.
63 B2 Phet Buri Thai.
63 B2 Phichit Thai.
141 D3 Philadelphia U.S.A.
136 C2 Philip U.S.A.
100 B2 Philippeville Belgium
100 A2 Philippine Neth.
64 B1 Philippines country Asia
64 B1 Philippine Sea N. Pacific Ocean
126 B2 Philip Smith Mountains U.S.A.
122 B3 Philipstown S. Africa
53 C3 Phillip Island Austr.
137 D3 Phillipsburg U.S.A.
123 C2 Phiritona S. Africa
63 B2 Phitsanulok Thai.
63 B2 Phnom Penh Cambodia
138 A2 Phoenix U.S.A.
49 G3 Phoenix Islands Kiribati
63 B2 Phon Thai.
62 B1 Phôngsali Laos
62 B2 Phônsavan Laos
62 B2 Phrae Thai.
63 A3 Phuket Thai.
62 A2 Phumiphon, Khuan Thai.
63 B2 Phumĭ Sâmraông Cambodia
123 C2 Phuthaditjhaba S. Africa
62 A2 Phyu Myanmar
108 A1 Piacenza Italy
110 C1 Piatra Neamţ Romania
151 D2 Piauí r. Brazil
108 B1 Piave r. Italy
117 B4 Pibor r. S. Sudan
117 B4 Pibor Post S. Sudan
108 A1 Picayune U.S.A.
152 B3 Pichanal Arg.
144 A2 Pichilingue Mex.
98 C1 Pickering U.K.
130 A1 Pickle Lake Can.
151 D2 Picos Brazil
153 B5 Pico Truncado Arg.
53 C3 Picton Austr.
150 B3 Piedras, Río de las r. Peru
145 C2 Piedras Negras Guat.
145 B2 Piedras Negras Mex.
93 I3 Pieksämäki Fin.
92 I3 Pielinen l. Fin.
136 C2 Pierre U.S.A.
105 C3 Pierrelatte France
123 D2 Pietermaritzburg S. Africa
110 B1 Pietrosa mt. Romania
128 C2 Pigeon Lake Can.
153 B4 Pigüé Arg.
92 I3 Pihtipudas Fin.
145 C3 Pijijiapan Mex.
136 C3 Pikes Peak U.S.A.
122 A3 Piketberg S. Africa
140 C3 Pikeville U.S.A.

103 D1 Piła Pol.
153 C4 Pilar Arg.
152 B2 Pilar Para.
53 C2 Pilliga Austr.
154 C1 Pilões, Serra dos *mts* Brazil
150 B3 Pimenta Bueno Brazil
153 C4 Pinamar Arg.
80 B2 Pınarbaşı Turkey
146 B2 Pinar del Río Cuba
103 E1 Pińczów Pol.
151 D2 Pindaré *r.* Brazil
106 B3 Pindos *mts* Greece *see* Pindus Mountains
111 B2 Pindus Mountains Greece
142 B2 Pine Bluff U.S.A.
50 C1 Pine Creek Austr.
136 B2 Pinedale U.S.A.
86 C2 Pinega Rus. Fed.
129 D2 Pinehouse Lake Can.
111 B3 Pineios *r.* Greece
128 C1 Pine Point (abandoned) Can.
136 C2 Pine Ridge U.S.A.
123 D2 Pinetown S. Africa
70 B2 Pingdingshan China
71 B3 Pingguo China
71 B3 Pingjiang China
70 A2 Pingliang China
71 C3 P'ingtung Taiwan
71 A3 Pingxiang *Guangxi* China
71 B3 Pingxiang *Jiangxi* China
70 B2 Pingyin China
151 D2 Pinheiro Brazil
101 D1 Pinneberg Ger.
145 C3 Pinotepa Nacional Mex.
88 C3 Pinsk Belarus
135 D3 Pioche U.S.A.
119 C3 Piodi Dem. Rep. Congo
103 E1 Pionki Pol.
103 D1 Piotrków Trybunalski Pol.
137 D2 Pipestone U.S.A.
131 C2 Pipmuacan, Réservoir *resr* Can.
154 B2 Piquiri *r.* Brazil
154 C1 Piracanjuba Brazil
154 C2 Piracicaba Brazil
155 D1 Piracuruca Brazil
154 C2 Piraçununga Brazil
111 B3 Piraeus Greece
154 C2 Piraí do Sul Brazil
154 C2 Pirajuí Brazil
154 B2 Piranhas Brazil
151 E2 Piranhas *r.* Brazil
155 D1 Pirapora Brazil
154 C1 Pires do Rio Brazil
151 D2 Piripiri Brazil
59 C3 Piru Indon.
108 B2 Pisa Italy
152 A2 Pisagua Chile
150 A3 Pisco Peru
102 C2 Písek Czech Rep.
79 D2 Pishin Iran
145 D2 Pisté Mex.
109 C2 Pisticci Italy
108 B2 Pistoia Italy
106 C1 Pisuerga *r.* Spain
134 B2 Pit *r.* U.S.A.
154 B2 Pitanga Brazil
155 D1 Pitangui Brazil
49 J4 Pitcairn Island *i.* Pitcairn Is
92 H2 Piteå Sweden
92 H2 Piteälven *r.* Sweden
110 B2 Pitești Romania
75 C2 Pithoragarh India
96 C2 Pitlochry U.K.
128 B2 Pitt Island Can.
141 D2 Pittsburg U.S.A.
141 D2 Pittsburgh U.S.A.

141 F7 Pittsfield U.S.A.
53 D1 Pittsworth Austr.
155 C2 Piumhi Brazil
150 A2 Piura Peru
90 C2 Pivdennyy Buh *r.* Ukr.
131 E2 Placentia Can.
135 B3 Placerville U.S.A.
146 C2 Placetas Cuba
139 C2 Plainview U.S.A.
154 C1 Planaltina Brazil
142 B2 Plaquemine U.S.A.
106 B3 Plasencia Spain
147 C4 Plato Col.
137 D2 Platte *r.* U.S.A.
141 E2 Plattsburgh U.S.A.
101 F1 Plau Ger.
101 F2 Plauen Ger.
101 F1 Plauer See *l.* Ger.
89 E3 Plavsk Rus. Fed.
129 E2 Playgreen Lake Can.
63 B2 Plây Ku Vietnam
153 B4 Plaza Huincul Arg.
139 D2 Pleasanton U.S.A.
54 B2 Pleasant Point N.Z.
104 C2 Pleaux France
130 B1 Pledger Lake Can.
54 C1 Plenty, Bay of *g.* N.Z.
136 C1 Plentywood U.S.A.
86 D2 Plesetsk Rus. Fed.
131 C1 Plétipi, Lac *l.* Can.
100 C2 Plettenberg Ger.
122 B3 Plettenberg Bay S. Africa
110 B2 Pleven Bulg.
109 C2 Pljevlja Montenegro
109 C2 Ploče Croatia
103 D1 Płock Pol.
109 C2 Pločno *mt.* Bos.-Herz.
104 B2 Ploemeur France
110 C2 Ploiești Romania
89 F2 Ploskoye Rus. Fed.
104 B2 Plouzané France
110 B2 Plovdiv Bulg.
88 B2 Plunge Lith.
88 C3 Plyeshchanitsy Belarus
99 A3 Plymouth U.K.
140 B2 Plymouth U.S.A.
147 D3 Plymouth (abandoned) Montserrat
88 C2 Plyussa Rus. Fed.
102 C2 Plzeň Czech Rep.
114 B3 Pô Burkina Faso
108 B1 Po *r.* Italy
77 E2 Pobeda Peak China/Kyrg.
142 B1 Pocahontas U.S.A.
134 D2 Pocatello U.S.A.
90 B1 Pochayiv Ukr.
89 D3 Pochep Rus. Fed.
89 D3 Pochinok Rus. Fed.
145 C3 Pochutla Mex.
141 D3 Pocomoke City U.S.A.
155 C2 Poços de Caldas Brazil
89 D2 Poddor'ye Rus. Fed.
91 D1 Podgorenskiy Rus. Fed.
109 C2 Podgorica Montenegro
82 G3 Podgornoye Rus. Fed.
83 H2 Podkamennaya Tunguska *r.* Rus. Fed.
89 E2 Podol'sk Rus. Fed.
109 D2 Podujevë Kosovo
  Podujevo Kosovo *see* Podujevë
122 A2 Pofadder S. Africa
89 D3 Pogar Rus. Fed.
109 D2 Pogradec Albania
65 B2 P'ohang S. Korea
48 E2 Pohnpei *atoll* Micronesia
110 B2 Poiana Mare Romania
118 C3 Poie Dem. Rep. Congo

118 B3 Pointe-Noire Congo
126 D2 Point Lake Can.
140 C3 Point Pleasant U.S.A.
104 C2 Poitiers France
74 B2 Pokaran India
75 C2 Pokhara Nepal
83 J2 Pokrovsk Rus. Fed.
91 D2 Pokrovskoye Rus. Fed.
138 A1 Polacca U.S.A.
103 D1 Poland *country* Europe
88 C2 Polatsk Belarus
61 C2 Polewali Indon.
118 B2 Poli Cameroon
102 C1 Police Pol.
109 C2 Policoro Italy
105 D2 Poligny France
64 B1 Polillo Islands Phil.
90 B1 Polis'ke Ukr.
103 D1 Polkowice Pol.
109 C3 Pollino, Monte *mt.* Italy
91 D2 Polohy Ukr.
123 C1 Polokwane S. Africa
123 D1 Polokwane *r.* S. Africa
90 B1 Polonne Ukr.
134 D1 Polson U.S.A.
91 C2 Poltava Ukr.
66 B2 Poltavka Rus. Fed.
91 D2 Poltavskaya Rus. Fed.
88 C2 Põlva Estonia
111 B2 Polygyros Greece
106 B2 Pombal Port.
102 C1 Pomeranian Bay Ger./Pol.
108 B2 Pomezia Italy
92 I2 Pomokaira *reg.* Fin.
110 C2 Pomorie Bulg.
  Pomorska, Zatoka *b.* Ger./Pol. *see* Pomeranian Bay
155 D1 Pompéu Brazil
139 D1 Ponca City U.S.A.
147 D3 Ponce Puerto Rico
127 F2 Pond Inlet Can.
106 B1 Ponferrada Spain
117 A4 Pongo *watercourse* S. Sudan
123 D2 Pongola *r.* S. Africa
128 C2 Ponoka Can.
84 D5 Ponta Delgada Arquipélago dos Açores
154 B3 Ponta Grossa Brazil
154 C1 Pontalina Brazil
105 D2 Pont-à-Mousson France
105 D2 Pontarlier France
102 B2 Pontcharra France
142 B2 Pontchartrain, Lake U.S.A.
106 B2 Ponte de Sor Port.
129 D3 Ponteix Can.
150 C3 Pontes e Lacerda Brazil
106 B1 Pontevedra Spain
140 B2 Pontiac *IL* U.S.A.
140 C2 Pontiac *MI* U.S.A.
61 B2 Pontianak Indon.
104 B2 Pontivy France
151 C1 Pontoetoe Suriname
129 E2 Ponton Can.
99 B3 Pontypool U.K.
108 B2 Ponziane, Isole *is* Italy
99 B3 Poole U.K.
  Poona India *see* Pune
52 B2 Pooncarie Austr.
150 A1 Poopó, Lago de *l.* Bol.
150 A1 Popayán Col.
83 I2 Popigay *r.* Rus. Fed.
52 B2 Popiltah Austr.
129 E2 Poplar *r.* Can.
137 E3 Poplar Bluff U.S.A.
118 B3 Popokabaka Dem. Rep. Congo
110 C2 Popovo Bulg.

103 E2	Poprad Slovakia
151 D3	Porangatu Brazil
74 A2	Porbandar India
126 B2	Porcupine r. Can./U.S.A.
108 B1	Poreč Croatia
54 B2	Porirua N.Z.
88 C2	Porkhov Rus. Fed.
104 B2	Pornic France
83 K3	Poronaysk Rus. Fed.
111 B3	Poros Greece
93 E4	Porsgrunn Norway
97 C1	Portadown U.K.
97 D1	Portaferry U.K.
140 B2	Portage U.S.A.
129 E3	Portage la Prairie Can.
128 B3	Port Alberni Can.
106 B2	Portalegre Port.
139 C2	Portales U.S.A.
128 A2	Port Alexander U.S.A.
128 B2	Port Alice Can.
134 B1	Port Angeles U.S.A.
51 D4	Port Arthur Austr.
139 E3	Port Arthur U.S.A.
96 A3	Port Askaig U.K.
52 A2	Port Augusta Austr.
147 C3	Port-au-Prince Haiti
131 E1	Port aux Choix Can.
73 D3	Port Blair India
52 B3	Port Campbell N.Z.
54 B3	Port Chalmers N.Z.
143 D3	Port Charlotte U.S.A.
147 C3	Port-de-Paix Haiti
128 A2	Port Edward Can.
155 D1	Poteirinha Brazil
151 C2	Portel Brazil
130 B2	Port Elgin Can.
123 C3	Port Elizabeth S. Africa
96 A3	Port Ellen U.K.
98 A1	Port Erin Isle of Man
122 A3	Porterville S. Africa
135 C3	Porterville U.S.A.
52 B3	Port Fairy Austr.
54 C1	Port Fitzroy N.Z.
118 A3	Port-Gentil Gabon
115 C4	Port Harcourt Nigeria
128 B2	Port Hardy Can.
131 D2	Port Harrison Can. see Inukjuak
131 B2	Port Hawkesbury Can.
50 A2	Port Hedland Austr.
99 A2	Porthmadog U.K.
131 E1	Port Hope Simpson Can.
140 C2	Port Huron U.S.A.
106 B2	Portimão Port.
53 C2	Portland N.S.W. Austr.
52 B3	Portland Vic. Austr.
141 E2	Portland ME U.S.A.
134 B1	Portland OR U.S.A.
128 A2	Portland Canal inlet Can.
97 C2	Portlaoise Ireland
139 D3	Port Lavaca U.S.A.
52 A2	Port Lincoln Austr.
114 A4	Port Loko Sierra Leone
113 K9	Port Louis Mauritius
53 D2	Port Macquarie Austr.
128 B2	Port McNeill Can.
131 D2	Port-Menier Can.
59 D3	Port Moresby P.N.G.
122 A2	Port Nolloth S. Africa
	Port-Nouveau-Québec Can. see Kangiqsualujjuaq
150 B2	Porto Acre Brazil
152 C4	Porto Alegre Brazil
151 B3	Porto Artur Brazil
151 C3	Porto dos Gaúchos Óbidos Brazil
150 C3	Porto Esperidião Brazil
108 B2	Portoferraio Italy
96 A1	Port of Ness U.K.
151 D2	Porto Franco Brazil
147 D3	Port of Spain Trin. and Tob.
108 B1	Portogruaro Italy
108 B1	Portomaggiore Italy
154 B2	Porto Mendes Brazil
152 C3	Porto Murtinho Brazil
151 D3	Porto Nacional Brazil
114 C4	Porto-Novo Benin
154 B2	Porto Primavera, Represa resr Brazil
151 C2	Porto Santana Brazil
155 E1	Porto Seguro Brazil
108 B2	Porto Tolle Italy
108 A2	Porto Torres Sardegna Italy
105 D3	Porto-Vecchio Corse France
150 B2	Porto Velho Brazil
150 A2	Portoviejo Ecuador
52 B3	Port Phillip Bay Austr.
52 A2	Port Pirie Austr.
96 A2	Portree U.K.
128 B3	Port Renfrew Can.
97 C1	Portrush U.K.
116 B3	Port Said Egypt
143 C3	Port St Joe U.S.A.
123 C3	Port St Johns S. Africa
123 D3	Port Shepstone S. Africa
99 C3	Portsmouth U.K.
141 E2	Portsmouth NH U.S.A.
140 C3	Portsmouth OH U.S.A.
141 D3	Portsmouth VA U.S.A.
97 C1	Portstewart U.K.
116 B3	Port Sudan Sudan
142 C3	Port Sulphur U.S.A.
99 B3	Port Talbot U.K.
106 B2	Portugal country Europe
97 B2	Portumna Ireland
105 C3	Port-Vendres France
48 F4	Port Vila Vanuatu
93 I3	Porvoo Fin.
65 B2	Poryŏng S. Korea
152 C3	Posadas Arg.
89 E2	Poshekhon'ye Rus. Fed.
92 I2	Posio Fin.
58 C3	Poso Indon.
151 D3	Posse Brazil
101 E2	Pößneck Ger.
139 C2	Post U.S.A.
	Poste-de-la-Baleine Can. see Kuujjuarapik
122 B3	Postmasburg S. Africa
109 C2	Posušje Bos.-Herz.
139 E1	Poteau U.S.A.
109 C2	Potenza Italy
151 D2	Poti r. Brazil
81 C1	Poti Georgia
115 D3	Potiskum Nigeria
141 D3	Potomac, South Branch r. U.S.A.
152 B2	Potosí Bol.
64 B1	Potran Phil.
138 C3	Potrero del Llano Mex.
101 F1	Potsdam Ger.
141 E2	Potsdam U.S.A.
141 D2	Pottstown U.S.A.
141 D2	Pottsville U.S.A.
131 E2	Pouch Cove Can.
141 E2	Poughkeepsie U.S.A.
98 B2	Poulton-le-Fylde U.K.
155 C2	Pouso Alegre Brazil
63 B2	Poŭthĭsăt Cambodia
103 D2	Považská Bystrica Slovakia
109 C2	Povlen mt. Serbia
106 B1	Póvoa de Varzim Port.
136 B2	Powell U.S.A.
135 D3	Powell, Lake resr U.S.A.
128 B3	Powell River Can.
154 B1	Poxoréu Brazil
	Poyang China see Poyang
71 B3	Poyang China
71 B3	Poyang Hu l. China
109 D2	Požarevac Serbia
145 C2	Poza Rica Mex.
109 C1	Požega Croatia
109 D2	Požega Serbia
79 D2	Pozm Tiāb Iran
103 D1	Poznań Pol.
106 C2	Pozoblanco Spain
108 B2	Pozzuoli Italy
60 B2	Prabumulih Indon.
102 C2	Prachatice Czech Rep.
63 A2	Prachuap Khiri Khan Thai.
155 E1	Prado Brazil
102 C1	Prague Czech Rep.
	Praha Czech Rep. see Prague
112 C5	Praia Cape Verde
139 C2	Prairie Dog Town Fork r. U.S.A.
140 A2	Prairie du Chien U.S.A.
60 A1	Prapat Indon.
154 C1	Prata Brazil
105 E3	Prato Italy
137 D3	Pratt U.S.A.
61 C2	Praya Indon.
63 B2	Preăh Vihéar Cambodia
89 F2	Prechistoye Rus. Fed.
129 D2	Preeceville Can.
88 C2	Preili Latvia
53 C2	Premer Austr.
105 C2	Prémery France
101 F1	Premnitz Ger.
102 C1	Prenzlau Ger.
63 A2	Preparis Island Cocos Is
63 A2	Preparis North Channel Cocos Is
63 A2	Preparis South Channel Cocos Is
103 D2	Přerov Czech Rep.
138 A2	Prescott U.S.A.
109 D2	Preševo Serbia
152 B3	Presidencia Roque Sáenz Peña Arg.
151 D2	Presidente Dutra Brazil
154 B2	Presidente Epitácio Brazil
64 B1	Presidente Manuel A Roxas Zamboanga del Norte Phil.
154 B2	Presidente Prudente Brazil
138 C3	Presidio U.S.A.
103 E2	Prešov Slovakia
141 F1	Presque Isle U.S.A.
101 F2	Pressel Ger.
98 B2	Preston U.K.
134 D2	Preston U.S.A.
96 B3	Prestwick U.K.
155 C1	Preto r. Brazil
123 C2	Pretoria S. Africa
111 B3	Preveza Greece
63 B2	Prey Vêng Cambodia
109 C2	Priboj Serbia
135 D3	Price U.S.A.
88 B3	Prienai Lith.
122 B2	Prieska S. Africa
103 D2	Prievidza Slovakia
109 C2	Prijedor Bos.-Herz.
	Prikaspiyskaya Nizmennost' lowland Kazakh./Rus. Fed. see Caspian Lowland
109 D2	Prilep Macedonia
91 D2	Primorsko-Akhtarsk Rus. Fed.
129 D2	Primrose Lake Can.
129 D2	Prince Albert Can.
122 B3	Prince Albert S. Africa

126 D2 Prince Albert Peninsula Can.
122 B3 Prince Albert Road S. Africa
126 C2 Prince Alfred, Cape Can.
122 A3 Prince Alfred Hamlet S. Africa
127 F2 Prince Charles Island Can.
55 E2 Prince Charles Mountains
Antarctica
131 D2 Prince Edward Island prov.
Can.
113 I11 Prince Edward Islands Indian
Ocean
128 B2 Prince George Can.
126 E2 Prince of Wales Island Can.
128 A2 Prince of Wales Island U.S.A.
126 D2 Prince of Wales Strait Can.
126 D1 Prince Patrick Island Can.
126 E2 Prince Regent Inlet sea chan.
Can.
128 A2 Prince Rupert Can.
51 D1 Princess Charlotte Bay Austr.
178 H2 Princess Royal Island Can.
128 B3 Princeton Can.
134 B2 Princeton U.S.A.
90 B1 Prineville U.S.A.
90 B1 Pripet r. Belarus/Ukr.
90 A1 Pripet Marshes Belarus/Ukr.
109 D2 Prishtinë Kosovo
Priština Kosovo see Prishtinë
101 F1 Pritzwalk Ger.
109 C2 Privlaka Croatia
89 F2 Privolzhsk Rus. Fed.
109 D2 Prizren Kosovo
151 C1 Professor van Blommestein
Meer resr Suriname
145 D2 Progreso Mex.
81 C1 Prokhladnyy Rus. Fed.
109 D2 Prokuplje Serbia
87 D4 Proletarskoye
Vodokhranilishche l. Rus. Fed.
126 C3 Prophet r. Can.
128 B2 Prophet River Can.
51 D2 Proserpine Austr.
89 E3 Protvino Rus. Fed.
110 C2 Provadiya Bulg.
141 E2 Providence U.S.A.
146 B3 Providencia, Isla de i.
Caribbean Sea
83 N2 Provideniya Rus. Fed.
135 D2 Provo U.S.A.
129 C2 Provost Can.
154 B3 Prudentópolis Brazil
126 B2 Prudhoe Bay U.S.A.
100 C2 Prüm Ger.
105 D3 Prunelli-di-Fiumorbo Corse
France
103 E1 Pruszków Pol.
110 C1 Prut r. Europe
91 C1 Pryluky Ukr.
91 D2 Prymors'k Ukr.
139 D1 Pryor U.S.A.
Prypyats' r. Belarus see Pripet
103 F2 Przemyśl Pol.
111 C3 Psara i. Greece
81 C1 Psebay Rus. Fed.
91 D3 Pshekha r. Rus. Fed.
88 C2 Pskov Rus. Fed.
88 C2 Pskov, Lake Estonia/Rus. Fed.
111 B2 Ptolemaïda Greece
109 C1 Ptuj Slovenia
150 A2 Pucallpa Peru
71 B3 Pucheng China
65 B2 Puch'ŏn S. Korea
103 D1 Puck Pol.
92 I1 Pudasjärvi Fin.
86 C2 Pudozh Rus. Fed.
Puducheri India see
Puducherry
73 B3 Puducherry India

145 C3 Puebla Mex.
136 C3 Pueblo U.S.A.
153 B4 Puelén Arg.
106 C2 Puente Genil Spain
153 A5 Puerto Aisén Chile
152 B2 Puerto Alegre Bol.
145 C3 Puerto Ángel Mex.
146 B4 Puerto Armuelles Panama
150 B1 Puerto Ayacucho Venez.
146 B3 Puerto Cabezas Nic.
150 B1 Puerto Carreño Col.
153 A5 Puerto Cisnes Chile
144 B2 Puerto Cortés Mex.
145 C3 Puerto Escondido Mex.
152 B2 Puerto Frey Bol.
150 B1 Puerto Inírida Col.
152 C2 Puerto Isabel Bol.
150 A2 Puerto Leguizamo Col.
144 A2 Puerto Libertad Mex.
146 B3 Puerto Limón Costa Rica
106 C2 Puertollano Spain
153 B5 Puerto Madryn Arg.
150 B3 Puerto Maldonado Peru
153 A5 Puerto Montt Chile
153 A6 Puerto Natales Chile
150 B1 Puerto Nuevo Col.
144 A1 Puerto Peñasco Mex.
152 C3 Puerto Pinasco Para.
147 C3 Puerto Plata Dom. Rep.
150 A2 Puerto Portillo Peru
64 A2 Puerto Princesa Phil.
147 D3 Puerto Rico terr. West Indies
158 B3 Puerto Rico Trench
Caribbean Sea
146 A3 Puerto San José Guat.
153 B6 Puerto Santa Cruz Arg.
144 B2 Puerto Vallarta Mex.
87 D3 Pugachev Rus. Fed.
74 B2 Pugal India
54 B2 Pukaki, Lake N.Z.
129 D2 Pukatawagan Can.
65 B1 Pukchin N. Korea
65 B1 Pukch'ŏng N. Korea
54 B1 Pukekohe N.Z.
65 B1 Puksubaek-san mt. N. Korea
108 B2 Pula Croatia
108 A3 Pula Sardegna Italy
152 B3 Pulacayo Bol.
77 C3 Pul-e Khumrī Afgh.
92 I3 Pulkkila Fin.
134 C1 Pullman U.S.A.
64 B1 Pulog, Mount Phil.
150 A2 Puná, Isla i. Ecuador
54 B2 Punakaiki N.Z.
123 D1 Punda Maria S. Africa
73 B3 Pune India
63 B1 P'ungsan N. Korea
121 C2 Púnguè r. Moz.
153 B4 Punta Alta Arg.
153 A6 Punta Arenas Chile
146 B3 Puntarenas Costa Rica
117 C4 Puntland reg. Somalia
150 A1 Punto Fijo Venez.
92 G2 Puolanka Fin.
75 C2 Puri India
100 B1 Purmerend Neth.
75 C2 Purnia India
75 C2 Puruliya India
150 B2 Purus r. Brazil/Peru
61 C2 Purwakarta Indon.
65 B1 Puryŏng N. Korea
65 B2 Pusan S. Korea
88 C2 Pushkinskiye Gory
Rus. Fed.
88 C2 Pustoshka Rus. Fed.
62 A1 Putao Myanmar

71 B3 Putian China
Puting China see De'an
61 C2 Puting, Tanjung pt Indon.
101 F1 Putlitz Ger.
60 B1 Putrajaya Malaysia
102 C1 Puttgarden Ger.
150 A2 Putumayo r. Col.
61 C1 Putusibau Indon.
91 C1 Putyvl' Ukr.
127 F2 Puvirnituq Can.
70 B2 Puyang China
104 C3 Puylaurens France
99 A4 Pwllheli U.K.
63 A2 Pyapon Myanmar
82 G2 Pyasina r. Rus. Fed.
87 D4 Pyatigorsk Rus. Fed.
91 C2 P'yatykhatky Ukr.
62 A2 Pye Myanmar
88 C3 Pyetrykaw Belarus
93 H3 Pyhäjärvi l. Fin.
93 H3 Pyhäjoki r. Fin.
92 I3 Pyhäsalmi Fin.
62 A2 Pyinmana Myanmar
65 B2 Pyŏksŏng N. Korea
65 B2 P'yŏnggang N. Korea
65 B2 P'yŏngsan N. Korea
65 B2 P'yŏngyang N. Korea
135 C2 Pyramid Lake U.S.A.
80 B3 Pyramids of Giza tourist site
Egypt
107 D1 Pyrenees mts Europe
111 B3 Pyrgos Greece
91 C1 Pyryatyn Ukr.
103 C1 Pyrzyce Pol.
88 C2 Pytalovo Rus. Fed.
111 B3 Pyxaria mt. Greece

Q

Qaanaaq Greenland see Thule
123 C3 Qacha's Nek Lesotho
68 C2 Qaidam Pendi basin China
74 A1 Qalāt Afgh.
78 B2 Qal'at Bishah Saudi Arabia
129 E1 Qamanirjuaq Lake Can.
Qamanittuaq Can. see
Baker Lake
79 C3 Qamar, Ghubbat al b. Yemen
78 B3 Qam Ḥadīl Saudi Arabia
77 C3 Qarshi Uzbek.
78 B2 Qaryat al Ulyā Saudi Arabia
127 H2 Qasigiannguit Greenland
79 D2 Qaşr-e Qand Iran
81 C2 Qaşr-e Shīrīn Iran
127 H2 Qassimiut Greenland
78 B3 Qa'tabah Yemen
79 C2 Qatar country Asia
116 A2 Qattara Depression Egypt
81 C1 Qazax Azer.
81 C2 Qazvīn Iran
127 H2 Qeqertarsuaq i. Greenland
127 H2 Qeqertarsuatsiaat Greenland
127 H2 Qeqertarsuup Tunua b.
Greenland
79 C2 Qeshm Iran
70 A3 Qianjiang Chongqing China
70 B2 Qianjiang Hubei China
65 A1 Qian Shan mts China
70 C2 Qidong China
68 B2 Qiemo China
71 A3 Qijiang China
68 C2 Qijiaojing China
127 G2 Qikiqtarjuaq Can.
74 A2 Qila Ladgasht Pak.
68 C2 Qilian Shan mts China

Qillak

127 I2 Qillak *i.* Greenland
70 B3 Qimen China
127 G1 Qimussersuaq *b.* Greenland
116 B2 Qina Egypt
70 C2 Qingdao China
68 C2 Qinghai Hu *salt l.* China
68 C2 Qinghai Nanshan *mts* China
70 A2 Qingyang *Gansu* China
71 B3 Qingyuan *Guangdong* China
65 A1 Qingyuan *Liaoning* China
       Qingzang Gaoyuan *plat.*
       China see Tibet, Plateau of
70 B2 Qingzhou China
70 B2 Qinhuangdao China
70 A2 Qin Ling *mts* China
       Qinting China see Lianhua
70 B2 Qinyang China
71 A3 Qinzhou China
71 B4 Qionghai China
68 C2 Qionglai Shan *mts* China
71 B4 Qiongshan China
69 E1 Qiqihar China
79 C2 Qīr Iran
66 B1 Qitaihe China
70 B2 Qixian China
       Qogir Feng *mt.* China/
       Pakistan see K2
81 D2 Qom Iran
       Qomolangma Feng *mt.*
       China/Nepal see
       Everest, Mount
76 B2 Qo'ng'irot Uzbek.
       Qong Muztag see Tacheng
77 D2 Qo'qon Uzbek.
76 B2 Qoraqalpog'iston Uzbek.
100 C1 Quakenbrück Ger.
63 B2 Quang Ngai Vietnam
63 B2 Quang Tri Vietnam
71 B3 Quanzhou *Fujian* China
71 B3 Quanzhou *Guangxi* China
108 A3 Quartu Sant'Elena *Sardegna*
        Italy
138 A2 Quartzsite U.S.A.
81 C1 Quba Azer.
53 C3 Queanbeyan Austr.
131 C2 Québec Can.
130 C1 Québec *prov.* Can.
101 E2 Quedlinburg Ger.
128 A2 Queen Charlotte Can.
128 B2 Queen Charlotte Sound
        sea chan. Can.
128 B2 Queen Charlotte Strait Can.
126 D1 Queen Elizabeth Islands Can.
126 E2 Queen Maud Gulf Can.
55 B2 Queen Maud Land *reg.*
       Antarctica
55 N1 Queen Maud Mountains
       Antarctica
52 B1 Queensland *state* Austr.
51 D4 Queenstown Austr.
54 A3 Queenstown N.Z.
123 C3 Queenstown S. Africa
121 C2 Quelimane Moz.
138 B2 Quemado U.S.A.
154 B2 Queréncia do Norte Brazil
145 B2 Querétaro Mex.
101 E2 Querfurt Ger.
128 B2 Quesnel Can.
128 B2 Quesnel Lake Can.
74 A1 Quetta Pak.
64 A2 Quezon Phil.
64 B1 Quezon City Phil.
120 A2 Quibala Angola
150 A1 Quibdó Col.
104 B2 Quiberon France
104 C3 Quillan France

153 C4 Quilmes Arg.
51 D2 Quilpie Austr.
153 A4 Quilpué Chile
120 A1 Quimbele Angola
152 B3 Quimili Arg.
104 B2 Quimper France
104 B2 Quimperlé France
137 D2 Quincy *IL* U.S.A.
141 E2 Quincy *MA* U.S.A.
107 C1 Quinto Spain
121 C2 Quionga Moz.
53 D2 Quirindi Austr.
121 C3 Quissico Moz.
120 A2 Quitapa Angola
150 A2 Quito Ecuador
151 E2 Quixadá Brazil
71 A3 Qujing China
52 A2 Quorn Austr.
79 C2 Qurayat Oman
77 C3 Qŭrghonteppa Tajik.
63 B2 Quy Nhơn Vietnam
71 B3 Quzhou China

R

103 D2 Raab *r.* Austria
92 H3 Raahe Fin.
100 C1 Raalte Neth.
61 C2 Raas *i.* Indon.
61 C2 Raba Indon.
114 B1 Rabat Morocco
48 E3 Rabaul P.N.G.
78 A2 Rābigh Saudi Arabia
131 E2 Race, Cape Can.
142 B3 Raceland U.S.A.
63 B3 Rach Gia Vietnam
140 B3 Racine U.S.A.
78 B3 Radā' Yemen
110 C1 Rădăuți Romania
140 B3 Radcliff U.S.A.
74 B2 Radhanpur India
130 C1 Radisson Can.
103 E1 Radom Pol.
103 D1 Radomsko Pol.
90 B1 Radomyshl' Ukr.
109 D2 Radoviš Macedonia
88 B2 Radviliškis Lith.
78 A2 Radwá, Jabal *mt.* Saudi Arabia
90 B1 Radyvyliv Ukr.
75 C2 Rae Bareli India
100 C2 Raeren Belgium
54 C1 Raetihi N.Z.
152 B4 Rafaela Arg.
118 C2 Rafaï C.A.R.
78 B2 Rafḩā' Saudi Arabia
79 C1 Rafsanjān Iran
64 B2 Ragang, Mount *vol.* Phil.
109 B3 Ragusa *Sicilia* Italy
59 C3 Raha Indon.
88 D3 Rahachow Belarus
74 B2 Rahimyar Khan Pak.
109 D2 Rahovec Kosovo
73 B3 Raichur India
75 C2 Raigarh India
128 C2 Rainbow Lake Can.
134 B1 Rainier, Mount *vol.* U.S.A.
130 A2 Rainy Lake Can./U.S.A.
129 E3 Rainy River Can.
75 C2 Raipur India
93 H3 Raisio Fin.
73 C2 Rajahmundry India
61 C1 Rajang *r.* Sarawak Malaysia
74 B2 Rajanpur India
73 B4 Rajapalayam India
74 B2 Rajasthan Canal India

74 B2 Rajgarh India
74 B2 Rajkot India
74 B2 Rajpur India
75 C2 Rajshahi Bangl.
54 B2 Rakaia *r.* N.Z.
90 A2 Rakhiv Ukr.
91 D1 Rakitnoye Rus. Fed.
88 C2 Rakke Estonia
88 C2 Rakvere Estonia
143 E1 Raleigh U.S.A.
48 F2 Ralik Chain *is* Marshall Is
74 B2 Ramgarh India
81 C2 Rāmhormoz Iran
       Ramlat Rabyānah *des.* Libya
       see Rebiana Sand Sea
110 C1 Râmnicu Sărat Romania
110 B1 Râmnicu Vâlcea Romania
89 E3 Ramon' Rus. Fed.
123 C1 Ramotswa Botswana
75 B2 Rampur India
62 A2 Ramree Island Myanmar
98 A1 Ramsey Isle of Man
99 D3 Ramsgate U.K.
75 C2 Ranaghat India
61 C1 Ranau *Sabah* Malaysia
153 A4 Rancagua Chile
75 C2 Ranchi India
93 F4 Randers Denmark
54 B2 Rangiora N.Z.
54 C1 Rangitaiki *r.* N.Z.
62 A2 Rangoon Myanmar
75 C2 Rangpur Bangl.
129 E1 Rankin Inlet Can.
53 C2 Rankin's Springs Austr.
96 B2 Rannoch Moor *moorland* U.K.
63 A3 Ranong Thai.
59 C3 Ransiki Indon.
61 C2 Rantaupanjang Indon.
60 A1 Rantauprapat Indon.
92 I2 Ranua Fin.
78 B2 Ranyah, Wādī *watercourse*
       Saudi Arabia
49 I4 Rapa *i.* Fr. Polynesia
136 C2 Rapid City U.S.A.
88 B2 Rapla Estonia
74 A2 Rapur India
49 H4 Rarotonga *i.* Cook Is
153 B5 Rasa, Punta *pt* Arg.
79 C2 Ra's al Khaymah U.A.E.
117 B3 Ras Dejen *mt.* Eth.
88 B2 Raseiniai Lith.
81 C2 Rasht Iran
74 A2 Ras Koh *mt.* Pak.
88 C2 Rasony Belarus
87 D3 Rasskazovo Rus. Fed.
79 C2 Ras Tannūrah Saudi Arabia
101 D1 Rastede Ger.
93 F3 Rätan Sweden
74 B2 Ratangarh India
63 A2 Rat Buri Thai.
62 A1 Rathedaung Myanmar
101 F1 Rathenow Ger.
113 B2 Rathlin Island U.K.
74 B2 Ratlam India
73 B3 Ratnagiri India
73 C4 Ratnapura Sri Lanka
90 A1 Ratne Ukr.
138 C1 Raton U.S.A.
96 D2 Rattray Head U.K.
101 E1 Ratzeburg Ger.
92 □B2 Raufarhöfn Iceland
54 C1 Raukumara Range *mts* N.Z.
93 H3 Rauma Fin.
61 C2 Raung, Gunung *vol.* Indon.
75 C2 Raurkela India
134 D1 Ravalli U.S.A.
81 C2 Rāvānsar Iran

108 B2	Ravenna Italy	
102 B2	Ravensburg Ger.	
74 B1	Ravi r. Pak.	
74 B1	Rawalpindi Pak.	
103 C1	Rawicz Pol.	
50 B3	Rawlinna Austr.	
136 B2	Rawlins U.S.A.	
153 B5	Rawson Arg.	
73 C3	Rayagada India	
69 E1	Raychikhinsk Rus. Fed.	
78 B3	Raydah Yemen	
87 E3	Rayevskiy Rus. Fed.	
134 B1	Raymond U.S.A.	
53 D2	Raymond Terrace Austr.	
139 D3	Raymondville U.S.A.	
145 C2	Rayón Mex.	
63 B2	Rayong Thai.	
78 A2	Rayyis Saudi Arabia	
104 B2	Raz, Pointe du pt France	
81 C2	Raanānah, Buhayrat ar l. Iraq	
110 C2	Razgrad Bulg.	
110 C2	Razim, Lacul lag. Romania	
110 B2	Razlog Bulg.	
104 B2	Ré, Île de i. France	
99 C3	Reading U.K.	
141 D2	Reading U.S.A.	
115 E2	Rebiana Sand Sea des. Libya	
66 D1	Rebun-tō i. Japan	
50 B3	Recherche, Archipelago of the is Austr.	
89 D3	Rechytsa Belarus	
151 E2	Recife Brazil	
123 C3	Recife, Cape S. Africa	
100 C2	Recklinghausen Ger.	
152 G3	Reconquista Arg.	
142 B2	Red r. U.S.A.	
131 E1	Red Bay Can.	
135 B2	Red Bluff U.S.A.	
98 C1	Redcar U.K.	
129 C2	Redcliff Can.	
52 B2	Red Cliffs Austr.	
128 C2	Red Deer Can.	
126 D3	Red Deer r. Can.	
129 D2	Red Deer Lake Can.	
134 B2	Redding U.S.A.	
99 C2	Redditch U.K.	
137 D2	Redfield U.S.A.	
130 A1	Red Lake Can.	
137 E1	Red Lakes U.S.A.	
134 C1	Red Lodge U.S.A.	
134 B2	Redmond U.S.A.	
137 D2	Red Oak U.S.A.	
106 B2	Redondo Port.	
159 B2	Red Sea Africa/Asia	
128 B1	Redstone r. Can.	
100 B1	Reduzum Neth.	
137 E2	Red Wing U.S.A.	
137 D2	Redwood Falls U.S.A.	
97 C2	Ree, Lough l. Ireland	
134 B2	Reedsport U.S.A.	
54 B2	Reefton N.Z.	
102 C2	Regen Ger.	
155 E1	Regência Brazil	
102 C2	Regensburg Ger.	
114 C2	Reggane Alg.	
109 C3	Reggio di Calabria Italy	
108 B2	Reggio nell'Emilia Italy	
110 B1	Reghin Romania	
129 D2	Regina Can.	
122 A1	Rehoboth Namibia	
101 F2	Reichenbach Ger.	
143 E1	Reidsville U.S.A.	
99 C3	Reigate U.K.	
105 C2	Reims France	
101 E1	Reinbek Ger.	
129 D2	Reindeer r. Can.	
129 E2	Reindeer Island Can.	

129 D2	Reindeer Lake Can.	
92 F2	Reine Norway	
100 C3	Reinsfeld Ger.	
123 C2	Reitz S. Africa	
122 B2	Reivilo S. Africa	
129 D1	Reliance Can.	
107 D2	Relizane Alg.	
79 C2	Remeshk Iran	
105 D2	Remiremont France	
100 C2	Remscheid Ger.	
102 B1	Rendsburg Ger.	
141 D1	Renfrew Can.	
60 B2	Rengat Indon.	
90 B2	Reni Ukr.	
52 B2	Renmark Austr.	
100 D2	Rennerod Ger.	
104 B2	Rennes France	
129 D1	Rennie Lake Can.	
108 B2	Reno r. Italy	
135 C3	Reno U.S.A.	
70 A3	Renshou China	
75 C2	Renukut India	
54 B2	Renwick N.Z.	
58 C3	Reo Indon.	
136 D3	Republican r. U.S.A.	
127 F2	Repulse Bay Can.	
150 A2	Requena Peru	
107 C2	Requena Spain	
154 B2	Reserva Brazil	
152 C3	Resistencia Arg.	
110 B1	Reşiţa Romania	
126 F2	Resolute Can.	
127 G2	Resolution Island Can.	
105 C2	Rethel France	
111 B3	Rethymno Greece	
113 K9	Réunion terr. Indian Ocean	
107 D1	Reus Spain	
102 B2	Reutlingen Ger.	
128 C2	Revelstoke Can.	
144 A3	Revillagigedo, Islas is Mex.	
128 A2	Revillagigedo Island U.S.A.	
75 C2	Rewa India	
134 D2	Rexburg U.S.A.	
92 □A3	Reykjanestá pt Iceland	
92 □A3	Reykjavík Iceland	
145 C2	Reynosa Mex.	
88 C2	Rēzekne Latvia	
	Rhein r. Ger. see Rhine	
100 C1	Rheine Ger.	
101 F1	Rheinsberg Ger.	
	Rhin r. France see Rhine	
100 C2	Rhine r. Europe	
140 B1	Rhinelander U.S.A.	
101 F1	Rhinluch marsh Ger.	
101 F1	Rhinow Ger.	
141 E2	Rhode Island state U.S.A.	
111 C3	Rhodes Greece	
111 C3	Rhodes i. Greece	
110 B2	Rhodope Mountains Bulg./Greece	
	Rhône r. France/Switz.	
105 C3	Rhône r. France/Switz.	
	Rhuthun U.K. see Ruthin	
98 B2	Rhyl U.K.	
154 C1	Rianópolis Brazil	
60 B1	Riau, Kepulauan is Indon.	
106 B1	Ribadeo Spain	
106 B1	Ribadesella Spain	
154 B2	Ribas do Rio Pardo Brazil	
121 C2	Ribáuè Moz.	
98 B2	Ribble r. U.K.	
154 C2	Ribeira r. Brazil	
154 C2	Ribeirão Preto Brazil	
104 C2	Ribérac France	
152 B2	Riberalta Bol.	
90 B2	Rîbniţa Moldova	
102 C1	Ribnitz-Damgarten Ger.	

140 A1	Rice Lake U.S.A.	
123 D2	Richards Bay S. Africa	
126 B2	Richardson Mountains Can.	
135 D3	Richfield U.S.A.	
134 C1	Richland U.S.A.	
140 A2	Richland Center U.S.A.	
53 D2	Richmond N.S.W. Austr.	
51 D2	Richmond Qld Austr.	
54 B2	Richmond N.Z.	
122 B3	Richmond S. Africa	
98 C1	Richmond U.K.	
140 C3	Richmond IN U.S.A.	
140 C3	Richmond KY U.S.A.	
141 D3	Richmond VA U.S.A.	
130 C2	Rideau Lakes Can.	
135 C3	Ridgecrest U.S.A.	
102 C1	Riesa Ger.	
100 D1	Rieste Ger.	
123 B2	Riet r. S. Africa	
101 D2	Rietberg Ger.	
108 B2	Rieti Italy	
136 B3	Rifle U.S.A.	
88 B2	Rīga Latvia	
88 B2	Riga, Gulf of Estonia/Latvia	
79 C2	Rīgān Iran	
134 D2	Rigby U.S.A.	
131 E1	Rigolet Can.	
93 H3	Riihimäki Fin.	
108 B1	Rijeka Croatia	
134 C2	Riley U.S.A.	
78 B2	Rimah, Wādī al watercourse Saudi Arabia	
103 E2	Rimavská Sobota Slovakia	
128 C2	Rimbey Can.	
100 D2	Rinteln Ger.	
131 D2	Rimouski Can.	
93 F3	Ringebu Norway	
93 E4	Ringkøbing Denmark	
92 G2	Ringvassøya i. Norway	
101 D1	Rinteln Ger.	
150 A2	Riobamba Ecuador	
150 B3	Rio Branco Brazil	
154 C3	Rio Branco do Sul Brazil	
154 B2	Rio Brilhante Brazil	
154 C2	Rio Claro Brazil	
153 B4	Río Colorado Arg.	
153 B4	Río Cuarto Arg.	
155 D2	Rio de Janeiro Brazil	
153 B6	Río Gallegos Arg.	
153 B6	Río Grande Arg.	
152 C4	Rio Grande Brazil	
144 B2	Río Grande Mex.	
139 D3	Rio Grande r. Mex./U.S.A.	
139 D3	Rio Grande City U.S.A.	
150 A1	Ríohacha Col.	
150 A2	Rioja Peru	
145 D2	Río Lagartos Mex.	
105 C2	Riom France	
152 B2	Río Mulatos Bol.	
154 B3	Rio Negro Brazil	
155 D1	Rio Pardo de Minas Brazil	
138 B1	Rio Rancho U.S.A.	
150 A2	Río Tigre Ecuador	
154 B1	Rio Verde Brazil	
145 C2	Río Verde Mex.	
154 B1	Rio Verde de Mato Grosso Brazil	
90 C1	Ripky Ukr.	
98 C2	Ripley U.K.	
107 D1	Ripoll Spain	
98 C1	Ripon U.K.	
66 D1	Rishiri-tō i. Japan	
93 E4	Risør Norway	
122 B2	Ritchie S. Africa	
63 A2	Ritchie's Archipelago is India	
134 C1	Ritzville U.S.A.	
152 B3	Rivadavia Arg.	

108 B1 Riva del Garda Italy
146 B3 Rivas Nic.
152 C4 Rivera Uru.
129 D2 Riverhurst Can.
52 B2 Riverina reg. Austr.
122 B3 Riversdale S. Africa
135 C4 Riverside U.S.A.
136 B2 Riverton U.S.A.
131 D2 Riverview Can.
104 C3 Rivesaltes France
131 D2 Rivière-du-Loup Can.
90 B1 Rivne Ukr.
54 B2 Riwaka N.Z.
78 B2 Riyadh Saudi Arabia
81 C1 Rize Turkey
70 D2 Rizhao China
105 C2 Roanne France
141 D3 Roanoke U.S.A.
143 E1 Roanoke r. U.S.A.
143 E1 Roanoke Rapids U.S.A.
52 A3 Robe Austr.
101 F1 Röbel Ger.
130 C1 Robert-Bourassa, Réservoir resr Can.
92 H3 Robertsfors Sweden
122 A3 Robertson S. Africa
114 A4 Robertsport Liberia
106 C2 Roberval Can.
50 A2 Robinson Ranges hills Austr.
52 B2 Robinvale Austr.
129 D2 Roblin Can.
128 C2 Robson, Mount Can.
108 B3 Rocca Busamba mt. Sicilia Italy
153 C4 Rocha Uru.
98 B2 Rochdale U.K.
154 B1 Rochedo Brazil
100 B2 Rochefort Belgium
104 B2 Rochefort France
137 E2 Rochester MN U.S.A.
141 E2 Rochester NH U.S.A.
141 D2 Rochester NY U.S.A.
140 B2 Rockford U.S.A.
51 E2 Rockhampton Austr.
54 C1 Rock Hill U.S.A.
50 A3 Rockingham Austr.
140 A2 Rock Island U.S.A.
136 B1 Rock Springs MT U.S.A.
139 C3 Rocksprings U.S.A.
136 B2 Rock Springs WY U.S.A.
136 C3 Rocky Ford U.S.A.
143 E1 Rocky Mount U.S.A.
128 C2 Rocky Mountain House Can.
124 G3 Rocky Mountains Can./U.S.A.
100 B3 Rocroi France
102 C1 Rødbyhavn Denmark
131 E1 Roddickton Can.
104 C3 Rodez France
89 F2 Rodniki Rus. Fed.
    Rodos Greece see Rhodes
    Rodos i. Greece see Rhodes
50 A2 Roebourne Austr.
50 B1 Roebuck Bay Austr.
123 C1 Roedtan S. Africa
100 B2 Roermond Neth.
100 A2 Roeselare Belgium
127 F2 Roes Welcome Sound sea chan. Can.
142 B1 Rogers U.S.A.
122 B3 Roggeveldberge esc. S. Africa
92 G2 Rognan Norway
134 B2 Rogue r. U.S.A.
88 B2 Roja Latvia
60 B1 Rokan r. Indon.
88 C2 Rokiškis Lith.
90 B1 Rokytne Ukr.
154 B2 Rolândia Brazil

137 E3 Rolla U.S.A.
51 D2 Roma Austr.
    Roma Italy see Rome
123 C2 Roma Lesotho
139 D3 Roma U.S.A.
143 E2 Romain, Cape U.S.A.
110 C1 Roman Romania
59 C3 Romang, Pulau i. Indon.
110 B1 Romania country Europe
91 C3 Roman-Kosh mt. Ukr.
69 D1 Romanovka Rus. Fed.
105 D2 Rombas France
64 B1 Romblon Phil.
108 B2 Rome Italy
143 C2 Rome GA U.S.A.
141 D2 Rome NY U.S.A.
99 D3 Romford U.K.
105 C2 Romilly-sur-Seine France
91 C1 Romny Ukr.
104 C2 Romorantin-Lanthenay France
99 C3 Romsey U.K.
96 □ Ronas Hill U.K.
151 C3 Roncador, Serra do hills Brazil
106 B2 Ronda Spain
154 B2 Rondon Brazil
154 B1 Rondonópolis Brazil
74 B1 Rondu Pak.
71 A3 Rong'an China
71 A3 Rongjiang China
62 A1 Rongklang Range mts Myanmar
    Rongmei China see Hefeng
93 F4 Rønne Denmark
55 P2 Ronne Ice Shelf Antarctica
101 D1 Ronnenberg Ger.
100 A2 Ronse Belgium
75 B2 Roorkee India
100 B2 Roosendaal Neth.
135 E2 Roosevelt U.S.A.
128 B2 Roosevelt, Mount Can.
55 K2 Roosevelt Island Antarctica
104 B3 Roquefort France
150 B1 Roraima, Mount Guyana
93 F3 Røros Norway
153 B4 Rosario Arg.
144 A1 Rosario Baja California Mex.
144 B2 Rosario Sinaloa Mex.
144 B2 Rosario Sonora Mex.
151 C3 Rosário Oeste Brazil
144 A2 Rosarito Mex.
109 C3 Rosarno Italy
104 B2 Roscoff France
97 B2 Roscommon Ireland
97 C2 Roscrea Ireland
147 D3 Roseau Dominica
137 D1 Roseau U.S.A.
134 B2 Roseburg U.S.A.
139 D3 Rosenberg U.S.A.
101 D1 Rosengarten Ger.
102 C2 Rosenheim Ger.
129 D2 Rosetown Can.
122 A2 Rosh Pinah Namibia
110 C2 Roșiori de Vede Romania
93 F4 Roskilde Denmark
89 D3 Roslavl' Rus. Fed.
109 C3 Rossano Italy
97 B1 Rossan Point Ireland
55 K1 Ross Ice Shelf Antarctica
131 D2 Rossignol, Lake Can.
89 C3 Rossland Can.
97 C2 Rosslare Ireland
114 A3 Rosso Maur.
105 D3 Rosso, Capo c. Corse France
99 B3 Ross-on-Wye U.K.
91 D1 Rossosh' Rus. Fed.
128 A1 Ross River Can.
55 K2 Ross Sea Antarctica

92 F2 Røssvatnet l. Norway
79 C2 Rostāq Iran
129 D2 Rosthern Can.
102 C1 Rostock Ger.
89 E2 Rostov Rus. Fed.
91 D2 Rostov-na-Donu Rus. Fed.
92 H2 Rosvik Sweden
138 C2 Roswell U.S.A.
59 D2 Rota i. N. Mariana Is
59 C3 Rote i. Indon.
101 D1 Rotenburg (Wümme) Ger.
102 C2 Roth Ger.
98 C1 Rothbury U.K.
98 C2 Rotherham U.K.
96 B3 Rothesay U.K.
53 C2 Roto Austr.
105 D3 Rotondo, Monte mt. Corse France
54 C1 Rotorua N.Z.
54 C1 Rotorua, Lake N.Z.
101 E2 Rottenbach Ger.
102 C2 Rottenmann Austria
100 B2 Rotterdam Neth.
102 C2 Rottweil Ger.
49 F3 Rotuma i. Fiji
105 C1 Roubaix France
104 C2 Rouen France
    Roulers Belgium see Roeselare
53 D2 Round Mountain Austr.
131 E2 Round Pond l. Can.
139 D2 Round Rock U.S.A.
134 E1 Roundup U.S.A.
96 C1 Rousay i. U.K.
130 C2 Rouyn-Noranda Can.
92 I2 Rovaniemi Fin.
91 D2 Roven'ki Rus. Fed.
91 D2 Roven'ky Ukr.
108 B1 Rovereto Italy
63 B2 Rôviêng Tbong Cambodia
108 B1 Rovigo Italy
108 B1 Rovinj Croatia
53 C1 Rowena Austr.
64 B1 Roxas Capiz Phil.
64 B1 Roxas Oriental Mindoro Phil.
64 A1 Roxas Palawan Phil.
52 A2 Roxby Downs Austr.
138 C1 Roy U.S.A.
140 B1 Royale, Isle i. U.S.A.
104 B2 Royan France
99 C2 Royston U.K.
90 C2 Rozdil'na Ukr.
91 C2 Rozdol'ne Ukr.
100 B3 Rozoy-sur-Serre France
87 D3 Rtishchevo Rus. Fed.
54 C1 Ruapehu, Mount vol. N.Z.
54 A3 Ruapuke Island N.Z.
78 B3 Rub' al Khālī des. Saudi Arabia
91 D2 Rubizhne Ukr.
77 E1 Rubtsovsk Rus. Fed.
135 C2 Ruby Mountains U.S.A.
66 C2 Rudnaya Pristan' Rus. Fed.
89 D3 Rudnya Rus. Fed.
76 C1 Rudnyy Kazakh.
101 E2 Rudol'fa, Ostrov i. Rus. Fed.
101 E2 Rudolstadt Ger.
119 D3 Rufiji r. Tanz.
153 B4 Rufino Arg.
121 B2 Rufunsa Zambia
70 C2 Rugao China
99 C2 Rugby U.K.
136 C1 Rugby U.S.A.
102 C1 Rügen i. Ger.
101 E2 Ruhla Ger.
88 B2 Ruhnu i. Estonia
100 C2 Ruhr r. Ger.
71 C3 Rui'an China
138 B2 Ruidoso U.S.A.

144	B2	Ruiz Mex.
119	D3	Rukwa, Lake Tanz.
96	A2	Rum i. U.K.
109	C1	Ruma Serbia
78	B2	Rumāh Saudi Arabia
117	A4	Rumbek S. Sudan
105	D2	Rumilly France
50	C1	Rum Jungle Austr.
54	B2	Runanga N.Z.
98	B2	Runcorn U.K.
120	A2	Rundu Namibia
68	B2	Ruoqiang China
130	C1	Rupert r. Can.
130	C1	Rupert Bay Can.
121	C2	Rusape Zimbabwe
110	C2	Ruse Bulg.
77	D3	Rushon Tajik.
136	C2	Rushville U.S.A.
53	C3	Rushworth Austr.
129	D2	Russell Can.
54	B1	Russell N.Z.
142	C2	Russellville AL U.S.A.
142	B1	Russellville AR U.S.A.
140	B3	Russellville KY U.S.A.
101	D2	Rüsselsheim Ger.
82	F2	Russian Federation country Asia/Europe
123	C2	Rustenburg S. Africa
142	B1	Ruston U.S.A.
98	B2	Ruthin U.K.
141	E2	Rutland U.S.A.
119	E4	Ruvuma r. Moz./Tanz.
79	C2	Ruweis U.A.E.
77	C1	Ruzayevka Kazakh.
87	D3	Ruzayevka Rus. Fed.
119	C3	Rwanda country Africa
89	E3	Ryazan' Rus. Fed.
89	F3	Ryazhsk Rus. Fed.
86	C2	Rybachiy, Poluostrov pen. Rus. Fed.
89	E2	Rybinsk Rus. Fed.
89	E2	Rybinskoye Vodokhranilishche resr Rus. Fed.
103	D2	Rybnik Pol.
89	E3	Rybnoye Rus. Fed.
99	D3	Rye U.K.
89	D3	Ryl'sk Rus. Fed.
67	C3	Ryotsu Japan
69	E3	Ryukyu Islands Japan
103	E1	Rzeszów Pol.
89	D2	Rzhev Rus. Fed.

S

79	C2	Sa'ādatābād Iran
101	E2	Saale r. Ger.
101	E2	Saalfeld Ger.
102	B2	Saarbrücken Ger.
88	B2	Saaremaa i. Estonia
92	I2	Saarenkylä Fin.
93	I3	Saarijärvi Fin.
102	B2	Saarlouis Ger.
80	B2	Sab' Ābār Syria
107	D1	Sabadell Spain
61	C1	Sabah state Malaysia
61	C2	Sabalana i. Indon.
155	D1	Sabará Brazil
108	B2	Sabaudia Italy
115	D2	Sabhā Libya
123	D2	Sabie r. Moz./S. Africa
145	B2	Sabinas Mex.
145	B2	Sabinas Hidalgo Mex.
131	D2	Sable, Cape Can.
143	D3	Sable, Cape U.S.A.
131	E2	Sable Island Can.
106	B1	Sabugal Port.
78	B3	Şabyā Saudi Arabia
76	B3	Sabzevār Iran
120	A2	Sachanga Angola
130	A1	Sachigo Lake Can.
65	B3	Sach'on S. Korea
126	C2	Sachs Harbour Can.
135	B3	Sacramento U.S.A.
138	B2	Sacramento Mountains U.S.A.
135	B2	Sacramento Valley U.S.A.
123	C3	Sada S. Africa
107	C1	Sádaba Spain
78	B3	Şa'dah Yemen
62	A1	Sadiya India
67	C3	Sadoga-shima i. Japan
107	D2	Sa Dragonera i. Spain
93	F4	Säffle Sweden
138	B2	Safford U.S.A.
99	D2	Saffron Walden U.K.
114	B1	Safi Morocco
86	D2	Safonovo Arkhangel'skaya Oblast' Rus. Fed.
89	D2	Safonovo Smolenskaya Oblast' Rus. Fed.
75	C2	Saga China
67	B4	Saga Japan
62	A1	Sagaing Myanmar
67	C3	Sagamihara Japan
75	B2	Sagar India
140	C2	Saginaw U.S.A.
140	C2	Saginaw Bay U.S.A.
106	B2	Segres Port.
146	B2	Sagua la Grande Cuba
141	F1	Saguenay r. Can.
107	C2	Sagunto Spain
76	B2	Sagyndyk, Mys pt Kazakh.
106	B1	Sahagún Spain
114	C3	Sahara des. Africa
		Saharan Atlas mts Alg. see Atlas Saharien
75	B2	Saharanpur India
75	C2	Saharsa India
114	B3	Sahel reg. Africa
144	B2	Sahuayo Mex.
78	B2	Şāhūq reg. Saudi Arabia
		Saïda Lebanon see Sidon
75	C2	Saidpur Bangl.
		Saigon Vietnam see Ho Chi Minh City
62	A1	Saiha India
69	D2	Saihan Tal China
67	B4	Saiki Japan
93	I3	Saimaa l. Fin.
144	B2	Sain Alto Mex.
96	C3	St Abb's Head U.K.
99	C3	St Albans U.K.
99	B3	St Aldhelm's Head U.K.
96	C2	St Andrews U.K.
131	E1	St Anthony Can.
134	D2	St Anthony U.S.A.
52	B3	St Arnaud Austr.
131	E1	St-Augustin Can.
131	E1	St-Augustin r. Can.
143	D3	St Augustine U.S.A.
99	A3	St Austell U.K.
104	C2	St-Avertin France
98	B1	St Bees Head U.K.
105	D3	St-Bonnet-en-Champsaur France
99	A3	St Bride's Bay U.K.
104	B2	St-Brieuc France
99	C3	St Catharines Can.
99	C3	St Catherine's Point U.K.
137	E3	St Charles U.S.A.
140	C2	St Clair, Lake Can./U.S.A.
105	D2	St-Claude France
137	E1	St Cloud U.S.A.
140	A1	St Croix r. U.S.A.
147	D3	St Croix i. Virgin Is (U.S.A.)
105	C2	St-Dizier France
131	D2	Ste-Anne-des-Monts Can.
105	D2	St-Égrève France
126	B2	St Elias Mountains Can.
131	D1	Ste-Marguerite r. Can.
129	E2	Sainte Rose du Lac Can.
104	B2	Saintes France
105	C2	St-Étienne France
108	A2	St-Florent Corse France
105	C2	St-Flour France
136	C3	St Francis U.S.A.
104	C3	St-Gaudens France
53	C1	St George Austr.
135	D3	St George U.S.A.
143	D3	St George Island U.S.A.
131	C2	St-Georges Can.
147	D3	St George's Grenada
97	C3	St George's Channel Ireland/U.K.
105	D2	St Gotthard Pass Switz.
113	F8	St Helena terr. S. Atlantic Ocean
122	A3	St Helena Bay S. Africa
122	A3	St Helena Bay S. Africa
98	B2	St Helens U.K.
134	B1	St Helens, Mount vol. U.S.A.
95	C4	St Helier Channel Is
100	B2	St-Hubert Belgium
141	E1	St-Hyacinthe Can.
140	C1	St Ignace U.S.A.
130	B2	St Ignace Island Can.
99	A3	St Ives U.K.
128	A2	St James, Cape Can.
131	C2	St-Jean, Lac l. Can.
104	B2	St-Jean-d'Angély France
104	B2	St-Jean-de-Monts France
130	C2	St-Jean-sur-Richelieu Can.
141	E1	St-Jérôme Can.
134	C1	St Joe r. U.S.A.
131	D2	Saint John Can.
141	F1	St John r. U.S.A.
147	D3	St John's Antigua
131	E2	St John's Can.
138	B2	St Johns U.S.A.
141	E2	St Johnsbury U.S.A.
137	E3	St Joseph U.S.A.
130	A1	St Joseph, Lake Can.
130	B2	St Joseph Island Can.
104	C2	St-Junien France
94	B2	St Kilda is U.K.
147	D3	St Kitts and Nevis country West Indies
		St Lawrence, Golfe du g. Can. see St Lawrence, Gulf of
151	C1	St-Laurent-du-Maroni Fr. Guiana
131	D2	St Lawrence inlet Can.
131	D2	St Lawrence, Gulf of Can.
83	N2	St Lawrence Island U.S.A.
104	B2	St Lô France
114	A3	St-Louis Senegal
137	E3	St Louis U.S.A.
137	E1	St Louis r. U.S.A.
147	D3	St Lucia country West Indies
123	D2	St Lucia Estuary S. Africa
104	B2	St-Malo France
104	B2	St-Malo, Golfe de g. France
122	A3	St Martin, Cape S. Africa
141	D2	St Marys U.S.A.
130	C2	St-Maurice r. Can.
104	B2	St-Nazaire France
104	C1	St-Omer France
129	C2	St Paul Can.
137	E2	St Paul U.S.A.

137 E2	St Peter U.S.A.
95 C4	St Peter Port Channel Is
89 D2	St Petersburg Rus. Fed.
143 D3	St Petersburg U.S.A.
131 E2	St-Pierre St Pierre and Miquelon
131 E2	St Pierre and Miquelon terr. N. America
104 B2	St-Pierre-d'Oléron France
105 C2	St-Pourçain-sur-Sioule France
131 D2	St Quentin Can.
105 C2	St-Quentin France
131 D2	St-Siméon Can.
129 E2	St Theresa Point Can.
130 B2	St Thomas Can.
105 D3	St-Tropez France
105 D3	St-Tropez, Cap de c. France
52 A3	St Vincent, Gulf Austr.
147 D3	St Vincent and the Grenadines country West Indies
100 C3	St-Vith Belgium
129 D3	St Walburg Can.
104 C2	St-Yrieix-la-Perche France
59 D1	Saipan i. N. Mariana Is
152 B3	Sajama, Nevado mt. Bol.
122 B2	Sak watercourse S. Africa
67 C4	Sakai Japan
67 B4	Sakaide Japan
78 B3	Sakākah Saudi Arabia
136 C1	Sakakawea, Lake U.S.A.
111 D2	Sakarya r. Turkey
66 C3	Sakata Japan
65 B1	Sakchu N. Korea
83 K3	Sakhalin i. Rus. Fed.
123 C2	Sakhile S. Africa
81 C1	Şäki Azer.
88 B3	Sakiai Lith.
69 E3	Sakishima-shotō is Japan
85 A3	Sakrivier S. Africa
122 B3	Sakon Nakhon Thai.
67 D3	Sakura Japan
91 C2	Saky Ukr.
93 G4	Sala Sweden
130 C2	Salaberry-de-Valleyfield Can.
88 B2	Salacgrīva Latvia
109 C2	Sala Consilina Italy
135 C4	Salada, Laguna salt l. Mex.
152 B4	Salado r. Arg.
145 C2	Salado r. Mex.
114 B4	Salaga Ghana
122 B1	Salajwe Botswana
115 D3	Salal Chad
78 A2	Salāla Sudan
79 C3	Şalālah Oman
145 B2	Salamanca Mex.
106 B1	Salamanca Spain
106 B1	Salas Spain
63 B2	Salavan Laos
59 C3	Salawati i. Indon.
104 C2	Salbris France
88 C3	Šalčininkai Lith.
106 C1	Saldaña Spain
122 A3	Saldanha S. Africa
88 B2	Saldus Latvia
53 C3	Sale Austr.
86 F2	Salekhard Rus. Fed.
73 B3	Salem India
137 E3	Salem MO U.S.A.
134 B2	Salem OR U.S.A.
96 B2	Salen U.K.
109 B2	Salerno Italy
98 B2	Salford U.K.
151 E2	Salgado r. Brazil
103 D2	Salgótarján Hungary
151 E2	Salgueiro Brazil
136 B3	Salida U.S.A.
111 C3	Salihli Turkey
88 C3	Salihorsk Belarus
121 C2	Salima Malawi
121 C2	Salimo Moz.
137 D3	Salina U.S.A.
108 B3	Salina, Isola i. Italy
145 C3	Salina Cruz Mex.
155 D1	Salinas Brazil
144 B2	Salinas Mex.
135 B3	Salinas U.S.A.
107 D2	Salinas, Cap de ses c. Spain
151 E2	Salinópolis Brazil
99 C3	Salisbury U.K.
141 D3	Salisbury MD U.S.A.
143 D1	Salisbury NC U.S.A.
99 B3	Salisbury Plain U.K.
151 D2	Salitre r. Brazil
92 I2	Salla Fin.
127 F2	Salluit Can.
75 C2	Sallyana Nepal
81 C2	Salmäs Iran
134 D1	Salmon U.S.A.
134 C1	Salmon r. U.S.A.
128 C2	Salmon Arm Can.
134 C2	Salmon River Mountains U.S.A.
100 C3	Salmtal Ger.
93 H3	Salo Fin.
87 D4	Sal'sk Rus. Fed.
122 B3	Salt watercourse S. Africa
138 A2	Salt r. U.S.A.
152 B3	Salta Arg.
145 B2	Saltillo Mex.
134 D2	Salt Lake City U.S.A.
154 C2	Salto Brazil
154 C2	Salto Uru.
155 E1	Salto da Divisa Brazil
154 B2	Salto del Guairá Para.
135 C4	Salton Sea salt l. U.S.A.
143 D2	Saluda U.S.A.
108 A2	Saluzzo Italy
151 E3	Salvador Brazil
79 C2	Salwah Saudi Arabia
62 A1	Salween r. China/Myanmar
81 C2	Salyan Azer.
102 C2	Salzburg Austria
101 E1	Salzgitter Ger.
101 D2	Salzkotten Ger.
101 E1	Salzwedel Ger.
144 B1	Samalayuca Mex.
66 D2	Samani Japan
64 B1	Samar i. Phil.
87 E3	Samara Rus. Fed.
61 C2	Samarinda Indon.
77 C3	Samarqand Uzbek.
81 C2	Sāmarrā' Iraq
81 C1	Şamaxı Azer.
119 C3	Samba Dem. Rep. Congo
61 C1	Sambaliung mts Indon.
75 C2	Sambalpur India
61 C1	Sambar, Tanjung pt Indon.
61 B1	Sambas Indon.
121 □E2	Sambava Madag.
90 A2	Sambir Ukr.
153 C4	Samborombón, Bahía b. Arg.
65 B2	Samch'ŏk S. Korea
81 C2	Samdi Dag mt. Turkey
119 D3	Same Tanz.
78 B2	Samirah Saudi Arabia
65 B1	Samjiyŏn N. Korea
49 G3	Samoa country S. Pacific Ocean
109 C1	Samobor Croatia
111 C3	Samos i. Greece
111 C3	Samothraki Greece
111 C2	Samothraki i. Greece
61 C2	Sampit Indon.
119 C3	Sampwe Dem. Rep. Congo
139 E2	Sam Rayburn Reservoir U.S.A.
80 B1	Samsun Turkey
81 C1	Samt'redia Georgia
63 B2	Samui, Ko i. Thai.
63 B2	Samut Songkhram Thai.
114 B3	San Mali
78 B3	Şan'ā' Yemen
118 A2	Sanaga r. Cameroon
81 C2	Sanandaj Iran
146 B3	San Andrés, Isla de i. Caribbean Sea
138 B2	San Andres Mountains U.S.A.
145 C3	San Andrés Tuxtla Mex.
139 C2	San Angelo U.S.A.
139 D3	San Antonio U.S.A.
135 C4	San Antonio, Mount U.S.A.
152 B3	San Antonio de los Cobres Arg.
153 B5	San Antonio Oeste Arg.
108 B2	San Benedetto del Tronto Italy
144 A3	San Benedicto, Isla i. Mex.
135 C4	San Bernardino U.S.A.
135 C4	San Bernardino Mountains U.S.A.
143 C3	San Blas, Cape U.S.A.
152 B2	San Borja Bol.
144 B2	San Buenaventura Mex.
64 B1	San Carlos Phil.
147 D4	San Carlos Venez.
153 A5	San Carlos de Bariloche Arg.
147 C4	San Carlos del Zulia Venez.
135 C4	San Clemente Island U.S.A.
104 C2	Sancoins France
150 A1	San Cristóbal Venez.
145 C3	San Cristóbal de las Casas Mex.
146 C2	Sancti Spíritus Cuba
61 C1	Sandakan Sabah Malaysia
93 E3	Sandane Norway
111 B2	Sandanski Bulg.
96 C1	Sanday i. U.K.
139 C2	Sanderson U.S.A.
150 B3	Sandia Peru
135 C4	San Diego U.S.A.
80 B2	Sandıklı Turkey
93 E4	Sandnes Norway
92 F2	Sandnessjøen Norway
118 C3	Sandoa Dem. Rep. Congo
103 E1	Sandomierz Pol.
89 E2	Sandovo Rus. Fed.
94 B1	Sandoy i. Faroe Is
134 C1	Sandpoint U.S.A.
71 B3	Sandu China
94 B1	Sandur Faroe Is
140 C2	Sandusky U.S.A.
122 A3	Sandveld mts S. Africa
93 F4	Sandvika Norway
93 G3	Sandviken Sweden
131 E1	Sandwich Bay Can.
129 D2	Sandy Bay Can.
51 E2	Sandy Cape Austr.
130 A1	Sandy Lake Can.
130 A1	Sandy Lake Can.
144 A1	San Felipe Baja California Mex.
145 B2	San Felipe Guanajuato Mex.
150 B1	San Felipe Venez.
144 A2	San Fernando Baja California Mex.
145 C2	San Fernando Tamaulipas Mex.
64 B1	San Fernando La Union Phil.
64 B1	San Fernando Pampanga Phil.
106 B2	San Fernando Spain
147 D3	San Fernando Trin. and Tob.

150 B1	San Fernando de Apure Venez.	
143 D3	Sanford FL U.S.A.	
141 C2	Sanford ME U.S.A.	
152 B4	San Francisco Arg.	
135 B3	San Francisco U.S.A.	
74 B3	Sangamner India	
83 J2	Sangar Rus. Fed.	
108 A3	San Gavino Monreale Sardegna Italy	
101 E2	Sangerhausen Ger.	
61 C1	Sangha r. Congo	
118 B3	Sangha r. Congo	
109 C3	San Giovanni in Fiore Italy	
64 B2	Sangir i. Indon.	
59 C2	Sangir, Kepulauan is Indon.	
65 B2	Sangju S. Korea	
61 C1	Sangkulirang Indon.	
73 B3	Sangli India	
118 B2	Sangmélima Cameroon	
121 C3	Sango Zimbabwe	
136 B3	Sangre de Cristo Range mts U.S.A.	
75 C2	Sangsang China	
144 A2	San Hipólito, Punta pt Mex.	
144 A2	San Ignacio Mex.	
130 C1	Sanikiluaq Can.	
71 A3	Sanjiang China	
135 B3	San Joaquin r. U.S.A.	
153 B5	San Jorge, Golfo de g. Arg.	
146 B4	San José Costa Rica	
64 B1	San Jose Nueva Ecija Phil.	
64 B1	San Jose Occidental Mindoro Phil.	
135 B3	San Jose U.S.A.	
144 A2	San José, Isla i. Mex.	
144 B2	San José de Bavicora Mex.	
81 B1	San Jose de Buenavista Phil.	
144 A2	San José de Comondú Mex.	
144 B2	San José del Cabo Mex.	
150 A1	San José del Guaviare Col.	
152 B4	San Juan Arg.	
146 B3	San Juan r. Costa Rica/Nic.	
147 D3	San Juan Puerto Rico	
135 D3	San Juan r. U.S.A.	
145 C3	San Juan Bautista Tuxtepec Mex.	
134 B3	San Juan Islands U.S.A.	
144 B2	San Juanito Mex.	
136 B3	San Juan Mountains U.S.A.	
153 B5	San Julián Arg.	
75 C2	Sankh r. India	
105 D2	Sankt Gallen Switz.	
105 D2	Sankt Moritz Switz.	
	Sankt-Peterburg Rus. Fed. see St Petersburg	
102 C2	Sankt Veit an der Glan Austria	
100 C3	Sankt Wendel Ger.	
80 B2	Sanliurfa Turkey	
138 D3	San Lorenzo Mex.	
106 B2	Sanlúcar de Barrameda Spain	
153 B4	San Luis Arg.	
145 B2	San Luis de la Paz Mex.	
138 A2	San Luisito Mex.	
135 B3	San Luis Obispo U.S.A.	
145 B2	San Luis Potosí Mex.	
144 A1	San Luis Río Colorado Mex.	
139 D3	San Marcos U.S.A.	
108 B2	San Marino country Europe	
108 B2	San Marino San Marino	
144 B2	San Martín de Bolaños Mex.	
153 A5	San Martín de los Andes Arg.	
153 B5	San Matías, Golfo g. Arg.	
70 B2	Sanmenxia China	
146 B3	San Miguel El Salvador	
152 B3	San Miguel de Tucumán Arg.	
145 C3	San Miguel Sola de Vega Mex.	

71 B3	Sanming China	
153 B4	San Nicolás de los Arroyos Arg.	
135 C4	San Nicolas Island U.S.A.	
123 C2	Sannieshof S. Africa	
103 E2	Sanok Pol.	
64 B1	San Pablo Phil.	
144 B2	San Pablo Balleza Mex.	
152 B3	San Pedro Arg.	
152 B3	San Pedro Bol.	
114 B4	San-Pédro Côte d'Ivoire	
144 A2	San Pedro Mex.	
138 A2	San Pedro watercourse U.S.A.	
106 B2	San Pedro, Sierra de mts Spain	
144 B2	San Pedro de las Colonias Mex.	
146 B3	San Pedro Sula Hond.	
108 A3	San Pietro, Isola di i. Sardegna Italy	
144 A1	San Quintín, Cabo c. Mex.	
153 B4	San Rafael Arg.	
108 A2	San Remo Italy	
146 B3	San Salvador El Salvador	
152 B3	San Salvador de Jujuy Arg.	
107 C1	San Sebastián Spain	
109 C2	Sanski Most Bos.-Herz.	
152 B2	Santa Ana Bol.	
146 B3	Santa Ana El Salvador	
144 A1	Santa Ana Mex.	
135 C4	Santa Ana U.S.A.	
144 B2	Santa Bárbara Mex.	
135 C4	Santa Barbara U.S.A.	
151 E3	Santa Bárbara, Serra de hills Brazil	
152 B3	Santa Catalina Chile	
150 B2	Santa Clara Col.	
146 C2	Santa Clara Cuba	
135 C4	Santa Clarita U.S.A.	
109 C3	Santa Croce, Capo c. Sicilia Italy	
152 B3	Santa Cruz r. Arg.	
152 B2	Santa Cruz Bol.	
64 B1	Santa Cruz Phil.	
135 B3	Santa Cruz U.S.A.	
145 C3	Santa Cruz Barillas Guat.	
155 E1	Santa Cruz Cabrália Brazil	
107 C2	Santa Cruz de Moya Spain	
114 A2	Santa Cruz de Tenerife Islas Canarias	
135 C4	Santa Cruz Island U.S.A.	
48 F3	Santa Cruz Islands Solomon Is	
152 B4	Santa Fe Arg.	
138 B1	Santa Fe U.S.A.	
154 B1	Santa Helena de Goiás Brazil	
193 B4	Santa Isabel Arg.	
154 B1	Santa Luisa, Serra de hills Brazil	
152 C3	Santa Maria Brazil	
144 B1	Santa Maria r. Mex.	
135 B4	Santa Maria U.S.A.	
123 D2	Santa Maria, Cabo de c. Moz.	
106 B2	Santa Maria, Cabo de c. Port.	
151 D2	Santa Maria das Barreiras Brazil	
109 C3	Santa Maria di Leuca, Capo c. Italy	
150 A1	Santa Marta Col.	
135 C4	Santa Monica U.S.A.	
151 D3	Santana Brazil	
106 C1	Santander Spain	
108 A3	Sant'Antioco Sardegna Italy	
108 A3	Sant'Antioco, Isola di i. Sardegna Italy	

107 D2	Sant Antoni de Portmany Spain	
131 C2	Santarém Brazil	
106 B2	Santarém Port.	
154 B1	Santa Rita do Araguaia Brazil	
153 B4	Santa Rosa Arg.	
152 C3	Santa Rosa Brazil	
135 B3	Santa Rosa CA U.S.A.	
138 C2	Santa Rosa NM U.S.A.	
146 B3	Santa Rosa de Copán Hond.	
135 B4	Santa Rosa Island U.S.A.	
144 A2	Santa Rosalía Mex.	
107 D2	Sant Francesc de Formentera Spain	
152 C3	Santiago Brazil	
153 A4	Santiago Chile	
147 C3	Santiago Dom. Rep.	
144 B2	Santiago Mex.	
146 B4	Santiago Panama	
64 B1	Santiago Phil.	
106 B1	Santiago de Compostela Spain	
144 B2	Santiago Ixcuintla Mex.	
144 B2	Santiago Papasquiaro Mex.	
107 D2	Sant Joan de Labritja Spain	
107 D1	Sant Jordi, Golf de g. Spain	
155 C2	Santo Amaro de Campos Brazil	
155 C2	Santo André Brazil	
152 C3	Santo Ângelo Brazil	
154 B2	Santo Antônio da Platina Brazil	
151 E3	Santo Antônio de Jesus Brazil	
150 B2	Santo Antônio do Içá Brazil	
155 C2	Santo Antônio do Monte Brazil	
147 D3	Santo Domingo Dom. Rep.	
138 B1	Santo Domingo Pueblo U.S.A.	
111 C3	Santorini i. Greece	
155 C2	Santos Brazil	
152 C3	Santo Tomé Arg.	
153 A5	San Valentín, Cerro mt. Chile	
146 B3	San Vicente El Salvador	
144 A1	San Vicente Mex.	
150 A3	San Vicente de Cañete Peru	
108 B2	San Vincenzo Italy	
108 B3	San Vito, Capo c. Sicilia Italy	
71 A4	Sanya China	
155 C2	São Bernardo do Campo Brazil	
152 C3	São Borja Brazil	
154 C2	São Carlos Brazil	
151 C3	São Félix Mato Grosso Brazil	
151 C2	São Félix Pará Brazil	
155 D2	São Fidélis Brazil	
155 D1	São Francisco Brazil	
151 C3	São Francisco r. Brazil	
154 C3	São Francisco, Ilha de i. Brazil	
154 C3	São Francisco do Sul Brazil	
152 C4	São Gabriel Brazil	
155 D2	São Gonçalo Brazil	
155 C1	São Gotardo Brazil	
155 C2	São João da Barra Brazil	
155 C2	São João da Boa Vista Brazil	
106 B1	São João da Madeira Port.	
155 D1	São João do Paraíso Brazil	
155 D2	São João Nepomuceno Brazil	
154 C2	São Joaquim da Barra Brazil	
154 C2	São José do Rio Preto Brazil	
155 C2	São José dos Campos Brazil	
154 C3	São José dos Pinhais Brazil	
155 C2	São Lourenço Brazil	
151 D2	São Luís Brazil	
154 C2	São Manuel Brazil	
154 C1	São Marcos r. Brazil	

151	D2	São Marcos, Baía de *b.* Brazil	77	D1	Saryarka *plain* Kazakh.	105	D2	Schaffhausen Switz.

São Marcos, Baía de

151 D2 São Marcos, Baía de *b.* Brazil
155 E1 São Mateus Brazil
155 C2 São Paulo Brazil
151 C2 São Raimundo Nonato Brazil
155 C1 São Romão Brazil
155 C2 São Sebastião, Ilha do *i.* Brazil
154 C2 São Sebastião do Paraíso Brazil
154 B1 São Simão Brazil
154 B1 São Simão, Barragem de *resr* Brazil
59 C2 Sao-Siu Indon.
113 F6 São Tomé São Tomé and Príncipe
155 C3 São Tomé, Cabo de *c.* Brazil
113 F6 São Tomé and Príncipe *country* Africa
155 C2 São Vicente Brazil
106 B2 São Vicente, Cabo de *c.* Port.
59 C3 Saparua Indon.
89 F3 Sapozhok Rus. Fed.
66 D2 Sapporo Japan
109 C2 Sapri Italy
81 C2 Saqqez Iran
81 C2 Sarāb Iran
63 B2 Sara Buri Thai.
109 C2 Sarajevo Bos.-Herz.
76 B1 Saraktash Rus. Fed.
141 E2 Saranac Lake U.S.A.
109 D3 Sarandë Albania
64 B2 Sarangani Islands Phil.
87 D3 Saransk Rus. Fed.
87 E3 Sarapul Rus. Fed.
143 D3 Sarasota U.S.A.
90 B2 Sarata Ukr.
136 B2 Saratoga U.S.A.
141 E2 Saratoga Springs U.S.A.
61 C1 Saratok *Sarawak* Malaysia
87 D3 Saratov Rus. Fed.
79 D2 Sarāvān Iran
61 C1 Sarawak *state* Malaysia
110 C2 Saray Turkey
111 C3 Sarayköy Turkey
79 D2 Sarbāz Iran
74 B2 Sardarshahr India
Sardegna *i.* Italy *see* **Sardinia**
108 A2 Sardinia *i.* Italy
92 G2 Sarektjåkkå *mt.* Sweden
77 C3 Sar-e-Pul Afgh.
158 B3 Sargasso Sea N. Atlantic Ocean
74 B1 Sargodha Pak.
115 D4 Sarh Chad
79 D2 Sārī Iran
81 D2 Sārī Iran
111 C3 Sarıgöl Turkey
81 C1 Sarıkamış Turkey
61 C1 Sarikei *Sarawak* Malaysia
51 D2 Sarina Austr.
65 B2 Sariwŏn N. Korea
111 C2 Sanyer Turkey
78 B2 Sark, Safrā' as *esc.* Saudi Arabia
77 D2 Sarkand Kazakh.
111 C2 Şarköy Turkey
59 C3 Sarmi Indon.
140 C2 Sarnia Can.
91 C1 Sarny Ukr.
60 B2 Sarolangun Indon.
111 B3 Saronikos Kolpos *g.* Greece
111 C2 Saros Körfezi *b.* Turkey
87 D3 Sarov Rus. Fed.
105 D2 Sarrebourg France
106 B1 Sarria Spain
107 C1 Sarrión Spain
105 D3 Sartène *Corse* France
103 D2 Sárvár Hungary

77 D1 Saryarka *plain* Kazakh.
76 B2 Sarykamyshskoye Ozero *salt l.* Turkm./Uzbek.
77 D2 Saryozek Kazakh.
77 D2 Saryshagan Kazakh.
82 F3 Sarysu *watercourse* Kazakh.
77 D3 Sary-Tash Kyrg.
75 C2 Sasaram India
86 D2 Sasebo Japan
129 D2 Saskatchewan *prov.* Can.
129 D2 Saskatchewan *r.* Can.
129 D2 Saskatoon Can.
83 I2 Saskylakh Rus. Fed.
123 C2 Sasolburg S. Africa
87 D3 Sasovo Rus. Fed.
114 B4 Sassandra Côte d'Ivoire
108 A2 Sassari *Sardegna* Italy
102 C1 Sassnitz Ger.
114 A3 Satadougou Mali
123 D1 Satara S. Africa
75 C2 Satna India
74 B2 Satpura Range *mts* India
63 B2 Sattahip Thai.
110 B1 Satu Mare Romania
63 B3 Satun Thai.
144 B2 Saucillo Mex.
93 E4 Sauda Norway
92 □B2 Sauðárkrókur Iceland
78 B2 Saudi Arabia *country* Asia
105 C3 Saugues France
105 C2 Saulieu France
130 B2 Sault Sainte Marie Can.
140 C1 Sault Sainte Marie U.S.A.
77 C1 Saumalkol' Kazakh.
59 C3 Saumlakki Indon.
104 B2 Saumur France
120 B1 Saurimo Angola
49 G3 Sava *r.* Europe
49 G3 Sava'i'i *i.* Samoa
91 E1 Savala *r.* Rus. Fed.
143 D2 Savannah *GA* U.S.A.
142 C1 Savannah *TN* U.S.A.
143 D2 Savannah *r.* U.S.A.
63 B2 Savannakhét Laos
130 A1 Savant Lake Can.
111 C3 Savaştepe Turkey
89 F2 Savino Rus. Fed.
86 D2 Savinskiy Rus. Fed.
108 A2 Savona Italy
93 I3 Savonlinna Fin.
92 I2 Savukoski Fin.
Savu Sea Indon. *see*
Sawu, Laut
74 B2 Sawai Madhopur India
62 A2 Sawankhalok Thai.
136 B3 Sawatch Range *mts* U.S.A.
53 D2 Sawtell Austr.
59 C3 Sawu, Laut *sea* Indon.
79 C3 Saywūn Yemen
69 D2 Saynshand Mongolia
141 D2 Sayre U.S.A.
144 B3 Sayula *Jalisco* Mex.
145 C3 Sayula *Veracruz* Mex.
128 B2 Sayward Can.
89 E2 Sazonovo Rus. Fed.
114 B2 Sbaa Alg.
98 B1 Scafell Pike *h.* U.K.
109 C3 Scalea Italy
96 □ Scapa Flow *inlet* U.K.
130 C2 Scarborough Can.
147 D3 Scarborough Trin. and Tob.
98 C1 Scarborough U.K.
64 A1 Scarborough Shoal *sea feature* S. China Sea
96 A2 Scarinish U.K.
Scarpanto *i.* Greece *see*
Karpathos

105 D2 Schaffhausen Switz.
100 B1 Schagen Neth.
102 C2 Schärding Austria
100 A2 Scharendijke Neth.
101 D1 Scharhörn *i.* Ger.
101 D1 Scheeßel Ger.
131 C1 Schefferville Can.
135 D3 Schell Creek Range *mts* U.S.A.
141 E2 Schenectady U.S.A.
101 E3 Scheßlitz Ger.
100 C1 Schiermonnikoog *i.* Neth.
108 B1 Schio Italy
101 F2 Schkeuditz Ger.
101 E1 Schladen Ger.
101 E2 Schleiz Ger.
102 B1 Schleswig Ger.
101 D2 Schloss Holte-Stukenbrock Ger.
101 D2 Schlüchtern Ger.
101 E3 Schlüsselfeld Ger.
101 D2 Schmallenberg Ger.
101 E3 Schneverdingen Ger.
101 E1 Schönebeck (Elbe) Ger.
101 E1 Schöningen Ger.
100 B2 Schoonhoven Neth.
59 D3 Schouten Islands P.N.G.
102 B2 Schwäbische Alb *mts* Ger.
102 C2 Schwandorf Ger.
61 C2 Schwaner, Pegunungan *mts* Indon.
101 E1 Schwarzenbek Ger.
101 F2 Schwarzenberg Ger.
122 A2 Schwarzrand *mts* Namibia
Schwarzwald *mts* Ger. *see*
Black Forest
102 C2 Schwaz Austria
102 C1 Schwedt an der Oder Ger.
101 E2 Schweinfurt Ger.
101 E1 Schwerin Ger.
101 E1 Schweriner See *l.* Ger.
105 D2 Schwyz Switz.
108 B3 Sciacca *Sicilia* Italy
95 B4 Scilly, Isles of U.K.
140 C3 Scioto *r.* U.S.A.
136 B1 Scobey U.S.A.
53 D2 Scone Austr.
55 R3 Scotia Ridge S. Atlantic Ocean
158 C8 Scotia Sea S. Atlantic Ocean
96 C2 Scotland *admin. div.* U.K.
128 B2 Scott, Cape Can.
123 D3 Scottburgh S. Africa
136 C3 Scott City U.S.A.
136 C2 Scottsbluff U.S.A.
142 C2 Scottsboro U.S.A.
96 B1 Scourie U.K.
141 D2 Scranton U.S.A.
98 C2 Scunthorpe U.K.
105 E2 Scuol Switz.
129 E2 Seal *r.* Can.
122 B3 Seal, Cape S. Africa
52 B3 Sea Lake Austr.
139 D3 Sealy U.S.A.
142 B1 Searcy U.S.A.
98 B1 Seascale U.K.
134 B1 Seattle U.S.A.
141 E2 Sebago Lake U.S.A.
144 A2 Sebastián Vizcaíno, Bahía *b.* Mex.
110 B1 Sebeş Romania
60 B2 Sebesi *i.* Indon.
88 C2 Sebezh Rus. Fed.
80 B1 Şebinkarahisar Turkey
143 D3 Sebring U.S.A.
128 B3 Sechelt Can.
150 A2 Sechura Peru
73 B3 Secunderabad India
137 E3 Sedalia U.S.A.

105 C2 Sedan France
54 B2 Seddon N.Z.
138 A2 Sedona U.S.A.
101 E2 Seeburg Ger.
101 E1 Seehausen (Altmark) Ger.
122 A2 Seeheim Namibia
104 C2 Sées France
101 E2 Seesen Ger.
101 E1 Seevetal Ger.
114 A4 Sefadu Sierra Leone
123 C1 Sefare Botswana
76 C3 Sefīd Kūh, Selseleh-ye mts
        Afgh.
60 B1 Segamat Malaysia
86 D2 Segezha Rus. Fed.
114 B3 Ségou Mali
106 C2 Segovia Spain
115 D2 Ségué Niger
114 B4 Séguéla Côte d'Ivoire
139 D3 Seguin U.S.A.
107 C2 Segura r. Spain
106 C2 Segura, Sierra de mts Spain
120 D3 Sehithwa Botswana
93 H3 Seinäjoki Fin.
104 C2 Seine r. France
104 B2 Seine, Baie de b. France
103 E1 Sejny Pol.
60 B2 Sekayu Indon.
114 B4 Sekondi Ghana
59 C3 Selaru i. Indon.
61 C2 Selatan, Tanjung pt Indon.
126 A2 Selawik U.S.A.
58 C3 Selayar, Pulau i. Indon.
98 C2 Selby U.K.
120 D3 Selebi-Phikwe Botswana
103 E3 Sélestat France
92 □A3 Selfoss Iceland
114 A3 Sélibabi Maur.
138 A1 Seligman U.S.A.
116 A2 Selima Oasis Sudan
111 C3 Selimiye Turkey
114 B3 Sélingué, Lac de l. Mali
89 D2 Selizharovo Rus. Fed.
93 E4 Seljord Norway
129 E2 Selkirk Can.
96 C3 Selkirk U.K.
128 C2 Selkirk Mountains Can.
142 C2 Selma AL U.S.A.
135 C3 Selma CA U.S.A.
89 D3 Sel'tso Rus. Fed.
150 A2 Selvas reg. Brazil
134 C1 Selway r. U.S.A.
129 D1 Selwyn Lake Can.
128 A1 Selwyn Mountains Can.
51 C2 Selwyn Range hills Austr.
60 B2 Semangka, Teluk b. Indon.
61 C2 Semarang Indon.
61 B1 Sematan Sarawak Malaysia
118 B3 Sembé Congo
81 C2 Semdinli Turkey
91 C1 Semenivka Ukr.
86 D3 Semenov Rus. Fed.
61 C2 Semeru, Gunung vol. Indon.
77 E1 Semey Kazakh.
89 E3 Semiluki Rus. Fed.
136 B2 Seminoe Reservoir U.S.A.
139 C2 Seminole U.S.A.
143 D2 Seminole, Lake U.S.A.
61 C1 Semitau Indon.
81 D2 Semnān Iran
61 C1 Semporna Sabah Malaysia
105 C2 Semur-en-Auxois France
150 B2 Sena Madureira Brazil
120 B2 Senanga Zambia
67 B4 Sendai Kagoshima Japan
67 D3 Sendai Miyagi Japan
114 A3 Senegal country Africa
114 A3 Sénégal r. Maur./Senegal
102 C1 Senftenberg Ger.
119 D3 Sengerema Tanz.
151 D3 Senhor do Bonfim Brazil
108 B2 Senigallia Italy
109 B2 Senj Croatia
92 G2 Senja i. Norway
122 B2 Senlac S. Africa
104 C2 Senlis France
63 B2 Senmonorom Cambodia
117 B3 Sennar Sudan
130 C2 Senneterre Can.
123 C3 Senqu r. Lesotho
105 C2 Sens France
109 D1 Senta Serbia
128 B2 Sentinel Peak Can.
123 C1 Senwabarwana S. Africa
75 B2 Seoni India
65 B2 Seoul S. Korea
155 D2 Sepetiba, Baía de b. Brazil
59 D3 Sepik r. P.N.G.
61 C1 Sepinang Indon.
131 D1 Sept-Îles Can.
59 C3 Seram i. Indon.
59 C3 Seram, Laut sea Indon.
60 B2 Serang Indon.
109 D2 Serbia country Europe
76 B3 Serdar Turkm.
89 E3 Serebryanyye Prudy Rus. Fed.
60 B1 Seremban Malaysia
119 D3 Serengeti Plain Tanz.
87 D3 Sergach Rus. Fed.
89 E2 Sergiyev Posad Rus. Fed.
74 A1 Serhetabat Turkm.
61 C1 Seria Brunei
61 C1 Serian Sarawak Malaysia
111 B3 Serifos i. Greece
80 B2 Serik Turkey
59 C3 Sermata, Kepulauan is Indon.
86 F3 Serov Rus. Fed.
120 B3 Serowe Botswana
106 B2 Serpa Port.
89 E3 Serpukhov Rus. Fed.
151 D3 Serra da Mesa, Represa resr
        Brazil
154 B1 Serranópolis Brazil
100 A3 Serre r. France
111 B2 Serres Greece
151 E3 Serrinha Brazil
155 D1 Sêrro Brazil
154 C2 Sertãozinho Brazil
61 C2 Seruyan r. Indon.
68 C2 Sêrxü China
120 A2 Sesfontein Namibia
108 B2 Sessa Aurunca Italy
108 A2 Sestri Levante Italy
105 C3 Sète France
155 D1 Sete Lagoas Brazil
92 G2 Setermoen Norway
93 E4 Setesdal val. Norway
115 C1 Sétif Alg.
67 B4 Seto-naikai sea Japan
114 B1 Settat Morocco
98 B1 Settle U.K.
106 B2 Setúbal Port.
106 B2 Setúbal, Baía de b. Port.
130 A1 Seul, Lac l. Can.
76 A2 Sevan, Lake Armenia
        Sevana Lich l. Armenia see
        Sevan, Lake
91 C3 Sevastopol' Ukr.
105 C3 Sévérac-le-Château France
130 B1 Severn r. Can.
122 B2 Severn S. Africa
99 B3 Severn r. U.K.
86 D2 Severnaya Dvina r.
        Rus. Fed.
83 H1 Severnaya Zemlya is Rus. Fed.
86 D2 Severnyy Nenetskiy
        Avtonomnyy Okrug Rus. Fed.
86 F2 Severnyy Respublika Komi
        Rus. Fed.
86 C2 Severodvinsk Rus. Fed.
86 C2 Severomorsk Rus. Fed.
91 D3 Severskaya Rus. Fed.
135 D3 Sevier r. U.S.A.
135 D3 Sevier Lake U.S.A.
        Sevilla Spain see Seville
106 B2 Seville Spain
128 A2 Sewell Inlet Can.
128 C2 Sexsmith Can.
144 B2 Sextín r. Mex.
86 G1 Seyakha Rus. Fed.
113 J7 Seychelles country Indian
        Ocean
92 □C2 Seyðisfjörður Iceland
91 C1 Seym r. Rus. Fed./Ukr.
83 L2 Seymchan Rus. Fed.
53 C3 Seymour Austr.
140 B3 Seymour IN U.S.A.
139 D2 Seymour TX U.S.A.
105 C2 Sézanne France
110 C1 Sfântu Gheorghe Romania
115 D1 Sfax Tunisia
        's-Gravenhage Neth. see
        The Hague
96 A2 Sgurr Alasdair h. U.K.
70 A2 Shaanxi prov. China
91 D2 Shabel'skoye Rus. Fed.
77 D3 Shache China
55 R1 Shackleton Range mts
        Antarctica
99 B3 Shaftesbury U.K.
75 C2 Shahdol India
77 C3 Shāh Fōlādī mt. Afgh.
75 B2 Shahjahanpur India
81 D2 Shahr-e Kord Iran
81 D2 Shāhrezā Iran
77 C3 Shahrisabz Uzbek.
89 E2 Shakhovskaya Rus. Fed.
91 E2 Shakhty Rus. Fed.
86 D3 Shakhun'ya Rus. Fed.
66 D2 Shakotan-misaki c. Japan
76 B2 Shalkar Kazakh.
69 C2 Shaluli Shan mts China
129 C2 Shamattawa Can.
139 C1 Shamrock U.S.A.
70 B2 Shancheng China
68 C2 Shandan China
70 B2 Shandong prov. China
70 C2 Shandong Bandao pen.
        China
121 B2 Shangani r. Zimbabwe
70 C2 Shanghai China
70 C2 Shanghai mun. China
71 B3 Shanghang China
70 A2 Shangluo China
71 B3 Shangrao China
70 B2 Shangshui China
70 C2 Shangyu China
69 E1 Shangzhi China
97 B2 Shannon r. Ireland
97 B2 Shannon, Mouth of the
        Ireland
71 B3 Shantou China
70 B2 Shanxi prov. China
71 B3 Shaoguan China
71 B3 Shaowu China
70 C2 Shaoxing China
71 B3 Shaoyang China
116 C2 Shaqrā' Saudi Arabia
90 B2 Sharhorod Ukr.
79 C2 Sharjah U.A.E.
88 C2 Sharkawshchyna Belarus

Shark Bay

50 A2 Shark Bay Austr.
78 A2 Sharm ash Shaykh Egypt
140 C2 Sharon U.S.A.
86 D3 Shar'ya Rus. Fed.
121 B3 Shashe r. Botswana/Zimbabwe
117 B4 Shashemené Eth.
134 B2 Shasta, Mount vol. U.S.A.
134 B2 Shasta Lake U.S.A.
89 E2 Shatura Rus. Fed.
129 D3 Shaunavon Can.
140 B2 Shawano U.S.A.
131 C2 Shawinigan Can.
139 D1 Shawnee U.S.A.
50 B2 Shay Gap (abandoned) Austr.
89 E3 Shchekino Rus. Fed.
89 E2 Shchelkovo Rus. Fed.
89 E3 Shchigry Rus. Fed.
91 C1 Shchors Ukr.
88 B3 Shchuchyn Belarus
91 D1 Shebekino Rus. Fed.
117 C3 Shebelē Wenz, Wabē r. Ethiopia/Somalia
140 B2 Sheboygan U.S.A.
91 D3 Shebsh r. Rus. Fed.
97 C2 Sheelin, Lough l. Ireland
98 C2 Sheffield U.K.
89 E2 Sheksna Rus. Fed.
89 E2 Sheksninskoye Vodokhranilishche resr Rus. Fed.
83 M2 Shelagskiy, Mys pt Rus. Fed.
131 D2 Shelburne Can.
134 D1 Shelby U.S.A.
140 B3 Shelbyville IN U.S.A.
142 C1 Shelbyville TN U.S.A.
83 L2 Shelikhova, Zaliv g. Rus. Fed.
129 D2 Shellbrook Can.
134 B1 Shelton U.S.A.
137 D2 Shenandoah U.S.A.
141 D3 Shenandoah r. U.S.A.
141 D3 Shenandoah Mountains U.S.A.
118 A2 Shendam Nigeria
86 D2 Shenkursk Rus. Fed.
65 A1 Shenyang China
71 B3 Shenzhen China
90 B1 Shepetivka Ukr.
53 C3 Shepparton Austr.
99 D3 Sheppey, Isle of i. U.K.
131 D2 Sherbrooke N.S. Can.
131 C2 Sherbrooke Que. Can.
116 B3 Shereiq Sudan
136 B2 Sheridan U.S.A.
139 D2 Sherman U.S.A.
100 B2 's-Hertogenbosch Neth.
96 ☐ Shetland Islands U.K.
76 B2 Shetpe Kazakh.
Shevchenko Kazakh. see Aktau
137 D1 Sheyenne r. U.S.A.
79 B3 Shibām Yemen
66 D2 Shibetsu Japan
77 C3 Shibirghān Afgh.
71 B3 Shicheng China
96 B2 Shiel, Loch l. U.K.
77 E2 Shihezi China
Shijiao China see Fogang
70 B2 Shijiazhuang China
74 A2 Shikarpur Pak.
67 B4 Shikoku i. Japan
66 D2 Shikotsu-ko l. Japan
86 D2 Shilega Rus. Fed.
75 C2 Shiliguri India
75 D2 Shillong India
89 F3 Shilovo Rus. Fed.
117 C3 Shimbiris mt. Somalia

67 C3 Shimizu Japan
73 B3 Shimoga India
67 B4 Shimonoseki Japan
96 C1 Shin, Loch l. U.K.
67 C4 Shingū Japan
123 D1 Shingwedzi S. Africa
123 D1 Shingwedzi r. S. Africa
119 D3 Shinyanga Tanz.
67 C4 Shiono-misaki c. Japan
138 B1 Shiprock U.S.A.
71 A3 Shiqian China
70 A2 Shiqian China
Shiquanhe China see Gar
Shiquan He r. China/Pak. see Indus
67 C3 Shirane-san mt. Japan
81 D3 Shīrāz Iran
66 D2 Shiretoko-misaki c. Japan
66 D2 Shiriya-zaki c. Japan
74 B2 Shiv India
Shivamogga India see Shimoga
75 B2 Shivpuri India
70 B2 Shiyan China
70 B2 Shizhong China
70 A2 Shizuishan China
67 C4 Shizuoka Japan
89 D3 Shklow Belarus
109 C2 Shkodër Albania
83 H3 Shmidta, Ostrov i. Rus. Fed.
135 C3 Shoshone U.S.A.
135 C3 Shoshone Mountains U.S.A.
123 C1 Shoshong Botswana
91 C1 Shostka Ukr.
70 B2 Shouxian China
138 A2 Show Low U.S.A.
91 C2 Shpola Ukr.
142 B2 Shreveport U.S.A.
99 B2 Shrewsbury U.K.
62 A1 Shuangjiang China
87 E4 Shubarkuduk Kazakh.
116 B1 Shubrā al Khaymah Egypt
89 D2 Shugozero Rus. Fed.
120 B2 Shumba Zimbabwe
110 C2 Shumen Bulg.
88 C2 Shumilina Belarus
89 D3 Shumyachi Rus. Fed.
126 A2 Shungnak U.S.A.
78 B3 Shuqrah Yemen
89 F2 Shushkodom Rus. Fed.
81 C2 Shushtar Iran
128 C2 Shuswap Lake Can.
89 F2 Shuya Rus. Fed.
89 F2 Shuyskoye Rus. Fed.
62 A1 Shwebo Myanmar
62 A1 Shwedwin Myanmar
62 A2 Shwegyin Myanmar
77 D2 Shyganak Kazakh.
77 C2 Shymkent Kazakh.
91 C2 Shyroke Ukr.
59 C3 Sia Indon.
74 A2 Siahan Range mts Pak.
74 B1 Sialkot Pak.
64 B2 Siargao i. Phil.
88 B2 Šiauliai Lith.
109 C2 Šibenik Croatia
83 I2 Siberia reg. Rus. Fed.
60 A2 Siberut i. Indon.
74 A2 Sibi Pak.
110 B1 Sibiu Romania
60 A1 Sibolga Indon.
61 C1 Sibu Sarawak Malaysia
118 B2 Sibut C.A.R.
64 B1 Sibuyan i. Phil.
64 B1 Sibuyan Sea Phil.
128 C2 Sicamous Can.
63 A3 Sichon Thai.

70 A2 Sichuan prov. China
70 A3 Sichuan Pendi basin China
105 D3 Sicié, Cap c. France
Sicilia i. Italy see Sicily
108 B3 Sicilian Channel Italy/Tunisia
108 B3 Sicily i. Italy
150 A3 Sicuani Peru
111 C3 Sideros, Akrotirio pt Greece
74 B2 Sidhpur India
107 D2 Sidi Aïssa Alg.
107 D2 Sidi Ali Alg.
114 B1 Sidi Bel Abbès Alg.
114 B1 Sidi Ifni Morocco
60 A1 Sidikalang Indon.
96 C2 Sidlaw Hills U.K.
99 B3 Sidmouth U.K.
134 B1 Sidney Can.
136 C1 Sidney MT U.S.A.
136 C2 Sidney NE U.S.A.
140 C2 Sidney OH U.S.A.
143 D2 Sidney Lanier, Lake U.S.A.
80 B2 Sidon Lebanon
154 B2 Sidrolândia Brazil
103 E1 Siedlce Pol.
100 C2 Sieg r. Ger.
100 C2 Siegen Ger.
63 B2 Siĕmréab Cambodia
108 B2 Siena Italy
103 D1 Sieradz Pol.
153 B5 Sierra Grande Arg.
114 A4 Sierra Leone country Africa
144 B2 Sierra Mojada Mex.
138 A2 Sierra Vista U.S.A.
105 D2 Sierre Switz.
111 B3 Sifnos i. Greece
107 C2 Sig Alg.
127 H2 Sigguup Nunaa pen. Greenland
103 E2 Sighetu Marmației Romania
110 B1 Sighișoara Romania
60 A1 Sigli Indon.
92 □B2 Siglufjörður Iceland
102 B2 Sigmaringen Ger.
100 B3 Signy-l'Abbaye France
106 C1 Sigüenza Spain
118 B3 Siguiri Guinea
88 B2 Sigulda Latvia
63 B2 Sihanoukville Cambodia
92 I3 Siilinjärvi Fin.
81 C2 Siirt Turkey
60 B2 Sijunjung Indon.
74 B2 Sikar India
114 B3 Sikasso Mali
137 F3 Sikeston U.S.A.
66 B2 Sikhote-Alin' mts Rus. Fed.
111 C3 Sikinos i. Greece
144 B2 Silao Mex.
75 D2 Silchar India
77 D1 Siletyteniz, Ozero salt l. Kazakh.
75 C2 Silgarhi Nepal
80 B2 Silifke Turkey
75 C1 Siling Co salt l. China
110 C2 Silistra Bulg.
80 A1 Silivri Turkey
93 F3 Siljan l. Sweden
93 E4 Silkeborg Denmark
88 C2 Sillamäe Estonia
142 B1 Siloam Springs U.S.A.
123 D2 Silobela S. Africa
88 B2 Šilutė Lith.
81 C2 Silvan Turkey
138 B2 Silver City U.S.A.
136 B3 Silverton U.S.A.
62 B1 Simao China
130 C2 Simard, Lac l. Can.
111 C3 Simav Turkey

111	C3	Sırnav Dağları mts Turkey
118	C2	Simba Dem. Rep. Congo
141	D2	Simcoe, Lake Can.
60	A1	Simeulue i. Indon.
91	C3	Simferopol' Ukr.
110	B1	Şimleu Silvaniei Romania
100	C3	Simmern (Hunsrück) Ger.
129	D2	Simonhouse Can.
51	C2	Simpson Desert Austr.
93	F4	Simrishamn Sweden
60	A1	Sinabang Indon.
116	B2	Sinai pen. Egypt
71	A3	Sinan China
65	B2	Sinanju N. Korea
62	A1	Sinbo Myanmar
150	A1	Sincelejo Col.
111	C3	Sındırgı Turkey
86	E2	Sindor Rus. Fed.
111	C3	Sinekçi Turkey
106	B2	Sines Port.
106	B2	Sines, Cabo de c. Port.
75	C2	Singahi India
60	B1	Singapore country Asia
61	C2	Singaraja Indon.
119	D3	Singida Tanz.
62	A1	Singkaling Hkamti Myanmar
61	B1	Singkawang Indon.
60	A1	Singkil Indon.
53	D2	Singleton Austr.
62	A1	Singu Myanmar
108	A2	Siniscola Sardegna Italy
109	C2	Sinj Croatia
116	B3	Sinkat Sudan
		Sinkiang Uighur Autonomous Region aut. reg. China see Xinjiang Uygur Zizhiqu
80	B1	Sinop Turkey
65	B1	Sinp'o N. Korea
61	C1	Sintang Indon.
100	B2	Sint Anthonis Neth.
100	A2	Sint-Laureins Belgium
147	D3	Sint Maarten terr. West Indies
100	B2	Sint-Niklaas Belgium
139	D3	Sinton U.S.A.
65	A1	Sinŭiju N. Korea
103	D2	Siófok Hungary
105	D2	Sion Switz.
137	D2	Sioux Center U.S.A.
137	D2	Sioux City U.S.A.
137	D2	Sioux Falls U.S.A.
130	A1	Sioux Lookout Can.
65	A1	Siping China
129	E2	Sipiwesk Lake Can.
60	A2	Sipura i. Indon.
93	F4	Sira r. Norway
		Siracusa Italy see Syracuse
51	C1	Sir Edward Pellew Group is Austr.
116	B1	Sirhān, Wādī an watercourse Saudi Arabia
79	C2	Sīrīk Iran
62	B2	Siri Kit, Khuan Thai.
128	B1	Sir James MacBrien, Mount Can.
79	C2	Sīrjān Iran
81	C2	Şırnak Turkey
74	B2	Sirohi India
74	B2	Sirsa India
115	D1	Sirte Libya
115	D1	Sirte, Gulf of Libya
88	B2	Širvintos Lith.
145	C2	Sisal Mex.
122	B2	Sishen S. Africa
81	C2	Sisian Armenia
129	D2	Sisipuk Lake Can.
63	B2	Sisŏphŏn Cambodia

105	D3	Sisteron France
75	C2	Sitapur India
123	D2	Siteki Swaziland
128	A2	Sitka U.S.A.
100	B2	Sittard Neth.
62	A2	Sittang r. Myanmar
62	A1	Sittwe Myanmar
61	C2	Situbondo Indon.
80	B2	Sivas Turkey
62	A1	Sivasagar India
111	C3	Sivash Turkey
80	B2	Siverek Turkey
80	B2	Sivrihisar Turkey
116	A2	Siwah Egypt
74	B1	Siwalik Range mts India/Nepal
105	D3	Six-Fours-les-Plages France
70	B2	Sixian China
123	C2	Siyabuswa S. Africa
109	D2	Sjenica Serbia
92	G2	Sjøvegan Norway
91	C2	Skadovs'k Ukr.
93	F4	Skagen Denmark
93	E4	Skagerrak str. Denmark/Norway
134	B1	Skagit r. U.S.A.
128	A2	Skagway U.S.A.
74	B1	Skardu Pak.
103	E1	Skarżysko-Kamienna Pol.
103	D2	Skawina Pol.
128	B2	Skeena r. Can.
128	B2	Skeena Mountains Can.
98	D2	Skegness U.K.
92	H3	Skellefteå Sweden
92	H3	Skellefteälven r. Sweden
97	C2	Skerries Ireland
111	B3	Skiathos i. Greece
97	B3	Skibbereen Ireland
92	□B2	Skíðadals-jökull glacier Iceland
98	B1	Skiddaw h. U.K.
93	E4	Skien Norway
103	E1	Skierniewice Pol.
115	C1	Skikda Alg.
52	B3	Skipton Austr.
98	B2	Skipton U.K.
93	E4	Skive Denmark
92	H1	Skjervøy Norway
111	B3	Skopelos i. Greece
89	E3	Skopin Rus. Fed.
109	D2	Skopje Macedonia
93	F4	Skövde Sweden
141	F2	Skowhegan U.S.A.
88	B2	Skrunda Latvia
128	A1	Skukum, Mount Can.
123	D1	Skukuza S. Africa
88	B2	Skuodas Lith.
96	A2	Skye i. U.K.
111	B3	Skyros i. Greece
111	B3	Skyros i. Greece
93	F4	Slagelse Denmark
97	C2	Slaney r. Ireland
88	C2	Slantsy Rus. Fed.
109	C1	Slatina Croatia
110	B2	Slatina Romania
129	C1	Slave r. Can.
114	C4	Slave Coast Africa
128	C2	Slave Lake Can.
82	G3	Slavgorod Rus. Fed.
109	C1	Slavonski Brod Croatia
90	B1	Slavuta Ukr.
90	C1	Slavutych Ukr.
91	D2	Slavyansk-na-Kubani Rus. Fed.
89	D3	Slawharad Belarus
103	D1	Sławno Pol.
97	A2	Slea Head Ireland
130	C1	Sleeper Islands Can.
97	D1	Slieve Donard h. U.K.
97	B1	Sligo Ireland

97	B1	Sligo Bay Ireland
93	G4	Slite Sweden
110	C2	Sliven Bulg.
110	C2	Slobozia Romania
128	C3	Slocan Can.
88	C3	Slonim Belarus
100	B1	Sloten Neth.
99	C3	Slough U.K.
103	D2	Slovakia country Europe
108	B1	Slovenia country Europe
91	D2	Slov"yans'k Ukr.
90	B1	Sluch r. Ukr.
103	D1	Słupsk Pol.
88	C3	Slutsk Belarus
97	A2	Slyne Head Ireland
131	D1	Smallwood Reservoir Can.
88	C3	Smalyavichy Belarus
88	C3	Smarhon' Belarus
129	D2	Smeaton Can.
109	D2	Smederevo Serbia
109	D2	Smederevska Palanka Serbia
91	C2	Smila Ukr.
88	C2	Smiltene Latvia
128	B2	Smithers Can.
143	E1	Smithfield U.S.A.
141	D3	Smith Mountain Lake U.S.A.
130	C2	Smiths Falls Can.
137	D3	Smoky Hills U.S.A.
92	E3	Smøla i. Norway
89	D3	Smolensk Rus. Fed.
110	B2	Smolyan Bulg.
130	B2	Smooth Rock Falls Can.
		Smyrna Turkey see İzmir
92	□B3	Snæfell mt. Iceland
98	A1	Snaefell h. Isle of Man
132	B2	Snake r. U.S.A.
134	D2	Snake River Plain U.S.A.
100	B1	Sneek Neth.
97	B3	Sneem Ireland
122	B3	Sneeuberge mts S. Africa
108	B1	Snežnik mt. Slovenia
91	C2	Snihurivka Ukr.
93	E3	Snøhetta mt. Norway
129	D1	Snowbird Lake Can.
98	A2	Snowdon mt. U.K.
		Snowdrift Can. see Łutselk'e
129	C1	Snowdrift r. Can.
138	A2	Snowflake U.S.A.
129	D2	Snow Lake Can.
52	A2	Snowtown Austr.
53	C3	Snowy r. Austr.
53	C3	Snowy Mountains Austr.
139	C2	Snyder U.S.A.
121	□D2	Soalala Madag.
117	B4	Sobat r. S. Sudan
89	F2	Sobinka Rus. Fed.
151	D3	Sobradinho, Barragem de resr Brazil
151	D2	Sobral Brazil
87	C4	Sochi Rus. Fed.
65	B2	Sŏch'ŏn S. Korea
49	I7	Society Islands Fr. Polynesia
150	A1	Socorro Col.
138	B2	Socorro U.S.A.
144	A3	Socorro, Isla i. Mex.
56	F6	Socotra i. Yemen
63	B3	Soc Trăng Vietnam
106	C2	Socuéllamos Spain
92	I2	Sodankylä Fin.
134	D2	Soda Springs U.S.A.
93	G3	Söderhamn Sweden
93	G4	Södertälje Sweden
116	A3	Sodiri Sudan
117	B4	Sodo Eth.
93	G3	Södra Kvarken str. Fin./Sweden
100	D2	Soest Ger.

110 B2	Sofia Bulg.	
	Sofiya Bulg. see Sofia	
68 C2	Sog China	
93 E3	Sognefjorden inlet Norway	
111 D2	Söğüt Turkey	
100 B2	Soignies Belgium	
105 C2	Soissons France	
90 A1	Sokal' Ukr.	
111 C3	Söke Turkey	
81 C1	Sokhumi Georgia	
114 C4	Sokodé Togo	
89 F2	Sokol Rus. Fed.	
101 F2	Sokolov Czech Rep.	
115 C3	Sokoto Nigeria	
115 C3	Sokoto r. Nigeria	
90 B2	Sokyryany Ukr.	
73 B3	Solapur India	
135 B3	Soledad U.S.A.	
89 F2	Soligalich Rus. Fed.	
99 C2	Solihull U.K.	
86 E3	Solikamsk Rus. Fed.	
87 E3	Sol'-Iletsk Rus. Fed.	
100 C2	Solingen Ger.	
92 G3	Sollefteå Sweden	
93 G4	Sollentuna Sweden	
101 D2	Solling hills Ger.	
89 E2	Solnechnogorsk Rus. Fed.	
60 B2	Solok Indon.	
48 E3	Solomon Islands country	
	S. Pacific Ocean	
48 E3	Solomon Sea S. Pacific Ocean	
105 D2	Solothurn Switz.	
101 D1	Soltau Ger.	
89 D2	Sol'tsy Rus. Fed.	
96 C3	Solway Firth est. U.K.	
120 B2	Solwezi Zambia	
111 C3	Soma Turkey	
117 C4	Somalia country Africa	
117 A4	Somaliland terr. Somalia	
120 B1	Sombo Angola	
109 C1	Sombor Serbia	
144 B2	Sombrerete Mex.	
140 C3	Somerset U.S.A.	
123 C3	Somerset East S. Africa	
126 E2	Somerset Island Can.	
122 A3	Somerset West S. Africa	
101 E2	Sömmerda Ger.	
75 C2	Son r. India	
65 C1	Sŏnbong N. Korea	
93 E4	Sønderborg Denmark	
101 E2	Sondershausen Ger.	
	Søndre Strømfjord inlet	
	Greenland see Kangerlussuaq	
62 B1	Sông Đa, Hồ resr Vietnam	
119 D4	Songea Tanz.	
65 B1	Sŏnggan N. Korea	
65 B1	Songhua Hu resr China	
	Sŏngjin N. Korea see	
	Kimch'aek	
63 B3	Songkhla Thai.	
65 B2	Sŏngnam S. Korea	
65 B2	Songnim N. Korea	
120 A1	Songo Angola	
121 C2	Songo Moz.	
69 E1	Songyuan China	
	Sonid Youqi China see	
	Saihan Tal	
89 E2	Sonkovo Rus. Fed.	
62 B1	Sơn La Vietnam	
74 A2	Sonmiani Pak.	
101 E2	Sonneberg Ger.	
138 A2	Sonoita Mex.	
144 A2	Sonora r. Mex.	
135 B3	Sonora CA U.S.A.	
139 C2	Sonora TX U.S.A.	
117 A4	Sopo watercourse S. Sudan	
103 D2	Sopron Hungary	

108 B2	Sora Italy	
130 C2	Sorel Can.	
51 D4	Sorell Austr.	
106 C1	Soria Spain	
90 B2	Soroca Moldova	
154 C2	Sorocaba Brazil	
87 E3	Sorochinsk Rus. Fed.	
59 D2	Sorol atoll Micronesia	
59 C3	Sorong Indon.	
119 D2	Soroti Uganda	
92 H1	Sørøya i. Norway	
92 G2	Sorsele Sweden	
64 B1	Sorsogon Phil.	
86 C2	Sortavala Rus. Fed.	
92 G2	Sortland Norway	
65 B2	Sŏsan S. Korea	
123 C2	Soshanguve S. Africa	
89 E3	Sosna r. Rus. Fed.	
153 B4	Sosneado mt. Arg.	
86 E2	Sosnogorsk Rus. Fed.	
86 D2	Sosnovka Rus. Fed.	
88 C2	Sosnovyy Bor Rus. Fed.	
103 D1	Sosnowiec Pol.	
91 D2	Sosyka r. Rus. Fed.	
145 C2	Soto la Marina Mex.	
118 B2	Souanké Congo	
104 C3	Souillac France	
	Soûl S. Korea see Seoul	
104 B2	Soulac-sur-Mer France	
104 B3	Soulom France	
	Soûr Lebanon see Tyre	
107 D2	Sour el Ghozlane Alg.	
129 D3	Souris Man. Can.	
131 D2	Souris P.E.I. Can.	
129 E3	Souris r. Can.	
151 E2	Sousa Brazil	
115 D1	Sousse Tunisia	
104 B3	Soustons France	
122 B3	South Africa, Republic of	
	country Africa	
99 C3	Southampton U.K.	
127 F2	Southampton Island Can.	
73 D3	South Andaman i. India	
52 A1	South Australia state Austr.	
130 B2	South Baymouth Can.	
140 B2	South Bend U.S.A.	
143 D2	South Carolina state U.S.A.	
156 B4	South China Sea N. Pacific	
	Ocean	
136 C2	South Dakota state U.S.A.	
99 C3	South Downs hills U.K.	
99 D3	Southend Can.	
99 D3	Southend-on-Sea U.K.	
54 B2	Southern Alps mts N.Z.	
50 A3	Southern Cross Austr.	
129 E2	Southern Indian Lake Can.	
159	Southern Ocean World	
143 E1	Southern Pines U.S.A.	
96 B3	Southern Uplands hills U.K.	
149 F6	South Georgia and the South	
	Sandwich Islands terr.	
	S. Atlantic Ocean	
96 A2	South Harris pen. U.K.	
129 E1	South Henik Lake Can.	
54 B2	South Island N.Z.	
65 B2	South Korea country Asia	
65 B2	South Korea country Asia	
135 B3	South Lake Tahoe U.S.A.	
55 Q4	South Orkney Islands S.	
	Atlantic Ocean	
136 C2	South Platte r. U.S.A.	
98 B2	Southport U.K.	
143 E2	Southport U.S.A.	
96 C1	South Ronaldsay i. U.K.	
123 D3	South Sand Bluff pt S. Africa	
129 D2	South Saskatchewan r. Can.	
129 E2	South Seal r. Can.	

55 P3	South Shetland Islands	
	Antarctica	
98 C1	South Shields U.K.	
117 A4	South Sudan country Africa	
54 B1	South Taranaki Bight b. N.Z.	
130 C2	South Twin Island Can.	
96 A2	South Uist i. U.K.	
53 D2	South West Rocks Austr.	
99 D2	Southwold U.K.	
109 C3	Soverato Italy	
88 B2	Sovetsk Rus. Fed.	
86 F2	Sovetskiy Rus. Fed.	
91 C2	Sovyets'kyy Ukr.	
123 C2	Soweto S. Africa	
66 D1	Sōya-misaki c. Japan	
90 C1	Sozh r. Europe	
110 C2	Sozopol Bulg.	
106 C1	Spain country Europe	
99 C2	Spalding U.K.	
135 D2	Spanish Fork U.S.A.	
97 B2	Spanish Point Ireland	
108 B3	Sparagio, Monte mt. Sicilia	
	Italy	
135 C3	Sparks U.S.A.	
140 A2	Sparta U.S.A.	
143 D2	Spartanburg U.S.A.	
111 B3	Sparti Greece	
109 C3	Spartivento, Capo c. Italy	
89 D3	Spas-Demensk Rus. Fed.	
89 F2	Spas-Klepiki Rus. Fed.	
66 B2	Spassk-Dal'niy Rus. Fed.	
89 F3	Spassk-Ryazanskiy Rus. Fed.	
111 B3	Spatha, Akrotirio pt Greece	
136 C2	Spearfish U.S.A.	
139 C1	Spearman U.S.A.	
137 D2	Spencer U.S.A.	
52 A2	Spencer Gulf est. Austr.	
98 C1	Spennymoor U.K.	
54 B2	Spenser Mountains N.Z.	
101 D3	Spessart reg. Ger.	
96 C2	Spey r. U.K.	
102 B2	Speyer Ger.	
100 C1	Spiekeroog i. Ger.	
100 B2	Spijkenisse Neth.	
128 C2	Spirit River Can.	
103 E2	Spišská Nová Ves Slovakia	
82 C1	Spitsbergen i. Svalbard	
102 C2	Spittal an der Drau Austria	
109 C2	Split Croatia	
129 E2	Split Lake Can.	
129 E2	Split Lake l. Can.	
134 C1	Spokane U.S.A.	
140 A1	Spooner U.S.A.	
102 C1	Spree r. Ger.	
122 A2	Springbok S. Africa	
131 E2	Springdale Can.	
142 B1	Springdale U.S.A.	
101 D1	Springe Ger.	
138 C1	Springer U.S.A.	
138 B2	Springerville U.S.A.	
136 C3	Springfield CO U.S.A.	
140 B3	Springfield IL U.S.A.	
141 E2	Springfield MA U.S.A.	
137 E3	Springfield MO U.S.A.	
140 C3	Springfield OH U.S.A.	
134 B2	Springfield OR U.S.A.	
123 C3	Springfontein S. Africa	
131 D2	Springhill Can.	
143 D3	Spring Hill U.S.A.	
54 B2	Springs Junction N.Z.	
98 C2	Spurn Head U.K.	
128 B3	Squamish Can.	
109 C3	Squillace, Golfo di g. Italy	
	Srbija country Europe see	
	Serbia	
109 C2	Srebrenica Bos.-Herz.	
110 C2	Sredets Bulg.	

83 L4	Sredinnyy Khrebet *mts* Rus. Fed.	
83 L2	Srednekolymsk Rus. Fed.	
	Sredne-Russkaya Vozvyshennost' *hills* Rus. Fed. *see* **Central Russian Upland**	
	Sredne-Sibirskoye Ploskogor'ye *plat.* Rus. Fed. *see* **Central Siberian Plateau**	
110 R7	Srednogorie Bulg.	
69 D1	Sretensk Rus. Fed.	
61 C1	Sri Aman *Sarawak* Malaysia	
	Sri Jayewardenepura Kotte *see* **Sri Lanka**	
73 B4	Sri Lanka *country* Asia	
73 C4	Srikakulam India	
68 A2	Srinagar India	
74 B1	Srinagar India	
73 B3	Srivardhan India	
101 D1	Stade Ger.	
101 E1	Stadensen Ger.	
100 C1	Stadskanaal Neth.	
101 D2	Stadtallendorf Ger.	
101 D1	Stadthagen Ger.	
101 E2	Staffelstein Ger.	
99 B2	Stafford U.K.	
99 C3	Staines U.K.	
91 D2	Stakhanov Ukr.	
	Stalingrad Rus. Fed. *see* **Volgograd**	
103 D3	Stalowa Wola Pol.	
99 C2	Stamford U.K.	
141 E2	Stamford CT U.S.A.	
139 D2	Stamford TX U.S.A.	
122 A1	Stampriet Namibia	
92 F3	Stamsund Norway	
123 C2	Standerton S. Africa	
140 C2	Standish U.S.A.	
153 C6	Stanley Falkland Is.	
136 C1	Stanley U.K.	
83 I3	Stanovoy Nagor'ye *mts* Rus. Fed.	
83 J3	Stanovoy Khrebet *mts* Rus. Fed.	
53 D1	Stanthorpe Austr.	
103 E1	Starachowice Pol.	
	Stara Planina *mts* Bulg./S.M. *see* **Balkan Mountains**	
89 D2	Staraya Russa Rus. Fed.	
89 D2	Staraya Toropa Rus. Fed.	
110 C2	Stara Zagora Bulg.	
103 D1	Stargard Szczeciński Pol.	
142 C2	Starkville U.S.A.	
91 D2	Starobil's'k Ukr.	
89 D3	Starodub Rus. Fed.	
103 D1	Starogard Gdański Pol.	
91 D2	Starokostyantyniv Ukr.	
91 D2	Starominskaya Rus. Fed.	
91 D2	Staroshcherbinovskaya Rus. Fed.	
91 D2	Starotitarovskaya Rus. Fed.	
89 F3	Starovur'yevo Rus. Fed.	
99 B3	Start Point U.K.	
88 C3	Staryya Darohi Belarus	
89 F3	Staryy Oskol Rus. Fed.	
101 E2	Staßfurt Ger.	
141 D2	State College U.S.A.	
143 D2	Statesboro U.S.A.	
143 D1	Statesville U.S.A.	
93 E4	Stavanger Norway	
87 D4	Stavropol' Rus. Fed.	
87 D4	Stavropol'skaya Vozvyshennost' *hills* Rus. Fed.	
52 B3	Stawell Austr.	
123 C2	Steadville S. Africa	
136 B2	Steamboat Springs U.S.A.	
101 E2	Stedten Ger.	
128 C2	Steen River Can.	
134 C2	Steens Mountain U.S.A.	
100 C1	Steenwijk Neth.	
126 D2	Stefansson Island Can.	
101 E3	Steigerwald *mts* Ger.	
129 C3	Steinbach Can.	
100 C1	Steinfurt Ger.	
120 A3	Steinhausen Namibia	
92 F3	Steinkjer Norway	
122 A2	Steinkopf S. Africa	
123 B2	Stella S. Africa	
105 D2	Stenay France	
101 E1	Stendal Ger.	
	Stepanakert Azer. *see* **Xankändi**	
131 E2	Stephenville Can.	
139 D2	Stephenville U.S.A.	
122 B3	Sterling S. Africa	
136 C2	Sterling CO U.S.A.	
140 B2	Sterling IL U.S.A.	
87 E3	Sterlitamak Rus. Fed.	
101 E1	Sternberg Ger.	
128 C2	Stettler Can.	
140 C2	Steubenville U.S.A.	
99 C2	Stevenage U.K.	
129 E3	Stevenson Lake Can.	
126 B2	Stevens Village U.S.A.	
128 B2	Stewart r. Can.	
126 B2	Stewart r. Can.	
54 A3	Stewart Island N.Z.	
127 F2	Stewart Lake Can.	
102 C2	Steyr Austria	
122 B3	Steytlerville S. Africa	
128 A2	Stikine r. Can.	
128 A2	Stikine Plateau Can.	
122 B3	Stilbaai S. Africa	
139 D1	Stillwater r. U.S.A.	
109 D2	Štip Macedonia	
96 C2	Stirling U.K.	
92 F3	Stjørdalshalsen Norway	
103 D2	Stockerau Austria	
93 G4	Stockholm Sweden	
98 B2	Stockport U.K.	
135 B3	Stockton U.S.A.	
98 C1	Stockton-on-Tees U.K.	
63 B2	Stœng Trêng Cambodia	
96 B1	Stoer, Point of U.K.	
98 B2	Stoke-on-Trent U.K.	
109 D2	Stol *mt.* Serbia	
109 C2	Stolac Bos.-Herz.	
100 C2	Stolberg (Rheinland) Ger.	
88 C3	Stolin Belarus	
101 F2	Stollberg Ger.	
101 D1	Stolzenau Ger.	
96 C2	Stonehaven U.K.	
129 F2	Stonewall Can.	
129 D2	Stony Rapids Can.	
92 G2	Storavan l. Sweden	
	Store Bælt *sea chan.* Denmark *see* **Great Belt**	
92 F3	Støren Norway	
92 F3	Storforshei Norway	
126 D2	Storkerson Peninsula Can.	
137 D2	Storm Lake U.S.A.	
93 E3	Stornosa *mt.* Norway	
96 A1	Stornoway U.K.	
86 F2	Storozhevsk Rus. Fed.	
90 B2	Storozhynets' Ukr.	
92 F3	Storsjön l. Sweden	
92 H2	Storslett Norway	
92 G2	Storuman Sweden	
99 C2	Stour r. *England* U.K.	
99 C3	Stour r. *England* U.K.	
130 A1	Stout Lake Can.	
88 C3	Stowbtsy Belarus	
97 C1	Strabane U.K.	
102 C2	Strakonice Czech Rep.	
102 C1	Stralsund Ger.	
122 A3	Strand S. Africa	
93 E3	Stranda Norway	
97 D1	Strangford Lough *inlet* U.K.	
96 B3	Stranraer U.K.	
105 D2	Strasbourg France	
140 C2	Stratford Can.	
54 B1	Stratford N.Z.	
139 C1	Stratford U.S.A.	
99 C2	Stratford-upon-Avon U.K.	
128 C2	Strathmore Can.	
96 C2	Strathspey *val.* U.K.	
102 C2	Straubing Ger.	
51 C3	Streaky Bay Austr.	
140 B2	Streator U.S.A.	
110 B2	Strehaia Romania	
153 B5	Stroeder Arg.	
101 D1	Ströhen Ger.	
109 C3	Stromboli, Isola i. Italy	
96 C1	Stromness U.K.	
92 G3	Strömsund Sweden	
96 C1	Stronsay i. U.K.	
53 D2	Stroud Austr.	
99 B3	Stroud U.K.	
100 C1	Strückhausen (Satörland) Ger.	
109 D2	Struga Macedonia	
88 C2	Strugi-Krasnyye Rus. Fed.	
122 B3	Struis Bay S. Africa	
109 D2	Strumica Macedonia	
122 B3	Strydenburg S. Africa	
111 B2	Strymonas r. Greece	
90 A2	Stryy Ukr.	
128 B2	Stuart Lake Can.	
130 A1	Stull Lake Can.	
89 E3	Stupino Rus. Fed.	
140 B2	Sturgeon Bay U.S.A.	
130 C2	Sturgeon Falls Can.	
130 A2	Sturgeon Lake Can.	
140 B2	Sturgis MI U.S.A.	
136 C2	Sturgis SD U.S.A.	
50 B1	Sturt Creek *watercourse* Austr.	
52 B1	Sturt Stony Desert Austr.	
123 C3	Stutterheim S. Africa	
102 B2	Stuttgart Ger.	
142 B2	Stuttgart U.S.A.	
92 □A2	Stykkishólmur Iceland	
90 B1	Styr r. Belarus/Ukr.	
155 D1	Suaçuí Grande r. Brazil	
116 B3	Suakin Sudan	
78 A3	Suara Eritrea	
109 C1	Subotica Serbia	
110 C1	Suceava Romania	
97 D2	Suck r. Ireland	
152 B2	Sucre Bol.	
154 B2	Sucuriú r. Brazil	
89 E2	Suda r. Rus. Fed.	
91 C3	Sudak Ukr.	
117 A3	Sudan *country* Africa	
130 B2	Sudbury Can.	
117 A4	Sudd *swamp* S. Sudan	
89 F2	Sudislavl' Rus. Fed.	
89 F2	Sudogda Rus. Fed.	
94 D1	Suðuroy i. Faroe Is.	
107 C2	Sueca Spain	
116 B2	Suez Egypt	
116 B2	Suez, Gulf of Egypt	
80 B2	Suez Canal Egypt	
141 D3	Suffolk U.S.A.	
116 B2	Sūhāj Egypt	
79 C2	Şuḩār Oman	
69 D1	Sühbaatar Mongolia	
101 E2	Suhl Ger.	
109 C1	Suhopolje Croatia	
70 B2	Suide China	
66 B2	Suifenhe China	
69 E1	Suihua China	
70 A2	Suining China	
70 B2	Suiping China	

70 B2	**Suiyang** China	
70 B2	**Suizhou** China	
74 B2	**Sujangarh** India	
74 B1	**Sujanpur** India	
74 A2	**Sujawal** Pak.	
60 B2	**Sukabumi** Indon.	
61 B2	**Sukadana** Indon.	
61 C2	**Sukaraja** Indon.	
89 E3	**Sukhinichi** Rus. Fed.	
89 F2	**Sukhona** r. Rus. Fed.	
62 A2	**Sukhothai** Thai.	
74 A2	**Sukkur** Pak.	
89 E2	**Sukromny** Rus. Fed.	
59 C3	**Sula, Kepulauan** is Indon.	
74 A1	**Sulaiman Range** mts Pak.	
	Sulawesi i. Indon. see **Celebes**	
150 A2	**Sullana** Peru	
137 E3	**Sullivan** U.S.A.	
139 D2	**Sulphur Springs** U.S.A.	
64 B2	**Sulu Archipelago** is Phil.	
64 A2	**Sulu Sea** N. Pacific Ocean	
101 E3	**Sulzbach-Rosenberg** Ger.	
79 C2	**Sumāil** Oman	
	Sumatera i. Indon. see **Sumatra**	
60 A1	**Sumatra** i. Indon.	
58 C3	**Sumba** i. Indon.	
61 C2	**Sumbawa** i. Indon.	
61 C2	**Sumbawabesar** Indon.	
119 D3	**Sumbawanga** Tanz.	
120 A2	**Sumbe** Angola	
96 □	**Sumburgh** U.K.	
96 □	**Sumburgh Head** U.K.	
61 C2	**Sumenep** Indon.	
67 D4	**Sumisu-jima** i. Japan	
131 D2	**Summerside** Can.	
140 C3	**Summersville** U.S.A.	
128 B2	**Summit Lake** Can.	
103 D2	**Šumperk** Czech Rep.	
81 C1	**Sumqayit** Azer.	
143 D2	**Sumter** U.S.A.	
91 C1	**Sumy** Ukr.	
75 D2	**Sunamganj** Bangl.	
65 B2	**Sunan** N. Korea	
79 C2	**Şunaynah** Oman	
52 B3	**Sunbury** Austr.	
141 D2	**Sunbury** U.S.A.	
65 B2	**Sunch'ŏn** N. Korea	
65 B3	**Sunch'ŏn** S. Korea	
123 C2	**Sun City** S. Africa	
60 B2	**Sunda, Selat** str. Indon.	
136 C2	**Sundance** U.S.A.	
75 C2	**Sundarbans** coastal area Bangl./India	
98 C1	**Sunderland** U.K.	
128 C2	**Sundre** Can.	
93 G3	**Sundsvall** Sweden	
123 D2	**Sundumbili** S. Africa	
60 B2	**Sungailiat** Indon.	
60 B2	**Sungaipenuh** Indon.	
60 B1	**Sungai Petani** Malaysia	
80 B1	**Süngülü** Turkey	
93 E3	**Sunndalsøra** Norway	
134 C1	**Sunnyside** U.S.A.	
135 B3	**Sunnyvale** U.S.A.	
83 I2	**Suntar** Rus. Fed.	
74 A2	**Suntsar** Pak.	
114 B4	**Sunyani** Ghana	
82 D2	**Suoyarvi** Rus. Fed.	
138 A2	**Superior** AZ U.S.A.	
137 D2	**Superior** NE U.S.A.	
140 A1	**Superior** WI U.S.A.	
140 B1	**Superior, Lake** Can./U.S.A.	
89 D3	**Suponevo** Rus. Fed.	
81 C2	**Sūq ash Shuyūkh** Iraq	
70 B2	**Suqian** China	
78 A2	**Sūq Suwayq** Saudi Arabia	
79 C2	**Şür** Oman	
74 A2	**Surab** Pak.	
61 C2	**Surabaya** Indon.	
61 C2	**Surakarta** Indon.	
74 B2	**Surat** India	
74 B2	**Suratgarh** India	
63 A3	**Surat Thani** Thai.	
89 D3	**Surazh** Rus. Fed.	
109 D2	**Surdulica** Serbia	
74 B2	**Surendranagar** India	
82 F2	**Surgut** Rus. Fed.	
64 B2	**Surigao** Phil.	
63 B2	**Surin** Thai.	
151 D1	**Suriname** country S. America	
	Surt Libya see **Sirte**	
	Surt, Khalīj g. Libya see **Sirte, Gulf of**	
60 B2	**Surulangun** Indon.	
89 F2	**Susanino** Rus. Fed.	
135 B2	**Susanville** U.S.A.	
80 B1	**Suşehri** Turkey	
131 D2	**Sussex** Can.	
101 D1	**Süstedt** Ger.	
100 C1	**Sustrum** Ger.	
83 K2	**Susuman** Rus. Fed.	
111 C3	**Susurluk** Turkey	
75 B1	**Sutak** India	
122 B3	**Sutherland** S. Africa	
99 C2	**Sutton Coldfield** U.K.	
66 D2	**Suttsu** Japan	
49 F4	**Suva** Fiji	
89 E3	**Suvorov** Rus. Fed.	
103 E1	**Suwałki** Pol.	
63 B2	**Suwannaphum** Thai.	
143 D3	**Suwannee** r. U.S.A.	
	Suweis, Qanâ el canal Egypt see **Suez Canal**	
65 B2	**Suwŏn** S. Korea	
79 C2	**Sūzā** Iran	
89 F2	**Suzdal'** Rus. Fed.	
70 B2	**Suzhou** Anhui China	
70 C2	**Suzhou** Jiangsu China	
67 C3	**Suzu** Japan	
67 C3	**Suzu-misaki** pt Japan	
82 B1	**Svalbard** terr. Arctic Ocean	
91 D2	**Svatove** Ukr.	
63 B2	**Svay Riĕng** Cambodia	
93 F3	**Sveg** Sweden	
88 C2	**Švenčionys** Lith.	
93 F4	**Svendborg** Denmark	
	Sverdlovsk Rus. Fed. see **Yekaterinburg**	
109 D2	**Sveti Nikole** Macedonia	
88 B3	**Svetlogorsk** Rus. Fed.	
88 B3	**Svetlyy** Rus. Fed.	
93 I3	**Svetogorsk** Rus. Fed.	
110 C2	**Svilengrad** Bulg.	
110 B2	**Svinecea Mare, Vârful** mt. Romania	
110 C2	**Svishtov** Bulg.	
103 D2	**Svitavy** Czech Rep.	
91 C2	**Svitlovods'k** Ukr.	
69 E1	**Svobodnyy** Rus. Fed.	
92 F2	**Svolvær** Norway	
88 C3	**Svyetlahorsk** Belarus	
143 D2	**Swainsboro** U.S.A.	
120 A3	**Swakopmund** Namibia	
52 B3	**Swan Hill** Austr.	
128 C2	**Swan Hills** Can.	
129 E2	**Swan Lake** Can.	
129 D2	**Swan River** Can.	
53 D2	**Swansea** Austr.	
99 B3	**Swansea** U.K.	
123 C2	**Swartruggens** S. Africa	
	Swatow China see **Shantou**	
123 D2	**Swaziland** country Africa	
93 G3	**Sweden** country Europe	
139 C2	**Sweetwater** U.S.A.	
136 B2	**Sweetwater** r. U.S.A.	
122 B3	**Swellendam** S. Africa	
103 D1	**Świdnica** Pol.	
103 D1	**Świdnik** Pol.	
103 D1	**Świebodzin** Pol.	
103 D1	**Świecie** Pol.	
129 D2	**Swift Current** Can.	
97 C1	**Swilly, Lough** inlet Ireland	
99 C3	**Swindon** U.K.	
102 C1	**Świnoujście** Pol.	
105 D2	**Switzerland** country Europe	
97 C2	**Swords** Ireland	
88 C3	**Syanno** Belarus	
89 D2	**Sychevka** Rus. Fed.	
53 D2	**Sydney** Austr.	
131 D2	**Sydney** Can.	
131 D2	**Sydney Mines** Can.	
91 D2	**Syeverodonets'k** Ukr.	
86 E2	**Syktyvkar** Rus. Fed.	
142 C2	**Sylacauga** U.S.A.	
75 D2	**Sylhet** Bangl.	
102 B1	**Sylt** i. Ger.	
111 C3	**Symi** i. Greece	
91 C2	**Synel'nykove** Ukr.	
109 C3	**Syracuse** Sicilia Italy	
136 C3	**Syracuse** KS U.S.A.	
141 D2	**Syracuse** NY U.S.A.	
77 C2	**Syrdar'ya** r. Asia	
80 B2	**Syria** country Asia	
80 B2	**Syrian Desert** Asia	
111 B3	**Syros** i. Greece	
87 D3	**Syzran'** Rus. Fed.	
102 C1	**Szczecin** Pol.	
103 D1	**Szczecinek** Pol.	
103 E1	**Szczytno** Pol.	
103 E2	**Szeged** Hungary	
103 D2	**Székesfehérvár** Hungary	
103 D2	**Szekszárd** Hungary	
103 E2	**Szentes** Hungary	
103 D2	**Szentgotthárd** Hungary	
103 D2	**Szigetvár** Hungary	
103 E2	**Szolnok** Hungary	
103 D2	**Szombathely** Hungary	

T

78 B2	**Tābah** Saudi Arabia	
76 B3	**Tabas** Iran	
81 D3	**Tābask, Kūh-e** mt. Iran	
150 B2	**Tabatinga** Brazil	
114 B2	**Tabelbala** Alg.	
129 C3	**Taber** Can.	
102 C2	**Tábor** Czech Rep.	
119 D3	**Tabora** Tanz.	
114 B4	**Tabou** Côte d'Ivoire	
81 C2	**Tabriz** Iran	
78 A2	**Tabūk** Saudi Arabia	
77 E2	**Tacheng** China	
102 C2	**Tachov** Czech Rep.	
64 B1	**Tacloban** Phil.	
150 A3	**Tacna** Peru	
134 B1	**Tacoma** U.S.A.	
152 C4	**Tacuarembó** Uru.	
138 B3	**Tacupeto** Mex.	
117 C3	**Tadjourah** Djibouti	
80 B2	**Tadmur** Syria	
129 E2	**Tadoule Lake** Can.	
65 B2	**Taegu** S. Korea	
65 B2	**Taejŏn** S. Korea	
65 B2	**Taejŏng** S. Korea	
65 B2	**T'aepaek** S. Korea	
69 E1	**Ta'erqi** China	
107 C1	**Tafalla** Spain	
152 B3	**Tafí Viejo** Arg.	

79 D2	Taftān, Kūh-e mt. Iran	
91 D2	Taganrog Rus. Fed.	
91 D2	Taganrog, Gulf of Rus. Fed./ Ukr.	
62 A1	Tagaung Myanmar	
64 B1	Tagaytay City Phil.	
64 B2	Tagbilaran Phil.	
64 B1	Tagudin Phil.	
64 B2	Tagum Phil.	
106 B2	Tagus r. Port./Spain	
60 B1	Tahan, Gunung mt. Malaysia	
115 C2	Tahat, Mont mt. Alg.	
69 E1	Tahe China	
49 I4	Tahiti i. Fr. Polynesia	
139 E1	Tahlequah U.S.A.	
135 B3	Tahoe, Lake U.S.A.	
135 B3	Tahoe City U.S.A.	
126 D2	Tahoe Lake Can.	
115 C3	Tahoua Niger	
79 C2	Tahrūd Iran	
128 B3	Tahsis Can.	
70 B2	Tai'an China	
71 C3	Taibei Taiwan	
	Taibus Qi China see Baochang	
54 C1	Taihape N.Z.	
70 C2	Tai Hu l. China	
52 A3	Tailem Bend Austr.	
71 C3	Tainan Taiwan	
155 D1	Taiobeiras Brazil	
60 B1	Taiping Malaysia	
71 B3	Taishan China	
153 A5	Taitao, Península de pen. Chile	
71 C3	T'aitung Taiwan	
92 I2	Taivalkoski Fin.	
92 H2	Taivaskero h. Fin.	
71 C3	Taiwan country Asia	
71 B3	Taiwan Strait China/Taiwan	
70 B2	Taiyuan China	
71 C3	Taizhou China	
71 C3	Taizhou Zhejiang China	
78 B3	Ta'izz Yemen	
77 D3	Tajikistan country Asia	
75 B2	Taj Mahal tourist site India	
	Tajo r. Port. see Tagus	
58 A1	Tak Thai.	
54 C1	Takaka N.Z.	
54 B4	Takamatsu Japan	
67 C3	Takaoka Japan	
54 B1	Takapuna N.Z.	
67 C3	Takasaki Japan	
122 B1	Takatokwane Botswana	
67 C3	Takayama Japan	
67 C3	Takefu Japan	
60 A1	Takengon Indon.	
63 B2	Takêv Cambodia	
63 B2	Ta Khmau Cambodia	
66 D2	Takikawa Japan	
128 B2	Takla Lake Can.	
128 A3	Takla Landing Can.	
77 E3	Taklimakan Desert China	
	Taklimakan Shamo des. China see Taklimakan Desert	
128 A2	Taku r. Can./U.S.A.	
63 A3	Takua Pa Thai.	
115 C4	Takum Nigeria	
88 C3	Talachyn Belarus	
74 B1	Talagang Pak.	
150 A2	Talara Peru	
59 C2	Talaud, Kepulauan is Indon.	
106 C2	Talavera de la Reina Spain	
153 A4	Talca Chile	
153 A4	Talcahuano Chile	
89 E2	Taldom Rus. Fed.	
77 D2	Taldykorgan Kazakh.	
59 C3	Taliabu i. Indon.	
64 B1	Talisay Phil.	

61 C2	Taliwang Indon.	
81 C2	Tall 'Afar Iraq	
143 D2	Tallahassee U.S.A.	
88 B2	Tallinn Estonia	
142 B2	Tallulah U.S.A.	
104 B2	Talmont-St-Hilaire France	
90 C2	Tal'ne Ukr.	
117 B3	Talodi Sudan	
91 E1	Talovaya Rus. Fed.	
126 E2	Taloyoak Can.	
88 B2	Talsi Latvia	
152 A1	Taltal Chile	
129 C1	Taltson r. Can.	
60 A1	Talu Indon.	
53 C1	Talwood Austr.	
114 B4	Tamale Ghana	
115 C2	Tamanrasset Alg.	
99 A3	Tamar r. U.K.	
145 C3	Tamazunchale Mex.	
114 A3	Tambacounda Senegal	
61 B1	Tambelan, Kepulauan is Indon.	
91 E1	Tambov Rus. Fed.	
145 C2	Tamiahua, Laguna de lag. Mex.	
143 D3	Tampa U.S.A.	
143 D3	Tampa Bay U.S.A.	
93 H3	Tampere Fin.	
145 C2	Tampico Mex.	
69 D1	Tamsagbulag Mongolia	
102 C2	Tamsweg Austria	
53 D2	Tamworth Austr.	
99 C2	Tamworth U.K.	
119 E3	Tana r. Kenya	
117 B3	Tana, Lake Eth.	
67 C4	Tanabe Japan	
92 I1	Tana Bru Norway	
61 C2	Tanahgrogot Indon.	
58 C3	Tanahjampea i. Indon.	
50 C1	Tanami Desert Austr.	
126 A2	Tanana U.S.A.	
108 A1	Tanaro r. Italy	
65 B1	Tanch'ŏn N. Korea	
64 B2	Tandag Phil.	
110 C2	Ţăndărei Romania	
153 C4	Tandil Arg.	
74 A2	Tando Adam Pak.	
74 A2	Tando Muhammad Khan Pak.	
114 B2	Tanezrouft reg. Alg./Mali	
119 D3	Tanga Tanz.	
119 C3	Tanganyika, Lake Africa	
	Tanger Morocco see Tangier	
101 E1	Tangermünde Ger.	
75 C1	Tanggula Shan mts China	
114 B1	Tangier Morocco	
75 C1	Tangra Yumco salt l. China	
70 B2	Tangshan China	
68 C2	Taniantaweng Shan mts China	
59 C3	Tanimbar, Kepulauan is Indon.	
64 B2	Tanjay Phil.	
60 A1	Tanjungbalai Indon.	
61 B2	Tanjungpandan Indon.	
60 B1	Tanjungpinang Indon.	
61 C1	Tanjungredeb Indon.	
61 C1	Tanjungselor Indon.	
74 B1	Tank Pak.	
115 C3	Tanout Niger	
75 C2	Tansen Nepal	
116 B1	Ţanţā Egypt	
119 D3	Tanzania country Africa	
69 E1	Taonan China	
138 B1	Taos U.S.A.	
114 B2	Taoudenni Mali	
88 C2	Tapa Estonia	
145 C3	Tapachula Mex.	

151 C2	Tapajós r. Brazil	
60 A1	Tapaktuan Indon.	
145 C3	Tapanatepec Mex.	
150 B2	Tapauá Brazil	
114 B4	Tapeta Liberia	
141 D3	Tappahannock U.S.A.	
74 B2	Tapti r. India	
150 B2	Tapurucuara Brazil	
154 A1	Taquari r. Brazil	
154 B1	Taquari, Serra do hills Brazil	
154 C2	Taquaritinga Brazil	
115 D4	Taraba r. Nigeria	
	Ţarābulus Libya see Tripoli	
61 C1	Tarakan Indon.	
88 A3	Taran, Mys pt Rus. Fed.	
54 B1	Taranaki, Mount vol. N.Z.	
106 C1	Tarancón Spain	
109 C2	Taranto Italy	
109 C2	Taranto, Golfo di g. Italy	
150 A2	Tarapoto Peru	
91 E2	Tarasovskiy Rus. Fed.	
150 A2	Tarauacá Brazil	
150 B2	Tarauacá r. Brazil	
48 F2	Tarawa atoll Kiribati	
77 D2	Taraz Kazakh.	
107 C1	Tarazona Spain	
77 C2	Tarbagatay, Khrebet mts Kazakh.	
96 A2	Tarbert Scotland U.K.	
96 B3	Tarbert Scotland U.K.	
104 C3	Tarbes France	
96 B2	Tarbet U.K.	
51 C3	Tarcoola Austr.	
53 D2	Taree Austr.	
110 C2	Târgovişte Romania	
110 B1	Târgu Jiu Romania	
110 B1	Târgu Mureş Romania	
110 C1	Târgu Neamţ Romania	
79 C2	Tarif U.A.E.	
152 B3	Tarija Bol.	
79 B3	Tarīm Yemen	
77 E3	Tarim Basin China	
77 E2	Tarim He r. China	
	Tarim Pendi basin China see Tarim Basin	
59 D3	Taritatu r. Indon.	
82 G2	Tarko-Sale Rus. Fed.	
114 B4	Tarkwa Ghana	
64 B1	Tarlac Phil.	
68 C2	Tarlag China	
92 G2	Tärnaby Sweden	
77 C3	Tarnak Rōd r. Afgh.	
110 B1	Târnăveni Romania	
103 E1	Tarnobrzeg Pol.	
103 E1	Tarnów Pol.	
75 C1	Taro Co salt l. China	
114 B1	Taroudannt Morocco	
108 B2	Tarquinia Italy	
107 D1	Tarragona Spain	
107 D1	Tàrrega Spain	
80 B2	Tarsus Turkey	
152 B3	Tartagal Arg.	
104 B3	Tartas France	
88 C2	Tartu Estonia	
80 B2	Ţarţūs Syria	
155 D1	Tarumirim Brazil	
89 F3	Tarusa Rus. Fed.	
108 B1	Tarvisio Italy	
81 D3	Tashk, Daryācheh-ye l. Iran	
	Tashkent Uzbek. see Toshkent	
131 D1	Tasiujaq Can.	
76 B1	Taskala Kazakh.	
77 E2	Taskesken Kazakh.	
54 B2	Tasman Bay N.Z.	
51 D4	Tasmania state Austr.	
54 B2	Tasman Mountains N.Z.	
156 D8	Tasman Sea S. Pacific Ocean	

103 D2 Tatabánya Hungary
90 B2 Tatarbunary Ukr.
83 K3 Tatarskiy Proliv str. Rus. Fed.
67 C4 Tateyama Japan
128 C1 Tathlina Lake Can.
78 B3 Tathlith Saudi Arabia
78 B2 Tathlīth, Wādī watercourse Saudi Arabia
53 C3 Tathra Austr.
62 A1 Tatkon Myanmar
128 B2 Tatla Lake Can.
103 D2 Tatra Mountains mts Pol./Slovakia
Tatry mts Pol./Slovakia see Tatra Mountains
154 C2 Tatuí Brazil
139 C2 Tatum U.S.A.
81 C2 Tatvan Turkey
151 D2 Taua Brazil
155 C2 Taubaté Brazil
101 D3 Tauberbischofsheim Ger.
54 C1 Taumarunui N.Z.
62 A1 Taunggyi Myanmar
62 A2 Taung-ngu Myanmar
62 A2 Taungup Myanmar
99 B3 Taunton U.K.
100 C2 Taunus hills Ger.
54 C1 Taupo N.Z.
54 C1 Taupo, Lake N.Z.
88 B2 Tauragé Lith.
54 C1 Tauranga N.Z.
80 B2 Taurus Mountains Turkey
111 C3 Tavas Turkey
86 F3 Tavda Rus. Fed.
106 B2 Tavira Port.
99 A3 Tavistock U.K.
63 A2 Tavoy Myanmar
111 C3 Tavşanlı Turkey
99 A3 Taw r. U.K.
140 C2 Tawas City U.S.A.
61 C1 Tawau Sabah Malaysia
64 A2 Tawi-Tawi i. Phil.
145 C3 Taxco Mex.
76 B2 Taxiatosh Uzbek.
77 D3 Taxkorgan China
96 C2 Tay r. U.K.
96 C2 Tay, Firth of est. U.K.
96 B2 Tay, Loch l. U.K.
128 B2 Taylor U.S.A.
139 D2 Taylor U.S.A.
140 B3 Taylorville U.S.A.
78 A2 Taymā' Saudi Arabia
83 H2 Taymura r. Rus. Fed.
83 H2 Taymyr, Ozero l. Rus. Fed.
Taymyr, Poluostrov pen. Rus. Fed. see Taymyr Peninsula
83 G2 Taymyr Peninsula Rus. Fed.
63 B2 Tây Ninh Vietnam
64 A1 Taytay Phil.
82 G2 Taz r. Rus. Fed.
114 B1 Taza Morocco
129 D2 Tazin Lake Can.
86 G2 Tazovskaya Guba sea chan. Rus. Fed.
81 C1 Tbilisi Georgia
91 E2 Tbilisskaya Rus. Fed.
118 B3 Tchibanga Gabon
118 B2 Tcholliré Cameroon
103 D1 Tczew Pol.
144 B2 Teacapán Mex.
54 A3 Te Anau N.Z.
54 A3 Te Anau, Lake N.Z.
145 C3 Teapa Mex.
54 C1 Te Awamutu N.Z.
115 C1 Tébessa Alg.
60 B2 Tebingtinggi Sumatera Selatan Indon.

60 A1 Tebingtinggi Sumatera Utara Indon.
114 B4 Techiman Ghana
144 B3 Tecomán Mex.
144 B2 Tecoripa Mex.
145 B3 Técpan Mex.
144 B2 Tecuala Mex.
110 C1 Tecuci Romania
68 C1 Teeli Rus. Fed.
98 C1 Tees r. U.K.
111 C3 Tefenni Turkey
61 B2 Tegal Indon.
146 B3 Tegucigalpa Hond.
115 C3 Teguidda-n-Tessoumt Niger
114 B4 Téhini Côte d'Ivoire
81 D2 Tehrān Iran
145 C3 Tehuacán Mex.
145 C3 Tehuantepec, Gulf of Mex.
145 C3 Tehuantepec, Istmo de isth. Mex.
99 A2 Teifi r. U.K.
76 C3 Tejen Turkm.
76 C3 Tejen r. Turkm.
Tejo r. Spain see Tagus
145 B3 Tejupilco Mex.
54 B2 Tekapo, Lake N.Z.
145 D2 Tekax Mex.
116 B3 Tekezé Wenz r. Eritrea/Eth.
111 C2 Tekirdağ Turkey
54 C1 Te Kuiti N.Z.
75 C2 Tel r. India
81 C1 Telavi Georgia
80 B2 Tel Aviv-Yafo Israel
145 D2 Telchac Puerto Mex.
128 A2 Telegraph Creek Can.
154 B2 Telêmaco Borba Brazil
99 B2 Telford U.K.
60 A2 Telo Indon.
86 E2 Telpoziz, Gora mt. Rus. Fed.
88 B2 Telšiai Lith.
61 B2 Telukbatang Indon.
60 A1 Telukdalam Indon.
60 B1 Teluk Intan Malaysia
130 C2 Temagami Lake Can.
61 C2 Temanggung Indon.
123 C2 Temba S. Africa
60 B2 Tembilahan Indon.
120 A1 Tembo Aluma Angola
99 B2 Teme r. U.K.
60 B1 Temerluh Malaysia
77 D1 Temirtau Kazakh.
53 C2 Temora Austr.
139 D2 Temple U.S.A.
97 C2 Templemore Ireland
145 C2 Tempoal Mex.
91 D2 Temryuk Rus. Fed.
153 A4 Temuco Chile
54 B2 Temuka N.Z.
145 C2 Tenabo Mex.
73 C3 Tenali India
63 A2 Tenasserim Myanmar
99 A3 Tenby U.K.
117 C3 Tendaho Eth.
105 D3 Tende France
108 A2 Tende, Col de pass France/Italy
73 D4 Ten Degree Channel India
67 C3 Tendō Japan
114 B3 Ténenkou Mali
115 C3 Ténéré, Erg du des. Niger
115 D2 Ténéré du Tafassâsset des. Niger
114 A2 Tenerife i. Islas Canarias
107 D2 Ténès Alg.
61 C2 Tengah, Kepulauan is Indon.
62 A1 Tengchong China
61 C2 Tenggarong Indon.

70 A2 Tengger Shamo des. China
71 B3 Tengxian China
119 C4 Tenke Dem. Rep. Congo
114 B3 Tenkodogo Burkina Faso
51 C1 Tennant Creek Austr.
142 C1 Tennessee r. U.S.A.
142 C1 Tennessee state U.S.A.
145 C3 Tenosique Mex.
53 D1 Tenterfield Austr.
155 D1 Teodoro Sampaio Brazil
155 D1 Teófilo Otoni Brazil
145 C3 Teopisca Mex.
144 B2 Tepache Mex.
54 B1 Te Paki N.Z.
144 B3 Tepalcatepec Mex.
144 B2 Tepatitlán Mex.
144 B2 Tepehuanes Mex.
109 D2 Tepelenë Albania
144 B2 Tepic Mex.
102 C1 Teplice Czech Rep.
89 E3 Teploye Rus. Fed.
144 B2 Tequila Mex.
108 B2 Teramo Italy
89 E3 Terbuny Rus. Fed.
108 B2 Terebovlya Ukr.
87 D4 Terek r. Rus. Fed.
151 D2 Teresina Brazil
155 D2 Teresópolis Brazil
63 A3 Teressa Island India
80 B1 Terme Turkey
108 B3 Termini Imerese Sicilia Italy
145 C3 Términos, Laguna de lag. Mex.
77 C3 Termiz Uzbek.
109 B2 Termoli Italy
59 C2 Ternate Indon.
100 A2 Terneuzen Neth.
108 B2 Terni Italy
90 B2 Ternopil' Ukr.
128 B2 Terrace Can.
130 B2 Terrace Bay Can.
122 B2 Terra Firma S. Africa
140 B3 Terre Haute U.S.A.
131 E2 Terrenceville Can.
100 B1 Terschelling i. Neth.
108 A3 Tertenia Sardegna Italy
107 C1 Teruel Spain
92 H2 Tervola Fin.
109 C2 Tešanj Bos.-Herz.
116 B3 Teseney Eritrea
66 D2 Teshio-gawa r. Japan
128 A1 Teslin Can.
128 A1 Teslin Lake Can.
154 B1 Tesouro Brazil
115 C3 Tessaoua Niger
121 C2 Tete Moz.
90 C1 Teteriv r. Ukr.
101 F1 Teterow Ger.
90 B2 Tetiyiv Ukr.
114 B1 Tétouan Morocco
109 D2 Tetovo Macedonia
152 B3 Teuco r. Arg.
144 B2 Teul de González Ortega Mex.
101 D1 Teutoburger Wald hills Ger.
Tevere r. Italy see Tiber
54 A3 Teviot N.Z.
51 E2 Tewantin Austr.
54 C2 Te Wharau N.Z.
139 E2 Texarkana U.S.A.
53 D1 Texas Austr.
139 D2 Texas state U.S.A.
139 E3 Texas City U.S.A.
106 B1 Texel i. Neth.
139 D2 Texoma, Lake U.S.A.
123 C2 Teyateyaneng Lesotho
89 F2 Teykovo Rus. Fed.
89 F2 Teza r. Rus. Fed.

75 D2 **Tezpur** India
62 A1 **Tezu** India
129 E1 **Tha-anne** r. Can.
123 C2 **Thabana-Ntlenyana** mt. Lesotho
123 C2 **Thaba Putsoa** mt. Lesotho
123 C1 **Thabazimbi** S. Africa
123 C2 **Thabong** S. Africa
63 A2 **Thagyettaw** Myanmar
62 D1 **Thai Bình** Vietnam
63 B2 **Thailand** country Asia
63 B2 **Thailand, Gulf of** Asia
62 B1 **Thai Nguyên** Vietnam
62 B2 **Thakhèk** Laos
63 A3 **Thalang** Thai.
74 B1 **Thal Desert** Pak.
101 E2 **Thale (Harz)** Ger.
62 B2 **Tha Li** Thai.
123 C1 **Thamaga** Botswana
116 C3 **Thamar, Jabal** mt. Yemen
79 C3 **Thamarit** Oman
130 B2 **Thames** r. Can.
54 C1 **Thames** N.Z.
99 D5 **Thames** est. U.K.
99 D3 **Thames** r. U.K.
63 A2 **Thanbyuzayat** Myanmar
62 A1 **Thandwè** Myanmar
62 B2 **Thanh Hoa** Vietnam
73 B3 **Thanjavur** India
63 A2 **Thanlyin** Myanmar
74 A2 **Thano Bula Khan** Pak.
62 B1 **Than Uyên** Vietnam
74 A2 **Thar Desert** India/Pak.
52 B1 **Thargomindah** Austr.
81 C2 **Tharthār, Buḩayrat ath** l. Iraq
111 B2 **Thasos** i. Greece
62 B1 **Thất Khê** Vietnam
62 A2 **Thaton** Myanmar
74 A2 **Thatta** Pak.
62 A1 **Thaungdut** Myanmar
62 A2 **Thayawadi** Myanmar
62 A2 **Thayetmyo** Myanmar
62 A1 **Thazi** Myanmar
146 C2 **The Bahamas** country West Indies
98 B1 **The Cheviot** h. U.K.
134 B1 **The Dalles** U.S.A.
99 C2 **The Fens** reg. U.K.
114 A3 **The Gambia** country Africa
The Great Oasis Egypt see Khārijah, Waḩāt al
79 C2 **The Gulf** Asia
100 B1 **The Hague** Neth.
129 E1 **Thelon** r. Can.
101 E2 **Themar** Ger.
96 A1 **The Minch** sea chan. U.K.
150 B2 **Theodore Roosevelt** r. Brazil
129 D2 **The Pas** Can.
111 B7 **Thermaikos Kolpos** g. Greece
136 B3 **Thermopolis** U.S.A.
53 C3 **The Rock** Austr.
130 B2 **Thessalon** Can.
111 B2 **Thessaloniki** Greece
99 D2 **Thetford** U.K.
131 C2 **Thetford Mines** Can.
62 A1 **The Triangle** mts Myanmar
131 D1 **Thévenet, Lac** l. Can.
99 D2 **The Wash** b. U.K.
139 D2 **The Woodlands** U.S.A.
142 B3 **Thibodaux** U.S.A.
129 E2 **Thicket Portage** Can.
137 D1 **Thief River Falls** U.S.A.
105 C2 **Thiers** France
119 D3 **Thika** Kenya
73 B4 **Thiladhunmathi** Maldives

75 C2 **Thimphu** Bhutan
105 D2 **Thionville** France
90 C1 **Thírsk** U.K.
73 B4 **Thiruvananthapuram** India
93 E4 **Thisted** Denmark
129 E1 **Thlewiaza** r. Can.
62 A2 **Thoen** Thai.
123 D1 **Thohoyandou** S. Africa
101 E1 **Thomasburg** Ger.
97 C2 **Thomastown** Ireland
143 D2 **Thomasville** U.S.A.
100 C2 **Thommen** Belgium
129 E2 **Thompson** Can.
128 E3 **Thompson** r. U.S.A.
134 C1 **Thompson Falls** U.S.A.
128 B2 **Thompson Sound** Can.
Thoothukudi India see Tuticorin
96 C3 **Thornhill** U.K.
55 C2 **Thorshavnheiane** reg. Antarctica
104 B2 **Thouars** France
128 C2 **Three Hills** Can.
63 A2 **Three Pagodas Pass** Myanmar/Thai.
114 B4 **Three Points, Cape** Ghana
73 B3 **Thrissur** India
63 B2 **Thu Dâu Môt** Vietnam
100 B2 **Thuin** Belgium
127 G1 **Thule** Greenland
121 B3 **Thuli** Zimbabwe
130 B2 **Thunder Bay** Can.
63 A3 **Thung Song** Thai.
101 E2 **Thüringer Becken** reg. Ger.
101 E2 **Thüringer Wald** mts Ger.
102 C1 **Thüringer Wald** mts Ger.
97 C2 **Thurles** Ireland
96 C1 **Thurso** U.K.
96 C1 **Thurso** r. U.K.
151 D2 **Tianguá** Brazil
70 B2 **Tianjin** China
70 B2 **Tianjin** mun. China
71 A3 **Tianlin** China
70 B2 **Tianmen** China
70 A2 **Tianshui** China
154 B2 **Tibagi** r. Brazil
118 B2 **Tibati** Cameroon
108 B2 **Tiber** r. Italy
Tiberias, Lake Israel see Galilee, Sea of
115 D2 **Tibesti** mts Chad
Tibet aut. reg. China see Xizang Zizhiqu
68 B2 **Tibet, Plateau of** China
Tibet Autonomous Region aut. reg. China see Xizang Zizhiqu
115 D2 **Tibīstī, Sarīr** des. Libya
52 B1 **Tibooburra** Austr.
144 A2 **Tiburón, isla** i. Mex.
114 B3 **Tichît** Maur.
114 A2 **Tichla** Western Sahara
145 D2 **Ticul** Mex.
114 A3 **Tidjikja** Maur.
100 B2 **Tiel** Neth.
65 A1 **Tieling** China
100 A2 **Tielt** Belgium
100 B2 **Tienen** Belgium
68 B2 **Tien Shan** mts China/Kyrg.
Tientsin China see Tianjin
93 G3 **Tierp** Sweden
145 C3 **Tierra Blanca** Mex.
145 C3 **Tierra Colorada** Mex.
153 B6 **Tierra del Fuego, Isla Grande de** i. Arg./Chile
154 C2 **Tietê** Brazil
Tiflis Georgia see Tbilisi

143 D2 **Tifton** U.S.A.
90 B2 **Tighina** Moldova
131 D2 **Tignish** Can.
150 A2 **Tigre** r. Ecuador/Peru
81 C2 **Tigris** r. Asia
145 C2 **Tihuatlán** Mex.
144 A1 **Tijuana** Mex.
91 E2 **Tikhoretsk** Rus. Fed.
89 D2 **Tikhvin** Rus. Fed.
89 D2 **Tikhvinskaya Gryada** ridge Rus. Fed.
54 C1 **Tikokino** N.Z.
81 C2 **Tikrīt** Iraq
83 J2 **Tiksi** Rus. Fed.
100 B2 **Tilburg** Neth.
152 B3 **Tilcara** Arg.
52 B1 **Tilcha (abandoned)** Austr.
114 C3 **Tillabéri** Niger
134 B1 **Tillamook** U.S.A.
63 A3 **Tillanchong Island** India
111 C3 **Tilos** i. Greece
52 B2 **Tilpa** Austr.
86 F2 **Til'tim** Rus. Fed.
89 E3 **Tim** Rus. Fed.
86 D2 **Timanskiy Kryazh** ridge Rus. Fed.
54 B2 **Timaru** N.Z.
91 D2 **Timashevsk** Rus. Fed.
114 B3 **Timbedgha** Maur.
50 C1 **Timber Creek** Austr.
114 B3 **Timbuktu** Mali
114 C2 **Timimoun** Alg.
111 B2 **Timiou Prodromou, Akrotirio** pt Greece
110 B1 **Timiş** r. Romania
110 B1 **Timişoara** Romania
130 B2 **Timmins** Can.
89 E2 **Timokhino** Rus. Fed.
151 D2 **Timon** Brazil
59 C3 **Timor** i. East Timor/Indonesia
58 C3 **Timor Sea** Austr./Indon.
93 G3 **Timrå** Sweden
75 C2 **Tingri** China
93 F4 **Tingsryd** Sweden
59 D2 **Tinian** i. N. Mariana Is
152 B3 **Tinogasta** Arg.
111 C3 **Tinos** Greece
111 C3 **Tinos** i. Greece
115 C2 **Tinrhert, Hamada de** Alg.
62 A1 **Tinsukia** India
107 D2 **Tipasa** Alg.
97 B2 **Tipperary** Ireland
109 C2 **Tirana** Albania
Tiranë Albania see Tirana
108 B1 **Tirano** Italy
90 B2 **Tiraspol** Moldova
111 C3 **Tire** Turkey
96 A2 **Tiree** i. U.K.
74 B1 **Tirich Mir** mt. Pak.
73 B3 **Tiruchchirappalli** India
73 B4 **Tirunelveli** India
73 B3 **Tirupati** India
73 B3 **Tiruppattur** India
73 B3 **Tiruppur** India
109 D1 **Tisa** r. Serbia
129 D2 **Tisdale** Can.
107 D2 **Tissemsilt** Alg.
152 B2 **Titicaca, Lake** Bol./Peru
75 C2 **Titlagarh** India
110 C2 **Titu** Romania
143 D3 **Titusville** U.S.A.
99 B3 **Tiverton** U.K.
108 B2 **Tivoli** Italy
79 C2 **Ţiwī** Oman
145 D2 **Tizimín** Mex.
107 D2 **Tizi Ouzou** Alg.

114	B2	Tiznit Morocco
145	C3	Tlacotalpán Mex.
144	B2	Tlahualilo Mex.
145	C3	Tlapa Mex.
145	C3	Tlaxcala Mex.
145	C3	Tlaxiaco Mex.
114	B1	Tlemcen Alg.
123	C1	Tlokweng Botswana
128	B2	Toad River Can.
121	□D2	Toamasina Madag.
60	A1	Toba, Danau l. Indon.
74	A1	Toba and Kakar Ranges mts Pak.
147	D3	Tobago i. Trin. and Tob.
59	C2	Tobelo Indon.
130	B2	Tobermory Can.
96	A2	Tobermory U.K.
129	D2	Tobin Lake Can.
60	B2	Toboali Indon.
86	F3	Tobol'sk Rus. Fed.
76	C1	Tobyl r. Kazakh./Rus. Fed.
151	D2	Tocantinópolis Brazil
151	D2	Tocantins r. Brazil
143	D2	Toccoa U.S.A.
108	A1	Toce r. Italy
152	A3	Tocopilla Chile
53	C3	Tocumwal Austr.
144	A2	Todos Santos Mex.
128	B3	Tofino Can.
96	□	Toft U.K.
49	G4	Tofua i. Tonga
59	C3	Togian, Kepulauan is Indon.
114	C4	Togo country Africa
74	B2	Tohana India
126	B2	Tok U.S.A.
116	B3	Tokar Sudan
69	E3	Tokara-rettō is Japan
91	E1	Tokarevka Rus. Fed.
49	G3	Tokelau terr. S. Pacific Ocean
91	D2	Tokmak Ukr.
77	D2	Tokmok Kyrg.
54	C1	Tokoroa N.Z.
68	B2	Toksun China
67	B4	Tokushima Japan
67	C3	Tōkyō Japan
121	□D3	Tôlañaro Madag.
154	B2	Toledo Brazil
106	C2	Toledo Spain
140	C2	Toledo U.S.A.
106	C2	Toledo, Montes de mts Spain
142	B2	Toledo Bend Reservoir U.S.A.
121	□D3	Toliara Madag.
58	C2	Tolitoli Indon.
108	B1	Tolmezzo Italy
104	B1	Tolosa Spain
145	C3	Toluca Mex.
87	D3	Tol'yatti Rus. Fed.
140	A2	Tomah U.S.A.
66	D2	Tomakomai Japan
106	B2	Tomar Port.
103	E1	Tomaszów Lubelski Pol.
103	E1	Tomaszów Mazowiecki Pol.
144	B3	Tomatlán Mex.
142	C2	Tombigbee r. U.S.A.
155	D2	Tombos Brazil
		Tombouctou Mali see Timbuktu
120	A2	Tombua Angola
123	C1	Tom Burke S. Africa
53	C2	Tomingley Austr.
58	C3	Tomini, Teluk g. Indon.
109	C2	Tomislavgrad Bos.-Herz.
50	A2	Tom Price Austr.
82	G3	Tomsk Rus. Fed.
93	F4	Tomtabacken h. Sweden
145	C3	Tonalá Mex.
150	B2	Tonantins Brazil
59	C2	Tondano Indon.
49	G4	Tonga country S. Pacific Ocean
49	G4	Tongatapu Group is Tonga
71	B3	Tongcheng China
70	A2	Tongchuan China
71	A3	Tongdao China
65	B2	Tongduch'ŏn S. Korea
100	B2	Tongeren Belgium
65	B2	Tonghae S. Korea
62	B1	Tonghai China
65	B1	Tonghua China
65	B2	Tongjosŏn-man b. N. Korea
62	B1	Tongking, Gulf of China/Vietnam
69	E2	Tongliao China
70	B2	Tongling China
52	B2	Tongo Austr.
71	A3	Tongren China
		Tongshan China see Xuzhou
		Tongtian He r. China see Yangtze
96	B1	Tongue U.K.
65	B3	T'ongyŏng S. Korea
69	E2	Tongyu China
65	A1	Tongyuanpu China
74	B2	Tonk India
63	B2	Tonle Sap l. Cambodia
135	C3	Tonopah U.S.A.
93	F4	Tønsberg Norway
135	D2	Tooele U.S.A.
52	B3	Tooleybuc Austr.
53	D1	Toowoomba Austr.
137	D3	Topeka U.S.A.
144	B2	Topia Mex.
144	B2	Topolobampo Mex.
86	C2	Topozero, Ozero l. Rus. Fed.
134	B1	Toppenish U.S.A.
111	C3	Torbalı Turkey
76	B3	Torbat-e Ḥeydarīyeh Iran
76	C3	Torbat-e Jām Iran
106	C1	Tordesillas Spain
107	C1	Tordesilos Spain
107	D1	Torelló Spain
101	E2	Torgau Ger.
76	C2	Torgay Kazakh.
100	A2	Torhout Belgium
		Torino Italy see Turin
154	B1	Torixoréu Brazil
106	B1	Tormes r. Spain
92	H2	Torneälven r. Sweden
127	G3	Torngat Mountains Can.
92	H2	Tornio Fin.
106	B1	Toro Spain
130	C2	Toronto Can.
119	D2	Tororo Uganda
		Toros Dağları mts Turkey see Taurus Mountains
99	B3	Torquay U.K.
106	B2	Torrão Port.
106	B1	Torre mt. Port.
107	D1	Torreblanca Spain
106	C1	Torrecerredo mt. Spain
106	B1	Torre de Moncorvo Port.
106	C1	Torrelavega Spain
106	C2	Torremolinos Spain
52	A2	Torrens, Lake imp. l. Austr.
107	C2	Torrent Spain
144	B2	Torreón Mex.
106	B2	Torres Novas Port.
106	B2	Torres Vedras Port.
107	C2	Torrevieja Spain
96	B2	Torridon U.K.
106	C2	Torrijos Spain
141	E2	Torrington CT U.S.A.
136	C2	Torrington WY U.S.A.
107	D1	Torroella de Montgrí Spain
94	B1	Tórshavn Faroe Is
108	A3	Tortolì Sardegna Italy
107	D1	Tortosa Spain
103	D1	Toruń Pol.
97	B1	Tory Island Ireland
89	D2	Torzhok Rus. Fed.
122	B2	Tosca S. Africa
108	B2	Toscano, Arcipelago is Italy
77	C2	Toshkent Uzbek.
89	D2	Tosno Rus. Fed.
152	B3	Tostado Arg.
101	D1	Tostedt Ger.
80	B1	Tosya Turkey
86	D3	Tot'ma Rus. Fed.
67	B3	Tottori Japan
114	B4	Touba Côte d'Ivoire
114	B1	Toubkal, Jebel mt. Morocco
114	B3	Tougan Burkina Faso
115	C1	Touggourt Alg.
105	D2	Toul France
105	D3	Toulon France
104	C3	Toulouse France
100	A2	Tournai Belgium
105	C2	Tournus France
151	E2	Touros Brazil
104	C2	Tours France
115	D2	Toussidé, Pic mt. Chad
122	B3	Touwsrivier S. Africa
66	D2	Towada Japan
134	D1	Townsend U.S.A.
51	D1	Townsville Austr.
77	E2	Toxkan He r. China
66	D2	Tōya-ko l. Japan
67	C3	Toyama Japan
67	C3	Toyota Japan
115	C1	Tozeur Tunisia
81	C1	T'q'varcheli Georgia
		Trâblous Lebanon see Tripoli
80	B1	Trabzon Turkey
106	B2	Trafalgar, Cabo de c. Spain
128	C3	Trail Can.
88	B3	Trakai Lith.
97	B2	Tralee Ireland
97	C2	Tramore Ireland
63	A3	Trang Thai.
59	C3	Trangan i. Indon.
55	I2	Transantarctic Mountains Antarctica
90	B2	Transnistria terr. Moldova
110	B1	Transylvanian Alps mts Romania
108	B3	Trapani Sicilia Italy
53	C3	Traralgon Austr.
63	B2	Trat Thai.
102	C2	Traunstein Ger.
140	C2	Traverse City U.S.A.
103	D2	Třebíč Czech Rep.
109	C2	Trebinje Bos.-Herz.
103	E2	Trebišov Slovakia
109	C1	Trebnje Slovenia
153	C4	Treinta y Tres Uru.
153	B5	Trelew Arg.
93	F4	Trelleborg Sweden
130	C2	Tremblant, Mont h. Can.
109	C2	Tremiti, Isole is Italy
134	D2	Tremonton U.S.A.
107	D1	Tremp Spain
103	D2	Trenčín Slovakia
153	B4	Trenque Lauquén Arg.
98	C2	Trent r. U.K.
108	B1	Trento Italy
141	D2	Trenton Can.
137	E2	Trenton MO U.S.A.
141	E2	Trenton NJ U.S.A.
131	E2	Trepassey Can.
153	B4	Tres Arroyos Arg.
155	C2	Três Corações Brazil
154	B2	Três Lagoas Brazil

153 A5 Tres Lagos Arg.
155 C1 Três Marias, Represa *resr* Brazil
155 C2 Três Pontas Brazil
153 B5 Tres Puntas, Cabo *c.* Arg.
155 D2 Três Rios Brazil
101 F1 Treuenbrietzen Ger.
108 A1 Treviglio Italy
108 B1 Treviso Italy
99 A3 Trevose Head U.K.
109 C2 Tricase Italy
53 C2 Trida Austr.
100 C3 Trier Ger.
108 B1 Trieste Italy
108 B1 Triglav *mt.* Slovenia
59 D3 Trikora, Puncak *mt.* Indon.
97 C2 Trim Ireland
73 C4 Trincomalee Sri Lanka
154 C1 Trindade Brazil
152 B2 Trinidad Bol.
147 D3 Trinidad *i.* Trin. and Tob.
136 C3 Trinidad U.S.A.
147 D3 Trinidad and Tobago *country* West Indies
131 E2 Trinity Bay Can.
111 B3 Tripoli Greece
80 B2 Tripoli Lebanon
115 D1 Tripoli Libya
113 D10 Tristan da Cunha *i.* S. Atlantic Ocean
108 B2 Trivento Italy
103 D2 Trnava Slovakia
109 C2 Trogir Croatia
109 C2 Troia Italy
100 C2 Troisdorf Ger.
131 C2 Trois-Rivières Can.
86 E2 Troitsko-Pechorsk Rus. Fed.
151 E2 Trombetas *r.* Brazil
123 C3 Trompsburg S. Africa
92 G2 Tromsø Norway
92 F3 Trondheim Norway
128 C2 Trout Lake Can.
128 B1 Trout Lake N.W.T. Can.
130 A1 Trout Lake Ont. Can.
99 B3 Trowbridge U.K.
142 C2 Troy *AL* U.S.A.
141 E2 Troy *NY* U.S.A.
105 C2 Troyes France
109 D2 Trstenik Serbia
89 D3 Trubchevsk Rus. Fed.
106 B1 Truchas Spain
79 C2 Trucial Coast U.A.E.
146 B3 Trujillo Hond.
150 A2 Trujillo Peru
106 B2 Trujillo Spain
147 C4 Trujillo Venez.
142 B1 Trumann U.S.A.
131 D2 Truro Can.
99 A3 Truro U.K.
138 B2 Truth or Consequences U.S.A.
103 D1 Trutnov Czech Rep.
93 F3 Trysil Norway
103 D1 Trzebiatów Pol.
68 B1 Tsagaannuur Mongolia
121 □D2 Tsaratanana, Massif du *mts* Madag.
110 C2 Tsarevo Bulg.
122 A2 Tses Namibia
122 B1 Tsetseng Botswana
68 C1 Tsetserleg Mongolia
122 B2 Tshabong Botswana
122 B1 Tshane Botswana
118 B3 Tshela Dem. Rep. Congo
118 C3 Tshikapa Dem. Rep. Congo
118 C3 Tshikapa *r.* Dem. Rep. Congo
123 D1 Tshipise S. Africa

118 C3 Tshitanzu Dem. Rep. Congo
118 C3 Tshuapa *r.* Dem. Rep. Congo
Tshwane S. Africa *see* Pretoria
87 D4 Tsimlyanskoye Vodokhranilishche *resr* Rus. Fed.
Tsingtao China *see* Qingdao
Tsining China *see* Ulan Qab
121 □D2 Tsiroanomandidy Madag.
123 C3 Tsomo S. Africa
67 C4 Tsu Japan
67 D3 Tsuchiura Japan
66 D2 Tsugarū-kaikyō *str.* Japan
120 A2 Tsumeb Namibia
122 A1 Tsumis Park Namibia
120 B2 Tsumkwe Namibia
67 C3 Tsuruga Japan
66 C3 Tsuruoka Japan
67 A4 Tsushima *is* Japan
Tsushima-kaikyō *str.* Japan/ S. Korea *see* Korea Strait
67 B3 Tsuyama Japan
122 C1 Tswelelang S. Africa
91 C2 Tsyurupyns'k Ukr.
Tthenaagoo Can. *see* Nahanni Butte
59 C3 Tual Indon.
97 B2 Tuam Ireland
91 D3 Tuapse Rus. Fed.
54 A3 Tuatapere N.Z.
96 A1 Tuath, Loch a' *b.* U.K.
138 A1 Tuba City U.S.A.
61 C2 Tuban Indon.
152 D3 Tubarão Brazil
102 B2 Tübingen Ger.
115 E1 Tubruq Libya
49 I14 Tubuai Fr. Polynesia
49 I4 Tubuai *i.* Fr. Polynesia
144 A1 Tubutama Mex.
152 C2 Tucavaca Bol.
128 B1 Tuchitua Can.
138 A2 Tucson U.S.A.
139 C1 Tucumcari U.S.A.
150 B1 Tucupita Venez.
151 D2 Tucuruí Brazil
151 D2 Tucuruí, Represa de *resr* Brazil
107 C1 Tudela Spain
106 B1 Tuela *r.* Port.
64 B1 Tuguegarao Phil.
106 B1 Tui Spain
59 C3 Tukangbesi, Kepulauan *is* Indon.
126 C2 Tuktoyaktuk Can.
88 B2 Tukums Latvia
145 C2 Tula Mex.
89 E3 Tula Rus. Fed.
145 C2 Tulancingo Mex.
133 C5 Tulare U.S.A.
138 B2 Tularosa U.S.A.
110 C1 Tulcea Romania
90 B2 Tul'chyn Ukr.
129 F1 Tulemalu Lake Can.
139 C2 Tullahoma U.S.A.
142 C1 Tullahoma U.S.A.
97 C2 Tullamore Ireland
104 C2 Tulle France
51 D1 Tully Austr.
139 D1 Tulsa U.S.A.
150 A1 Tumaco Col.
123 C2 Tumahole S. Africa
Tumakuru India *see* Tumkur
93 G4 Tumba Sweden
118 B3 Tumba, Lac *l.* Dem. Rep. Congo
53 C3 Tumbarumba Austr.
150 A2 Tumbes Peru

128 B2 Tumbler Ridge Can.
57 A2 Tumby Bay Austr.
65 B1 Tumen China
150 B1 Tumereng Guyana
64 A2 Tumindao *i.* Phil.
73 B3 Tumkur India
74 A2 Tump Pak.
151 C1 Tumucumaque, Serra *hills* Brazil
53 C3 Tumut Austr.
99 D3 Tunbridge Wells, Royal U.K.
80 B2 Tunceli Turkey
53 D2 Tuncurry Austr.
119 D4 Tunduru Tanz.
110 C2 Tundzha *r.* Bulg.
128 B1 Tungsten (abandoned) Can.
115 D1 Tunis Tunisia
114 C1 Tunisia *country* Africa
150 A1 Tunja Col.
92 F3 Tunnsjøen *l.* Norway
Tuoji China *see* Huangshan
154 B2 Tupã Brazil
154 C1 Tupaciguara Brazil
142 C2 Tupelo U.S.A.
152 B3 Tupiza Bol.
76 B2 Tupkaragan, Mys *pt* Kazakh.
83 H2 Tura India
86 F3 Tura *r.* Rus. Fed.
78 B2 Turabah Saudi Arabia
83 J3 Turana, Khrebet *mts* Rus. Fed.
54 C1 Turangi N.Z.
76 B2 Turan Lowland Asia
78 A1 Turayf Saudi Arabia
88 B2 Turba Estonia
74 A2 Turbat Pak.
150 A1 Turbo Col.
110 B1 Turda Romania
Turfan China *see* Turpan
111 C3 Turgutlu Turkey
80 B1 Turhal Turkey
107 C2 Turia *r.* Spain
108 A1 Turin Italy
86 F3 Turinsk Rus. Fed.
90 A1 Turiys'k Ukr.
119 D2 Turkana, Lake *salt l.* Eth./Kenya
80 B2 Turkey *country* Asia/Europe
77 C2 Turkistan Kazakh.
76 C3 Türkmenabat Turkm.
76 B2 Türkmenbaşy Turkm.
76 B2 Turkmenistan *country* Asia
147 C2 Turks and Caicos Islands *terr.* West Indies
93 H3 Turku Fin.
135 B3 Turlock U.S.A.
54 C2 Turnagain, Cape N.Z.
100 B2 Turnhout Belgium
129 D2 Turnor Lake Can.
110 B2 Turnu Măgurele Romania
68 B2 Turpan China
77 D2 Turugart Pass China/Kyrg.
142 C2 Tuscaloosa U.S.A.
142 C2 Tuskegee U.S.A.
73 B4 Tuticorin India
120 B3 Tutume Botswana
49 F3 Tuvalu *country* S. Pacific Ocean
78 B2 Tuwayq, Jabal *hills* Saudi Arabia
78 B2 Tuwayq, Jabal *mts* Saudi Arabia
78 A2 Tuwwal Saudi Arabia
144 B2 Tuxpan Nayarit Mex.
145 C2 Tuxpan Veracruz Mex.
145 C3 Tuxtla Gutiérrez Mex.
62 B1 Tuyên Quang Vietnam
63 B2 Tuy Hoa Vietnam

80	B2	Tuz, Lake *salt l.* Turkey
		Tuz Gölü *salt l.* Turkey *see*
		Tuz, Lake
81	C2	Tuz Khurmātū Iraq
109	C2	Tuzla Bos.-Herz.
91	E2	Tuzlov *r.* Rus. Fed.
89	E2	Tver' Rus. Fed.
98	B1	Tweed *r.* U.K.
122	A2	Twee Rivier Namibia
135	C4	Twentynine Palms U.S.A.
131	E2	Twillingate Can.
134	D2	Twin Falls U.S.A.
137	E1	Two Harbors U.S.A.
129	C2	Two Hills Can.
139	D2	Tyler U.S.A.
83	J3	Tynda Rus. Fed.
93	F3	Tynset Norway
80	B2	Tyre Lebanon
111	B3	Tyrnavos Greece
52	B3	Tyrrell, Lake *dry lake* Austr.
108	B2	Tyrrhenian Sea France/Italy
87	E3	Tyul'gan Rus. Fed.
86	F3	Tyumen' Rus. Fed.
83	J2	Tyung *r.* Rus. Fed.
99	A3	Tywi *r.* U.K.
123	D1	Tzaneen S. Africa

U

120	B2	Uamanda Angola
150	B2	Uaupés Brazil
155	D2	Ubá Brazil
155	D1	Ubaí Brazil
151	E3	Ubaitaba Brazil
118	B3	Ubangi *r.* C.A.R./Dem. Rep.
		Congo
67	B4	Ube Japan
106	C2	Úbeda Spain
154	C1	Uberaba Brazil
154	C1	Uberlândia Brazil
106	B1	Ubiña, Peña *mt.* Spain
123	D2	Ubombo S. Africa
63	B2	Ubon Ratchathani Thai.
119	C3	Ubundu Dem. Rep. Congo
150	A2	Ucayali *r.* Peru
74	B2	Uch Pak.
66	D2	Uchiura-wan *b.* Japan
83	J3	Uchur *r.* Rus. Fed.
128	B3	Ucluelet Can.
74	B2	Udaipur India
91	C1	Uday *r.* Ukr.
93	F4	Uddevalla Sweden
92	G2	Uddjaure *l.* Sweden
100	B2	Uden Neth.
74	B1	Udhampur India
108	B1	Udine Italy
89	E2	Udomlya Rus. Fed.
62	B2	Udon Thani Thai.
73	B3	Udupi India
83	K3	Udyl', Ozero *l.* Rus. Fed.
67	C3	Ueda Japan
58	C3	Uekuli Indon.
118	C2	Uele *r.* Dem. Rep. Congo
101	E1	Uelzen Ger.
119	C2	Uere *r.* Dem. Rep. Congo
87	E3	Ufa Rus. Fed.
119	D3	Ugalla *r.* Tanz.
119	D2	Uganda *country* Africa
89	E2	Uglich Rus. Fed.
89	D3	Ugra Rus. Fed.
103	D2	Uherské Hradiště
		Czech Rep.
101	E2	Uichteritz Ger.
96	A2	Uig U.K.

120	A1	Uíge Angola
65	B2	Ŭijŏngbu S. Korea
135	D2	Uinta Mountains U.S.A.
120	A3	Uis Mine Namibia
65	B2	Ŭisŏng S. Korea
123	C3	Uitenhage S. Africa
100	C1	Uithuizen Neth.
74	B2	Ujjain India
59	F3	Ujung Pandang Indon.
62	A1	Ukhrul India
86	E2	Ukhta Rus. Fed.
135	B3	Ukiah U.S.A.
127	H2	Ukkusissat Greenland
88	B2	Ukmergė Lith.
90	C2	Ukraine *country* Europe
		Ulaanbaatar Mongolia *see*
		Ulan Bator
68	C1	Ulaangom Mongolia
69	D1	Ulan Bator Mongolia
		Ulanhad China *see* Chifeng
69	E1	Ulanhot China
87	D4	Ulan-Khol Rus. Fed.
70	B1	Ulan Qab *Nei Mongol* China
69	D1	Ulan-Ude Rus. Fed.
75	D1	Ulan Ul Hu *l.* China
65	B2	Ulchin S. Korea
		Uleåborg Fin. *see* Oulu
88	C2	Ülenurme Estonia
69	D1	Uliastai China
68	C1	Uliastay Mongolia
59	D2	Ulithi *atoll* Micronesia
53	D3	Ulladulla Austr.
96	B2	Ullapool U.K.
98	B1	Ullswater *l.* U.K.
65	C2	Ullŭng-do *i.* S. Korea
102	B2	Ulm Ger.
65	B2	Ulsan S. Korea
96	□	Ulsta *i.* U.K.
97	C1	Ulster *reg.* Ireland/U.K.
52	B3	Ultima Austr.
111	C3	Ulubey Turkey
111	C2	Uludağ *mt.* Turkey
126	D2	Ulukhaktok Can.
123	D2	Ulundi S. Africa
77	E2	Ulungur Hu *l.* China
50	C2	Uluru *h.* Austr.
98	B1	Ulverston U.K.
87	D3	Ul'yanovsk Rus. Fed.
136	C3	Ulysses U.S.A.
90	C2	Uman' Ukr.
86	C2	Umba Rus. Fed.
59	D3	Umboi *i.* P.N.G.
92	H3	Umeå Sweden
92	H3	Umeälven *r.* Sweden
127	I2	Unnivviip Kangertiva *inlet*
		Greenland
126	D2	Umingmaktok (abandoned)
		Can.
123	D2	Umlazi S. Africa
117	A3	Umm Keddada Sudan
78	A2	Umm Lajj Saudi Arabia
117	B3	Umm Ruwaba Sudan
115	E1	Umm Sa'ad Libya
134	B2	Umpqua *r.* U.S.A.
120	A2	Umpulo Angola
154	B2	Umuarama Brazil
109	C1	Una *r.* Bos.-Herz./Croatia
155	E1	Una Brazil
154	C1	Unaí Brazil
78	B2	'Unayzah Saudi Arabia
136	C1	Underwood U.S.A.
89	D3	Unecha Rus. Fed.
53	C2	Ungarie Austr.
52	A2	Ungarra Austr.
127	G2	Ungava, Péninsule d' *pen.*
		Can.
127	G3	Ungava Bay Can.

90	B2	Ungheni Moldova
		Unguja *i.* Tanz. *see* Zanzibar
		Island
154	B3	União da Vitória Brazil
150	B2	Unini *r.* Brazil
142	C1	Union City U.S.A.
122	B3	Uniondale S. Africa
141	D3	Uniontown U.S.A.
79	C2	United Arab Emirates *country*
		Asia
95	C3	United Kingdom *country*
		Europe
132	D3	United States of America
		country N. America
129	D2	Unity Can.
96	□	Unst *i.* U.K.
101	E2	Unstrut *r.* Ger.
89	E3	Upa *r.* Rus. Fed.
119	C3	Upemba, Lac *l.* Dem. Rep.
		Congo
122	B2	Upington S. Africa
134	B2	Upper Alkali Lake U.S.A.
128	C2	Upper Arrow Lake Can.
134	B2	Upper Klamath Lake U.S.A.
128	B1	Upper Liard Can.
97	C1	Upper Lough Erne *l.* U.K.
93	G4	Uppsala Sweden
78	B2	'Uqlat aş Şuqūr Saudi Arabia
		Urad Qianqi China *see*
		Xishanzui
76	B2	Ural *r.* Kazakh./Rus. Fed.
53	D2	Uralla Austr.
87	E3	Ural Mountains Rus. Fed.
76	B1	Ural'sk Kazakh.
		Ural'skiy Khrebet *mts*
		Rus. Fed. *see* Ural Mountains
119	D3	Urambo Tanz.
53	C3	Urana Austr.
129	D2	Uranium City Can.
86	F2	Uray Rus. Fed.
98	C1	Ure *r.* U.K.
86	D3	Uren' Rus. Fed.
144	A2	Ures Mex.
76	C2	Urganch Uzbek.
100	B1	Urk Neth.
111	C3	Urla Turkey
81	C2	Urmia, Lake *salt l.* Iran
		Uroševac Kosovo *see* Ferizaj
144	B2	Uruáchic Mex.
151	D3	Uruaçu Brazil
144	B3	Uruapan Mex.
150	A3	Urubamba *r.* Peru
151	C2	Urucara Brazil
151	D2	Uruçuí Brazil
151	C2	Urucurituba Brazil
152	C3	Uruguaiana Brazil
153	C4	Uruguay *country* S. America
		Urumchi China *see* Ürümqi
68	C2	Ürümqi China
53	D2	Urunga Austr.
110	C2	Urziceni Romania
64	B4	Usa Japan
82	A2	Usa *r.* Rus. Fed.
111	C3	Uşak Turkey
82	G1	Ushakova, Ostrov *i.* Rus. Fed.
77	E2	Usharal Kazakh.
77	D2	Ushtobe Kazakh.
153	B6	Ushuaia Arg.
86	E2	Usinsk Rus. Fed.
88	C3	Uskhodni Belarus
89	E3	Usman' Rus. Fed.
86	D2	Usogorsk Rus. Fed.
104	C2	Ussel France
66	B2	Ussuriysk Rus. Fed.
108	B3	Ustica, Isola di *i.* Sicilia Italy
83	H3	Ust'-Ilimsk Rus. Fed.
86	E2	Ust'-Ilych Rus. Fed.

103 D1 Ustka Pol.
83 I1 Ust'-Kamchatsk Rus. Fed.
77 E2 Ust'-Kamenogorsk Kazakh.
86 F2 Ust'-Kara Rus. Fed.
86 E2 Ust'-Kulom Rus. Fed.
83 I3 Ust'-Kut Rus. Fed.
91 D2 Ust'-Labinsk Rus. Fed.
88 C2 Ust'-Luga Rus. Fed.
86 E2 Ust'-Nem Rus. Fed.
83 K2 Ust'-Nera Rus. Fed.
83 K2 Ust'-Omchug Rus. Fed.
83 H3 Ust'-Ordynskiy Rus. Fed.
86 E2 Ust'-Tsil'ma Rus. Fed.
86 D2 Ust'-Ura Rus. Fed.
76 B2 Ustyurt Plateau Kazakh./ Uzbek.
89 E2 Ustyuzhna Rus. Fed.
89 D2 Usvyaty Rus. Fed.
135 D3 Utah state U.S.A.
135 D3 Utah Lake U.S.A.
93 I4 Utena Lith.
123 C2 uThukela r. S. Africa
141 D2 Utica U.S.A.
107 C2 Utiel Spain
128 C2 Utikuma Lake Can.
100 B1 Utrecht Neth.
106 B2 Utrera Spain
92 I2 Utsjoki Fin.
67 C3 Utsunomiya Japan
87 D4 Utta Rus. Fed.
62 B2 Uttaradit Thai.
Uummannaq Greenland see Dundas
177 H2 Uummannaq Fjord inlet Greenland
93 H3 Uusikaupunki Fin.
139 D3 Uvalda U.S.A.
119 D3 Uvinza Tanz.
68 C1 Uvs Nuur salt l. Mongolia
67 B4 Uwajima Japan
78 A2 'Uwayriḍ, Ḥarrat al lava field Saudi Arabia
116 A2 Uweinat, Jebel mt. Sudan
83 H3 Uyar Rus. Fed.
115 C4 Uyo Nigeria
152 B3 Uyuni, Salar de salt flat Bol.
76 C2 Uzbekistan country Asia
104 C2 Uzerche France
105 C3 Uzès France
90 C1 Uzh r. Ukr.
90 A2 Uzhhorod Ukr.
109 C2 Užice Serbia
89 E3 Uzlovaya Rus. Fed.
111 C3 Üzümlü Turkey
111 C2 Uzunköprü Turkey

V

123 B2 Vaal r. S. Africa
123 C2 Vaal Dam S. Africa
123 C1 Vaalwater S. Africa
92 H3 Vaasa Fin.
103 D2 Vác Hungary
152 C3 Vacaria Brazil
154 B2 Vacaria, Serra hills Brazil
135 D3 Vacaville U.S.A.
74 B2 Vadodara India
92 I1 Vadsø Norway
105 D2 Vaduz Liechtenstein
94 B1 Vágar i. Faroe Is
94 B1 Vágur Faroe Is
103 D2 Váh r. Slovakia
49 F3 Vaiaku Tuvalu
88 B2 Vaida Estonia
136 B3 Vail U.S.A.

79 C2 Vakīlābād Iran
108 B1 Valdagno Italy
89 D2 Valday Rus. Fed.
89 D2 Valdayskaya Vozvyshennost' hills Rus. Fed.
106 B2 Valdecañas, Embalse de resr Spain
93 G4 Valdemarsvik Sweden
106 C2 Valdepeñas Spain
153 B5 Valdés, Península pen. Arg.
153 A4 Valdivia Chile
130 C2 Val-d'Or Can.
143 D2 Valdosta U.S.A.
128 C2 Valemount Can.
105 C3 Valence France
107 C2 Valencia Spain
150 B1 Valencia Venez.
107 D2 Valencia, Golfo de g. Spain
100 A2 Valenciennes France
136 C2 Valentine U.S.A.
64 B1 Valenzuela Phil.
150 A1 Valera Venez.
109 C2 Valjevo Serbia
88 C2 Valka Latvia
93 H3 Valkeakoski Fin.
100 B2 Valkenswaard Neth.
91 D2 Valky Ukr.
55 D2 Valkyrie Dome Antarctica
145 D2 Valladolid Mex.
106 C1 Valladolid Spain
93 E4 Valle Norway
145 C2 Vallecillos Mex.
150 B1 Valle de la Pascua Venez.
150 A1 Valledupar Col.
145 C2 Valle Hermoso Mex.
135 B4 Vallejo U.S.A.
152 A3 Vallenar Chile
85 H5 Valletta Malta
137 D1 Valley City U.S.A.
134 B2 Valley Falls U.S.A.
128 C2 Valleyview Can.
107 D1 Valls Spain
129 D3 Val Marie Can.
88 C2 Valmiera Latvia
88 C3 Valozhyn Belarus
154 B2 Valparaíso Brazil
153 A4 Valparaíso Chile
105 C3 Valréas France
59 D3 Vals, Tanjung c. Indon.
74 B2 Valsad India
122 B2 Valspan S. Africa
91 D1 Valuyki Rus. Fed.
106 B2 Valverde del Camino Spain
81 C2 Van Turkey
81 C2 Van, Lake salt l. Turkey
141 F1 Van Buren U.S.A.
128 B3 Vancouver Can.
134 B1 Vancouver U.S.A.
128 B3 Vancouver Island Can.
140 B3 Vandalia U.S.A.
123 C2 Vanderbijlpark S. Africa
128 B2 Vanderhoof Can.
88 C2 Vändra Estonia
93 F4 Vänern l. Sweden
93 F4 Vänersborg Sweden
121 □D3 Vangaindrano Madag.
Van Gölü salt l. Turkey see Van, Lake
138 C2 Van Horn U.S.A.
59 D3 Vanimo P.N.G.
83 K3 Vanino Rus. Fed.
104 B2 Vannes France
59 D3 Van Rees, Pegunungan mts Indon.
122 A3 Vanrhynsdorp S. Africa
93 H3 Vantaa Fin.
49 F4 Vanua Levu i. Fiji

48 E3 Vanuatu country S. Pacific Ocean
140 C2 Van Wert U.S.A.
122 B3 Van Wyksvlei S. Africa
122 B2 Van Zylsrus S. Africa
75 C2 Varanasi India
92 I1 Varangerfjorden sea chan. Norway
92 I1 Varangerhalvøya pen. Norway
109 C1 Varaždin Croatia
93 F4 Varberg Sweden
109 D2 Vardar r. Macedonia
93 E4 Varde Denmark
92 J1 Varde Norway
100 D1 Varel Ger.
88 B3 Varėna Lith.
108 A1 Varese Italy
155 C2 Varginha Brazil
93 I3 Varkaus Fin.
110 C2 Varna Bulg.
93 F4 Värnamo Sweden
155 D1 Várzea da Palma Brazil
86 C2 Varzino Rus. Fed.
Vasa Fin. see Vaasa
88 C2 Vasknarva Estonia
110 C1 Vaslui Romania
93 G4 Västerås Sweden
93 G3 Västerdalälven r. Sweden
88 A2 Västerhaninge Sweden
93 G4 Västervik Sweden
108 B2 Vasto Italy
90 C1 Vasyl'kiv Ukr.
104 C2 Vatan France
108 B2 Vatican City Europe
92 □B3 Vatnajökull Iceland
110 C1 Vatra Dornei Romania
93 F4 Vättern l. Sweden
138 B2 Vaughn U.S.A.
105 C3 Vauvert France
49 G4 Vava'u Group is Tonga
88 B3 Vawkavysk Belarus
93 F4 Växjö Sweden
86 E1 Vaygach, Ostrov i. Rus. Fed.
101 D1 Vechta Ger.
110 C2 Vedea r. Romania
100 C1 Veendam Neth.
100 B1 Veenendaal Neth.
129 C2 Vegreville Can.
106 B2 Vejer de la Frontera Spain
93 E4 Vejle Denmark
109 D2 Velbŭzhdki Prokhod pass Bulg./Macedonia
100 B2 Veldhoven Neth.
109 C2 Velebit mts Croatia
100 C2 Velen Ger.
109 C1 Velenje Slovenia
109 D2 Veles Macedonia
106 C2 Vélez-Málaga Spain
155 D1 Velhas r. Brazil
109 D2 Velika Plana Serbia
88 C2 Velikaya r. Rus. Fed.
89 D2 Velikiye Luki Rus. Fed.
89 D2 Velikiy Novgorod Rus. Fed.
86 D2 Velikiy Ustyug Rus. Fed.
110 C2 Veliko Tŭrnovo Bulg.
108 B2 Veli Lošinj Croatia
89 D2 Velizh Rus. Fed.
86 D2 Vel'sk Rus. Fed.
101 E1 Velten Ger.
91 D1 Velykyy Burluk Ukr.
108 B2 Venafro Italy
154 C2 Venceslau Bráz Brazil
104 C2 Vendôme France
89 E3 Venev Rus. Fed.
Venezia Italy see Venice
150 B1 Venezuela country S. America
150 A1 Venezuela, Golfo de g. Venez.

108 B1 Venice Italy
143 D3 Venice U.S.A.
108 B1 Venice, Gulf of Europe
100 C2 Venlo Neth.
100 C2 Venray Neth.
88 B2 Venta r. Latvia/Lith.
88 B2 Venta Lith.
123 C3 Venterstad S. Africa
99 C3 Ventnor U.K.
88 B2 Ventspils Latvia
135 C4 Ventura U.S.A.
139 C3 Venustiano Carranza, Presa resr Mex.
107 C2 Vera Spain
145 C3 Veracruz Mex.
74 B2 Veraval India
108 A1 Verbania Italy
108 A1 Vercelli Italy
105 D3 Vercors reg. France
92 F3 Verdalsøra Norway
154 B1 Verde r. Goiás Brazil
154 B2 Verde r. Mato Grosso do Sul Brazil
144 B2 Verde r. Mex.
138 A2 Verde r. Mex.
155 D1 Verde Grande r. Brazil
101 D3 Verden (Aller) Ger.
154 B1 Verdinho, Serra de mts Brazil
108 A2 Verdon r. France
105 D2 Verdun France
123 C2 Vereeniging S. Africa
106 B1 Verín Spain
91 D3 Verkhnebakanskiy Rus. Fed.
92 J2 Verkhnetulomskiy Rus. Fed.
91 E1 Verkhniy Mamon Rus. Fed.
89 E3 Verkhov'ye Rus. Fed.
90 A2 Verkhovyna Ukr.
83 J2 Verkhoyanskiy Khrebet mts Rus. Fed.
129 C2 Vermilion Can.
137 D2 Vermillion U.S.A.
130 A2 Vermillion Bay Can.
141 E2 Vermont state U.S.A.
135 E2 Vernal U.S.A.
128 C2 Vernon Can.
139 D2 Vernon U.S.A.
143 D3 Vero Beach U.S.A.
111 B2 Veroia Greece
108 B1 Verona Italy
104 C2 Versailles France
104 B2 Vertou France
123 C2 Verulam S. Africa
100 B2 Verviers Belgium
105 C2 Vervins France
105 D3 Vescovato Corse France
87 F3 Veselaya, Gora mt. Rus. Fed.
91 C2 Vesele Ukr.
105 D2 Vesoul France
92 F2 Vesterålen is Norway
92 F2 Vestfjorden sea chan. Norway
94 B1 Vestmanna Faroe Is
92 E3 Vestnes Norway
108 B2 Vesuvius vol. Italy
89 E2 Ves'yegonsk Rus. Fed.
93 G4 Vetlanda Sweden
86 D3 Vetluga Rus. Fed.
100 A2 Veurne Belgium
105 D2 Vevey Switz.
91 D1 Veydelevka Rus. Fed.
80 B1 Vezirköprü Turkey
151 D2 Viana Brazil
106 B1 Viana do Castelo Port.
Viangchan Laos see Vientiane
62 B1 Viangphoukha Laos
111 C3 Viannos Greece
154 C1 Vianópolis Brazil
108 B2 Viareggio Italy

93 E4 Viborg Denmark
109 C3 Vibo Valentia Italy
107 D1 Vic Spain
144 A1 Vicente Guerrero Mex.
108 B1 Vicenza Italy
105 C2 Vichy France
142 B2 Vicksburg U.S.A.
155 D2 Viçosa Brazil
52 A3 Victor Harbor Austr.
50 C1 Victoria r. Austr.
52 B3 Victoria state Austr.
128 B3 Victoria Can.
153 A4 Victoria Chile
113 K7 Victoria Seychelles
139 D3 Victoria U.S.A.
119 D3 Victoria, Lake Africa
52 B2 Victoria, Lake Austr.
62 A1 Victoria, Mount Myanmar
59 D3 Victoria, Mount P.N.G.
120 B2 Victoria Falls Zambia/Zimbabwe
126 D2 Victoria Island Can.
50 C1 Victoria River Downs Austr.
122 B3 Victoria West S. Africa
135 C4 Victorville U.S.A.
110 C2 Videle Romania
92 □A2 Víðidalsá Iceland
153 B5 Viedma Arg.
153 A5 Viedma, Lago l. Arg.
100 B2 Vielsalm Belgium
101 E2 Vienenburg Ger.
103 D2 Vienna Austria
105 C2 Vienne France
104 C2 Vienne r. France
62 B2 Vientiane Laos
100 C2 Viersen Ger.
104 C2 Vierzon France
144 B2 Viesca Mex.
109 C2 Vieste Italy
62 B2 Vietnam country Asia
62 B1 Viêt Tri Vietnam
64 B1 Vigan Phil.
108 A1 Vigevano Italy
106 B1 Vigo Spain
73 C3 Vijayawada India
92 □B3 Vík Iceland
129 C2 Viking Can.
106 B2 Vila Franca de Xira Port.
106 B1 Vilagarcía de Arousa Spain
106 B1 Vilalba Spain
106 B1 Vila Nova de Gaia Port.
107 D1 Vilanova i la Geltrú Spain
106 B1 Vila Real Port.
106 B1 Vilar Formoso Port.
155 D2 Vila Velha Brazil
150 A3 Vilcabamba, Cordillera mts Peru
92 G3 Vilhelmina Sweden
150 B3 Vilhena Brazil
88 D2 Viljandi Estonia
88 B3 Viļaka Latvia
88 B2 Vilkaviškis Lith.
83 H1 Vil'kitskogo, Proliv str. Rus. Fed.
144 B1 Villa Ahumada Mex.
106 B1 Villablino Spain
102 C2 Villach Austria
144 B2 Villa de Cos Mex.
152 B4 Villa Dolores Arg.
145 C3 Villa Flores Mex.
145 C2 Villagrán Mex.
145 C3 Villahermosa Mex.
144 A2 Villa Insurgentes Mex.
152 B4 Villa María Arg.
152 B3 Villa Montes Bol.
144 B2 Villanueva Mex.
106 B2 Villanueva de la Serena Spain

106 C2 Villanueva de los Infantes Spain
152 B3 Villa Ocampo Arg.
108 A3 Villaputzu Sardegna Italy
152 C3 Villarrica Para.
106 C2 Villarrobledo Spain
152 B3 Villa Unión Arg.
144 B2 Villa Unión Durango Mex.
144 B2 Villa Unión Sinaloa Mex.
150 A1 Villavicencio Col.
152 B3 Villazon Bol.
107 C2 Villena Spain
104 C3 Villeneuve-sur-Lot France
142 B2 Ville Platte U.S.A.
105 C2 Villeurbanne France
102 B2 Villingen Ger.
88 C3 Vilnius Lith.
91 C2 Vil'nohirs'k Ukr.
91 D2 Vil'nyans'k Ukr.
100 B2 Vilvoorde Belgium
88 C3 Vilyeyka Belarus
83 J2 Vilyuy r. Rus. Fed.
93 G4 Vimmerby Sweden
153 A4 Viña del Mar Chile
107 D1 Vinaròs Spain
140 B3 Vincennes U.S.A.
55 G3 Vincennes Bay Antarctica
141 D3 Vineland U.S.A.
62 B2 Vinh Vietnam
63 B2 Vinh Long Vietnam
139 D1 Vinita U.S.A.
90 B2 Vinnytsya Ukr.
55 O2 Vinson Massif mt. Antarctica
93 E3 Vinstra Norway
108 B1 Vipiteno Italy
64 B1 Virac Phil.
129 D3 Virden Can.
104 B2 Vire France
120 A2 Virei Angola
155 D1 Virgem da Lapa Brazil
138 A1 Virgin r. U.S.A.
123 C2 Virginia S. Africa
137 E1 Virginia U.S.A.
141 D3 Virginia state U.S.A.
141 D3 Virginia Beach U.S.A.
135 C3 Virginia City U.S.A.
147 D3 Virgin Islands (U.K.) terr. West Indies
147 D3 Virgin Islands (U.S.A.) terr. West Indies
63 B2 Virôchey Cambodia
109 C1 Virovitica Croatia
100 B3 Virton Belgium
88 B2 Virtsu Estonia
109 C2 Vis i. Croatia
88 C2 Visaginas Lith.
135 C3 Visalia U.S.A.
74 B2 Visavadar India
64 B1 Visayan Sea Phil.
93 G4 Visby Sweden
126 D2 Viscount Melville Sound sea chan. Can.
151 D2 Viseu Brazil
106 B1 Viseu Port.
73 C3 Vishakhapatnam India
88 C2 Viški Latvia
109 C2 Visoko Bos.-Herz.
103 D1 Vistula r. Pol.
108 B2 Viterbo Italy
49 F4 Viti Levu i. Fiji
83 I3 Vitim r. Rus. Fed.
155 D2 Vitória Brazil
151 D3 Vitória da Conquista Brazil
106 C1 Vitoria-Gasteiz Spain
104 B2 Vitré France
105 C2 Vitry-le-François France
89 D2 Vitsyebsk Belarus

105	D2	Vittel France
108	A3	Vittoria *Sicilia* Italy
108	B1	Vittorio Veneto Italy
106	B1	Viveiro Spain
144	A2	Vizcaíno, Sierra *mts* Mex.
110	C2	Vize Turkey
73	C3	Vizianagaram India
100	B2	Vlaardingen Neth.
87	D4	Vladikavkaz Rus. Fed.
89	F2	Vladimir Rus. Fed.
66	B2	Vladivostok Rus. Fed.
109	D2	Vlasotince Serbia
100	D1	Vlieland *i.* Neth.
110	A2	Vlissingen Neth.
109	C2	Vlorë Albania
102	C2	Vöcklabruck Austria
101	D2	Vogelsberg *hills* Ger.
119	D3	Voi Kenya
105	D2	Voiron France
131	D1	Voisey's Bay Can.
109	C1	Vojvodina *prov.* Serbia
92	J3	Voknavolok Rus. Fed.
		Volcano Bay Japan *see*
		Uchiura-wan
89	E2	Volga Rus. Fed.
89	F2	Volga *r.* Rus. Fed.
87	D4	Volgodonsk Rus. Fed.
87	D4	Volgograd Rus. Fed.
89	D2	Volkhov Rus. Fed.
89	D1	Volkhov *r.* Rus. Fed.
101	E2	Volkstedt Ger.
91	D2	Volnovakha Ukr.
90	B2	Volochys'k Ukr.
91	D2	Volodars'ke Ukr.
90	B1	Volodars'k-Volyns'kyy Ukr.
90	B1	Volodymyrets' Ukr.
90	A1	Volodymyr-Volyns'kyy Ukr.
89	E2	Vologda Rus. Fed.
89	E2	Volokolamsk Rus. Fed.
91	D1	Volokonovka Rus. Fed.
111	B3	Volos Greece
88	C2	Volosovo Rus. Fed.
89	D2	Volot Rus. Fed.
89	E3	Volovo Rus. Fed.
87	D3	Vol'sk Rus. Fed.
114	C4	Volta, Lake *resr* Ghana
155	D2	Volta Redonda Brazil
87	D4	Volzhskiy Rus. Fed.
92	⌐C2	Vopnafjörður Iceland
88	C3	Voranava Belarus
86	F2	Vorkuta Rus. Fed.
88	B2	Võrnsi *i.* Estonia
89	E3	Voronezh Rus. Fed.
89	E3	Voronezh *r.* Rus. Fed.
91	E1	Vorontsovka Rus. Fed.
91	D2	Vorskla *r.* Rus. Fed.
88	C2	Võrtsjärv *l.* Estonia
88	C2	Võru Estonia
122	B3	Vosburg S. Africa
105	D2	Vosges *mts* France
89	E2	Voskresensk Rus. Fed.
93	E3	Voss Norway
83	H3	Vostochnyy Sayan *mts* Rus. Fed.
86	E3	Votkinsk Rus. Fed.
154	C2	Votuporanga Brazil
100	B3	Vouziers France
92	J2	Voynitsa Rus. Fed.
91	C2	Voznesens'k Ukr.
93	E4	Vrådal Norway
66	B2	Vrangel' Rus. Fed.
		Vrangelya, Ostrov *i.* Rus. Fed.
		see Wrangel Island
109	D2	Vranje Serbia
110	C2	Vratnik *pass* Bulg.
110	B2	Vratsa Bulg.
109	C1	Vrbas *r.* Bos.-Herz.
109	C1	Vrbas Serbia
122	A3	Vredenburg S. Africa
122	A3	Vredendal S. Africa
100	B3	Vresse Belgium
109	D1	Vršac Serbia
122	B2	Vryburg S. Africa
123	D2	Vryheid S. Africa
89	D1	Vsevolozhsk Rus. Fed.
		Vučitrn Kosovo *see* Vushtrri
109	C1	Vukovar Croatia
91	E1	Vulaņļil Rus. Fed.
123	C2	Vukuzakhe S. Africa
109	B3	Vulcano, Isola *i.* Italy
63	B2	Vung Tau Vietnam
109	D2	Vushtrri Kosovo
74	B2	Vyara India
		Vyatka Rus. Fed. *see* Kirov
89	D2	Vyaz'ma Rus. Fed.
93	I3	Vyborg Rus. Fed.
88	C2	Vyerkhnyadzvinsk Belarus
87	D3	Vyksa Rus. Fed.
90	B2	Vylkove Ukr.
90	A2	Vynohradiv Ukr.
89	D2	Vypolzovo Rus. Fed.
89	D2	Vyritsa Rus. Fed.
91	D2	Vyselki Rus. Fed.
90	C1	Vyshhorod Ukr.
89	D2	Vyshniy-Volochek Rus. Fed.
103	D2	Vyškov Czech Rep.
86	C2	Vytegra Rus. Fed.

W

114	B3	Wa Ghana
100	B2	Waal *r.* Neth.
100	B2	Waalwijk Neth.
128	C2	Wabasca *r.* Can.
128	C2	Wabasca-Desmarais Can.
140	B3	Wabash *r.* U.S.A.
117	C4	Wabē Gestro Wenz *r.* Eth.
129	E2	Wabowden Can.
143	D3	Waccasassa Bay U.S.A.
101	D2	Wächtersbach Ger.
139	D2	Waco U.S.A.
115	D2	Waddān Libya
		Waddeneilanden *is* Neth. *see*
		West Frisian Islands
100	B1	Waddenzee *sea chan.* Neth.
128	D2	Waddington, Mount Can.
100	B1	Waddinxveen Neth.
129	D2	Wadena Can.
137	D1	Wadena U.S.A.
74	A2	Wadh Pak.
116	B2	Wadi Halfa Sudan
116	B3	Wad Medani Sudan
70	C2	Wafangdian China
100	B2	Wageningen Neth.
127	F2	Wager Bay Can.
53	C3	Wagga Wagga Austr.
137	D2	Wahoo U.S.A.
137	D1	Wahpeton U.S.A.
54	B2	Waiau *r.* N.Z.
59	C3	Waigeo *i.* Indon.
58	B3	Waikabubak Indon.
52	A2	Waikerie Austr.
54	B2	Waimate N.Z.
75	B3	Wainganga *r.* India
58	C3	Waingapu Indon.
129	C2	Wainwright Can.
54	C1	Waiouru N.Z.
54	B2	Waipara N.Z.
54	C1	Waipawa N.Z.
54	B2	Wairau *r.* N.Z.
54	C1	Wairoa N.Z.
54	B2	Waitaki *r.* N.Z.
54	B1	Waitara N.Z.
54	B1	Waiuku N.Z.
119	E2	Wajir Kenya
67	C3	Wakasa-wan *b.* Japan
54	A3	Wakatipu, Lake N.Z.
129	D2	Wakaw Can.
67	C4	Wakayama Japan
136	D3	WaKeeney U.S.A.
54	B2	Wakefield N.Z.
98	C2	Wakefield U.K.
48	F1	Wake Island N. Pacific Ocean
66	D1	Wakkanai Japan
123	D2	Wakkerstroom S. Africa
103	D1	Wałbrzych Pol.
53	D2	Walcha Austr.
100	C1	Walchum Ger.
103	D1	Wałcz Pol.
99	B2	Wales *admin. div.* U.K.
53	C2	Walgett Austr.
119	C3	Walikale Dem. Rep. Congo
135	C3	Walker Lake U.S.A.
52	A2	Wallaroo Austr.
90	B2	Wallasey U.K.
134	C1	Walla Walla U.S.A.
101	D3	Walldürn Ger.
53	C2	Wallendbeen Austr.
49	G3	Wallis and Futuna Islands *terr.* S. Pacific Ocean
96	□	Walls U.K.
98	B1	Walney, Isle of *i.* U.K.
99	C2	Walsall U.K.
136	C3	Walsenburg U.S.A.
101	D1	Walsrode Ger.
143	D2	Walterboro U.S.A.
120	A3	Walvis Bay Namibia
119	C2	Wamba Dem. Rep. Congo
52	B1	Wanaaring Austr.
54	A2	Wanaka N.Z.
54	A2	Wanaka, Lake N.Z.
130	B2	Wanapitei Lake Can.
154	B3	Wanda Arg.
66	B1	Wanda Shan *mts* China
62	A1	Wanding China
54	C1	Wanganui N.Z.
53	C3	Wangaratta Austr.
65	B1	Wangqing China
62	A1	Wan Hsa-la Myanmar
71	B4	Wanning China
100	B2	Wanroij Neth.
99	C3	Wantage U.K.
70	A2	Wenyuan China
70	A2	Wanzhou China
73	B3	Warangal India
101	D2	Warburg Ger.
50	B2	Warburton Austr.
52	A1	Warburton *watercourse* Austr.
75	B2	Wardha India
96	C1	Ward Hill U.K.
128	B2	Ware Can.
101	F1	Waren Ger.
100	C2	Warendorf Ger.
53	D1	Warialda Austr.
122	A2	Warmbad Namibia
135	C3	Warm Springs U.S.A.
134	C2	Warner Lakes U.S.A.
143	D2	Warner Robins U.S.A.
152	B2	Warnes Bol.
52	B3	Warracknabeal Austr.
53	C2	Warrego *r.* Austr.
53	C2	Warren Austr.
142	B2	Warren AR U.S.A.
140	C2	Warren OH U.S.A.
141	D2	Warren PA U.S.A.
97	C1	Warrenpoint U.K.
137	E3	Warrensburg U.S.A.
122	B2	Warrenton S. Africa
115	C4	Warri Nigeria
98	B2	Warrington U.K.

52	B3	Warrnambool Austr.
103	E1	Warsaw Pol.
		Warszawa Pol. *see* Warsaw
103	C1	Warta r. Pol.
53	D1	Warwick Austr.
99	C2	Warwick U.K.
135	C3	Wasco U.S.A.
136	C1	Washburn U.S.A.
141	D3	Washington DC U.S.A.
137	E2	Washington IA U.S.A.
140	D3	Washington IN U.S.A.
137	E3	Washington MO U.S.A.
143	D1	Washington NC U.S.A.
140	C2	Washington PA U.S.A.
134	B1	Washington state U.S.A.
141	E2	Washington, Mount U.S.A.
140	C3	Washington Court House U.S.A.
74	A1	Washuk Pak.
130	C1	Waskaganish Can.
129	E2	Waskaiowaka Lake Can.
122	A2	Wasser Namibia
130	C2	Waswanipi, Lac l. Can.
58	C3	Watampone Indon.
141	E2	Waterbury U.S.A.
97	C2	Waterford Ireland
97	C2	Waterford Harbour Ireland
137	E2	Waterloo U.S.A.
123	C1	Waterpoort S. Africa
141	D2	Watertown NY U.S.A.
136	D2	Watertown SD U.S.A.
140	B2	Watertown WI U.S.A.
141	F2	Waterville U.S.A.
99	C3	Watford U.K.
136	C1	Watford City U.S.A.
129	D2	Wathaman r. Can.
139	D1	Watonga U.S.A.
129	D2	Watrous Can.
119	C2	Watsa Dem. Rep. Congo
140	B2	Watseka U.S.A.
118	C3	Watsi Kengo Dem. Rep. Congo
128	B1	Watson Lake Can.
135	B3	Watsonville U.S.A.
59	C3	Watubela, Kepulauan is Indon.
59	D3	Wau P.N.G.
117	A4	Wau S. Sudan
53	D2	Wauchope Austr.
140	B2	Waukegan U.S.A.
139	D2	Waurika U.S.A.
140	B2	Wausau U.S.A.
99	D2	Waveney r. U.K.
137	E2	Waverly U.S.A.
143	D2	Waycross U.S.A.
137	D2	Wayne U.S.A.
143	D2	Waynesboro GA U.S.A.
141	D3	Waynesboro VA U.S.A.
143	D1	Waynesville U.S.A.
74	B1	Wazirabad Pak.
98	C1	Wear r. U.K.
139	D2	Weatherford U.S.A.
135	B2	Weaverville U.S.A.
130	B1	Webequie Can.
117	C4	Webi Shabeelle r. Somalia
137	D1	Webster U.S.A.
137	E2	Webster City U.S.A.
55	Q2	Weddell Sea Antarctica
100	B2	Weert Neth.
53	C2	Wee Waa Austr.
100	C2	Wegberg Ger.
103	E1	Węgorzewo Pol.
101	F3	Weiden in der Oberpfalz Ger.
70	B2	Weifang China
70	C2	Weihai China

53	C1	Weilmoringle Austr.
101	E2	Weimar Ger.
70	A2	Weinan China
51	D1	Weipa Austr.
53	C1	Weir r. Austr.
140	C2	Weirton U.S.A.
62	B1	Weishan China
101	E2	Weißenfels Ger.
102	C2	Weißkugel mt. Austria/Italy
103	D1	Wejherowo Pol.
128	C1	Wekweètì Can.
140	C3	Welch U.S.A.
117	B3	Weldiya Eth.
123	C2	Welkom S. Africa
99	C2	Welland r. U.K.
51	C1	Wellesley Islands Austr.
53	C2	Wellington Austr.
54	B2	Wellington N.Z.
122	A3	Wellington S. Africa
137	D3	Wellington U.S.A.
153	A5	Wellington, Isla i. Chile
53	C3	Wellington, Lake Austr.
128	B2	Wells Can.
99	B3	Wells U.K.
134	D2	Wells U.S.A.
50	B2	Wells, Lake imp. l. Austr.
54	B1	Wellsford N.Z.
98	D2	Wells-next-the-Sea U.K.
102	C2	Wels Austria
99	B2	Welshpool U.K.
123	C2	Wembesi S. Africa
130	C1	Wemindji Can.
134	B1	Wenatchee U.S.A.
71	B4	Wencheng China
114	B4	Wenchi Ghana
70	C2	Wendeng China
101	E1	Wendisch Evern Ger.
117	B4	Wendo Eth.
134	D2	Wendover U.S.A.
71	B3	Wengyuan China
71	C3	Wenling China
71	A3	Wenshan China
52	B2	Wentworth Austr.
71	C3	Wenzhou China
123	C2	Wepener S. Africa
122	B2	Werda Botswana
101	F2	Werdau Ger.
101	F1	Werder Ger.
101	F3	Wernberg-Köblitz Ger.
101	E2	Wernigerode Ger.
101	D2	Werra r. Ger.
53	D2	Werris Creek Austr.
101	D3	Wertheim Ger.
100	C2	Wesel Ger.
101	E1	Wesendorf Ger.
101	D1	Weser r. Ger.
101	D1	Weser sea chan. Ger.
51	C1	Wessel, Cape Austr.
51	C1	Wessel Islands Austr.
123	C2	Wesselton S. Africa
80	B2	West Bank terr. Asia
140	B2	West Bend U.S.A.
99	C2	West Bromwich U.K.
100	C2	Westerburg Ger.
100	C1	Westerholt Ger.
50	B2	Western Australia state Austr.
116	A2	Western Desert Egypt
73	B3	Western Ghats mts India
114	A2	Western Sahara terr. Africa
100	A2	Westerschelde est. Neth.
100	C1	Westerstede Ger.
100	C2	Westerwald hills Ger.
153	B6	West Falkland i. Falkland Is
140	B3	West Frankfort U.S.A.
100	B1	West Frisian Islands is Neth.
147	D2	West Indies is Caribbean Sea

96	A1	West Loch Roag b. U.K.
128	C2	Westlock Can.
100	B2	Westmalle Belgium
142	B1	West Memphis U.S.A.
140	C3	Weston U.S.A.
99	B3	Weston-super-Mare U.K.
143	D3	West Palm Beach U.S.A.
137	E3	West Plains U.S.A.
97	B2	West Point Ireland
54	B2	Westport N.Z.
129	D2	Westray Can.
96	C1	Westray i. U.K.
100	B1	West-Terschelling Neth.
140	C3	West Virginia state U.S.A.
53	C2	West Wyalong Austr.
134	D2	West Yellowstone U.S.A.
59	C3	Wetar i. Indon.
128	C2	Wetaskiwin Can.
101	D2	Wetzlar Ger.
59	D3	Wewak P.N.G.
97	C2	Wexford Ireland
129	D2	Weyakwin Can.
129	D3	Weyburn Can.
101	D1	Weyhe Ger.
99	B3	Weymouth U.K.
54	C1	Whakatane N.Z.
129	E1	Whale Cove Can.
96	□	Whalsay i. U.K.
54	B1	Whangarei N.Z.
98	C2	Wharfe r. U.K.
139	D3	Wharton U.S.A.
128	C1	Wha Ti Can.
136	B2	Wheatland U.S.A.
138	B1	Wheeler Peak NM U.S.A.
135	D3	Wheeler Peak NV U.S.A.
140	C2	Wheeling U.S.A.
98	B1	Whernside h. U.K.
128	B2	Whistler Can.
98	C1	Whitby U.K.
142	B2	White r. U.S.A.
50	B2	White, Lake imp. l. Austr.
131	E2	White Bay Can.
136	C1	White Butte mt. U.S.A.
52	B1	White Cliffs Austr.
128	C2	Whitecourt Can.
134	D1	Whitefish U.S.A.
98	B1	Whitehaven U.K.
97	D1	Whitehead U.K.
128	A1	Whitehorse Can.
142	B3	White Lake U.S.A.
135	C3	White Mountain Peak U.S.A.
116	B3	White Nile r. Africa
86	C2	White Sea Rus. Fed.
134	D1	White Sulphur Springs U.S.A.
143	D2	Whiteville U.S.A.
114	B3	White Volta r. Burkina/Ghana
138	B2	Whitewater Baldy mt. U.S.A.
130	B1	Whitewater Lake Can.
129	D2	Whitewood Can.
96	B3	Whithorn U.K.
54	C1	Whitianga N.Z.
135	C3	Whitney, Mount U.S.A.
51	D2	Whitsunday Island Austr.
52	A2	Whyalla Austr.
100	A2	Wichelen Belgium
137	D3	Wichita U.S.A.
139	D2	Wichita Falls U.S.A.
96	C1	Wick U.K.
138	A2	Wickenburg U.S.A.
97	C2	Wicklow Ireland
97	D2	Wicklow Head Ireland
97	C2	Wicklow Mountains Ireland
98	B2	Widnes U.K.
101	D1	Wiehengebirge hills Ger.
100	C2	Wiehl Ger.

103 D1 Wieluń Pol.
Wien Austria *see* Vienna
103 D2 Wiener Neustadt Austria
100 B1 Wieringerwerf Neth.
100 C2 Wiesbaden Ger.
100 C1 Wiesmoor Ger.
103 D3 Wieżyca *h.* Pol.
99 C3 Wight, Isle of *i.* U.K.
96 B3 Wigtown U.K.
100 B2 Wijchen Neth.
52 B2 Wilcannia Austr.
123 C3 Wild Coast S. Africa
123 C7 Wilge *r.* S. Africa
100 D1 Wilhelmshaven Ger.
141 D2 Wilkes-Barre U.S.A.
55 H3 Wilkes Land *reg.* Antarctica
129 D2 Wilkie Can.
138 B2 Wilcox U.S.A.
100 B2 Willebroek Belgium
147 D3 Willemstad Curaçao
52 B3 William, Mount Austr.
52 A1 William Creek Austr.
138 A1 Williams U.S.A.
141 D3 Williamsburg U.S.A.
128 B2 Williams Lake Can.
140 C3 Williamson U.S.A.
141 D2 Williamsport U.S.A.
143 F1 Williston U.S.A.
122 B3 Williston S. Africa
136 C1 Williston U.S.A.
128 B2 Williston Lake Can.
135 B3 Willits U.S.A.
137 D1 Willmar U.S.A.
122 B3 Willowmore S. Africa
123 C3 Willowvale S. Africa
50 B3 Wills, Lake *imp. l.* Austr.
52 A3 Willunga Austr.
52 A2 Wilmington Austr.
141 D3 Wilmington DE U.S.A.
143 E2 Wilmington NC U.S.A.
100 D2 Wilnsdorf Ger.
143 E1 Wilson U.S.A.
53 C3 Wilson's Promontory
pen. Austr.
100 B3 Wiltz Lux.
50 B2 Wiluna Austr.
99 C3 Winchester U.K.
140 C3 Winchester KY U.S.A.
141 D3 Winchester VA U.S.A.
98 B1 Windermere *l.* U.K.
120 A3 Windhoek Namibia
137 D2 Windom U.S.A.
51 D2 Windorah Austr.
136 B2 Wind River Range *mts* U.S.A.
53 D2 Windsor Austr.
130 B2 Windsor Can.
147 D3 Windward Islands
Caribbean Sea
147 C3 Windward Passage Cuba/Haiti
53 D2 Winfield U.S.A.
100 A2 Wingene Belgium
53 D2 Wingham Austr.
120 B1 Winisk *r.* Can.
130 B1 Winisk (abandoned) Can.
130 B1 Winisk Lake Can.
63 A2 Winkana Myanmar
129 E3 Winkler Can.
114 B4 Winneba Ghana
140 B2 Winnebago, Lake U.S.A.
134 C2 Winnemucca U.S.A.
136 C2 Winner U.S.A.
142 B2 Winnfield U.S.A.
137 E1 Winnibigoshish, Lake U.S.A.
129 E3 Winnipeg Can.
129 E3 Winnipeg *r.* Can.
129 E2 Winnipeg, Lake Can.
129 D2 Winnipegosis, Lake Can.

141 E2 Winnipesaukee, Lake U.S.A.
142 B2 Winnsboro U.S.A.
137 E2 Winona MN U.S.A.
142 C2 Winona MS U.S.A.
100 C1 Winschoten Neth.
101 D1 Winsen (Aller) Ger.
101 E1 Winsen (Luhe) Ger.
138 A1 Winslow U.S.A.
143 D1 Winston-Salem U.S.A.
101 D2 Winterberg Ger.
143 D3 Winter Haven U.S.A.
100 C2 Winterswijk Neth.
105 D2 Winterthur Switz.
51 D2 Winton Austr.
54 A3 Winton N.Z.
52 A2 Wirrabara Austr.
99 D2 Wisbech U.K.
140 A2 Wisconsin *r.* U.S.A.
140 B2 Wisconsin *state* U.S.A.
140 B2 Wisconsin Rapids U.S.A.
Wisła *r.* Pol. *see* Vistula
101 E1 Wismar Ger.
98 D2 Withernsea U.K.
100 B1 Witmarsum Neth.
99 C3 Witney U.K.
123 D2 Witrivier S. Africa
101 F2 Wittenberg, Lutherstadt Ger.
101 E1 Wittenberge Ger.
101 E1 Wittenburg Ger.
101 E1 Wittingen Ger.
100 C3 Wittlich Ger.
100 C1 Wittmund Ger.
101 F1 Wittstock Ger.
120 A3 Witvlei Namibia
101 D2 Witzenhausen Ger.
103 D1 Władysławowo Pol.
103 D1 Włocławek Pol.
53 C3 Wodonga Austr.
59 C4 Wokam *i.* Indon.
99 C3 Woking U.K.
101 F2 Wolfen Ger.
101 E1 Wolfenbüttel Ger.
101 D2 Wolfhagen Ger.
136 B1 Wolf Point U.S.A.
101 E1 Wolfsburg Ger.
100 C3 Wolfstein Ger.
131 D2 Wolfville Can.
102 C1 Wolgast Ger.
102 C1 Wolin Pol.
129 D2 Wollaston Lake Can.
129 D2 Wollaston Lake Can.
126 D2 Wollaston Peninsula Can.
53 D2 Wollongong Austr.
101 C2 Wolmirsleben Ger.
101 E1 Wolmirstedt Ger.
100 C1 Wolvega Neth.
99 B2 Wolverhampton U.K.
65 B2 Wŏnju S. Korea
65 B2 Wŏnsan N. Korea
53 C3 Wonthaggi Austr.
52 A2 Woocalla Austr.
51 C1 Woodah, Isle *i.* Austr.
99 D2 Woodbridge U.K.
136 B3 Woodland Park U.S.A.
50 C2 Woodroffe, Mount Austr.
51 C1 Woods, Lake *imp. l.* Austr.
129 E3 Woods, Lake of the Can./U.S.A.
53 C3 Woods Point Austr.
131 D2 Woodstock N.B. Can.
140 C2 Woodstock Ont. Can.
54 C2 Woodville N.Z.
139 D1 Woodward U.S.A.
53 D2 Woolgoolga Austr.
52 A2 Woomera Austr.
140 C2 Wooster U.S.A.
122 A3 Worcester S. Africa

99 B2 Worcester U.K.
141 E2 Worcester U.S.A.
102 C2 Wörgl Austria
98 B1 Workington U.K.
98 C2 Worksop U.K.
136 B2 Worland U.S.A.
101 D3 Worms Ger.
99 C3 Worthing U.K.
137 D2 Worthington U.S.A.
58 C3 Wotu Indon.
59 C3 Wowoni *i.* Indon.
83 N2 Wrangel Island Rus. Fed.
128 A2 Wrangell U.S.A.
96 B1 Wrath, Cape U.K.
136 C2 Wray U.S.A.
122 A2 Wreck Point S. Africa
98 B2 Wrexham U.K.
136 B2 Wright U.S.A.
63 A2 Wrightmyo India
128 B1 Wrigley Can.
103 D1 Wrocław Pol.
103 D1 Września Pol.
70 B2 Wu'an China
70 A2 Wuhai China
70 B2 Wuhan China
70 B2 Wuhu China
Wujin China *see* Changzhou
115 C4 Wukari Nigeria
62 B1 Wuliang Shan *mts* China
59 C3 Wuliaru *i.* Indon.
71 A3 Wumeng Shan *mts* China
130 B1 Wunnummin Lake Can.
101 F2 Wunsiedel Ger.
101 D1 Wunstorf Ger.
62 A1 Wuntho Myanmar
100 C2 Wuppertal Ger.
123 A3 Wuppertal S. Africa
101 F2 Wurzbach Ger.
101 D3 Würzburg Ger.
101 F2 Wurzen Ger.
68 C2 Wuwei China
70 A2 Wuxi Chongqing China
70 C2 Wuxi Jiangsu China
Wuxing China *see* Huzhou
71 A3 Wuxuan China
Wuyang China *see* Zhenyuan
69 E1 Wuyiling China
71 B3 Wuyishan China
71 B3 Wuyi Shan *mts* China
70 A1 Wuyuan China
71 A4 Wuzhishan China
70 A2 Wuzhong China
71 B3 Wuzhou China
53 C2 Wyangala Reservoir Austr.
52 D3 Wycheproof Austr.
99 B3 Wye *r.* U.K.
50 B1 Wyndham Austr.
142 B1 Wynne U.S.A.
129 D2 Wynyard Can.
136 B2 Wyoming *state* U.S.A.
103 E1 Wyszków Pol.
140 C3 Wytheville U.S.A.

X

117 D3 Xaafuun Somalia
62 B2 Xaignabouli Laos
121 C3 Xai-Xai Moz.
145 C3 Xalapa Mex.
70 A1 Xamba China
62 A1 Xamgyi'nyilha China
62 B1 Xam Nua Laos
120 A2 Xangongo Angola
81 C2 Xankändi Azer.
111 B2 Xanthi Greece

Xapuri

150	B3	Xapuri Brazil
107	C2	Xàtiva Spain
		Xiaguan China see Dali
71	B3	Xiamen China
70	A2	Xi'an China
70	A3	Xianfeng China
		Xiangjiang China see Huichang
71	B3	Xiangtan China
70	B2	Xiangyang China
70	B2	Xiantao China
70	A2	Xianyang China
70	B2	Xiaogan China
69	E1	Xiao Hinggan Ling mts China
70	C2	Xiaoshan China
62	B1	Xichang China
145	C2	Xicohténcatl Mex.
71	A3	Xifeng Guizhou China
75	C2	Xigazê China
83	I4	Xilinhot China
70	B2	Xincai China
68	C2	Xinghai China
70	B2	Xinghua China
71	B3	Xingning China
70	B2	Xingping China
70	B2	Xingtai China
151	C2	Xingu r. Brazil
71	A3	Xingyi China
71	B3	Xinhua China
68	C2	Xining China
		Xinjiang Uygur Autonomous Region aut. reg. China
		Xinjiang Uygur Zizhiqu
75	C1	Xinjiang Uygur Zizhiqu aut. reg. China
		Xinjiang China see Jingxi
65	A1	Xinmin China
71	B3	Xinning China
70	B2	Xintai China
70	B2	Xinxiang China
70	B2	Xinyang China
70	B2	Xinyi China
71	C3	Xinying Taiwan
71	B3	Xinyu China
69	D2	Xinzhou Shanxi China
70	B2	Xinzhou Shanxi China
71	C3	Xinzhu Taiwan
106	B1	Xinzo de Limia Spain
		Xiongshan China see Zhenghe
68	C2	Xiqing Shan mts China
151	B3	Xique Xique Brazil
70	A1	Xishanzui China
71	A3	Xiushan China
71	B3	Xiuying China
70	B2	Xixia China
		Xixón Spain see Gijón
68	B2	Xizang Zizhiqu aut. reg. China
76	B2	Xo'jayli Uzbek.
70	B2	Xuancheng China
71	A3	Xuanwei China
70	B2	Xuchang China
		Xucheng China see Xuwen
117	C4	Xuddur Somalia
		Xujiang China see Guangchang
71	B3	Xun Jiang r. China
71	B3	Xunwu China
107	C2	Xúquer, Riu r. Spain
71	B3	Xuwen China
71	A3	Xuyong China
70	B2	Xuzhou China

Y

117	B4	Yabêlo Eth.
69	D1	Yablonovyy Khrebet mts Rus. Fed.
143	D2	Yadkin r. U.S.A.
75	C2	Yagodnina China
89	E2	Yagnitsa Rus. Fed.
118	B3	Yagoua Cameroon
128	C3	Yahk Can.
144	B2	Yahualica Mex.
80	B2	Yahyalı Turkey
67	C4	Yaizu Japan
134	B1	Yakima U.S.A.
114	B3	Yako Burkina Faso
66	D2	Yakumo Japan
126	B3	Yakutat U.S.A.
83	J2	Yakutsk Rus. Fed.
91	D2	Yakymivka Ukr.
63	B3	Yala Thai.
53	C3	Yallourn Austr.
111	C2	Yalova Turkey
91	C3	Yalta Ukr.
65	A1	Yalu Jiang r. China/N. Korea
67	D1	Yamagata Japan
67	B4	Yamaguchi Japan
		Yamal, Poluostrov pen. Rus. Fed. see Yamal Peninsula
86	F1	Yamal Peninsula Rus. Fed.
53	D1	Yamba Austr.
117	A4	Yambio S. Sudan
111	E3	Yambol Bulg.
86	G2	Yamburg Rus. Fed.
62	A1	Yamethin Myanmar
114	B4	Yamoussoukro Côte d'Ivoire
90	B2	Yampil' Ukr.
75	C2	Yamuna r. India
75	D2	Yamzho Yumco l. China
83	K2	Yana r. Rus. Fed.
70	A2	Yan'an China
150	A3	Yanaoca Peru
78	A2	Yanbu' al Baḥr Saudi Arabia
70	C2	Yancheng China
50	A3	Yanchep Austr.
70	B2	Yangcheng China
71	B3	Yangchun China
65	A1	Yangdok N. Korea
71	B3	Yangjiang China
		Yangôn Myanmar see Rangoon
70	B2	Yangquan China
71	B3	Yangshuo China
70	C3	Yangtze r. China
69	D2	Yangtze, Mouth of the China
70	B2	Yangzhou China
65	B3	Yanji China
137	D2	Yankton U.S.A.
83	K2	Yano-Indigirskaya Nizmennost' lowland Rus. Fed.
83	K2	Yanskiy Zaliv g. Rus. Fed.
53	C1	Yantabulla Austr.
70	C2	Yantai China
118	B3	Yaoundé Cameroon
59	D2	Yap i. Micronesia
59	D3	Yapen i. Indon.
59	D3	Yapen, Selat sea chan. Indon.
144	A2	Yaqui r. Mex.
51	D2	Yaraka Austr.
86	D3	Yaransk Rus. Fed.
48	F2	Yaren Nauru
78	B3	Yarīm Yemen
77	D3	Yarkant He r. China
75	C2	Yarlung Zangbo r. China
131	D2	Yarmouth Can.
86	F2	Yarono Rus. Fed.
89	E2	Yaroslavl' Rus. Fed.
66	B2	Yaroslavskiy Rus. Fed.

53	C3	Yarram Austr.
89	D2	Yartsevo Rus. Fed.
89	E3	Yasnogorsk Rus. Fed.
63	B2	Yasothon Thai.
53	C2	Yass Austr.
111	C3	Yatağan Turkey
129	E1	Yathkyed Lake Can.
67	B4	Yatsushiro Japan
150	B2	Yavari r. Brazil/Peru
75	B2	Yavatmal India
67	B4	Yavoriv Ukr.
81	D2	Yazd Iran
142	B2	Yazoo City U.S.A.
111	B3	Ydra i. Greece
63	A2	Ye Myanmar
77	D3	Yecheng China
144	B2	Yécora Mex.
89	E3	Yefremov Rus. Fed.
89	E2	Yegor'yevsk Rus. Fed.
117	B4	Yei S. Sudan
86	F3	Yekaterinburg Rus. Fed.
77	D1	Yekibastuz Kazakh.
89	E3	Yelets Rus. Fed.
114	A3	Yélimané Mali
96	□	Yell i. U.K.
128	C1	Yellowknife Can.
70	B2	Yellow River r. China
69	E2	Yellow Sea N. Pacific Ocean
136	C1	Yellowstone r. U.S.A.
136	A2	Yellowstone Lake U.S.A.
88	C3	Yel'sk Belarus
78	B3	Yemen country Asia
86	E2	Yemva Rus. Fed.
91	D2	Yenakiyeve Ukr.
62	A1	Yenangyaung Myanmar
62	B1	Yên Bái Vietnam
114	B4	Yendi Ghana
111	C3	Yenice Turkey
111	C3	Yenifoça Turkey
68	C1	Yenisey r. Rus. Fed.
53	C2	Yeoval Austr.
99	B3	Yeovil U.K.
53	E2	Yeppoon Austr.
83	I2	Yerbogachen Rus. Fed.
81	C1	Yerevan Armenia
77	D1	Yereymentau Kazakh.
87	D3	Yershov Rus. Fed.
		Yertis r. Kazakh./Rus. Fed. see Irtysh
65	B2	Yesan S. Korea
77	D1	Yesil' Kazakh.
111	C3	Yeşilova Turkey
99	A3	Yes Tor h. U.K.
53	C3	Yetman Austr.
62	A1	Ye-U Myanmar
104	B2	Yeu, Île d' i. France
91	C2	Yevpatoriya Ukr.
91	D2	Yeya r. Rus. Fed.
91	D2	Yeysk Rus. Fed.
88	C2	Yezyaryshcha Belarus
71	A3	Yibin China
70	B2	Yichang China
69	E1	Yichun Heilong. China
71	B3	Yichun Jiangxi China
110	C2	Yıldız Dağları mts Turkey
80	B2	Yıldızeli Turkey
70	A2	Yinchuan China
65	B3	Yingchengzi China
71	B3	Yingde China
70	C1	Yingkou China
70	B2	Yingshan Hubei China
70	A2	Yingshan Sichuan China
70	B2	Yingtan China
77	E2	Yining China
117	B4	Yirga Alem Eth.

70 B2 Yishui China
68 C2 Yiwu China
71 B3 Yiyang China
71 A3 Yizhou China
92 I2 Yli-Kitka l. Fin.
92 H2 Ylitornio Fin.
92 H3 Ylivieska Fin.
61 C2 Yogyakarta Indon.
118 B2 Yoko Cameroon
67 C3 Yokohama Japan
115 D4 Yola Nigeria
67 D3 Yonezawa Japan
71 B3 Yong'an China
71 B3 Yongchun China
70 A2 Yongdeng China
65 B3 Yŏngdŏk S. Korea
71 C3 Yongkang China
62 B1 Yongsheng China
71 B3 Yongzhou China
71 B3 Yongzhou China
150 A1 Yopal Col.
50 A3 York Austr.
98 C2 York U.K.
137 D2 York NE U.S.A.
141 D3 York PA U.S.A.
51 D1 York, Cape Austr.
52 A3 Yorke Peninsula Austr.
52 A3 Yorketown Austr.
98 C2 Yorkshire Wolds hills U.K.
129 D2 Yorkton Can.
87 D3 Yoshkar-Ola Rus. Fed.
97 C3 Youghal Ireland
53 C2 Young Austr.
52 A3 Younghusband Peninsula Austr.
140 C2 Youngstown U.S.A.
114 B3 Youvarou Mali
77 F2 Youyi Feng mt. China/Rus. Fed.
80 B2 Yozgat Turkey
134 B2 Yreka U.S.A.
76 C2 Yrgyz Kazakh.
Yr Wyddfa mt. U.K. see Snowdon
105 C2 Yssingeaux France
93 F4 Ystad Sweden
Ysyk-Köl Kyrg. see Balykchy
77 D2 Ysyk-Köl salt l. Kyrg.
92 □A3 Ytri-Rangá r. Iceland
62 B1 Yuanjiang China
62 B1 Yuan Jiang r China
62 B1 Yuanmou China
133 B3 Yuba City U.S.A.
66 D2 Yūbari Japan
145 C3 Yucatán pen. Mex.
146 B2 Yucatan Channel Cuba/Mex.
50 C2 Yuendumu Austr.
71 B3 Yueyang China
86 F2 Yugorsk Rus. Fed.
83 L2 Yukagirskoye Ploskogor'ye plat. Rus. Fed.
128 A1 Yukon admin. div. Can.
126 A2 Yukon r. Can./U.S.A.
71 B3 Yulin Guangxi China
70 A2 Yulin Shaanxi China
62 B1 Yulong Xueshan mt. China
138 A2 Yuma AZ U.S.A.
136 C2 Yuma CO U.S.A.
80 B2 Yunak Turkey
71 B3 Yuncheng China
71 B3 Yunfu China
62 B1 Yunnan prov. China
52 A2 Yunta Austr.
71 B3 Yunyang China
150 A3 Yurimaguas Peru
77 E3 Yurungkax He r. China

71 C3 Yu Shan mt. Taiwan
68 C2 Yushu China
Yushuwan China see Huaihua
81 C1 Yusufeli Turkey
77 E3 Yutian China
62 B1 Yuxi China
66 D2 Yuzhno-Kuril'sk Rus. Fed.
83 K3 Yuzhno-Sakhalinsk Rus. Fed.
91 C2 Yuzhnoukrayins'k Ukr.
69 D2 Yuzhou China
104 C2 Yvetot France

Z

100 B1 Zaandam Neth.
69 D1 Zabaykal'sk Rus. Fed.
78 B3 Zabid Yemen
76 C3 Zābol Iran
79 D2 Zāboli Iran
144 B3 Zacapu Mex.
144 B2 Zacatecas Mex.
145 C3 Zacatepec Mex.
145 C3 Zacatlán Mex.
111 B3 Zacharo Greece
144 B2 Zacoalco Mex.
145 C2 Zacualtipán Mex.
109 C2 Zadar Croatia
63 A3 Zadetkyi Kyun i. Myanmar
89 E3 Zadonsk Rus. Fed.
106 B2 Zafra Spain
109 C1 Zagreb Croatia
Zagros, Kūhhā-ye mts Iran see Zagros Mountains
81 C2 Zagros Mountains Iran
79 D2 Zāhedan Iran
80 B2 Zahlé Lebanon
78 B3 Zahrān Saudi Arabia
Zaïre country Africa see Congo, Democratic Republic of the
109 D2 Zaječar Serbia
89 E3 Zakharovo Rus. Fed.
81 C2 Zākhō Iraq
111 B3 Zakynthos Greece
111 B3 Zakynthos i. Greece
103 D2 Zalaegerszeg Hungary
110 B1 Zalău Romania
78 B2 Zalim Saudi Arabia
117 A3 Zalingei Sudan
78 A2 Zalmā, Jabal az mt. Saudi Arabia
128 C2 Zama City Can.
120 C2 Zambeze r. Moz.
120 C2 Zambezi r. Africa
120 B2 Zambezi Zambia
120 B2 Zambia country Africa
64 B2 Zamboanga Phil.
64 B2 Zamboanga Peninsula Phil.
106 B1 Zamora Spain
144 B3 Zamora de Hidalgo Mex.
103 F1 Zamość Pol.
75 B1 Zanda China
100 B2 Zandvliet Belgium
140 C3 Zanesville U.S.A.
81 C2 Zanjān Iran
75 B1 Zanskar Mountains India
Zante i. Greece see Zakynthos
119 D3 Zanzibar Tanz.
119 D3 Zanzibar Island Tanz.
89 E3 Zaokskiy Rus. Fed.
115 C2 Zaouatallaz Alg.
89 D2 Zapadnaya Dvina r. Europe
89 D2 Zapadnaya Dvina Rus. Fed.
68 B1 Zapadnyy Sayan reg. Rus. Fed.
139 D3 Zapata U.S.A.

92 J2 Zapolyarnyy Rus. Fed.
91 D2 Zaporizhzhya Ukr.
101 E2 Zappendorf Ger.
80 B2 Zara Turkey
145 B2 Zaragoza Mex.
107 C1 Zaragoza Spain
74 A1 Zarah Sharan Afgh.
76 B3 Zarand Iran
76 C3 Zaranj Afgh.
88 C2 Zarasai Lith.
89 E3 Zaraysk Rus. Fed.
150 B1 Zarara Venez.
115 C3 Zaria Nigeria
90 B1 Zarichne Ukr.
81 D3 Zarqān Iran
66 B2 Zarubino Rus. Fed.
103 D1 Zary Pol.
115 D1 Zarzis Tunisia
123 C3 Zastron S. Africa
69 E1 Zavitinsk Rus. Fed.
103 D1 Zawiercie Pol.
77 E2 Zaysan, Lake Kazakh.
Zaysan, Ozero l. Kazakh. see Zaysan, Lake
90 B1 Zdolbuniv Ukr.
93 F4 Zealand i. Denmark
100 A2 Zeebrugge Belgium
123 C2 Zeerust S. Africa
50 C2 Zeil, Mount Austr.
101 F2 Zeitz Ger.
88 B3 Zelenogradsk Rus. Fed.
82 E1 Zemlya Aleksandry i. Rus. Fed.
82 F1 Zemlya Vil'cheka i. Rus. Fed.
107 D2 Zemmora Alg.
145 C3 Zempoaltépetl, Nudo de mt. Mex.
65 B1 Zengfeng Shan mt. China
105 D2 Zermatt Switz.
91 E2 Zernograd Rus. Fed.
102 C2 Zeulenroda Ger.
101 D1 Zeven Ger.
100 C2 Zevenaar Neth.
83 J3 Zeya Rus. Fed.
79 C2 Zeydābād Iran
83 J3 Zeyskoye Vodokhranilishche resr Rus. Fed.
103 D1 Zgierz Pol.
88 B3 Zhabinka Belarus
76 A2 Zhalpaktal Kazakh.
77 C1 Zhaltyr Kazakh.
76 B2 Zhanakala Kazakh.
76 B2 Zhanaozen Kazakh.
Zhangde China see Anyang
71 C3 Zhanghua Taiwan
71 B3 Zhangjiajie China
70 B1 Zhangjiakou China
71 B3 Zhangping China
71 B3 Zhangpu China
71 B3 Zhangye China
71 B3 Zhangzhou China
87 D4 Zhanibek Kazakh.
71 B3 Zhanjiang China
71 B3 Zhao'an China
71 B3 Zhaoqing China
71 A3 Zhaotong China
75 C1 Zhari Namco salt l. China
77 E2 Zharkent Kazakh.
89 D2 Zharkovskiy Rus. Fed.
77 E2 Zharma Kazakh.
90 C2 Zhashkiv Ukr.
Zhayyk r. Kazakh./Rus. Fed. see Ural
71 C3 Zhejiang prov. China
82 F1 Zhelaniya, Mys c. Rus. Fed.
89 E3 Zheleznogorsk Rus. Fed.
76 B2 Zhem r. Kazakh.
70 A2 Zhenba China

71	A3	Zheng'an China
71	B3	Zhenghe China
70	B2	Zhengzhou China
70	B2	Zhenjiang China
71	A3	Zhenyuan China
91	E1	Zherdevka Rus. Fed.
86	D2	Zheshart Rus. Fed.
77	D2	Zhetysuyskiy Alatau mts China/Kazakh.
77	C2	Zhezkazgan Karagandinskaya Oblast' Kazakh.
77	C2	Zhezkazgan Karagandinskaya Oblast' Kazakh.
68	C2	Zhigang China
83	J2	Zhigansk Rus. Fed.
		Zhi Qu r. China see Yangtze
76	C1	Zhitikara Kazakh.
88	D3	Zhlobin Belarus
90	B2	Zhmerynka Ukr.
74	A1	Zhob Pak.
83	L1	Zhokhova, Ostrov i. Rus. Fed.
75	C2	Zhongba China
		Zhonghe China see Xiushan
70	A2	Zhongning China
71	B3	Zhongshan China
		Zhongshan China see Liupanshui
70	A2	Zhongwei China
		Zhongxin China see Xamgyi'nyilha
76	C2	Zhosaly Kazakh.
70	B2	Zhoukou China
70	C2	Zhoushan China
91	C2	Zhovti Vody Ukr.
65	A2	Zhuanghe China
70	B2	Zhucheng China
89	D3	Zhukovka Rus. Fed.
89	E2	Zhukovskiy Rus. Fed.
70	B2	Zhumadian China
		Zhuoyang China see Suiping
71	B3	Zhuzhou Hunan China
71	B3	Zhuzhou Hunan China
90	A2	Zhydachiv Ukr.
88	C3	Zhytkavichy Belarus
90	B1	Zhytomyr Ukr.
103	D2	Žiar nad Hronom Slovakia
70	B2	Zibo China
103	D1	Zielona Góra Pol.
62	A1	Zigaing Myanmar
71	A3	Zigong China
114	A3	Ziguinchor Senegal
144	B3	Zihuatanejo Mex.
103	D2	Žilina Slovakia
83	H3	Zima Rus. Fed.
145	C2	Zimapán Mex.
121	B2	Zimbabwe country Africa
114	A4	Zimmi Sierra Leone
110	C2	Zimnicea Romania
115	C3	Zinder Niger
78	B3	Zinjibār Yemen
103	D2	Zirc Hungary
62	A1	Ziro India
79	C2	Zīr Rūd Iran
103	D2	Zistersdorf Austria
145	B3	Zitácuaro Mex.
103	C1	Zittau Ger.
87	E3	Zlatoust Rus. Fed.
103	D2	Zlín Czech Rep.
89	D3	Zlynka Rus. Fed.
89	E3	Zmiyevka Rus. Fed.
91	D2	Zmiyiv Ukr.
89	E3	Znamenka Orlovskaya Oblast' Rus. Fed.
91	E1	Znamenka Tambovskaya Oblast' Rus. Fed.
91	C2	Znam"yanka Ukr.
103	D2	Znojmo Czech Rep.
91	D1	Zolochiv Kharkivs'ka Oblast' Ukr.
90	A2	Zolochiv L'vivs'ka Oblast' Ukr.
91	C2	Zolotonosha Ukr.
89	E3	Zolotukhino Rus. Fed.
121	C2	Zomba Malawi
80	B1	Zonguldak Turkey
105	D3	Zonza Corse France
114	B4	Zorzor Liberia
115	D2	Zouar Chad
114	A2	Zouérat Maur.
109	D1	Zrenjanin Serbia
89	D2	Zubtsov Rus. Fed.
105	D2	Zug Switz.
81	C1	Zugdidi Georgia
106	B2	Zújar r. Spain
100	C2	Zülpich Ger.
121	C2	Zumbo Moz.
145	C3	Zumpango Mex.
138	B1	Zuni Mountains U.S.A.
71	A3	Zunyi China
109	C1	Županja Croatia
105	D2	Zürich Switz.
100	C1	Zutphen Neth.
115	D1	Zuwārah Libya
90	C2	Zvenyhorodka Ukr.
121	C3	Zvishavane Zimbabwe
103	D2	Zvolen Slovakia
109	C2	Zvornik Bos.-Herz.
114	B4	Zwedru Liberia
123	C3	Zwelitsha S. Africa
103	D2	Zwettl Austria
101	F2	Zwickau Ger.
100	C1	Zwolle Neth.
83	L2	Zyryanka Rus. Fed.

Acknowledgements

pages 34-35
Climatic map data:
Kottek, M., Grieser, J., Beck, C., Rudolf, B., and Rubel, F., 2006: World Map
of the Köppen-Geiger climate classification updated.
Meteorol. Z., 15, 259–263.
http://koeppen-geiger.vu-wien.ac.at

pages 36-37
World land cover map data:
© ESA 2010 and UCLouvain
Arino, O., Ramos, J., Kalogirou, V., Defourny, P., Achard, F., 2010.
GlobCover 2009. ESA Living Planet Symposium 2010, 28th June - 2nd July, Bergen, Norway, SP-686, ESA,
www.esa.int/due/globcover
http://due.esrin.esa.int/prjs/Results/20110202183257.pdf

pages 38-39
Population map data:
Center for International Earth Science Information Network (CIESIN), Columbia University; and Centro Internacional de Agricultura
Tropical (CIAT). 2005. Gridded Population of the World Version 3 (GPWv3). Palisades, NY: Socioeconomic
Data and Applications Center (SEDAC), Columbia University.
Available at: http://sedac.ciesin.columbia.edu/gpw
http://www.ciesin.columbia.edu

Cover
Yosemite Valley: © zschnepf/Shutterstock